The End of the European Era

SIXTH EDITION

THE NORTON HISTORY OF MODERN EUROPE

The Foundations of Early Modern Europe, 1460–1559, *2d edition*
EUGENE F. RICE, JR. and ANTHONY GRAFTON
The Age of Religious Wars, 1559–1689, *2d edition*
RICHARD S. DUNN
Kings and Philosophers, 1689–1789
LEONARD KRIEGER
Eighteenth-Century Europe: Tradition and Progress, *1715–1789*
ISSER WOLOCH
The Revolutionary Era, *1789–1850, 3d edition*
CHARLES BREUNIG and MATTHEW LEVINGER
The Age of Nationalism and Reform, *1850–1890, 2d edition*
NORMAN RICH
The End of the European Era, 1890 to the Present, *6th edition*
FELIX GILBERT and DAVID CLAY LARGE

The End of the European Era
1890 to the Present

SIXTH EDITION

FELIX GILBERT

Late of the Institute for Advanced Study

DAVID CLAY LARGE

Montana State University

W. W. Norton & Company
New York · London

W. W. Norton & Company has been independent since its founding in 1923, when William Warder Norton and Mary D. Herter Norton first published lectures delivered at the People's Institute, the adult-education division of New York City's Cooper Union. The firm soon expanded its program beyond the Institute, publishing books by celebrated academics from America and abroad. By midcentury, the two major pillars of Norton's publishing program— trade books and college texts—were firmly established. In the 1950s the Norton family trans- ferred control of the company to its employees, and today—with a staff of four hundred and a comparable number of trade, college, and professional titles published each year—W. W. Norton & Company stands as the largest and oldest publishing house owned wholly by its employees.

The text of this book is composed in Electra, with the display set in Weiss.
Composition by Binghamton Valley Composition.
Manufacturing by the Courier Companies—Westford division.
Production manager: Eric Pier-Hocking.

Cover painting: *The Strand by Night*, 1937, by Christopher Richard Wynne Nevinson (1889–1946). © Bradford Art Galleries and Museums, West Yorkshire, UK/The Bridgeman Art Library.

Library of Congress Cataloging-in-Publication Data

Gilbert, Felix, 1905-1991.
    The end of the European era : 1890 to the present / Felix Gilbert,
David Clay Large.—6th ed.
        p. cm.—(The Norton history of modern Europe)
    Includes bibliographical references and index.
    ISBN 978-0-393-93040-5 (pbk.)
    I. Large, David Clay. II. Title.

D443.G473 2009
940.5—dc22

                                    2008045590

W. W. Norton & Company, Inc., 500 Fifth Avenue, New York, NY 10110
www.wwnorton.com

W. W. Norton & Company Ltd., Castle House, 75/76 Wells Street, London W1T 3QT

1 2 3 4 5 6 7 8 9 0

Contents

Part II   The Peace That Failed

Part III   Rebuilding Europe

Part IV   Resurgent Europe

Maps

Preface

In the six years that have elapsed since the last revision of this textbook, Europe and the world around it have changed significantly; it is the primary task of this sixth edition of *The End of the European* Era to explicate those changes.

To this end, I have re-crafted Chapter 16, now titled Continental Drift, to encompass key developments on the domestic scene in the major European nations from the early 1990s to the present. From the vantage point of 2008, it has become much clearer that the monumental transformations of the late twentieth century—the collapse of Communism, the end of the Cold War, the reunification of Germany—have brought with them not only opportunities but also challenges. We will also see that various alterations in national leadership across Europe did not necessarily result in improvements in governmental performance. And in some cases—most notably Russia—the most recent change at the top has dealt a major blow to prospects for liberalization and democratization.

In addition, this sixth edition contains a completely new chapter, titled Europe and the Challenges of Globalization. This concluding chapter examines how individual European governments and the expanded European Union have addressed such overlapping issues as immigration and migration, economic globalization, environmental degradation and climate change, and terrorist violence. Of course, none of these problems applies exclusively to Europe; and therefore I have tried to show how the task of meeting the challenges of the new twenty-first century has affected Europe's relations with the non-European world, especially the United States.

The European Union may have grown significantly in size since *The End of the European Era* was last revised, but this book, alas, cannot expand commensurately; it needs to be transportable in an average-sized backpack. I have therefore compressed detail in earlier sections of the text where possible. Along with the trimming, however, I have also tried to enliven the discussion with infusions of new insights derived from the most recent scholarship.

As with the fifth edition, I have had to undertake this task of revision without the guiding hand of Professor Felix Gilbert, who died in 1991. But once again, I trust that the changes I have made are consistent with the course he laid out in the early editions of the book.

David Clay Large
Montana State University

PART I

EUROPE'S APOGEE

CHAPTER 1

The Beginning of a New Century

ONE AFTERNOON early in the twentieth century, a member of the British aristocracy, a great landowner, stood with one of his guests on the terrace extending along the back of his large country house. In the valley at their feet lay farms, cottages, a railway, a coal mine, and streets dense with workers. Beyond this valley was a hill, with another large country house on top of it. Pointing to this house, the host said to his guest: "You see, there is no one between us and them."

This is a revealing story. In earlier centuries it might have been natural for great landowners to feel themselves far removed from the servants and agricultural laborers who lived and worked in their houses and on their estates and to have considered them of no account. But in the twentieth century, as the monopoly of power slipped out of the hands of the landowning classes, and those living in the neighborhood were no longer as dependent, this undisguised feeling of superiority seemed inappropriate and even perverse. At the same time, however, this story points up the reasons for social and political tensions and instability in the twentieth century; in times of great changes a ruling class has difficulty not only in permitting others to participate in power but, still more, in recognizing that such a change is going on.

A RISING POPULATION

The story of our landowner is a striking example of the inability of the upper classes to realize one of the main changes in this period: the increasing role of the industrial urban population and the decline of the agrarian sector. Between 1871, when the unification of Germany altered the map of Europe and established a new balance of power, and 1914, when the outbreak of the First World War occurred and European political life was molded into new forms, the population of Europe rose by more than 150 million and, if Russia is included, totaled almost 450 million people. In the first decade after 1870 this growth of population was still slow and gradual, but it accelerated from the 1880s on. There

Traffic on one of the main streets of Paris, the Boulevard des Italiens, in 1909, before the widespread use of the automobile.

was a close connection, of course, between industrialization and population growth, and therefore, the population rise was greatest in Germany, where at that time industrialization was achieving full speed. The German population grew between 1890 and 1910 from 49 million to 65 million, or by more than 25 percent. The population of Great Britain, where industrialization had come earlier into full stride, amounted in 1914 to 42 million and had grown between 1890 and 1914 by 7.8 million, by a still considerable growth rate of 18 percent. Even the countries of the Mediterranean area, which for a long time had lagged behind the northern European countries, began to grow with great speed; for instance, from 31 million in 1890, Italy had grown to 36 million in 1910. The two greatest contrasts were between Russia and France: Russia's population increased rapidly, and it certainly was the most populous great European power; France, however, was the only European state whose population did not increase during this period. In discussing the developments of European foreign policy at this time one must keep in mind that while until 1914 no great frontier changes occurred with regard to the great European powers, their internal strength in relation to each other was in a state of flux.

Perhaps even more startling than increases in population was the migration that took place within the various European states. Before the Industrial Revolution economic life had been primarily agrarian, and agriculture remained the dominant occupation far into the twentieth century in Eastern and Southeastern Europe. In the two Western European countries—England and France—in which industrialization had begun to develop at the end of the eighteenth century, the relation between the number of people occupied in industry and agriculture remained roughly the same from the middle of the nineteenth century until 1914; in England only 10 percent of the population were engaged in agriculture. In France, where, even in the times of the First Industrial Revolution, agriculture had remained highly important, it continued to absorb 40 percent of the population.

In Italy, the greater part of the population was occupied in agriculture, but the percentage of those employed in industry and commerce grew steadily especially from the nineties on. By the turn of the century industry represented 20.2 percent of the gross national product; eight years later, 26.1 percent. But the most striking change in social structure occurred in Germany. In the middle of the nineteenth century about 70 percent of the German population was engaged in agriculture. By the nineties, this figure had been reduced to 35 percent and continued to decline. These statistics are interesting from still another point of view: despite the decrease of Germans employed in agriculture in percentages of the entire population, their absolute number did not decrease. This means that the population growth that took place in these decades was exclusively an increase in the industrial labor force. Although in other countries this development is less clear, it remains true that most of the population growth fed industrialization.

These demographic developments had one consequence which was noticeable without any study of statistical figures: the increase in the number and the size of big cities. Whereas in 1850 there had not been more than fourteen European cities with more than two hundred thousand inhabitants, this figure had risen to thirty-eight by 1910. In Great Britain and France, the rate of urban growth had begun to slow down by the end of the nineteenth century. Nevertheless, Greater London grew from 5 million inhabitants in 1880 to 7 million in 1914; Paris, from 2 million to almost 3 million. Cities in those countries that entered the industrial age in the fifty years before the First World War grew even more dramatically. Berlin, with about five hundred thousand inhabitants in 1866, had more than 2 million in 1914. Barcelona and Milan, the industrial capitals of Spain and Italy, both surpassed five hundred thousand by 1914. Most significant was the rise in population and the growth of urban settlements in the great coal- and iron-mining districts. In northern France, the city of Lille doubled its population between 1850 and 1914. By 1914 Lille had two hundred thousand inhabitants, and the population in neighboring cities so increased that northeastern France began to form one megalopolis. The same phenomenon could be observed in Germany in the Ruhr area, where, for example, Essen, Gelsenkirchen, Bochum, and Mülheim began to run into one another, and the same was happening in the coal-mining districts of upper Silesia around Kattowitz. Russia entered the industrialization race last. But

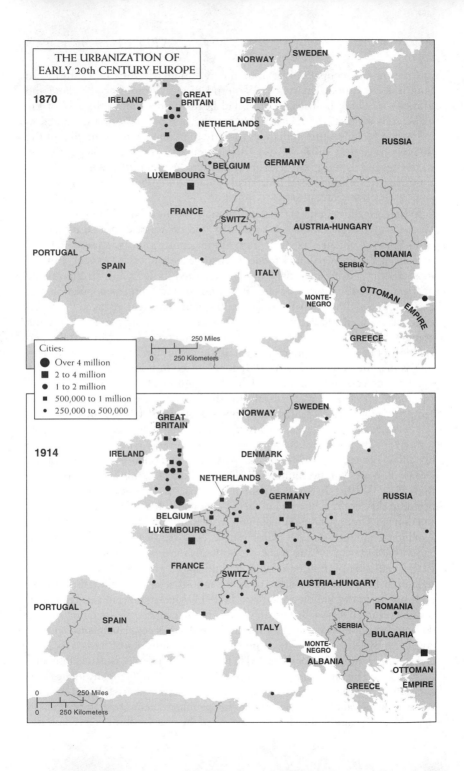

THE URBANIZATION OF
EARLY 20th CENTURY EUROPE

1870

Cities:
- Over 4 million
- 2 to 4 million
- 1 to 2 million
- 500,000 to 1 million
- 250,000 to 500,000

1914

NORWAY
SWEDEN
IRELAND
GREAT
BRITAIN
DENMARK
NETHERLANDS
RUSSIA
BELGIUM
GERMANY
LUXEMBOURG
FRANCE
SWITZ.
AUSTRIA-HUNGARY
PORTUGAL
SPAIN
ITALY
ROMANIA
SERBIA
MONTE-
NEGRO
OTTOMAN EMPIRE
GREECE

0   250 Miles
0   250 Kilometers

GREAT
BRITAIN
NORWAY
SWEDEN
IRELAND
DENMARK
NETHERLANDS
GERMANY
RUSSIA
BELGIUM
LUXEMBOURG
FRANCE
SWITZ.
AUSTRIA-HUNGARY
PORTUGAL
SPAIN
ITALY
ROMANIA
SERBIA
BULGARIA
MONTE-
NEGRO
ALBANIA
OTTOMAN
EMPIRE
GREECE

0   250 Miles
0   250 Kilometers

there, urban development was rapid. In 1863, Russia had only three cities with more than one hundred thousand inhabitants: St. Petersburg, Moscow, and Kiev; forty years later there were more than fifteen. Around the coal and iron mines of the Donets Basin and in the oil areas of the Caucasus densely populated districts developed.

INTELLECTUAL DISQUIET
AND CULTURAL REVOLT

These shifts in the European social structure are easy to recognize at a later time after they have been reflected in events and can be elucidated with statistical data. But although the specific nature of the changes that occurred were not clearly grasped by contemporary Europeans, they were aware that developments were taking place that cast doubt on the validity of the assumptions and values that had dominated the nineteenth century. Their doubts grew slowly and gradually until, at the end of the century, particularly in the 1890s, movements in literature, art, and philosophy arose, in revolt against traditional attitudes and approaches. Sometimes explicitly, sometimes only implicitly, those classes of society that had been the supporters and protagonists of the established culture came under attack.

Perhaps the most striking indication of widespread intellectual uneasiness was the spread of criticism and demands for reform of those institutions which by their very nature acted as the defenders of the existing order: the churches. In the Catholic and Protestant churches single individuals—Albert de Mun in France; the Catholic Bishop Ketteler and the Protestant court preacher Adolf Stöcker in Germany—organized movements that concentrated on the workers, recognizing that the uninterest, if not rejection of Christianity, on the workers' part was closely connected with the misery in which they lived. The most important document expressing the need for religion to take an interest in the situation of industrial workers was the encyclical of Pope Leo XIII, *Rerum Novarum*, issued in 1891. The encyclical had a practical purpose: the approval and encouragement of the formation of Christian trade unions. But its theoretical assumptions are no less significant. Not unlike Karl Marx, the pope envisaged as the outcome of industrialization an increasing number of people living in dependence and misery and an accumulation of wealth in the hands of a very few rich people. The pope expressed the view that under these circumstances the state had the right to interfere and to initiate social legislation to protect the workers against exploitation and ameliorate their economic condition. The encyclical was sharply critical of liberalism, in particular, of laissez-faire economics, and of the underlying assumption that a good society could be achieved by giving free play to the forces of the individual.

Criticism of those attitudes and values which had dominated the rise of the liberal bourgeoisie to influence and power was also a feature of new movements in literature and art. The recognized leader of the modern drama was the Norwegian Henrik Ibsen (1828–1906), whose perfectly constructed, provocative plays appeared in the eighties and nineties and were produced all over Europe. In his dramas, Ibsen attacked the many injustices in the social life of his time; the inferior and dependent position of women and the ruthlessness of men in the pursuit of social advance were favorite themes. But almost all of Ibsen's plays were also directed against what he considered a more basic and more general defect of his society: the hypocrisy of the bourgeois, who in order to preserve the outward appearance of respectability built his life on lies, ruthlessly condemning those who had sinned against the accepted moral code and even destroying them.

Ibsen was the great model and teacher for two dramatists who, in Germany and England, dominated the stage from the nineties almost to the middle of the twentieth century: Gerhart Hauptmann (1862–1946) and George Bernard Shaw (1856–1950). Hauptmann gained his reputation in the nineties with a play called *The Weavers*. It presented the revolt of Silesian weavers in the first part of the nineteenth century against the introduction of machines and factories and contained a strong revolutionary message directed against the bourgeoisie for disregarding the human misery that accompanied their chase after money. In Hauptmann's plays of this early period the chief themes are the contrasts between the ruling group and the poor and the human tragedies resulting from the insistence on the preservation of conventional morality; Hauptmann was a socialist who agitated for the overthrow of the existing order. George Bernard Shaw was also a socialist, but a Fabian socialist, who believed in the possibility of establishing a better social order by reforms rather than by revolution. Shaw's plays were mostly comedies. At first he selected as themes certain features of modern society—for example, prostitution and militarism—and built the entire play around bitter satiric criticism of them. His later work was lighter, aimed at teasing the prejudices of the ruling classes. The earlier and later plays differed so much in their tone that Shaw himself called them, in a collected edition, "unpleasant and pleasant plays."

These modern playwrights abandoned the tradition of heroizing verse dramas; they were "naturalists." Their people spoke on the stage as they were assumed to speak in real life. This social realism had had its first triumphs in another literary genre, the novel. Émile Zola (1840–1902), the master of this technique, continued to publish into the twentieth century, depicting the social changes brought about by industrialization. But the main focus of the younger novelists was given to the phenomenon of the decline of the ruling group; this decline was considered most strikingly reflected in the disintegration of the family as an institution—the tendency of later generations to enjoy wealth rather than to increase it, the accompanying decline in morals or acceptance of an aristocratic behavior by the bourgeoisie. At the end of the 1890s Thomas Mann (1875–1955) wrote the novel *Buddenbrooks*, in which this process of bourgeois decline is pictured with the deepest psychological understanding; this novel has become the most famous example of many novels with the same theme. Hauptmann, Shaw, Mann, who in the last decade of the nineteenth century made names for themselves with works that outraged and shocked the ruling classes, were thirty years later almost classics; all three received the Nobel Prize for Literature before the end of the 1920s.

If the fame of these writers has grown in the course of the twentieth century, they were not the most widely known or appreciated literary figures in the 1890s or at the beginning of the twentieth century. These were the years of the "cult of decadence," and attention was focused on the representatives of this attitude. The writers and poets of this aestheticizing trend were no less antagonistic to conventional bourgeois morality than Hauptmann or Shaw, but if the latter had confidence in the coming of a freer life and society, the protagonists of aestheticism saw only decline as result of industrialization and of the emergence of the masses. Understanding for art and beauty had been lost; if it still existed, it was the privileged possession of a selected few with finer perceptions and greater sensitivity than the average person. This view was most provokingly flaunted by Oscar Wilde (1854–1900); his comedies dominated the London theater in the 1890s. There is irony in the fact that Wilde and his plays were the vogue, applauded by those whom, quite intentionally, he attacked and ridiculed.

The fashionable admiration of decadence passed quickly, but a neoromantic trend remained strong in literature. Poets and writers believed that the cultural achievements of past aristocratic ages were greater than those of the modern world and that in order to show the potentialities of life, you must not depict the reality of the contemporary world but resuscitate the image of a better past. Many of these literary works were set to music because the connection of word and music heightened the feeling of being transposed to a more ideal world. The greatest masters of this neoromanticism were the Belgian Maurice Maeterlinck (1874–1949), whose *Bluebird*, indicating the search for a never attainable goal, became a symbol of the entire movement, and the Austrian Hugo von Hofmannsthal (1874–1929), whose poems, published when he was nineteen, made him the embodiment of poetic youth all over Europe. It is characteristic that the main works of these two poets became operas: Maeterlinck's *Pelléas et Mélisande* became the most successful composition of the French composer Claude Debussy (1862–1918); Hofmannsthal's evocation of the eighteenth-century Viennese aristocracy *Der Rosenkavalier*, the masterwork of Richard Strauss (1864–1949).

Remote as these romantic evocations of a better past might appear from the modern industrial world, they had their impact on the political climate of the twentieth century; unintentionally they were an important ingredient in the ideology of the political groups and parties that opposed the trend toward progressivism and socialism and the nourished notions from which Fascism and racism would spring. The neoromantic idealization of a past aristocratic age was not only linked to achievements in the cultural sphere but also viewed as tied to a heroic style of life that despised material comfort and was willing to lead a strenuous life in the service of higher ideals. The most eloquent preacher of this aspect of neoromanticism was the Italian writer and poet Gabriele d'Annunzio (1863–1938). The unrealistic contents of his novels—presenting men ruthlessly but selflessly serving great causes, leading lives devoted to passion and beauty— are redeemed by sudden scenes of psychological insight and a rich and powerful language. Now half forgotten, he was one of the most widely read and most influential writers at the end of the 1890s and the beginning of the twentieth century.

When d'Annunzio had his great successes, the philosopher Friedrich Nietzsche (1844–1900), whose writings were disregarded and almost unknown when they appeared, had suddenly become a widely read and much-discussed author. D'Annunzio's heroes are echoes of Nietzsche's Superman; with d'Annunzio the process began in the course of which Nietzsche's Superman became the embodiment of a ruthless pursuit of power. Actually, the ideas that Nietzsche connected with this concept were much more sophisticated. He believed that Christian morality, with its praise of humility, was frustrating the development of man's powers and suffocating human creativity and that not an idealized and invented picture of man, only a recognition of his natural instincts and drives, could constitute the basis of a true ethical code and of a new society of equality. His aim was not the creation of a world of men recklessly striving for power but a new ethics.

In Nietzsche's writing his criticism of modern morality and convention was expressed in a literary, almost poetic form. It constituted the immense importance of Sigmund Freud that he gave scientific proof to the notions that formed an element in the various literary and philosophical trends of the period: that man was oppressed by a conventional morality which had lost its original justification and was now becoming only frustrated and inhibited and that this suppression of man's instincts was an element in the oppression and injustice of the social world. Of course, Freud's teaching began to exert influence only much later, but it is significant that the book that would make him most widely known, his _Interpretation of Dreams_, was a work of the last decade of the nineteenth century and appeared in the first year of the twentieth century.

Although many, in either hopeful or fearful expectation, believed in the coming of a crisis that would result in the end of a period of civilization, certainly not all, perhaps not even very many Europeans shared these feelings. Although the belief in progress, so strong in the eighteenth century and in most of the nineteenth century, had been shaken, it had not been extinguished; the conviction remained alive that on the basis of the achievements of the past, in a continuous

Noted Viennese psychoanalyst Sigmund Freud.

process, a better future could be attained. Such expectations received strength and confirmation from the discoveries of science that were steadily extended over all fields of human life. In celebration of the beginning of the new century, H. G. Wells wrote a number of articles, then assembled in a book under the title *Anticipation of the Reaction of Mechanical and Scientific Progress upon Human Life and Thought*. Wells painted a glowing picture of the world that, on the basis of new discoveries and their industrial exploitation, lay before humanity in the twentieth century: better health, better living conditions, availability of goods from all parts of the globe, a regulation of economic life that would permit greater leisure and full employment. Wells certainly expressed the ideas of wide groups of the European middle classes about the outlook of the future more correctly than the poets and philosophers of cultural pessimism. There were not only those who felt threatened by the rise of the new industrial world or those who aimed for a revolution because they felt suppressed and excluded, but also those who looked to the coming of the twentieth century with pride and expectation.

THE SECOND INDUSTRIAL REVOLUTION
AND THE GLOBAL DIMENSIONS OF
EUROPEAN POLITICS

Hopes for a revolution, fears of cultural and social decline because of the emergence of a mass civilization, expectations for steady material progress—all these views became magnified and intensified by the developments in the economic sphere that occurred during the last decade of the nineteenth century. From the end of the Napoleonic era, one long deflationary trend, only briefly interrupted in the middle of the century, characterized European economic developments, but this changed by 1896. An increasing supply of money, stimulated by the discovery of large new gold fields in South Africa and the Klondike, allowed new investments and spurred industrial activities. A new development, which has been called the Second Industrial Revolution, began. The foundation for this "revolution" had been laid in the previous decades: the discovery of a new process to produce basic steel that possessed neither the hardness of pig iron nor the corrosiveness of wrought iron. The advances then made propelled the development of two new industries: the electrical and chemical industries. These new industries brought about a startling transformation of the external conditions of life: lighting and heating, streetcars, subways, railroads. All made living and working in extensive urban centers possible and created the preconditions for the development of the large cities. But these innovations also affected the economy of the countryside, changing the forms of production and the marketing of agricultural products. The chemical industry completed this process through industrial manufacturing of fertilizers; the dyestuffs it produced diminished the costs and enlarged the availability of textile and cleaning products; the development of synthetic fibers perfected the transition to mass production of clothing materials.

However, the influence these new industries exerted on the process of manufacturing and their by-products were as important as the new goods they brought onto the market. First, they were instrumental in opening new sources of energy and widening energy distribution. Power stations allowed a more rational and economic location of factories at points close to the needed mineral resources or to the market. Then, within the factory, electricity stimulated the creation and the use of precision instruments that accelerated and mechanized labor. Output would be increased by augmenting the number of workers without special training. Although the potential of oil as a source of energy had been known, the chemical industry converted it into a fuel, which from the first years of the twentieth century was increasingly used in warships and in ocean liners.

Advancements in the fields of steel production, electricity, and chemistry all contributed to the invention of what must be considered the most characteristic phenomenon of the Second Industrial Revolution: the internal-combustion engine. The automobile and later the airplane were the most dramatic evidence of the coming of a new age widely different from the world of the nineteenth century.

A crucial factor in the Second Industrial Revolution was that it created the possibility of industrialization in countries that, because of a lack of coal and iron, had seemed destined to remain mainly agricultural. With the development of an electrical and chemical industry the possession of coal and iron resources became less of a necessity. Of course, although all European countries were now able to participate in industrialization, the extent and degree of their participation differed and depended on their geographical situation, their social and economic structure, and the extent and character of public education. In practice this new situation meant that Great Britain, which during a good part of the nineteenth century had possessed a monopoly on the European and almost on the world market, now began to meet stiff competition. The chief competitor was the newly unified Germany, with its rich deposits of coal and iron in the Ruhr and Silesia and its burgeoning electrical and chemical industries. The changed situation is reflected in the transition from free trade to protective tariffs to which, with the exception of Great Britain, all European countries became converted in the latter part of the nineteenth century. The various continental countries were concerned that the advantages Great Britain possessed as a first-comer in the age of industrialization would slow down or impede the industrial development in their countries. Great Britain not only was now excluded from the German market but also met competition from Germany, France, and other European countries on the world markets.

This new wave of protectionism meant that the Second Industrial Revolution had repercussions on international relations and foreign policy. It stimulated interest in the regions that could supply raw materials for domestic industries. Indeed, during the last quarter of the 1890s and the first fourteen years of the twentieth century more than eleven million square miles were added to the colonial possessions of the great European powers. These new colonial possessions lay in Africa and in southwest Asia. The islands in the South Pacific aroused the ambitions of France, Germany, and Great Britain; there European powers met a new rival in the United States. Yet despite some diplomatic crises, the wrangles ended with a peaceful division of the spoils among the competing powers. In Africa at the beginning of the twentieth century only Ethiopia, the Boer Republics, and Morocco—states that had a long history of independence—remained sovereign, and competition for control over these areas was sharp, lasting far into the twentieth century.

From the economic point of view the creation of a colonial empire was hardly more important than the domination of areas that—politically independent, or at least independent by standards of international law—could serve as markets for industrial products. Until the Second Industrial Revolution these countries had been economically dominated by Great Britain. Now Germany entered a contest with Great Britain in South Africa, and British economic influence in

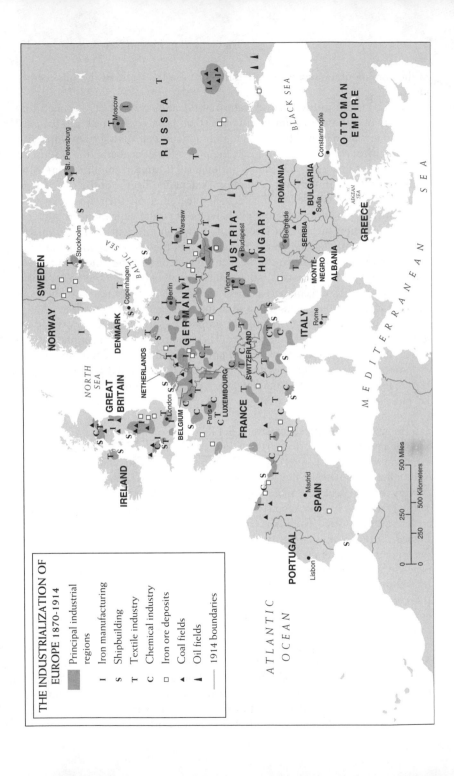

THE INDUSTRIALIZATION OF
EUROPE 1870-1914

Principal industrial
regions

I   Iron manufacturing
S   Shipbuilding
T   Textile industry
C   Chemical industry
□   Iron ore deposits
▲   Coal fields
◀   Oil fields
—   1914 boundaries

China became disputed not only by the industrialized nations of Europe but also by the United States and by a new industrial power, Japan. The greatest prize, however, which for economic and strategic reasons all the great powers tried to win, was the "sick man of Europe," the Ottoman Empire. Politically debilitated, it seemed unable to put up much resistance to economic penetration and control by a foreign power.

THE STRUCTURE OF SOCIETY

Although the extension of European power and control over the entire globe appeared to be the most striking feature of the Second Industrial Revolution, the home market remained for the industrialized countries of Europe more important than finding outlets for production beyond their frontiers. While within each European nation the nature of the problems involved in adjusting the new to the old or the old to the new varied, the process was crucially difficult in all of them. The anecdote with which this chapter began, about the inability or unwillingness of the aristocratic landowner to recognize the existence of a large working class, is an almost comical indication of the difficulties involved in becoming aware of the emergence of a new social structure. The industrial worker was the decisive new element in this structure, and the integration of the industrial labor force into the existing order the most crucial issue.

The Workers

Whereas in previous centuries a number of social groups—household servants, serfs and half-free peasants, craftsmen, artisans—had formed the weakest class of society, at the end of the nineteenth century, the industrial workers—the proletariat—were in the lowest and most endangered position. During the early years of industrialization, the workers had experienced insecurity and misery. With the economic improvement of the late nineteenth century, wages began to rise, and the workers' living standards improved gradually. Nevertheless, better wages and the possibility of somewhat better food and clothing did not eliminate the hardships which formed part of the existence of the proletariat.

Industry, particularly as it developed in the First and Second Industrial Revolutions, meant removal of work in the home to work in factories and decline in small enterprises and rise in large enterprises employing more than fifty people. Factory workers had to live close to their workplace and to each other, and the industrial centers, in which the workers lived, grew in an entirely unplanned way. Housing for the masses that streamed into these centers was controlled by private builders, speculators, or absentee landlords.

In Great Britain people continued to live in one-family houses, but these small houses now accommodated numerous families and soon became overcrowded, unsanitary slums. In other countries workers were housed in apartment buildings four to six stories high, each floor containing five or six apartments. Built side by side with no intervening space, centered on small dark courtyards, these buildings had no gardens or green areas and were bounded by treeless streets.

The factories were generally large structures without adequate air or light. Working conditions began to improve after the first cruel years of the beginning of industrialization. Even at best, however, sanitary conditions in the factories were appalling, and little was done to ensure the safety of the workers from occupational hazards. Safety precautions, particularly in the coal mines, were neglected. In Russia, Italy, and Spain there were no laws against the employment of children or women nor were their working conditions different from those of male adults. Economic crises, frequent dismissal of workers, and a considerable rate of unemployment were regarded as unavoidable. No provision was made for these recurring periods of hardship, and wages were so low that the workers were unable to accumulate savings to fall back on in these times. In the oil fields of the Caucasus, workers like the young Iosif Vissarionovich Dzhugashvili, who later would take the name of Josef Stalin (1879–1953), were imprisoned in barracks for eight hours during the night and worked during the day under police supervision. The young Aneurin Bevan (1897–1960), after the Second World War one of the inspiring leaders of the British Labor party, grew up in the misery of a Welsh coal-mining village. One of his brothers was killed in what Bevan was always to regard as an avoidable mine accident, and his mother died of starvation. A picture of life in a worker's house, of the desperate struggles of mothers for food for their children, of the lack of medical care, of the men's escape into drunkenness, of the recruitment of teenagers to work in the mines is given by D. H. Lawrence in his novel *Sons and Lovers* (1913). This British writer, with his message of a free life, grew up amid the collieries of a Midlands mining village.

People living under such conditions were naturally inclined to regard the world that permitted such misery with hostility. Realizing their economic and social weaknesses, many workers placed their hope in organizing themselves and formed trade unions in the expectation that unified action would improve their common lot. In the 1890s the trade union movement began to make great strides; by 1905 the British unions, which had developed earlier than those on the Continent, had more than three million members; in Germany one and a half million workers were unionized; and in France, one million. These figures sound impressive; actually not even 25 percent of the adult industrial workers in these countries belonged to unions. Nevertheless, the trade unions benefited the entire working population because employers were gradually forced to provide better conditions in order to keep their workers.

The main activities of the trade unions were directed toward improving the material situation of the workers by collective bargaining, by granting financial assistance to strikers when negotiations failed, and by collecting benefit funds with which the unemployed, the sick, and the aged could be supported. But unions also attempted to equip the workers for the struggle for

Working-class housing in the East End of London, 1912.

social betterment: They organized training schools, set up educational courses, arranged holiday excursions. They made the lives of the workers more meaningful, liberating them from a sense of helpless isolation by providing a sense of community.

The union movement was especially important for Europe's working-class women. Until the last decades of the nineteenth century, trade unions had been an exclusively male preserve, but male factory workers began to understand that their own economic advancement would be stalled if women workers continued to be paid so much less than men that they held the men back. Starting in the late 1880s, British and continental unions began recruiting women in large numbers, thus enhancing their own power as well as that of their new female members. Largely because of union backing, women gained shorter working hours and protective legislation. Unfortunately, however, female servants and pieceworkers proved hard to unionize, meaning that few gains were achieved in those fields. Moreover, even in industry women continued to receive lower wages than males for comparable work, though the disparity was less egregious than before.

It was soon noticed that the trade unions exerted considerable influence on the minds of the workers. Ministers and priests became aware of the extent to which these organizations were successfully competing with the churches. The encyclical *Rerum Novarum*, in which Pope Leo XIII expressed approval of the attempts to form Christian trade unions, arose from this concern. Although the Catholic trade unions never were as powerful as the "free" trade unions, they became a significant political and social factor in Germany and Austria.

Yet the continued existence of trade unions was by no means secure. They had to fight for recognition, which was achieved only gradually: in Great Britain between 1870 and 1876; in France in 1884; in Germany after 1890. In some countries only local trade unions or trade unions for particular industrial activities were permitted. In Russia trade unions remained illegal until 1906. Few countries recognized the right of collective bargaining. Strikes and picketing were frequently prohibited. Since the activities by which the trade unions tried to improve the lot of their members met with limited success only, many workers came to feel that a real improvement of their situation required a change in the entire political system: Action in the economic sphere had to be complemented by action in the political sphere. Many trade union leaders shared this view and took a leading role in political movements that attempted to organize the workers for revolution.

The last quarter of the nineteenth century saw the formation in almost all European countries of political parties which called themselves Socialist or Social Democratic. These parties shared the main tenets of the political creed which Karl Marx (1818–1883) had formulated. Before the First World War the most powerful socialist party was the German Social Democratic Party. Its program, named after Erfurt, the town where it was adopted in 1891, was written with the cooperation of the aged Friedrich Engels (1820–1895), Marx's friend and collaborator. The Erfurt Program, subsequently the model for the programs of all the European socialist parties, was based on a few clear and simple tenets. Fundamental was the Marxist assumption that every society consisted of classes determined by economic interests, and every political struggle was actually a struggle between different economic classes. Thus, no improvement of the economic situation of the workers could be expected without a political revolution in which the workers would wrest power from the capitalist ruling group. By this transfer of power the means of production would fall into the hands of the proletariat, private property would be replaced by common possession of all goods, and the results of labor could be distributed to the benefit of all. Everyone would receive according to his needs.

Such possibilities were presented not as an unrealistic utopia but as the sequence of events that scientific investigation had proved to be necessary and inevitable. Because under capitalism wealth was becoming increasingly concentrated among fewer and fewer people, and more and more people were being pushed down into the proletariat, fewer people would have the means to buy goods and to stimulate the economy; consequently, the economic crises that were considered to be inherent in the capitalist system would become progressively more frequent and severe. However, the Marxists urged the workers not to stand idly by waiting for the final crisis and the collapse of capitalism. The capitalists would defend themselves by force, so the workers had to strive for a position from which they could seize power. They were to work for a democratization of political life in capitalist society, in order to undermine the existing state and to defeat the last stand of capitalism. Since capitalism dominated the world, its overthrow presupposed an international revolution. In 1889 the socialist parties of all countries therefore formed an alliance, the International, and representatives from these parties met regularly. Although the decisions of the International were recommendations only and not binding on the individual socialist parties, the International did create the impression of a great supranational force working toward a single goal.

The socialist doctrine had obvious attractions for the workers who were outsiders in the prewar society. But the doctrine had inner contradictions: If society had to be entirely transformed, was it meaningful to work for its democratization? If the collapse of capitalism was historically inevitable, what justification was there for forming political parties and for undertaking a political struggle? These contradictions became the more puzzling because the actual political and economic situation in the prewar years did not develop according to the Marxian scheme. Economic crises did not become more frequent or more serious. Indeed, no serious economic crises arose between 1890 and 1914; in general there was an upward trend in the standard of living on the Continent. By 1900 the wages of skilled workers were almost double those of unskilled workers, and the skilled workers were able to accumulate some reserves.

The growth of socialist parties and of trade unions led to the creation of large bureaucratic apparatuses. They employed numerous officers; they acquired publishing houses and newspapers; some of their leaders were elected to parliaments. Consequently, many party and trade union officers became more interested in keeping their organizations alive than in risking their existence by political action. Some socialists suggested that evolution rather than revolution was the way to socialism. Since the workers would slowly become a majority, it might be possible, they thought, to achieve the transition to socialism gradually, by a democratic process. The originator of this theory was a German socialist, Eduard Bernstein (1850–1932), who had been impressed by improvements in the situation of the working classes in Great Britain during the nineteenth century. Revisionism, as the movement was called, was particularly influential in Great Britain and Germany, countries with highly developed industrial systems, where the workers received some of the benefits of economic progress. In Spain, France, and Russia, where industrialization was still in its infancy and where the governments looked with disfavor upon demands of the workers that might retard the process of industrialization, socialists rejected the entire doctrine of Revisionism. In the meetings of the International, the views of the Revisionists were debated, but they never became official socialist doctrine. The demand for revolution was maintained.

The Ruling Group in Europe

If the Second Industrial Revolution brought into the political scene a new element that tended to oppose the existing political order, the established ruling group also had difficulty maintaining its position in an industrialized society or in adjusting to it. The European ruling group—to a lesser degree in Great Britain, still strongly in Central and Eastern Europe—carried the traces of the past: of its origin in an agrarian society, of feudal and hierarchical ideas.

Around the turn of the century, there were only two republics in Europe: France and Switzerland. The prevalent form of government was the monarchy. The degree to which monarchical rulers possessed actual political power varied. But whether or not they had sufficient power to exert real influence on state policy, the monarchs were justified in considering themselves the most important persons in the European political arena.

Members of ruling dynasties could marry only members of other ruling dynasties, unless they were willing to relinquish their status and rights. At the beginning of the twentieth century even the members of the British royal family, who with the ruling monarch's permission might marry commoners, were for the most part married to members of princely families. Religion somewhat separated the dynasties into two groups. Almost all of the Catholic princes were related to the Habsburgs and the Bourbons. The Protestant ruling families, into which the Eastern Orthodox rulers, particularly the Russian tsars, also tended to marry, were tied together through the numerous small German dynasties, which provided marriageable princes and princesses for almost any contingency. In the nineteenth century the remarkable fertility of the admirable couple Victoria and Albert had bound the Protestant rulers still more tightly together. Thus the British king Edward VII was the uncle both of the German emperor William II and of Alexandra, the wife of the Russian tsar, Nicholas II. The birthdays, wed-

A royal jamboree. King Edward VII of Great Britain and his son, later King George V, the German emperor William II, the Spanish king Alfonso XIII, and their wives.

dings, and funerals of monarchs were not only state occasions but also family reunions. It was natural that at the wedding of the daughter of William II in 1912 the tsar and tsarina of Russia and the king and queen of England would come to Berlin and that almost all of Europe's rulers would be present at the funerals of Queen Victoria in 1901 and of her son Edward VII in 1910.

After the death of Queen Victoria, the oldest ruling monarch in Europe was the emperor Francis Joseph of Austria-Hungary; born in 1830, he had ascended the throne in 1848. He was venerated as a kind of patriarch by all the rulers, and his seventieth birthday in 1900, his eightieth in 1910, and the sixtieth jubilee of his reign in 1908 were all occasions for royal meetings. Visits among cousins were frequent. The German emperor often met with the tsar. Edward VII, in order to lose weight and to remain in shape for the gastronomic feasts which he loved, regularly visited the spa of Marienbad, and when he passed through Germany, it would have been impolite for him not to arrange a meeting with his nephew William II, though there was little love between them. On their travels the monarchs were accompanied by high officials, and, unavoidably, political subjects were discussed. Most of all, this network of princely relations and connections gave the monarchs a feeling of solidarity against the common danger of revolution, although, as the First World

The innovative Le Bon Marché department store in Paris, circa 1880.

War would show, this feeling of standing together against a common danger did not guarantee peace.

The existence of a monarchy presupposed the existence of a ruling group closely connected with the throne. In the eighteenth century, the princes of continental Europe had become absolute by gaining direct control of the armed forces and by allying themselves with the landowning nobility. This alliance of the monarchs with the army and the landed aristocracy lasted into the twentieth century. Although by that time an elected parliament had become an influential factor in politics, the arbiter of social status remained the court, with its officialdom of ministers, chamberlains, masters of ceremonies—all nobles and mostly descendants of the oldest families. The monarchs kept up their special closeness to the army by insisting on a voice in the promotion of officers. Moreover, the monarchs stood in particularly intimate relation to certain regiments, the guard regiments. These were stationed in or near the palace or capital; in them the heirs of the throne and other princes received their military education. The officers of these regiments, almost exclusively the sons of aristocratic families, were among the few who were on familiar terms with members of the royal families. Thus, in the monarchy a landed aristocracy with military values and a military code of honor continued to set the social standard.

The eminence of a landed aristocracy, which had been justified by the economic and political conditions of previous centuries, seemed an anomaly in the twentieth century, when industry and commerce became dominating factors in economic life. The heads of the large banks, the owners and managers of the great industrial enterprises were the creators of the prosperity and power of a nation. But even in those countries in which industrialization was most advanced, agriculture retained an important place in the economy. In many parts of Europe the possessor of a large landed estate was still very wealthy. Although the Dohnas, an old noble family with vast estates in East Prussia, were not as rich as the Krupps, the great armament manufacturers of the Ruhr, they were still among the richest families of Germany. The estates of the Esterházy and Károlyi families in Hungary yielded incomes that permitted the owners to indulge themselves in every luxury resort of Europe. The fabulous wealth of the Russian aristocracy came from agriculture; a Prince Yussupov even as a teenager traveled in his special train through Europe. Moreover, many of the aristocrats had lands from which coal, the most precious raw material of the time, was mined. Lord Derby of the Stanley family in England, the Princes Pless and Henckel-Donnersmarck in Germany, and the Hohenlohes in Bohemia were landowners and industrialists at the same time. Moreover, in France, Italy, and Germany the cultivation of vineyards and the installation of breweries yielded the owners of landed estates an income often equal to that of the great bankers and captains of industry.

There remained tensions, however, between the industrial and agricultural sectors of European society. The less well-situated members of the nobility looked with envy and disdain on the increasing wealth of the bourgeoisie. The owners of smaller industrial enterprises usually retained many of the antiaristocratic views of the early nineteenth century, when the bourgeoisie had been struggling against the Old Regime. Yet between the upper strata of the landed aristocracy and the wealthiest members of the industrial and commercial society there were many links; gradually these two elements came to be joined together in a single ruling group.

A preindustrial, antimodern element persisted in the European society of the early twentieth century. The code of honor of the nobility—its concern for rank and for gentlemanly behavior—the social preeminence of the military profession, and the prestige of the life of leisure, along with a certain contempt for money-making activities—all were characteristic of the period. Symbolic was the importance of the horse in this society. It would be reasonable to assume that in a technical and industrial age the horse, previously important for agriculture, transport, and war, would become obsolete. But horse racing remained the most elegant sport, its great events honored by the presence of royalty. Establishing a stable of racehorses was the surest way for a wealthy man to advance into the upper strata of society. Admission to membership in the jockey clubs, founded for the promotion of horse racing, was a sign of having entered the Upper Ten Thousand, as the ruling group was called. In the armies the guard-cavalry regiments were the most elegant: the blue and red tunics and helmets with drooping horsehair plumes of the English Royal Horse Guards; the black caps with death's heads and fur-trimmed jackets of the Prussian "black" hussars; the light blue coats and the golden froggings of the Austrian imperial chasseurs—these were the uniforms of the cream of the European armies. In all Europe, cavalry regiments were maintained in a strength hardly compatible with the changes in warfare that the technical age required and strategic thinkers envisaged. Soon after the First World War had started, the uselessness of these trappings became obvious: colorful uniforms were replaced by drab gray, horses bred and trained for the cavalry were left behind, and cavalrymen had to fight as foot soldiers.

The Middle Classes

The social group usually considered to have been the driving force in the development of industrial society was the "middle classes." Before the Second Industrial Revolution, this social group was usually united in aims, interests, and beliefs; the Second Industrial Revolution, though chiefly the work of this social group, shattered its unity. The term *middle classes* remains appropriate only if it is understood as comprising that part of the population that belonged neither to the upper strata of society nor to the proletariat.

The lack of coherence and of unity in this social group is reflected in its being frequently divided into an upper middle class and a lower middle class. Before the Second Industrial Revolution, the term *middle classes* was applied to a segment of society whose members possessed economic independence. Merchants, artisans, craftsmen, shop owners—though they might differ in wealth—had a common bond of interests that distinguished them clearly from the other classes of society: they were urban, free, masters of their own business. Industrialization favored concentration and bigness in economic life. Some shop owners or artisans succeeded in adjusting to the times; they developed their business or trade into a small factory or chain stores. Nevertheless, the small family-owned factory, in most countries, was soon changed into a joint-stock company or absorbed by larger companies working in the same field. Moreover, the income of a member of the managerial top echelon, of a director or manager of a large factory or bank, exceeded that of the owner of a small enterprise struggling to remain independent. Together with the best-paid members of the so-called free professions—doctors, lawyers, teachers—the high-level employees of the industrial concerns and of the banks now formed the upper bourgeoisie, and their ambition was to advance to the head of their enterprises and to rise into the ruling group.

Not only had the economic gap widened immensely between the industrial entrepreneurs and managers and the artisans, craftsmen, and shop owners, but the latter group had to struggle for survival against competition from factory-produced goods and department stores. But they did not entirely disappear; over some shops, particularly those of wine merchants or butchers or greengrocers, signs still proclaimed ownership in the same family extending over centuries. One would find relatively prosperous shop owners or artisans chiefly in small towns; in the big cities their existence became increasingly precarious. For a while it seemed that "tossed about between the hope of entering the ranks of the wealthy class, and the fear of being reduced to the state of proletarians or paupers," they would "finally disappear in the face of modern industry"—that had been the prognosis of Marx and Engels in the middle of the nineteenth century— but this view overestimated the rapidity and thoroughness with which modern industry would remove all remnants of preindustrial society. Further, industrialization itself led to the expansion of the lower middle classes.

Industrial life required in increasing numbers what came to be called white-collar workers; they were needed in commerce and factories, but also in public service, in which the economic and demographic growth entailed an expanding bureaucracy; the number of post office and railroad employees, police officers, and administrative officials rose steadily. Similarly, the need grew for doctors, lawyers, and teachers. The increase in demand made these professions so attractive and rewarding that they quickly became overcrowded. As supply outraced demand, wide differences appeared in the financial position within the professional group. The great corporate and criminal lawyers and the renowned medical specialists had very high incomes and certainly belonged to the upper bourgeoisie; many lawyers and doctors, however, had to scrape by on meager earnings.

This emergence of a new lower middle class as a consequence of industrialization can be most clearly and strikingly observed in Germany, where industrialization advanced most suddenly and most rapidly. In 1914, at the time of the outbreak of the First World War, the number of industrial workers exceeded thirteen million, but the number of people who can be considered as belonging to the lower middle classes was almost half as large; among them there were two million white-collar employees and two million low- and middle-rank civil servants.

It is clear that the lower middle classes formed a heterogenous group, widely differing in occupation, income, and social status, easier to define in negative than in positive terms. They were not workers; they had a higher income and, to a certain extent—through fixed salaries, pension rights, etc.—greater economic security. Moreover, they, or at least their children, had the possibility of social mobility.

Until far into the nineteenth century, men engaged in economic activities had no need for higher education. But the new industrial society required highly trained specialists—economists, engineers, chemists—and gradually the educational system in all European countries began to change. There was an improvement in primary education, but the really significant changes took place in the secondary schools and the universities. Secondary schools introduced programs concentrating on natural sciences and modern languages. In the universities, which formerly had served to train a limited number of lawyers, doctors, teachers, and civil servants, emphasis began to shift away from a general education in arts and letters toward scientific training and technical instruction; technical colleges were founded; like the universities, they received the right to grant higher degrees. Philosophers and historians no longer dominated the universities, as they

Members of a women's boating club from Royal Holloway College, London, strike a proud pose (1890s).

had in the early and middle decades of the nineteenth century; the admired leaders of academic life were the great scientific discoverers—men like Helmholtz, Pasteur, Lister.

The wealthy upper group of the leaders of industrial and commercial life was small, and entry in their circle was difficult, yet not impossible. It could be gained through technical expertise—in chemistry and physics, in economics, in engineering. The best, almost the only, means for economic and social advancement was the possession of special knowledge and techniques for which the degree of a university or a technical college was prerequisite. This was the road on which middle-class parents wanted their sons to proceed. It was a difficult road, however, because it demanded some financial resources to send their sons to preparatory schools and to maintain them during their years of university study. Despite the value of the university degree, the number of those who enjoyed a higher education remained small; statistics from the year 1913 show that in the various countries of Europe before the First World War the number of university students among each *ten thousand* of the population ranged between seven and eleven.

We have focused here on the professional and educational opportunities for middle-class *men* because women, even from the best families, rarely enjoyed similar prospects for advancement. Although by the last quarter of the nineteenth century many European nations were providing some free primary education for girls, they resisted opening secondary and advanced education to women on the ground that the professions accessed by such training belonged to the male domain. Fully aware that without better education their chances of making significant contributions to society would be forever limited to arenas like charity work, women from professional families began fighting for the right to attend secondary schools and universities along with their brothers. Their struggle was hindered by the fact that many women agreed with the conventional wisdom that too much education was "bad" for females because it would render them unfit for their traditional roles as wives and mothers. In the Catholic countries, where middle- and upper-class girls were generally educated by nuns, efforts to enroll young women in the public secondary schools were perceived as anticlerical, as in part they were.

Despite these impediments, some signal successes were achieved. After privately training girls to pass university exams taken by men, the English educational reformer Emily Davies (1830–1921) managed to get women's colleges opened at Cambridge University. (However, female students at Cambridge, and later at Oxford, were not allowed actually to take degrees at these universities until after World War I.) The state of Baden in Germany established that nation's first academic high school for girls in 1893, while the University of Baden became the first German university to admit women in 1900. The prestigious Friedrich-Wilhelm University in Berlin followed suit in 1908, and by 1914 there were 4,126 women studying in German universities. Women were admitted to Russian universities in 1876, but then banned from 1881 to 1905 because a woman had been involved in the assassination of Tsar Alexander II in 1881. France opened its public secondary schools to girls in the 1890s but restricted them to non-university-preparatory curricula, with the result that only the graduates of the country's very few private preparatory schools could go on to university studies. In 1913 there were 4,254 women enrolled in French universities, compared with 37,783 men. Thus, if the percentage of university students relative to the general population was low in all European countries, it was especially low for women.

Women found it particularly hard to gain admission to Europe's medical schools since even men who believed that ladies were capable of doing advanced university work drew the line at medicine. This field, they insisted, belonged exclusively to the male preserve. F. D. Maurice, a liberal English clergyman who had helped found colleges for women, insisted that there was no point in educating women in fields for which neither nature nor God had suited them. As he put the matter, "The more pains we take to call forth and employ the faculties which belong characteristically to each sex, the less it will be intruding upon the province which, not the convention of the world, but the will of God assigned to the other." Divine will notwithstanding, a few women managed to force their way into medical classes in Britain, France, and Spain in the last decades of the nineteenth century, though they were not allowed to take degrees. In Spain, male students threw mud at the first female medical students, and in France, the first woman who tried to become an intern was burned in effigy by her classmates. By the eve of the First World War, however, women were represented (albeit still underrepresented) in the classes of most major European medical schools, with Russia boasting the largest number owing to its chronic shortage of doctors.

THE WANING OF POLITICAL CONSENSUS

The decline of liberalism not only was of importance for those who had believed in the liberal tenets but also implied a change in the climate of political thought. Certainly liberalism had never exerted an uncontested rule over the minds of the people of the nineteenth century, but the conservative attitude had been mainly defensive, insisting on the importance of traditional values and the maintenance of a hierarchical social order. Certain basic liberal ideas—the necessity of a constitution, the representation of the people by a legislative body, and a guarantee of fundamental individual rights—had been accepted also by the conservatives. The extent to which a basic liberal outlook had become an ingredient of all political thinking could still be seen at the end of the nineteenth and the beginning of the twentieth century when the condemnation of Captain Alfred Dreyfus in France in secret military court proceedings in the 1890s and, in the following decade, the execution of the anarchist Francisco Ferrer in Spain without sufficient proof of his participation in revolutionary activities aroused excitement and indignation all over the Western world.

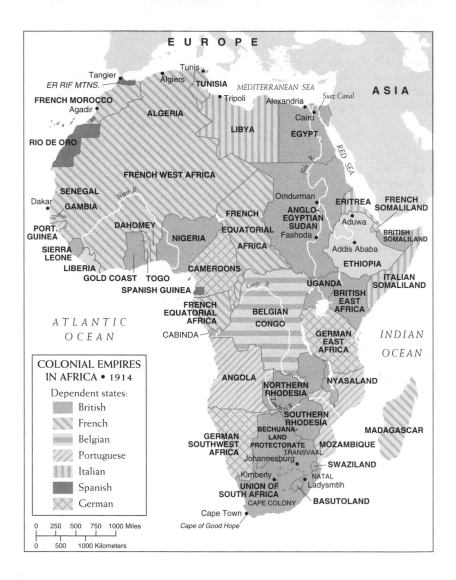

EUROPE

Tangier

ER RIF MTNS.

FRENCH MOROCCO
Agadir

RIO DE ORO

Tunis

Algiers

TUNISIA   MEDITERRANEAN SEA

Tripoli   Alexandria   Suez Canal

ALGERIA

LIBYA   Cairo

EGYPT

ASIA

RED SEA

FRENCH WEST AFRICA

Niger R.

SENEGAL

Dakar   GAMBIA

PORT.
GUINEA

SIERRA
LEONE

LIBERIA

DAHOMEY

GOLD COAST   TOGO

SPANISH GUINEA

NIGERIA

FRENCH
EQUATORIAL
AFRICA

Omdurman

ANGLO-
EGYPTIAN
SUDAN
Fashoda

ERITREA   FRENCH
            SOMALILAND

Aduwa

BRITISH
SOMALILAND

Addis Ababa

ETHIOPIA

CAMEROONS

FRENCH
EQUATORIAL
AFRICA

CABINDA

Congo R.

BELGIAN
CONGO

UGANDA

ITALIAN
SOMALILAND

BRITISH
EAST
AFRICA

ATLANTIC
OCEAN

GERMAN
EAST
AFRICA

INDIAN

OCEAN

COLONIAL EMPIRES
IN AFRICA • 1914

Dependent states:

British

French

Belgian

Portuguese

Italian

Spanish

German

ANGOLA

Zambezi R.

GERMAN
SOUTHWEST
AFRICA

NORTHERN
RHODESIA

SOUTHERN
RHODESIA

BECHUANA-
LAND
PROTECTORATE

Johannesburg

Kimberly

UNION OF
SOUTH AFRICA

CAPE COLONY

Cape Town

Cape of Good Hope

NYASALAND

MADAGASCAR

MOZAMBIQUE

TRANSVAAL

SWAZILAND

NATAL
Ladysmtih

BASUTOLAND

0   250   500   750   1000 Miles

0   500   1000 Kilometers

A weakening of liberal beliefs did not yet find expression in direct doubts or in direct rejection of basic liberal tenets, but it became noticeable in hesitations and tensions about the consequences of liberalism for practical politics. We have mentioned already that in the last quarter of the nineteenth century, in order to counter the advantages inherent in Britain's industrial headstart, the European powers converted to protectionism and thereby began to abandon the liberal free trade doctrine.

Another fundamental economic doctrine of liberalism was noninterference of the state in economic life, but here again the maintenance of a principle was in conflict with the situation and the interests existing in the new industrial society. There were humanitarian reasons that demanded government action for the maintenance of hygienic standards in factories, limitation of working hours, protection of women and children against exploitation—in short, an active role of the state in the regulation of industrial life. If such demands might appear to be in the interest of the workers, the industrial leaders were no less eager for government action: they endorsed protective tariffs; they wanted the state to prohibit strikes or at least to protect strikebreakers. The leaders of heavy industry were interested in government contracts for the production of guns and warships. Moreover, the great armament concerns—Krupp in Germany, Schneider-Creusot in France, Skoda in Austria—were anxious to sell their goods all over the world and for this kind of business frequently needed the support of their governments. The frontiers between economics and politics became increasingly blurred.

The main shock to the liberal tenets, however, was administered by the rise of socialism, with its rejection of a free competitive economy and its threat of revolution. If an underlying trend in the liberal age had been extension of

The white rulers administer justice to their black subjects, the German Cameroons, 1911.

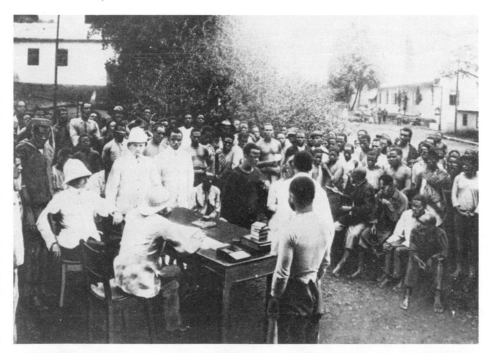

suffrage and widening democratization, questions arose whether this kind of policy might not lead to the suppression of that right which formed the point of departure and the paramount aim of all liberal thought: freedom of the individual. Although the movements for removing inequalities in voting and for universal suffrage did not stop, they slowed down, and there was little inclination to limit the powers of the upper houses of parliaments, whose members generally gained their seats either by heredity or by weighted elections in which the wealthier classes preserved control. The march of democracy seemed to falter.

What changed the political climate at the end of the nineteenth century was not only the weakening of the hold of liberal ideas but even more the emergence of new ideas contradictory to basic liberal notions. It has been said that the liberals committed a fatal sin by accepting and promoting imperialism. Of course, the notion that industrialists and bankers had the right to pursue and to extend their business all over the globe corresponded to the liberal notions of free trade, but the form this economic expansion took—colonialism and market control in less developed countries—created a situation in which the Europeans became a superior class above the indigenous peoples whose fate they controlled. This, in itself, represented a violation of the liberal notion of equality or equal dignity of rational man. It was unavoidable that a rationalization of this elitist attitude was undertaken. The crucial elements in this process of rationalization were Social Darwinism and racism. Darwin was interpreted to have suggested that it was not only natural but almost desirable that the stronger rule over the weaker. Racism provided justification for the rule of white Europeans over the black, brown, and yellow populations of the globe—the "lesser breeds" as Kipling defined them.

The gaping moral chasm between high-sounding claims of "elevating" subject peoples and the grim realities of their exploitation was perhaps most brutally revealed in the Congo, where Belgium's King Leopold II seized a huge territory to be plundered for its ivory and (later) rubber. Advertising his personal fiefdom as a model of enlightened administration, Leopold in fact presided over an enterprise whose genocidal cruelty, when its full extent was exposed, shocked the conscience of the Western world. Joseph Conrad's *Heart of Darkness* (1902), that haunting account of "civilized" man run amok, was fittingly set in Leopold's Congo.

Racist doctrine not only served to exculpate imperialist expansion but also began to make an impact in the domestic policy of the various European countries. Racism often took the form of anti-Semitism. Indeed, anti-Semitism, not as the social attitude of individuals but as a political movement, gained a certain mass appeal in these years. Racism also underlay the acceptance of the notion that birth or race made one segment of society superior to others; this view rationalized the exclusion of large groups—like the workers—from the right to participate in government. Differences in social status were believed to follow from natural selection, from having "better blood"; the existence of a ruling group, of an elite, in every society was not an accident but a natural necessity.

These ideas were cultivated by small groups. As presented in the novels of Maurras and Barrès, two of the most widely read French writers of this time, for example, they seemed mainly to imply an aesthetic disdain of the mass culture of the big cities. Their emergence, however, was an ominous sign of the reawakening of an authoritarianism, no longer moderated by tradition and religion as in the age of absolutism, and of contempt for the life of individuals belonging to another race or a lower class who were judged to be of little value.

As racism developed and became wedded to nationalism, it endowed nationalism with an explosive and aggressive character. In the first half of the nineteenth century, the expression of nationalism and the demands of national unification were part of a broad liberal political program; it was assumed that united by their belief in the same human values, the various nation-states would live harmoniously together as one great family. But with the weakening of the faith in liberalism and democratization, nationalism served to emphasize what was unique and different in each nation. *Emergence of nationalism*

The situation was paradoxical. Europe dominated the world more than ever before or ever after. But the forces that held European society together had become increasingly tenuous. The mass of the working population had no part

A Congolese native being strangled in the coils of King Leopold II's vicious rubber empire, *Punch* magazine, 1906.

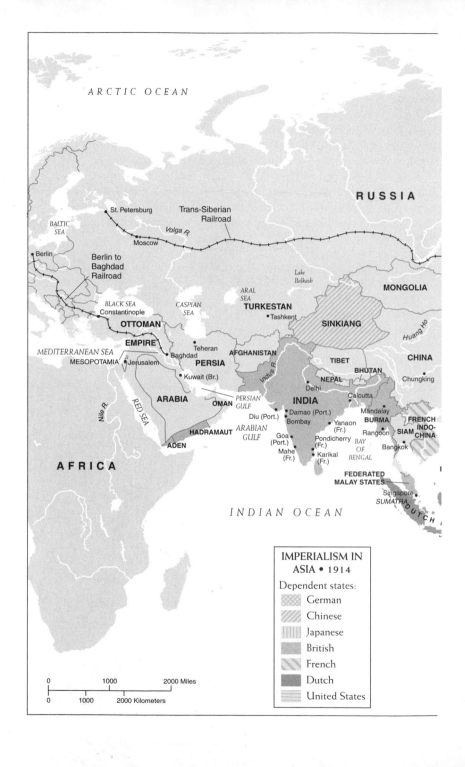

ARCTIC OCEAN

RUSSIA

St. Petersburg   Trans-Siberian
Railroad

BALTIC
SEA   Volga R.

Moscow

Berlin   Berlin to
          Baghdad
          Railroad

Lake
Balkash

ARAL
SEA

MONGOLIA

BLACK SEA   CASPIAN   TURKESTAN
Constantinople   SEA   •Tashkent

SINKIANG

OTTOMAN

Huang Ho

EMPIRE   •Teheran
MEDITERRANEAN SEA   Baghdad   AFGHANISTAN   TIBET   CHINA
MESOPOTAMIA   •Jerusalem   PERSIA   BHUTAN
                                          NEPAL Chungking
            •Kuwait (Br.)   Indus R.
                              Delhi
ARABIA   PERSIAN   INDIA   Calcutta
OMAN   GULF
                  Diu (Port.) •Damao (Port.)   Mandalay
                    Bombay •Yanaon   BURMA   FRENCH
HADRAMAUT ARABIAN   (Fr.)   INDO-
                  GULF   Goa   Pondicherry Rangoon SIAM CHINA
ADEN   (Port.) (Fr.) BAY   Bangkok
                  Mahe •Karikal OF
                  (Fr.)   (Fr.) BENGAL

Nile R.
RED SEA

AFRICA

FEDERATED
MALAY STATES

INDIAN OCEAN

Singapore
SUMATRA

IMPERIALISM IN
ASIA • 1914

Dependent states:

German

Chinese

Japanese

British

French

Dutch

United States

0   1000   2000 Miles

0   1000   2000 Kilometers

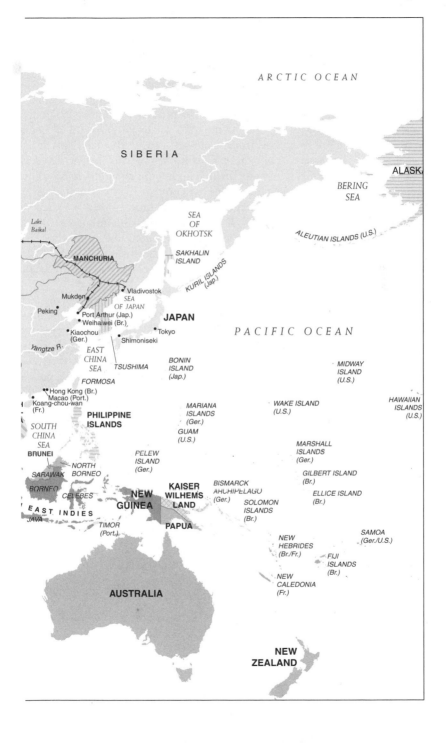

in the government and believed in an internationalism encompassing the whole world and extinguishing all national boundaries. At the other end of the social hierarchy, royalty and aristocracy still formed a supranational element united by personal relationships and a common style of life. But the most important constituents in the social life of the period, the industrial and commercial groups, became more and more closely tied to the nation-state and placed their hopes on its strength and on its support in the competition against others. This development formed the basis for the picture of the interconnection between domestic and foreign policy that Lenin presented in his famous pamphlet *Imperialism, the Highest Stage of Capitalism.* According to Lenin, the industrial and financial forces in each country were united in one large combine, and the few men at its head determined the foreign policy of the nation. After the undiscovered and unexplored areas of the world had been divided among the great powers, a period of world wars was inevitable because the states would clash with one another in their efforts to increase their markets and stave off economic crises at home.

It was a picture that was widely overdrawn. Neither did Lenin's view of the relation of business and government—business as commanding the governments—correspond to reality; frequently it was the reverse, the government ordering business to make investments to justify political demands. Nor was the business of one country always opposed to the business of another country; the trend toward a supranational cooperation of economic corporations was already noticeable in the period before the First World War. But even if the clash among the European powers was not unavoidable, international tension and the possibility of war formed an integral element of the political atmosphere of Europe at the beginning of the twentieth century.

CHAPTER 2

Politics and Society, 1890–1914

GENERALIZATIONS IN HISTORY are dangerous. When closely examined, historical events and developments almost invariably reveal aspects that are individual and unique. For a true picture of the past, a grasp of the general pattern of development must be combined with an understanding of the individual features that in each country modified the pattern and gave to each nation's history its particular shape. Thus, after a broad survey of the factors determining the course of European history at the beginning of the twentieth century, we now turn our attention to the developments in the individual European nations. In their constitutional developments, the Western European states differed decisively from those in Central and Eastern Europe. In Western Europe, elected parliaments determined the character of the governments and the course of their policies. By contrast, the monarchs in the Central and Eastern European great power states—Germany, Austria-Hungary, and Russia—had strong policy-making influence, though the extent of that influence and the constitutional arrangements in these countries differed.

GREAT BRITAIN

From the Victorian to the Edwardian Age

Of the great powers, Great Britain had advanced furthest in democratic evolution and in industrialization. Having made progress while preserving continuity, Britain gave the impression of remarkable political and social stability. The "miracle of its constitution"—the British two-party system, British parliamentarianism—seemed to offer an example of how the problems and tensions of the twentieth century could be overcome.

Yet at the close of the nineteenth century even in Britain one epoch seemed to come to an end and a new one to begin. Queen Victoria died in 1901. She was succeeded by her son King Edward VII (ruled 1901–1910). No more striking contrast can be imagined than that between the strict and dignified queen and her flamboyant heir. Edward indulged in all the pleasures of a gilded society. He was devoted to beautiful women and good food. In his youth he gambled; in later years he played bridge from afternoon until late at night during his weekend visits to the country houses of the British rich. He had a stable of racehorses, and he was also a motorist. Together with his wife, Queen Alexandra, one of the great beauties of the age, the king was the recognized social leader of an ostentatiously opulent and luxurious society.

The sudden change from the dignified and aloof court of Victoria to the pleasure-loving and indulgent court of Edward VII had the effect not of impairing the position of the monarchy but of strengthening it. During Victoria's reign the bourgeoisie through hard work—slowly and steadily—had transformed Great Britain into the leading industrial country of the world. By the turn of the century this work was done and its fruits could be enjoyed. Edward was the perfect representative of this stage of British economic development, and he was extremely popular.

With the wisdom of hindsight it is easy to see that the British economic position in the first decade of the twentieth century was not as brilliant as it appeared. In the last quarter of the nineteenth century the tempo of British economic development had slowed down. Between 1885 and 1913, the rate of increase in Britain's industrial production was 2.11 percent, while Germany's increased by 4.5 percent and that of the United States by 5.2 percent. The actual output of steel, iron, and coal, the chief sources of Britain's strength as an industrial and commercial power, was still very high. But Great Britain was no longer the leading producer of these goods. By 1906 it had been overtaken by the United States in the production of steel, iron, and coal and by Germany in the production of steel. Similarly, in the development of innovations connected with electricity, the motorcar, and chemicals Britain lagged behind Germany and the United States. Besides, these two countries possessed more modern industrial equipment than Great Britain. Other aspects of economic life were more favorable. In the shipping industry, in textile production, and as a center of trade Britain remained the leading power. Above all, during its period of economic growth, Britain had made immense investments in foreign countries, which now paid off and generated new investment possibilities. Thus, it was the world's greatest capital market. Its banks enjoyed enormous prestige. The gold standard and the pound were almost synonymous. But Britain did not produce as much as it imported, although the receipts from its foreign investments concealed this deficit in the balance of trade. The basis for the economic difficulties it had to face after the First World War, and still more threateningly after the Second World War, had already been laid.

The golden glimmer of the Edwardian era was an evening glow, but few were aware of this. To most people, London was the capital of the world in the decades before the First World War, the embodiment of a luxurious style of life unequaled since the Roman Empire. The harmoniousness of the ruling group confirmed this impression of stable prosperity. Conflicts between the attitudes of a feudal and authoritarian military class and that of a bourgeois society did not exist in Great Britain. The British people had successfully fought against the standing army, which they viewed as an instrument of princely absolutism, and their insular position made conscription unnecessary. Moreover, the economic basis of a military caste—agriculture—had been almost eliminated. If in the first half of the nineteenth century the repeal of the corn laws and the establishment of free trade had signified the victory of the industrial and commercial classes over agricultural interests, this development was completed by the agricultural crisis of the 1880s. In a country unprotected by tariffs, competition against grain imported from Russia or America became impossible; the cultivation of grain was virtually abandoned, and the soil was used for grazing, dairy farming, or fruit farming. But the landowners remained wealthy. Many found that their soil was rich in coal; industrial settlements sprang up on their land, and they drew large incomes from rents. Landowners frequently became involved in industrial and financial activities. The amalgamation of the rising classes of businessmen with the old aristocratic ruling group represented no problem in Britain: "While business men were becoming peers, peers were becoming business men, so that when the new rich reached the Upper House they found themselves on familiar ground."[1]

The Politics of the Ruling Class

Politics mirrored this homogeneity of the ruling class. Although strife between the Unionists, as the Conservatives were officially named, and the Liberals was quite vehement, the social composition of the leadership in each of the parties was very much alike. After William Gladstone's resignation in 1894 and the short-lived Liberal government under Lord Rosebery, the Conservatives held power for ten years, from 1895 to 1905: until 1902 the Marquess of Salisbury (1830–1903) was prime minister; from 1902 to 1905 Salisbury's nephew Arthur Balfour (1848–1930). In both parties, descendants of the aristocratic families who had ruled Britain in previous centuries continued to be prominent. Salisbury and Balfour were Cecils; Greys and Ponsonbys were to be found on the councils of the Liberals. The leadership of both parties included aristocrats with industrial and financial connections, like the Liberal Rosebery, who was married to a Rothschild, and the Conservative earl of Derby, who had large coal mine holdings. In both parties, businessmen played significant roles. Conservative and Liberal politicians enjoyed the same strictly classical education. Attendance at one of the great public schools—Eton, Harrow, Rugby—followed by Oxford or Cambridge was the usual background for a political career and almost a requirement for it; prominence in the debating society of one of the two universities marked a young man for political success. In this period, Oxford's Balliol College was the breeding ground of statesmen. Its master, Benjamin Jowett, the translator of Plato, attracted the most brilliant minds to his college and infused them with the idea that public service was the duty of the social elite.

The British ruling class had no doubt of the nation's right to rule over other peoples, to maintain the empire, and to continue imperial expansion despite the increasing competition of other states. The most important leaders of both parties were conscious imperialists. The Conservative government of Salisbury used the occasion of Queen Victoria's Diamond Jubilee in 1897 to glorify Britain's world-spanning empire. But Liberals like Rosebery and Haldane were equally enthusiastic advocates of Britain's imperial role. Conservatives might be more concerned with maintaining their nation as the world's foremost power, while Liberals might emphasize its mission of guiding the colonial peoples to self-government and the other blessings of British society, but leaders of both parties were firmly resolved not to be content with what Britain possessed and to compete actively for the African and Asian lands that were up for grabs.

This was the time when the visionary dream of a British Empire in Africa reaching from the Cape to Cairo made its impact on British policy. The first consequence was a serious clash between the British and the French. Seeking

The colonial mission led by France's Colonel Marchand, whose forces almost came to blows with the British at Fashoda in 1898.

to enlarge their African holdings, the French had organized two expeditions, one starting from Ethiopia in the east and moving west, the other moving from Lake Chad to the east. They were to meet in the upper Nile Valley and there establish the French claim to this area, the possession of which would link French Somaliland in the east with the French colonies of Algeria in the north and Senegal in the west. This empire would cut straight across the continuous territory stretching from the Cape to Cairo that was sought by the British. Hence they quickly decided on countermeasures. They ordered General Herbert Kitchener (1850–1916) to move up the Nile into the Sudan, which, since the defeat of General Gordon in 1885, had remained in the control of the Mahdi. In 1898 the army of the Mahdi was overcome in two battles, at the Atbara River (April 8) and at Omdurman (September 2), and "the whole mass of the dervishes dissolved into fragments and into particles and streamed away into the fantastic mirages of the desert," according to a description of the Battle of Omdurman by a participant, the young supernumerary lieutenant Winston Churchill. Kitchener moved quickly ahead along the upper Nile, for the French expedition under Colonel Jean Baptiste Marchand, coming from the west, had reached Fashoda, in the southeastern Sudan, and had planted a French flag there on July 10, 1898. With a few of his troops Kitchener sailed up the Nile, arriving at Fashoda on September 18. He asked Marchand to withdraw; Marchand refused. Kitchener and Marchand conferred and agreed to await the decision of their home governments; then they drank whiskey and soda together. Public opinion in Great Britain was so enraged by the French audacity in placing obstacles in the path of the British imperial plans that even if the government had wanted to make concessions, it could not have done so. The French were faced with the alternative of going to war against Great Britain or giving in. On November 3 the French government decided to surrender and ordered the unconditional evacuation of Fashoda.

The Labor Movement and Social Reform

The Diamond Jubilee of Queen Victoria in 1897 and Omdurman and Fashoda in 1898 represented the apex of British imperial power. Nevertheless, the coherence of society, the grasp of the ruling classes over the mass of the nation, was less firm and secure than one might have expected as a result of the unbroken success of British policy in the nineteenth century. Although Great Britain had passed the worst hardships and sufferings that accompanied industrialization in its early stages, misery among the masses of the working population was still great. The sacrifice of agriculture to industry, accelerated by a severe agricultural crisis in the 1880s, had forced small farmers and farmhands to migrate to the cities, thus increasing the number of unskilled workers. Housing conditions in the great industrial centers were bad. In the East End of London, families of eight or ten people often lived in one room.

From the middle of the 1890s to the outbreak of the First World War no severe economic crisis occurred in Great Britain. But wages, which had been steadily rising until the turn of the century, then began to stagnate—while prices increased. Moreover, the shadow of unemployment hovered perpetually over the industrial workers. At the end of their lives they were almost unavoidably dependent on charity and the very insufficient provisions of the Poor Law. The trade unions, which supplied almost the only protection the workers had, were handicapped by their limited financial means, and their rights were not clearly determined. Hence a new, more militant spirit arose in the trade unions: The conviction grew that a change of the economic system to provide collective ownership and control over production, distribution and exchange was necessary and that to effect this change, labor had to enter the political arena as an independent force. The driving personality in the new movement was James Keir Hardie (1856–1915), a Scottish miner and trade union organizer. Whereas previously trade union men elected to Parliament had joined the Liberals, Keir Hardie and his friends had succeeded by 1900 in persuading the trade unions to finance and to support at the forthcoming elections a slate of candidates who would represent the interests of the workers in Parliament. The Labor Party, then called the Labor Representation Committee, had come into life.

This development was helped by a movement among middle-class British intellectuals whose social consciences were deeply stirred by the contrast between the wealth of the ruling group and the misery of the workers. Calling themselves Fabians after the Roman dictator Fabius, whom they admired because he had waited patiently for the right moment but then had struck hard, the influential members of this movement were rather disparate. Among them were reform-minded radicals like Annie Besant, successful literary figures like the novelist H. G. Wells, and George Bernard Shaw, at that time not yet a dramatist but a music and literary critic, and scholars like the political scientist Graham Wallas. But the guiding spirit was that of a husband and wife whose closeness of aims is well testified to by the fact that they are usually named together as the Webbs. Sidney Webb (1859–1947) began as a civil servant but soon decided to devote himself to the problems of industrial society. Beatrice Webb (1858–1943) was a woman of great beauty from a socially prominent family who had a sensitive social conscience. From sporadic welfare activities, in which she had engaged as a young woman, she went forward to serious scientific study of social problems and became one of the great pioneers in the field of social reform in industrial society. One of the Webbs' most lasting achievements was the founding of the London School of Economics, later a division of the University of London, which has been particularly devoted to the investigation of political and social problems in the modern world. The Fabians believed that the march of modern society was irrevocably set toward greater democratization. But democratization could be complete only if it was economic as well as political. And economic democratization meant socialization: the public authorities—local, regional, or central—were to have the right to organize basic industries and to determine how capital income would be used. Fabianism was socialism but not Marxism. It did not presuppose a revolution that would give all power to one class, the proletariat, and it did not advocate the end of the national state.

For a while the Fabians tried to convince the leaders of the existing political parties that they ought to adopt the Fabian program. Sidney Webb, who disapproved of spending money on clothes or jewels, permitted Beatrice to buy a new dress if doing so might make political leaders willing to listen to the Fabian program. But when both Conservative and Liberal leaders proved unresponsive, some of the Fabians turned to the idea of establishing a third party, which would realize socialism in Britain. They joined forces with Keir Hardie's Labor Representation Committee, and their ideas soon began to dominate the young Labor Party. This alliance has remained in force in the Labor Party ever since, but by the late twentieth century, with the advent of Tony Blair's "New Labor," the trade unionist influence weakened considerably.

Both the Conservatives and the Liberals were aware that the founding of an independent Labor Party was a threat to the two-party system. They recognized that they had to make a greater effort to satisfy the demands of the laboring classes. Ever since Disraeli had coined the slogan "Tory Democracy," a wing of the Conservative Party had placed emphasis on social reform. This movement received new impetus when in 1886 Joseph Chamberlain (1836–1914), with a group of followers, broke with Gladstone and the Liberals and joined the Conservatives. Chamberlain, coming from industrial Birmingham, had made a name for himself as an advocate of radical reforms. As lord mayor of Birmingham he had introduced "municipal socialism"; he had improved public services and made them less expensive by placing streetcars, street lighting, and public utilities under the administration of the city government. Chamberlain had also modernized party politics by creating wards with party organizers who would get the masses to the polls. For a politician of this outlook "Conservative" seemed hardly the right label, and following his alliance with the Conservatives, they were officially named Unionists.

A similar tendency toward social reform could be observed in the Liberal Party. Nonconformists and radicals had always formed a strong element in this party. Such Liberals felt that leaders like Rosebery and the imperialists did not represent the true Liberal tradition, and many thought they ought to oppose the imperial expansionism which oppressed other peoples. They believed that the Liberal Party ought to concentrate on domestic problems and work toward the solution of the Irish question by seeking to obtain for Ireland its own government and parliament, home rule. The members of this group were sometimes called Little Englanders because of their doubts about the value of the empire. Their most respected leader, Sir Henry Campbell-Bannerman (1836–1908), had held high government office under Gladstone and was regarded as Gladstone's authentic heir, the man who would continue his reform policy. Among this group a new leader arose in a young lawyer and brilliant orator from Wales, David Lloyd George (1863–1945), whose political passion was fired by the misery which he saw among the Welsh mine workers.

Imperialism versus Domestic Reform

The tensions between the imperialists and the domestic reformers were sharpened by Britain's conflict with the Boer republics in South Africa. In Salisbury's government Joseph Chamberlain had become secretary for the colonies. Partly because he saw little chance to move his Conservative colleagues toward social reform and partly because of the demands of his office, Chamberlain turned his great energies to the realization of an empire extending from the Cape to Cairo. French ambitions for the upper Nile Valley had been thwarted at Fashoda, but Transvaal and the Orange Free State, the independent Boer republics in southern Africa, still remained a barrier to these plans. A conflict between these independent states and Great Britain seemed unavoidable; its outbreak was accelerated by the discovery of gold in the Transvaal. The Boers feared that the immigrants streaming to the Transvaal in search of quick riches would soon outnumber them, limiting Boer political influence, and, since most of the immigrants (known as Uitlanders) were British, that they might decide to make the Boer republics part of the British Empire. There is no doubt that Cecil Rhodes, the dominating figure in the British Cape Colony, aimed at an absorption of the Boer republics by the empire. He believed that the unrest created by the tension between Boers and Uitlanders might provide the opportune moment. In 1896 he organized an invasion by a small force of 470 men under the leadership of Dr. Leander Starr Jameson, an adventurer. The expectation was that the march of this force into the interior of the Transvaal would give the signal for a rebellion in Johannesburg by the Uitlanders against the Boers. But no such upheaval occurred; Jameson and his men were quickly defeated and surrendered to the Boers. Rhodes's responsibility for the raid was incontestable, and he was forced to resign as prime minister of the Cape Colony. But the much-discussed question was whether Chamberlain, the British colonial secretary, had previous knowledge of the raid. The British government immediately declined all responsibility for the raid, and a committee of the House of Commons gave Chamberlain a clean bill of health. But doubts about Chamberlain's role were never entirely removed, and recent investigations have revealed that he knew much more about what was planned than he admitted at the time.

People outside England had no doubt that the Jameson Raid was a British defeat. The German emperor, William II, sent a telegram to the president of the Transvaal republic, Paul Kruger, congratulating him upon his success "in restoring peace and in maintaining the independence of the country against attacks from without." This message, which rubbed salt in Britain's wounds, may have been unwise politically, but in giving vent to his indignation about British ruthlessness, William expressed the feelings not only of the German nation but of all the European continent. The Jameson Raid and the telegram of the German emperor made war between the Boers and Great Britain almost certain. To the British, conquest of the Boer republics had become a matter of prestige. On the other hand, the raid confirmed the Boers in their fear of the influence of the immigrants, while at the same time the public acknowledgment of the Boers' right to independence encouraged them to resist the British. Hence they continued their discriminatory policy against the Uitlanders, while the British took up the cause of these new immigrants and insisted that they should receive the right to vote. When negotiations proved fruitless, Britain sent troop reinforcements to the Cape Colony, and on the demand of the Boers for withdrawal of these troops, the British cut off all discussion. In October 1899 war broke out between the Boer republics (Transvaal and the Orange Free State) and the British.

The Boer War followed a pattern common to many colonial wars. The resistance of the indigenous forces proved to be more effective than had been expected, and initially the British had severe losses. But when the full force of the British was brought into play, the difference in strength proved decisive. Where the Boer War differed from most other colonial engagements was in the severity of the reverses suffered by the invading British forces, which were first repulsed, then encircled at Ladysmith and Kimberley and there besieged. They were relieved only at the end of February 1900, after large reinforcements from England had arrived and a change in command had taken place. The British offensive ended with the conquest and annexation of the Transvaal in September 1900. But military action continued for another year and a half. The Boers engaged in guerrilla warfare, and Kitchener, the British commander, proceeded against them ruthlessly, burning the farms of Boer guerrillas and interning the women and children of Boer soldiers in specially constructed camps. Finally, on May 31, 1902, a peace treaty was signed in which the Boers acknowledged British sovereignty.

The Boer War placed unexpected demands on the British people. Since the colonial army was not sufficiently large, troops had to be sent from England; three hundred fifty thousand men were needed to subdue sixty thousand Boers. In England families grew increasingly anxious over the fate of relatives and friends whose lives had been unexpectedly endangered by a colonial war. Moreover, all over Europe there was an outburst of fury against Great Britain. This sudden revelation of their unpopularity was a great surprise to the British, and although the European governments did not take any common action against them, they began to fear that their country might be confronted by a combination of all the continental powers. Thereafter British foreign policy gradually began to veer away from "splendid isolation" and into an acceptance of cooperation with other states. The Boer War had shown the obsoleteness and clumsiness

Le Petit Journal

Le Petit Journal
Le Supplément Illustré

SUPPLÉMENT ILLUSTRÉ
Huit pages CINQ centimes

ABONNEMENTS

Dixième année

DIMANCHE 19 NOVEMBRE 1899

Numéro 470

LE LION ANGLAIS ET LE TAUREAU BOER

A French cartoon showing the British lion being butted by a Boer bull with the head of Afrikaner President Paul Krueger, 1899.

of British military organization and raised serious doubts about the aims of British policy and the efficiency of British political processes.

Was the imperial expansion worth the loss of life and the expenditure of money exacted by the Boer War? At first, the opponents of the policy that had led to war were shouted down and socially boycotted. But as the conflict dragged on, the politicians who had resisted the wave of imperialist enthusiasm—men like Campbell-Bannerman and Lloyd George—gained in political stature. They found increasing support for their arguments that attention should be focused on domestic problems. Events confirmed the view that internal tensions were reaching a dangerous state. The newly militant trade unions had encountered fierce resistance by employers and had retaliated with local strikes against the employment of "free," or nonunion, labor. The tenseness of this situation was aggravated by the Taff Vale decision (1901), which asserted that a trade union was financially liable for damage caused by all strikes in which its members took part. Indignation among the working population was immense because the decision underlined the precarious position of the trade unions and the helplessness of the working classes. The government also lost popularity as a result of the measures it instituted for reform in education. The need for such reform was generally recognized. Great Britain had only a limited number of elementary schools maintained by the state—that is, by the counties and towns. More than half the children of England and Wales received their elementary education at voluntary schools that were unable to maintain reasonable standards. The Education Act of 1902 placed all these schools under county and town control so that they were forced to adhere to recognized standards; if necessary, they would receive financial support from local taxes. The measure undoubtedly represented a great improvement in English education. But because it implied that tax money would be used to support Anglican and Roman Catholic schools, it aroused the vehement opposition of an important segment of the British population, the nonconformists.

The Triumph of the Liberal Party

The final cause for the end of ten years of Conservative rule was a split among the Conservatives themselves. Joseph Chamberlain had not abandoned his original radicalism when he turned from internal reforms to imperial expansion. On the contrary, he regarded a resolute imperial policy as a means for improving the lot of the masses. He believed that his country's continued economic prosperity depended on the expansion of opportunities to emigrate to the colonies. He advocated protective tariffs that would limit foreign competition in the British market and, by giving preferences to the British colonies, would tie the empire together as a great economic unit. To promote these aims, Chamberlain organized the Tariff Reform League, and to devote himself to this campaign, he left the government. In Prime Minister Balfour's view, British public opinion was not ready to accept protective tariffs. In a country dependent on the importation of agricultural goods the first result of protection would be an increase in the price of food, which would place another burden on the masses. Split over the tariff question, the Conservatives seemed to lack an economic policy, while the Liberals adhered to the hallowed tradition of free trade. Unable to control his own party, Balfour resigned in December 1905, and the Liberals took over. Campbell-Bannerman became prime minister, not without the displeasure of the imperialist elements in his own party. But he reconciled them by giving them strong representation in the cabinet. Sir Edward Grey (1862–1933) became foreign secretary; Herbert Asquith (1852–1928), chancellor of the exchequer; and Haldane, secretary of state for war. The radical wing of the reformers was also well represented. Lloyd George became president of the Board of Trade, and John Burns (1858–1943), president of the Local Government Board. The new government was an incongruous mixture of imperialists and social reformers. But at this time Great Britain was still prosperous enough to attempt simultaneously to maintain a powerful position in foreign affairs and to undertake reforms at home. In the elections of January 1906 the Liberals gained a sweeping victory, but it was a sign of the times that the new Labor Party gained twenty-nine seats.

Ten years of Liberal rule followed the Conservative defeat of 1906. This decade saw the accomplishment of reforms that had a wide-ranging effect. The first years of the new government did not give the impression that the change of government was different from those of earlier years—namely, that the outs were in and the ins were out. The Liberal government was chiefly occupied with redressing those measures of the Conservatives that had aroused passionate indignation and with repairing defects in the machinery of government that recent events had revealed. By giving self-government to the Transvaal, the Liberal government contributed to healing the wounds of the Boer War. The Taff Vale decision was annulled; a Trades Disputes Act legalized peaceful picketing and relieved trade unions from liability for damages caused by their members. Haldane carried through an army reform that fully proved itself in the First World War. The army was divided into two parts, an expeditionary force ready for immediate action on the Continent and a territorial force into which were merged traditional organizations such as the volunteers and the yeomanry. Moreover, Haldane created a general staff as had existed in Prussia since the nineteenth century and was regarded to be responsible for German military superiority. Like other successful military reforms, these measures also resulted in financial economies.

Even so, the results of the first years of Liberal rule were somewhat meager. The reason was that many measures the government advocated—among them changes in the Education Act that would have removed the objections of the nonconformists—were rejected by the House of Lords, controlled by the Conservatives. Moreover, Asquith, chancellor of the exchequer, pursued a traditional line in his financial policy and was disinclined to finance social experiments. This situation changed in 1908 when Asquith succeeded the dying Campbell-Bannerman as prime minister and Lloyd George took Asquith's place as chancellor of the exchequer.

A sudden acceleration in the policy of reform could be traced in part to this dynamic figure. Lloyd George was a Welshman of immense energy, of great ambition, impatient to get things done, and anxious always to be in the public eye. Moreover, he was the leader of the radicals in the Liberal Party, and he considered the success of the Labor Party in the elections of 1906 an indication that if the government remained relatively inactive, a good part of the radical supporters of the Liberals would desert to Labor. Therefore, Lloyd George resolutely used the power of the purse for social reform. The most important feature of this reform was the National Insurance Act (1911), patterned after the social legislation that Bismarck had sponsored in Germany. Contributions made on a compulsory basis by workers, employers, and the state were to provide payments to workers in case of sickness and unemployment. Social reforms were to be paid for by means of a revised system of taxation that placed the chief burden for the expenses of the new programs on the wealthy classes. Thus, Lloyd George's first budget, that of 1909, represented a radical departure. He raised the

Radicals of the Edwardian
era. Lloyd George and
Churchill on the way to the
House of Commons on
Budget Day, 1910.

death duties, made a sharp distinction between earned and unearned income,
and introduced a supertax to be levied on the possessors of large incomes. He
also increased the taxes on tobacco and liquor. *For Su at at of 63*

Lloyd George emphasized the novel character of his budget by introducing it
with a four-hour speech. Opposition formed at once. The Conservatives were
particularly upset by a suggestion that later proved to be impractical and was
abandoned: the taxing of increases in land value. Since much of the wealth of
the British landowners came from estates having mineral resources like coal,
this tax was regarded as a direct attack on the position of the propertied classes.

The Conservatives fought the budget vigorously, and when it reached the
House of Lords, it was rejected. Since the Liberals had been constantly blocked
in their legislative proposals by the Lords, they were deeply aroused by this further frustration of their plans, particularly since tradition had established that the
handling of finance bills was primarily a function of the House of Commons.
The rejection of the budget by the House of Lords was regarded as a breach of
the constitution.

As a next step the Liberal government introduced the Parliament bill, designed
to eliminate the House of Lords as a partner equal to the House of Commons in
the law-making process. If it passed, the House of Lords would be able only to

delay legislation, not to veto it absolutely. The great problem that faced the Liberal government was how to persuade the House of Lords to agree to its own diminution of power. This issue began to become more important than the details of the budget.

The debate over the Parliament bill was conducted with an animosity previously unknown in English political life. On one occasion Prime Minister Asquith was prevented from speaking in the House of Commons by a group of diehards shouting, "Traitor," and drowning his voice in hoots and jeers. The struggle lasted for over two years and ended only after two dissolutions of the House of Commons, new elections, and the threat that the government would create enough Liberal peers to get the proposal through the House of Lords. The final vote, on August 10, 1911, took place under immense excitement because the outcome seemed uncertain; the bill was passed only after thirty-seven Conservatives and thirteen bishops decided not to abstain and cast their votes with the government.

*Intensification of Internal Conflicts: Women's Rights
and the Irish Question*
    Edward VII died on May 6, 1910, in the midst of the struggle over the Parliament bill. With his death, British life seemed to lose some of its splendor. His son and successor, King George V (ruled 1910–1936), was a much less glamorous figure; in a sense his somberness corresponded to the dark and threatening atmosphere that prevailed in Great Britain in the two or three years before the outbreak of the First World War.

Even after passage of the Parliament bill it became evident that the conflicts and problems that had existed before were still there and unsolved; moreover, the bitterness the struggle had engendered gave a sharp edge to all political conflicts.

This was especially true of the long-simmering conflict over women's right to vote. In Great Britain women had attained in 1894 the right to vote in municipal and county elections, but they were excluded from national elections. Believing this exclusion to be arbitrary and unjust, British women, backed by some members of the Labor Party, mounted an impassioned campaign for national suffrage. They presented their demands in the election meetings of various parties and continued their propaganda by distribution of leaflets, street demonstrations, and petitions to Parliament. It is perhaps questionable whether the movement for women's rights would have made such an impact had it not been led initially by women of such boundless energy as Emmeline Pankhurst and her daughters, Christabel and Sylvia. The Pankhursts looked and dressed like ladies, but when their patience wore thin, they were increasingly prepared to adopt "unladylike" methods to get their point across. As Emmeline Pankhurst herself said, "The argument of the broken pane of glass is the most valuable argument of modern politics." Clashes between militant suffragettes and the

Suffragettes are arrested after a demonstration before Buckingham Palace.

police led to the mass arrest of middle-class ladies, an unprecedented development on the British scene. When the court gave the accused the choice between
fines and prison, the suffragettes frequently chose the latter; there they went on
hunger strikes, to which the government replied with forced feeding. Pictures
showing police roughness in handling women demonstrators or women prisoners resisting forced feeding caused outcries about police brutality. Ironically, as
home secretary Herbert Gladstone, the former prime minister's son, was responsible for the behavior of the police although himself in favor of women's right to
vote. Yet until 1911 the outbreaks of violence remained sporadic, because as
long as the fight on the Parliament bill continued, the suffragettes hoped that
frequent elections would finally result in a Parliament that would give them the
vote. But when the struggle over the Parliament bill had ended and Parliament
showed no sign of widening the franchise, a systematic policy of militant
demonstrations was adopted by the Women's Social and Political Union
(WSPU), as the organization of the suffragettes was called. Targets of attack were
no longer only the Parliament building or government offices; disturbances were
extended to all spheres of life in the hope of achieving the surrender of the ruling male politicians. For instance, on March 1, 1912, 150 well-dressed women
marched along the main shopping streets in the center of London—Oxford and
Regent streets—and, with hammers concealed in their handbags, smashed the

windows of the large department stores in the vicinity: Burberry, Liberty's, Marshall and Snelgrove. This was the beginning of a concerted campaign of destruction that included cutting telegraph wires, burning railroad cars, smashing exhibits in the Tower of London, slashing pictures in the National Gallery, and setting fire to private homes of prominent politicians. A tragic culmination was reached at the Epsom Derby on June 4, 1913, when one of the most active suffragettes, Emily Davison, threw herself in front of the king's horse, ending her life. Those who retrieved her body found a banner inscribed with VOTES FOR WOMEN sewn into her coat. Militant suffragette actions continued until the outbreak of the First World War, but it can be questioned whether they were not becoming counterproductive. People who might have been neutral began to turn against the suffragettes, and their demonstrations began to meet counterdemonstrations. Moreover, among the suffragettes themselves, opposition arose, and while Emmeline and Christabel Pankhurst, who were most insistent on continuing the violence, remained leaders at the core of the movement, several splinter groups pursuing a more conciliatory policy were formed. It is difficult to say whether without the war, when women had to take over many of the jobs men had done, the aims of the suffragettes would have been realized in the near future. However, it is clear that if the movement had not directed public attention to the question of the female franchise, the war would not have brought about female suffrage. Women received it in the Representation of the People Act of 1918.

The Irish question became urgent because of the intricacies of the English parliamentary situation. Gladstone's home rule proposals in the nineteenth century had always been wrecked by the resistance of the House of Lords. The Irish nationalists therefore, under the leadership of John Edward Redmond, supported the Liberal government in its attempt to curtail the power of the House of Lords. The support of the Irish nationalists became crucial when, in the various elections held to clarify the trends of public opinion in the struggle over the Lords, the Liberals lost their majority and kept government control only with the help of the Irish nationalists. After the struggle was over, the nationalists asked to receive their reward; a home rule bill was drafted by the government in 1912. But this proposal led to a critical situation because of changes in Ireland since the times of Gladstone's abortive home rule legislation. Although the Conservative government, which had followed Gladstone, opposed home rule, the Conservatives had been aware of the need to allay misery and discontent in Ireland. By a Land Purchase Act they had made it possible for the tenants on the large estates to become owners of the land they cultivated, and a certain amount of self-administration on the local level was introduced.

These measures coincided with the beginning of the movement for an Irish cultural renaissance. The Irish people, now economically less oppressed and more conscious of their national identity, became increasingly resentful that almost all the high positions in the administration of Ireland were in the hands of Protestant

Englishmen. Despite the improvements brought about by the Conservative government, the demand for home rule had gained in strength rather than diminished. Moreover, the stress on Irish Catholic traditions made home rule less acceptable to the English Protestants in Ireland who were particularly strong in Ulster. "Home rule is Rome rule" was the Protestant slogan, and they formed organizations of volunteers ready to resist the introduction of home rule. One of their most influential and most passionate leaders was a prominent lawyer, one of the great orators of the time, Sir Edward Carson. What is astonishing is that the appeal for rebellion that Carson and other Ulstermen uttered was defended and encouraged by the leaders of the Conservative Party in England. Clearly the Conservatives regarded home rule legislation as a way to get rid of the Liberal government.

The Asquith government tried to effect a compromise, according to which the status quo might be maintained in the northern Protestant section and that part of the country be excluded from home rule. But since neither the Irish nationalists nor the Ulstermen were pleased with such a compromise, no agreement about the frontier to be drawn between home rule Ireland and Ulster could be reached. By the spring of 1914 the period of delay that the House of Lords was still able to interpose was over, the home rule bill had passed through all the

A violent protest. The suffragette Emily Davison throwing herself in front of the king's horse at the Derby on June 4, 1913. At this time action photographs were rare and usually obtained only by chance.

parliamentary stages, and a most explosive situation had come about. Officers of a regiment stationed in Ulster, most of them Conservative, many of them descended from the Protestant Irish, demanded a pledge from the government that they would not be asked to coerce Ulster; otherwise they preferred to resign. Weapons to equip volunteer formations were landed in the north and south of Ireland. Only the outbreak of the First World War prevented a test of the resolve and power of the government to carry through its Irish policy. In contrast to the question of the women's vote, however, the war did not bring about a solution to the Irish problem. Although in a patriotic outburst all the divided forces—Irish nationalists and Ulstermen—expressed their willingness to defend Great Britain against Germany, the conflict continued to smolder. It would explode two years later in an uprising known as the Easter Rebellion of 1916.

The Waning of Confidence

The violence that accompanied the suffragette cause and the agitation for home rule legislation occurred because these movements lay outside the traditional constitutional framework. In both movements one finds reflected the feeling that parliamentary institutions did not function properly under the pressures of the rapidly changing world of the twentieth century. The fight of the people against the Lords gave further impetus to the notion that the existing institutions were a hindrance to full democracy. In the years before the war the statistics of a contemporary best seller were frequently quoted: in Great Britain, with a total population of 45 million people, 38 million had hardly more than half the national income, whereas one hundred twenty-five thousand rich had more than a third. Although these figures were estimates and exaggerated, the popularity of this pamphlet revealed the growing resentment existing toward British class society. This view was particularly strong among the workers, and in the years before the outbreak of the First World War their discontent was well grounded. Prices had increased in consequence of the inflationary process that had been set in motion with the discovery of the South African gold fields, and although the wages of the workers had also increased, they had not risen enough to compensate for the rise in prices. Industrialists were hesitant to raise wages because of the competition of Germany and the United States on the world market. The impression of class rule, of suppression of workers by the rich, established ruling group, was also reinforced by a court decision that denied trade unions the right to collect political contributions. Consequently, the Labor Party, which the trade unions saw as representing their interests, was weakened and unable to repeat in subsequent elections the success it had had in the elections of 1906. Confidence in attaining better economic conditions by means of parliamentary action through the Labor Party was shaken.

Disillusionment about the efficacy of the pressure exerted by their party led elements of the labor movement to look favorably upon other recipes for correcting the ills of their economic situation. They became attracted by the idea, which reached Britain from the Continent, particularly from France, that direct action—strikes—was the appropriate weapon for workers seeking to improve their situation. Thus, economic and political motives lay behind a number of strikes in 1911 and 1912. The most notable were a seamen's strike, a general railway strike, a strike of the coal miners, and a strike of the dockers. Most of them were accompanied by violence, looting, and sabotage of the machinery in the factories. Frequently troops had to be used since the police were not able to keep order. Some of the strikes were ended quickly by concessions on the part of the employers. The miners' strike resulted in the introduction of the Miners' Minimum Wage Act, a tacit admission by the government of the hardships faced by the mine workers. But some of the strikes simply collapsed, partly because the wage lag began to be made up and partly because the public, tired of economic unrest, began to turn sharply against the trade unions.

The attitude of the Liberal government in these labor disputes was ambiguous. Whereas Lloyd George demonstrated his sympathy for the cause of the workers, others were more inclined to propose legislation that would forbid strikes in essential services like the railroads. There was also no agreement on the question of how far the government should go in fixing and enforcing minimum wages.

Irritation about the restlessness of the workers and hesitancy to spend money on social reforms was also increased by tension on the international scene. Churchill, who in the earlier years of the Liberal government had been Lloyd George's strongest ally in supporting social reforms and the beginnings of a welfare policy, had become first lord of the admiralty. As such he favored the building of large warships, the so-called dreadnoughts. This brought him in conflict with Lloyd George. Asquith, the prime minister, succeeded in effecting a compromise and preventing a breakup of the government, but it was evident that the tension between the imperialists and the radical wing of the Liberal government was again coming into the foreground. After the First World War, when the problems of government intervention in economic life and social reforms once more would dominate political discussion, the Liberal Party would split and gradually become eliminated as decisive factor in British political life. But even before the war its failure to develop a clear, unified program caused cracks within the party that reflected larger uncertainties in the nation.

FRANCE

Social Basis of French Parliamentarianism

During the decade before the First World War France was the most democratic of the powers on the Continent. France too had a parliamentary system. The head of the state, the president, had little power, and the executive arm of the government, led by a prime minister, was dependent on the confidence of elected representatives—the Senate and the Chamber of Deputies. In a formal sense, France was even more democratic than Great Britain, for the French upper house, the Senate, was elected, whereas in Britain membership in the upper house was hereditary. However, the voting system by which French senators were chosen favored rural districts and the well-to-do, so the Senate functioned as a conservative counterweight to the more liberal Chamber of Deputies.

In contrast to the British system, French political life was not characterized by the dominance of a two-party system. The French parliament was composed of a large number of small parties; every government was a coalition, and governments changed frequently. In the twenty-four years between 1890 and 1914 there were forty-three governments and twenty-six prime ministers. Yet these statistics are deceptive; stability was greater than the figures imply. The multiplicity of French political parties was not a reflection of irreconcilable internal tensions. The French population was socially quite homogeneous. France was a country of small businessmen and farmers. Industrial enterprises were generally limited in size and frequently family-owned. Until the First World War more than half the entire population was occupied in agriculture, which accounted even in 1890 for more than a third of the national income. The multifariousness of the political groupings was chiefly a reflection of tiny differences in economic interests and of variations stemming from local and regional particularities. Politicians moved easily from one party to the other. The center of the political spectrum formed the basis of almost all governments. A number of the same politicians were to be found in almost every cabinet, although they were usually assigned different ministries each time a change in government took place. The various governments differed mainly in whether the center ruled with support of the left or with support of the right.

Ironically, the strength of the center in French politics was an indication that France was lagging in the industrial race. France had entered the industrial age almost simultaneously with Great Britain. But after the spurt given by the French Revolution and Napoleon, the rate of industrial growth slowed down in the nineteenth century, and France trailed far behind the United States and Germany. By its accumulated wealth the nation remained a great financial power. However, the French were inclined to invest their capital not in industrial enterprises but, more cautiously, in public loans. In the market for government loans French banks played a particularly great role. The heavy industries were mainly centered in the northeast, where there were rich coal mines and a textile industry, and in Lorraine, which had valuable iron ore deposits. Thus, the problems arising from modern industrialization were concentrated in relatively small areas and aroused little interest in the rest of the country. Health and safety precautions in industrial enterprises, particularly in the mines, were unsatisfactory. Trade unions had finally been legalized in 1884 but remained very much restricted in their activities.

France had an active Socialist Party, but it was small, and many of its deputies could not have been elected without support from the rural population. Thus, the Socialists, despite theoretical radicalism, were inclined to be conciliatory in practice. Since the workers could not expect much from parliamentary action, theories that recommended direct action and emphasized the efficacy of purely economic weapons, such as strikes, were appealing. As the propagandist of the myth that the general strike was the proper instrument for the overthrow of capitalism, Georges Sorel became an influential figure among radical intellectuals through his book titled *Reflections on Violence* (1908). His views increased the appeal of syndicalism, a revolutionary doctrine that preached direct action with the goal of building a new society through the cooperation of the trade unions of individual factories. Syndicalism was popular among workers in France and spread from there to Italy and Spain. Among the workers of these countries it was a serious competitor to Marxian socialism.

The Republican Regime versus Monarchist Traditions

Because the progress of industrialization in France was slow, political life was not dominated by social conflicts. The main divisions were ideological; they concerned issues the French Revolution had raised. It has been said that after the French Revolution there were two Frances: an aristocratic, monarchical France and a republican France. Defeat in the Franco-Prussian War had strengthened the feeling of malaise about the unavoidable decline of the deeply divided nation. The republic, which had been born in the times of the heroic resistance at the end of the Franco-Prussian War, was now beset by scandals and corruption and appeared unable to give an impulse to a regeneration of power. The enemies of the republican and revolutionary tradition felt justified in their conviction that the democratic form of the French government was the reason for the decline of their nation's power and that what France needed was a more authoritarian regime. Moreover, the enemies of the republic were firmly entrenched in two institutions: the army and the church.

In the last decade of the nineteenth century a crucial event brought about an open confrontation of the two Frances. This was the Dreyfus Affair, whose influence on French thinking was so profound that digesting and absorbing it took decades. The importance of the events beginning in 1894 became clear only slowly. On October 15, 1894, Alfred Dreyfus (1859–1935), a captain on the French general staff, was placed under arrest for high treason. After some weeks Dreyfus was found guilty at a secret military trial, and a few days later, on January 5, 1895, he was sentenced in a solemn ceremony in the courtyard of the general staff building; he was deprived of his rank, his sword was broken, and he was sent for life to Devils Island, in French Guiana. The trial had been full of legal irregularities. The main proof used against Dreyfus was a small piece of blue paper, which became famous as the *bordereau*. Found by a cleaning woman in the wastepaper basket of the German military attaché, it contained information about the French army, and handwriting experts maintained that it had been written by Dreyfus.

A republican and a Jew, Dreyfus had been an outsider among the aristocratic and Catholic officers of the French general staff; his fellow officers were

A scene from the trial of Captain Alfred Dreyfus before the Council of War at Rennes, 1899.

easily convinced, therefore, that if a traitor was among them, it could only be Dreyfus. He belonged to a wealthy Alsatian family, who made every effort to obtain a new trial. A few journalists and lawyers who opposed the military caste were active on Dreyfus's behalf. But for a long while no one could make headway.

In 1896 the counterespionage section of the French general staff received a new chief, Colonel Georges Picquart, who must be considered the true hero of the Dreyfus Affair. Picquart noticed that the removal of Dreyfus had not ended the leakage of military secrets. He also became aware that the handwriting of the *bordereau* was much more similar to that of Walsin Esterhazy, another member of the general staff, than to that of Dreyfus. Moreover, Esterhazy, a playboy and a gambling addict, was in continuous financial difficulties. But when Picquart insisted on proceedings against Esterhazy, nobody on the general staff was willing to listen to him, and he was transferred from Paris to Algiers. Before leaving Paris, he confidentially informed a few people of his suspicions about Esterhazy. Now a number of influential voices joined the campaign for Dreyfus. Among them were Georges Clemenceau (1841–1929), a journalist and politician, and the novelist Anatole France. Still, this was not a popular cause. The Socialist leader Jean Jaurès (1859–1914) was for a long time doubtful of Dreyfus's innocence, and when he finally became convinced that a miscarriage of justice had occurred and was ready to take up the fight, he met reluctance and hesitation in his own party. The Socialist leaders doubted that their adherents, the workers, would perceive a connection between their own interests and the cause of a wealthy Jewish officer.

It is hard to say what would have happened if the army leaders had not got rattled and overplayed their hand. In order to quell once and for all the agitation for Dreyfus, they ordered a trial of Esterhazy, and he was acquitted. Picquart, one of the witnesses against Esterhazy, was arrested and imprisoned. This arbitrary procedure provoked one of the great political documents of modern times—*J'accuse* (1898). In this open letter addressed to the president of the republic, Émile Zola (1840–1902) stated the case against the army leaders briefly and concisely, singling out the responsible officers by name and devoting to each of them a single paragraph beginning *"J'accuse."* The publication led to proceedings against Zola, and rightly expecting that he would be condemned, he fled to England, where he continued the fight. Zola's intervention represented the turning point in the Dreyfus Affair. Immense public interest had been aroused, and every step taken in the proceedings was carefully scrutinized. It emerged that in order to strengthen the case against Dreyfus, documents had been falsified. Colonel Hubert Henry, who had done this falsification, committed suicide; Esterhazy fled to England. Under these circumstances the highest court of appeal on June 3, 1899, set aside the previous condemnation of Dreyfus and ordered a new trial. But the military were unwilling to accept the humiliation of the rehabilitation of Dreyfus. It was widely assumed that the officers were preparing a coup d'état to overthrow the republican regime.

This threat against the existing regime made all the adherents of the republic realize that they had to act and to act quickly. For the first time in European history Socialists declared their willingness to support a bourgeois government. On June 22, 1899, René Waldeck-Rousseau, a member of a well-known family that was both republican and Catholic and a man who had proved himself an able administrator in previous governments, formed a coalition government reaching from the right of center to the left. When the new trial culminated in a grotesque verdict that confirmed Dreyfus's guilt while conceding him "extenuating circumstances," the Waldeck-Rousseau government was strong enough to pardon him.

In the course of the affair the personal fate of Dreyfus became relatively insignificant. When Dreyfus accepted pardon from the Waldeck-Rousseau government, Charles Péguy, a young French writer, wrote: "We would have died for Dreyfus. Dreyfus did not die for Dreyfus." In Péguy's opinion, Dreyfus was no Dreyfusard; he should have continued to insist on his full rehabilitation because the fight had involved irreconcilable principles and ought therefore to have ended with the full victory of the right principles over the wrong ones—of the republican over the authoritarian ideas.

The obstinacy of the anti-Dreyfusards, which appeared to be stupid, if not downright criminal, becomes more comprehensible when the affair is seen as a struggle for principles. The most influential advocate of a monarchical revival in France was Charles Maurras (1868–1952), who fought for his idea in a number of brilliantly written essays and articles, notably his *Enquête sur la monarchie* (1900). But Maurras's concept of monarchy had little to do with the institution as it had existed in France. In his view, monarchy, army, and church were necessary because they formed and maintained discipline and order. Discipline and order were the conditions of national strength. National power and vitality depended on the completeness with which the individual was willing to identify and subordinate himself to the national organization of which he was part. Against the revolutionary doctrines of individual rights, Maurras set the idea of a hierarchically organized society. Therefore, to him the question of Dreyfus's actual guilt or innocence was unimportant. The individual had to be sacrificed if his rehabilitation would damage the prestige of institutions, like the army, which were essential for the life of the nation.

The Dreyfus Affair gave to the republic and to the republicans a prestige they had never possessed before. High courage had been necessary to defend Dreyfus, for the affair had aroused violent emotions. If Zola had not fled to England, he might have been assassinated. Dreyfus's lawyer was shot at, stones were thrown at windows in the houses of Dreyfus supporters, and the police were very slow in protecting the Dreyfusards. But after the affair was over, the individuals who had risked their careers and their lives for the sake of justice were highly esteemed. In the following decades most of those who played a leading role in French politics were men who had first attracted public attention as defenders of Dreyfus: Clemenceau, Briand, Millerand, Viviani, Caillaux, Blum.

As a result of the Dreyfus Affair, the political right acquired an ideology; the left received a new sense of direction, becoming aware that the aims of the French Revolution had not been realized, that the social problems inherent in the rise of industrial society involved new tasks to which the structure of government must be adapted. It was characteristic that the history of the French Revolution, previously a rather neglected field of study, now became a topic of scholarly interest. Indicative was the establishment of a chair for the history of the French Revolution at the Sorbonne.

The Consolidation of the Republic

Obviously, progress toward a more democratic society could be achieved only if those institutions that had shown themselves open enemies of the government and obstructed its policy were deprived of power. The chief target was the army, which was now brought under civilian control: promotions to the rank of general in the army were taken out of the hands of a military council and placed in those of the minister of war, a civilian. He was inclined to favor those officers whom he considered to be reliable republicans. But while this measure did eliminate the danger of an antirepublican military coup, it also had the effect of splitting the officer corps into monarchist and republican groups. Moreover, the influence of political considerations did not always bring the most capable generals into the forefront; for instance, the selection of Maurice Gamelin (1872–1958), an officer popular among republican politicians but of moderate military gifts, as commander in chief at the beginning of the Second World War demonstrates the disadvantages of these political appointments.

The other force that had shown itself openly hostile to the republic was the church, and the attempts at curbing its influence became the crucial issue in French politics in the first decade of the twentieth century. Education policy provided the chief battleground. A large number of French schools were controlled by Roman Catholic religious orders, which provided most of the teaching personnel. Even before the Dreyfus Affair the government had undertaken to build additional state schools and to increase their attractiveness by offering free primary education. The religious orders, however, continued to control a great many schools. After the Dreyfus Affair the government decided on a policy of reducing the number and influence of these schools. The means the government used was a more rigid interpretation of the law regulating the existence of associations. Religious orders were declared to be associations; to exist legally, they had to obtain authorization, which required a legislative act. In 1902, Waldeck-Rousseau, whose policy had been to limit the influence of the church on education, but who had not been anxious to eliminate all Catholic schools, resigned and was succeeded by Émile Combes (1835–1921), a fanatic anti-Catholic. Combes decided to refuse authorization to most of the religious orders. They had no choice but to leave France. The measures against the orders were vehemently denounced by the church and the entire Catholic clergy and provoked widespread demonstrations against the government all over France. The possibilities of a compromise between the anti-Catholic political powers and the church began to disappear. In 1904 a law was passed that prohibited all teaching by religious orders. The relations between France and the Vatican were broken off, and remained severed until just after the First World War, when the religious orders were permitted to return.

The educational policy of the government could not be confined to eliminating the influence of the church. The vacuum had to be filled, and the importance of infusing education with republican ideals was apparent. New schools had to be created; more teachers had to be trained, and they had to be guided by new educational ideas. The center from which the government's educational philosophy spread was the École Normale Supérieure, which prepared the future professors of high schools and universities. It provided an anticlerical, secular education, inspired by a belief in human rights and scientific progress. Whether taught directly at the École Normale Supérieure or by professors trained there, schoolteachers became the protagonists of the spirit of the Third Republic. Many novels describe the situation in the villages where the aristocratic landowner and the priest represented the Old Regime, while the mayor and the school teacher embodied the spirit of the French Revolution.

The Rise of New Tensions

The governments that carried through the rehabilitation of Dreyfus and the separation of church and state—those of Waldeck-Rousseau and Combes—were broadly based left-center coalitions, and their measures were prepared by the *cartel des gauches*, a committee including representatives of all the center and leftist parties. But the years from 1906 to the outbreak of the First World War saw the breakup of the coalition and a sharp division of French political life into right and left. One reason for this split was that the French Socialists—not unlike the British Labor Party—wanted to be rewarded for their support of the government in the years of crisis by measures of social reform. Although France remained far behind Germany, Great Britain, and the United States in industrial activity, the economic upswing that had begun in 1896 had given a spur to the French economy. But this surge of industrialization revealed the retrograde and outdated character of labor conditions and labor legislation—that is, lack of security regulations in factories; long working hours, even for women and children; and no collective bargaining. Chances of effective parliamentary pressure were not good because only a quarter of the entire population was employed in industry. Consequently, the appeal of direct action by strike was great. Indeed, a variety of strikes followed upon each other. Among the most important was a miners' strike, which resulted from a mining disaster for which the workers held the mine owners responsible. The lack of firm wage scales and fixed terms of employment in public enterprises led first to a strike of the postal workers and in 1911 to a strike of the railroad workers. Under Clemenceau, the government reacted with remarkable severity. In the miners' strike troops were sent in to protect strikebreakers. The postal strike was met with sharpening the law forbidding state employees to strike. In the case of the railroad strike, the trains were kept rolling by the government ordering military mobilization so that the railroad workers were conscripted as soldiers and forced to work under military command.

Why did the government proceed in such a repressive manner? There is an old proverb that "Frenchmen wear their hearts on the left and their pocketbooks on the right." The government was aware that if it extended its ideological struggle against the right into a costly policy of social reform, it would lose much support. Moreover, memories of the Paris Commune of 1871 still haunted many Frenchmen, warning them against concession to radical workers. But a decisive reason was the situation in foreign policy: The struggle with Germany over Morocco had come to the fore in 1905, leading to a grave crisis in 1911, which was temporarily eased only after 1911. The government did not want the impression to spread that France was unable to act and to resist because of internal unrest.

Yet the external danger also had the effect of increasing the differences between left and right. The French military leaders, supported by the right, maintained that in order to compensate for Germany's greater strength and manpower, it was necessary to extend conscription from two to three years. The left, particularly the socialists, of whom many were pacifists, opposed this measure on principle and were especially incensed because the financing of the military service required higher taxes and diverted to the military outlays that could have been used for social reform. At this time it became clear that the introduction of an income tax was a necessity. The left demanded that the burden of such a tax be distributed so the rich would carry their appropriate share. Joseph Caillaux, the finance minister, indeed proposed a tax reform scheme that provided for a graduated income tax. But because middle- and upper-class Frenchmen would not accept the proposed revisions, only the expansion of conscription, not new tax revenues, came into effect. The victory of the right seemed complete when in January 1913 their chief leader, Raymond Poincaré (1860–1934), a successful lawyer from Lorraine, who had proved himself to be a good administrator, was elected president of the republic. Yet, as the elections to the Chamber of Deputies in the following spring showed, a countertrend soon set in. Even after the consolidation of the republic achieved in the years of the Dreyfus Affair and the struggle with the church, France seemed still to be a very unstable factor in European politics.

Foreign Policy

Actually France had succeeded in strengthening its position in the European balance of power. In the years of the Dreyfus Affair and the struggle over the separation of church and state, the conduct of foreign policy had been almost independent of the domestic party struggles. From 1898 to 1905 the foreign ministry had been held by one man—Théophile Delcassé (1852–1923).

France had already aquired an extended colonial empire, and there was no pronounced economic interest in further colonial expansion. Although France did participate in the imperialist race of the 1890s, it quickly abandoned this policy after the setback at Fashoda. It retained, however, a serious concern in the countries on the North African shore across the Mediterranean: Tunisia and Morocco. This interest was political and strategic rather than economic because in case of war the control of these countries by another power might make the transport of troops from Algeria to France impossible and might even open France to an attack from the south. In the interest of securing domination in this area the French were willing to abandon other colonial claims. They conceded to the British their rights in Egypt and recognized the Italian demands on Tripoli. In compensation, Great Britain and Italy acknowledged France's predominant interest in Morocco. Since neither of these states had claims on Morocco, their concrete gains from these agreements were greater than those of France. But the ties with Great Britain and Italy gave France increased weight in Europe. This was the chief aim of French foreign policy: the nation was to become again a factor to be reckoned with in Europe. In the pursuit of this policy, financial strength was a precious asset. By means of loans France was able to establish close ties with Russia. French firms invested widely in Russian private industry, particularly in mining and metallurgy. Indeed, one-third of all foreign investments in nongovernmental enterprises in Russia were of French origin. But the French banks also took up a substantial proportion of Russian government loans. At the time of the outbreak of the First World War, almost half the loans the Russian government issued were held by foreigners, and the French people held 80 percent of this amount.

Thus, France had again become powerful in European politics, a situation disadvantageous to Germany, which since the war of 1870–1871 had attempted to keep France isolated. Indicative of the tension between the two states, between 1871 and the outbreak of the First World War no official visit between French and German statesmen ever took place. Whether the maintenance of such a rigidly hostile posture was unavoidable or whether after France had reasserted its position in Europe some gradual lessening of the tension could have been effected remains an open question. There were French financial circles interested in economic cooperation with Germany. Left-wing groups would have liked the government to spend less on defense and more on social reform. Moreover, the French Socialists were pacifists, and their leader, Jean Jaurès, gave eloquent voice to their ideals. Yet there was deep emotional resistance to

The French Socialist leader Jean Jaurès speaking to a crowd in front of the banners and symbols of the French Revolution.

any attempt at reconciliation with Germany. Throughout this period, on the Place de la Concorde in Paris, where each large French city was represented by a statue, the statue of Strasbourg remained veiled in black. The French did not envisage a war to reconquer Alsace-Lorraine, but there was strong feeling that as long as Germany held Alsace-Lorraine, cooperation between the two states was impossible. French foreign policy, it was felt, ought to hold the line against Germany. This indeed remained the prevailing tendency of that policy and was probably the decisive factor explaining why, after the war broke out, the deep cleavage that separated left from right did not prevent general support of the war effort. It is significant that Jaurès was assassinated by a nationalist on the day the war began because the murderer assumed that he was to make a speech opposing the war. Ironically, the speech Jaurès had prepared was intended to support the government in its resistance to the Germans.

ITALY

Italian national unification had primarily been the work of the middle class in northern and southern Italy. Although Italy was politically unified, the social differences between northern and central Italy and southern Italy, the Mezzogiorno, where a firmly entrenched feudal nobility remained all powerful, had never been bridged. Rising industrial activity intensified this regional contrast and contributed to the growth of a revolutionary-minded lower class. Marxist and syndicalist ideas had a stronghold over the industrial workers, while discontent spread among the poor peasants and agricultural workers. Not only industrial but also agricultural strikes and occupation of land by agricultural workers and peasants happened frequently in this period. In the quarter of a century before the outbreak of the First World War, Italy was perhaps changing more rapidly than any other great European power.

The outstanding figure among Italian statesmen in the last decades of the nineteenth century was Francesco Crispi (1819–1901), one of the heroes of the Risorgimento period. Crispi decided to turn Italian energies to colonial expansion, a policy that corresponded with Italy's ambition to be a great power. Many Italians still lived under the rule of the Habsburg empire in South Tyrol, Gorizia, and Istria. Crispi, however, wanted to turn Italian nationalist ambitions away from these areas because he was anxious to avoid a clash with Austria-Hungary and its ally, Germany. Moreover, Italian colonial expansion might overcome the feeling that Italian policy had reached a dead end. Crispi decided to enter the race with the other great powers for the control of African areas that had not yet been subjected to European rule; because Italy had a small colonial possession along the Red Sea, he wanted to extend its rule in the area to neighboring Ethiopia. In 1896, against the better judgment of his military advisers, Crispi ordered the advance into Ethiopia of troops stationed in neighboring Eritrea. Crispi miscalculated his opponent's military strength. The Ethiopians were good warriors; they had received some training from French officers and had been equipped with guns by the French. At Adua, in difficult mountainous terrain, the Italian army of twenty thousand men—half of them Italians, half of them natives—encountered a well-directed force of about a hundred thousand Ethiopians. The Italians were completely defeated; about six thousand were killed, two thousand wounded, and two thousand taken prisoner. When the news of the defeat reached Rome, the Crispi government resigned amid immense public demonstrations demanding the immediate end of the African adventure. Crispi's successor, Antonio Rudinì (1839–1908), accordingly made peace with Emperor Menelik (1844–1913), thus recognizing the independence of Ethiopia. Italy's status among the European states plunged. Instead of solidifying Italian national unity, the attempt to become a world power had only increased discontent, and the Ethiopian adventure was followed by years of unrest.

Moreover, the protective tariffs adopted by France had provoked Italian countermeasures, and the ensuing tariff war diminished Italian exports and impeded industrial expansion by cutting off loans from French banks. Unemployment rose in the industrial areas, and in May 1898 bread riots broke out in Milan, barricades were erected in the streets, and order was restored only after some fighting and a declaration of martial law. A general, Luigi Pelloux (1839–1924), became prime minister. He ruled by royal decree and tried to establish a military dictatorship. He was defeated in the elections of 1900, and a month later King Humbert, who had appointed Pelloux and had supported his dictatorial policy, was assassinated.

Thereafter, the situation quieted; the radical left had overplayed its hand. Railway strikes in 1902 and a general strike in 1904 aroused widespread indignation. They appeared inspired by political motives rather than by economic hardships and were viewed as an attempt at revolution. In consequence, all the moderate forces drew more closely together; the threat of revolution even led to a softening of the hostility between the Italian state and Roman Catholicism. Pope Pius X now permitted Catholics to enter the party struggle because the safety of the society order was threatened. In the elections of October 1904 the radical left suffered harsh defeat.

One of the reasons for greater calm in the domestic situation was the economic upswing that had taken place in Europe since 1896 and made itself felt in Italy in a quickening of the tempo of industrialization. It has been said that during the period from 1896 to 1914 Italy had its Industrial Revolution. In the 1890s the Banca d'Italia was founded and assumed the role of a central bank. It had the sole right to issue currency and thus could control and regulate the money supply and provide money for industry. Newly established stability in the money market led immediately to the founding of a number of commercial banks, frequently with the strong participation of foreign, particularly German, capital; they became active in the financing of industrial enterprises.

The political situation in Italy also took a turn toward stability. In 1903, Giovanni Giolitti (1842–1928) became prime minister. Giolitti came from the north and had started his career in government service, but he was soon elected deputy and proved himself to be an unusually clever parliamentarian, whose tactical skill assured a remarkable degree of political stability. He considered the modernization of economic life the primary task in the Italian situation. Giolitti was prime minister three times—1903–1905, 1906–1909, 1911–1914; even when out of office, he remained the dominant political figure. Under his influence, the government took an active part in promoting the process of industrialization. It ordered military equipment from Italian suppliers even if the price was higher and the quality lower. It started an ambitious program of railroad building after the railroads, previously privately owned, had been taken over by the state, and it gave direct subsidies to key enterprises like the merchant marine to stimulate the various activities involved in shipbuilding. Giolitti's policy of industrialization had remarkable results. In the twenty years before the outbreak of the First World War the share of industry in the national production increased from 20 percent to 25 percent and the national income grew by approximately 50 percent.

Giolitti was aware that economic progress demanded a favorable social climate. He initiated numerous measures of social reform. Trade unions were legalized, and collective bargaining was promoted. Minimum standards for hygienic conditions in factories were set, and working conditions for women and children were improved.

The beneficial effects of Giolitti's regime on Italian economic life were undeniable, but the means by which he carried out his policy were questionable, subjecting him to criticisms that he exerted a corrupting influence in Italian politics and that his regime was really a dictatorship. From the point of view of parliamentary support, Giolitti was in a difficult situation. The traditional ruling group was opposed to his social policy, and the socialists were disinclined to cooperate with a capitalist and monarchical government. In order to attain his aims, Giolitti ruled with fluctuating majorities, which he created by means of a political maneuver called *trasformismo*. Unlike other European countries where electoral districts were large and frequently sent two or three representatives to the national parliament, Italian electoral districts were small and elected only one deputy; consequently, he was dependent for reelection on the good opinion of the inhabitants of his district rather than on his party. By granting a deputy special advantages for the district he represented, Giolitti got the votes of deputies who did not belong to the government party or who even belonged to parties opposed to the government. Ideals and principles became a façade behind which deputies bargained for political and material advantages. Giolitti's sacrifice of principles for tactical advantages emerged most starkly in his treatment of the Mezzogiorno. He did not extend his policy of economic and social reforms into the south; he made no attempt to institute agrarian reform there, to dissolve the latifundia (large agricultural estates) and provide land for the numerous peasants living in abject poverty. This gained him the votes of the deputies of the south, but it also meant that the great landowners, allied with the church, remained all powerful and that in Sicily the Mafia—which, according to private and official investigations, had ordered and approved fraud, violence, and even murder—maintained its influence. Giolitti even made some concession to church interests by facilitating religious education in those localities where parents demanded it. In practice, this meant that the schools in the south were controlled by priests, themselves only half educated and of no great help in educating others. The gap between the Italian north and the Italian south was considerably widened: Whereas in parts of the north the illiteracy rate was reduced to 11 percent, in the south it remained over 90 percent. This policy actually damaged Giolitti's own economic aims: The great majority of the people of the south could not be employed in work that demanded even a minimum of skills, nor did they have the money to buy industrial goods. The internal market, which had an impact on the entire industrial development of Italy, was retarded by the south.

Of course, Giolitti was aware of the need to secure a broader parliamentary base for his regime, and he had a left-center government in mind with Socialist participation. Many of his social measures were directed toward gaining the support of the trade unions, which exerted great power in the Socialist Party; with their help Giolitti believed he would be able to overcome the traditional Marxist resistance against collaboration in a capitalist system. Giolitti thought he was so near to this goal that he proclaimed in parliament that the Socialists had "put Marx in the attic." He felt that this policy would be sealed by the government carrying an electoral reform through in 1912 that raised the number of voters from 3.5 million to 8 million and made universal suffrage of males over thirty years old a reality. Only male illiterates who had done no military service (and women) were denied the right to vote.

But in the Socialist Party the groups opposing the assumption of governmental responsibility proved stronger than once thought. The trade unions were competing in most northern provinces with the chambers of labor in which all the workers of a particular area were joined. These chambers of labor were radical and revolutionary in their outlook because their membership also included the badly paid workers of small industries and in some areas, like the Romagna, the agricultural workers, for whom nothing had been done by Giolitti's reforms. The reformist wing of the Socialist Party had the upper hand only for a brief period. In general, the radical wing, which had anarchist tendencies and argued for revolutionary actions, strikes, and sabotage, set the tone. At the party congress of 1912, the radicals gained control. One of their leaders, Benito Mussolini, became editor of Avanti, the official paper of the Socialist Party.

This triumph of the Socialist left over the Socialist right was also influenced by events in the area of diplomacy and war. The wound inflicted on Italian self-esteem by the defeat at Adua had never fully healed. These resentments found expression in a nationalist political movement organized by Enrico Corradini. Corradini ascribed these military humiliations to the lack of heroism inherent in democracy and parliamentary government. The powerful spokesman of this movement was Gabriele d'Annunzio, Italy's most famous writer, who proclaimed the need for one great man to rule the country. He found many adherents among the younger generation. Even if the nationalist movement remained numerically rather weak, a feeling that Italy had to assert itself as a great power was widespread. When the French began to claim Morocco, Italy began an economic penetration of Tripoli. The view that the conquest of Tripoli was necessary extended even into Socialist ranks; if Giolitti had wanted to refrain from this action, he would hardly have been able to do so.

However, the great masses of the Socialist Party were not willing to accept the view of their moderate leaders that the economic improvement expected to result from the creation of a colony in North Africa was worth a war. The majority of the Socialist Party condemned the war as imperialist and felt hardened in the attitude of refusing cooperation with the capitalist government.

If Giolitti had hoped that by undertaking this war he would gain support on the right, he was also disappointed. The nationalists considered the war chiefly proof that movements and actions outside parliament were needed and could be effective. The election in 1913 based on the new law establishing universal suffrage did not create a secure parliamentary basis for a reform government but demonstrated the strength of radicalism on the left and on the right. When the First World War came, the liberal state was in a serious crisis.

GERMANY

Constitution and Social Structure

The authoritarian system of the German Empire (Reich) was primarily a product of its historical development in the preceding century. Because the unification of Germany had been accomplished by Prussia, the political structure of the German Reich bore a Prussian pattern.

Prussia had successfully withstood the middle-class revolution of the nineteenth century. Its constitution was highly authoritarian; the army was outside civilian control, under direct command of the king, and the Prussian parliament was elected by a method that guaranteed control to the great landowners from east of the Elbe, the Junkers.

The Prussian monarch and the Prussian leaders did not want to see their system of government submerged in a wider imperial structure. Hence the German Empire became not a unitary state but a federal state composed of twenty-five individual states. With the exception of three free cities, the rulers of these states were princes; the government of each of these states appointed a delegate to a federal council, the Bundesrat, which met in Berlin under the chairmanship of the delegate appointed by the Prussian king, who regularly designated the Prussian prime minister for this post. It was as president of this federation of princes that the king of Prussia held the title of German emperor. Since the number of votes that each state possessed within the council was determined by its geographical extent and the size of its population, the Bundesrat was dominated by Prussia.

The leaders of Prussian policy at the time of German unification had to take into account, however, that the chief resistance to unification had come from the princely rulers of the German states and the groups bound to them through interest or loyalty. The chief protagonists of unification had been the masses of the people, particularly the middle class. Thus, in order to check separatist tendencies that might come into the foreground in the Bundesrat, a parliament—the Reichstag—was created, with members elected on the basis of a most progressive voting system: universal suffrage of all males above twenty-five years of age.

Legislation for the Reich had to be passed by both the Bundesrat and the Reichstag. The areas over which the Reich could decide and legislate were strictly limited: foreign affairs, naval affairs, the mail and the telegraph, customs, colonies. It also had the right to establish common standards for the administration of justice and military affairs, although the armies remained under the control of the rulers of the individual states and were placed under a unified command only in wartime. The Reich was to receive a certain percentage of the taxes raised by the states, and it had the right to levy indirect taxes.

Although the tasks of the Reich were limited, they were extended enough to require governmental agencies, and the manner in which the federal administration was organized reinforced the dominating position of Prussia. The control and supervision of the federal administration were entrusted to the chairman of the Bundesrat, who was expected to explain and to defend new legislation in the Reichstag. Since this chairman was always the Prussian prime minister, he combined in his person two functions. As head of the federal administration he had the title of chancellor—*Reichskanzler*—and had under him a number of high officials, "secretaries," who administered the various areas under federal control: foreign affairs, naval affairs, colonies, and so on. As Prussian prime minister he directed Prussian policy and presided over the Prussian cabinet, composed of "ministers": of the interior, of war, of education, of finance, and so on. This arrangement gave the chancellor a remarkable amount of independence. He was appointed by the Prussian king and could be removed neither by the Bundesrat nor by the Reichstag. Despite the strength of his position, the chancellor could more easily prevent a new departure in politics than initiate one. He could frustrate measures of which he disapproved by playing against each other the Reich and Prussia, the Bundesrat and the Reichstag. But he had to maneuver carefully to move these different forces in the same direction. Thus, the complicated political structure of the Reich led to strange contradictions. It made it possible for Prussia to take the leading role without having to give up its system of government and its autonomy. But in providing guarantees against meddling in Prussian affairs, the constitution of the Reich also secured the other German states against interference in their systems of government. Hence within the German Empire great political diversity existed. In contrast to the conservative north, the southern German states—Bavaria, Württemberg, Baden—were liberal, even democratic, and they had parliamentary governments. The majority of the German population was Protestant, but the Catholic minority was very considerable; in 1900 there were 35 million Protestants and 20 million Roman Catholics in Germany. Some of the German states were prevailingly Protestant; in others Catholicism had an important political influence.

The complex constitution doubtless required of the Reich's leaders great art in balancing the divergent forces that constituted the German Empire. The unified Reich was Otto von Bismarck's creation, and its constitution had been tailored to his forceful but prudent personality. He was also favored by the fact that in the first decade after unification, an equilibrium of social forces still existed; the conflict between the interests of agriculture and industry was still muted. But toward the close of the nineteenth century the conditions for a successful functioning of the German constitution began to disappear. Bismarck was dismissed in 1890, and the rapid and striking change in the German social structure upset the delicate balance of social forces. Germany had become a highly industrialized and commercial country.

At the outbreak of the First World War, Germany's merchant marine was the second largest in the world, surpassed only by that of Great Britain. By then too Germany was the third-largest coal-producing power—behind the United States and only slightly behind Great Britain. Germany produced considerably more pig iron and steel than any other European power, Great Britain included, and almost half as much as the United States. Germany's rich mineral resources favored the development of an armament industry. Krupp, the leading German armament manufacturer, together with Skoda in Austria and the French firm of Schneider-Creusot, dominated the armament market of the world. The electrical and chemical industries also flourished. Some of the German dyestuffs and pharmaceuticals enjoyed a kind of monopoly on the world market. In contrast to the United States and the British Empire, Germany produced much more than could be consumed on the domestic market. Between 1887 and 1912 the value of German exports increased 185 percent. Germany's rise as an industrial world power thus involved a rapid penetration into foreign markets. Until 1880 it had traded almost exclusively with other European countries; thereafter Germany began to exchange goods increasingly with other continents.

The mineral resources on which industrial development was based could be found in almost every part of the nation. Most important was the Ruhr, where coal and iron were available. In the southwest, in the areas of Alsace and Lorraine ceded by France in 1871, were iron and potash; in the east, Upper Silesia was rich in coal; and in central Germany, lignite deposits served the electrical and chemical industries. Thus, the impact of industrialization was felt all over the country. Since industrial development in Germany started later than in Great Britain and in France, large capital investments were needed to facilitate competition with the more advanced nations. Such quantities of capital could be provided only by banks, not by the industrial entrepreneurs themselves or by private financiers. In German economic development, banking and industrial enterprises became closely interconnected. This alliance promoted the formation of big companies possessing greater efficiency than smaller ones that produced the same goods. In some fields the large enterprises achieved a monopoly; in others a few big industrial companies banded together in cartel agreements that enabled them to fix prices and delimit markets. The members of a cartel could establish high price levels at home to maintain profits while they attempted to conquer foreign markets by "dumping" goods there at low prices. For this reason the German government not only permitted monopolies and cartels but even gave legal protection to cartel agreements; violators could be brought to court and punished.

The rapid development of Germany into a great economic power and the accompanying rise in wealth in almost all groups of the population had a dangerously intoxicating effect on the German upper and middle classes. Most of them succumbed to the fatal fascination of the idea of becoming a "world power." Germany ought to have a navy; it ought to have colonies; German passenger ships had to be the largest and fastest. German bankers and industrialists were convinced that wherever they found the opportunity for economic

The Krupp gun factory in Essen in 1904.

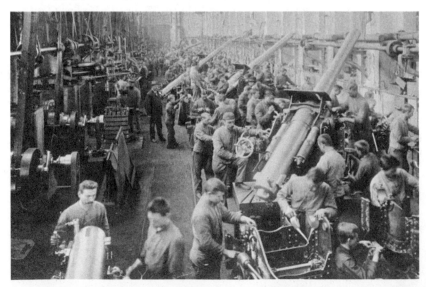

penetration—in Turkey, in China, or anywhere else—they ought to make use of it, regardless of the claims, rights, or interests of other nations. Since Germany was a latecomer on the world scene, they felt, it had to be pushy to gain its due "place in the sun," as William II characterized his realm's political ambitions.

Nevertheless, industrial development in Germany did not progress without conflicts. Wherever industrial and agrarian interests clashed, the Junkers were able to put up strong resistance, for they dominated the political system of Germany's most powerful state. Moreover, the transition to industrialization was unavoidably accompanied by social tensions, and the gap between entrepreneur and workers was widened by the resentment that Bismarck's repressive antisocialist laws had created. After these laws had lapsed, and as a consequence of the rapid progress of industrialization, the socialists made great strides. The Social Democrats increased their number of deputies in the Reichstag from 35 in 1890 to 110 in 1911 and became the strongest political party. Although by then the Social Democratic Party and the allied trade unions had become big bureaucracies inclined to move slowly and cautiously, the Marxian view of the need for a revolution remained dominant among the workers, especially since the government continued to proceed vigorously against all subversive agitation and propaganda.

After 1890 instability was further increased as the role the constitution assigned to the emperor—but as had actually been filled by Bismarck—had fallen to a monarch who wanted to rule but lacked the qualities necessary for doing so.

The Empire under William II

In the public mind, particularly in those countries that fought against Germany in the First World War, William II (ruled 1888–1918) is usually pictured as the prototype of the warlord: imperious, brutal, barbarian. Indeed, William did like to appear in full military panoply, preferably in the uniform of an officer of the cuirassier guards, in silvery, shining mail and a helmet crowned by a golden eagle. He talked to his ministers and to his people as an officer talks to his soldiers, giving them orders and commands. William felt himself the heir and successor of the absolutist Hohenzollern kings of the eighteenth century. He believed that his power came from God and considered himself, as he said in one of his bombastic speeches, "an instrument of God." Most of all, he felt obliged to maintain the Prussian military tradition. He was hardly aware that the army was no longer an army of mercenaries, the personal property of the monarch, but was now based on general conscription. Addressing a Berlin regiment about the socialist opposition, he told the soldiers that they would have to shoot their fathers and mothers if he ordered them to do so. Because he disapproved of modern dances, he forbade all men in uniform to dance the tango when it became popular in 1913. Since the inner organization of the army and the appointment of officers were entirely outside civilian control, William had some legal justification for believing he could demand absolute obedience.

Cartoon from
Simplicissimus, satirizing
William II's priorities:
"His Majesty has no time
for Europe. His Majesty is
designing a uniform for
service chaplains."

Nevertheless, he wanted to be more than the preserver of an absolutist tradition. He wanted to be a modern monarch who would lead Germany into a new era of history. He surrounded himself not only with members of the Prussian aristocracy but also with industrialists and bankers. Although in his youth William had participated in meetings of an anti-Semitic group, he was later inclined to favor wealthy Jews and to grant them titles, to the great disgust of the Prussian aristocracy. He was fascinated by discoveries in the natural sciences and delighted in bestowing decorations on outstanding scientists and occasionally ennobling them. He preached enthusiastically the need for making Germany a world power. William was a zealous reader of Alfred Mahan and accepted his view that sea power was the crucial factor in the struggle of nations and the competition for empire.

This combination of Prussian authoritarianism with faith in technological progress and capitalist expansion corresponded to the inclinations of the German bourgeoisie. In the earlier years of his reign William II was extremely popular. But he also had many opponents, and their number increased over the years. His adversaries and critics were to be found not only among the socialists, who condemned the entire regime, but also among those who knew him best. Some considered him the gravedigger of the German monarchy. They were aware of his superficiality. His various intellectual and aesthetic enthusiasms were short-lived, and he was incapable of sustained effort and serious work. Nervous and restless, he traveled continually from one place to another and expected to be constantly entertained. Most of all, despite his martial appearance and powerful gestures, William II was weak, easily influenced by men with stronger wills, especially when they presented their ideas in amusing and flattering forms. Military men, industrialists, bankers, and courtiers could sway the emperor.

Although he failed to provide unifying direction to the nation, William II was unwilling to concede to his chancellors that decisive influence which Bismarck had possessed. Each chancellor had to struggle against military, naval, and personal influences, and the course of German policy became erratic.

Of Bismarck's successors, the first, Count Leo von Caprivi (chancellor from 1890 to 1894), was a military man; the others were civil servants. Prince Chlodwig von Hohenlohe (from 1894 to 1900) had been the administrative head of Alsace-Lorraine; Bernhard von Bülow (from 1900 to 1909) came from the diplomatic corps; Theobald von Bethmann-Hollweg (from 1909 to 1917) from the Prussian administration. The appointment of civil servants to high positions of political leadership emphasized the independence of the government from parliamentary influence. But as we have seen, although the role of the Reichstag was limited, its approval of new legislation and taxation was necessary. The Social Democrats, as opponents of the entire system, always voted against the government, which therefore had to seek support from the parties to the right of the socialists. These were of greatly varying political shadings. The Conservatives spoke chiefly for the agrarian interests, while the Center Party included members of every stratum of society since its unifying bond was religion, Roman Catholicism. The bourgeois world was represented by two groups: the National Liberals, who championed the interests of heavy industry, and the Progressives, supported by small entrepreneurs and white-collar workers and retaining the nineteenth-century ideal of a liberal and democratic Germany.

Cooperation among parties of such varied interests was difficult to achieve. The government usually had the support of the Conservatives and the National Liberals, although their alliance—one between agricultural and industrial interests—had not been easy to achieve. The crucial problem had been of an economic nature. There was the conflict between the landowner's demand for protective tariffs against American and Russian grain and the industrialist's desire for low food prices, which would allow low wages and facilitate competition on the world market. At the beginning of the reign of William II, under Bismarck's successor, Caprivi, agricultural tariffs were lowered in the interest of industrial expansion. But the Junkers forced Caprivi's fall, and the government changed its course and embarked on a policy of agricultural protection, buying the agreement of the National Liberals by concessions to industrial interests.

One of these concessions was the execution of a major program to build a fleet of battleships. The origin of the naval program has to be ascribed to William II's envy and admiration of Great Britain and to the influence of Admiral von Tirpitz on the emperor. But support for the program was not lacking. It provided heavy industry with a continuous flow of government orders; in the eyes of the industrialists this was an advantage that might outweigh the disadvantages of protective tariffs. Likewise, the Conservatives considered protective tariffs a compensation for their abandonment of opposition to a large fleet.

The cooperation of industrial and agrarian leaders with the government not only served parliamentary purposes but was also intended to defend and maintain the social order against the subversive Social Democratic movement. Schools (elementary schools, as well as the *Gymnasium*, which was required for admission to the university) were state institutions, and the teachers were commanded to fight Social Democratic ideas by emphasizing patriotism and Christian piety in their teaching. Moreover, attainment of any position of importance in the civil service was dependent on demonstrating full acceptance of "official" values. Although Jews were legally freed from all restrictions, they were not appointed to positions in the civil service. Civil servants sitting on the boards examining candidates for admission to the civil service gave much weight to the political reliability of the candidates. But the crucial factor in this process of selecting civil servants was the introduction of the reserve officer. It was almost impossible to become a member of the civil service without being a reserve officer. In Germany, every male was obligated to two years of military service, but those who had received a higher education needed to serve only one year. To become a reserve officer after this one year was like becoming a member of a club. The decision to make someone a reserve officer depended on the active officers of the regiment in which the potential reserve officer had served; these officers would accept only those who shared their standards of behavior. But to be a reserve officer had still wider implications; it was a virtual requirement to be counted as a member of court society and the higher social circles. Thus, influence in Germany, particularly in Prussia, depended on adjustment to the behavior and the values that dominated the higher civil service and the officer corps of the army, groups in which the nobility played the decisive role. The feudal and militaristic values of the Prussian nobility remained powerful. In Germany, therefore, aristocratic values were not replaced by bourgeois values; instead, the German high bourgeoisie became feudalized.

Although the German ruling group was not willing to permit democratization of German political life, the administration was both efficient and anxious to show that it was concerned with the well-being of the citizens. The bureaucracy was incorrupt; the police, although perhaps overzealous, maintained order and peace. The government was not despotic. On the contrary, the Germans prided themselves on living in a society ruled according to law—in a Rechtsstaat. In court proceedings, legal forms were strictly observed, and the individual could be sure of having his rights carefully protected.

If intellectual life in Berlin and in Prussia was stifled by the narrowness and the conservatism of the outlook of the Prussian ruling group, a livelier and freer intellectual climate could be found in other parts of Germany. If Berlin was the political capital, Munich was the center of modern movements such as Expressionism in German art and literature.

Nevertheless, the existing system made any opposition to the prevailing militaristic tendencies futile. This was strikingly shown in 1913, when popular demonstrations took place in the Alsatian town of Zabern against the troops stationed there. In an arbitrary extension of their functions, the military authorities placed the town under martial law. William II's response was to congratulate the officer responsible for this energetic behavior. All the protests of political moderates did not help. Yet the authoritarian behavior of the emperor in the Zabern Affair increased and intensified doubts about the viability of continuing the kind of regime that existed in Germany. On the local level, particularly in municipal administrations, a collaboration between socialists and progressive bourgeois parties began to develop. The Catholic Center Party started to activate the role of the Reichstag and to prepare, in cooperation with the progressives and socialists, a transition to a parliamentary system. Whether without the war and defeat these tendencies could have won out over the coalescence of powerful economic interests and deeply ingrained traditions, which supported the existing authoritarian regime, is impossible to say.

The amalgamation of the outlook of the rich industrial and financial bourgeoisie with feudal military traditions had a dangerous effect on foreign policy. In Germany's struggle for a "place in the sun," the accent was very much on power politics. Wherever some acquisition of territory seemed possible—in Africa or China or the Pacific—Germany raised claims, and these widespread claims brought about conflicts of interest with almost all the other major European states. The influence of the Prussian Conservatives made it certain that Germany would remain the strongest military power in Europe. But the building of a first-rank navy, combined with the economic competition arising from Germany's growing industrial strength, complicated German relations with Great Britain, traditionally the strongest naval power. Moreover, in order not to endanger the alliance between agrarian and industrial interests, the government tended to yield to their pressures. Thus, for example, it supported the building of the Baghdad Railway in Turkey by German financial groups, thereby stepping into an area that previously Great Britain and Russia had regarded as exclusively theirs. Because of its ambitious rush into world politics, Germany became exposed to pressure from all sides.

THE HABSBURG MONARCHY

Of the seven great European powers that existed at the turn of the century, Austria-Hungary alone failed to survive the First World War. Even before that conflict, the Habsburg monarchy, including the most different nationalities— Germans, Magyars, Slovaks, Croatians, Czechs, Romanians, Italians, Poles—was

"The Lieutenant the Day before Yesterday, Yesterday and Today," a caricature from *Simplicissimus*. The caption was presented in slang that is difficult to reproduce in English. The lieutenant says, "Yesterday, gambled at the jockey club, improved my finances; then champagne nothing but champagne."

an anachronism. Much of the time, despite feeble and inconsistent attempts at constitutional forms and parliamentarism, it was ruled dictatorially. Satirizing the monarchy in his seminal novel, *The Man without Qualities* (1932), Robert Musil labeled it "Kakania"—a pun on the terms *K und K* (kaiserlich und königlich*, or imperial and royal) and *kaka* (excrement). The anachronistic nature of this monarchy gave to Austria-Hungary, and particularly to the Vienna of the prewar years, a peculiar attraction. Aristocratic and cosmopolitan Vienna seemed to preserve a refined cultural tradition that was disappearing in the rest of Europe. Vienna was the center of the music world, attracting the most famous singers to its opera and the best orchestra conductors and composers. Johannes Brahms might be seen sitting next to the wife of Johann Strauss, and while Strauss was conducting his waltzes, Brahms wrote on Mrs. Strauss's fan: "Unfortunately not by Johannes Brahms." The best German actors and actresses performed in the Burgtheater. Vienna was the center of literary trends exploring the complexities of human psychology, and in the coffeehouses the representatives of this modern literary approach—Arthur Schnitzler and Hermann Bahr—might be found talking respectfully to a fragile youth, not yet twenty years old, who had just become famous as the author of a small volume of exquisite poems: Hugo von Hofmannsthal, later to write the libretto of Richard Strauss's *Rosenkavalier* (1911). Then there were the elegant Baroque palaces, from which issued carriages drawn by beautiful horses taking their noble and wealthy owners—the Liechtensteins, the Esterházys, the Schwarzenbergs—to Vienna's famous park, the Prater. They all contributed to making the life of the Vienna court the most brilliant in Europe, and because of the scandals in which the wild young Habsburg archdukes became involved, it was also the most romantic.

The embodiment of this anachronism was Emperor Francis Joseph (ruled 1848–1916). In 1900 he had ruled for more than fifty years, and he would go on ruling into the First World War. Musil wrote that the emperor was like one of those distant stars whose light has already gone out by the time it reaches earth. Having lived through political and personal disasters—having been forced to abandon part of his heritage to Italy, having been pushed out of Germany, having lost his son by suicide and his wife by assassination—he still continued to get up every morning at five to begin the study of the files on his desk and went on to preside over his court, in which the most rigid etiquette was observed. It is typical of the strength as well as the weakness of this regime that when in June 1914 Francis Joseph's nephew and presumptive heir Francis Ferdinand and his morganatic wife were assassinated at Sarajevo, the event that precipitated the outbreak of World War I a little over a month later, the emperor's primary reaction was not sorrow about the death of a close relation but relief that the murders had averted the danger that the son of this misalliance might become ruler of Austria-Hungary. Oblivious to the political chaos likely to ensue from the assassination, Franz Joseph said upon hearing the news from Sarajevo: "A higher Power has restored the order that I was unhappily unable to maintain."

The Dual Monarchy

The Habsburg empire became known as the Dual Monarchy. In one part—the Empire of Austria—the Germans predominated; in the other—Hungary—the Magyars. These two parts had in common only the person of the emperor, foreign policy, customs policy, and the army. But Austria was not purely German, nor was Hungary purely Magyar, and the maintenance of German or Magyar rule over the subordinate nationalities became more difficult from decade to decade. The widening distribution of printed materials—newspapers and literary works—made the various nationalities conscious of their particular cultural heritage. Industrialization drew many peasants into the cities and gave them economic strength. Social tensions inherent in the general economic changes of this period were heightened by the resistance against German and Magyar rule. Both parts of the Austrian-Hungarian monarchy had constitutions, but they were of a very different character.

The great problem for the Dual Monarchy, and in a very acute form for its Austrian half, was created by the rise of nationalism. Order was difficult, if not impossible, to maintain if all these various nationalities remained dissatisfied and oppressed, but any concession to them aroused the resistance of the Germans, who were accustomed to being the ruling nationality and to serving as government officials in this entire part of the Habsburg empire. Thus, the constitution of Austria was very complicated. The Reichsrat (the parliament) had a voting system that favored the propertied classes, particularly the landowners,

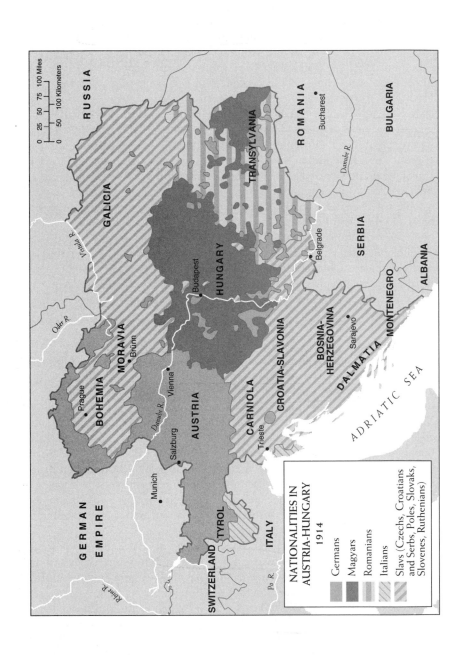

NATIONALITIES IN
AUSTRIA-HUNGARY
1914

Germans
Magyars
Romanians
Italians
Slavs (Czechs, Croatians
and Serbs, Poles, Slovaks,
Slovenes, Ruthenians)

RUSSIA

GERMAN EMPIRE

ROMANIA

Bucharest

BULGARIA

GALICIA

TRANSYLVANIA

Vistula R.

Oder R.

HUNGARY

Budapest

SERBIA

Belgrade

ALBANIA

MORAVIA

Brünn

BOHEMIA

Prague

MONTENEGRO

BOSNIA-HERZEGOVINA

Sarajevo

DALMATIA

Vienna

Danube R.

AUSTRIA

CARNIOLA

CROATIA-SLAVONIA

Salzburg

Munich

Trieste

ADRIATIC SEA

SWITZERLAND

TYROL

ITALY

Po R.

Rhine R.

Danube R.

0 25 50 75 100 Miles

0 50 100 Kilometers

who were regarded as reliable support of the government. Moreover, each nation had a quota, a fixed number of deputies, so that all nationalities had a voice, but the quota of Germans was so large that they remained dominant. As could be expected, the other nationalities demanded a greater share. Moreover, the Germans were split into a liberal and a Conservative-Catholic group. Consequently, each legislative proposal became the subject of endless bargaining.

A dramatic crisis occurred at the end of the nineties when the prime minister, in an attempt to pacify the Czechs and gain their support, issued a series of decrees ordering that in districts with a mixed German and Czech population, officials must be able to use both languages. The Germans were vehemently opposed because while most Czechs knew German, most Germans did not know Czech and were therefore in danger of losing positions in the administration. Violent demonstrations arranged by German nationalists proclaiming German racial superiority took place in Vienna and most of the larger cities of German-speaking Austria. There were clashes between the army and demonstrators; under the pressure of this agitation the prime minister was dismissed and his language decrees were withdrawn.

Not without awareness of the difficulties inherent in Austria's nationality problems, the constitution provided that cabinet and crown had the power of temporary emergency legislation when the Reichsrat was not meeting, and during much of the following decade Austria was ruled on the basis of a rather doubtful application of this emergency provision. Since the eighteenth century Austria had been ruled almost uninterruptedly by bureaucrats who were highly competent in carrying out administrative tasks, but administrative routine did not suffice for the needs of modern industrial society. The government gave cautious support to industrial development, especially by furthering the construction of railroads and making gradual progress in social legislation. But it was evident that to keep pace with the developments in the other European countries, Austria needed economic and financial measures and reforms for which parliamentary approval was needed. Thus, in 1907 the government gave in to the pressure of liberal and nationalistic forces and decreed the introduction of an electoral reform that, although maintaining quotas for the various nationality groups, provided universal male suffrage. The government believed that the main protagonists of nationalism were the middle classes in the towns, whereas workers and peasants to whom the vote was now given were loyal to the monarchy or at least interested in maintaining the unity of a wide economic area. It is ironic that in the Habsburg monarchy, which in many respects must be regarded as a remnant of the Middle Ages and of absolutism, the Social Democrats supported the government; they too believed that the industrial development would suffer if the various nationalities became autonomous or even independent because then the middle classes would rule, hindering industrial development and preventing improvement of the workers' situation.

In contrast to the Austrian part of the Dual Monarchy, Hungary had a functioning parliamentary system, but voting was restricted in such a way that Magyars and great landowners could be assured of a majority. The ruling group, which through protective tariffs remained economically prosperous, began to consider its ties with the Habsburg monarchy—which required financial expenses for common obligations like defense and foreign policy—as a burden. The Independence Party, which had existed since the Revolution of 1848, again began to exert greater influence under the leadership of Franz Kossuth, son of the hero of the Hungarian revolt, Ludwig Kossuth. The demand of the party that caused a clash with the government in Vienna was the request to separate the Hungarian regiments from the rest of the army. The Hungarian government proposed that these regiments have their own insignia and that the language of military command for them be Hungarian instead of German. When Francis Joseph rejected these demands, regarding them as direct interference with his powers, the Magyars refused to recognize the government the emperor had appointed. This Magyar revolt was broken by the threat of the emperor to introduce universal suffrage, which would have destroyed both the Magyar domination and the power of the landowners. The Hungarian leaders realized that they had gone too far. Henceforth Hungarian politics was controlled by men who knew that Magyar rule in Hungary was inextricably tied to the maintenance of the empire as a whole and might suffer from changes or a general upheaval.

It may be the inherent logic of a fundamentally illogical situation that some of the most energetic leaders in the Habsburg empire turned away from ideas of domestic change and reform and came to believe that the empire could best be maintained by a policy of expansion. Their hope was that the pride aroused by military successes might form a bond among the various nationalities. But Austria-Hungary was without access to an ocean; world politics, sea power, and colonies had no attraction. As in previous centuries, the Balkans were the crucial area for Habsburg foreign policy. Because of the relationship between some of the Balkan nations and the peoples in Austria-Hungary, the nationalism of the Balkan states created unrest and dissatisfaction among the minorities living in the Dual Monarchy; at the same time, the Austrian concern with the Balkans kept alive the tension with Russia, which had its own ambitions in this area.

RUSSIA

The Autocracy in Practice

Tense and unstable though the situation was in many European countries, the only state in which the tensions led to a full-scale revolution before the First World War was Russia. In its political development, Russia was less advanced than any other European nation; at the end of the nineteenth century it was still ruled by an absolute monarch. Moreover, the man who held this formidable power was in character the most insignificant of all the monarchs of his time. The diary of Tsar Nicholas II (ruled 1894–1917), with its monotonous notices about the weather and visits of relations, even on days when the fate of his coun-

Tsar Nicholas II and the tsarina in
their coronation robes.

try and dynasty was being decided, gives the impression that for this monarch
the world was confined to the precincts of his palaces. Like other weak and stupid men, he clung with a desperate obstinacy to the few ideas with which he had
been indoctrinated in his youth, and primary among these was the conviction
that the absolute power he had inherited should be left, intact and unlimited, to
his son.

Nicholas was easily dominated by stronger personalities who shared this
belief. In the first ten years of his reign he was under the influence of the procu-
rator of the Holy Synod, Konstantin Pobedonostsev (1827–1907), who had been
his tutor and who in his religious zeal expected that the salvation of Russia
would be achieved by shutting the nation off from all liberal Western ideas. In
the tsar's later years he was dominated by his wife and the monk Rasputin. The
tsarina believed that Rasputin possessed healing powers that could keep her
hemophilic son alive. Since Rasputin's grasping and corrupting manners were
generally resented and despised, the tsarina also felt that he could be kept at
court only if the tsar remained an autocrat. Thus, it was in the interest of both
the tsarina and Rasputin to reinforce the tsar's absolutist notions. But since many
ministers opposed Rasputin's political ideas and he was frequently able to force
the dismissal of his opponents, Rasputin's presence at the court represented a
serious political issue. In rejecting the attacks against Rasputin, the tsar and
tsarina convinced themselves that their "friend" was a "holy man," through
whom they heard the "voice of the people."

It was hardly feasible for one man to govern the immense Russian Empire at
the beginning of the twentieth century. The real ruler of Russia was a gigantic
bureaucracy—slow, clumsy, uncontrolled, and corrupt. If administrators of talent
and energy did emerge—as did, for instance, Count Sergei Witte (1849–1915),

finance minister between 1892 and 1903, and, after the Revolution of 1905, Peter Stolypin (1863–1911), prime minister between 1906 and 1911—they soon found themselves entangled in bureaucratic intrigues. Furthermore, the tsar became distrustful of the new ideas advocated by such men and saw in their popularity a threat to his power. Thus, neither Witte nor Stolypin enjoyed the full support of the tsar, and he was soon anxious to get rid of them. The obvious weakness of an absolutist system in modern times was augmented by the tsar's personal defects.

The Drive toward Industrialization

The problems the Russian government faced were staggering. Russia was predominantly agricultural, but after the Crimean War it became clear that the nation would have to develop industries to remain a great power. It did possess the natural resources necessary for industrialization: coal and iron in the Donets Basin, oil in the Caucasus, cotton in Turkestan. But the obstacles to industrialization were also formidable. Before 1860, Moscow, St. Petersburg, and Kiev were the only great cities; Russia lacked the social strata which in other countries provided the capital and the skills needed for industrial development. Most of the capital therefore had to come from abroad. In 1900 more than 50 percent of the capital of Russian industrial companies was foreign; about 90 percent of the capital invested in mining and over 60 percent of the capital in metal industries were foreign. The Royal Dutch Oil Company led in the exploitation of Caucasian oil; British capital played a major role in the development of the iron industry in Ukraine.

A requisite for industrial development was the improvement of communications through the construction of a countrywide network of railroads. In the wide steppes of Russia, some of them hardly inhabited or explored, railroad construction was a complicated and difficult task that naturally fell to the state and gave it a direct share in the development of the iron and coal industries. Thus, the government was an important entrepreneur. The capital necessary for its enterprises was derived from loans, and they again were largely taken up by foreign banks, particularly the French. Almost 50 percent of all the interest paid on Russian state loans went out of Russia.

Obtaining the manpower needed for industrialization was difficult. One of the principal motives behind Alexander II's famous emancipation of the serfs in 1861 had been to make it possible for peasants to emigrate to the urban areas to become industrial workers. But this purpose was partly defeated by details in the emancipation regulations. The former serfs had to pay for the land that had been granted to them. To fulfill this obligation, village committees, mirs, were formed; these undertook to make the payments, but they needed men to work the land and were unwilling to permit emigration to the cities. In order to move to the industrial centers, the peasants either had to give up all claims to land or had to return for the harvest, spending only part of the

Early industrialization in Russia. Foundry workers in St. Petersburg, 1890.

Serfs & ulster, city

year in the cities. Unable to work continuously in industry, they remained unskilled and had to take any job given to them. Their wages were extremely low; in 1880 Russian workers in Moscow received only 25 percent as much as their British counterparts. The workers were housed in barracks, awakened by bells, marched to the factories, and marched back again after work, and then the gates of the barracks were closed. These conditions created unrest and dissatisfaction; when the workers returned to their villages and families, they gave vent to their feelings and spread revolutionary propaganda among the rural population. Moreover, Russia's industrialization suffered from the ills common to the beginnings of industrialization in all countries: the absence of health and safety precautions in the factories and of limitations on working hours, even for women and children. For instance, in the textile industries, workers were expected to work twelve to fifteen hours a day. There was no collective bargaining and no right to strike. In addition, the change in Russian social life brought about by industrialization was deeply upsetting. With the sudden eruption of big cities, industrialization in Russia was not only an economic event but an emotional experience.

Russia was the home of many nationalities. The great masses of the population in the center of the country were Russians, but the situation in the outlying districts was very different. In the west the population was Polish; in the north the Finns had been annexed to Russia only in the early nineteenth century; in the Baltic states German nobles ruled as landowners over Estonians, Latvians, and Lithuanians. The Caucasus was populated by Georgians. Most of these national groups, particularly the Poles and the Finns but also the inhabitants of the Baltic states, had formed part of the European world at the time when Russia was still isolated. Hence they were very different from the Russians in their social structure and their intellectual outlook. They had old medieval towns and a middle class. They had been active in trade and industry; the manufacture of textiles, for example, had been carried on in Poland while Russia was still purely agrarian. They had old universities, and their intellectual life was oriented toward the West. The Poles were Catholics; the Finns and the Balts were Lutherans. Religious differences reinforced the tensions arising from differences of nationality. All these non-Russians, close to the West in their outlook, felt humiliated by the absence of institutions the West possessed: constitutional government and self-administration. On the other hand, the Russian government feared that granting a constitution and self-administration would increase the centrifugal tendencies in these areas, and it was brutal enough to make various attempts at Russification, demanding the use of the Russian language and placing obstacles in the way of all churches that were not Orthodox. Moreover, the great landowners were favored at the expense of the rest of the population. All these policies only increased national feeling and social tension.

The Opposition

The usual outlets for political dissatisfaction, the usual means for testing the strength of opposition, were absent in Russia. Political parties were not permitted. Even associations like trade unions did not exist. A few professional organizations enjoyed approval, but even their meetings were supervised. There was rigorous censorship. Some critical views and plans for change and reform might be inserted in larger theoretical treatises, where they escaped the eyes of the censor, but political literature or even newspapers expressing criticism of the government had to be secretly printed and distributed. Frequently such publications were the work of exiles and were smuggled over the frontiers.

Switzerland and Great Britain were the chief destinations of Russian political émigrés. *Iskra* ("The Spark"), the main organ of the Russian Social Democratic Party, which was an underground organization, was edited and printed in Switzerland. The party's first congress, at Minsk in 1898, had resulted in the arrest of some of the leaders, and the next one, in 1903, was held first in Brussels and then in London; it was attended largely by exiles. One of the chief points of debate of the 1903 congress concerned the organization of the party: whether it should be limited to people who were active revolutionaries or should also admit those who were just sympathizers. Clearly, a small party could be directed and controlled from the outside, whereas a larger organization would be affected by the changing moods in Russia and would be less serviceable as an instrument for conspiratorial activities. The dispute also involved a broader issue. Would the overthrow of absolutism be immediately followed by a socialist state, or would socialism have to be preceded by a bourgeois liberal regime? The division on this point was the Russian version of the split in European socialism between the orthodox Marxists and the Revisionists.

The advocates of a small revolutionary party were led by Vladimir Ilich Lenin (1870–1924), a young émigré who had escaped from Siberia to Switzerland and had attracted attention by a number of brilliant articles in *Iskra*. In a vote that was of doubtful validity because a number of the principal members of the congress were absent, Lenin's faction won out, and thereafter it called itself the Bolsheviks ("majority group"). Lenin's leadership was soon bitterly attacked, and the control of the party came into the hands of his opponents, the Mensheviks ("minority group"); the Bolsheviks, led by Lenin, essentially became a socialist splinter faction. The policy of the Mensheviks, aiming at closer collaboration with other opposition elements, seemed much more realistic than that of the Bolsheviks because the workers were only a small part of the population. Dissatisfaction was not restricted to them; it was particularly strong among the peasantry. The Social Revolutionaries, who worked chiefly among the rural population, were almost more powerful than the Social Democrats. A successful revolution seemed more likely to come about through collaboration between peasants and workers than through the exclusive efforts of the proletariat on which Lenin wanted to rely.

All these opposition movements worked underground. The threat of punishment, usually exile to Siberia, hung over the head of everyone involved. Violence was the only effective expression of dissatisfaction with the government. Attempts on the lives of high officials and of members of the ruling dynasty were frequent. To discover prohibited meetings, investigate forbidden activities, and detect conspiracies, a large police force was a necessity. The police department was one of the most extended and most feared institutions of the Russian bureaucracy. The police were said to have spies in every block of houses. They infiltrated opposition groups, and the revolutionaries countered by offering themselves as spies to the police to find out about police plans. In some cases it seems impossible to establish whether a man was a police spy or a genuine revolutionary. When Prime Minister Stolypin, who had become unpopular with the reactionaries of the court, was assassinated in 1911, it was widely believed that the police had had some hand in the act. These rumors were characteristic of the atmosphere of suspicion and insecurity that permeated the entire Russian political scene.

Yet if belonging to the Russian ruling group had dangers, there were also compensations. It has been said that anyone wanting to taste the full sweetness and pleasure of life at the end of the nineteenth century should have lived among the Russian nobility. In Russia at this time landownership meant great wealth because recent innovations in transportation facilitated the export of Russian wheat to other European countries, and wheat prices were rising. The aristocrats lived in palaces in St. Petersburg and Moscow. During the year they moved from their great city palaces to their estates and to the Crimea; they traveled in private railroad cars to the Riviera, to Paris, and to London. A characteristic expression of the luxury of the Russian nobility was the popularity of the works of Fabergé, miniature sculptures constructed of precious jewels, which the members of the aristocracy found fashionable and amusing to give one another as Easter presents.

If the Russian aristocrats appeared to indulge in senseless luxuries, one reason was that they too suffered from the distrust of the absolutist ruler and his bureaucrats and were excluded from responsible participation in political life. Thus, it should not be assumed that all the members of the Russian nobility were frivolous and unaware of the seriousness of their country's political situation. Leo Tolstoy, with his radical ideas of returning to a life of pristine Christian virtues, was one such exception. Moreover, Russian aristocrats were active in the *zemstvos*, regional councils established by Alexander II, which represented the nearest approach to local self-administration in Russia. Many tried to work in the zemstvos for improvements in the economic situation and attempted to extend the sphere of activities of the zemstvos, legally limited to local and charitable tasks, to political matters. But they were always rebuffed by the government.

The Russo-Japanese War and the Revolution of 1905

Resentment about the continued absolutism of the tsars permeated almost all strata of society, and though the opposition groups differed in their concrete aims, only a spark was needed to unite them in a general revolutionary explosion. This spark was provided by the Russian defeats in the Russo-Japanese War, which was caused by Russia's attempt to expand its influence in the Far East at the expense of Japan. The war started on February 8, 1904, with a surprise attack by Japanese torpedo boats against the Russian Far Eastern squadron anchored in the harbor of Port Arthur. The subsequent defeat of the Russian land forces in the Battle of Mukden was a great surprise. Few had foreseen that a great European power could succumb to attack by an Asian state. With the wisdom of hindsight, one can recognize the reasons for the Japanese victory. The Japanese had been prepared for the war, while the supplying and strengthening of Russian forces in the Far East had been slow and difficult because the Trans-Siberian Railway had only one track and did not yet extend to the Pacific. Before Russia could bring the full weight of its military forces into play, the Russians agreed to accept the mediation of President Theodore Roosevelt of the United States in arranging a peace with Japan. A treaty with the Japanese was signed on September 5, 1905, in Portsmouth, New Hampshire.

The Russo-Japanese War placed an immense strain on the Russian system of transportation, and the provisioning of the great urban centers broke down.

Bread prices soared, and the wages of the workers proved insufficient. Spontaneous strikes broke out in many places. When on January 9, 1905, a procession of workers approached the Winter Palace of the tsar to submit to him their grievances, the way was blocked by troops, whose commander lost his head and fired on the masses. This Bloody Sunday set in motion the revolution. A general strike was declared in St. Petersburg, and most industrial centers followed suit. The workers combined into unions; the professional organizations, which had been allowed a supervised existence, now became politically active, electing new leaders and drawing up programs of political reform. The zemstvos formulated political demands. The general cry was for the creation of a parliamentary government based on universal suffrage.

Progress toward this goal was achieved in stages. In March, the tsar was forced to declare that a consultative assembly would be established. In August he conceded that this assembly would be elected, but he insisted that suffrage would be limited and the power of this assembly, the Duma, would be purely deliberative. Then a new wave of strikes and revolutionary outbreaks occurred. In October, under the pressure of a breakdown of public order, with cities like St. Petersburg and Moscow in the hands of the workers, the tsar made a further concession: The Duma would be elected on the basis of a wide franchise, and it would have legislative functions. Civil liberties would be guaranteed. The change in the political system was indicated by the appointment of a prime minister; this office was given to Count Witte. But revolutionary agitation among the workers continued, and peasant unrest began to spread. In the southern parts of Russia peasants burned the houses of landowners and occupied the land. Under the threat of this peasant revolt, the tsar, on Witte's advice, in December conceded universal and secret suffrage. But this was his last concession. Troops returning from the Far East bolstered the government; the leaders of the workers in St. Petersburg were arrested, and an insurrection of the workers in Moscow was defeated. Boris Pasternak's *Doctor Zhivago* (1957) contains a graphic description of the Cossacks riding down the masses in Moscow in the winter of 1905.

The Revolution of 1905 did not seal the fate of tsarism. It might be called a turning point that did not turn. A constitutional system was introduced. Although universal suffrage was not maintained and the voting structure favored the wealthier classes, large groups of the population were willing to cooperate with the government to make the constitution work. Moreover, the peasants were freed from making further payments for their land, and under Stolypin the dissolution of the mirs opened the way to an agricultural development based on private ownership; wealthy peasants—kulaks—began to appear. But the tsar, far from welcoming these developments, obstructed them in every way. In March 1906 he dismissed Witte, whom he believed to have made unnecessary concessions; Stolypin, who came to office later in 1906, had lost the tsar's favor by the time he was assassinated in 1911. Whenever possible, Nicholas appointed reactionary ministers. He openly bestowed his favor on the most reactionary groups, among them the Black

"Bloody Sunday," January 9, 1905. Demonstrators are fired on by troops outside the Winter Palace.

Hundreds, who with the support of the troops embarked on barbaric punitive actions against the peasants. The tsar also encouraged anti-Semitic pogroms. As before, the influence of the crown remained the chief target of all liberal forces.

Actually, the tsar might have utilized the revolution and its consequences to broaden the basis of support for his government. Through the summer of 1905 almost all social groups except for the extreme reactionaries had favored the revolutionary movement. This unified front broke down in the autumn, as agrarian unrest continued and the workers began to fight more openly for a socialist republic. Liberal aristocrats, professional groups, the middle classes—all were by then satisfied with the concessions made by the tsar in the October decree. Revolutionary activity between October and December faltered because it began to lose general support and became restricted to workers and peasants. For a moderately liberal policy the tsar could have counted on the backing of a large segment of society.

Except for the Paris Commune of 1871, previous revolutions had been bourgeois in character. The Russian Revolution of 1905 can be regarded as the first socialist revolution. It showed the immense importance of the general strike as a political weapon. Moreover, it revealed new techniques for effecting a social revolution. For the first time workers' councils, composed of men elected by the workers of the various factories, exerted a directing influence upon events and in certain critical periods functioned as an effective government. The leading spirit of the workers' council in St. Petersburg was a young socialist writer named Leon Trotsky. Like Lenin, he realized that in revolutionary times these workers' councils could serve as the authority that could prevent chaos and at the same time keep power in the hands of the proletariat.

The Russian Revolution of 1905 had a great impact all over Europe. Fear of revolution became tangible in the political atmosphere; governments became more concerned about maintaining their authority and their prestige than they had ever been before. The result was an increase in tensions within the nations of Europe and also a more intensive pursuit of success in foreign policy. Further, the dangers and opportunities in the international arena were abruptly expanded, for the sudden revelation of Russia's weakness changed the entire European scene.

CHAPTER 3

The First World War

LIKE THE DECKS of a ship floundering in heavy weather, the European political scene shifted and heaved uncertainly in the decade preceding the outbreak of the First World War. The great powers stumbled from one diplomatic crisis to the next as they contended, not very adroitly, with the demands that one of their number, Germany, was making for a "place in the sun." To complicate matters, the continuing decline of a former great power, the Ottoman Empire, opened a dangerous power vacuum in the Balkans. Nationalist animosities took on increasing virulence as opinion makers across the Continent pilloried rival nations and warned of imminent war. Many Europeans began to believe that some sort of military conflict was inevitable, and some actually pined for it. What they ultimately got, however, was something almost no one had bargained for: a war of such scope, duration, and devastation that it completely altered the political and even the cultural landscape of twentieth-century Europe.

THE RIGIDIFICATION OF THE ALLIANCE SYSTEM

The year 1905 was crucial in the unfolding of a new European diplomacy. The events of that year decided the division of the European state system into two opposing blocs. Alliances between the great powers of Europe had been in existence since the nineteenth century. Primary among them was the Triple Alliance among Germany, Austria-Hungary, and Italy; this was followed in the 1890s by the Russo-French alliance. But some flexibility, some room for maneuvering between alliances and powers, had remained. Although after Bismarck's fall the Reinsurance Treaty, through which he had tried to maintain good relations with Russia, had not been renewed, collaboration between Germany and Russia, chiefly by means of an assumed friendship and an actual familial relationship between the tsar and William II, had not entirely ceased. Most important, Great Britain was not bound by any alliance.

The rigidification of the existing compacts in 1905 did not occur overnight. Great Britain had been surprised by the reaction the Boer War had aroused on the Continent. The Boers clearly enjoyed the sympathy of the peoples on the Continent, and English defeats were viewed with a certain glee. To avoid a common stand of the great powers against them and to reinforce the security of their empire, the English needed to abandon their policy of "splendid isolation" and seek the backing of a great continental power.

The most likely potential partner of Britain was Germany, which was stronger than Britain's closest continental neighbor, France. Moreover, the interests of Great Britain and Russia, France's ally, clashed in Persia, on the northern frontier of India, and in China. However, if Britain was unpopular in Germany, Germany was no less unpopular in Britain. The British saw the German advances into Africa, China, and the South Seas as the actions of a spoiled and brutal young man who wanted to grab everything he could lay his hands on. In the eyes of the leaders of British policy, two actions of the German government posed a special danger: the construction of a powerful navy and the financing and building of the Baghdad Railway. When the German naval program began, there was probably little awareness of what its later consequences would be. Because sea power was regarded as essential for effective participation in world politics, the navy soon became popular among the German bourgeoisie; in contrast to the predominantly aristocratic officers of the army, naval officers came mainly from bourgeois families. The popular backing for the navy was efficiently promoted by the secretary of the navy, Admiral von Tirpitz, who established a special office that edited pamphlets, helped to organize navy leagues, and arranged meetings where speakers discussed the importance of naval power. This office was the forerunner of all later propaganda ministries. In 1898 the Reichstag had sanctioned a navy bill that was a new departure for Germany in that it proposed not only cruisers that might defend the German coast but also battleships fit for combat on the open sea; the bill provided for the building of eleven battleships and five first-class cruisers by 1905. The German Navy envisaged here was still small. However, two years later, in 1900, Tirpitz carried through the adoption of a second bill, which would expand the building program, calling for the construction of thirty-eight battleships to be completed in twenty years. The anti-British tendency of this second bill was evident. Tirpitz's goal was a fleet of such strength that the British would hesitate to attack Germany.

Likewise, the German project for a railroad to Baghdad developed from innocuous beginnings into an enterprise with dangerous political consequences. The capital needed and the financial risks involved were so large that the Deutsche Bank, the German financial house interested in the undertaking, obtained concessions for the project from the Turkish government in 1899 almost by default of other competitors. The leaders of the Deutsche Bank tried without success to obtain the cooperation of financiers of other countries for this enterprise. The only serious opponents of the project were the Russians. The French supported the Germans, and the British raised no objections; both Great

Britain and France were anxious to bar Russian expansion in the Near East and to involve Germany in the preservation of Turkey. However, their attitude changed when, almost unavoidably, the construction of the railroad gave Germany economic and then political control in Turkey.

If these German enterprises lowered the attractiveness of an understanding with Germany, all such attempts were cut off by the attitude of the German political leaders. The German statesmen in power, especially Chancellor Bernhard von Bülow (1849–1929) and his political adviser, Friedrich von Holstein, felt sure that Britain could turn to no other power. Thus, Germany could refuse to be satisfied with an agreement that merely delimited German and British colonial interests and wait until the time was ripe to demand a defensive alliance.

But the British government, having no intention of going that far, turned to France, and the result was the Entente Cordiale, concluded on April 8, 1904. Formally, this treaty was an agreement on all the issues concerning colonies that had occasioned disputes between Great Britain and France; the chief points were that France abandoned all its claims in Egypt and Britain recognized that France had a dominating interest in Morocco and promised diplomatic support of French plans for achieving control of Morocco. A year later what was a limited temporary agreement had become a close political partnership.

The developments that took place in 1905 were preceded by a change in the position of Russia. Throughout the nineteenth century the contrast between Great Britain and Russia had been a basic factor in European foreign policy; it was axiomatic that "bear and whale could never come together." Significantly, when the British government abandoned the policy of "splendid isolation," the first agreement it concluded was an alliance that recognized Japan's special interest in Korea. But the primary British interest in this treaty was to strengthen the barrier against any further Russian advance in the Far East. When the Russo-Japanese War broke out two years later, the Russians feared that Great Britain might enter the war on the Japanese side—especially after an incident in the North Sea in which Russian ships sailing from the Baltic to the Far East had mistakenly fired on British trawlers. Consequently, the Russians began to set great store on a benevolent neutrality of Germany and began to seek German support. This situation appeared to the German statesmen an ideal opportunity to reassert German predominance on the Continent. They persuaded themselves that because Russia, involved in the Far East, could not come to the assistance of France, this was the right moment to humiliate the French and show them that their Entente Cordiale with Great Britain was without value. They believed that German superiority and French helplessness would be strikingly demonstrated if they halted the French penetration into Morocco.

THE CRISES OF 1905–1914

The First and Second Moroccan Crises

The first Moroccan crisis started when William II, on a Mediterranean trip in March 1905, debarked briefly in Tangier and solemnly declared that the Germans were willing to maintain the independence of Morocco. When the French protested, the Germans demanded an international conference to adjudicate the dispute, fully expecting the conference to demonstrate France's isolation and impotence. The French at first rejected this demand but eventually agreed to the conference after being assured of British backing for their position. Thus, when the conference convened in the Spanish port of Algeciras in January 1906, it was not France but Germany that was in an almost isolated position. A test vote on a minor question revealed that Russia, France, Britain, Italy, and even the United States all sided with France; only Austria-Hungary voted with Germany. This suggested that if Germany decided to unleash a war with France, it would now be opposed by every great power but Austria. Chancellor von Bülow realized that Germany had to give in. The final agreement was couched in diplomatic language, but Germany's defeat was evident: France would be the dominant power in a nominally independent Morocco. More important, France could be assured of not standing alone against an increasingly aggressive Germany. Indeed, the conference was significant primarily for what it revealed about the diplomatic constellation in Europe. At Algeciras, the powers that would confront one another in the First World War found themselves for the first time grouped in opposing camps.

Germany, however, did not fully grasp the implications of the first Moroccan crisis and in the summer of 1911 again tried to bully France, thereby provoking a second Moroccan crisis and suffering a new diplomatic defeat. Following an outbreak of internal struggles in Morocco, Germany dispatched a gunboat to the Moroccan port of Agadir, allegedly to protect German commercial interests threatened by France's intervention to suppress the disruptions. This move alarmed the British more than the French since London worried that Germany might try to establish a naval base at Agadir, which could threaten Gibraltar. Lloyd George delivered a stern warning to Germany in a speech at Mansion House on July 21, 1911. Although the French government consented to negotiate with the Germans, it was unprepared to yield much since it knew it had the support of Britain. In the agreement that was eventually signed, France gained a free hand in Morocco, and Germany received a part of the French Congo connecting the German Cameroons with the Congo River, a small compensation for Berlin. Again, moreover, Germany had failed to intimidate the French or to drive a wedge between the Entente powers; on the contrary, its gunboat diplomacy had succeeded only in confirming the other nations' perception of Germany as a dangerously aggressive new power.

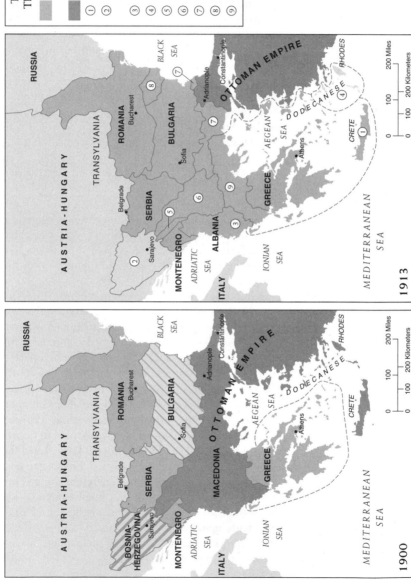

THE RESULTS OF
THE BALKAN WARS

Independent Balkan
states

Ottoman Empire

① To Greece, 1908
② Annexed by
   Austria-Hungary, 1909
③ New state, 1912
④ To Italy, 1912
⑤ To Montenegro, 1913
⑥ To Serbia, 1913
⑦ To Bulgaria, 1913
⑧ To Romania, 1913
⑨ To Greece, 1913

1913

RUSSIA

AUSTRIA-HUNGARY

TRANSYLVANIA

ROMANIA

Bucharest

BULGARIA

Sofia

SERBIA

Belgrade

Sarajevo

MONTENEGRO

ALBANIA

GREECE

Athens

ITALY

ADRIATIC
SEA

IONIAN
SEA

MEDITERRANEAN
SEA

AEGEAN
SEA

DODECANESE

CRETE

RHODES

BLACK
SEA

Adrianople

Constantinople

OTTOMAN EMPIRE

0   100   200 Miles
0   100   200 Kilometers

1900

RUSSIA

AUSTRIA-HUNGARY

TRANSYLVANIA

ROMANIA

Bucharest

BULGARIA

Sofia

SERBIA

Belgrade

Sarajevo

BOSNIA-
HERZEGOVINA

MONTENEGRO

MACEDONIA

GREECE

Athens

ITALY

ADRIATIC
SEA

IONIAN
SEA

MEDITERRANEAN
SEA

AEGEAN
SEA

DODECANESE

CRETE

RHODES

BLACK
SEA

Adrianople

Constantinople

OTTOMAN EMPIRE

0   100   200 Miles
0   100   200 Kilometers

War and Crisis in the Balkans

In 1908, Germany's Austrian ally took an important step in strengthening its influence in the Balkans by annexing the Turkish provinces of Bosnia and Herzegovina. The Germans put pressure on Turkey, now under the control of a revolutionary new regime led by the modernizing "Young Turks," to accept the annexations. The country that was most indignant over the Austrian action was Serbia. Because the peoples of Bosnia and Herzegovina were primarily South Slavs, the Serbs felt that they, not the Austrians, ought to rule these provinces. Encouraged by Russian backing, Serbia made military preparations, and Austria followed suit. Finally, in March 1909, the German government sent a sharp note to Russia demanding that it abandon its support of Serbia and recognize Austria's annexation of Bosnia and Herzegovina. Still reeling from its loss in the Russo-Japanese war, St. Petersburg gave in.

However, the possibility of avoiding war if tensions continued in the Balkans became increasingly less likely. After the Agadir crisis the focus of tension shifted to the east. From 1912 onward the affairs of the Ottoman Empire and the national aspirations of the Balkan nations evoked one crisis after the other. The prelude was the war that began in September 1911 between Turkey and Italy. All the great powers had recognized that Tripoli was in the Italian sphere of interest; when France finally absorbed Morocco, the Italian government decided to take action and proclaimed the annexation of Tripoli. Turkey answered with a declaration of war against Italy. The Italians won a quick victory, but in the meantime the Tripolitan War triggered action in the Balkans. Serbia and Bulgaria believed that if they did not take action before the end of Turkey's conflict with Italy, they might miss an opportunity for driving the Turks out of Europe. They succeeded in getting the support of Montenegro and Greece, and war against Turkey broke out in October 1912. The Turkish troops in the Balkans were defeated in a number of battles in which the Bulgarian and Serbian soldiers proved themselves to be excellent warriors.

But a diplomatic settlement was much more difficult to achieve than military victory. There was dissension among the victors about drawing the frontiers after the war had assured the end of Turkish rule in Europe. The two areas about which disposition had to be made were Macedonia and Albania.

Bulgaria, Greece, and Serbia all demanded parts of Macedonia, and the claims of Greece and Bulgaria were particularly irreconcilable because both were anxious to control the northern coast of the Aegean Sea. The result was a second Balkan war, in which Greece, Serbia, Romania, and Turkey rallied against Bulgaria. The outcome of this war determined that only a very small part of Macedonia fell to Bulgaria. Most of Macedonia was divided between Serbia and Greece, and the Turks regained Adrianople. The division of Macedonia among three powers remained a cause for tension and conflict among them almost until the end of the Second World War.

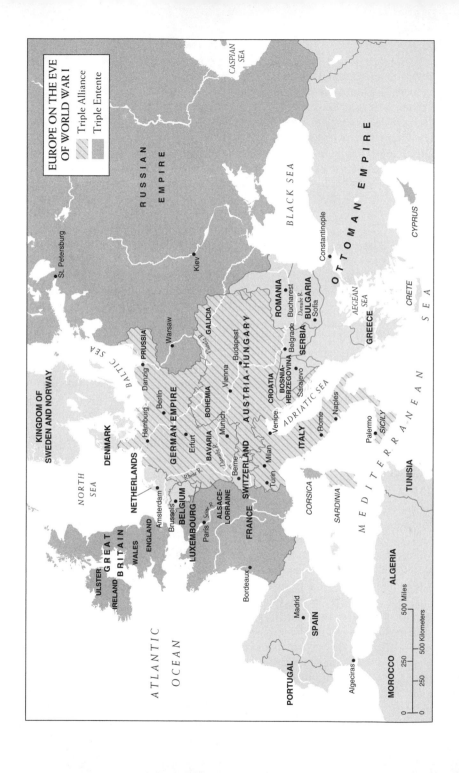

EUROPE ON THE EVE
OF WORLD WAR I

Triple Alliance

Triple Entente

The Serbs were less successful in their demand for Albanian territory that would give them a direct access to the Adriatic Sea. The great powers, meeting with the Balkan nations and Turkey in London, forced Serbia and Montenegro to accept the creation of an independent Albania. Serbia remained cut off from the Adriatic.

In the meetings in London, Russia had backed the claims of Serbia, whereas Austria-Hungary advocated those of Bulgaria and together with Italy sharply opposed the Serbian demand for access to the Adriatic Sea. To underline the seriousness with which they looked upon the situation, both Russia and Austria-Hungary made some military preparations. Great Britain and Germany cooperated to obtain a peaceful solution of the conflict. Nevertheless, the Balkan wars accumulated new explosive material that the compromise worked out by the great powers in London concealed rather than eliminated. Turkey, in need of military reorganization, called in a German general, but this move evoked violent Russian protests because it appeared to be a further step in the establishment of German control over Turkey. Both Russia and Austria indicated that in the negotiations about the final resettlement of the Balkan wars they should have received stronger support from their respective friends, Great Britain and Germany. Consequently, in both Britain and Germany the government leaders felt that their alliances might be endangered if in the next emergency they did not give stronger support to their allies. But the most dangerous consequence of the Balkan wars was that all the resentment of Serbian nationalism was now focused on the Habsburg

The murder at Sarajevo. *Above:* Archduke Francis Ferdinand on his visit to Bosnia a few hours before his assassination. *Right:* The police seizing the assassin, Gavrilo Princip.

monarchy. The Serbs had considered the Austrian annexation of Bosnia and Herzegovina in 1908 to be a blow to Serbia's aspirations to become the home of all South Slavs. Now, in 1913, Austria-Hungary had again been the chief obstacle to Serbia's ambitions and had deprived it of the fruits of victory: access to the Adriatic Sea. To the nationalistic Serbs the Habsburg monarchy was an old, evil monster that prevented their nation from becoming a great and powerful state. On June 28, 1914, a young Serbian nationalist, Gavrilo Princip, assassinated the heir to the Habsburg monarchy, the archduke Francis Ferdinand, and his wife at Sarajevo.

THE OUTBREAK OF THE FIRST WORLD WAR

The events of the five weeks between the assassination of the archduke Francis Ferdinand and the outbreak of the First World War have been more carefully investigated than almost any others in world history. An endless number of books and articles have reviewed and probed all aspects of the question of responsibility for the outbreak of the war: whether the Serbian government had knowledge of the plans for the assassination of the archduke; whether Germany encouraged Austria-Hungary to take action against Serbia and deliberately instigated a general war in 1914; whether France believed this crisis would be a favorable opportunity for starting a war in order to regain Alsace-Lorraine and therefore stiffened the attitude of its Russian ally; whether military requirements restricted and eliminated the freedom of decision of the political leaders; and whether British policy was mistaken in not taking a clear stand. On this last point, the British historian Niall Ferguson has argued that Sir Edward Grey, Britain's foreign secretary, unnecessarily antagonized the Germans by taking an all-too-clear stance in favor of France. Had Grey worked diplomatically to clear a more prominent place for the Germans at the table of world power, Ferguson's argument goes, the First World War and all the catastrophes it brought in its wake might have been averted. This is an intriguing proposition, but like all the other "what if?" alternative scenarios surrounding the outbreak of World War I, it remains pure speculation.

At any rate, it is probable that the responsible leaders of the Serbian government did not know about the plans for the attempt on the life of the archduke. On the other hand, the assassination was the work not of an individual but of a group of Bosnian and Serbian nationalists, who were encouraged and promoted by a Serbian secret society, the Black Hand, in which the chief of the intelligence department of the Serbian general staff was a leading figure. However, when in an ultimatum of July 23, 1914, the Austrian government accused Serbian government officials of being involved in the plot, it had no proof, based its accusation on falsified documents, and did not mention the Black Hand, specifying only individuals and organizations that in truth had nothing to do with the assassination. Thus, the assassination was consciously used by the Austrian government for the purposes of power politics: to remove the threat Serbia represented to the existence of the Habsburg monarchy. As further proof that this was Austria's intention, although the Serbian government accepted almost all the demands of the exceedingly harsh and humiliating ultimatum, the Austrian minister in Belgrade, acting on instructions given to him before he had received the Serbian note, declared the Serbian answer unsatisfactory and left Belgrade, making war between the two states inevitable.

However, without the certainty of German backing, the Austrian leaders would not have embarked on the war against Serbia. Actually, Austrian governmental circles were divided in their views on the course to follow; influential men, notably the Hungarian prime minister, Tisza, were opposed to any action that might lead to war. However, the German government urged the Austrians to resolute action against Serbia, and Tisza's hesitations were overcome when he was given proof that Germany desired Austria to proceed against Serbia and had promised support if other powers became involved in the conflict.

The Germans encouraged Austria because they regarded the death of the heir to the Habsburg throne as a danger signal foreshadowing a possible collapse of the Habsburg monarchy, which would leave Germany without allies. The Germans hoped that a successful show of strength against Serbia might revitalize the Habsburg monarchy. Since the assassination of the archduke and his wife had aroused general indignation and widespread sympathy for the Austrian emperor, there seemed to be a chance that the war between Austria and Serbia might remain localized. However, from the outset, the Germans were aware that the Austrian action against Serbia ran the risk of a general war in which Russia, France, and Great Britain might be allied against Germany and Austria, and the justifiable indictment against the German leaders might be made that they willingly accepted this risk. Their attitude was the result of a variety of circumstances. A predominant part of the German ruling group was obsessed with the idea that the future belonged to the great world powers and that Germany would become a world power only through a war that would show it to be equal to the strongest and would gain for the German people and for German economic expansion a broader territorial basis than it possessed. Moreover, if war was long delayed, Germany's chances for ascending to the small circle of world powers might be missed forever. Once Russia, with its large population and great mineral resources, became fully developed, it would tower over all its neighbors, and Germany's opportunities for development would disappear. From a purely military point of view too, time seemed to be running against Germany. In a few years Russia's recovery from losses and defeat and France's three-year conscription law would tilt the military balance against Germany. Historical speculations, economic expansionism, and military calculations reinforced one another to create a climate in which war became acceptable. Such considerations guided the policy of the German government.

Chancellor Bethmann-Hollweg was an earnest and responsible man inclined to pessimism, and he was aware that the consequences of a world war were unforeseeable. Yet he encouraged Austria to take action, and he gave the Austrian statesmen a free hand, fully conscious of the risk that a great European conflict might result. Bethmann-Hollweg was not simply bowing to the demands of the military, who carried such a powerful weight in imperial Germany; he was himself among those who saw the growing Russian power as a threat to Germany's future, and he had an almost fatalistic belief that a world war was coming. In 1914 Germany's chances would be better than in later years. In the last critical days, when the prophesied world war threatened to become reality, Bethmann-Hollweg seems to have become frightened by his own courage, and he made some desperate attempts to keep the conflict between Austria and Serbia localized, but in his heart he must have been aware that these efforts were condemned to failure.

If for no other reason, these last attempts could not succeed because the Austrians had wasted in an almost incredible manner the sympathy the assassination had aroused. They sent their ultimatum to Serbia only on July 23—after more than three weeks—when the excitement about the murder of the archduke had begun to die down. The reason for the delay was Austrian dilatoriness (*Schlamperei*), although they rationalized these delays by maintaining that the harvest in Hungary had to be gathered in before they could call the men to arms. In the end, there was a further postponement of three days because the French president, Poincaré, was visiting the tsar and the Austrians did not want to present the ultimatum until Poincaré had left Russia, so that the Russian and French governments would not be able to agree immediately upon joint action.

Poincaré and the French prime minister were in St. Petersburg from July 20 to July 23, 1914. It is not known what they said in private to their Russian hosts about the course that ought to be pursued in the approaching crisis between Austria-Hungary and Serbia. In their public declarations, the French and Russian statesmen emphasized the close bonds uniting the Russian Empire and the French republic, and this must have strengthened the Russian will to oppose the Austrian action. In the following critical week the French ambassador in Russia certainly encouraged the Russian government to take a firm line. The Russians were in a better military position than they had been in 1908: their army had been built up, and transport had been improved by the development of the railroad system in western Russia. Unquestionably, the Russian rulers, under the pressure of an excited public and of military men eager to avenge the defeat of 1905, felt unable to accept another diplomatic setback and decided to prevent Austria from encroaching upon Serbian integrity and sovereignty. On July 24, they were informed of the contents of the Austrian ultimatum, and they decided that if Austria took action against Serbia, they would institute partial mobilization, which meant mobilization of the military districts close to the Austrian border. But on July 30, after Austria had rejected the Serbian answers, had

Russian infantry marching to the Petrograd train station, 1914.

declared war against Serbia, and had mobilized part of its forces, the Russian government persuaded the tsar to declare a general mobilization. The reasons for this change of plan were in part technical. The Russian general staff believed that after a partial mobilization was under way, it would be difficult and slow to organize a general mobilization. It also seems clear, however, that this step must have been necessitated by Russian-French military agreements. The Russians and the French had some general knowledge of the German war plans. They were aware that at the outset most of the German military forces would be concentrated against France and that the possibility of successful French resistance depended on a quick advance of Russian troops into Germany.

After the Russians had ordered a general mobilization on July 30, the military timetables the various general staffs had worked out began to dominate political action. The Russian action impelled the German military leaders to demand immediate mobilization and to urge full mobilization on Austria. According to the military plans agreed on by the German and Austrian chiefs of staff, the Austrian armies were to slow down the Russian advances toward Germany while the bulk of the German Army, engaged in the attempt to knock France out of the war, would be unable to protect Germany's eastern frontier. With the Russians mobilizing, Austrian general mobilization, which would make possible quick counteraction, was required, but it was also necessary that the German campaign against France be started immediately and ended in time for German troops to be moved from the west to the east before the Austrian resistance against the superior Russian forces broke down. Thus, the German military leaders were anxious to terminate all further diplomatic negotiations so they could invade France. Neither the monarchs of the three empires—Francis Joseph, Nicholas II, and William II—nor their chief civilian advisers had the courage to resist the military leaders who declared that without mobilization their campaign plans would be ruined and the existence of their nations would be endangered. Germany sent an ultimatum to Russia demanding immediate cessation of military preparations, and when no satisfactory answer had been received, declared war on Russia, on August 1. This move was followed on August 3 by a declaration of war against France, which the Germans justified with the palpably false statement that French forces had violated the German frontier.

The irrevocability of the military timetables condemned to failure the last-minute attempts of Sir Edward Grey, the British foreign secretary, to halt mobilization and convoke a conference. British diplomacy had worked hard to save the peace, but the question has been raised of whether it followed the right tactics. Could peace have been maintained if at an early stage of the crisis Grey had declared that Great Britain would back France and Russia in case of war? An early British commitment might have gained time for a conference. Austria might have hesitated to take action against Serbia, and Russia, secure in the promise of British help, might have been less anxious to order general mobilization. Those who defend Grey's attitude argue that an assurance of British support might have had the contrary effect of encouraging Russia and France to assume an aggressive attitude. Moreover, Grey's defenders question whether a British declaration would have deterred Germany from its course because the Germans did expect Britain to enter the war but not soon enough to save France from defeat.

Moreover, Grey might have hesitated to make any definite statement on what Britain would do in case of war because he could not be sure whether the British people would follow his lead. British public opinion was split on the issue. Decision was brought about only by the German invasion of Belgium on August 3. Belgium's neutrality had been guaranteed by an international treaty to which Germany was a party, and this violation of international law by Germany convinced both the British government and the British people of the necessity of entering the conflict. War was declared on August 4.

During the critical week before the German violation of Belgian neutrality, the Conservatives had favored the participation of Britain because of its ties with France and its interest in maintaining the balance of power. The Labor Party opposed intervention. This view was shared by the radical wing of the Liberal Party; thus, the Liberals lacked any uniform policy on the issue. The Liberal government, like the Liberal Party, was divided; even after the violation of Belgian neutrality two members of the government resigned to demonstrate their opposition to Britain's participation. In the debates and discussions on this issue Sir Edward Grey favored British entry into the war but maintained that Britain had a free hand and was not obligated to support France and Russia. Formally he was right, in that a binding political alliance had not been concluded. The agreements between the British and French general staffs were purely military. Nevertheless, Grey's contention that Britain was free to choose its course was questionable. On the basis of the conversations between the two general staffs, the French could expect the arrival of a British expeditionary force on French soil. No general staff would make such arrangements without informing its government and having its approval. In denying the existence of a commitment to France, Grey either was incredibly naïve about the possibility of separating political and military planning or was bending the truth to avoid arousing the resentment of the radicals in his party. The French ambassador in London, Paul Cambon, in demanding a British declaration of war against Germany, said that the British answer to this request would show whether "the word 'honor' will not have to be stricken out of the British vocabulary." Grey himself felt immensely relieved when, after the invasion of Belgium, the cabinet decided to enter the war. Waverers were won over by the argument that Britain's participation had now become a moral necessity.

The European Attitude toward War in 1914

The First World War revealed the frightfulness of warfare in the industrial age. But the terrible losses in human life and material resources caused by the war have colored and distorted the interpretation of the events of July and August 1914. The discussion of the origins of the First World War has been dominated by the question of guilt: historical research has been essentially an effort to determine the distribution of guilt among the individuals and nations involved. It should therefore be emphasized that in 1914 war was not considered a crime but was regarded as a legitimate, though unpleasant and dangerous, instrument of politics.

Certainly a few people did have some notion of the changes in warfare brought about by the enormously increased destructiveness of modern weapons. Courageous and far-seeing individuals had tried to arouse the public to the dangers of modern war by organizing pacifist movements. The destructiveness of war had also been underlined by the two international peace conferences held in The Hague in 1899 and 1907. But these conferences had been concerned with the limitation of armaments and with the humanizing of war rather than with its abolition. Up to 1914 no attempt had been made to prohibit war itself. Moreover, almost everyone was convinced that because the European economy had become a complex integrated structure, a war could last only a few weeks or months and would be quickly decided in a few great battles. Nobody in 1914 was able to envisage the possibilities that would become stark reality in the next few years.

If government leaders hesitated to embark on the adventure of military conflict, they were not deterred by fear of being stamped as criminals. Rather, after the experiences of the Franco-Prussian War and the Russo-Japanese War, they saw lurking behind each war the danger of revolution. They were aware that they might unleash forces the existing ruling group might be unable to control. The governments of the European nations had another equally weighty reason for refraining from obvious aggression: their armies were based on conscription of the male population. It seemed difficult, if not impossible, to ask people to abandon civilian life and peaceful occupations when the necessity of war was not obvious. Separated by a deep rift from the bourgeois world, the workers were thought to be unwilling to accept war unless convinced that an attack had been made on a peaceful country by external enemies.

Thus, in the summer of 1914 all the European governments were eager to appear as the innocent victims of aggression. In the course of the First World War this moralistic element, this insistence on the righteousness of one's own cause, grew steadily in emphasis. Increasing hatred of the enemy bolstered internal strength. It helped stiffen the will to resist and minimized social and political friction. The war became a struggle of good against evil, which had to be fought through until the enemy was completely destroyed.

The fear in government circles that the lower classes would resist mobilization had been primarily caused by the declaration of the Socialist Second International that the workers ought to respond to a call to arms with a general strike. Actually none of the European socialist parties heeded the recommendation of the Second International. Each of them backed the war policy of its government. Not only did opposition fail to materialize, but the outbreak of war was greeted with an almost delirious enthusiasm. This astonishing response points to causes of war that went deeper than the calculations and miscalculations of foreign ministers and diplomats.

In most European countries the war seemed like a liberation from an unbearable situation. The feeling that political developments had reached a dead end was widespread among the ruling groups—not only in tsarist Russia and in Austria-Hungary, where the governments were involved in a desperate struggle to maintain outmoded forms of rule, but all over Europe. In Great Britain, the reforms of the Liberal government did not mitigate social tensions; labor conflicts and strikes had been particularly vehement in the years immediately before the outbreak of the war. Furthermore, although an attempt to solve the Irish question could no longer be postponed, the situation in Ireland endangered the authority of the government. In France, politics had again become polarized between right and left, which opposed each other with renewed vehemence. In Italy, impatience with the government's cautious policy of industrialization and democratization had stirred up extreme antiparliamentary movements on the right and left. In Germany, the elections to the Reichstag in 1912, from which the Social Democrats emerged as the strongest political party, had demonstrated that the masses could not be reconciled to their lack of political power by orderly administration and measures of social welfare. The years before the First World War are usually regarded as having been full of sun and light in contrast to the darkness that descended on Europe in 1914. But actually the unrest in the years immediately preceding the outbreak of the war was great. This does not mean that the conflict was unavoidable. The war that began in 1914 was not an imperialist war in the sense that the economic interests of the various European nations were bound to clash. The economic expansion over the entire globe had increased both competition and cooperation among the financial and industrial companies of the various countries; in general, businessmen were no advocates of war. Also, despite strikes and violence, the possibility of an immediate revolution did not threaten the governments of those European states with enough reliable military and police forces to keep order; these included Great Britain, Germany, and France. Therefore, these nations did not need to take recourse to war to stave off their overthrow. But industrialization had created and was creating problems that steadily mounted and that no form of government—neither authoritarianism nor parliamentarianism—seemed to be able to solve. There originated a longing for a turn of events that would make all these intractable problems disappear. To some politicians, weary of seeing their nation divided into hostile camps, war seemed to promise the restoration of a common purpose.

THE NATURE OF TOTAL WAR

As time has passed since the days of August 1914, it has become increasingly clear that the outbreak of the First World War meant the end of an age. To be sure, if we consider carefully the developments of the decades preceding the war, we can distinguish trends and tendencies that were steering European politics and social life into new waters. But the First World War reinforced these trends and thus accelerated the tempo of change.

It would be a mistake to assume that the new era began only in 1918, with the end of hostilities. The First World War was not just a violent interlude separating the old era from the new. The new age came about during the war years, and what happened between 1914 and 1918 helps make the period that followed comprehensible.

Most immediately apparent were the changes effected by the conflict itself, by innovations in the techniques and the conduct of the war. When the European powers mobilized in the radiant late-summer days of 1914, the troops marching through the streets to the railroad stations, accompanied by jubilant crowds, offered an impressive and colorful sight. Flowers were strewn before the men who were expected to return triumphant after a few weeks. Flags flew, bands played, and the soldiers went singing into the war. In the first months, military action was conducted in a traditional manner. Extended columns of infantry marched along the roads. The cavalry scouted enemy positions; officers led their men to storm a town or village. But after the initial battles in the west the lines became weirdly silent. Soldiers dug themselves into deep trenches fortified by barbed wire; a no-man's-land between the opposing positions was illuminated at night by rockets, intended to reveal any enemy patrols trying to penetrate the lines. The graceful, elegant horses of the cavalry became superfluous. Reconnaissance was most efficient from the air, and sometimes these scouting planes armed with machine guns engaged in air battles. Pilots became the popular war heroes. The infantry soldier, clad in mud-colored gray or khaki, still had his rifle and bayonet, but his most valuable weapons were the hand grenade, the spade, and the machine gun. Before the war was over, poison gas was being directed against enemy lines, and tanks moved clumsily over fields and trenches.

The changes in sea warfare were no less considerable. With one exception—the indecisive meeting of the British and German fleets at Jutland (1916)—no naval battles took place. Warships were used to protect convoys against the attacks of submarines, which became the supreme weapon in the struggle for control of the seas.

These changes indicate that in the twentieth century war was becoming more than the struggle of armed forces; not without reason does the term *total war* appear. To maintain a flow of the weapons that had become decisive, the continuous functioning of a sophisticated industrial complex was required. When the war broke out, only a very few had an inkling of the importance of a steady supply of raw materials and manpower, and it took some time for political and military leaders to be convinced of this fact.

It is important to remember too that although World War I was primarily a European conflict, the soldiers who fought in it included men from the European

British colonial troops posing with a British officer.

nations' colonies, dominions, and dependencies. Thousands of Senegalese, Indians, and Canadians supplemented Allied forces on the western front. Australians and New Zealanders took the lion's share of casualties in the ill-fated Gallipoli campaign in western Turkey. The First World War spread to such distant outposts of European colonization as Egypt, Mesopotamia, Persia, Africa, and the central Pacific. Japan attacked German holdings in China. The entry of the United States in 1917 of course added yet another non-European dimension to this truly global conflict, the devastating consequences of which crucially weakened the old European nations, opening the way for the rising new powers of the non-European world.

Yet perhaps the most important change to emerge from the carnage of the First World War was a new attitude toward war itself on the part of the soldiers obliged to fight it. The glaring contrast between the glittering phrases used by politicians and publicists to justify the slaughter and the grim realities of daily life in the trenches—thigh-high mud, voracious lice, corpse-fattened rats, cadavers and body parts strewn across no-man's-land—led to a heightened sense of irony about the entire martial enterprise. From the Great War emerged a generation much less inclined to see war as a brilliantly sporting and noble affair, a kind of armed version of the Olympic Games. Though of course, there continued to be those who romanticized the war experience, the majority of war memoirs and war novels produced in the 1920s depicted the action (at least for the ground soldiers) as mechanically and anonymously brutal, as the martial equivalent of dehumanizing factory work.

The Home Front

In the question of manpower, the crucial problem was to reconcile military and industrial needs. Miners and steelworkers might be perfectly suited for military service, but they possessed the skills and the physical abilities needed in mines and industry. Priorities had to be established. As the war dragged on and casualties became heavy, the tapping of new sources of manpower became a constant concern of the governments. The age limits for military service were extended, and women were employed in jobs previously reserved for men, working in offices and factories, as streetcar conductors and farmhands.

The increased presence of women in the work force affected the lives of middle-class women more than those of the proletariat because the latter had been working outside the home for years. Some working-class women, however, now took on white-collar jobs that had previously been closed to them. Despite the obvious need for women to take the place of men called to the front, many males opposed the hiring of females even when the women promised to leave their jobs when the war was over. Although women's wages went up during the war both in absolute terms and in comparison to men's earnings, females still made less than men for doing essentially the same work. For example, women employed in metallurgy in Paris before the war earned about

War enthusiasm in 1914. Young men, volunteering for military service, marching on Unter den Linden, Berlin's main street.

45 percent of what their male counterparts brought home; by 1918 that ratio had risen to 84 percent.

Every industry not immediately serving military ends had to be reduced to a minimum. One reason was the need for conserving manpower; another, the scarcity of raw materials. Before the conflict no European country had been self-sufficient. France, which had been less dependent on imports than other European powers, soon lost this advantageous position because a great part of its most industrialized regions was occupied by the Germans. International trade, through which raw materials had been obtained in peacetime, was interrupted by military action. Moreover, the importation of raw materials represented a drain on the gold reserves of each country because the manufacture of the exports that had brought in foreign currency was no longer possible. Strict control over raw materials—their conservation, collection, and distribution to factories according to military needs—became necessary.

Maintenance of the supply of food was the most burning problem, not only in great industrial countries like Great Britain and Germany, which in peacetime had relied on imported wheat and other foodstuffs, but also in agrarian countries like Austria and France, where conscription denuded the land of agricultural workers. Moreover, the transportation of food to the urban centers was difficult because the railroads were overtaxed by military needs. All the governments resorted to rationing, which usually began with bread and meat, then extended to other foodstuffs, and finally included clothes, soap, and so on. Thus, manpower, raw materials, consumer goods all were placed under government control.

Ministries for directing economic activities were established. Strikes were outlawed; working hours, prolonged. Scarcity of goods drove prices upward, and price regulations became necessary to avoid a sharpening of the conflict between rich and poor with damaging consequences for civilian morale. Price regulations, however, were acceptable to employers only if they were supplemented by wage controls. In the planning and executing of such measures, governments sought the support of industrialists and trade union leaders, since their consent was necessary in carrying out these measures. Governments became deeply involved in the functioning of economic life in all its aspects. Certainly government intervention in economic affairs and government regulation of economic life were more thorough in some countries than in others—more complete in Germany and Great Britain than in Austria-Hungary, Russia, and Italy, with their ineffective bureaucracies. Nevertheless, the subjection of economic activities to government regulation all over Europe represented a radical break with the notion that the economy could function only when free from government intervention. Unquestionably, rationing and government regulations were the only possible means of assuring the existence of all the people. Even so, on the Continent, particularly in Russia, Austria, and Germany, these measures provided hardly a subsistence minimum; people were hungry and easily exhausted, and black markets, from which the wealthy added to their rations, resulted in a spread of corruption and a decline in morale.

One telling index of the growing morale problem on the home front was the rising frustration of women, who shouldered the primary burdens of running households in the face of mounting prices for food, fuel, and other necessities. Thus, it is not surprising that women began taking to the streets in all the belligerent nations to demand more equitable distribution of resources and the enforcement of government price controls. In Germany, where the "civil truce" on the home front broke down earliest, proletarian women in Berlin engaged in riots against high food prices as early as October 1915. In one such instance a group of women descended on a butter store whose owner had jacked up his prices. When he responded to their complaints by telling them that they'd soon be paying six marks for a pound of butter and "eating shit for dessert," they beat him up and smashed his windows. In addition to the trials of sustaining their families on the home front, women faced the threat, and all too often the horrible reality, of losing their husbands and sons on the battlefield. Upon learning that her son Peter had been killed on the western front in October 1914, the German artist Käthe Kollwitz confided to her diary: "There is in our lives a wound which will never heal. Nor should it." Kollwitz later sculpted a modern pietà consisting of a mother mourning her dead child, a work that became a

Because of the manpower shortage on the home front, women were employed in a gun factory.

poignant symbol for all mothers who lost children in the carnage of twentieth-century warfare.

As the suffering of Europe's women made manifest, the devastation of World War I increasingly encompassed the entire life of each nation. To be sure, airplane construction was not yet advanced enough to permit mass bombing. A few raids by airplanes over enemy cities and a few flights of the big German airship the Zeppelin over the English east coast and London were more effective in inspiring terror than in inflicting serious damage. But they were signs of the form of wars to come.

The chief instrument used to throttle the economic life of the enemy was the blockade. The British controlled the North Sea and prevented Germany from receiving supplies from the other side of the Atlantic. The Germans suddenly recognized that their strongest weapon in sea warfare was the submarine, and they declared the entire British Isles to be blockaded territory and claimed the right to search and sink all ships approaching British ports.

Given the crucial importance of the home front in the First World War, the governments did all they could to maintain their people's morale. In all countries censorship was used, both to prevent the spreading of news that might be helpful to the enemy and to control and direct all news media toward the strengthening of civilian morale. It was as a consequence of the First World War

Käthe Kollwitz, painter and sculptress.

that "propaganda" came to be a pejorative term; all governments installed propaganda offices, and all of them falsified news. One of the chief duties of the war propaganda offices was to discredit the enemy, to paint him in the darkest colors, so that the populace would become convinced that defeat would mean the destruction of all that was worth living for. The practice of viewing the war as a struggle against evil increased steadily. Anti-German propaganda was particularly effective because the conduct of the Germans provided a factual basis for reports of their atrocities. The brutal behavior of the German armies in Belgium was undeniable. Because they had expected to pass through unmolested, the Belgian resistance infuriated them. The suddenness of the German invasion made it impossible for the Belgians to mobilize, and many fought in civilian clothes, identified as soldiers only by armbands. This practice was accepted in international law, but the Germans considered all those fighting out of uniform to be franc-tireurs (civilian terrorists), to be shot when captured. The impression that the entire civilian population of Belgium was resisting made the Germans jittery; they took hostages and executed them when they found opposition. In the last week of August the London *Times* called the Germans Huns, in reference to events in Louvain. There, in the belief that sniping had occurred and that Louvain was full of franc-tireurs, the Germans shot a large number of citizens and set the town on fire. The famous old library of the university was entirely destroyed. The "vandalism of Louvain" was soon aggravated by the "crime of Rheims." In September 1914 the Germans, convinced that the tower of the Cathedral of Rheims served as a French observation post, fired on the cathedral, severely damaging the roof and the nave. Even if the tower was being used, the destruction wrought on a great monument of European art was indefensible. The Germans provided further food for propaganda against them by their ruthless occupation policy in Belgium. They executed Edith Cavell, a nurse who had helped British and French soldiers to escape over the borders into the neutral Netherlands, ignoring the fact, recognized by some of their own occupation officers, that as head of a hospital she had selflessly worked to mitigate the sufferings of soldiers of all nations and deserved mercy rather than justice. Another incident, called by President Wilson "one of the most distressing and I think one of the most unjustifiable incidents of the present war," was the deportation of more than a hundred thousand Belgian workers into Germany.

The War Aims

Nurtured by propaganda and publicly proclaimed by all governments was the notion that the enemy was evil and that his defeat would create the foundation for a better world. This ideological and moralistic view made impossible a negotiated peace aimed at reestablishing a balance of power and restoring international collaboration. Each side was convinced that the war could end only with the complete defeat of the enemy, so that an entirely new world could be created. Each therefore attempted to present its war aims in generalized idealistic terms showing that victory would serve the interest of all mankind. Formulation of such war aims was relatively easy for Great Britain, France, and their allies in the last two years of the conflict. The war was declared to be a struggle for a new world order based on the principles of democracy and national self-determination, its purpose succinctly summarized in the famous slogan "To make the world safe for democracy." As long as Russia, with its authoritarian government, was a member of the coalition against Germany, the assertion about fighting for democracy had a hollow sound. But after the overthrow of the tsar in March 1917 the notion of a struggle between democracy and authoritarianism gained meaning, particularly since the overthrow coincided with the entrance into the war against Germany of the greatest democracy in the world, the United States. The fact that men and women of all classes contributed to the military effort gave force to the demand that they should have the right to decide the political fate of their country. Where before the First World War the demand for suffrage for women had been regarded as utopian and even ridiculous, and the request for women's suffrage had inspired a movement of some strength only in Great Britain, now this demand became more urgent, and its justification was much more generally recognized. In Great Britain, Germany, and the United States, female suffrage was achieved soon after the war. In Italy and France its adversaries were able to delay giving women the vote until after the Second World War. But even there the final victory of female suffrage was never seriously in doubt.

It was difficult for Germany and its allies to place the war on a broad ideological level. The German Social Democratic Party had been the largest and best organized of all socialist parties. Socialist approval of the money bills required for the financing of the war was the most striking and also the most surprising example of the abandonment of revolutionary internationalism by Social Democrats in favor of defense of the homeland. The German government gained the support of socialist and progressive forces without taking them into the government. Thus, during most of the war Germany continued to be ruled by the members of the conservative bureaucracy. Their innate resistance to liberal and democratic reforms was reinforced by the military, whose power now increased immensely. William II, who even in peacetime had failed to exercise steady leadership, did not dare challenge the men of the hour. Thus, the German military leaders Paul von Hindenburg (1847–1934) and Erich Ludendorff (1865–1937) began to exert—if not in form, at least in fact—a military dictatorship. As allies of the Conservatives they resisted political reforms, and the tensions that had existed in peacetime reemerged during the last two years of the war, expressing themselves in a bitter struggle about war aims. In the early weeks of the war, when the German advance in France appeared irreversible, industrialists and their Conservative allies insisted that the results of the war must be acquisition of a secure foundation for German world hegemony. Germany ought to keep Belgium and the valuable French steel and coal mines of the Longwy-Briey Basin. Later in the war, when the Germans occupied broad territorial stretches in the east, demands arose to annex these agricultural areas so that the German food supply would be secured for all time. Until almost the final months of the war, leaders of heavy industry and Conservatives supported by the military under Ludendorff asserted the need to fight for total victory so that Germany could attain these expansionist goals. When a quick victory proved elusive, however, those who opposed such war aims—whether they considered them unrealistic or immoral—began to raise their voices. Annexationists were confronted by those who believed that peace ought to be concluded on the basis of the status quo and that every effort should be made to reach a peace of understanding. Thus, in Germany from the second year of the war on, the united front which had been established in August 1914 began to show fissures, which became deeper month by month.

THE TIDES OF BATTLE

The Expanding Theater of War

The conflict that took place between 1914 and 1918 is rightly called a world war, for it assumed global dimensions. At the start, however, it was confined to the great European powers: Great Britain, France, Russia, Germany, and Austria–Hungary. Only two of the smaller European states participated from the outset in this struggle of the great powers: Serbia, whose conflict with Austria had led to the explosion, and Belgium, which had been forced to resist by the German violation of its internationally guaranteed neutrality. The first non-European power, Japan, entered the war in August. But its military contribution was limited to the conquest and occupation of the German colonial possessions in the Far East. A real enlargement of the theater of war took place with the entry of Turkey on the

German side in November 1914. Turkey occupied a key position. By allying itself with the Western powers and Russia, it could have closed the ring around the Central Powers, as Austria and Germany were called, and ensured coordinated action against them from the west, east, and south. On the other hand, as an ally of Germany and Austria, Turkey could prevent the shipping of supplies to Russia through the Mediterranean and the Black Sea. Hence a fierce diplomatic struggle for the favors of Turkey took place in Constantinople, but the hold that Germany had developed over Turkey through the building of the Baghdad Railway, reinforced by the appearance of two German naval ships in the Dardanelles, proved to be the stronger. The entry of Turkey extended the war into Mesopotamia and Persia, where British and Russian forces on the one hand and Turkish troops under German command on the other fought with alternating success. To relieve the pressure on Turkey, Germany and Austria became anxious to establish direct communication with the Ottoman Empire. Promising the cession of large parts of Macedonia, now in Serbian hands, they persuaded Bulgaria to enter the war in October 1915. In counteraction, the Allies—France, Great Britain, and Russia—induced Romania in August 1916 and then Greece in June 1917 to declare war on the Central Powers, although by that time Serbia had succumbed to the joint attacks from the west and the north, so that the Central Powers dominated a broad connected stretch of territory from the North Sea to Mesopotamia and the Suez Canal. However, in 1915 the Allies had gained an important partner in Italy. Originally the Italians had declared themselves to be neutral because in their view the Austrians had started the war and had not acted in self-defense, requiring Italian assistance under the Triple Alliance. The Italians were courted by both sides, but the Central Powers could not make any promises that outweighed Italy's interest in using this war for the liberation of people of Italian nationality living under

The German military high command: Hindenburg, William II, Ludendorff.

Austrian rule. The Allies, in a secret agreement concluded in London in April 1915, promised Italy, in addition to the Austrian provinces inhabited by Italians, a wide expanse on the eastern side of the Adriatic Sea, including northern Albania; the Dodecanese in the Aegean Sea; and—if Turkey was partitioned—a part of Asia Minor. Later even Portugal and San Marino entered the war; by 1917, with exception of the Scandinavian countries, the Netherlands, Switzerland, and Spain, all the European nations were engaged on one side or the other. With the entry of the United States in April 1917, the war finally took on a global character. Then a number of Latin American states, among them Brazil, declared war on Germany, and others, such as Bolivia, Peru, and Ecuador, severed relations with Germany. In Asia, China and Siam and, in Africa, Liberia joined the coalition against the Central Powers. In many of these cases the reason for participation was purely economic. The rupture with Germany served to tighten loopholes in the blockade, to prevent the transference of German capital, and to permit the confiscation of German assets. In any event, the war had become global.

The small size of the area occupied by the Central Powers in comparison with the vast extent of the territory represented by their enemies might lead one to believe that the defeat of the Central Powers was almost inevitable. But the actual fact is that many times Germany seemed near victory, and the German collapse in 1918 was sudden and unexpected.

Stalemate in the West

When the war broke out, the German general staff planned to defeat France within six weeks and then to turn against Russia. A quick victory in the west was to be attained by concentrating almost all the German forces against France, most of them on the right wing, which was to advance in a great wheeling movement through Belgium and northern France and then turn south and finally east, trapping the French forces in a gigantic ring. The strategy used by Hannibal in his defeat of the Romans at Cannae was to be repeated on an immensely enlarged scale. This was the famous Schlieffen Plan, named after the German chief of staff who had conceived it about 1905. The plan failed; the German advances were halted in the Battle of the Marne, which takes its place as one of the decisive battles of history. There were many reasons for the failure. First, the Belgian resistance delayed the German advance. Also, the Germans had not counted on the appearance of a British expeditionary corps which, although thrown back in the battles of Mons and Le Cateau, seriously retarded their movement forward. Alexander von Kluck, the commander of the German First Army, operating on the extreme right, believed that the presence of the British forces made it impossible to include Paris in the wide encircling movement that had been envisaged. He ordered his troops to turn sharply to the south, leaving Paris at their right. This gave the French their opportunity. Although forced to retreat throughout August, the

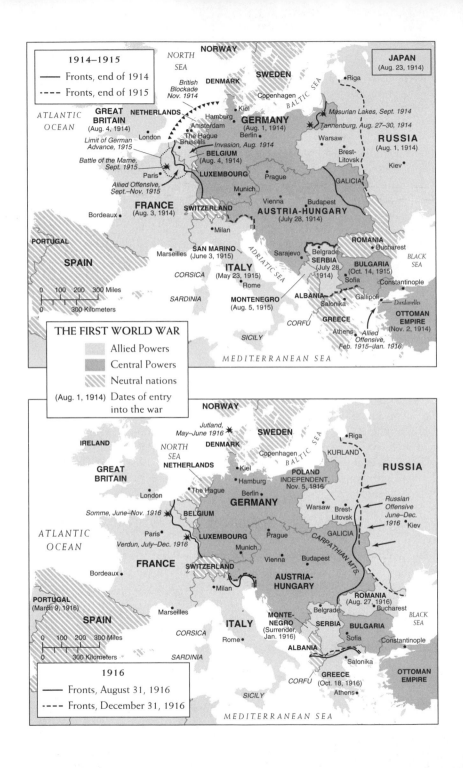

1914–1915

— Fronts, end of 1914

---- Fronts, end of 1915

NORTH SEA

NORWAY

JAPAN
(Aug. 23, 1914)

British Blockade Nov. 1914

DENMARK

SWEDEN

BALTIC SEA

•Riga

ATLANTIC OCEAN

GREAT BRITAIN
(Aug. 4, 1914)

NETHERLANDS

•Kiel

Copenhagen

Masurian Lakes, Sept. 1914

Hamburg

GERMANY
(Aug. 1, 1914)

Amsterdam

Tannenburg, Aug. 27–30, 1914

Limit of German Advance, 1915

London

The Hague

Brussels — *Invasion, Aug. 1914*

Berlin•

•Warsaw

RUSSIA
(Aug. 1, 1914)

Battle of the Marne, Sept. 1915

BELGIUM
(Aug. 4, 1914)

Brest-Litovsk•

•Kiev

Allied Offensive, Sept.–Nov. 1915

Paris•

LUXEMBOURG

•Prague

GALICIA

Munich•

FRANCE
(Aug. 3, 1914)

SWITZERLAND

Vienna

Budapest

Bordeaux •

•Milan

AUSTRIA-HUNGARY
(July 28, 1914)

PORTUGAL

SAN MARINO
(June 3, 1915)

ROMANIA

•Bucharest

SPAIN

Marseilles•

ADRIATIC SEA

Sarajevo•

Belgrade•

SERBIA
(July 28 1914)

BULGARIA
(Oct. 14, 1915)

BLACK SEA

CORSICA

ITALY
(May 23, 1915)

•Sofia

Constantinople

0 100 200 300 Miles

•Rome

0   300 Kilometers

SARDINIA

MONTENEGRO
(Aug. 5, 1915)

ALBANIA

•Salonika

Gallipoli

Dardanelles

OTTOMAN EMPIRE
(Nov. 2, 1914)

THE FIRST WORLD WAR

Allied Powers

Central Powers

Neutral nations

(Aug. 1, 1914) Dates of entry into the war

CORFU

GREECE

Athens•

Allied Offensive, Feb. 1915–Jan. 1916

SICILY

MEDITERRANEAN SEA

NORWAY

Jutland, May–June 1916

SWEDEN

•Riga

IRELAND

NORTH SEA

DENMARK

Copenhagen•

KURLAND

BALTIC SEA

GREAT BRITAIN

NETHERLANDS

•Kiel

POLAND INDEPENDENT, Nov. 5, 1916

RUSSIA

•Hamburg

London•

The Hague•

Berlin•

•Warsaw

Brest-Litovsk•

Russian Offensive June–Dec. 1916

Somme, June–Nov. 1916

BELGIUM

GERMANY

•Kiev

ATLANTIC OCEAN

Paris•

LUXEMBOURG

•Prague

GALICIA

Verdun, July–Dec. 1916

Munich•

CARPATHIAN MTS.

FRANCE

SWITZERLAND

Vienna

Budapest

Bordeaux •

•Milan

AUSTRIA-HUNGARY

PORTUGAL
(March 9, 1916)

ROMANIA
(Aug. 27, 1916)

•Bucharest

SPAIN

Marseilles•

Belgrade•

BLACK SEA

0 100 200 300 Miles

CORSICA

ITALY

Rome •

MONTE-NEGRO
(Surrender, Jan. 1916)

SERBIA

BULGARIA

0   300 Kilometers

SARDINIA

•Sofia

Constantinople

ALBANIA

1916

— Fronts, August 31, 1916

---- Fronts, December 31, 1916

•Salonika

CORFU

GREECE
(Oct. 18, 1916)

Athens•

OTTOMAN EMPIRE

SICILY

MEDITERRANEAN SEA

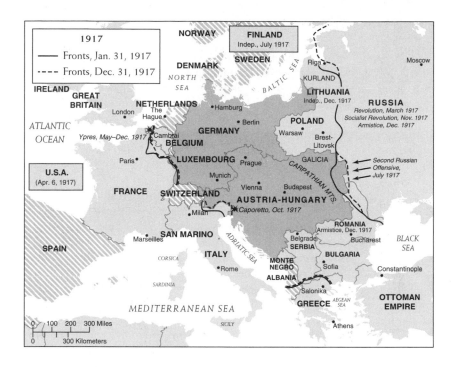

1917

— Fronts, Jan. 31, 1917
---- Fronts, Dec. 31, 1917

NORWAY

FINLAND
Indep., July 1917

DENMARK

SWEDEN

Riga

Moscow

KURLAND

NORTH SEA

BALTIC SEA

IRELAND

GREAT BRITAIN

London

NETHERLANDS
The Hague

*Hamburg

LITHUANIA
Indep., Dec. 1917

RUSSIA
Revolution, March 1917
Socialist Revolution, Nov. 1917
Armistice, Dec. 1917

ATLANTIC OCEAN

Ypres, May–Dec. 1917

*Berlin

POLAND

•Cambrai

GERMANY

Warsaw•

Brest-Litovsk

BELGIUM

Paris•

LUXEMBOURG

Prague

GALICIA

CARPATHIAN MTS.

U.S.A.
(Apr. 6, 1917)

Munich

Vienna

Budapest

Second Russian
Offensive,
July 1917

FRANCE

SWITZERLAND

AUSTRIA-HUNGARY

•Milan

✷Caporetto, Oct. 1917

ROMANIA
Armistice, Dec. 1917

SPAIN

Marseilles•

SAN MARINO

Belgrade•

Bucharest•

BLACK SEA

ADRIATIC SEA

SERBIA

BULGARIA

CORSICA

ITALY

MONTE-NEGRO

Sofia

Constantinople

•Rome

ALBANIA

SARDINIA

Salonika•

OTTOMAN EMPIRE

MEDITERRANEAN SEA

SICILY

GREECE

AEGEAN SEA

•Athens

0 100 200 300 Miles

0   300 Kilometers

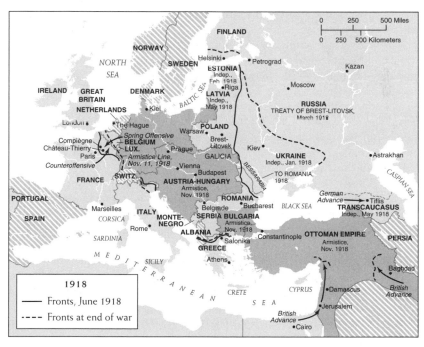

NORWAY

FINLAND

Helsinki•

•Petrograd

Kazan•

NORTH SEA

SWEDEN

ESTONIA
Indep.,
Feb. 1918
•Riga

•Moscow

IRELAND

GREAT BRITAIN

DENMARK

BALTIC SEA

LATVIA
Indep.,
May 1918

RUSSIA
TREATY OF BREST-LITOVSK,
March 1918

NETHERLANDS

•Kiel

London•

The Hague•

POLAND
Warsaw•

Compiègne•
Château-Thierry•

Spring Offensive
BELGIUM
LUX.

Brest-Litovsk

Kiev•

Paris•

•Prague

UKRAINE
Indep., Jan. 1918

•Astrakhan

Counteroffensive

Armistice Line,
Nov. 11, 1918

Vienna•

GALICIA

BESSARABIA

TO ROMANIA,
1918

CASPIAN SEA

FRANCE

SWITZ.

AUSTRIA-HUNGARY
Armistice,
Nov. 1918

Budapest•

PORTUGAL

ROMANIA

German
Advance

•Tiflis

SPAIN

Marseilles•

ITALY

MONTE-NEGRO

Belgrade•

•Bucharest

BLACK SEA

TRANSCAUCASUS
Indep., May 1918

CORSICA

SERBIA BULGARIA
Armistica,
Nov. 1918

Rome•

ALBANIA

Constantinople•

OTTOMAN EMPIRE
Armistice,
Nov. 1918

PERSIA

SARDINIA

SICILY

Salonika•

GREECE

Baghdad•

MEDITERRANEAN SEA

Athens•

CRETE

CYPRUS

•Damascus

British
Advance

British
Advance

•Jerusalem

•Cairo

1918

— Fronts, June 1918
---- Fronts at end of war

0   250   500 Miles

0   250   500 Kilometers

French Army had not disintegrated. The commander of the French forces, Joseph Joffre, was an adherent of the doctrine of continuous attack and had been less concerned with arranging a defensive position than with seizing an opportunity to attack. Kluck's move to the south made it possible for Joffre to attack the German flank and rear. A famous episode of the ensuing battle was that under orders from the commandant of Paris, the city's taxi drivers transported men directly from Paris to the front. On September 9, Kluck's army was ordered to retreat from the Marne to the Aisne. The German campaign plan had failed.

The German military command contributed to the defeat. It had watered down the original Schlieffen Plan; the right wing was weaker than it ought to have been. Moreover, the German Army on the left had been engaged in a battle in Lorraine and could therefore spare no troops to reinforce the right wing at the decisive moment. Helmuth von Moltke, the German chief of staff, following the precepts of his uncle, the great strategist of the nineteenth century, gave his field commanders freedom of decision. But he followed this principle too literally and too slavishly. There was little leadership from above, nor was there much communication among the various German commanders. Thus, between the First German Army, operating on the extreme right, and the Second German Army, operating farther left, a gap opened at the critical time when the French counterattack began. Moltke, alarmed by the dangers that might result from French advances into this gap, ordered retreat.

Whatever responsibility for the outcome of the Battle of the Marne one assigns to the energy and courage of the French and British generals or to the mistakes committed by the German military leaders, the entire Schlieffen Plan was probably not feasible; the distances involved in encircling the armed forces of an entire nation were too large to be covered by foot soldiers, at least with the speed and precision required for success. In the Second World War such gigantic encirclement maneuvers were frequently carried out with success, but by then the armies were fully motorized, and communications more easily established and maintained.

The Battle of the Marne was followed by a race for the Channel ports. Each side tried to regain freedom of movement by outflanking the other, but despite a bloody struggle along the seacoast in Flanders, neither was dislodged. The front now became stabilized: it began at the North Sea, in Flanders, bulged out into France, with Germany retaining control of important French industrial areas; and then swung back to the Franco-German frontier along Alsace-Lorraine, ending at the Swiss border. The armies dug in. For the next four years, until the spring of 1918, the lines remained almost unchanged, although sporadic and bloody attempts were made to end the stalemate and break through the enemy's lines. In February 1916, the Ger-

The political and military leaders of Great Britain and France. Haig, Joffre, Lloyd George are shown on the left. Foch, Haig, Clemenceau, and Weigand are shown on the right.

mans launched an attack on Verdun. This was intended to be a battle of attrition. The Germans wanted to draw the flower of the French Army into this battle and destroy the morale of the French troops. But in June, when the battle was broken off, the German losses were hardly less great than the French and the German territorial gains were insignificant. In July 1916 the French and the British attacked along the Somme; again, only small territorial gains had been made by November, when the battle at the Somme got stuck in the mud. The French and British attempted a breakthrough in the spring of 1917 by simultaneous attacks at two different points, Arras and along the Aisne; the general responsible for this offensive was the French commander in chief Robert Nivelle. His main success was the conquering of the Chemin des Dames, a height in the center of the front line, but the losses were so terrible that mutiny broke out in the French Army, and General Henri Philippe Pétain (1856–1951), who was called in to replace Nivelle, decided on a purely defensive conduct of the war in the west. However, the British commander, Douglas Haig, believed that Nivelle's offensive had failed because of tactical mistakes and that he, Haig, could do better. Despite great doubts in the British cabinet, Haig ordered an offensive in Flanders, around Ypres, which began on July 31 and lasted until November. Again the territorial gains were small, and the casualties staggering. The rain and mud of autumn slowed down every step so that the advancing troops offered easy targets. Passchendaele, as this battle is usually called, together "with the Somme and Verdun, will always rank as the most gigantic, tenacious, grim, futile and bloody fight ever waged in the history of war"[1]—an entirely useless slaughter. If any further proof was needed, Passchendaele showed that new weapons and new methods had to be introduced if the superiority of the defense over the offense was to be overcome.

German Success in the East

The failure at Verdun sufficiently proved to the Germans the futility of an offensive in the west. Those German military leaders who had believed since the failure in the Battle of the Marne that victory could be obtained only through defeat of Russia now gained the upper hand. The most influential and effective representatives of this view were Hindenburg and Ludendorff. They had acquired immense popularity in Germany because in August and September 1914, in the battles of Tannenberg and the Masurian Lakes, they had defeated and annihilated two Russian armies advancing into East Prussia. Hindenburg's and Ludendorff's responsibility for these victories is somewhat diminished by the fact that they arrived—Hindenburg from retirement, Ludendorff from the west—when the German commanders on the spot had already made the arrangements for the battles. Nevertheless, Hindenburg and Ludendorff, as saviors of Germany from the Russian barbarians, became popular heroes. In September 1914, Hindenburg was made commander in chief of the German armies in the east, and in 1916 he became chief of staff, with Ludendorff as his main assistant. The German conduct of the war in the east was brilliant. In 1915 a great offensive was started in Galicia, which the Russians had occupied, and soon the operations extended over the entire eastern frontier; by the time military activity halted in the fall the lines reached from the eastern part of Galicia straight to the north, with the Central Powers having conquered Poland, Lithuania, and Courland.

These German victories were facilitated by the Russians' lack of munitions and equipment. At the beginning of 1915 the British had made an ingenious attempt to open a direct route to Russia through the Dardanelles. This operation—the Gallipoli campaign—failed mainly through lack of cooperation between the naval and the land forces. Thus, materials could be sent to the Russians only through Siberia; the Russians were forced to rely on their own resources for the 1916 summer campaign, which became the last military enterprise of tsarist Russia.

Why Men Fought

As the war dragged on, with the irony between the politicians' glittering phrases and the horrible realities of life on the battlefields becoming ever more apparent, backers of the war began understandably to worry that the soldiers might simply opt out of the struggle, through either mutiny or mass desertion. Serious mutinies did occur in the French Army in 1917, and desertion helped

[1] David Lloyd George, *War Memoirs*, vol. IV (London, 1934), p. 2110.

undermine the Russian war effort in 1917 and the German fighting capacity in 1918. On the whole, however, the soldiers of World War I continued on with the grim business of industrialized slaughter despite ever-mounting losses and growing doubts that the conflict would accomplish the purposes for which it was supposedly being fought. How do we explain this willingness to keep on killing when the chances for victory seemed greatly outweighed by the chances of getting killed? How do we explain the seemingly suicidal readiness to go "over the top" into a withering hail of enemy machine-gun fire or to stay put in the trenches under earsplitting barrages that could bury you alive—if they did not first blow you to pieces?

Undoubtedly, harsh discipline at the front helped deter desertion, mutiny, and malingering. Soldiers faced the prospect of execution (with the added indignity of dishonor) if they abandoned their duty or fomented resistance to their superiors. In the British Army, where discipline was especially draconian, some 3,080 troopers were sentenced to death for desertion, though only 346 actually had their sentences carried out. The French organized hasty trials and executions for some of the mutineers of 1917.

Even fear of punishment, however, would probably not have been sufficient to keep desertion and mutiny figures so low without the weight of other factors. One of these was the respect that enlisted men tended to harbor for their immediate superiors—junior officers and NCOs—at the front. (By contrast, front soldiers generally despised the staff officers at the rear, who were too busy ordering suicidal attacks to "muck it up" with the troops in the trenches.) Respect for frontline officers as a morale-sustaining factor, however, has also been exaggerated, not least by the officers themselves in their memoirs. After all, many junior officers hardly got to know their men before being killed or transferred to other units.

A more compelling source of discipline perhaps was the loyalty that soldiers typically felt for their buddies, whom they did not want to let down and before whom they were loath to appear as cowards. Yet such "primary group" loyalty also had its limits since units were constantly being rearranged and restaffed as a result of the mounting losses. Comrades of today were likely to be gone, often literally, tomorrow.

While the much-celebrated comradeship of the trenches was often fleeting, national loyalty was not, and patriotism, buttressed by religion, should not be underestimated as a morale factor, however much such feelings were abused by nationalistic blowhards. In the First World War, men really did fight passionately for God and country, though the exact nature and degree of their loyalties differed significantly from case to case. Australians and New Zealanders, for example, typically harbored a stronger sense of identity with their own lands than with the mother country of Britain. Similarly, many Slavic soldiers in the Austrian Army identified more closely with their regional homelands than with the Habsburg empire.

"An army cannot fight on an empty stomach," insists a well-known military dictum, and mundane matters like food, clothing, and billets played crucial roles in the maintenance of morale in the First World War (as, in fact, in any war). Nor should we forget the importance of tobacco, drugs, and alcohol, which quieted the nerves, sedated the conscience, and on occasion stimulated the urge to kill. As the British military historian John Keegan has pointed out, extra rations of strong navy rum were doled out to British soldiers just before they went over the top; in some cases, the leading wave of attackers was thoroughly drunk. Recalling this bizarre state of affairs, one British medical officer opined: "Had it not been for the rum ration, I do not think we should have won the war."

By befogging the brain, rum and other drugs helped men do their duty, but some apparently needed no intoxicants to kill; they simply enjoyed doing it. The lust for killing, though as old as warfare itself, has generally been played down as a morale-boosting factor in modern war, no doubt because it harbors such discouraging implications for our civilization. It would undoubtedly be too much to contend that the majority of soldiers in the First World War (or, for that matter, in the Second, which involved more pronounced racial and ideological hatreds) took an active delight in killing, but Niall Ferguson is probably right when he lists "the joy of war" among the factors that kept the conflict going for so long. Although many soldiers spoke and wrote, no doubt truthfully, of their repugnance for the business of killing, others openly celebrated the war experience in all its cruelty. Ernst Jünger, the brilliant German novelist, discovered an ethereal beauty in the corpse-strewn landscape of the western front, while Julian Grenfell, an aristocratic British cavalry officer, found, like his ancestors in previous battles, that there was nothing like a little shooting and sticking to cheer a fellow up. "I *adore* war," he wrote in a letter during the conflict. "It is like a big picnic without the objectlessness of a picnic. I've never been so well or happy."

1917: THE TURNING POINT OF THE WAR

From the end of 1915 on, the war assumed a new face. The expectation that it would end quickly had faded, and the patriotic fervor with which news about the progress of military events had been greeted in all countries at the outset was replaced by a questioning sobriety; heavy casualties and economic hardships had brought the reality of war into almost every home.

Living conditions of the civilian population in Germany plunged to their nadir in the winter of 1916–1917. There was a scarcity of coal and hence little heat. Rations of meat and butter were exiguous. In the memories of those who lived through those months, the winter was recalled as the turnip time, since this was the one abundantly available food. Turnips were publicly praised as an excellent substitute for potatoes, vegetables, and almost any kind of victual. The shock of this winter led to better planning in the following war winters, so that even if the situation did not fundamentally change, it appeared less desperate. In Austria lack of food in the big urban centers, primarily Vienna, was caused by inadequate transportation, since the railroads were needed to transfer troops from one theater of war to another. It was compounded by the unwillingness of Hungarian landowners and peasants to sell their products in Austria at low, controlled prices.

In almost all countries, radical groups were gaining in strength within the socialist parties. These groups opposed the support that the socialists were giving the war efforts of the governments. In Austria an event occurred that exemplified this phenomenon: On October 21, 1916, the Austrian prime minister was assassinated by Friedrich Adler, son of the leader of the Austrian Social Democrats. Adler considered this deed a protest against the continuation of the war and against his father's leadership of the Socialist Party, which supported the war policy of the government. There is no doubt that Friedrich Adler was giving expression to a widespread feeling of war weariness. When Emperor Francis Joseph died in November 1916, his successor, Emperor Charles, tried to negotiate a peace. His attempts were unsuccessful because Austria could not escape the encircling clasp of the German armies. But Austria became a less and less willing ally of Germany.

Trench warfare. This was taken during the Battle of the Somme, 1916.

In England and France, shortages, although very noticeable, contributed less to a rising wave of discontent than the lack of military success, particularly the failure in the Battle of the Somme. In France this debacle, together with the heavy sacrifices in manpower during the defense of Verdun, produced a defeatist mood that expressed itself in local mutinies; a change in the high command, making Pétain commander in chief, sufficed to reestablish discipline, but political dissatisfaction continued to grow, until finally, in November 1917, Georges Clemenceau became prime minister, an appointment that meant, as was generally recognized, ruthless organization of all possible resources for complete victory. In Great Britain the bad news about the Battle of the Somme had come after other disappointing reports: the Easter Rebellion in Ireland and the indecisive clash with the German high-seas fleet in the Battle of Jutland. These difficulties and failures were increasingly ascribed to the dilatoriness of the government in introducing conscription; its unwillingness to impose stringent economic measures; and Prime Minister Herbert Asquith's incapacity to accelerate production of weapons and munitions and in general to mobilize the empire. In December 1916, Asquith was replaced as prime minister by Lloyd George; like the appointment of Clemenceau in France ten months later, this meant that the war would be carried through to final victory. It also indicated that the English had realized too that the views about the nature of war, which had been heard in prewar days, had been erroneous. Modern war was totalitarian and demanded extreme measures and efforts.

THE REVOLUTION IN RUSSIA

Developments in Russia were different from those in England. In Russia too the view began to develop that a successful outcome of war required measures that went beyond the purely military sphere, that the entire civilian life had to be organized and directed according to the needs of the war. But in Russia these demands for a new, more energetic leadership resulted in what was to become the most crucial and most important event of the First World War: the overthrow of tsarism and the Bolshevik conquest of power. The Somme offensive in the summer of 1916 formed part of a great strategic plan to subject Germany to Allied attacks from all sides, west and east. The Russians took their share by attacking the southern section of the Austrian-German lines and succeeded in reaching the heights of the Carpathian Mountains. But there they were halted and forced to retreat—partly because of immense losses in manpower and partly because of a breakdown in the transportation of supplies. Moreover, in this campaign, as in previous campaigns during the war, the Russians lacked ammunition. The failure of this offensive—called the Brusilov offensive, after the commander of the Russian troops—resulted in a general outcry that only a new government that had the confidence of the Duma and contained leaders of the various political parties would have the authority to take the necessary measures to increase industrial production and secure a food supply for the army and the workers in the industrial centers. Only a broadly based government would inspire enough confidence in the people to maintain their belief in a successful outcome of the war. Such demands ran counter to the deeply ingrained absolutist inclinations of the tsar and the tsarina, who considered the appointment of ministers to lie entirely in their hands. A personal motive for the resistance of the tsar and particularly of the tsarina to any encroachment on the tsar's autocracy and to the formation of a more broadly based, liberal government was their awareness that one of the first demands of such a government would be the removal of the corrupt Rasputin from the court; they believed his presence was needed to keep their hemophilic son alive.

Thus, the tsarina insisted on maintaining the tsar's powers intact so that only men in favor of Rasputin would be members of the government. The result was a succession of incompetent and corrupt ministers, moreover, of men suspected to be germanophiles since it was well known that Rasputin opposed the entire war. People from different classes and of different political opinions—conservatives and liberals, grand dukes and foreign ambassadors—joined in attempts to persuade the tsar to install a parliamentary regime. Rasputin was assassinated by a member of the imperial family and a leading conservative politician, in the hope that his removal would weaken the resistance of the tsar against the change in the government system. Actually the opposite happened. The tsar closed himself in and became almost inaccessible to the influence of political circles. As the pressure grew, he went to the military headquarters, where it was almost impossible to reach him. Thus, when bread riots broke out in Petrograd and the guard regiment joined the rebelling masses, the tsar found no defenders, not even among the military, and was forced to submit to the demands for abdication. He and his family were made prisoners, first in Tsarkoe Selo, the tsar's summer residence near the capital; from there they were brought to Siberia and then back to the Urals. In July 1918, when monarchist troops approached the Urals, the tsar and tsarina and their children were executed. They had borne their fall from power with an astonishing fatalism; it seems almost as if they believed in the unavoidability of the fulfillment of one of Rasputin's prophecies—namely, that when he died, tsarist Russia would also perish.

The tsar had abdicated in favor of his brother Michael. But Michael also resigned the throne, aware that support for a continuation of the dynasty was weak. Thus, the Duma established a provisional government composed of the chief leaders of all the bourgeois parties and tolerated by the moderate socialists, the Mensheviks, who were inclined to cooperate with the liberal bourgeoisie and to support the war for democracy.

The government came to power in a difficult situation, and from then on, throughout the next six months, events proceeded with confusing speed. For the members of the government the continuation and intensification of the war effort were paramount. But such policy needed the support of the masses and the overthrow of tsarism had raised their hopes: the workers expected the realization of socialism; the peasants, the acquisition of more land through partitioning the great estates. These demands had great weight. Workers' councils had been formed in the factories and soldiers' councils in the armies, in which representatives of peasants were a crucial factor. Execution of the measures of the provisional government was widely dependent on these soviets (councils) of workers and soldiers. Clearly, conservative and liberal members of the provisional government lacked enthusiasm for these radical demands. They declared that decisions about such fundamental changes should be left to a constituent assembly, elected on the basis of universal suffrage for men and women above eighteen years of age; war conditions, however, made such elections difficult. But the continuation of the war depended on intensified cooperation of workers and peasants, and these groups, disgruntled because of the postponement of socialization and land distribution, had to be assured that reforms would be coming. Aleksandr Kerensky, a socialist politician, who mainly by his rhetorical gifts had become vice president of the Petrograd Soviet, was appointed minister of justice. A deep inner contrast was implanted in the

Lenin addressing a crowd in Moscow's Red Square in October 1917.

provisional government. Unavoidably, Kerensky's influence grew because he represented the main link to the increasingly restless and discontented mass of workers and peasants. In July, Kerensky became prime minister. But the growing influence of the left in the government aroused resistance among conservatives and liberals and particularly generated indignation among officers and generals, because they saw army discipline disintegrating before their eyes. The result was military action on the part of Lavr Kornilov, the commander in chief of the army, in order to restore discipline and order. He was opposed by Kerensky. A famous scene in the Russian film *October* (1927), by Sergei Eisenstein, which celebrated the Bolshevik Revolution, shows the workers of Petrograd destroying the railroad tracks on which Kornilov's troops were expected to arrive. It should be added that Kornilov's order to his troops to advance against Petrograd had found little obedience. But Kornilov's attempt, although abortive, undermined Kerensky's own position. It was considered an indication of the weakness and the halfheartedness of the provisional government that reactionary activities could have reached such a strength that counterrevolutionaries were able to attempt a coup. It had become clear that the adoption of a policy centering on continuation of the war left the former ruling group in a strong position and revealed itself to be incompatible with the attainments of the goals of the workers and peasants. The hour of the Bolsheviks had come.

An event that occurred when Lenin arrived on the night of April 3, 1917, at Petrograd's Finland Station revealed itself now in its full significance. The Germans had permitted Lenin to travel from Switzerland, where he was in exile, through Germany to Russia, in hope that as leader of the radical Bolsheviks opposed to the war he would interfere with the work of the war-minded provisional government. When Lenin arrived, and was solemnly received in the waiting room formerly reserved for the imperial family by the Menshevik leaders of the Petrograd Soviet, he immediately rejected the invitation of these Menshevik leaders to cooperate in the defense of the revolution against enemies from within and from without. Addressing the assembled masses, Lenin declared that the revolution had not solved the fundamental problems of the Russian proletariat and that the task ahead was to turn the bourgeois revolution into a proletarian socialist revolution. Thus, at the outset Lenin established the line the Bolsheviks should follow and that separated them from all other parties. The real revolution that would give the proletariat monopoly of power was still to come, and every effort must be made to bring it about as soon as possible. This aim could not be attained in wartime since war left power in the hands of the army and the bourgeoisie. The war therefore must be immediately ended. Peace and revolution were complementary to each other. But he also addressed the workers of other countries, reminding them of the Marxist tradition of international revolution and antimilitarism.

The demand for peace implied a propagandistic appeal to the Russian soldiers.

And there can be no doubt that the soldiers were anxious to return home and participate in the expected land distribution. The Bolsheviks were also aware that the accomplishment of the task they had set themselves meant primarily gaining control over Russia's administrative and industrial center, Petrograd. Before the conquest of power, adherents of the Bolsheviks among the Russian population were not numerous. Even among the industrial workers, the Bolsheviks had less support than their socialist rivals, the Mensheviks. Petrograd was divided into a number of districts, each with its own workers' council. While the Mensheviks dominated the Petrograd municipal government, the Bolsheviks worked at the grass roots in the district soviets and thus came to control certain sections of the city. This was their base for revolutionary action.

In the period from April, when Lenin returned to Russia and assumed leadership of the Bolshevik party, until October 24 (Russian calendar; November 9, Gregorian calendar), when the Bolsheviks seized power, Lenin's line of policy frequently seemed unrealistic. Even among prominent Bolsheviks, there were those who believed that it would be better to cooperate with the Mensheviks and to defend the gains that had been obtained through the overthrow of tsarism than to work for a dictatorship of the proletariat under Bolshevik control. Such considerations gained in strength when an attempt to seize power in July failed miserably. There were even temporary defections. But the turning point came when Kornilov's putsch (attempted governmental overthrow) revealed the weakness of Kerensky and his provisional government. Then doubts and hesitations disappeared, and a definite trend toward a more energetic and revolutionary government became noticeable even among those workers who were adherents of the Mensheviks.

Lenin, who, since the abortive Bolshevik putsch in July, was in hiding, urged immediate action. But those who were in closer touch with the mood of the Petrograd population decided to synchronize the renewed attempt to seize power with the meeting of the all-Russian Congress of Soviets, which was to assemble on October 25. Although the members of this congress were by no means all Bolsheviks, they were all socialists and would approve of the demise of the Kerensky government and the taking over of power by a socialist government. Indeed, the Bolshevik coup d'état, brilliantly organized by Trotsky, met almost no serious resistance. Kerensky was unable to mount a military counteroffensive, and the ministers of the provisional government who had remained in Petrograd were forced to surrender. On the next day the all-Russian Congress of Soviets met; under protest of a group of Mensheviks, the congress legitimized the creation of a revolutionary Bolshevik government.

Lenin's strategy appeared brilliantly justified. He possessed undisputed authority in the new government, whose members called themselves not ministers but people's commissars. But Lenin needed all his authority to steer the government through the next months and years. The people's commissars immediately took a number of steps indicating that a new socialist era had come. One of their first decrees ordered the partition of the large estates and distribution of the land among the peasants without compensation for the former owners. All banks were nationalized and control over the factories was given to the workers. To underline the break with the bourgeois capitalist system, private bank accounts were confiscated, church property was seized, and secret diplomatic documents—among them agreements with the Allies about territorial changes to be forced upon the enemies—were published.

The Bolshevik government was beset by more urgent problems, however, than those of internal reforms. For the Allies were aware that the Bolshevik seizure of power meant Russia's withdrawal from the war; thus, they gave their protection to the adversaries of the Bolsheviks—officers, monarchists, bourgeois politicians—who, at the fringes of the Russian Empire, began to organize resistance. On the other hand, the conclusion of peace, the cornerstone of the policy of the new regime, could not come from a one-sided proclamation but demanded negotiations with the Central Powers. Although the German and Austrian governments agreed with the Russian government that peace ought to be based on the principle of national self-determination, they gave this principle a peculiar interpretation. They insisted that Poland, Finland, and the Baltic states ought to be separated from Russia and remain under German and Austrian control and

Bolshevik soldiers marching through Red Square in 1917.

that Ukraine, almost the entire south of European Russia, become an independent state. The peace negotiations, which were conducted at Brest-Litovsk, offered a strange spectacle: on the one side were the delegations of the Central Powers, led by masters of the diplomatic craft who were advised by high-ranking military officers; on the other side were the Russians, led by the young revolutionary hero Leon Trotsky and among whose delegates were a peasant and a sailor. Trotsky proclaimed the need for a peace without annexations and indemnities and exposed the rulers of the Central Powers as ruthless annexationists, against whom he appealed to the solidarity of the workers of all countries; but his rejection of the demands of the Central Powers was futile. Lenin was fully aware from the beginning that Russia had to give in, and after a brief show of resistance, the Bolshevik government did so. The acceptance of this humiliating peace increased the indignation of all the bourgeois elements against the Bolsheviks, whose Russian antagonists were now augmented by the Social Revolutionaries, a radical party that represented the peasants. The Social Revolutionaries had so far cooperated with the Bolsheviks because of their policy of land distribution, but since a good part of the strength of the Social Revolutionaries lay in Ukraine, they bitterly resented handing over this region to Germany. For Germany the war in the east seemed over. But for the Bolsheviks the end of the war with the Central Powers meant the beginning of civil war.

DECISION IN THE WEST

In the early spring of 1918 the Central Powers seemed in a brilliant position. They had freed themselves from the danger of a two-front war. Half a year later the German high command was to declare to its government that the war must be considered lost, and in November 1918, a Germany transformed by revolution into a republic agreed to an armistice that could only lead to a peace dictated by the Western powers. What had happened to bring about this reversal of fortune?

All of Germany's successes in the east could not outweigh the fact that its strongest adversaries were in the west and that victory was impossible without defeating them. It seemed clear that action at sea would be required to subdue Great Britain, the most formidable of the Western enemies. Early in the war, a naval blockade to deprive Germany of raw materials had been instituted by Britain and France. In international law a distinction is made between contraband—munitions and raw materials needed for the manufacture of military equipment—and noncontraband, notably food and clothing. Only contraband is subject to confiscation by a blockading power. But the British refused to recognize this distinction. No ships of any neutral power were permitted to go to a German port, and imports into the Scandinavian countries and the Netherlands were limited to quantities that assured the goods would be used in the importing countries and not be reshipped to Germany.

A *New Combatant: The United States*

The British violation of recognized international law created serious trouble between the United States and Great Britain. But the United States finally sided with Great Britain against Germany because the Germans too violated international law—flagrantly and even more brutally than the British. The Germans felt that they could counterbalance the British blockade by a more effective form of economic warfare, a submarine blockade. Submarines could not remove goods or people from merchant ships; they could only sink the ships. The Germans declared the waters surrounding the British Isles to be a war zone in which all enemy vessels carrying goods might be sunk. In May 1915 a German submarine torpedoed the *Lusitania*, a British passenger liner; almost twelve hundred people drowned, among them 188 American citizens. While it was true that the *Lusitania* carried ammunition, the death of more than one thousand civilians, many from neutral countries, seemed incredibly brutal. Indignation in the United States mounted. After a severe warning by President Wilson, the Germans relented, and for two years they modified their conduct of submarine warfare. But pressure against Chancellor Bethmann-Hollweg and his advisers who advocated caution in using the submarine steadily mounted. It was difficult for the public to bear the hardships of the British blockade when Germany was believed to be in possession of a weapon with which it could retaliate. Moreover, the German Navy had built many new submarines, and the naval high command, supported by experts anxious to please the admirals, maintained that Great Britain could be starved out and forced to surrender in a short time. Hindenburg and Ludendorff gave full support to the demands of the navy. On January 31, 1917, the Germans proclaimed the resumption of unrestricted submarine warfare. President Wilson severed diplomatic relations with Germany, and provoked by the sinking of American ships, the United States declared war on Germany on April 6, 1917.

The effect of America's entry into the war was immense. British shipping losses, especially since the declaration of unrestricted submarine warfare, had risen dangerously. In April 1917 alone, eight hundred seventy-five thousand tons of shipping were sunk. By organizing a convoy system, the British had tried to master this threat. But the entry of the United States into the war made the German submarine warfare an evident failure because thereafter the number of ships convoyed and the number of ships protecting the convoys was increased steadily. Convoys of ships transporting food, war materials, and troops arrived safely in Britain, and the rate of shipping construction soon exceeded the rate of loss. Moreover, the entry of the United States into the war blunted the uplift in morale that the breakdown of Russia would otherwise have produced in Germany. Indeed, Wilson's insistence on a just and democratic peace increased internal tension in Germany and gave a particularly sharp edge to the debate on war aims. The demand grew for a guarantee that the war would not be fought to achieve the aims and ambitions of the ruling group but would be terminated as

A German cartoon celebrating the successes of Reich submarines in World War I.

soon as the existence of the German people was no longer threatened. Both at home and abroad, distrust of the policy of the German leaders was reinforced by the impression created by the peace of Brest-Litovsk and its aftermath. In the areas separated from Russia, the Central Powers established regimes controlled by small wealthy groups: German landowners in the Baltic States, a small pro-German clique in Ukraine. German princes were placed on the thrones of such newly established states as Lithuania, Courland, and Finland. The behavior of the Germans in this area helped to give a wide echo to Trotsky's words during the peace negotiations that the Central Powers conducted the war not in the interest of the people but of a small exploitative ruling group.

Despite the apparent military advantage of the Central Powers at the beginning of 1918, their situation had grave weaknesses. The brutal German policy in the east kept the conquered areas restless and in revolt. Large military forces had to remain in the east, and the transportation of food, especially of wheat from Ukraine, met many obstacles. Increasingly, the governments of the Central Powers were being criticized as overweening in their ambitions and unwilling or unable to terminate the war. The Allies had become strong enough to mount offensives at various fronts. In the fall of 1917 the British had thrown the Turks back from the Egyptian frontier and advanced into Palestine, taking Jerusalem on

Caporetto: The result of machine-gun fire on the southern front.

December 8, 1917. Greece's entry into the war in June 1917 had made possible an offensive against Bulgaria. On the other hand, in October 1917, Austrian and German troops had broken the Italian front in the Battle of Caporetto, brilliantly described by Ernest Hemingway in A *Farewell to Arms* (1929). To stem the panic among Italian troops, Italian military police were ordered to shoot every tenth man of any formation that was fleeing. Significantly, even the German victory at Caporetto did not eliminate Italy from the war. The British and French were able to send in enough reinforcements to reconstruct an Italian front along the Piave.

Thus, at the beginning of 1918, despite the Treaty of Brest-Litovsk, Germany was not in an unassailable position, able to wait for the Allies to force the issue. The arrival of American troops and increasing disaffection within Germany necessitated action leading to a quick end to the war. The German military leaders responded with an offensive in the west that they believed, with the help of reinforcements from the east, would bring victory. But in its outcome this offensive, which started on March 21, 1918, was no different from previous ones in the west. Initially, territorial gains were large. But when the German soldiers advanced beyond the zone where they enjoyed protection from their artillery, they again found that in trench warfare defense was superior to attack, and the German offensive got stuck. German attacks in other areas of the front lacked even the force of the March offensive. The Germans were halted—by the French at Compiègne and by the Americans and the French at Château-Thierry. Starting in July 1918, the Allies, now led by Ferdinand Foch, commander in chief of all the armies in France, began to attack. Their advances were powerfully supported by use of the tank, a new weapon that brought an element of movement into the war of position. At the same time, the Allied armies in Salonika and the Italians at the Piave began to advance, and both the Bulgarian and the Austrian fronts collapsed; Bulgaria and Austria asked for peace.

At this point Ludendorff urged the German government to seek an armistice. German political leaders now lost all confidence in the German high command, and the German people and the troops were no longer willing to accept the leadership of the military or of the rulers who had supported them. Revolution spread from town to town. By November 9 all the German princes, William II included, had abdicated, and on November 11 the armistice was signed. The First World War was at an end.

CONSEQUENCES OF THE FIRST WORLD WAR

When the news of the armistice reached London, Big Ben, silenced during the war, rang out again. In London and Paris people danced on the streets and embraced one another. It was as if people had suddenly awakened from an oppressive, terrifying nightmare and the world again appeared in its true colors and shapes. But the notion that one could now return to the life that had existed before August 1914 was a deception. The world war had created burdens that perdured well into the postwar period.

There was, of course, the pressing burden of mourning. In addition to the millions of corpses brought home from the various battlefronts or buried in named graves on foreign fields, there were some 3 million soldiers unaccounted for—men who been reduced to unrecognizable body parts or who had simply vanished in the killing grounds. An English chaplain proposed a symbolic burial of one of those unknown soldiers to memorialize all the missing dead. This became the inspiration for the "Unknown Soldier" tombs instituted after the war by virtually all the nations that had maintained armies in the field.

Then there were the huge economic burdens to contend with. The costs of the war had been enormously high. In 1917, for example, the German war expenditure amounted to two-thirds of the total German national income of prewar years. Only a small part of these vast sums had been obtained through taxation. In Germany, the war had been financed through inflationary printing of paper money and internal loans (war loans); for the Allies, a particularly important source of funds was the United States. By means of loans the European countries paid for the war materials they bought from the United States; cash payments would have quickly exhausted their gold reserves.

Thus, in addition to the waste of capital and resources, there was a decline of the European economic position in comparison to that of the United States.

The European powers were transformed from creditor nations into debtor nations. By the end of the war Great Britain's indebtedness to the U.S. government amounted to $3,696,000,000; that of France to $1,970,000,000; and that of Italy to $1,031,000,000. Altogether, the Allied powers of Europe owed the United States more than $7,000,000,000. In addition, many loans were made in the period just after the end of the war; when the debt of the Allied nations to the United States was funded in 1922, the total indebtedness amounted to $11,656,932,900. The center of the world money market began to move from London to New York.

As a further consequence of the First World War, European investments in non-European countries diminished, and the opportunities of the European states for influencing economic development in other continents were lessened. Most German assets outside Europe were confiscated by the governments of the countries in which they were located. Before the United States entered the war, loans were not easily obtainable, and Great Britain therefore paid for goods with gold and procured the necessary foreign exchange by mobilizing foreign securities held by British citizens. British and European holdings in non-European countries were thus considerably reduced. Moreover, because the European countries geared their industrial production to the war effort, their export trade ceased almost entirely, with the result that economic life in the non-European parts of the world was reoriented. For instance, before the First World War, the British and to a somewhat lesser degree the Germans dominated international trade with the states of Latin America. At that time agriculture was the economic mainstay of these countries, and manufactured goods were obtained from abroad. In the postwar period Latin American trade with the United States, and investments by American firms in Latin America, increased steadily. The American economic influence accelerated industrial progress: the chief American investments were in mining, and American capital played a leading part in the development of oil fields in Venezuela, Peru, Colombia, and Ecuador. Now these countries were set toward industrialization, and in the 1920s they achieved a remarkable prosperity. Economic development in India was similar. During the war the government actively promoted industrial growth so that India could supply equipment for the troops fighting in Mesopotamia and the Near East. The Tata Iron and Steel Company in Bihar became the largest steelworks in the world, producing almost a million tons annually. Production figures around the world revealed the diminished economic role of the European continent. In 1925 the world output of manufactured goods was 20 percent higher than in 1913; this rise can be attributed primarily to the expansion of production in the non-European world.

While the consequences of these structural shifts emerged only gradually, economic difficulties of a temporary character arose immediately. Industrial production, which had been geared to the war effort, had to be changed over to peaceful uses. This was necessarily a slow but urgent process, for there were thousands of demobilized soldiers returning home seeking work. In almost all European countries war was followed by a period of unemployment, an inappropriate reward for those who, a few months earlier, had been praised as the heroic defenders of their countries.

In the budgets of all European countries the payment of pensions to those who had been wounded in the war and to the widows and children of those who had been killed formed a significant part of governmental expenses. Instead of diminishing, taxes increased, and at the same time the possibilities of making changes in government expenses and of applying them to social or political purposes decreased.

Budgetary constraints occurred at a time when governments were expected to do more for the people than ever before. The war had shown that governments could direct economic life into the channels that served government interests. It was hard to grasp why now, with war over, unemployment could not be prevented and the situation of the lower classes improved. Orators had proclaimed the end of the war a victory for democracy; as a result of the sacrifices total war had imposed on all elements of the population, the right of the lower classes to determine their own fates was generally recognized and had led to a broadening of suffrage all over Europe—although it varied in extent in different countries. It was an important aspect in the political situation of the postwar years that the expectations of what government could and ought to do had increased, whereas the governments had become more confined in the means they had at their disposal for action.

The contrast between expectations and reality was a pervasive element in the entire intellectual atmosphere. The end of the war was believed to bring about a totally new era; the return to the routine of daily life, even more drab than it had been in the prewar era, seemed like a mockery of the sufferings people had undergone. The British poet Siegfried Sassoon had written:

> You're quiet and peaceful, summering safe at home;
> You'd never think there was a bloody war on! . . .
> O yes, you would . . . why, you can hear the guns.
> Hark, Thud, thud, thud,—quite soft . . . they never cease
> Those whispering guns—

These lines reveal how the hard reality of war had raised doubts about the beliefs society had held before the war. War poetry shows the change of mind of the writers who wanted to communicate the war experience. If the poems and writings of the earlier years of the war were expressed in traditional patriotic terms, treating the soldier's craft as proper for young men and praising death on the battlefield as a fitting and beautiful end of life, the later poems and writings were—with their descriptions of horror, suffering, and destruction—an accusation against the war. For many writers, traditional language and imagery not only were insufficient to express what they felt but also seemed to conceal reality and to lie by describing unheard-of suffering and passion in mundane words and forms. To express the desperation of one's heart—whether aroused by the war or by the hopelessness of life—one must use words or images that arouse in the reader the same feelings one has; this is not achieved with logically composed sentences or realistic and formal drawings that contain a moral meaning or prescription. Although their beginnings lie in the years before 1914, Expressionism in literature and nonrepresentational art became the dominant intellectual trends with the First World War, a further sign of the break the war represented in European life.

The war also had a profound effect on manners and morals, especially on the manners and morals of women. Having become accustomed to going out alone or with other women during the war, young women in the postwar period continued to stroll the streets without male escorts. More than likely these "new" women would be dressed in skirts that ended not at the ankle, which was the prewar fashion, but just below the knee. Corsets were discarded in favor of brassieres, an innovation that conservatives (male and female alike) found shocking. Abandoned along with the corsets was the effulgent Rubenesque look of the Belle Époque; now the thing was to be svelte, and diets became de rigueur. So too, for the fashionable set, did "bobbed" hair and cosmetics, which before the war had been associated with prostitutes. The new look in fact signaled freer attitudes toward sex that had been fostered during the war by what a British official called "the freedom from home restraints of large numbers of young persons of both sexes." After all, with young men being killed or mutilated by the millions on the battlefields, it had not seemed to make much sense to hold true to the old ideals of chastity and self-restraint. The handsome hero home today might be gone forever tomorrow—or at least a vital part of him. Contraceptive use, abortions, and illegitimate births all had gone up during the war, and like women's hemlines, they did not come down when the fighting was over.

The changes and developments in the economic, political, and intellectual spheres made reconstruction of social life and adjusting the new to the old extremely difficult, but the task was immensely more complicated because the war had taken so dreadful a toll on human life. More than any other phenomenon, the greatest problem after the First World War was that an entire generation had been lost.

In Western Europe the losses and casualties of the First World War were considerably larger than those suffered by the same states in the Second World War. Altogether, about 8.5 million men were dead. More than twice that number were wounded, many of them maimed for life. The total number of casualties, including killed, wounded, and missing, is figured as 37.5 million. The greatest number of war dead and wounded—about 6 million—was suffered by Germany. France's losses were 5.5 million, but with a population less than two-thirds that of Germany, France suffered proportionately more in the First World War than

War crimes. The Cathedral of Rheims after artillery bombardment.

any other European belligerent. Australia, with fifty-nine thousand killed out of a population of 5 million, had the highest proportion of fatalities of all. Moreover, combined Australian and New Zealand casualties—62 percent of those who served—were the highest of all the units from the Anglo-Saxon world. The losses in single battles were horrendous. In the Battle of Verdun the Germans and the French each lost more than three hundred thousand men. Passchendaele cost the British two hundred forty-five thousand men. An entire generation rotted on the battlefields. Modern warfare does not lead to a survival of the strongest or the best. Many who might have been leaders in the coming decades never returned from the war.

In considering the developments following the slaughter, one should remember that the usual transition from one generation to the next did not take place in the interwar period. It is true that at the end of the 1920s a few men of the war generation did advance to political leadership: Anthony Eden in Great Britain, Édouard Daladier in France, Heinrich Brüning in Germany. But the distinction they enjoyed as members of the war generation emphasizes how few of those who could become national leaders survived. Benito Mussolini and Adolf Hitler made a great play over having been frontline soldiers fighting in the trenches. They pretended to be the representatives of the generation the old men tried to keep down and to suffocate. Exaggerated as such claims were, the leading statesmen of Europe, far into the 1930s and almost up to the Second World War, were for the most part men who had come into positions before the First World War. Moreover, because the memory of the events and experiences of this war persisted long after 1918, people continued to look upon the wartime military leaders as father figures to whom they could entrust their fate. Instead of fading away, the generals, the Hindenburgs and the Pétains—whether victorious or defeated—remained important personages on the political scene. There was a strange incongruity between the new issues the First World War had created and the aged political leaders whose task it was to grapple with these problems.

PART II

THE PEACE THAT FAILED

CHAPTER 4

Peacemaking

THE STATESMEN AND THEIR AIMS

THE TWO decades from 1919 to 1939 are frequently called the interwar years. It needs to be emphasized, however, that such a characterization is obviously the result of hindsight. When the statesmen of the victorious powers assembled in Paris in January 1919, they expected, and were expected, to make a settlement that would establish peace for all time; moreover, the hope of their succeeding in what they had set out to do died only gradually. It became clear only in the thirties that what had been attained was not a lasting peace, that the threat of war still hung over the world. Though the peacemakers failed to achieve what the war-tired people of Europe yearned for, it must be said in their defense that they confronted a task of immeasurable complexity. The war had begun as a European conflict but had developed into a global war; consequently, although it was generally agreed that the settlement ought to be of a global character, some regarded the elimination of potentially explosive rivalries in Europe as the paramount task. This central difference was intensified by other differences. Some of the statesmen and diplomats—mainly those whose eyes were focused on the European part of the settlement—believed in reaching their goal by traditional methods; others believed in an entirely new approach to the problems of international relations. If we look at the personalities of the leaders assembled in Paris at the end of 1918, these differences become very evident.

Arthur Balfour, the British foreign secretary, had attended the Berlin Congress of 1878 and regarded the proceedings in Paris with the detachment of an old man; as a diplomat of the old school he was chiefly concerned with the reestablishment of a balance of power. But Balfour's attitude was an exception. The prevailing mood at the Paris Peace Conference was that of nineteenth-century nationalism. This emotion burned, for example, in the French prime minister, Georges Clemenceau, for whom the French defeat in 1870–1871 was still a personal unforgotten experience, so that his main concern now was to

The leaders of the French Army, Foch and Joffre, lead the victory parade along the Champs Élysées after signing the peace in 1919.

make a resumption of the Franco-German duel impossible. The principal representatives of nationalism, however, were the leaders and delegates of those nations that as a result of the war had emerged from the rule of, or dependence upon, other powers and now strove to establish independent national states. Nikola Pašić (c. 1845–1926), the Serbian Bismarck, and Eleutherios Venizelos (1864–1936), the popular and influential Greek statesman, worked for the fulfillment of Greek and Serbian national aims; they wanted to create a greater Serbia and a greater Greece. The Czech and Polish representatives, Eduard Beneš (1884–1948) and Ignace Paderewski (1860–1941), based the demands for their new states on the new principle that each nationality had the right to self-determination. But they could be obdurate and ruthless when the interests of their nations clashed with those of others.

At the same time, advocates of the "new diplomacy"—those who aimed at overcoming old conflicts and tensions by building a supranational organization and strengthening international law—were also strongly represented. They came chiefly from non-European countries, as did General Jan Christian Smuts (1870–1950), the influential South African statesman. The leader of these idealists was of course Woodrow Wilson (1856–1924). For the first time, an American president went to Europe while in office. Wilson was enthusiastically and tumultuously received in Paris, in London, and in Rome. He was welcomed as the savior who would bring about a new and better age. And though many of the leaders of the European states may have been skeptical, Wilson had numerous adherents among the younger members of their delegations. However, the variety of views and approaches represented at the Paris Peace Conference made it unavoidable that the settlement that would result could not be a full realization of Wilsonian ideals, but a compromise in which the principles of a new diplomacy would be watered down by considerations of power politics and nationalist passions.

The Paris Peace Conference opened officially on January 18, 1919, and reached its high point with the signing of the peace treaty with Germany in the Hall of Mirrors in Versailles on June 28, 1919. Like the Congress of Vienna after the defeat of Napoleon, the Paris Peace Conference was not only a political but also a social event. Paris was crowded; the delegations of the various nations included politicians, military men, and experts in law, finance, geography, and history, and they mixed socially with the great French literary figures of this period.

A large number of committees were formed to discuss, to negotiate, and finally to draft the articles settling the new frontiers, adjusting the legal and economic problems arising from these territorial changes, and determining the amounts and methods of payment of reparations. But the final decisions were made by the Big Four: Wilson, Lloyd George, Clemenceau, and Orlando—the president of the United States and the prime ministers of Great Britain, France, and Italy. They had difficulties in arriving at agreement. The chief contrast was between Wilson, proponent of a new diplomacy, and Clemenceau, concerned only about France's security, which in his opinion meant keeping Germany powerless. Orlando, in general inclined to follow Wilson's lead, was adamant where Italy's territorial demands were concerned. Lloyd George, after he had in his speeches before the British elections taken an extremely hard line

The Big Four at the Paris Peace Conference: Lloyd George, Orlando, Clemenceau, and Wilson.

toward Germany, was now less concerned about the issues than about obtaining agreements and results.

In the settlements arrived at in the end, each of the Big Four had to give in somewhat. Although their willingness to compromise secured the conclusion of peace treaties and the establishment of a League of Nations, their prestige in their own countries suffered greatly from the concessions they had to make, and all were displaced as leaders of their governments.

THE SETTLEMENTS IN EASTERN EUROPE

The main business of the Paris Peace Conference was the conclusion of treaties with the enemy states: Turkey, Bulgaria, Austria-Hungary, and Germany. These settlements bear elegant-sounding and historic names because they were signed in various palaces in the suburbs of Paris. The short-lived Treaty of Sèvres (1920) terminated the war with Turkey. The Treaty of Neuilly (1919) established peace with Bulgaria. The situation resulting from the disintegration of the Habsburg empire was resolved by the Treaty of St. Germain (1919) with Austria and the Treaty of Trianon (1920) with Hungary. The most important of the peace settlements was the Treaty of Versailles (1919), ending the war with Germany.

These treaties dealt with two main issues. One was political, the drawing of new frontiers on the basis of the principle of national self-determination; as those who formulated these treaties soon became aware, the application of the principle of national self-determination proved to be much more complex and difficult than had been assumed. The other issue was of an economic nature: the reparations question, the fixing of sums to be paid in compensation for the damages and losses incurred during the war. This issue caused tension and friction in international relations throughout the entire next decade.

The Treaty of Sèvres and the Birth of Modern Turkey

The Treaty of Sèvres was the last treaty arranged at the Paris Peace Conference, signed only on April 20, 1920. It is treated here first because in several respects it has a character very different from that of the other treaties. First, it dealt not strictly with Europe but with a non-European part of the world. Furthermore, the principles that were supposed to determine the political settlement in Europe were not applied to the Ottoman Empire; the victors dealt with the Ottoman Empire as if it were a colony. But this high-handed treatment of an old nation conscious of its great past necessarily produced a strong reaction. Hence this treaty—or, to be exact, the failure of this treaty—became closely connected with the rise of anti-imperialism and anticolonialism in the Near East and with Russia's efforts to emancipate the nonwhite races from the tutelage of the great capitalist powers of the West. In the settlement of the peace with Turkey, the last chapter of one story, that of the First World War, is immediately joined with the first chapter of a new story, that of the anti–European revolt.

During the war, the Western powers had made a number of agreements concerning the partitioning of the Ottoman Empire. There had been a general understanding that the Arab portions would be separated from Turkey, but the arrangements made by the Allies during the war also envisaged a partition of the Turkish heartland of Asia Minor. Even after the collapse of tsarism had made the details of this agreement obsolete, the notion of a partition was maintained. In April 1919, the Italians appeared in Adalia, in southern Asia Minor, and a month later the Greeks landed in Smyrna. The Greek occupation bore, to quote from an official report of an investigating committee, "more resemblance to a conquest and a crusade than to any civilizing mission." An Allied force controlled Constantinople and its surrounding areas.

In the Treaty of Sèvres, Smyrna and Thrace were given to Greece, large areas in Asia Minor were assigned to Italy and France as their spheres of interest, and Constantinople was internationalized. The sultan, residing in occupied Constantinople, signed the treaty under protest. But the foreign advances into Asia Minor encountered a vehement Turkish reaction, and Turkish nationalism found a leader in a hero of the First World War, Mustafal Kemal Pasha (1881–1938), who began to organize resistance in the interior of the country. Kemal Pasha set up a countergovernment in Angora (now Ankara) and refused to recognize the treaty. To enforce the treaty, the Allies permitted the Greeks to advance from Smyrna into the interior. The Turco-Greek war, lasting from 1920 to 1922, ended with the complete defeat of Greece. The Turkish success was chiefly due to the brilliant military and political leadership of Kemal. But Turkey was also aided by supplies from Bolshevik Russia, which was glad to help this revolt against the dominance of the Western powers. Most important, instead of rallying to the support of Greece, the Allies were competing against one another. Italy resented the increase of Greek power in Asia Minor, and France wanted to limit the British influence in the Near East. Hence Italy and France were willing to withdraw from Asia Minor when they received the promise of economic concessions by the Turks. Only the British, particularly the prime minister, Lloyd George, remained passionate supporters of the Greeks. But although Lloyd George was inclined toward active intervention to assist the Greeks and to hold Constantinople, the British people were too tired of war to accept this policy. Left alone, the Greeks were defeated, and in the summer of 1923 the Treaty of Lausanne, replacing the Treaty of Sèvres, was concluded. The Turks lost most of the Aegean Islands, some to Italy, others to Greece. The Straits remained demilitarized and open to ships of all nations, but the Turks regained the strip of European territory, including Adrianople, that they had possessed before the First World War. They were again complete rulers of all Asia Minor, including Constantinople.

Kemal now became the creator of a modern state. Because the last sultan had opposed the nationalist movement, the sultanate was abolished, and Turkey became a republic. The capital became Ankara, a city in the interior of Asia Minor, because Constantinople was too much imbued with the political and social institutions of the past and too close to the guns of the great powers. For a while, the position of caliph, the spiritual head of all Muslims, was maintained and left in the hands of an Ottoman prince. But when the caliphate became a rallying point of anti-secular Islamist forces it was also abolished. This was a crucial step in the modernization of Turkey. Now all the habits, customs, and laws rooted in religious dogma could be abolished. One visible sign of this change was the abolition of the fez; Kemal justified it with the following statement: "It was necessary to abolish the fez which sat on the heads of our nation as an emblem of ignorance, negligence, fanaticism, hatred of progress and civilization, to accept in its place the hat, the headgear used by the whole civilized world and in this way to show that the Turkish nation in its mentality as in other respects in no way diverges from civilized social life." The removal of the caliphate also made possible the adoption of a new legal code, no longer embodying the notions of the Muslim religion; the Swiss legal code was taken as the model. Polygamy became illegal; the introduction of civil marriage, which also allowed divorce and gave equal rights to both parties, implied a complete change in the position of women. An important further step, made possible by the removal of the hold of the Muslim religion, was the introduction of the Latin alphabet and compulsory school attendance, which the orthodox Muslim clerics had forbidden.

Kemal Atatürk in Western dress.

All these reforms were due to Kemal's initiative. Officially he was president of the Turkish republic and adopted the name Kemal Atatürk. As such he had the right to appoint the prime minister, who was Ismet Pasha, one of Kemal's companions-in-arms (he took the name Inönü). The various legislative measures passed through a parliament elected by universal suffrage, but since only one party, Kemal's People's Party, existed, the parliament offered no resistance to Kemal's wishes and twice gave him emergency powers facilitating the execution of the reforms.

During Kemal's lifetime Turkey was hardly a parliamentary democracy in the Western pattern; in economic life the influence of Soviet Russia was strong. In the times of economic difficulties at the end of the twenties, the foreign trade of the country was placed under government control, and in 1934 a five-year plan helped by a Russian loan and Russian advisers was introduced. This plan served the development of a basic industrial potential by building iron and steelworks and the development of consumer industries by building paper, glass, and, most of all, textile factories. The problems created by this emphasis on statism came to the forefront only after Kemal's death.

The Treaties of Neuilly, Trianon, and St. Germain
and Developments in Southeastern and Eastern Europe
The immediate purpose of the treaties of Neuilly, Trianon, and St. Germain was to conclude peace with Bulgaria, Hungary, and Austria. But these treaties involved the settlement of the entire area of Eastern Europe, from the Aegean Sea in the south to the Baltic Sea in the north. The political, territorial, and economic questions with which the treaties had to deal were extremely complex. For one thing, the area was inhabited by a large number of different nationalities, with relations between some of them poisoned by the fact that before the First World War certain groups, such as the Magyars and the Germans, had dominated the others. Moreover, the reorganization of this area cut deeply into the existing economic structure. Austria-Hungary, which the treaties of Trianon and St. Germain destroyed, had formed a natural economic unit that was now torn into parts. The various sovereign states among which the territory of the former Danube monarchy was divided needed financial resources, and the settlements therefore involved a distribution among them of the economic assets of the former Austria-Hungary.

The victors believed that the application of the principle of national self-determination would not only guarantee peace among the states of this region but also allow, in an area previously ruled by authoritarian governments, the functioning of democratic political institutions. After fifteen years, with the exception of Czechoslovakia, not one of the states created or reorganized at the Paris Peace Conference remained a democracy. What were the reasons for this situation? What were the weaknesses in the peace settlement that allowed developments so different from those envisaged at the end of the war?

TERRITORIAL CHANGES AS A RESULT OF WORLD WAR I

—— Line of Treaty of Brest-Litovsk

Territories Lost

By Russia

By Austria-Hungary

By Germany

By Bulgaria

Plebiscite areas

—— 1914 boundaries

Murmansk

WHITE SEA

FINLAND

SWEDEN

NORWAY

Oslo

Helsinki

Petrograd

Stockholm

NORTH SEA

Moscow

DENMARK

BALTIC SEA

UNITED

KINGDOM

USSR

NETHERLANDS

EAST PRUSSIA

Minsk

London

Hamburg

Danzig

The Hague

Berlin

Warsaw

Brest-Litovsk

BELGIUM

GERMANY

POLAND

Kiev

Paris

SAAR

Prague

Kraków

Lemberg

UKRAINE

LUXEMBOURG

ALSACE-LORRAINE

Munich

Vienna

FRANCE

SWITZ.

Budapest

Geneva

AUSTRIA-HUNGARY

Trieste

Milan

Venice

Fiume

ROMANIA

ADRIATIC

Belgrade

Bucharest

BLACK SEA

Marseilles

ITALY

SERBIA

BULGARIA

Barcelona

MONTENEGRO

Sofia

CORSICA

Rome

SEA

Tirane

Constantinople

SARDINIA

Naples

ALBANIA

TURKEY (OTTOMAN EMPIRE)

GREECE

AEGEAN SEA

MEDITERRANEAN

CORFU

SICILY

Athens

Tunis

ALGERIA

TUNISIA

MALTA (Br.)

CRETE

SEA

0   250   500 Miles

0   250   500 Kilometers

TERRITORIAL SETTLEMENTS AFTER WORLD WAR I

— 1926 boundaries

New independent nations

Demilitarized zone

Murmansk

WHITE SEA

FINLAND

SWEDEN

NORWAY

Oslo

Helsinki

Petrograd

Stockholm

NORTH SEA

ESTONIA

Moscow

DENMARK

LATVIA

BALTIC SEA

LITHUANIA

USSR

UNITED KINGDOM

NETHERLANDS

Danzig (Free state)

EAST PRUSSIA

London

Hamburg

The Hague

Berlin

Warsaw

Brest-Litovsk

BELGIUM

GERMANY

POLAND

Kiev

Paris

SAAR

Prague

Kraków

Lemberg

UKRAINE

LUXEMBOURG

ALSACE-LORRAINE

Munich

CZECHOSLOVAKIA

FRANCE

Vienna

Budapest

SWITZ.

AUSTRIA

HUNGARY

Geneva

ROMANIA

Milan

Trieste

Venice

Fiume

Belgrade

Bucharest

BLACK SEA

Marseilles

YUGOSLAVIA

Barcelona

ITALY

BULGARIA

CORSICA

Rome

Sofia

ADRIATIC SEA

Constantinople

SARDINIA

Naples

ALBANIA

GREECE

AEGEAN SEA

TURKEY

MEDITERRANEAN

CORFU

Athens

SICILY

ALGERIA

Tunis

TUNISIA

MALTA (Br.)

CRETE

0   250   500 Miles

0   250   500 Kilometers

SEA

It is easy to understand that democracy was a weak plant in those defeated countries that had to cede territories and pay damages. Actually, the conditions to which Bulgaria had to submit were not very harsh: some minor border revisions in favor of Serbia, Romania, and Greece (see map), payment of reparations, and the reduction of its army to twenty thousand men. Although not crippling, these conditions were sufficiently hard to keep alive in the proud and ambitious Bulgarian nation a feeling of resentment against neighboring Romania and Yugoslavia (the enlarged kingdom of Serbia). The officers of the diminished Bulgarian Army were particularly eager for revenge. They kept a protecting hand over Macedonian nationalists, who, dissatisfied because Macedonia had not been established as an independent state but had been divided between Yugoslavia and Greece, had fled to Bulgaria and operated from Bulgarian soil against Yugoslavia. Bulgarian officers allied to Macedonian nationalists vehemently opposed any policy that implied recognition of the peace settlement and hence clashed with those who wanted to concentrate on domestic reforms.

Discredited by defeat, Bulgaria's leaders were replaced when the war ended. King Ferdinand abdicated in favor of his son Boris (ruled 1918–1943), and a new party, the Agrarian Party, came into power. The Agrarian leader, Aleksandr Stamboliski, advocated cooperation among the peasants of southeastern Europe and aimed at a Balkan federation in which Serbians and Bulgarians would be reconciled. In Bulgaria, he introduced land reforms, dividing the extended agrarian estates. Although the number of large landowners hurt by these measures was small, Stamboliski's agrarian program was widely considered a step toward Communism, especially since many members of his party expressed sympathy for the Bolshevik social and economic policy. Hence the Bulgarian bourgeoisie, the military, and the king all became upset by Stamboliski's reforms. But since he had a firm grip over the peasants, who formed 80 percent of the Bulgarian population, he could not be removed by democratic means. His enemies therefore resorted to violence. In the early summer of 1923 his government was overthrown by a military coup. Stamboliski was captured by Macedonian terrorists, cruelly mutilated, tortured, and finally killed. This military coup ended democracy in Bulgaria. Behind the façade of a series of impotent bourgeois governments, Macedonian nationalists and Bulgarian officers, sometimes in alliance, sometimes quarreling, maintained control and terrorized the country. Finally, in 1935, King Boris, who had played an important role behind the scenes all along, came into the foreground and established a dictatorship, supported by the army and the police.

In the peace settlements Hungary suffered more extensive territorial losses than Bulgaria and Austria. The Treaty of Trianon provided that in addition to paying reparations and limiting its army to thirty-five thousand men, Hungary would have to cede to Czechoslovakia, Yugoslavia, and Romania three-quarters of its former territory, with two-thirds of its population. These harsh conditions could hardly arouse in the defeated nation great enthusiasm for the principles, such as democracy, advocated by the victors. Moreover, through a change of regime in the last stages of the war, the Hungarians had expected to gain the favor of the Western democracies. Two weeks before the end of the war they had pronounced the union with Austria dissolved and had declared themselves independent. Power had been taken over by Count Mihály Károlyi, who as an enemy of Tisza and a sympathizer with democratic Western ideas, had been a lonely figure among the Hungarian aristocrats. Károlyi had immediately taken steps to initiate a radical land reform; he himself ceded his own vast landholdings—more than fifty thousand acres—to his peasants for distribution among them, and his government began to arrange for the dissolution of large estates. Károlyi also supported the convocation of a constitutional assembly, to be elected by universal and secret suffrage of men and women. But the elections for this assembly never took place. Károlyi, who had opposed Austria-Hungary's participation in the war, was a sincere believer in Wilsonian principles, and his popularity declined when the victors treated Hungary not as a newly arisen nation but as a defeated enemy and supported the claims of Yugoslavia, Romania, and Czechoslovakia to Hungarian territory. Under these circumstances Károlyi felt that he could no longer be useful, and in March 1919 he resigned in favor of the radicals of the left. From March to August 1919, Hungary was a Communist republic, with Béla Kun as the leading political figure. Although representing a small extremist minority, the government of Béla Kun originally enjoyed broad support. The Hungarians hoped and expected that with the help of Bolshevik Russia they might be able to repulse Romanian and Czechoslovakian encroachments on what they regarded as Hungarian territory. Officers and soldiers of the old Habsburg army served under Kun, whose government was careful not to antagonize the non-Communist groups of society. The great landed estates were collectivized, but the management of these collectives was frequently entrusted to the former landowners or their administrators; thus, at first the old ruling group and the bourgeoisie were willing to tolerate the Communist government. However, after a few initial military successes, the Kun government was forced by Allied pressure to evacuate Slovakia, and Romanian troops, backed by the French, advanced toward Budapest. Realizing that even the Communists were unable to save the territorial integrity of Hungary, the old ruling group and the bourgeoisie withdrew their support from Kun and rallied around a former officer of the Austro-Hungarian navy, Admiral Miklós Horthy (1868–1957). The Communists tried to retain power through terrorist measures, but under the pressure of external and internal foes their regime collapsed; Kun fled to Russia, where he was later executed in one of Stalin's purges. Horthy and his reactionary supporters took over; by the autumn of 1919 the old ruling group was in power again in Hungary, and Communists, those suspected of radical views, spokesmen for workers and peasants, and particularly Jews were rounded up, tortured, and killed. After some months the terror ended, and political life returned to its prewar pseudoconstitutionalism. Horthy reigned as regent. Legally, the monarchy was restored, but Hungary's neighbors vetoed the return of the last Habsburg ruler as king, so the throne remained empty. Parliament was reestablished, but the right to vote remained limited, and the elections were managed by the group in power. The landowners, large and small, were all-powerful in Hungary until the Second World War. Horthy and his group had bought the assistance of the Allies against the Communists by accepting the Treaty of Trianon, which was signed on June 4, 1920. Yet indignation about the treaty was immense. Hungarians resented the reduction of their nation to a minor power. Moreover, the loss of many of Hungary's former markets created great difficulties for industry and agriculture. The constant aim of Hungarian foreign policy was to change the peace settlement and to regain the areas that once had been under the crown of St. Stephen. During the interwar period, Hungary remained a constant factor of unrest and was the natural ally of any power seeking to revise the peace settlement.

In contrast to Bulgaria and Hungary—nations with strong national traditions—the Austria that emerged from the First World War had little relationship to the Austria of the Habsburgs. Since its territory was limited to the German-speaking part of the Habsburg empire, it became a small country, with about 6.5 million inhabitants. One German-speaking area, South Tyrol, was given to Italy. And the unwillingness of the South Tyroleans to adjust themselves to Italian rule created continual friction between Austria and Italy. In other respects, the Austrians had little cause to resent the manner in which their frontiers were drawn. The complaint they could make against the Treaty of St. Germain was that their nation was not permitted to join Germany, that it was deprived of the right of self-determination. This prohibition against Anschluss, or joining together of Austria and Germany, created a festering wound, for though the enthusiasm of the Austrians to become part of the German Reich may have been limited, there was doubt whether as a separate state Austria was economically viable. Vienna, formerly the capital of an empire, was one of the world's larger cities, much too large now for the small state of which it was the capital. After the war the inhabitants of Vienna formed a third of the entire population of Austria. This disproportion between the rural and the urban populations created constant economic difficulties and political tensions. In Vienna, the socialists prevailed and established an effective municipal administration. The rest of the country was conservative and Catholic, and this outlook dominated the government of the republic. Thus, the political situation was inherently unstable, and when in the 1930s economic difficulties and pressure from the north endangered Austrian independence, the rulers dared no longer trust the fate of Austria to the outcome of popular elections but turned to dictatorial forms of government.

Bulgaria, Hungary, and Austria had fought as allies of Germany. What was in store for the people on the victors' side? Serbia and Romania had fought against the Central Powers, while Poles and Czechs, although not organized as independent political units before the war and suppressed under the authoritarian regimes of the Hohenzollerns and the Habsburgs, had gained the favor of the victors by forming volunteer brigades fighting on the Allied side. The representatives of these nations—Serbia, Romania, Poland, and Czechoslovakia—were admitted as full participants to the Paris Peace Conference. These countries are called the successor states because their territories, either entirely or partly, had formed part of the Habsburg empire before the war (see map). Romania and Poland received border extensions toward the east in order to keep Communism as far as possible away from Europe.

But while the principle of national self-determination formed the basic justification for establishing these nations as independent states, the population in this geographical area was strongly intermingled; the application of the principle of self-determination to this area was complicated and raised as many problems as it was assumed to solve.

A case in point is Yugoslavia, the enlarged kingdom of Serbia. The new name was intended to indicate that all the people living in this state were South Slavs—Yugoslavs—members of the various branches of the South Slav family. But though they were all South Slavs, the Serbs, Croatians, and Slovenes of Yugoslavia regarded themselves as distinct national groups, and this attitude created problems that impeded the working of democracy there. The Serbs and their leader, Pašić, considered themselves the creators of this new national state and were not ready to share power with the others. They clamored for a Greater Serbia, not for a federal state of several nationalities. Because a federal principle was rejected by the government, the Croatians refused to take seats in the constituent assembly elected in November 1919, and in their absence a constitution was adopted establishing a centralized state dominated by the Serbs. The consequent resentment of the Croatians and Slovenes was reinforced by religious contrasts and social friction. While the Serbs were Greek Orthodox, the Croatians and Slovenes were largely Roman Catholic. Moreover, the great majority of the Croatians were peasants, while the controlling element among the Serbs was a bourgeoisie favoring industrialization. When in 1928 the political leader of the Croatians was assassinated, disintegration threatened, and the king, relying on the support of the army, ended parliamentary rule and established a military dictatorship. The ensuing quiet in the political scene was deceiving, for although the Croatians were forcibly suppressed, they remained dissatisfied. Throughout the 1930s the choice seemed to be between political disintegration and the continuation of a brutal dictatorship.

Democracy did not long survive either in Poland or in Romania. There was no nationality problem in these countries, for the minority peoples (some Magyars and Germans in Transylvania) were powerless. A virulent anti-Semitism existed in both states; governments even tried to gain popularity by permitting and stimulating anti-Semitic disturbances. But the Jews carried little political weight and could defend themselves only by economic means. In Poland, as in many countries, a primary source of unrest and dissatisfaction was the agrarian problem. New regulations limited the maximum area a single owner could hold to a hundred hectares (or well over two hundred acres), with a total of four hundred hectares permitted in the eastern border region. But the application of these laws encountered the obdurate resistance of the Polish nobility, who owned immense landed estates, and the laws remained chiefly unenforced. The landowners found allies in the members of the bourgeoisie, who feared Communist influences among peasants and workers and were reluctant to allow them greater power. The deadlock resulting from this division of Polish political life into two hostile camps provided the opportunity for a coup d'état in 1926. Its leader was Józef Piłsudski (1867–1935), who was recognized as a patriot and military hero by all groups of society. He had struggled for Polish independence under tsarism, he had organized a Polish legion during the First World War, and with its help he had established an independent Polish government in the last phase of the war. In 1920, as leader of the Polish Army, he had stopped the Russian advance before Warsaw and saved the country from Bolshevism. In his early years Piłsudski had been a socialist, and when he undertook the military coup of 1926, he was supported by the workers of Warsaw, who expected that he would reactivate the stalled movement toward democracy and social reform. But Piłsudski disappointed them. Once in power, he allied himself with the bourgeoisie and the landowners, and the rule of these relatively small groups inevitably led to restrictions on liberty. In 1935 a constitution was forced upon the people that gave the president and the government unlimited powers. In the same year Piłsudski died, and power now remained in the hands of his confidants, chiefly men who had been officers in his Polish Legion during the First World War. This group of colonels, less selfless than Piłsudski and not beyond corruption, ruled in Poland in the years before the outbreak of the Second World War.

In Romania, the Liberal Party, which represented the wealthy urban bourgeoisie, had ruled under the leadership of the Bratianu family since the latter part of the nineteenth century and had been a determining factor in steering Romania to the Allied side. The end of the war saw democratic reforms: a widened suffrage and secret ballot. But the territorial acquisitions of Romania after the war—Bessarabia and Transylvania, mainly agricultural regions—increased social tensions and sharpened the conflict between parties representing the interests of the peasants, anxious for agrarian reforms and protective tariffs, and the Liberal Party, representing commercial and industrial interests that favored low tariffs so that Romania's industrial products, particularly oil, could be easily sold on foreign markets. Thus, the Liberal Party could keep power only by introducing an electoral change providing that a party receiving 40 percent of the vote would get 50 percent of the seats in parliament. But even rigging elections could not keep the Liberals in power after their energetic leader, Ion Bratianu, died in 1927. With a deterioration of the economic situation, the peasants became more radicalized and aggressive. Their leader, Iuliu Maniu, who had succeeded in uniting the peasant parties of Bessarabia and Transylvania under his leadership, became prime minister in 1928. Maniu was a man of stubborn democratic honesty but not much of a politician. In 1930, he recalled King Carol to Romania from exile. The king had abdicated in favor of his young son Michael, and gone into exile rather than give up his liaison with Magda Lupescu, a relationship that had begun before Carol's marriage to a Greek princess and continued after his marriage, shocking his people. The condition for his return in 1930 was that Lupescu would not return with him. However, the king did not keep his promise and came into conflict with Maniu, who soon resigned. Maniu's intractable nature served a more admirable purpose after the Second World War, when he came to power again and tried in vain to stave off the Communist takeover; he died in prison in 1953, having been condemned in 1947 to hard labor for life. But in 1930 the stubbornness that led him to resign did damage; it began a period of political instability in which rigged elections became the chief means to securing power, as the government alternated between the Liberals and the peasant parties. Because the king had to give permission to dissolve parliament, his power steadily increased; gradually the abolition of the parliament and the establishment of a dictatorship appeared to be the simple solution for getting things done. But by the time the royal dictatorship was established in Romania, Fascism and Nazism had already appeared on the scene; imitating the Italian and German leaders, Carol tried to establish a one-party system. He believed that he was riding the wave of the future, and certainly the Romanian dictatorial regime was not far behind Fascism and Nazism in brutality and terror.

Only in Czechoslovakia did democracy continue to function throughout the entire interwar period. Like Yugoslavia, Czechoslovakia included people of several different nationalities: Czechs, Slovaks, Ruthenians, Germans. If in Czechoslovakia nationality conflicts were less sharp than in Yugoslavia, one reason may be found in the developments that preceded the foundation of the state. During the war, leaders of the Czechs and the Slovaks, among them Tomáš Masaryk (1850–1937), an internationally known scholar of proved political courage and integrity, formed a committee that propagandized the cause of Czech independence and organized a military force fighting on the side of the Allies. Even before the war ended, the Allies recognized this committee as a provisional government. From the outset Czechs and Slovaks had worked together on this committee, and they were aware of the need for building a state based on cooperation among different nationalities. Thus, when parties were formed and parliamentary elections took place, the largest and most important political parties—the Social Democrats and the Agrarian Party—included members of all nationalities, from all parts of the republic. One of the first measures of the new state, the dismemberment of the large landed estates, created among the peas-

Czech President Tomás Masaryk salutes a military parade, circa 1920.

ants throughout the country a vested interest in the maintenance of the new republic. Furthermore, since Czechoslovakia had coal and iron mines and modern brewing and textile industries, its economy was better balanced between industry and agriculture than that of any other country in this area. Finally, as president of the republic, Masaryk, himself a Slovak, worked steadily for fairness toward all sections of the population. As a professor at the University of Prague before the war, Masaryk had educated the intellectual elite of the entire area, and he enjoyed immense respect and authority. Nonetheless, Czechoslovakia was by no means free of internal tensions. The Ruthenian and Slovak parts of the country were chiefly agrarian, and their inhabitants believed that the government neglected the agrarian sector of the economy in favor of the industrial parts in Bohemia. Moreover, most of the Ruthenians and Slovaks were Roman Catholic; their antagonism to the administration was sharpened by friction that developed between the anticlerical government and the Roman Catholic Church. Finally, many of the Germans living in Czechoslovakia, particularly in the Sudeten area, had before 1918 regarded themselves as the ruling element of the population; they accepted their sudden demotion with bad grace. But these centrifugal forces became dangerous and destructive to Czech democracy only when in the second part of the 1930s they were supported and stimulated by an outside power—Nazi Germany.

Thus, in the Balkans and in the former Habsburg empire, two groups of powers developed as a result of the war. On the one hand were the defeated—Bulgaria and Hungary—both dissatisfied with the peace settlement; on the other were the victors—Romania, Czechoslovakia, and Yugoslavia—that wished to maintain the status quo and formed a little entente to defend the situation created by the peace settlement. The antagonism between these two groups in foreign affairs increased the internal political instability of the various states because it prevented economic cooperation. An attempt to obtain through a Danube federation the economic cohesion formerly provided by the empire was in vain. The defeated saw in such an organization an effort to stabilize the status quo. The victors feared that it might be a first step toward the restoration of the Habsburg monarchy. In the end, each country directed its economic policy toward autarky in the hope that it could become independent of its neighbors. The artificial stimulation of industry resulted in stiff competition and low prices—a precarious and vulnerable economic situation.

The situation in the Balkans and eastern Europe held two particular dangers for the stability of Europe as a whole. Democracy there had succumbed because of contrasts between nationalities, conflicts between a radical peasantry and a bourgeoisie anxious to foster industrialization, resistance of a landowning class to agrarian reform, and fear of revolution and of Communism. The dictatorial or pseudodictatorial regimes that followed the democratic governments clamped the lid on these problems; they did not solve them. Thus, they were themselves unstable, and having come to power by force, they were threatened by force. They would rather take risks than endanger their position by retreat.

If the great powers of Europe had been united, they might have been able to work out a common policy for this area that would have improved the economic situation and relieved tension. But the great European powers were divided, and each side sought support among the eastern European states, with the result that the antagonisms in eastern Europe deepened. On the other hand, the prestige of the great powers became tied up with the fortunes of their Balkan allies, and the conflicts over the Balkan area placed a severe handicap on all attempts to overcome tensions among the great powers.

THE TREATY OF VERSAILLES

Although the Paris Peace Conference reorganized the map in extensive areas of Europe, the main attention, then and subsequently, focused on that part of the settlement that arranged the peace with the Western powers' principal enemy—Germany. This treaty was signed at Versailles on June 28, 1919, in the Hall of Mirrors, where in 1871 the German Empire had been proclaimed. Its territorial provisions included the return of Alsace-Lorraine to France and the cession of areas with Polish populations—notably Poznán and the larger part of West Prussia—to Poland, so that a stretch of territory under Polish sovereignty, the so-called Polish Corridor, would separate East Prussia from the rest of Germany. Danzig, a German seaport at the northern end of the Polish Corridor, was established as a free city under supervision of the League of Nations; the intention was to guarantee Poland unimpeded access to the Baltic Sea. Memel, at the northern tip of East Prussia, was also placed under the League of Nations; later it was seized by Lithuania. Plesbiscites were ordered in Schleswig and Upper Silesia and the southern part of East Prussia, and as a result of these, Germany had to give up some additional territory, although only the loss of the rich coal mines of Upper Silesia was of significance. Finally, Germany had to relinquish its colonies. Altogether, 13.1 percent of Germany's prewar territory and 10 percent of its population in 1910 were lost.

These territorial arrangements were complemented by clauses dealing with military and economic matters. The German army was limited to a hundred thousand officers and men, all volunteers. It was not to utilize aircraft, tanks, or aggressive weapons, and their production was prohibited. Artillery, aircraft, and tanks still in German possession were to be handed over to the victors. Also the German Navy was to be surrendered to the British; however, the Germans had succeeded in scuttling most of their ships. In the future the German Navy was to be restricted to twelve ships, none more than ten thousand tons; submarines were forbidden. The general staff and the officers' schools were to be abolished. Finally, as a guarantee for the fulfillment of the military clauses, the Rhineland would be occupied by Allied forces for up to fifteen years and would remain permanently demilitarized.

The Allies had great difficulty in reaching agreement about the economic aspects of the settlement. In the end, Article 231 of the Treaty of Versailles stated that the Germans must accept "responsibility of Germany and her allies for causing all the loss and damage to which the Allied and Associated Governments and their nationals have been subjected as a consequence of the war imposed upon them by the aggression of Germany and her allies." The far-reaching nature of this formulation was obvious. It might be interpreted as requiring Germany to finance pensions for officers, demobilization payments, and compensations for the wounded and maimed. The exact determination of how much, on the basis of this article, Germany would have to pay was difficult to reach, and no figure was specified in the treaty because the amount the experts believed Germany could pay was very different from the sum the people in the victorious countries had been led to expect. The treaty did state that in the next few years Germany was to pay $5 billion, pending a definite settlement in 1921. However, the treaty included various provisions that weakened the German economy and hence reduced the nation's subsequent capacity to make payments. Germany had to hand over to the Allies most of its merchant marine, a quarter of its fishing fleet, and a good part of its railroad stock. For five years Germany had to build annually two hundred thousand tons of shipping for the victors. It had to make yearly deliveries of coal to France, Italy, and Belgium and to pay the costs of the occupation of the Rhineland by the Allied armies. In addition, France received economic control over the Saar area, rich in coal and iron. For fifteen years this area was to be administered by the League of Nations; then a plebiscite was to decide its fate.

The strong moral condemnation of Germany and the German people that was contained in Article 231, with its statement that the war had been caused by German aggression, was also implied in other arrangements. Germany was not permitted to join the League of Nations; the Germans were to hand over their former political and military leaders to the Allies so that they could be judged by an international court for their crimes against international morality; the political union of Austria and Germany was prohibited—that is, the German-speaking people were not permitted to exert the principle of national self-determination. The impression that the Germans were treated as outcasts was reinforced by the manner in which the treaty was presented to them. The German delegation that had come to Versailles on April 29 was kept in isolation behind barbed wire. On May 7, the treaty was presented to the Germans without previous negotiations, and after they had received it, only an exchange of written notes took place. On June 16, the Allies presented an ultimatum in which they declared that they would resume hostilities if the Germans had not agreed to sign the treaty within a week. They did so on June 23, and five days later the ceremony in the Hall of Mirrors took place.

The harshness of the Treaty of Versailles has been sharply criticized and is frequently mentioned as a reason for the rise of Nazism in Germany. It is probably more correct to say that the fault of the Treaty of Versailles was that it was a compromise, neither fully generous nor totally destructive. The French wanted to destroy German unity, or at least to separate the Rhineland from Germany, and to keep Germany disarmed and economically weak in the foreseeable future. Great Britain and the United States were opposed to these French aims, partly because they considered them immoral, partly because they regarded them as impossible to realize. All the victorious powers were agreed that if the conditions were unbearably harsh, Germany might throw itself into the arms of the Bolsheviks, and Communism might penetrate into the center of Europe. Thus, the French aims were resisted by Great Britain and the United States. But to persuade the French to abandon their plans, the British and the Americans had to make concessions. The result was a treaty that *appeared* to cripple Germany but in fact left it relatively strong, especially since Germany managed to evade paying most of its World War I debts.

In view of the hatreds aroused in the war, perhaps nothing better than the Treaty of Versailles could have been arranged. By and large, it did establish frontiers according to the principle of national self-determination. And the necessity of revising and mitigating the military and economic clauses of the treaty was soon accepted. But the impression received by the Germans in the summer of 1919, when the treaty was presented to them, was that of unrelenting harshness. This impression was particularly strong because they believed that they had been assured generous treatment. The Germans thought they had laid down their arms under the condition that the peace treaty would be concluded on the basis of Wilson's Fourteen Points. Actually, at the signing of the armistice, the Germans were hardly in a position to make conditions. Their armies were in full retreat, their people were in revolt, and further resistance was hopeless.

BEGINNINGS OF THE WEIMAR REPUBLIC

When in October 1918 the German front in the west began to weaken, a new German government was formed, headed by Prince Max of Baden, a man of humane outlook and liberal principles whose activities on behalf of prisoners of war had earned him a high reputation even in the non-German world. His task as chancellor was to direct the political transition of Germany; the military failure had compromised the existing ruling group in the eyes of the German people. The constitutional changes made during October transformed Germany into a parliamentary democracy. Its government was made dependent on a vote of confidence in the Reichstag. The introduction of universal suffrage in Prussia meant that the dominating influence of the Junkers on the policy of the Reich was broken. Moreover, the leaders of the political parties of the center and left of center—the parties that had always urged a democratization of German political life—entered the government. Given time, perhaps the government could have persuaded the world that a new democratic Germany had arisen. But these changes and reforms took place under the shadow of imminent military catastrophe. When Prince Max of Baden formed his government, Ludendorff, despairing of the military situation, demanded the opening of negotiations that would lead to an immediate ending of hostilities. The government therefore informed President Wilson of its readiness for peace negotiations based on the Fourteen Points. An exchange of notes followed, lasting through October. Because the European Allies distrusted the sincerity of this sudden conversion to democracy at the moment of defeat, Wilson demanded clear proof of the change in Germany. But meanwhile the government's appeal to Wilson was having an immense impact on the German people. They became suddenly aware of what had been concealed by optimistic military communiqués: the fact that the war was lost. The belief became widespread that the old leaders ought to give up power so that Wilson and his allies would have undeniable proof of the change in Germany. When William II hesitated to abdicate, mutinies—first in the navy—broke out. Unrest spread in the cities. Demonstrations and strikes indicated that the government could no longer rely on police or military force. On November 9, 1918, a republic for Germany was proclaimed in Berlin. Two days later the armistice was signed.

The revolution within Germany threw power into the laps of the socialists.

But if they wanted to use the fall of the monarchy for a transformation of their country into a socialist state, the chaotic situation in Germany frustrated them. The socialists themselves were divided, and the next month saw a struggle between moderates and radicals. The moderate majority of the Social Democratic leaders, known as Majority Socialists to distinguish them from the dissident Independent Socialists, believed that radical social changes would result in the dissolution of the Reich, especially since separatist movements had begun to arise in Bavaria and the Rhineland. The Majority Socialists pushed the radicals out of the government, and the latter resumed revolutionary action. The driving force toward this revolutionary action was an extreme leftist organization, the Spartacus group, from which later the German Communist party developed. In the winter of 1918–1919 its leaders were Karl Liebknecht and Rosa Luxemburg, both of whom had been influential in the socialist movement before the First World War. There was fierce street fighting in Berlin, particularly vehement in the last weeks of 1918 and the first weeks of 1919. Uprisings spread in the Ruhr area and in Hamburg, and in April a Soviet republic was established in Bavaria. All these revolutionary movements were defeated.

To fight off the radical left, the Majority Socialists felt constrained to accept help from the elements to their right. They were particularly anxious to gain control over an organized military force. Immediately after the proclamation of the republic in November 1918, Friedrich Ebert (1871–1925), the leader of the socialists and head of the new federal government, approached Field Marshal von Hindenburg and General Wilhelm Groener of the military high command—the latter having replaced Ludendorff—and the generals agreed to cooperate with the socialist leaders to maintain German unity.

The alliance between the Majority Socialists and the military high command had important consequences. Following Hindenburg's example, the German civil servants recognized the legitimacy of the new government and placed their services at its disposal. The resulting administrative continuity helped overcome the difficulties of demobilization and eased the transition to a peacetime economy. But the support of the military high command for military action against the extremists on the left did not prevent the outbreak of civil war and had a fatal influence on future developments. When the troops returned to German soil from the occupied territories in the west and east, discipline dissolved; they left the ranks and went to their homes. This created a critical situation in the last months of 1918. The high command responded by starting to organize volunteer units (Freikorps) in which former officers had a leading role; these Freikorps played their part in the fight against the extremists. The weight of the conservative allies pushed the government strongly in the direction of ending the revolutionary situation in which councils of workers and soldiers interfered in the process of government. The government was urged to arrange as soon as possible elections through which the bourgeoisie and the

Karl Liebknecht
(*center*) and Rosa
Luxemburg.

more conservative part of the population could make their voices heard. At the end of January 1919, when most of the revolutionary movements of the radical left had been defeated, elections to a constituent assembly took place. The new assembly met in Weimar on February 6, 1919.

However, the shotgun wedding between the socialists and the high command had consequences that extended far beyond the winter of 1918–1919 and stultified the development of democracy in Germany. Because the socialists relied on the old civil servants, the republic was obligated to preserve the rights these functionaries had possessed under the empire. Thus, during the entire existence of the republic its administrative apparatus was in the hands of conservative, usually monarchist, civil servants who could not be dismissed and who exerted a controlling influence on the admission of new members to their ranks. Furthermore, when the new 100,000–man army was created, the task of selecting its officer corps remained in the hands of the officers of the old general staff. This reliance on conservative forces prevented the destruction or even the weakening of the powerful position of the landowners and industrialists. Promises of agrarian reform, made in the initial burst of revolutionary enthusiasm, were not kept. The industrialists fended off all attempts at socialization, although the trade unions did gain the assurance that employers would accept the principle of collective bargaining and refrain from obstructing the functioning of the unions in the factories. It has been argued that the socialists were unable to undertake a thorough transformation of German society because if they had acted against the bourgeoisie, the resulting conflict would have destroyed the unity of the Reich. But the unity of the Reich withstood severe crises in the following years. The fact is that most of the leaders of the Majority Socialists were bureaucrats rather than revolutionaries and did not know what to do with the power that had fallen to them.

In November 1918, the German people were ready for far-reaching changes, as shown by the elections that took place when reaction had already begun to set in. In the constituent assembly, those who advocated democratization of German political life obtained a striking majority: 328 deputies out of a total of 423. Within this republican group the moderate socialists, with 165 members, were strongest, but lacking a majority, they had to collaborate with the two bourgeois republican parties, the Catholic Center Party and the left-liberal Democratic Party, which together were not quite as strong as the socialists. Thus, the constitution resulting from the deliberations of this assembly established not a socialist system but a parliamentary democracy. All power was concentrated in the hands of a parliament (the Reichstag), elected through secret ballot by all men and women of at least twenty-one years of age, on the basis of proportional representation. The federal government of the republic was given more power than had been enjoyed by its counterpart in the empire; a provision gave the right to raise direct taxes to the federal government, which then assigned funds to the various states. As in the United States, the president—the head of the republic—was to be elected directly by the people. The government, with a chancellor as its head, was responsible to the Reichstag. Thus, both the Reichstag and the president could claim to represent the people and to enjoy democratic legitimation. When they clashed, the door was opened for the overthrow of parliamentary democracy. In emergency situations the president had the right to rule by decree without previous approval of the parliament, and no law ever defined what an emergency situation was.

Despite internal conflicts and economic misery, the changes in the forms of political life and the emergence of new political leaders raised hopes in Germany. But when the draft of the peace treaty was handed to the German delegation in Versailles, these hopes turned into disappointment and vehement indignation. In the face of violent opposition, the treaty was accepted in the Reichstag by a small majority consisting of the moderate socialists and the Center Party. A resumption of hostilities, as the military leaders admitted, was impossible. And it was feared that an occupation of Germany by the Allied armies might result in the disintegration of the Reich. The acceptance of the peace treaty led to a strengthening of the monarchical right and the radical left, the right accusing the republican government of a lack of feeling for national honor, the left advocating cooperation with Bolshevik Russia as a means of "liberation." After the summer of 1919 those parties that were the protagonists of a democratic republic and the true authors of the new constitution—the Center Party, the Democratic Party, and the Majority

Socialists—did not again constitute a majority in the Reich. It has been said about the rise of the Nazis that as long as there were free elections in Germany, the Nazis never gained a majority among the voters. This is true. But it must also be said that after 1919, during the fourteen years of the Weimar Republic, those parties that were convinced supporters of the republican regime never had a clear majority either.

THE LEAGUE OF NATIONS

The war had been conducted in Europe, Africa, and Asia, and in its last phase, Latin American states had entered the war, implying that more was expected from the Paris Peace Conference than treaties drawing new frontiers in central and eastern Europe. People from all parts of the globe looked hopefully to the Paris Peace Conference; in their opinion, the chief task of the statesmen assembled in Paris was the establishment of the principles, rules, and organization that—by recognizing the changes the rise of non-European states had brought about—would guarantee a peaceful world order. This feeling for the need of a new world order expressed itself in the establishment of the League of Nations.

In contrast to the nineteenth-century concert of a few great European powers, the League was expected to embrace all the states of the world, and large and small were to have the same voice. The idea of the League owed its origin to a widespread rejection of prewar diplomacy, which with its concern for the balance of power, its eagerness for secret treaties and systems of alliances, and its insistence on strong armaments was considered to have been responsible for the outbreak of the First World War. During the war the need for a new diplomacy was particularly emphasized by writers and politicians of the Anglo-Saxon countries, and their ideas found an eloquent advocate in President Woodrow Wilson, who incorporated them in his peace program.

At the most critical time of the war, when Russia had made peace with the Central Powers, Wilson had given Allied morale a great lift by providing a persuasive justification of the war. The Allies were fighting for the creation of a new world. Boundaries should be drawn according to the principle of national self-determination so that conflicts over expansion would not arise. Freedom of the seas and removal of economic restrictions should raise the level of economic well-being in all nations and bind them together in cooperation. The single states should establish democratic forms of government so that the peaceful intentions of the people would prevail over the designs of small authoritarian, militaristic groups. Abolition of secret treaties and open diplomacy would further assure the coming of a peaceful era in international relations, and a world-embracing organization of nations would supervise the maintenance of this new order. Wilson summarized these democratic war aims in his so-called Fourteen Points, which made a deep impression all over the world.

At the Paris Peace Conference, Wilson regarded the organization of the

League of Nations as his most important task; in return for agreement to this project he was willing to make many concessions, for he was convinced that if the League were established, it would be able in the course of time to rectify any errors in the peace treaties.

The life of the League was short. Its first meeting took place in 1920, and its last in 1939, although the official dissolution did not occur until April 18, 1946. Since the League did not succeed in preventing war, it can hardly be called a success; nevertheless, as the first attempt to create a world-embracing organization of states for the preservation of peace it represented a landmark. Its original members came from every part of the globe. Moreover, in the League Assembly, which met regularly every year, each member—whether great or small—had the same rights. The executive business was entrusted to a Council whose composition did preserve something of the old idea of the rule of the world by great powers: Great Britain, France, Italy, and Japan were its permanent members. But the Council also included a number of elected temporary members (originally four, later this number was steadily enlarged), and among them there regularly were representatives from Latin America, from Asia, and from the British dominions. Recognition of the equality of all nations and of their right to self-rule was also reflected in the fact that German and Ottoman territories in Asia and Africa that the victors had taken over were retained by them only as mandates, to be administered under supervision of the League of Nations with the aim of gradually preparing their inhabitants for full independence.

Nevertheless, the League failed to prevent aggression and to preserve peace. The reasons can be traced to its beginnings. Although it claimed to be a world-encompassing organization, it was not. President Wilson was unable to overcome American fears that membership in the League might lead to involvement in "foreign quarrels," and the United States remained outside the League.

But the failure of the League has to be explained by more than its lack of comprehensiveness. Even those states that had participated in the founding of this organization and belonged to it from the beginning were hesitant to agree to arrangements that would limit their sovereignty. Thus, from the outset the League's chances of success in preserving peace were limited, for it had no "teeth." Membership involved commitments to avoid war, to respect the territorial integrity of other powers, and to submit disputes to investigation, arbitration, and settlement by the Permanent Court of International Justice in The Hague or by the Council of the League. If a government refused to honor these commitments and became an aggressor, the members of the League were to apply economic sanctions—to sever all economic intercourse with the aggressor state. Clear prescriptions for military action against the offender did not exist. Moreover, in questions of conflicts between states, decisions by the Council of the League required unanimity and were therefore almost impossible to obtain.

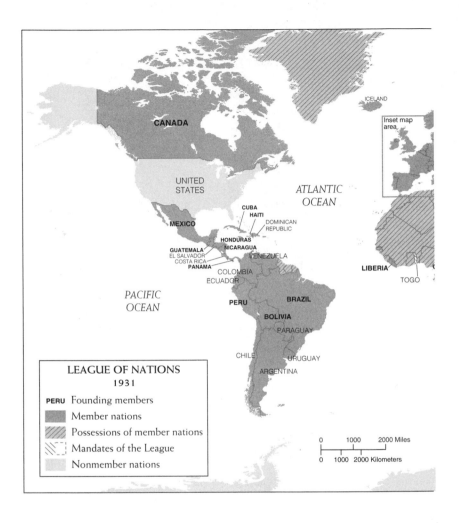

ICELAND

Inset map area

CANADA

UNITED STATES

ATLANTIC OCEAN

CUBA
HAITI
DOMINICAN REPUBLIC

MEXICO

HONDURAS
GUATEMALA   NICARAGUA
EL SALVADOR
COSTA RICA
PANAMA   VENEZUELA
COLOMBIA
ECUADOR

LIBERIA

TOGO

PACIFIC OCEAN

PERU   BRAZIL

BOLIVIA

PARAGUAY

CHILE   URUGUAY

ARGENTINA

LEAGUE OF NATIONS
1931

PERU Founding members

Member nations

Possessions of member nations

Mandates of the League

Nonmember nations

0   1000   2000 Miles

0   1000   2000 Kilometers

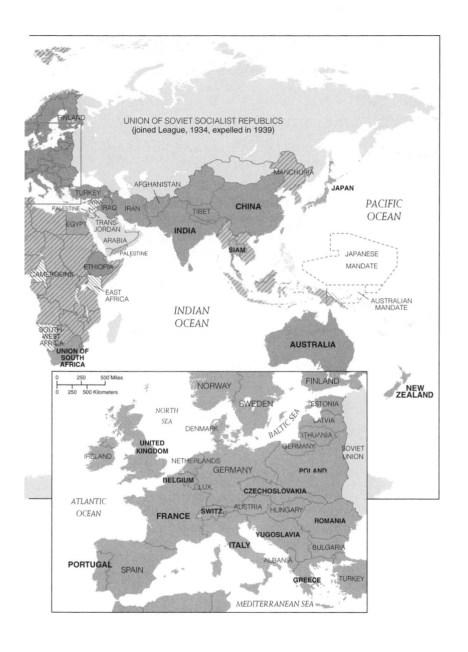

UNION OF SOVIET SOCIALIST REPUBLICS
(joined League, 1934, expelled in 1939)

FINLAND

AFGHANISTAN

MANCHURIA

JAPAN

TURKEY

SYRIA
PALESTINE
IRAQ   IRAN   TIBET   CHINA

PACIFIC
OCEAN

EGYPT   TRANS-
JORDAN

INDIA

ARABIA

PALESTINE   SIAM

JAPANESE
MANDATE

ETHIOPIA

CAMEROONS

EAST
AFRICA

INDIAN
OCEAN

AUSTRALIAN
MANDATE

SOUTH
WEST
AFRICA

UNION OF
SOUTH
AFRICA

AUSTRALIA

NEW
ZEALAND

0   250   500 Miles
0   250   500 Kilometers

NORWAY

FINLAND

NORTH
SEA

SWEDEN

ESTONIA

DENMARK

BALTIC SEA

LATVIA

LITHUANIA

UNITED
KINGDOM

GERMANY

SOVIET
UNION

IRELAND

NETHERLANDS

GERMANY

POLAND

BELGIUM

LUX.

CZECHOSLOVAKIA

ATLANTIC
OCEAN

FRANCE   SWITZ.   AUSTRIA   HUNGARY

ROMANIA

YUGOSLAVIA

ITALY

BULGARIA

PORTUGAL   SPAIN

ALBANIA

GREECE   TURKEY

MEDITERRANEAN SEA

The most effective work of the League was done in promoting international cooperation in the technical and economic spheres. Its greatest successes were achieved by its health organization, which helped control epidemics, standardize drugs and vaccines, promote worldwide studies on nutrition, and improve health services in Asia. The Economic Section of the League provided valuable analyses and statistics. The League Organization on Communications and Transit furthered collaboration concerning such matters as electric power and inland navigation. The International Labor Organization, working under the League, had some success in improving working conditions.

SOVIET RUSSIA AND THE PEACE SETTLEMENT

The League lacked effectiveness not only because the United States, which had been expected to play a leading role, refused to participate but also because Germany and Russia, two important powers, were excluded. Germany, as we shall discuss, was later permitted to join the League, but the exclusion of Russia, a country that covered an immense amount of the globe, was of lasting significance. The events in Russia, from the time of the Bolshevik conquest of power in 1917 to the end of the Russo-Polish War in 1920, were an important factor, if only a negative one, in shaping the world that emerged from the Paris peace settlement.

Adherents of a Wilsonian peace were aware of the difficulties created by the absence of Russia, and several attempts were made—for instance, through a mission of the American diplomat William Bullitt—to contact the leaders of Russia. But these efforts were not followed up energetically, for every attempt to come to an understanding with Russia immediately aroused the opposition of the influential groups in France and Great Britain that advocated intervention to overthrow the Bolshevik regime.

The Bolsheviks had started their rule with a number of startling and, to the rest of the world, shocking measures and decrees. They retained civil servants who accepted the new government, but they also gave positions in the bureaucracy to reliable party members without demanding examinations or special knowledge. Likewise, courts were staffed by judges who lacked legal training. Thus, the obstacles a conservative bureaucracy usually places in the path of a revolutionary regime were immediately removed—to the horror of the rest of Europe, which regarded civil servants as members of an exclusive higher order.

The economic measures the Bolsheviks instituted—confiscation of private accounts, nationalization of the banks, abolition of private trade, handing over the factories to the workers, making all land government property—were meant to signify the abolition of capitalism. Most of them, however, were soon somewhat modified. Larger estates were divided up, but the peasants remained in possession of their land, although they were forced to give certain quotas of their production to the government for distribution among other sectors of the population. The chaos that resulted when the workers directed the factories was soon replaced by planning. In 1921, after the civil war had ended, there was even an openly acknowledged change from the early Communism to the New Economic Policy (NEP), which permitted a remarkable amount of freedom of trade within the country. However, heavy industry, transportation, and the credit system remained nationalized, and foreign trade remained a government monopoly. Russia had abandoned the principles of capitalist economy, and the government's grip over economic life was firm enough to permit an enforcement of stricter controls at any time. Moreover, the original measures confiscating bank accounts, socializing factories, and nationalizing land had completely impoverished the middle classes and the nobility. The appropriation of industrial enterprises and the repudiation of state loans also hit foreigners—individuals, banks, governments—who had investments in Russia. In all further negotiations with the Bolshevik leaders, the claims of these foreign investors for compensation and for the repayment of debts contracted by tsarist Russia formed an insurmountable obstacle. In particular, the French, because of the large loans they had given to the tsarist government, for a long time remained adamant in refusing contact with the Bolshevik regime until they had received compensation for their losses.

But these conflicts over financial matters were only one aspect of the differences between Bolshevik Russia and the rest of the world. The Bolsheviks rejected all the liberal and democratic values for which the Western powers had claimed to be fighting. Like the tsars, the Bolsheviks refused to permit freedom of the press and freedom of expression. The Russian leaders pursued a sharply antireligious policy, and church property was confiscated. Furthermore, attempts to establish a democratic basis for the regime were soon abandoned. After their seizure of power the Bolshevik leaders had been proclaimed to be the legitimate Russian government by a Congress of Soldiers' and Workers' Councils (Soviets). But the previous government had ordered elections to a constituent assembly that would create a final constitution, and before seizing power, the Bolsheviks had accused the government of delaying these elections; they therefore felt constrained to let them take place. But the voting, on November 25, 1917, left the Bolsheviks still a minority. When the constituent assembly opened on January 18, 1918, it declared that because the voter lists had been made out before the Bolshevik Revolution, the constituent assembly "represented the old order." With the help of troops, the assembly was dissolved. The soviets remained the popular basis of the regime. Within the soviets, the Bolsheviks, who now had the support of the great majority of the industrial proletariat, shared power with the left-wing Social Revolutionaries, who represented the peasants.

The dissolution of the constituent assembly sharpened internal tensions. The Bolsheviks saw themselves surrounded by enemies within the nation. In

December 1917 they had established the All-Russian Extraordinary Commission (Cheka) for the purpose of "combating counterrevolution and sabotage." With the organization of the Cheka, terror became a consciously used, openly recognized instrument of government. In the summer of 1918 the Bolshevik leaders broke with their only partner in government, the Social Revolutionaries. As representatives of the peasant population, the Social Revolutionaries had opposed the acceptance of the Treaty of Brest-Litovsk, which deprived Russia of Ukraine, one of its most important agricultural areas. In an effort to nullify this treaty and to effect a break with Germany, Social Revolutionaries on July 6, 1918, assassinated the German ambassador in Moscow. There remain puzzling questions about this event. It is difficult to understand how the murderers could get easy access to the ambassador, and it has been suggested that the Bolsheviks themselves, who had received information about the plans of the Social Revolutionaries, made this possible. Even if not true, such rumors were indicative of the confused and desperate situation in Moscow at this time. The Bolsheviks succeeded, however, in defeating the attempt of the Social Revolutionaries to overthrow the government to which the assassination had given the signal. But the struggle went on. Like the revolutionaries of tsarist times, the Social Revolutionaries tried to shake the regime through a series of assassinations. On August 30, 1918, Lenin himself was severely wounded. The Bolshevik answer was increased terror, directed by the Cheka. Exact figures about the number of victims of this Red Terror are lacking. From Bolshevik sources we know that at the beginning of September in Petrograd, 512 "counterrevolutionaries and White guards" were shot in one day. Many were killed not for the commission of a specific crime, but because as members of the propertied classes they were regarded as enemies of the state. The indignation of the non-Russian world was great; representatives of foreign powers in Petrograd and Moscow protested, accusing the Bolsheviks of "barbarous oppression" and "unwarranted slaughter" that aroused "the indignation of the civilized world."

In the fall of 1918, when the weapon of terror was unleashed with utter ruthlessness, the Bolshevik position was precarious. The conflict with the Social Revolutionaries intensified the civil war. When the Peace of Brest-Litovsk was signed on March 3, 1918, British and French troops were sent to such harbors as Arkhangel'sk and Vladivostok to prevent supplies and ammunitions that the Allies had sent to Russia from falling into the hands of the Germans. In these areas occupied by the Allies, and therefore beyond Bolshevik control, the enemies of the Bolsheviks had assembled and began to launch an attack against them. From the north and from the east, later also from the Baltic states and from Ukraine, tsarist generals advanced, halfheartedly supported by the Western powers. For two years, from 1918 to 1920, civil war raged. The Bolsheviks had the advantage of controlling the interior lines, which permitted them to

1917 ОКТЯБРЬ 1920

A Russian poster. The Bolshevik
knight slaying the capitalist dragon.

move their troops rapidly from one threatened frontier to another. On the Bolshevik side, the military hero of this civil war was Leon Trotsky, the commissar
of war. He succeeded in organizing an efficient and disciplined Red Army. He
personally appeared at the most threatened points of the front, living in a railroad car that moved from one endangered sector to the other. Moreover, the
leaders of the White Russians, as the opponents of the Bolsheviks were called,
were disunited. Some, like Admiral Aleksandr Kolchak, who advanced
through Siberia into eastern Russia, wanted to restore the tsarist regime. Others realized the necessity for a more liberal and democratic program. Against
the White Russians with their contradictory aims, the Bolsheviks were able to
keep the support of large parts of the population. The peasants feared that if
the White Russians were victorious, they would have to return the land they
had seized to its former owners. The assistance the White Russians received
from Great Britain and France, though minor and insufficient, made the Bolsheviks appear to be defenders of Russian national interest against foreign
intervention. Officials of previous governments placed themselves at the service of the Bolsheviks and, strictly supervised by political commissars, were
used by them as "technical experts." Bolshevik attempts—with the help of
native Communist parties—to reconquer Finland, the Baltic states, and
Poland failed. But in the rest of the former tsarist territories, the Bolsheviks
gained control.

In the first two years of the civil war, however, the situation of the Soviet regime often seemed desperate. But the Bolshevik leaders were convinced time was on their side. For the European war was drawing to a close. The German government was tottering. Dissatisfaction was widespread in other countries, and there was some reason to assume that the end of the war would be accompanied by revolution in several European states. At this time the Russian leaders could not imagine that Russia could become a socialist country while the rest of the world remained capitalist. As Lenin had proclaimed at the Finland Station, they supposed the Bolshevik Revolution in Russia to be the first step of a revolutionary process that would extend over the whole globe. They believed that their own position depended quite as much on the spread of the revolution into other countries as on their staying in power in Russia. Thus, while involved in a deadly struggle within Russia, they established a Communist International, intended to stimulate revolution elsewhere. The First Congress of the Communist International, or Comintern, took place in Moscow in March 1919; it was a rather tame affair, for the only delegates from abroad were a few leaders of extremist groups that had split off from the socialist parties. More important was the Second Congress of the Communist International, which met in Moscow in August 1920. Including representatives of the extreme left from a large number of countries, this congress gave a more definite form to the organization of the Communist International.

The establishment of the Communist International had far-reaching consequences. One of these was a definite split within the various Marxist-inspired workers' movements. Even before the First World War, most of the socialist parties in Europe had included a left and a right—a revolutionary and a revisionist wing—but the unity of a socialist movement had been maintained. From 1919 on, there were two different Marxist parties: Socialists and Communists. Moreover, the structure of the Communist International was essentially different from that of the Second Socialist International. In the latter, the socialist parties of the various nations remained sovereign; the organization that included them all—the Second International—gave advice only. In the Communist International, supreme authority was held by the World Congress of the Communist Parties, which met every year, or more precisely, by an executive committee this congress elected. The decisions of this congress or its executive committee were binding upon all Communist parties; they had to follow the "line" laid down by the Communist International. The influence of the Russian Bolsheviks was predominant because the headquarters of the executive committee were in Moscow and its permanent secretary, Grigori Zinoviev, was a Bolshevik leader. One of the basic principles of the Communist International was that all Communist parties must regard the maintenance, defense, and strengthening of the Bolshevik regime in Russia as their paramount aim. The goal of the Communist International was world revolution, and the Communist parties in the various countries were to build up support

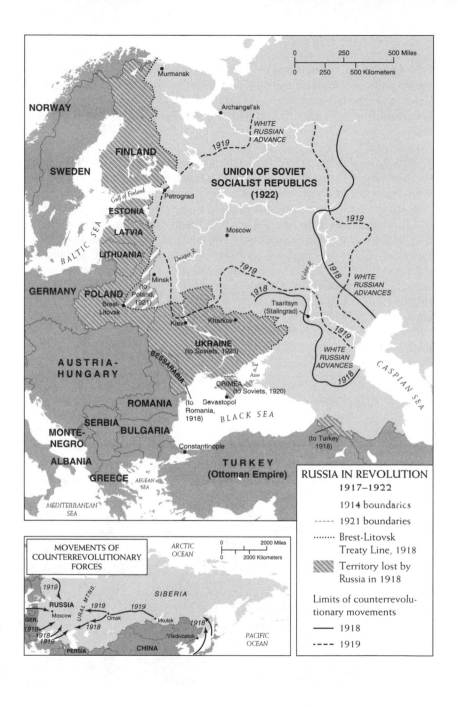

RUSSIA IN REVOLUTION
1917–1922

—— 1914 boundaries

----- 1921 boundaries

········· Brest-Litovsk
Treaty Line, 1918

▨ Territory lost by
Russia in 1918

Limits of counterrevolu-
tionary movements

—— 1918

---- 1919

for the revolutionary movement by forming special youth organizations, Communist trade unions, and the like, all subject to the same discipline as the Communist parties themselves. Whether these organizations would work openly and freely or secretly and illegally, or whether open and clandestine organizations would work side by side, was to be determined by the situation in each country.

At the time of its formation the Communist International had as its chief goal the overthrow of the governments in the great capitalist states of western Europe. From the beginning, however, the Communist leaders were aware that the European nations drew much of their strength from the control they exerted over the non-European parts of the world. Therefore, the undermining of European rule over colonial areas was from the outset an openly declared aim of the Communist International. Its first manifesto, issued on April 6, 1919, already included the statement that "the colonial question in its fullest extent has been placed on the agenda. . . . Colonial slaves of Africa and Asia! The hour of proletariat dictatorship in Europe will also be the hour of your own liberation." This point was emphasized and elaborated in 1920, when special "theses on the national and colonial question" were presented. It was proclaimed that "our policy must be to bring into being a close alliance of all national and colonial liberation movements with Soviet Russia. . . . The task of the Communist International is to liberate the working people of the entire world. In its ranks the white, the yellow

Lenin speaking to troops leaving Moscow for the front in the civil war, 1920. Trotsky is standing on the steps to the right of the podium. In later years, under Stalin, this picture was frequently reproduced, but on Stalin's orders, Trotsky was cut from the picture.

and the black-skinned peoples—the working people of the entire world—are fraternally united."

The existence of a government and of an organization like the Communist International, which not only stood outside the League of Nations but was its bitter enemy, was a crucial factor in weakening the power of Europe in relation to the non-European world. As a result of the First World War, a change in the relationship between whites and nonwhites, between European rulers and colonial peoples, had taken place. Men of different races had fought side by side; the distance whites had kept from other races diminished. Where native movements for autonomy or independence had existed they gained a stronger impetus, and where nationalism had been sleeping it was now awakened. The Bolshevik antagonism to the world established in the Paris Peace Conference strengthened these movements decisively; indigenous peoples were aware that they were not the only ones who did not want to recognize the international order organized and controlled by the European powers. Although in the twenties these movements still seemed no serious threat to the great European colonial powers, they gradually gained in weight, and as we shall see, with the thirties, when the entire settlement of the Paris Peace Conference became threatened, they were a factor of significance in the consideration of the governments on the policy to be followed.

But when the Paris Peace Conference met, the increase in pressure against the colonial empires exerted by the Communist International appeared of small practical significance. Of much greater immediate importance was that just at the time of unofficial negotiations about the possibility of contacts with Russia, the threat of a Communist revolution in Europe did appear to have some reality behind it. Communist revolts broke out in various parts of eastern and central Europe. From March to August 1919 the Communists, under Béla Kun, ruled in Hungary. Throughout April 1919 a Soviet republic existed in Bavaria. Communists were fought in Berlin and in the industrial Rhineland. The danger that the Bolsheviks would gain a foothold in central Europe, together with the Bolshevik repudiation of private enterprise, their use of terror, and their doubtful chances of survival against counterrevolutionary advances gave those who opposed all negotiations with the Communists easily the upper hand. Unavoidably, the settlement agreed upon in Paris took an anti-Russian aspect: the Paris Peace Conference adopted the policy of constructing a stout dam against the Bolsheviks in eastern Europe, a *cordon sanitaire* which would separate Bolshevik Russia from the democratic states. Finland had acquired independence by its own efforts. But the various Baltic nations—Estonia, Latvia, Lithuania—needed and received support in their resistance to Russian attempts at reconquest. Because it was believed that Poland and Romania could become firm bulwarks against Communism, these states were given former Russian territory by the makers of the peace settlement, even in violation of the principle of national self-determination. Romania received what had been Russian Bessarabia; Poland tried to push its eastern frontiers as far as possible into Russia and claimed the entire Ukraine. Although the Russo-Polish War of 1920 stemmed the Polish advance, western diplomatic help and economic aid gave the Poles a border extending far into Russian territory.

CHAPTER 5

The Era of Stabilization

DURING THE First World War and in the arrangements of peace afterward, France and Great Britain had been allies and, despite tensions and disputes over particular issues, had been close collaborators. Soon, however, differences in policy and outlook between the two nations became noticeable and exacerbated. These differences extended over the globe—for example, in the Near Eastern crisis of 1922, the British backed the Greeks, while the French favored the Turks—but the crucial issue in this deterioration of relations was a European issue, the divergences of Britain and France regarding the treatment of Germany. At the center of the dispute was the fulfillment of the arrangements made in the Treaty of Versailles: whether harsh or mild methods should be used. Lack of agreement between France and Britain had its impact on Germany, creating unrest and endangering the existence of the newly created republic. This unstable situation in the center of Europe had an unsettling effect on the entire continent.

UNREST AND CHAOS IN GERMANY: 1919–1924

Problems connected with the execution of the peace treaty dominated the policy of the Weimar Republic throughout its existence. In the first five years after the signing of the Treaty of Versailles the two principal issues concerned the reduction of the army to a hundred thousand men and the payment of reparations. These questions kept alive the conflicts that had developed over the acceptance of the peace treaty. Opponents of the treaty urged a purely negative obstructionist policy, suggesting that changes in the world situation would make enforcement of the terms impossible. The republican parties believed that a show of willingness to fulfill the clauses of the peace treaty was needed because it might help embark on further negotiations and might gain sympathy for Germany in such negotiations.

The most vehement opponents of adherence to the military clauses were the career officers, who had in the defense minister, the socialist Gustav Noske, an all-too-trusting chief. The general staff continued to function in disguised form as a section of the defense ministry. The military assisted the formation of unofficial, secret military organizations, provided them with weapons, and participated in their training. Among the men used by the army for keeping alive the military spirit was a corporal named Adolf Hitler, whose oratorical gifts seemed suited for this task.

The wave of military obstructionism reached its high point in March 1920, when the reduction of the army to its accepted size could no longer be delayed. In a putsch organized by a former imperial civil servant, Wolfgang Kapp, the generals attempted to overthrow the government. Although the government had to flee Berlin, a general strike forced the putschists to surrender. The army was reduced to its prescribed strength, and the illegal military organizations gradually disbanded. But the disorder of the Kapp Putsch led to Communist revolts, particularly in the Ruhr area, that could be suppressed only with the help of the military. The republican government therefore felt unable to take advantage of its victory over the rightists for a purge of the army of monarchist elements. The new hundred-thousand-man army, the Reichswehr, remained firmly in the hands of the old officers' group.

German soldiers occupying government headquarters in Berlin during the Kapp Putsch; that they are in revolt against the republican government is shown in their display of the war flag of imperial Germany.

The Treaty of Versailles had left determination of the exact amount of reparations and the details of their payment to later negotiations. These questions were thrashed out in a number of meetings and conferences which showed a wide gap between Allied demands and the Germans' estimate of their ability to pay; this disagreement served to maintain a poisoned atmosphere between the adversaries. An agreement that was submitted to Germany in the form of an ultimatum, and to which Germany felt forced to submit, was finally reached at a conference in London in May 1921: The amount of damages for which reparations were required was fixed at 132 billion marks ($31.5 billion), due in annual installments of 2 billion marks (close to $500 million).

All the German political parties were convinced that their country could not pay this sum. But German politicians disagreed on how a reduction could be achieved. Once again the rightist parties advocated obstruction; the republican parties were in favor of making some payments and deliveries, in the hope that they would lead to the opening of negotiations and to economic cooperation. The most prominent protagonist of this fulfillment policy was Walter Rathenau (1867–1922). Rathenau was an uncommon figure. An aesthete who was close to many figures of modern art and literature and a writer who in a number of widely read books had discussed the impact of modern technology on human existence, he was also a man of action who had proved his practical abilities as chairman of the great German electricity trust. Rathenau was also a good German patriot. At the beginning of the war he had suggested that the government inventory all raw materials—a most necessary measure—and had been entrusted with the task. In the difficult postwar situation Rathenau again put himself at the disposal of the government, serving as minister of reconstruction (May 1921) and subsequently as foreign minister (February 1922). His primary aim was to halt the inflationary trend of the German economy by substituting deliveries of goods for payments in gold; he hoped that economic cooperation, particularly between German and French industry, would gradually lead to a feasible reparations settlement. However, Rathenau was not master in his own Foreign Ministry, in which influential officials believed that Western pressure on their nation would be weakened only if Germany exerted some counterpressure; they favored close connections with Soviet Russia. On April 16, 1922, when no improvement in the reparations arrangements seemed obtainable, Rathenau, the advocate of a Western orientation in German foreign policy, was persuaded to conclude at Rapallo a treaty with Russia that provided for closer political and economic collaboration with the East. Nevertheless, because the German public regarded Rathenau as the embodiment of a policy of concessions to the victor, he became the chief target of the extremists of the right. On June 24, 1922, he was assassinated by members of a secret organization consisting chiefly of former officers who sought to eliminate as traitors the principal exponents of the fulfillment policy. Rathenau's assassination was only one in a long chain of political murders. Early in 1919, Karl Liebknecht and Rosa

Luxemburg, who as leaders of the Spartacus group had been involved in the extremist revolt against the Majority Socialists, had been killed without trial after falling into the hands of the military. Matthias Erzberger, the leader of the Center Party who had signed the armistice, had been assassinated in 1921, and in 1922 an attempt had been made on the life of the socialist Philipp Scheidemann, who in November 1918 had proclaimed the republic in Berlin from the balcony of the Reichstag building. The members of the judiciary were conservative and nationalistic and refrained from probing the nationalistic organizations to which the murderers belonged.

With Rathenau's elimination, the pendulum swung to the side of those who favored a purely negative policy of refusal; even a complete collapse of the German currency should not be considered disastrous since it would demonstrate Germany's inability to pay. In previous years, the government, under the pressure of heavy industry, had not been averse to increasing the circulation of paper money because the depreciation of the mark helped the export trade and underlined the German inability to pay the demanded reparations. Now, in early 1923, a government of experts under the business leader Heinrich Cuno, supported by the parties of the right, deliberately refused to make the deliveries to which Germany was obligated. The French reaction was quick and sharp. French troops moved into the Ruhr area, so that the mines of the district would now produce for France. But encouraged by the German government, the miners refused to work and embarked on a policy of passive resistance. To provide

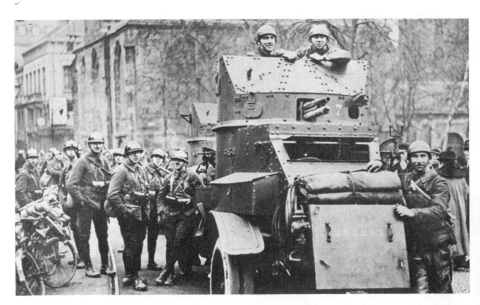

The occupation of the Ruhr area in 1923. French troops enter Essen.

the money the workers needed to live on, the German presses began to turn out currency with accelerated speed, and the mark plunged to unimaginable depths. At the beginning of 1923, the American dollar, which in 1914 had been the equivalent of 4.2 marks, brought 1,800 marks. By the fall of 1923 one American dollar was worth 4.2 trillion marks. Currency of this sort had no real value. When people received their wages, they hastened to transform them into goods before their buying power diminished even further. Workers were hard hit because their wages, although steadily increased, did not keep up with the rising prices. Civil servants, with fixed salaries that only slowly adjusted to the upward trend, were in dire straits. Those dependent upon pensions, rents, or investment in government loans existed by selling whatever pieces of value they possessed. That the middle classes, usually a stabilizing social force, suffered most gravely and became embittered and increasingly radical was a fatal blow to the prestige of the republican regime. The inflation had a deeply demoralizing effect. While most people did not understand what was going on, those who did were able to make great amounts of money. Boys of seventeen and eighteen left school, turned to financial speculation, and quickly earned ten times as much as their fathers, who had been slowly working their way up through the bureaucratic hierarchy.

Conditions in Germany became chaotic. Separatist movements sprang up in the Rhineland. In Saxony the radical left came into power. Bavaria was dominated by Bavarian monarchists and radical rightist organizations led by Ludendorff and Hitler. If a unified Reich and an ordered social life were to be maintained, the printing of money would have to be stopped, the passive resistance in the Ruhr would have to be abandoned, and Germany would have to resume reparations payments.

The necessity for admitting defeat was realized not only by those who had advocated the fulfillment policy but also by a leader of the right-wing German People's party, Gustav Stresemann (1878–1929). Stresemann looked like a typical German petit bourgeois. Before 1914 he had been an enthusiastic admirer of William II, and as a member of the Reichstag during the war years he had been a rabid nationalist and annexationist and supported the high command in all its demands. But Stresemann had been deeply shaken by the way the military leaders had deceived themselves and the German people about their chances in the war. He became convinced that a reorganization of German political life on a democratic basis was unavoidable, and when the republican German Democratic party failed to accept him, he founded his own party, which aimed at the restoration of the monarchy but accepted the parliamentary system of government. In asserting the hopelessness of the contest over the Ruhr, Stresemann risked his popularity, but he was aware that by assuming leadership in this matter, he was opening the door to a positive role for himself in the political life of the Weimar Republic. In a number of speeches made all over Germany during the early summer of 1923, he prepared the public for the necessity of abandoning the Ruhr struggle. In August 1923 he became chancellor, with the program of stabilizing the German currency and resuming the fulfillment policy. As a first step he ended the passive resistance in the Ruhr. He was helped by the fact that the chaotic situation that had developed in central Europe was having a damaging economic effect throughout the Continent. All the great powers now recognized that for the sake of their own economic stability some compromise about German reparations payments had to be worked out; they agreed to the reopening of the question by a committee of experts headed by an American, Charles G. Dawes, and the formation of the Dawes Committee represents the beginning of a period of stabilization in European life.

THE ROAD TO THE REPARATIONS SETTLEMENT

The formation of the Dawes Committee and, even more, the acceptance of the Dawes Plan did much to heal the rift between Great Britain and France that had steadily widened in the first five years after the Paris Peace Conference. But whereas France, in the years immediately following the war, at least insofar as European affairs were concerned, had been predominant from the middle of the twenties on, Britain's role was decisive. Under British influence, after the unrest of the immediate postwar years, the second part of the twenties became an era of stabilization. To understand these developments, which include the formation of the Dawes Committee, the acceptance of the Dawes Plan, and the shift in political weight from France to England, we must turn our attention to the developments within these two countries in the years following the war.

France

The end of the First World War was a high point in French history. Alsace-Lorraine had been regained and the defeat in the Franco-Prussian War of 1870–1871 had been revenged. The First World War had been won by Allied forces under the command of a French general, Marshal Foch. The French Army was looked upon as the first army of the world. Before the First World War the German Army had formed the model for the military forces of many of the smaller states, but now French officers became instructors in the newly organized states, and the officers and soldiers in these new armies wore uniforms patterned after French uniforms.

It was in recognition of the role France had played in the war that the peace conference met in Paris. With statesmen and politicians from all over the globe assembling there, Paris could claim, at least for the duration of the conference, to be capital of the world. Through their presence in Paris, men from all over the world learned that with Marcel Proust, Paul Claudel, André Gide, and Paul Valéry a new generation of significant French writers had emerged and that French civilization was entering a new era of greatness.

But there was a reverse side to this picture of a France radiant in the joy of victory. The nation had lost 1,320,000 military men and 250,000 civilians in the war. Because the French birthrate was low, these losses would be replaced only slowly, and it was evident that in the number of males of military age France would remain inferior to Germany. Moreover, for four years the northern part of the country had been a theater of war, and on their retreat in 1918 the Germans had devastated much of this area, in which France's most important industries were situated. French finances, like those of other belligerents, had suffered from the war. Despite foreign loans, chiefly from the United States but also from Great Britain, France had been forced to print money; by the end of the war, more than five times as much money was in circulation as in 1914, and prices were three and a half times as high as they had been before the war.

It is not astonishing that a country that had suffered as much as France would expect that its material losses would be paid for by the defeated opponent, Germany. The French were not overly concerned about the hardships which such demands would cause in German economic life. Inferior to Germany in manpower and in natural resources, France advocated the use of Germany's economic resources for rebuilding the economy of the victors, a measure that would weaken Germany's competitive capacities. And if the pressure on Germany also destroyed the unity of the Reich, this was not a development the French would regret.

A military mentality was reflected in the elections that took place in November 1919. Known as *horizon bleu* elections, after the color of French uniforms, they resulted in a great victory of the conservative *bloc national*, which obtained two-thirds of the seats in the Chamber of Deputies: 437 out of 613. The *cartel des gauches*, led by Édouard Herriot (1872–1957), and the Socialists lost heavily. This swing to the right was not purely the result of nationalist enthusiasm caused by victory; in France almost more than in any other country the coming to power of the Bolsheviks in Russia had aroused deep fears and hostility. The Bolshevik repudiation of the French prewar loans to Russia had provided the French bourgeoisie with some practical experience of what a revolution could involve. Alarm was reinforced by a change in the French economic system. The war had started a trend toward concentration in industry, with large corporations overshadowing the small family enterprises characteristic of the prewar economy. The acquisition of Lorraine, with its rich iron ore mines, strengthened the position of heavy industry within the industrial structure. A new social force in French political life emerged as membership in the Confédération Générale du Travail, the most important trade union organization, soared from six hundred in 1914 to 2 million in 1920. In recognition of the strength of the workers, the government under Clemenceau pushed through an eight-hour day and legal status for collective agreements before the 1919 elections. But this courting of labor appeared dangerous to the other strata of society because in 1919 the French Socialist party was still in close contact with the Bolsheviks. Only in

1920, at the Socialist congress in Tours, did the party split: the larger group declared its adherence to the Communist International; the smaller, under Léon Blum, remained loyal to the Second Socialist International as it had been reconstructed after the war.

In the triumphant *bloc national* the most influential leader was Raymond Poincaré. His term as president of the republic ended in February 1920, but he was elected to the Senate and continued political activities. As president he had supported Foch, who advocated separation of the Rhineland from Germany, and he had been hostile to Clemenceau because of the latter's willingness to make concessions to the British and the United States and to content himself with a long-term occupation of the Rhineland. Poincaré favored the most adamant enforcement of the Treaty of Versailles. When the negotiations about reparations dragged on, he took over as prime minister and foreign minister, in 1922, and embarked on a policy that, disregarding the more accommodating approach of the British, was intended to force Germany to make the reparations payments agreed upon—albeit under protest on Germany's part—in London in 1921. A strong motive for this policy was the difficult financial situation in which France found itself. The war had been financed with loans that demanded repayment. The French people resisted anything more than a small raise in taxation, so that the government revenues amounted to a mere fraction of expenditures and the government was forced to finance its expenses by selling bonds. Reconstruction of the devastated and destroyed areas of the country placed a further burden on government finances. The money needed for this purpose was raised by loans, underwritten by the German reparations payments. When Germany balked at meeting the payments, the French deficit soared.

Poincaré's policy, designed to break down the German resistance to reparations payments, culminated in the invasion of the Ruhr. Poincaré's immediate aim was to have the coal and steel mines of the Ruhr working for the French government so that with the profits made from the sale of the Ruhr coal and steel, the cost of reconstruction of the destroyed areas could be paid. He also envisaged this combination of military and economic pressure to strengthen the centrifugal forces in the Reich and perhaps lead to the foundation of a separate republic in the Rhineland.

The French occupation of the Ruhr proved to be a failure. The Reich remained unified, and the passive resistance organized by the German government was so effective that all work in the mines ceased. It is true that the expenses involved in this passive resistance—that is, paying miners for not working in the mines—led to bankruptcy. After nine months, in September 1923, the Germans were forced to end the passive resistance and declare their intentions to resume payments and deliveries under the Versailles Treaty. But the expenses involved in the Ruhr adventure had also deteriorated the French economic situation. The French franc declined rapidly in value, and speculators expected it to go the way of the German mark. A loan by American bankers, particularly

J. P. Morgan and Company, stopped the run on the franc, but the French government had to accept the establishment of an international committee of experts, the Dawes Committee, which would assess the German economic situation and the possibilities for reparations.

The result of all this was a reaction against Poincaré's policy in the French republic. Evidently the French became aware of the "painful impression of intransigence"—to quote from a note to the French government by the British foreign secretary George Curzon—which French policy had made all over the world. In the elections of the year following the Ruhr occupation, the *cartel des gauches* won; Poincaré resigned. The new prime minister was Édouard Herriot, and the foreign minister in the government of the left was Aristide Briand (1862–1932).

Briand remained foreign minister from 1925 to 1932. The early years of his political career, when he had been feared as a radical for his role in effecting the separation of church and state, were far behind him. He had subsequently served in many French cabinets, as minister of education, minister of justice, and prime minister. As prime minister during the German offensive against Verdun, Briand had experienced the horrors of this battle, and his interests in the postwar years turned toward foreign affairs and the problems of peace. Briand was no less convinced than his predecessors that France needed guarantees against attack, but he hoped to achieve them through agreements and alliances embedded in a system of collective security that would automatically align the members of the League of Nations against any aggressor. Briand was a great orator, and his speeches, always high points at meetings of the League of Nations in Geneva, created a great deal of international goodwill for France. Nevertheless, the acceptance of his foreign policy in France represented a resigned acknowledgment of the limitations of French power. Despite victory in war, and despite possession of the great European army, France was not able to go it alone in foreign policy during the postwar years.

Great Britain

Although Great Britain came to advocate a more lenient treatment of Germany than France, the British people did not have any sympathy for the Germans at the end of the war. Indeed, the hatred had grown so strong that it took years before personal contacts between the British and German people were resumed. The elections that took place in December 1918, and in which for the first time women were entitled to vote, were known as khaki elections, for the campaign and the voting both reflected the spirit of the khaki-clad soldier. In the campaign, the government promised to prosecute William II and all those Germans responsible for war atrocities and to make Germany pay the entire costs of war. With Lloyd George, the prime minister, assuring the people that he would "exact the last penny we can get out of Germany up to the limit of her capacity," the government gained an overwhelming victory, winning 478 seats while the opposition secured only 87. The government was a coalition of Conservatives (still called Unionists) and of Liberal adherents of Lloyd George and reflected the nationalist mood of this period in that the Conservatives, with 335 seats, were much stronger than their Liberal coalition partners.

Nevertheless, in Great Britain the expectations for the postwar world were different from those in France. The French had achieved concrete gains, such as the recovery of Alsace-Lorraine, and nurtured concrete aims, notably liberation from the incubus of German superiority and aggression. The British had much vaguer notions. They expected a peaceful world and a better life for all the people in the British Isles. The idea of a new order in international affairs went hand in hand with demands for reform in domestic life. The crucial importance of making the postwar world an era of social reforms was reflected in the address of the king at the opening of the postwar Parliament: "The aspirations for a better social order which have been quickened in the hearts of my people by the experience of the war must be encouraged by prompt and comprehensive action. . . . [S]ince the outbreak of the war every party and every class have worked and fought together for a great ideal . . . we must continue to manifest the same spirit. We must stop at no sacrifice of interest or prestige to stamp out unmerited poverty, to diminish unemployment, to provide decent homes, to improve the nation's health, and to raise the standard of well-being throughout the country." These notions were underlined by Lloyd George in a speech in the House of Commons in February 1919 in which he stated that there was no member in the House who was not pledged to the cause of social reform. "If we fail, history will condemn not merely the perfidy but the egregious folly of such failure."

The war effort had involved all classes of British society, and those who had participated in the war now expected fulfillment of their needs in peacetime. The government had given women of thirty and over the right to vote and extended the male suffrage by removing property qualifications. But its record in instituting social reforms was unsatisfactory, despite such steps as the extension of unemployment insurance to almost all workers earning less than five pounds a week. The most important issue in postwar Britain was housing. Building had stopped during the war years, and it was estimated that at least 300,000 new houses were needed within one year after the war. But two years later the housing policy of the government had produced only 14,594 new houses, and when in 1923 budgetary cutbacks ended government subsidies for home construction, the shortage of houses was even worse than it had been in 1918. Slums remained an indelible and spreading blot on English industrial centers.

The disappointment of the expectations that victory and the promises of the government had aroused raised questions also about the past. It transformed enthusiasm for the wartime statesmen into doubts and criticism and aroused skepticism about the policy pursued toward Germany.

The failure to achieve social reform was partly a failure of the government but also due in part to circumstances beyond its control. For one thing, the government was made up of prima donnas. Besides Lloyd George, who had acquired immense authority because of his war leadership, there were such formidable figures as the former prime minister Arthur Balfour; Alfred Milner of South African fame; and George Curzon, a former viceroy of India. Also included were the stars of a younger generation, among them the arrogant and witty F. E. Smith (later earl of Birkenhead); Winston Churchill; and Austen Chamberlain, Joseph Chamberlain's son and political heir. These and other leaders seemed more interested in maneuvering against one another for public favor than in carrying out a unified policy. Their ambitions and intrigues were fed by the press, particularly by the newspapers belonging to the press "Lords"—Northcliffe, Rothermere, Beaverbrook—who themselves were eager for a political role.

As a coalition of Conservatives and Liberals the government was beset by conflicting principles whenever it strove to establish a definite line of policy. The old conflict about free trade revived, with the Liberals eager to maintain an open trade policy and the Conservatives favoring preferential tariffs for the members of the British Empire. There was also a conflict over the maintenance of government control over economic life within Great Britain. Without the possibility of some such control, the Liberals' demands for an active policy of social reforms could not be carried out. The Conservatives, however, used their strength in the House of Commons to force Lloyd George to abolish the economic restrictions and regulations introduced during wartime.

Other problems confronted the government. The turmoil the war had raised did not easily subside; instead, unrest was widespread through the British Empire. The peace conference, the question of the intervention in Russia, and the struggle in the Near East absorbed much of the attention of British statesmen. Closer to home, a settlement of the Irish question, which had disturbed British political life for almost a century, could no longer be postponed. During the war, the government had hesitated to take energetic steps toward the introduction of home rule in Ireland, and the result had been a rebellion at Easter time in 1916. It was quickly defeated, but the ruthlessness of its suppression destroyed the influence of the moderates in Ireland. The dominating force in Irish policy now became the Sinn Fein; the name, which means "we ourselves," indicated that the goal of this group was complete independence. The Sinn Fein engaged in guerrilla warfare: British officers were attacked, manor houses belonging to those opposed to independence were burned, banks were robbed. To replace Irishmen who had resigned, the police force was strengthened by recruits from England, derisively called the Black and Tans after the colors of their uniform. Their brutality aroused indignation even in England.

The Conservatives believed that dealings with the Sinn Fein should start only after the Black and Tans had reestablished order. But the Liberals wanted to enter negotiations immediately, and their view prevailed. In December 1921, a treaty was signed that divided Ireland into a northern part, Ulster, which remained within the United Kingdom; and a southern part, the Irish Free State,

Easter uprising of the Sinn-Fein movement in April 1916, kicking off the Irish Civil War.

with dominion status. Some members of the Sinn Fein, led by Eamon de Valera (born 1882), were not content with this arrangement; they fought bitterly against the moderate Irish government and finally attained power. In 1937, they succeeded in gaining complete independence for the Irish Free State.

The most serious blow to all plans of social reform was an economic depression that engulfed Britain in 1921. The pent-up demand for goods that had not been available during the war had resulted in a boom that soon led to overexpansion and overspeculation. In consequence, a great rise in prices immediately after the war was suddenly followed by a decline, which led to a shrinking of production and a diminution of buying power. In 1921, British exports to France fell by 65.2 percent and to the United States by 42.6 percent from the previous year's level. Altogether, British exports in 1921 were less than half of what they had been in 1920. The nadir of this depression was reached in June 1921, with 23.1 percent (2,185,000) of Britain's workers unemployed. The full extent of this misery was not reflected in this figure, however. Certain industries suffered more than others, and in some localities unemployment climbed to 40 percent or 50 percent of the labor force. After 1922 the situation improved, but not until the outbreak of the Second World War did the number of unemployed in Britain drop below 1 million. One of the permanent features in British economic life became the dole, the benefits the unemployed received under the Unemployment Insurance Act. They were strictly limited to two periods of sixteen weeks each and were paid only to those who proved to be in need. Unemployment and the dole seemed strange compensation for the hardships and sacrifices of a victorious war.

The 1920s in Great Britain became a time of disillusionment. The most flamboyant of the war leaders lost much of their appeal. Winston Churchill had to struggle hard to maintain his place in politics. Lloyd George aroused the greatest distrust. In 1922, in a famous speech in the Carleton Club, the very heart of the Conservative Party, Stanley Baldwin, then president of the Board of Trade, said of Lloyd George that he was "a great dynamic force" but that a dynamic force could be "a very terrible thing." The Conservatives then voted against continuation of the coalition, and Lloyd George never returned to a position in the government.

The view that no victory could compensate for the losses and damages of war became widespread. Pacifist organizations proliferated. Expenditure for the armed forces became unpopular. The government required the military services to base their budget estimates on the assumption that "the British Empire will not be engaged in any general war during the next ten years and that no expeditionary force will be required." Disarmament was regarded as the panacea.

The country that profited most from this change of view was Germany. It was believed that wartime propaganda had painted an exaggerated and false picture of Germany. Back in 1919 John Maynard Keynes's *Economic Consequences of the Peace* had opened the attack on the peace settlement, and now German demands for revision of the Treaty of Versailles began to find a hearing in Great Britain.

Because so many young men had been lost in the war, the older men remained in power much longer than their counterparts in the prewar days. It seemed impossible to make a dent in their closed ranks. Viewing the traditions and customs of political life with disgust, young men turned away from politics. Rejection of accepted forms and values became characteristic of the most gifted writers and artists of the new generation. The great literary monument of the disillusionment and desperation of the postwar world in England was T. S. Eliot's *The Waste Land* (1922).

The abandonment, in pursuit of victory, of attitudes deeply rooted in liberal beliefs and the disillusionment of the postwar era aroused skepticism toward the traditions and the achievements of the past, and this changed political mood played a role in what, from the point of view of political history, might be regarded as the most striking event in the years after the war, the rise of the Labor Party. In 1914 the replacement of the Liberal Party by the Labor Party would have been regarded as most improbable. The war had favored the chances of the Labor Party. With the ousting of Asquith as prime minister in 1916 and his replacement by the dynamic Lloyd George, the Liberal Party had been split into two hostile groups. Moreover, the war had strengthened the power of the Labor Party. The shift of industries to war production and the need for using all available manpower required cooperation of the government with trade unions. The unions' power and therefore also their appeal had increased. By 1919, the membership of the trade unions had almost doubled and amounted to more than 8 million. To assure the support of the workers, two leading figures in the Labor Party, Arthur Henderson and John Robert Clynes, had entered the war government, and their moderate stance on issues like wages and working laws disproved the thesis that Labor leaders were wild radicals who could not be entrusted with government responsibility. On the other hand, the kind of opposition to the war that had existed in the Liberal Party in 1914 continued to dominate the thinking of some groups in the Labor Party. Most prominent among the opponents of the war was Ramsay MacDonald (1866–1937).

An intellectual who looked like a peer of the realm, MacDonald was rather removed from the down-to-earth trade union leaders who dominated the party organization. But MacDonald showed remarkable courage during the war, struggling against the tide of national hysteria and sponsoring meetings at which conscientious objectors expressed their pacifist views. MacDonald argued eloquently that the war would have meaning only if it were the beginning of a changed and better world. In 1917, he greeted the Russian Revolution as an inspiration for labor movements all over the globe and advocated the formation of workers' and soldiers' councils in Britain.

In the disillusionment of the postwar years Labor benefited from contrast to the Conservatives and Liberals, as it represented the possibility of change; at the same time, the war seemed to have proved that Labor was able to govern. This worked to Labor's advantage in the elections held in December 1923. The coalition government under Lloyd George had been succeeded by a Conservative government, headed first by Bonar Law (1858–1923) and then by Stanley Baldwin (1867–1947). Baldwin decided on new elections to get a mandate for the realization of the old Conservative demand for protective tariffs, which he believed would alleviate unemployment. In the elections, the Conservatives remained the strongest party, but they lost their majority. The Liberals and Labor combined had more votes than the Conservatives, and since Labor held more seats than the Liberals, Ramsay MacDonald was asked by King George V to form the government. Because this first Labor government lacked a majority and needed the support of the Liberals, its potential for action was strictly limited and its accomplishments were meager. A housing act, providing state subsidies for the building of houses with controlled rents, was the main domestic achievement. In foreign affairs, the government established diplomatic relations with Soviet Russia and promptly signed a commercial treaty with the Russians. Storms of protest greeted these moves. On a minor issue—the somewhat questionable dropping of the prosecution of a Communist journalist—the Liberals voted against the government, and in the elections that followed, Labor was defeated. This loss was chiefly due to anti-Communist hysteria. The middle classes, which had been upset by MacDonald's negotiations with Soviet Russia, were turned decisively against Labor by the publication during the election campaign of a letter allegedly written by Zinoviev, the head of the Communist International, outlining a strategy for revolution in England. Although a clever falsification, the letter did compromise the Labor Party. The Labor government lasted only ten months, but its tenure, though short, established Labor as the alternative to the Conservatives. Moreover, although Labor's domestic record had been unexciting, it could claim that in foreign affairs its rule had been an undisputed success, a success primarily attributed to Ramsay MacDonald. Mac-Donald had been foreign secretary as well as prime minister, and it was while he was foreign secretary that agreement on the reparations question was achieved.

When Labor came to power, a committee of experts, the Dawes Committee, was examining the reparations question, but still not settled was whether the states involved, and particularly France, would consider the result of the committee's deliberations binding on them. In a letter to Poincaré in February 1924, MacDonald made a statement almost undiplomatic in its frankness: "It is widely felt in England that, contrary to the provisions of the Treaty of Versailles, France is endeavoring to create a situation which gains for it what it failed to get during the allied peace negotiations. . . . The people in this country regard with anxiety what appears to them to be the determination of France to ruin Germany and to dominate the continent without consideration of our reasonable interests and future consequences to European settlement." MacDonald clearly implied that England expected France to accept the report of the experts and was not willing to bargain about this. The French people could have little doubt about the dangerous consequences of British hostility for French economic life in times of rising inflationary pressure. Fortunately for MacDonald, Herriot and the *cartel des gauches* came into power in May 1924, and the new government participated in a conference in London over which MacDonald presided. There were long and difficult negotiations, but finally the liquidation of the Ruhr occupation by a gradual withdrawal of French troops was conceded by Herriot. On the basis of the report of the Dawes Committee an agreement on reparations was signed on August 31 by all powers concerned.

The policy of MacDonald was not very different from that of the Conservative foreign secretaries who preceded and followed him. But Labor and Conservatives arrived at the same policy from somewhat different points of departure. Mac-Donald's approach was idealistic. He had been an opponent of the war, and he wanted to liquidate the consequences of the war as quickly and as thoroughly as possible as a prerequisite for building a peaceful international order. The Conservatives were more realistic; in the main, they had become a party of businessmen. They were concerned about the deterioration and the difficulties of the

British economic situation. They were unhappy about the weakness and the collapse of the German mark since the cheapness of the German goods made them fierce competitors on the world market. They regarded a stabilization of the economic conditions in central Europe as necessary for Britain's own recovery.

Moreover, financial circles in the United States, which had been exerting a great influence on British economic policy since the war, were demanding a settlement of the reparations question. In the first months of 1923, Stanley Baldwin, then chancellor of the exchequer, had negotiated an agreement with the American government on the repayment of the loans Britain had received from the United States during the war. Officially, the American government maintained that there was no connection between German reparations and the repayment of war loans given to the Allies. But it was evident that the European states would not repay their war debts until they received reparations from Germany. Thus, a settlement of the reparations question that would allow an economic recovery of Europe was in the American interest and became a common goal of the two English-speaking countries. American financial circles were willing to assume a positive role. An American, Charles Dawes, chaired the committee of experts that was reexamining the reparations question. The American financial circles were ready to make the proposals of the report work by giving a loan. It was this active interest and assistance that gave Europe the possibility of a breathing space.

BRITAIN AS EUROPE'S LEADER: 1925–1929

The era of stabilization that Europe enjoyed in the second part of the twenties was achieved in two steps. The first step to placing economic life on a firm basis was an agreement on reparations in accordance with the Dawes Plan. The next step was the conclusion of a political agreement among the principal European powers, embodied in the Locarno treaties, arranged in Locarno, Switzerland, in October 1925 and signed in London on December 1, 1925.

After abandoning passive resistance in the Ruhr, Germany stabilized its currency by introducing a new basic unit, the Rentenmark, equivalent to a trillion of the old marks. This was an operation on paper, purely an elimination of a number of zeros. It assumed some reality because the president of the German Reichsbank managed to obtain credits from British banks and a loan from the Bank of England. On the other hand, the Reichsbank started a strictly deflationary policy by refusing to give any further credits to the German government or to German economic enterprises. The printing of money had ended. However, renewed pressure for reparations payments would have restored the inflationary trend if the stabilization of the German currency had not been complemented by the acceptance of the Dawes Plan.

The Dawes Plan fixed the German reparations payments for the next five years; the installments were then gradually to increase as Germany's economy

The architects of the Locarno treaties: from left to right, Stresemann, Austen Chamberlain, and Briand.

recovered with the aid of a large foreign loan. An American commissioner was to make certain that Germany paid to the limits of its capacity. He was to control the remittance of reparations and to establish the transfer of payments in gold. It would be in his power to exert a far-reaching influence on German economic life, for he would supervise the policy of the Reichsbank and the financial administration of the railroads as well as other state-run enterprises. The presence of this commissioner assured the Germans of a hearing if the payments envisaged in the Dawes Plan went beyond their capacity. Furthermore, the existence of the accompanying foreign loan meant that the financial interests of other nations were connected with German economic recovery and prosperity.

John Maynard Keynes (1883–1946) described the reparations settlement as follows: "Reparations and interallied debts are being mostly settled on paper and not in goods. The United States lends money to Germany, Germany transfers its equivalent to the allies, the allies pass it back to the United States government. Nothing real passes—no one is a pennyworse." In this brilliant satirical summary Keynes did not mention one issue that would become highly important in the following years. The loans had to be repaid with interest, and the Germans had to earn this interest through exports. Because German wages had been low since the end of the war and because the world economy was again expanding, after the economic nadir of 1921, the earnings of German exports were sufficient to pay the scheduled amount of reparations and the interest on the loans. The system functioned for a number of years, but it ran into trouble when the requisite combination of low German wages and world prosperity began to disappear. With the establishment of international interest in the economic recovery of Germany, it became important for the victors of the First World War to tie Germany also to the political settlement made at the Paris Peace Conference. To the Germans this meant a chance to regain a place among the great powers. These were the considerations that underlay the arrangements made at Locarno. The most important of them was a treaty concluded by Great Britain, Germany, France, Belgium, and Italy. Germany recognized that its western frontier, as defined in the Treaty of Versailles, was permanent. If there were to be an "unprovoked attack" by Germany against France or by France against Germany, the victim would be helped by Great Britain and Italy; especially noteworthy was the stipulation that not only a violation of the frontiers but also a "flagrant violation" of the demilitarization of the Rhineland was regarded as an act of aggression. This stipulation became important after the occupation of the Rhineland had ended in 1930, for six years later, when German troops marched into the Rhineland, the expressions "flagrant violation" and "unprovoked attack" became loopholes through which remilitarization of the Rhineland was condoned. Although nobody could deny that the Germans had broken the Locarno treaties, it was argued that this violation was neither "flagrant" nor "unprovoked." But in 1925 the general opinion was that the frontiers between Germany, France, and Belgium—and the permanent demilitarization of the Rhineland—were now recognized as final.

This treaty, the core of the Locarno arrangements, was complemented by a number of other agreements. Treaties concluded by Germany with France, Belgium, Poland, and Czechoslovakia established that all disputes that could not be resolved by diplomatic negotiations would be submitted to arbitration. Moreover, agreements between France and Poland and France and Czechoslovakia determined that if Germany refused arbitration, these states would assist each other against Germany by force of arms if necessary. Finally, Germany was to be admitted to the League of Nations and receive a permanent seat on the Council of the League. Germany declared, however, that if the League imposed military sanctions on some state, Germany's participation would be limited by its military and geographical situation because military clauses of the Treaty of Versailles had left the country too weak to join in military actions. Practically, this meant that Germany would not have to participate in military action against Soviet Russia.

To what extent did the Locarno agreements change the existing political situation, and who gained an advantage from them? Germany's admission to the League of Nations and acquisition of a permanent seat on the Council meant that Germany was again recognized as an equal of other nations and as a great European power. For the Germans, abandonment of the claims to Alsace-Lorraine on their western frontier and the acknowledgment of restrictions on the exercise of sovereignty in the Rhineland were painful. However, there was no comparable acceptance of the permanence of the eastern borders; Germany abjured the use of force for revising these frontiers but was not prevented from urging such revision. Moreover, Germany was able to maintain its special relationship with Russia, which had been established in 1922 with the Treaty of Rapallo; in April 1926, in the Treaty of Berlin, the two states confirmed the Treaty of Rapallo. Germany had not opted between East and West. It certainly was in no worse a bargaining position than before, perhaps in a better one.

France also had not lost. Ever since the end of the First World War, France had been insisting that its security demanded a firm alliance with the United States and Great Britain against Germany. Now it had finally obtained assurances of aid from Great Britain. To be sure, the Locarno treaty was not a special Franco-British alliance, just a guarantee of the existing frontiers of both France and Germany. But since nobody expected France to want to change the frontiers, it actually amounted to a promise of British support in case of a German attack. France would have liked a similar guarantee of the eastern frontiers of Germany. But the demilitarization of the Rhineland, coupled with France's military alliances with Poland and Czechoslovakia, had left Germany militarily powerless, unable to expand either to the east or to the west. Thus, the Locarno treaties did not weaken the French position. If anything, they reinforced French military security.

For both France and Germany two ways were open. They could regard the Locarno arrangements as a new departure, the beginning of a cooperation that slowly and gradually might remove distrust and create a European community. Or they could fall back into antagonistic positions, their relative strength neither weakened nor increased.

The Locarno agreements were bitterly criticized in Germany and France. Briand and Stresemann, the foreign ministers who had concluded them, were accused of having abandoned essential national interests. Each of these men trusted the other and was convinced of the other's goodwill. But each had to demonstrate to his people that the treaties had advantages for their nation. To bring about a gradual recognition of these advantages, much could be done by Great Britain. If Britain cautiously balanced France against Germany and Germany against France by opposing every resurrection of German military power and every French attempt to use its military strength for keeping Germany economically weak, it might help to bring the old antagonists together. For a number of years Britain did indeed follow this course.

When the Locarno treaties were signed in London, the portrait of Viscount Castlereagh was brought down from an attic in the British Foreign Office and hung in the room in which the solemn ceremony took place. The gesture was appropriate. Castlereagh had been banished to the attic because during the period of Britain's splendid isolation his policy of cooperation with the great European powers had seemed contradictory to the British tradition. But his aim of maintaining peace and stability in Europe by a diplomacy based on conferences with the Continent's leading statesmen appeared very similar to the policy that Austen Chamberlain, the British foreign secretary, was now pursuing. Indeed, the effect of the Locarno agreements was not limited to the mitigation of tensions between Germany and France. Their main effect was to reestablish a concert of the great European powers, thereby restoring some order within Europe and extending the influence of the European powers through the entire world.

ITALY AND RUSSIA IN THE TWENTIES

The regulation of the reparations question and the political stabilization through the Locarno treaties implied a reaffirmation of those political values in the name of which the war had been conducted, most of all democracy, and a reaffirmation of the leadership of the two great European powers on which the chief burden of the victory had lain: France and Great Britain. The agreements of 1924 and 1925 of course meant that Germany should be drawn into this constellation, although as we have indicated, the question remained of to what extent and how completely this aim was attained. But there was still the further question of how those powers that had remained excluded or had opposed the Paris peace settlement would react to the establishment of a new concert of Europe and whether even if they accepted the situation which the Locarno treaties had created, they would cooperate or would mainly tolerate it and wait for an opportunity to change it or overthrow it. This question refers to Italy and Russia.

The Rise of Fascism in Italy

Italy had fought in the First World War on the Allied side; when the Paris Peace Conference convened, Orlando, the Italian prime minister, was one of the four men (the Big Four) who presided over the new organization of the globe—along with Wilson, Lloyd George, and Clemenceau. Nevertheless, in the postwar world Italy did not regard itself as a victorious power; it was anxious to see the peace treaties modified and tended to support revisionist movements. This separation from the other Allies, already evident at the Paris Peace Conference, had its roots in the events accompanying Italy's entry into the war in 1915.

Unlike the other great powers, which were drawn into the hostilities in consequence of a chain of events over which they had lost control, Italy entered the war deliberately, with the aim of aggrandizement. In the secret Treaty of London of 1915, Great Britain, France, and Russia had promised Italy wide territorial gains. But the fulfillment of this treaty had encountered difficulties at the Paris Peace Conference, especially with regard to the extended Austrian territories Italy was to receive: the Trentino and South Tyrol up to the Brenner Pass, Trieste, Istria, the islands along the Dalmatian coast, and a great part of Dalmatia. These acquisitions were intended to give Italy security against the Habsburg empire, which in 1915 nobody expected to disappear. But when the war ended,

Austria-Hungary no longer existed, and adherence to the arrangements of the Treaty of London was incompatible with the principle of self-determination for it would have placed more than a million Yugoslavs under Italian rule. Nevertheless, the Italians occupied Austrian territory up to the line assigned to them in the treaty of 1915, and when the Paris Peace Conference convened, they insisted on their pound of flesh—the fulfillment of the treaty. Aware, however, of the obstacles that in these changed circumstances the execution of the early promises would encounter, the Italians intimated that they might be willing to accept less if they were given Fiume, which had not been assigned to them in the Treaty of London. But Fiume had a large Yugoslav population, and the Yugoslavs vehemently refused this Italian demand since they did not want to see the two good ports on the eastern side of the Adriatic Sea—Trieste and Fiume— in Italian hands. The question of Fiume became one of the stumbling blocks at the Paris Peace Conference. President Wilson's appeal to the Italian people to accept the principle of self-determination was rejected. For three weeks the Italian delegates absented themselves from the negotiations. Even after their return the Fiume question remained undecided.

The Paris Peace Conference allowed Italy to extend its frontiers to the Brenner Pass and to take over the Istrian Peninsula, including the city of Trieste. Italy thus acquired all the Habsburg territories that had been regarded as *Italia irredenta* in the prewar years, but the government, to get backing for its additional claims, had whipped up nationalist excitement to such a degree that the joy over the fulfillment of these national aspirations was overshadowed by disappointment over the failure to obtain Fiume and Dalmatia. All over Italy people spoke of "the mutilated victory."

In Italy the parliamentary system was in a serious crisis before 1914. The disappointing results of the war reanimated and reinforced contempt for the feebleness of parliamentary politics. The strong radical movements that had developed on the left and the right in response to the government's failure to address itself to the miseries of the south or to give reality to Italy's claim of being a great power once again asserted themselves. Nationalist organizations of an antiparliamentary character sprang up everywhere. The fiery poet Gabriele d'Annunzio became an influential political leader in Italy. In the fall of 1919, while the negotiations over Fiume were still going on, he organized a troop of volunteers who seized power in Fiume. There they remained until December 1920. By then Italy's foreign minister, Count Carlo Sforza (1873–1952), had negotiated a treaty according to which Fiume became an independent city-state, and in compensation Italy received a number of islands on the Dalmatian coast. Now Italian troops turned d'Annunzio and his volunteers out of Fiume. But d'Annunzio had exposed the weak and vacillating character of the Italian government, which first made great demands and then hesitated to enforce them. Among the nationalist leaders of this period, the most efficient was the former Socialist leader Benito Mussolini (1883–1945), who had left the Socialist Party because it had resisted Italian entry into the war. He had served in the war as a volunteer and was now seeking a platform from which to reenter political life. On March 23, 1919, in a building on the Piazza San Sepolcro in Milan, he founded his own organization, the Fasci di Combattimento, whose members came to be known as Fascists.

Resentment over thwarted nationalist aims was fed by economic misery and discontent. In Italy more than 50 percent of the country's tax revenues came from consumer taxes, which fell off when the war caused a decrease in the production of consumer goods. An attempt was made to finance the Italian war effort through internal and foreign loans, and when these proved insufficient, the government resorted to printing paper money. The consequence was inflation; in 1920 the lira had less than a fifth of its prewar value. The financial problems were increased by a growing deficit in the balance of trade.

During the war, when most of the male population was conscripted, agricultural production had been maintained on a satisfactory level through the efforts of women, children, and the elderly. But no work had been done for amelioration of the soil; the soil was exhausted. After the war Italy had to import not only coal and oil but also great quantities of grain.

Most directly hit by the inflation were the members of the middle classes: people with fixed incomes, such as civil servants, landlords prevented by law from raising rents, and rentiers who had invested their money in government bonds. But economic distress was also felt by the rural classes and the workers. After the war, more than 50 percent of all Italians were engaged in agriculture. Nine-tenths of those who owned land possessed less than three acres, not nearly enough even for subsistence. And a great part of the rural population was entirely landless, working for wages on the great estates. During the war the government had promised a redistribution of the land; rumors—many exaggerated—about what had been done in Russia stimulated the impatience of the Italian peasants and raised their expectations. The war also increased unrest among the industrial workers. Hitherto industrial activity had largely taken the form of very small enterprises, employing fewer than ten workers. But during the war large-scale industrial establishments had become much more numerous. The wartime need for the production of guns, planes, cars, and ships led to the formation of great industrial complexes engaged in steel production, engineering, and shipping. Ansaldo employed more than one hundred thousand workers, but Iloa, Fiat, and others were also enterprises of remarkable size. These big industries were closely allied with the great Italian banks—the Banca Commerciale and the Banca di Sconto—and this combination of industrial and commercial interests developed into a powerful factor in Italian politics. The depreciation of the Italian currency facilitated the export of Italian industrial products and increased the wealth of the entrepreneur, whereas the wages of the workers could not keep up with the inflationary rise of prices. These economic difficulties, coupled with news about the workers' "paradise" in Russia, intensified the demand for social reform by the workers, and the long-standing influence of syndicalism and anarchism contributed to their radicalization. Dissatisfaction among the rural and industrial proletariat erupted in direct action. In dramatic fashion, bands of peasants and agricultural workers, marching to the accompaniment of martial music and the pealing of church bells, occupied uncultivated land belonging to the great landowners. In cities and towns, strikes increased. The strike wave reached its high point in the summer of 1920, when dismissals in the metallurgical industries led to an occupation of the factories by the workers in industrial regions. However, these demonstrations had no long-lasting effect. The police removed the peasants from the land they had appropriated, and the workers, lacking raw materials, capital, and salesmen, were unable to keep the industries going and evacuated the factories. Nevertheless, the political activity of peasants and workers contributed significantly to the transformation of the Italian party system. Before the war, the Italian political parties were rather loose in structure; the individual deputy owed his election to his reputation and his standing in his own district, not to his party label. After the war, the Socialists, in close alliance with the trade unions, built an efficient, centrally directed organization. Furthermore, Pope Benedict XV gave permission for the foundation of a Catholic political party, and the Catholic People's Party appeared on the scene. Eager for mass support, it looked beyond the Catholic bourgeoisie for adherents, seeking to attract the peasants of the south and the industrial workers, among whom Catholic trade unions began to compete with socialist trade unions. The guiding spirit of the Catholic People's Party was a Sicilian priest, Don Luigi Sturzo, whose experience in the stagnant Italian south had made him aware of the need for social—particularly agrarian—reform. The influence of the two mass parties—the Socialists and the Catholic People's Party—was strengthened by the adoption of the proportional voting system, which the government had introduced as a concession to the demands for reform: the number of deputies allowed each party was determined by the total number of votes received by the party throughout Italy. The bourgeois parties of the center and the left, Liberals and Democrats, were seriously threatened. This was the situation when the Fascists came to power in October 1922.

Mussolini's claim that Fascism saved Italy from Bolshevism is palpably untrue. If there ever was danger of a successful Communist takeover in Italy after the First World War—and this is most doubtful—the revolutionary wave had certainly passed its crest by the spring of 1921. The new mass parties, now firmly entrenched, did not advocate revolution. However, they did agree on the need for far-reaching social and economic reform. Reform was deeply feared by the industrialists and landowners, still suffering from the shock of the occupation of factories and land by workers and peasants. In their anxiety, they turned to the opponents of parliamentary democracy, hoping to gain support in their fight against reform. Mussolini's Fascists offered themselves as a most suitable instrument. Throughout Italy the party had formed paramilitary organizations, consisting chiefly of young unemployed war veterans. In the industrial centers of the north, these Fascist organizations made themselves popular with the bourgeoisie by protecting strikebreakers and disrupting socialist street demonstrations. In the rural areas they supported the landowners anxious to prevent the formation of unions of farm workers, or to break them up where they existed. The young Fascists were ruthless but effective. Moreover, Mussolini, their leader, inspired some confidence; he was a journalist of gifts and a remarkable orator. Although his boasts of intensive study of Marx and Nietzsche were considerably exaggerated, his acquaintance with Marxist thought and modern philosophy was sufficient to give his writings and speeches intellectual respectability. Through his advocacy of Italy's entry into the war and through his war service he had demonstrated his patriotism, but Mussolini was too much of a Marxist to believe that the world could stand still and be satisfied with the same old ideas. He was therefore not only a nationalist but also a revolutionary activist. This combination constituted his strength in the eyes of the Italian upper classes. On the one hand, Mussolini seemed to have a hold over the masses, who were threatening to get out of control; on the other, he seemed to share their own nationalist ideals and their rejection of international socialism. They expected that Mussolini might develop his organization into a counterforce to the new mass parties. Leaders of the old political groups, such as Giolitti, regarded Mussolini's rise with benevolence. They believed that he would be useful and that cooperation with him would be feasible.

The test came with the Fascist seizure of power—the March on Rome on October 27, 1922. The version of this event the Fascists later spread was that the Fascist organizations had converged on Rome and the government, faced by this revolutionary force, capitulated. Actually, negotiations about Fascist participation in the government had been going on for some time. Leaders of various political parties were willing to form a coalition government that included the Fascists. To clinch these negotiations, Mussolini organized the March on Rome; his paramilitary organizations approached the capital from four directions. The government felt sure that it could defeat this Fascist revolt with the help of the army, and the king was willing to sign the order declaring a state of siege. But on the night of October 27 he changed his mind—it is not clear why—either because he had received an exaggerated report of the Fascist military strength, as he maintained after the fall of Mussolini, or because he had been informed about the unwillingness of the army to attack the Fascist squadrons. When Mussolini heard of the king's attitude, he was no longer content with a subordinate partnership in a coalition government and insisted that he be made prime minister. Only after this demand had been granted did he come to Rome; arriving on October 30, he appeared before the king and was commissioned to form a government. The Fascist organizations now entered Rome and held a victory parade. The March on Rome shows all the features characteristic of Mussolini's policy in the first decade of Fascist rule: on the one hand, the dramatic gesture directed toward the outside world; on the other, cautious preparation and careful calculation.

In the first years of his regime Mussolini's policy was rather ambiguous. The Fascist paramilitary organizations became a militia paid by the state and were effectively used to eliminate opposition. Mussolini placed Fascists in key positions in his administration, and they controlled the police. However, his government included not only Fascists but also liberals, conservatives, and some members of the Catholic People's Party, and the parliament continued to function. Mussolini's main difficulties at the beginning were created by the diversity, almost the contrasts, among his supporters. Conservatives and liberals cooperated with him because his government promised a "normalization" of Italian life, a reestablishment of stability, of social and political order, and tranquillity. On the other hand, a good amount of the violence had been committed by the Fascist *squadri*, the Fascist paramilitary organization; their aggressiveness and ruthlessness were a chief instrument in intimidating the farm workers and in breaking strikes—briefly, in achieving order and "normalization."

At the outset, Mussolini's system of government seemed to be formed after the model of Giolitti's parliamentary dictatorship in the prewar years. However, because the mass of workers and peasants had become more vocal and better organized, such a parliamentary dictatorship was much more difficult to maintain. Accordingly the men in power had fewer hesitations to use ruthless and brutal methods. Moreover, Mussolini was determined to remain in power—not only because normalization required guarantees of stability at the top but also because of his love of power. The difficulty was that Mussolini had given repeated assurances that he would remain within the framework of the constitution in his conduct of affairs. He found a way around this difficulty by introducing a measure that provided a change in the electoral law: under the threat of a second wave of revolution he forced the parliament to accept the so-called Acerbo Law. This stated that the party with the largest number of votes would receive two-thirds of the seats in the Chamber of Deputies. The Acerbo Law of 1923, more than the March on Rome, represented the end of parliamentary power, the forsaking of the constitution. It removed all obstacles in the way of a dictatorial regime. In the election of 1924 the government received a very strong vote, which, by means of the Acerbo Law, was transformed into a two-thirds majority. The government had 356 of the 535 seats in the chamber.

The manner in which Mussolini had proceeded unified the opposition. Opponents of the government were still able to make themselves heard from the tribune of the parliament and from there attacked Fascist brutality and the falsified election returns. Mussolini ordered his henchmen to beat up some of the prominent opposition leaders so that they would be unable to appear in parliament or at least would be intimidated. One of the main opponents of the Fascist

Benito Mussolini during the March on Rome, October 1922.

regime was a young, highly respected Socialist deputy, Giacomo Matteotti; in his writings and speeches Matteotti had presented extended proof of Fascist terrorist acts. In particular, he had demonstrated how violence had been used to intimidate voters in the recent election, and his revelations had been highly compromising to several members of the Fascist hierarchy. Matteotti suddenly disappeared; his body was later fished out of the Tiber. It soon became known that Matteotti had been assassinated, his abduction and murder instigated by prominent Fascists close to Mussolini.

Although there was no proof that Mussolini ordered Matteotti's death, the murder was a manifestation of the atmosphere of brutality and violence that had developed with the toleration and encouragement of government leaders. The excitement over these disclosures was immense. The parliamentary opposition—about a hundred deputies, among them the various Socialist groups, some members of the Catholic People's Party, and left-wing liberals—demanded the dissolution of the Fascist militia and refused to have any contact with the Fascists, members of a party including murderers. They therefore withdrew from the Chamber of Deputies and set up their own counterparliament on the Aventine. The demands of the opposition were strongly supported by the large Italian newspapers, which called for Mussolini's resignation. He seems to have thought of retirement, but the king, whom the opposition expected to take the initiative in dismissing Mussolini, did not act. Mussolini remained in power, and he now took the initiative. He said in a famous speech: "I declare that I and I alone assume the political, moral, and historical responsibility for all that has happened. . . . If Fascism has been a criminal association, if all the acts of violence have been the result of a certain historical, political, and moral climate, the responsibility for this is mine." Mussolini now steered energetically toward a one-party system and a totalitarian dictatorship.

The powers of parliament were increasingly curtailed and finally almost eliminated. It could no longer overthrow a government by a vote of lack of confidence. Its members could not propose a question for discussion; the head of the government determined the subjects to be debated in parliament. The position of the head of the government, or prime minister, was raised above that of other members of the cabinet. He was to appoint and dismiss the ministers and to direct their work. Neither individually nor collectively could the ministers remonstrate against his decisions. The prime minister also became almost independent of the crown, for if it should be necessary to appoint a new head of the government, the king was now obliged to choose him from a list of candidates put together by the Great Council of the Fascist Party. Thus, the Fascist Party became an officially recognized institution and the decisive element in Italian political life. Soon it was the only legal political party; the other parties, having become entirely impotent, were forcibly dissolved. Since the list of candidates the voters could accept or reject was put together by the Great Council of the Fascist Party, only Fascists were elected to the Chamber of Deputies. The Fascist Party was carefully organized at local and provincial levels as well as nationally; all party officials were appointed, not elected. The highest authority in the party was the Great Council, consisting of about thirty members selected by Mussolini as his most loyal followers.

Mussolini was at once the prime minister—chief executive of the government—and the leader (*duce*) of the party. Through the channels of the party organization, local party officers reported to him about the efficiency and loyalty of government officials. By "supervising"—or informing on—administrative functionaries at all levels, the Fascists held a heavy club over the heads of civil servants, who soon saw the futility, if not the danger, of questioning the actions of party members. Little or nothing was done when members of the Fascist militia committed acts of violence. Terror became an instrument of rule. Many prominent political leaders of the pre-Fascist era went into exile. Some who remained in Italy were physically attacked and gravely wounded; some were imprisoned without trial or banished to small islands in the Mediterranean or to isolated villages in the Calabrian mountains.

Police supervision, reinforced by terror, was supplemented as a means of control by censorship, introduced immediately after the assassination of Matteotti. The censorship laws created so many obstacles in the way of privately owned and independent newspapers that these publications began to disappear. The owners were forced to sell them. Some were taken over by the government; local papers were bought cheaply by local party officials. Censorship extended to every aspect of literature and scholarship. Writers and scholars were forced either to desist from writing on contemporary issues or to promote Fascist ideas. And the Fascists were very conscious of the importance and value of propaganda. They offered great spectacles to the masses; they embodied their doctrine in slogans, which appeared on posters all over the country; they impressed intellectuals by demonstrating interest in modern literary and artistic movements, such as Futurism; and by having the railroads run on time, they showed foreigners that order had been restored.

Mussolini was aware that it was questionable how effective these instruments of control would be against unemployment and economic misery. Despite repeated assertions in his speeches that Fascism represented neither capitalism nor Marxian socialism, but rather a new social system, Mussolini kept close to the financial and industrial leaders who had helped him into power. Thus, after Fascist extremism had done its job, weakening and destroying possible centers of political opposition, Mussolini insisted on introducing stricter discipline among the *squadri* of the Fascist Party, and it was decreed that party officers would be appointed, not elected. Moreover, Mussolini did not permit the party to infiltrate the bureaucracy. Although the party officers exercised political supervision over the civil servants, party and state were kept apart. This fundamentally conservative attitude was particularly noticeable in the regime's economic policy.

Mussolini's famous corporate state, which was supposed to realize the new Fascist ideas in social and economic life, actually served the purposes of the wealthier classes. According to the charter that established this corporate state, the employers and employees of each branch of industry were to form a corporation; for each corporation, committees including representatives of the employers, the employees, and the government would decide questions of wages, working hours, and the like. The decisions of the committees were to be binding, and therefore, strikes were forbidden. But since only Fascist trade unions were permitted to exist, the union leaders who represented the workers in the committees followed the line set by the government representatives, who usually sided with the industrialists. The economic recovery that took place all over Europe in the 1920s caused a reduction in unemployment and disguised the fact that the workers had become powerless. Moreover, impressed by Mussolini's claim to have saved his country from Bolshevism, both Italian and foreign bankers regarded Fascist Italy as trustworthy and stable and gave loans to the Fascist government, which provided additional stimulus to Italian economic life.

The respectability of the regime and its popularity among the various groups of Italian society were also increased by the reconciliation, sealed in the Lateran Treaty of February 11, 1929, of the Italian state with the Roman Catholic Church. Mussolini had initiated negotiations with the Vatican almost immediately after coming to power. In the 1929 agreement the pope was recognized as the independent ruler of a small state—Vatican City—and the church received a large financial sum as restitution for the expropriations at the time of Italy's unification. The relations between the church and the state were regulated by a *concordate*, which declared Roman Catholicism to be the official religion of the state, permitted the pope to appoint the Italian bishops after he had received the approval of the government for his candidates, guaranteed religious education in schools, and made a religious marriage ceremony mandatory. Two days after the conclusion of the Lateran Treaty, Pius XI (pope from 1922 to 1939) declared that he regarded Mussolini as "a man sent by Providence."

Reconciliation with the church may seem a strange step for one who in earlier years had flaunted his atheism and his contempt for the church. But with the adoption of Fascism, Mussolini had accepted the view that the politician should not be bound by a system or principles. He emphasized the novelty of Fascist ideas, but when he came to power, it was by no means clear what these new Fascist ideas actually were. In later years, when attempts were made to formulate the system of Fascism, this lack of a consistent framework of thought was justified by the assertion that thought independent from action did not exist.

It has always been easier to discover what Fascism rejected than what it stood for. In their statements about Fascist concepts of politics and government, Mussolini and his adherents emphasized that Fascism stood against the individualistic and rationalistic philosophy of the French Revolution. The law of politics, like the law of nature, was struggle; continued existence required continued growth and could be achieved only through action, not thought. Nations were living, viable units in politics, and man's function was to be an instrument in the hands of his nation's leader. Having turned from socialism and internationalism to nationalism, Mussolini preached the subordination of the individual to the nation with the excessive zeal of a convert. But he was also aware that the pursuit of a strictly nationalistic policy offered the best opportunity to conceal the contradictions of a regime that claimed to be revolutionary but actually defended and maintained the status quo. Thus, personal inclination and political calculation combined to make the conduct of a forceful foreign policy, expressive of national egotism, the cornerstone of Mussolini's rule.

Mussolini disliked collective action and stabilization and wanted a fluid situation in which, by making use of the changing relations among various states, Italy could advance its own national interests. He stressed that Italy was not a satisfied nation, but "a nation hungry for land because we are prolific and intend to remain so." Mussolini always emphasized his disbelief in eternal peace and stressed that Italy must possess not only a powerful army and navy but also "an air force that dominates the skies." He set the new tone of Italian foreign policy as early as 1923, when he used the assassination of a group of Italian officers on the Greek-Albanian border as pretext for an ultimatum to Greece. He demanded an indemnity of 50 million lire, an inquiry with the assistance of the Italian military attaché, ceremonial apologies, and funeral honors. When the Greeks hesitated to comply, he bombarded and occupied the island of Corfu, evacuating it only after the Greeks, on the advice of the great powers, had given in to the Italian demands. The tangible result of Mussolini's first adventure in foreign policy was small and could have been obtained without force. But his aim had been to show the Italians that their state was no longer ruled by a weak, timid, internationally minded government, and he used every opportunity to demonstrate that Italy had embarked on a new active course in foreign policy. He was proud to have shown with his action in the Corfu incident that Italy had freed itself from the tutelage of Great Britain and France.

But in the 1920s the bark of Fascism was more threatening than its bite. Mussolini was careful to avoid moves that might lead to serious complications, such as a conflict with one of the great powers. He was aware that Italy was a much weaker state. Moreover, the Italian economy was in need of foreign loans. When Great Britain, France, and Germany initiated the negotiations that resulted in the Locarno treaties, Mussolini kept aloof from them because of his disapproval of the League of Nations and of collective action. But when these negotiations neared completion, he rushed to Locarno and participated in the signing of the documents. He was not willing to arouse displeasure that might have repercussions on Italy's economic position. Moreover, he was anxious to demonstrate that Italy was one of the great European powers. One might add that one year after Matteotti's murder, Mussolini's position was still not secure enough to arouse further resentment in other countries by obstructing a policy of pacification. But if in the second half of the twenties he did not directly oppose the stabilization at which the other European powers were aiming, neither did he abandon his hostility to democracy and peace and his dreams of Italy as a great expansionist power. Still, in the 1920s he took some concrete steps toward expansion through the establishment of an Italian protectorate over Albania. The fateful consequences of his emphasis on action and national prestige became apparent only in the 1930s when the Nazis had come to power in Germany and pursued an aggressive course. Then Mussolini was hoist with his own petard. He did not want to appear less virile and martial than the Fascist leader of Germany. By then the prosperity of the 1920s had passed, and Italians had begun to notice how little the Fascist regime had changed the economic and social life of their nation. The only way out, it seemed to Mussolini, was to tie the fortunes of his country to the rising power of Nazi Germany.

The Stabilization of Communism in Russia

FROM LENIN TO STALIN

The main achievement of the Bolsheviks in the first three years of their rule was survival. Under the exigencies of the civil war many of the original measures intended to create the new socialist society in the economic and institutional field had to be abandoned. Under the high-sounding name of the New Economic Policy (NEP) a certain amount of freedom of trade in agrarian products, of personal ownership of land, and of private entrepreneurship in industry and commerce had been restored—all, however, on a small scale. The question was how and when the march toward socialism could be taken up again. Lenin was aware that because the proletariat had not come to power in a highly industrialized society, the introduction of socialism involved very special problems: It meant the construction of a completely new society in which socialism could function. But in addition to this most fundamental task, a variety of practical issues arose that demanded immediate answers: Was the foreign trade monopoly compatible with the need for foreign currency and for increased commerce? To what extent was it possible in Russia, which contained many different nationalities, to have both realization of the principle of national self-determination and a strong central government? What was the role of the trade unions? Could they, as representatives of the workers, be entrusted with the managing of the factories? Finally, what status and roles would be accorded to women, who had helped bring the Bolsheviks to power by demonstrating en masse against the tsarist system?

On all these questions vehement debates took place among the Bolshevik leaders, but in all of them Lenin's views prevailed. The trade unions were not subordinated to the economic administration of the government. They remained independent but mainly as schools of Communism, since the workers themselves could not yet run the economy. In the question of nationalities, the establishment of Soviet Russia as a federal state was crucial; although unity was maintained by means of cooperation among the Communist parties ruling in the different federal states, the federalist structure was meant to provide a guarantee against overt Russian chauvinism, which Lenin regarded as a detestable legacy of tsarism and as involving the danger of a purely bureaucratic rule. Despite economic disadvantages, the government's foreign trade monopoly was strictly maintained, a requisite for avoiding inroads of capitalist behavior.

At least in principle, women were granted full emancipation and absolute equality, in accordance with Lenin's commitment to the political, legal, social, and economic liberation of Russia's females. A series of decrees and laws gave women equal status in marriage, the courts, and property ownership. The separation of church and state eliminated religious-based limitations on their freedom, such as restrictions on divorce. A Women's Department of the Communist Party was established to translate these laws into reality through education, mobilization, and social work. This mission, however, quickly became bogged down in the mire of economic misery and internal strife that attended the birth of Communist rule in Russia. In the mixed economy of the NEP women were generally the first to feel the pinch of job cutbacks. Moreover, not all of Lenin's colleagues shared his enlightened views on gender relations, and as the leader's health and strength weakened, more traditionalist views came to the fore. Male preeminence remained the rule not just in Soviet society at large but also in the party, which had few females in leadership positions.

Immediately after Lenin's death in 1924, it was decided that his embalmed body be placed in a mausoleum on the square before the Kremlin so that contemporaries and later generations could show their respect. It was a decision considered by those who had been closest to Lenin entirely contradictory to his ideas and character. His widow opposed the suggestion by saying: "If you want to honor the name of Vladimir Ilyich, build crèches, kindergartens, houses, schools, libraries, medical centers, hospitals, homes for the disabled, etc., and above all, let us put his precepts into practice." But the decision was made, and the Lenin cult began. One of the originators and most active propagandists of the cult was the man who would succeed Lenin, Joseph Stalin.

Born as Josif Djugashvili on December 6, 1878, in the Russian imperial border state of Georgia, the man who would rechristen himself "Stalin" ("man of steel") hardly seemed destined by origin or upbringing to become a major player on the stage of world history. His father, an alcoholic cobbler, often beat him; his mother hoped and prayed that he might become a priest in the Russian Orthodox Church. Small of stature, he had a pockmarked face, bandy legs, and one arm shorter than the other. His only intellectual attainment seemed to be a prodigious memory, which won him promotion to a seminary school in the Georgian capital of Tiflis. It thus appeared that he might become a priest after all, just as his mother had envisaged.

Recent biographies of Stalin, while admitting that he might have developed "pathological" traits in later life, have stressed the extent to which he worked calmly and deliberately within Russia's revolutionary Social Democratic movement to promote his own advancement. Stalin's cause was undoubtedly helped by the fact that many of his contemporaries underestimated his intellect, dismissing him as a semiliterate savage when in fact he wrote fairly cogently on a wide variety of subjects. Yet it must also be emphasized that Stalin's rapid rise within the ranks of Russia's fledgling Bolshevik Party was a team effort, involving timely assistance from fellow radicals who thought (mistakenly) they could use him for their own purposes.

Stalin's advancement to supreme leader of the new Soviet state also owed much to the help of his would-be partners in power—along with some luck. In May 1922, Lenin suffered a stroke, and from that time until his death on January 21, 1924, he was able to work only intermittently. In his last years Lenin clashed with Stalin but was no longer able to follow up the orders by which he tried to curb him. He inserted in his last will a statement that Stalin was too ruthless and should be removed from office. But Lenin's suggestion was not carried out; many of the Bolshevik leaders were more in fear of Trotsky than of Stalin. They preferred to ally themselves with the solid and plodding Stalin against the brilliant but erratic Trotsky, whom they regarded as an unstable intellectual. Thus, when Lenin's will was read in a meeting of the Central Committee of the Communist Party, a great majority—forty against ten—voted to suppress publication of the passage directed against Stalin. Among those who favored Stalin over

Trotsky were Grigori Zinoviev and Lev Kamenev, two leading members of the Bolshevik Central Committee. Twelve years later, Zinoviev and Kamenev would be executed on trumped-up charges of treason following the first of Stalin's infamous show trials. Such were the rewards of helping the "man of steel" to power.

In the early years of Bolshevik rule, Stalin held a number of positions, highest in the official hierarchy being that of the people's commissar of nationalities. In this office he was instrumental in effecting the transformation of Russia into the federal Union of Soviet Socialist Republics; in 1922 the members of the union were Russia, Byelorussia, Ukraine, and Transcaucasia; to these, subsequently the Uzbek and Turkmen republics were added. The major fields of governmental activity—foreign policy, international trade, defense, economic planning, the organization of justice and education—were under federal control, but within this framework the governments of the various Soviet republics could adjust the school system, the administration of justice, the organization of agriculture to the particular needs and demands of their regions and citizens.

Stalin was also the general secretary of the Central Committee of the Communist Party; it was about this position that Lenin was primarily concerned, because Stalin's ruthlessness seemed to him to endanger the Communist Party's coherence and enthusiasm. As general secretary of the Central Committee, Stalin, as Lenin wrote, "concentrated an enormous power in his hands." Understanding of the key role played by the general secretary of the Central Committee of the Communist Party requires some acquaintance with the constitutional structure of Soviet Russia. The basic elements of the Bolshevik government were the councils of the workers and peasants. These existed on local, provincial, and regional levels, the higher councils consisting of members deputized by the lower councils. Every two years an all-union congress of councils elected a Central Executive Committee, composed of two chambers, one representing the people, the other the governments of the member republics of the Soviet Union. This Central Executive Committee met every year, roughly fulfilling the role of a European parliament. It appointed the Council of People's Commissars, which exercised the highest executive power. The government thus appeared to be a pyramidal structure, rising from a broad base to a small peak. But the twelve people's commissars who directed policy were almost independent of the elected body that had appointed them. One reason was that the infrequent and relatively short meetings of the all-union congress of councils and the Central Executive Committee did not allow true supervision of the people's commissars, who had to make important decisions daily. Another reason was that the people's commissars drew their strength from their prominent position in the Communist Party, for it was the party that was the controlling element within the Soviet structure. Legally every man in the Soviet Union earning his livelihood through productive labor had the right to vote. But the lists of council candidates for whom the people could vote were assembled by the Communist Party.

The Communist Party was relatively small, comprising not more than 1 percent of the population; in 1930 the party had 1,192,000 members. In sharp contrast to the pyramidal structure of the council system, the party was directed from above, by a Central Committee of about twenty of the most prominent Communists. The most brilliant and active of these concentrated on work in a special committee, the Politburo, which laid down the general lines of Russian and Communist policy; Stalin, however, immersed himself in the drudgery of party administration. As general secretary of the Central Committee of the Communist Party he had a decisive voice in determining admission to the party and promotion within its ranks. Since the party determined who could be council candidates, he thus exerted control over personnel throughout the government. The result was that he knew intimately the rank-and-file Communists, and they, being dependent on him for promotion, were willing to accept his leadership.

The firm hold over the party organization represented Stalin's main strength in the struggle to succeed Lenin. But because of his role in the party organization, Stalin not only could count on many adherents but also knew well what the rank and file of the party were feeling and thinking. The great mass of party members were no longer the old Bolsheviks of tsarist times, well versed in Marxist thought and able to think independently about the problems of socialism. Since the Bolshevik seizure of power, many young people, frequently without substantial knowledge of the party's history, many of them only semiliterate, had joined the party. Stalin was aware that for them the Lenin cult fulfilled an important need, setting before them an example how a true socialist had acted. In 1924, Stalin himself published lectures titled *The Foundations of Leninism* in which, using an endless number of quotations from Lenin, he summarized what he considered the essence of Lenin's teachings. Although pedestrian and certainly much less sophisticated than the writings on Leninism and revolutionary strategy by other Bolshevik leaders like Trotsky, Bukharin, or Zinoviev, Stalin's lectures made a great impact because they codified Lenin's thought in a simple and clear system. Further, they were essential to Stalin's standing in the party, for he needed to prove that he was not only a Bolshevik fighter and organizer but also, like his competitors for Lenin's succession, a recognized theoretician.

The struggle for Lenin's succession dominated the Russian political scene in the years following Lenin's death. Although chiefly of a personal nature, the struggle was connected with a policy decision of crucial importance. When the Bolsheviks came to power, they had expected that their revolution would soon be followed by revolutions in the industrialized countries of Europe, first in Germany. All were convinced that the Bolshevik regime would not be able to remain in power if Russia were the only country in which the capitalist system was overthrown. It is by no means clear that Lenin ever changed his mind on the subject or ever lost hope that the revolution would also break out

This picture of Lenin and Stalin is of great importance; under Stalin it was used to show his close relationship with Lenin. In fact, the photograph was doctored, Stalin having been inserted into the frame.

in the West. The year 1923, when it became clear that Lenin's death was imminent, was also when the end of inflation in Germany terminated the revolutionary ferment in central Europe; any hope that the revolution might spread beyond the Russian borders was crushed. Trotsky, as organizer of the 1917 revolt in Petrograd and as hero of the civil war, was much better known than Stalin and was the latter's main rival to succeed Lenin. It seemed impossible to Trotsky to maintain an isolated socialist state within a capitalist world. He advanced the idea of the permanent revolution: that it was the chief function of Bolshevism in Russia, even if as a result, the Bolshevik regime in Russia might be destroyed, to organize and support revolutionary movements all over the world because this would precipitate a new political and economic crisis that would end in a world revolution. At first, Stalin shared this view. But when, after some hesitation, he had convinced himself of the solidity of the capitalist regimes in the face of Communist attacks, he set his course firmly toward the construction of a new Russian society able to stand on its own. During the Fourteenth Communist Party Congress, in March 1925, Stalin obtained official approval of the doctrine of "socialism in one country."

Other Bolshevik leaders found abandonment of the idea of world revolution more difficult. Many of them, during long years in exile, had established close relations with extremists in other countries. Stalin had been outside Russia just once—and then for a few weeks—and had no real acquaintance with social and industrial developments in other countries. Moreover, some of the Bolshevik leaders, such as Grigori Zinoviev, head of the Communist International, and Karl Radek, were motivated by ideological considerations in contrast to the empirical Stalin, who was aware that concentration on an economic transformation in Russia would strengthen his own position since an increasing number of party officials would be needed to direct and control the process.

Opposition to Stalin's policy of socialism in one country became pronounced only after it was evident that it resulted in the creation of an immense new bureaucracy. Trotsky, for instance, attacked Stalin because instead of leading to the disappearance of the state, in accordance with Marxist theory, his course of action resulted in an aggrandized bureaucratic machinery. But Stalin's views had become the accepted "line" of the Communist Party, and Stalin stamped Trotsky's opposition as antirevolutionary and subversive. In 1927, Trotsky was divested of all his functions and expelled from the party, with seventy-five other leading members of the opposition. Exiled to Siberia, he continued his agitation there. In 1929, he was expelled from Russia and found refuge in Mexico. Eleven years later he was assassinated by a man unquestionably acting on Stalin's orders.

SOCIALISM IN ONE COUNTRY

Pursuit of the policy of socialism in one country resulted in a major social upheaval accompanied by economic hardship and suffering. The golden age that theoretically was supposed to follow the defeat of capitalism seemed still far away, and the Bolshevik leaders were anxious to emphasize that a truly Communist society could become reality only after the capitalist system had been overthrown all over the world; at the moment they were at work to create a system of transition, a socialist society.

The underlying aim of socialism in one country was to transform Russia into a highly industrialized state, able to compete with more advanced countries, such as Great Britain and the United States, and capable of putting up a good fight against aggression by capitalist nations. In Russia, industrialization also involved a transformation of agriculture, which had to be more efficient so that the increasing number of industrial workers in the cities could be fed and a surplus could be produced for export, which alone could provide needed foreign currency. The vast changes had to be accomplished without impairment of the fundamental principle of a socialist regime—control of the state over economic life—and without the help of private or foreign capital. To achieve these aims the Russians devised a method that was entirely novel: the drafting of an economic plan that encompassed all fields of economic activity in all parts of the country. Thus, in the following years, Russian life was dominated by the efforts to achieve the goals set in two five-year plans. The first was initiated in 1928, but as the Russian leadership proudly proclaimed, it was carried out in four years, so the second Five-Year Plan could begin in 1932.

During the Second World War, Winston Churchill once asked Stalin if he had found the stresses of the war as bad as those arising from carrying through the policy of the collective farms. " 'Oh, no,' he said, 'the Collective Farm policy was a terrible struggle.'"[1] The Russian economic planners ordered collectivization of agriculture primarily because it would facilitate the use of modern methods and machines that would increase production. But collectivization was expected also to strengthen the grip of the government over rural life. The somewhat wealthier peasants, the kulaks, who had been favored by Stolypin's reforms and later had flourished under the New Economic Policy, became disenchanted with the Bolshevik regime in the course of the 1920s. Because rationing and fixed food prices made agricultural production unremunerative, many peasants refused to deliver their produce to the cities and limited production to their own personal needs. When the government decided on collectivization, the kulaks regarded this policy as a direct attack on their property rights and on their very existence, and they resisted in all possible ways. They burned collective farms, they destroyed tractors and other agricultural machinery, and when integration into the collective farm system finally became unavoidable, they slaughtered their animals; almost 3 million horses and cattle— nearly half their entire stock—were killed. The government then decided to eliminate the kulaks as a class and incited the poorer peasants against them, assisting this class warfare with police and military forces. The land owned by kulaks was confiscated, their houses were transformed into clubs or schools, and an estimated 2 million were deported to remote areas, where they were used as forced labor.

The requirements for modernizing agriculture were important in determining the plans set up for industry. For example, the annual production of tractors increased from six thousand at the beginning of the first Five-Year Plan to one hundred fifty thousand at its end. Next to the needs of agriculture those of defense were most influential in shaping the industrialization program. The emphasis was on heavy industry. Large new cities sprang up in the vicinity of coal and iron mines. Magnitogorsk, in the midst of rich mineral deposits in the southern Urals, owed its existence to the five-year plans. At the end of the first Five-Year Plan it had about sixty-five thousand inhabitants; seven years later the population had grown to more than one hundred fifty thousand. The concentration on heavy industry necessarily limited the production of consumer goods; for instance, the Five-Year Plan envisaged a shoe industry that would give each person two new pairs every three years. This paucity of consumer goods meant that wages could be kept down and that the general standard of living remained low.

[1] Winston S. Churchill, *The Second World War*, vol. IV. *The Hinge of Fate* (Boston, 1950), p. 498.

From the point of view of the planners, the shortage in consumer goods had the advantage that workers were unable to spend all their wages and would place some of their earnings in the state bonds that helped finance industrialization. The five-year plans were also financed by the profits of the state stores and by taxes, notably a turnover tax, a form of sales tax.

Although Russian pronouncements and statistics tended to paint an exaggerated picture of the success of the five-year plans, the main goals were undoubtedly achieved. Russia was transformed from an agrarian into an industrial country. In 1932, 70.7 percent of the Russian national product came from industry. In addition, as a consequence of the centralized organization of Russian economic life, private enterprise disappeared almost completely.

The Soviet rulers, as firm believers in the theories of Marx, regarded intellectual achievements as a superstructure resting on the economic system; they attached great importance to intellectuals and their training. They were aware that an industrial society required a large corps of trained personnel—technicians, engineers, doctors, economists, teachers—and that the great bulk of the people ought to have an education that would enable them to handle modern machinery. Hence the Bolshevik regime established schools all over the country to eliminate illiteracy, which at the time of the revolution was widespread; in 1923, 27 million people in Russia still could neither write nor read.

Workers took evening courses to prepare for university study; universities proliferated, emphasizing technical subjects and the natural sciences. With the reduction of illiteracy, publishing activities grew in extent and importance; newspapers and periodicals dispensed knowledge useful for increasing industrial and agricultural productivity, and they also spread propaganda. The Russian rulers recognized that the work the masses were forced to do and the privations they were asked to undergo were made bearable only by the conviction that the end result would be a life safer and better than ever before. The Russian people had to be sure, however, that their leaders were steering toward this goal with utmost speed on the only possible route. Confidence in the state's leaders was emphasized; Stalin was shown to be omniscient and farseeing. What was later called the personality cult began to develop.

The vast transformation of Russian society under Stalin naturally embraced the female component of the population; indeed, the lives of women were more profoundly altered in these years than at any other time in Russian history. The government's push for rapid industrialization and economic modernization brought a dramatic rise in women's upward mobility, giving them greater educational and professional opportunities than ever before. Traditional male occupations like medicine, science, engineering, and architecture were now open to women—even to women of the lower classes. Female literacy increased from 42.4 percent in 1926 to 81.6 percent in 1939, while the proportion of women attending institutions of higher learning rose from 31 percent to 51 percent. In roughly the same period the number of women workers jumped from about 3 million in 1928 to over 13 million in 1940. On the other hand, the regime's pursuit of a higher birthrate put pressure on women to breed as well as to work and brought an end to the liberal abortion policy that had characterized the earlier Soviet period. If Lenin's Russia had exalted the woman as rebel and warrior, Stalin's Russia celebrated her as mother, establishing special awards for patriotic producers of large families. Thus, even while women were exploring new territories in the workplace, they were expected to retain their traditional roles in the home and nursery. The Soviet male's working day typically ended in the bar with a bottle of vodka; the Soviet woman's ended back home with a bottle of baby formula and a broom.

The years of the transformation into an industrial society have been called Russia's Iron Age. In this period, life in Russia was very different in spirit from what it had been for a brief time after the Bolsheviks came to power. Daring revolutionary intellectuals like Trotsky and Radek were now replaced by careful bureaucrats and technical experts. The experiments in avant-garde art and literature that had been promoted by Anatoli Lunacharsky, commissar for education under Lenin, were now abandoned, and the government required artists to provide easily understandable, realistic representations of the achievements of the five-year plans and of other events showing Russia's progress under Bolshevism. The fight of the militant atheists against religion was continued because the influence of the church formed an obstacle to the modernization of rural life. Free love and divorce, however, were no longer encouraged, as they had been in the first years of Bolshevik rule. It was hoped, however, that after the successful completion of the two five-year plans the production of consumer goods would be increased and the disciplined monotony that had become customary would gradually give way to an easier and more varied life. Furthermore, on June 12, 1936, *Pravda* ("Truth"), the most widely distributed official newspaper, published the draft of a new constitution, which seemed to indicate the beginning of a period in which the Soviet citizens would possess enlarged, well-defined rights.

Of course, those rights never materialized; instead the rights and freedoms of Soviet citizens were further narrowed as Stalin continued to consolidate his dictatorship. Part of that consolidation involved an expansion of the political police (OGPU), which was now placed under the Commissariat for Internal Affairs (NKVD) and given the authority to arrest people without charge. Increasingly, Stalin saw enemies everywhere—enemies he defined as "terrorists" out to undercut or reverse the gains made by the USSR. In a 1931 interview, Stalin insisted that he had initially betrayed the Soviet working class by showing too much leniency to these counterrevolutionary "terrorists." He promised not to make that mistake again: from now on, no more Mr. Nice Guy.

THE AMBIGUITY OF THE WEIMAR REPUBLIC

Considering that even after the Locarno Treaty resistance to the settlement created in Paris was muted rather than extinguished, the position of Germany was decisive for what the future might bring. We have explained that the treaties of Locarno must be viewed as providing a new starting point rather than a solution—that the question was whether Germany would consider the situation created at Locarno merely as a breathing space, intending to later embark on a policy aimed at overthrowing the existing order, or whether Germany now recognized the status quo and was willing to maintain it, or at least to rely for revisions on the mechanism that existed at the League of Nations for such a purpose. These questions are closely connected, almost identical with the question of whether authoritarian Germany had been transformed into a democratic society.

Clearly there was a change in the German political climate after the acceptance of the Dawes Plan and the conference of Locarno. Until then, events had crowded upon each other; a long procession of personalities had come forward and then disappeared from the scene after a short time. There had been strikes and unrest, sometimes developing into civil war, in Berlin, in Bavaria, in the Rhineland, and in Saxony. There were moments when it seemed questionable whether the federal government could enforce its authority in all parts of the Reich, especially since the army and the judiciary kept their protecting hands over secret military organizations bitterly hostile to the republic. In critical situations, like that of the Ruhr occupation, hostility to the Western powers created an alliance—called National Bolshevism—between the extreme right and the extreme left.

The social and economic chaos of the immediate postwar years had taken place in a new political framework. Germany had become a republic, with a parliamentary system. The functions of the Reich had been enlarged at the expense of the members of the federation. General suffrage and the parliamentary system had also been introduced in the individual German states, so that, for instance, Prussia had a government headed by a Social Democrat until 1932. The position of the trade unions had been legally fortified, and as a result of the influence of the Social Democrats, governmental intervention and arbitration in labor conflicts secured a fair hearing for the cause of the trade unions.

But only after the years of continuous unrest and emergencies were over was it possible to test whether the changed constitutional forms would become a reality because they reflected a social transformation, the evolution of a democratic society and of a liberal spirit.

It should be emphasized that the parliamentary system never really functioned in Germany. Along with the Communists on the extreme left and some small parties on the extreme right there were five important political parties in Germany during the 1920s: three republican—the Social Democratic Party, the

Democratic Party, and the Catholic Center Party—and two monarchist—the German People's Party and the German Nationalist Party. No single party ever had a majority. The governments changed frequently; several of them were minority governments or governments of experts, ruling with ever-shifting majorities. Those based on a parliamentary majority, such as the two governments of the Great Coalition, in 1923 and 1928, were possible only with right-wing support; these governments included—in addition to the three republican parties (Social Democrats, Democrats, Center Party)—the monarchist German People's Party. The governments of Heinrich Brüning and Franz von Papen, preceding Hitler's rise to power, ruled by presidential emergency decrees, without a secure parliamentary basis. The tenuousness of the hold of the republican regime became evident in 1925, when Friedrich Ebert, the leader of the Social Democrats, died and popular elections for a new president of the republic were held. The people elected Field Marshal von Hindenburg, who received eight hundred thousand votes more than Wilhelm Marx, the moderate Catholic who was the candidate of the republican parties. The Communist candidate, Ernst Thälmann, won almost 2 million votes. The republican center was weaker than the combined forces of the right and the left.

That after many prosperous decades of monarchical authoritarianism, belief in the value of a monarchical form of government and distrust in parliaments and parliamentarianism had not completely waned in Germany is not astonishing. Inflation had impoverished the middle classes, and many of them considered the failure of the new leaders to ward off economic catastrophe clear proof of the inferiority of democracy and parliamentarianism. Antiparliamentary movements and attitudes found strong support in the bureaucracy and the army, in which the men of the former ruling group remained dominant. They could not be deposed under the constitution, and they chose publicly to advocate a return to the traditional values of discipline, hierarchical order, and selfless state service, emphasizing not merely their differences from the new leaders but also the superiority of the old over the new.

However, changes in the economic situation of Germany played a decisive role in strengthening the antidemocratic and antiparliamentary right in Germany. During the twenties, German economic life was on the rise. As devastating as the consequences of the inflation had been in many spheres of life, the loss of value of the currency also had an advantageous side. Export of German goods was facilitated because they would be sold at lower prices, and many industrial enterprises could pay off their debts. With the profits from exports and new investments after the stabilization, the German industrial apparatus became thoroughly modernized. But the German economy also had weaknesses; one was agriculture.

Overseas competition, combined with modernization in the United States, had weakened the postwar agricultural situation all over Europe. The situation in Germany was particularly bad because even in the decades before the war

German agrarians had been chiefly concerned with the production of grain and were unwilling or unable to change to a more specialized production of marketable goods, like fruits and vegetables; they had relied on protective tariffs and government support. After the war the situation became more critical. Wartime needs had exhausted the soil. Low profits and inflation prevented the formation of capital needed for modernization, and without modernization, transition to a more specialized production was impossible. Moreover, the climate of the republic was less favorable to the demands of the agrarians than the Hohenzollern monarchy had been. Because the agrarian reform, which had been promised to the returning soldiers in the first weeks of the revolution, did not take place, the crisis in German agriculture continued, and agricultural policy remained the subject of a bitter dispute. The Junkers, left in possession of their estates, demanded protective tariffs and government subventions. The socialists, who had become a powerful factor in the republic, as representatives of the workers, were interested in cheap food prices and therefore had little sympathy for protective tariffs. The great landowners—mostly members of the high nobility and, as such, monarchists—became the protectors and patrons of rightist and monarchical antiparliamentarian political parties and were inclined to give their support to antirepublican organizations.

The impact of agrarian opposition was immensely strengthened because the landowners had allies among an important group of German industrialists. Germany's share of world industrial production declined from its prewar level of 14.3 percent to 11.6 percent in the postwar period. But, considering the rise in industrial production in non-European countries, like Japan and the United States, this decline was actually quite an achievement. Germany certainly did better than Great Britain. But a good part of German economic recovery had to be ascribed to the success of the electrical and chemical industries, particularly on the export market. German heavy industry lost ground to heavy industry in non-European countries. Since it could no longer manufacture armaments, heavy industry focused increasingly on the domestic market and joined the agrarians in the demand for high protective tariffs. The nationalistic inclinations of the industrialists were reinforced by their economic interests; they would reap great direct advantages from removal of the disarmament clauses of the Versailles Treaty. The parties of the right therefore were no longer chiefly agrarian but also represented strong industrial interests; moreover, in appealing to times of past splendor, in contrast to the civilian drabness of the present, they exerted a powerful emotional appeal among wide groups of the bourgeoisie. After a slow and modest beginning immediately after the revolution, the nationalists soon became a factor that would not be left out of account. Almost all the coalition governments, therefore, which ruled in Germany—either to keep their right-wing partner the German People's Party satisfied or to draw some of the popular support away from the right—felt forced to make concessions to the nationalists. They publicly repudiated the war guilt clauses of the Versailles Treaty; in a clear circumvention of the disarmament clauses they embarked on building pocket battleships, which were smaller and less heavily armed than conventional battleships. Soon after the Dawes Plan had begun functioning, they demanded— probably prematurely—its revision. It is evident that these continued German demands made the French distrustful of German sincerity in concluding the Locarno treaties, and the French sharply opposed these revisionist aims. For several years the foreign ministers of Germany and France, Stresemann and Briand, succeeded in avoiding a serious break. But Franco-German relations remained precarious.

Although after 1920 the three republican parties never again had the majority in the Reichstag, they remained in the twenties the strongest bloc. But they were on the defensive. In the turmoil of defeat and under the threat of national disintegration, the chances for agrarian reform and for socialization had been missed; only a few had even recognized the necessity of ending the rule of the Junkers in the east and the curtailing of the power of the Ruhr industrialists for the creation of a new democratic society. Further, the Dawes Plan presupposed the maintenance of the existing economic structure. Consequently, the left-wing parties, particularly the socialists, became primarily concerned with defending and improving the material interests of their constituencies. The vision of a new social order was lost in the bargaining over more wages and tariffs, social insurance payments, strikes, and arbitration.

However, German life did assume a new shape in one area—that is, culture. Frustrated in more far-reaching plans, liberals and socialists were anxious to demonstrate that culturally, at least, a new era had begun. The municipal governments of many of the big German cities were in the hands of the socialists, who were responsible for building schools, hospitals, public offices, and, most of all, low-cost housing for workers and other low-income groups. This work was frequently entrusted to architects like Walter Gropius, the founder of the Bauhaus, who created a new functionalist style by subordinating architectural design to a building's purposes. Apartment houses in Frankfurt, Berlin, Düsseldorf, Stuttgart, and Dessau became showplaces of what was then considered daring modern architecture. The liberal or socialist ministers of education in federal states ruled by the left, most of all in Prussia, supported the modern tendencies in art and literature, which had been fought by conservative ministers of education under the empire. The turmoil and the insecurity of these years created an excitement that was a spur to artistic and intellectual experiments. Furthermore, inflation had somehow shaken the belief in traditional values. And, as we have seen, some people profited considerably from speculations during the inflationary period. They put their money into things of lasting worth, such as works of art; they spent freely and quickly, anticipating the rapid depreciation of paper money. Thus, masking the grimness of the social reality, there was a glittering façade, particularly in Berlin and other large cities. The amusement industry flourished. Art exhibitions, operas, theaters, and concerts were well

Modern architecture in Germany. The Bauhaus in Dessau.

attended. There was much experimentation in opera, drama, and art. In the early twenties the first plays of the young Bertolt Brecht appeared on the German stage; the opera *Wozzeck*, by Alban Berg, had its first triumph; movies like *The Cabinet of Dr. Caligari* demonstrated the possibilities inherent in this new art form. The absence of social stability fostered cynicism as well as sharpening social criticism—both evident in the drawings and paintings of George Grosz. Even after the economic crisis of the immediate postwar period had been overcome, a critical spirit remained alive, and eagerness for experimentation continued. Brecht's *Threepenny Opera*, with a musical score by Kurt Weill, was notable not only for its new dramatic style but also for its condemnation of corrupt bourgeois society and values. It proved an immense success, playing in Berlin continuously from 1928 until the rise of the Nazis. The intellectual atmosphere of Berlin after the First World War was electrifying; it attracted journalists, writers, and artists from all over the world. Such figures as Sinclair Lewis, Dorothy Thompson, Stephen Spender, Christopher Isherwood, and Ilya Ehrenburg were to look back nostalgically upon life in Berlin in the 1920s as one of their great experiences.

But because of their rejection of traditional forms of art and their conscious cultivation of contacts with the most advanced intellectual movements in other countries, these cultural activities aroused opposition among many Germans. Conservatives regarded them as further proof that the Weimar regime represented a break with German tradition and was an alien element in German history. The monarchist and nationalist elite met annually in August in Bayreuth, where under the sharp eyes of that inexorable guardian of tradition Richard Wagner's widow, Cosima, they listened to *The Ring of the Nibelung* in the exact, and overdone, production first seen in the nineteenth century. The distance widened between Berlin, the modern capital of the republic, and the rural areas, far removed from the rapid changes of modern life. This alienation of Berlin and other large urban centers from the rest of the country strengthened the appeal that in later years Nazi propaganda against the Weimar "system" would have among wide circles of the population.

BRAVE NEW WORLD

The revival of a spirit of enterprise and progress in the later part of the 1920s is not sufficiently described and explained by referring only to the somewhat precarious stabilization of the political situation. This revival occurred in the context of far-reaching developments in science and technology that transformed many aspects of human existence. The war had given powerful impetus to these developments, and they continued long after its end.

This change and progress are symbolized by an event in the most prosperous year of the twenties. On May 21, 1927, after a daring and lonely flight, Charles Lindbergh arrived on the Paris airfield of Le Bourget. He had accomplished the first nonstop flight over the Atlantic in an eastward direction. No other event in the twenties caught the imagination of the world to the same extent. This is not difficult to explain. Lindbergh's feat touched the heart of the twentieth century in two ways: human pride in the continued existence of individual heroism and in advances in science and technology.

The use of the airplane as a regular means of transportation was the most visible evidence of the changes technology had brought about. In the case of the airplane,

Lindbergh's plane, *The Spirit of St. Louis*, landing at Le Bourget, Paris, May 21, 1927.

the war had been decisive in effecting a quick transition from the experimental stage to general use. Because of the airplane's role in the war, the great potential of aviation had been recognized. Passenger service was installed between London and Paris in 1919 and between Amsterdam and London a year after Lindbergh's flight. Soon all larger European cities had airfields and were connected by scheduled commercial flights. While Lindbergh's achievement pointed toward the development of a regular transatlantic air service, this was delayed until more than ten years later, on the eve of the outbreak of the Second World War.

The impact of the First World War on developments in transportation and communication was far-reaching in many ways. The First World War was not a motorized war. Tanks appeared only in the final phase of the conflict; larger military units, if not marching on foot, were transported by rail. Smaller groups, however, particularly officers, moved around in automobiles; the resulting increase in automobile construction prepared for the postwar expansion of the auto industry, particularly the building of mass-produced, small, relatively inexpensive cars, which made it possible for a broad stratum of society to own automobiles, although possession of a car was still the exception rather than the rule in Europe.

The use of wireless communication in the First World War opened the way for entirely new developments in this area. After the war, experiments in wireless communication were begun, financiers invested heavily, and the radio industry was established. The primitive earphones of wartime were replaced by sensitive receiving instruments; radio stations were equipped to present programs throughout the day. Each European state had a public broadcasting company working under government control; international conventions stipulated the wavelengths each country was entitled to use. In 1927, wireless telephone service was initiated between England and the United States.

The effects of the First World War on industrial life extended in a variety of directions. The war was of particular importance for the development of the chemical industry, which continued to grow in importance. The most significant consequence of wartime needs was probably the discovery that atmospheric nitrogen could be made into ammonia, an essential ingredient for the manufacture of both explosives and fertilizers. Their production was no longer dependent on imports from those countries—primarily Chile—that possessed deposits of natural sodium nitrates. Actually, without the industrial production of sodium nitrates, Germany could not have carried on the war for a great length of time. The chemical industry also benefited from the challenge to create substitutes for goods that could not be produced during wartime because of difficulties in obtaining raw materials.

Although a process for the manufacture of synthetic fibers was discovered in the nineteenth century and production of rayon had started before 1914, the war, by reducing the possibilities of importing silk and increasing the need for material to cover airplane wings, stimulated the output of a more durable viscose rayon. After the war, the production of artificial silk became one of the most quickly developing industrial areas, increasing from 1920 to 1925 at the rate of 45 percent per year. Rayon was economically cheaper than natural silk. It was used for a variety of purposes; for instance, as shorter skirts became the fashion in women's clothes, the sales of rayon stockings soared. Although in almost all European countries the chemical companies accelerated the manufacture of artificial fibers, their production was especially significant in Germany and Italy—in Germany because it helped regain for the German chemical industry the leading role it had played before the war; in Italy because this industry did not require the raw materials that Italy did not possess, coal and iron, but only electricity, which Italian waterpower could provide.

Technology and inventions that make scientific discoveries applicable to practical uses frequently follow the original discoveries at a wide distance. The advances in transportation and communication and in the chemical industry were based on scientific discoveries that had been made a long time before, certainly before 1914. On the other hand, the scientific discoveries of the twenties had their impact—an impact of revolutionary character—on the life of humanity only twenty years later, during and after the Second World War. But the 1920s were one of the great epochs in the history of science.

The "understanding of atomic physics . . . had its origins at the turn of the century and its great synthesis and resolutions in the nineteen twenties."[2] Thus did J. Robert Oppenheimer, one of the principals in this scientific revolution, characterize the main stages of its development. Its great events at the turn of the century were Max Planck's publication in 1900 of "On the Theory of the Law of Energy Distribution in a Normal Spectrum," which presented the thesis of the quantum theory, and Albert Einstein's publication in 1905 of the papers that set forth the special theory of relativity. By 1903 the need for a new theoretical outlook had been confirmed by experiments in which Pierre and Marie Curie isolated radium and Antoine Henri Becquerel recognized the extent of radioactivity. After the First World War the implications of these theories and discoveries were explored by a score of young scientists. The great centers of this absorbing intellectual adventure were Copenhagen, where Niels Bohr, the guiding spirit of the entire field of atomic research, worked; Göttingen, where Max Born, James Franck, and David Hilbert maintained the tradition of this university as a center of mathematics and natural science; and Cambridge, where Ernest Rutherford continued his study of radioactivity and then, together with Sir James Chadwick, turned to the investigation of the composition of the atom. There was a lively exchange among all these groups, and the common achievement of these scientists from many countries was the genesis of a new physical worldview. Although it did not invalidate the classical Newtonian physics, this new perspective limited its applicability.

[2] J. Robert Oppenheimer, *Science and the Common Understanding* (New York, 1953), p. 35.

The creative excitement of these decades was caused by the necessity of revising the basic assumptions of classical physics, notably the supposition that through observation and experiments it is possible to establish the laws that demonstrate the causal connection determining the processes of nature. When Planck showed that certain incongruities in the radiation of energy occur, that it is transmitted from one body to another not in continuous waves but in flashes, like a stream of bullets of fixed size ("quantum"), his theory suggested that the assumption of complete continuity in the process of nature was untenable. Nature is discontinuous; a certain sequence of events will probably result from the release of a quantum of energy, but it is not predetermined. Similarly, Einstein's demonstration in his theory of relativity of the bonds between the dimensions of space and of time forced a reexamination of the value of the material provided by observation. It was found that when measurements of a small elementary particle like the electron focus on speed, measurements of its precise position become uncertain, while measurements of position reduce precision in the measurement of speed. The conclusion was that an element of uncertainty remains in the description of nature.

The disclosure that discontinuity and uncertainty are inherent in nature nullified the expectation of earlier scientists that immutable laws would someday be discovered that could explain all known phenomena. The work of the physicist became limited to the exploration of relations among the phenomena. But this limitation actually gave the investigator scope for greater creative efforts.

The basis for this change in theoretical assumptions that was worked out in the 1920s and 1930s was concrete investigation; the intellectual speculations were accompaniments of the discoveries resulting from a study of the atom. Already in the nineteenth century there had been some research showing that the atom did not form an indivisible basic unit of matter, as had been assumed. The investigations of the twentieth century gradually revealed that the atom is composed of a very small nucleus (usually consisting of positively charged protons and electrically neutral neutrons) surrounded by negatively charged electrons. The problem was that despite the radioactivity of certain elements, which ought to have led to a loss of energy, their atoms remained stable. The explanation of this fact with the help of the new theoretical insights led to the discovery of nuclear energy.

The general public understood as little as, or perhaps even less than, we do today about the discoveries and advances in science. The terms *relativity* and the *principle of uncertainty* were used in everyday language and were often believed to have meanings of a philosophical nature, but such vague general associations as were connected with these terms only revealed that even the educated had no real conception of their exact scientific meaning. Still, the interest in these notions indicates something of the public's awareness of living in an age of great scientific advance. Scientific advances and innovations, however, not only arouse enthusiasm but also instill fear. The security that humans receive from feeling they live in a well-known world begins to disappear and people become aware not only of new opportunities but also of new dangers, not only of widening horizons but also of new means of control. The fears these great strides in science produced were not restricted to those segments that are generally opposed to change; others too raised questions about the consequences of the new inventions and whether they would be beneficial.

The new means of communication had diminished the distance that in the previous century had separated private life and the world of politics and business. With voices from radio present in the home, the individual was subjected to a constant barrage of demands from the world outside. Powerful propaganda efforts had been exerted during the First World War to keep spirits from sagging on the home front; the citizen was constantly encountering posters urging service in the army or the buying of war bonds or warning about enemy spies. After the war, the technical devices of propaganda were taken up by advertisers in print, on billboards, in the cinema, and on the radio. The radio especially could be placed in the service of mass control; it was a powerful means of manipulating the emotions of the general public.

The changes wrought in the environment by science, technology, and industry created new possibilities for the conduct of public affairs. But these developments were not widely used in the political sphere until the 1930s; the extent to which their potential was realized depended on the particular situation in each country, especially on the strength of its political tradition. For example, although the technique of radio "fireside chats" contributed to the popularity of Franklin Delano Roosevelt, its imitation by Gaston Doumergue, then French prime minister, was regarded as a sign of arrogance and authoritarianism and played a role in the downfall of his government. It was natural that those political movements that arose in opposition to the established political structure were most ready to use new political techniques. Mussolini and Hitler both stressed that they were leaders of modern movements. Mussolini liked to be photographed piloting an airplane; Hitler was frequently seen in his Mercedes-Benz. In the Western democracies there was much admiration for the courage of Neville Chamberlain, prime minister of Great Britain, when in September 1938—to meet Hitler in Berchtesgaden—he entered an airplane for the first time in his life, with an umbrella on his arm. But the Nazis and Fascists considered Chamberlain's reluctance to use modern means of transportation contemptible, a sign of the backwardness of the democracies.

Since the eighteenth century, science has been connected with "enlightenment," with the hopes for the establishment of a better—that is, more rational—world order. It was difficult therefore to realize that science could also be an oppressive force, serving to control human minds in whatever way was advantageous to those holding the means of communication. The first clear warning against a facile optimism that scientific progress would lead to a world that was rationally organized and in which life would be made happier appeared in 1932, in Aldous Huxley's *Brave New World*. This utopian novel is a powerful demonstration of the inner emptiness that might accompany a life completely organized and freed from emotional complexities and complications, and in which all right to choice or decision has been lost. But Huxley's novel appeared when a new mood had begun to develop in Europe, as it had become clear that the years of stability and prosperity were over.

CHAPTER 6

The Economic Crisis and the Rise of Nazism

THE WORLD ECONOMIC CRISIS

AFTER A few years the stability achieved in 1925 was shattered by the world economic crisis. The impact of this crisis was all the more powerful because as the 1920s passed, people had gradually become confident that the wounds left by the First World War could be healed, that the prosperity of the years before 1914 would again be reached, and that the march toward progress that the war had interrupted could be resumed. The economic crisis destroyed these expectations and hopes; the prewar world now appeared irretrievably lost, and many were convinced that the new course of events was leading inexorably downhill and would end in a holocaust more dangerous and devastating for the continuity of European life than the First World War had been. Thus, the decade of the 1930s was a period full of anxiety and insecurity. A full recovery from the world economic crisis had still not occurred when the Second World War broke out in 1939.

The really acute phase of the economic breakdown lasted from 1929 to 1933; before its underlying causes are discussed, it might be well to recapitulate the dramatic events of these years. The actual beginning of the crisis was the collapse of the New York Stock Exchange under a wave of speculation in the last week of October 1929, although some danger signs pointing to a decline in production had appeared earlier. In Europe the high point of the crisis occurred in the summer of 1931. In May 1931, the most important Austrian bank, the Kreditanstalt, which was controlled by the Austrian Rothschilds, declared itself unable to fulfill its obligations. This failure shook confidence in the solvency of banks in Germany; there was an accelerated recall of money from them, and the main German banks soon found themselves insolvent and were forced to close. They were able to reopen only with the help of a government guarantee. In this critical economic situation the payment of international debts was clearly impossible, and the American president Herbert Hoover (1874–1964) suggested a one-year moratorium on reparations and war debts; after tedious negotiations, this was agreed upon in August. But the moratorium came too late to remedy the British financial situation, which had been seriously impaired by the economic collapse in central Europe. On September 21, 1931, Britain abandoned the gold standard; this event seemed to mark the end of an epoch, for hitherto the pound had enjoyed the reputation of being as good as gold. In the next years the level of economic activity remained low, although from 1934 on, slowly and gradually recovery began, especially in the industrial countries. Agricultural prices remained depressed, and the Balkan states, which were dependent on the export of agricultural products, continued to suffer severely. Moreover, France, which at the outset had seemed unaffected by the crisis, began to experience economic difficulties in 1932, and the French recession played its part in retarding recovery in the rest of Europe.

To understand the nature of this economic catastrophe—its severity, length, and spread—one must realize that two factors were at work. First, there was the decline in production, which led to a decrease in trade and created unemployment; second, there was the financial crisis.

The decline in production set in from what was a rather low plateau, for after the First World War production had remained sluggish. By 1929, the prewar level had indeed been reached, but the rate of economic growth ought to have been much larger in relation to the increased population, even though the rate of population growth was small. Moreover, the European share in world trade

Depression in Britain. Unemployed men queuing up in London in response to a job offer.

was less than it had been in 1914, as European nations faced competition from the rising economies of the non-European nations. To the diminished share of Europe in non-European markets, the elimination of Russia from the world economic system must be added as a further restricting and damaging factor.

The economic boom in the second part of the 1920s was built on a narrow base. The limited amount of population growth restricted sales possibilities, especially since unemployment, which had been high in the years immediately after the war, was never entirely eliminated. Profits were attained through modernization of production rather than as the result of new investments and market expansion. The boom lacked the strength to resist any serious blow.

Even before 1929, falling prices for agricultural goods indicated the onset of an unfavorable economic trend. This decline in prices immediately affected the peasant countries of southeastern Europe—especially Romania, Bulgaria, and Yugoslavia—where, by tradition or as a result of agrarian reforms after the war, small farms with rather high production costs were the prevailing form of landownership. For the farmers of these countries the falling agricultural prices made competition in the European market outside the Balkans impossible. Even within these Balkan states the price of wheat fell by almost half. Since the prices of industrial goods did not decline to the same degree, the people of these countries were caught in a disparity between industrial and agricultural prices— a "price scissors"—and they were unable to purchase manufactured goods from industrial countries. Hence, a shrinking of industrial production throughout Europe took place, and it was aggravated by the widespread introduction of protective measures against foreign goods, by which each country tried to defend its own industries at the expense of all others.

This crisis in production took an extraordinary and dramatic form because its difficulties were compounded by a financial crisis. Its center was Wall Street, where in 1929 a speculative boom ended in a stock market crash that ushered in a long depression. The American economic collapse had its immediate repercussions in Europe, particularly in Germany. American loans had been granted not only to the German government for the settlement of reparations but also to many private and semipublic enterprises within Germany—industrial companies, public utilities, and municipal governments. Foreign capital had been drawn into Germany by high interest rates, which the German economy had been able to sustain because labor costs were relatively low. With the stock market crash, the influx of American money ended and American banks demanded the repayment of loans as soon as they became due. In a time of shrinking production and declining prices the abrupt withdrawal of American loans was a severe blow to the German businessmen who, relying on the continuous availability of American capital, had used money borrowed on short terms for long-term investments. Despite being warned against this unsound practice by men like Schacht, the president of the Reichsbank, neither German businessmen nor foreign bankers had been able to resist the allure of easy gains.

With the withdrawal of American money from the German economy, the liquid reserves of German banks and businesses came under steadily increasing pressure. In addition, because loans from abroad had to be repaid in foreign currency, the withdrawal endangered the German currency by absorbing the gold reserves of the Reichsbank; by 1931 they amounted to only 10 percent of what they had been before the onset of the crisis. These developments reached their culmination in the summer of 1931, when the German public, becoming aware of the catastrophic financial situation, started a run on the banks. Because Germany had been the center for the investment of foreign money, the difficulties of the German banks meant great losses for the banks of other countries, particularly Great Britain and the United States. The result was a general restriction of credit, with capital for investments difficult or even impossible to obtain. The consequent lack of new investments prolonged the depression and slowed down recovery.

At this time, the view of John Maynard Keynes that in periods of depression new money ought to be pumped into the economy was regarded as a dangerous heresy by almost all economists. A deflationary policy marked by a balanced budget, with expenses limited to the absolute minimum, was the economists' prescription for the handling of both public and private finances in times of crisis; they did not realize that unemployment reinforced the depression because people without money could not buy goods. The generally sluggish economic development of the 1920s had created pockets of unemployment all over Europe; with the depression the numbers of unemployed increased rapidly. In Great Britain, almost 3 million were jobless in 1931; in Germany at the beginning of 1933, industrial production was half of what it had been in 1929, while there were three times as many—6 million—unemployed.

The economic crisis was a turning point in the interwar years because it changed the political climate and the political constellation in Europe. Even when economic life became less turbulent, there was no return to the situation that had existed before 1929.

With the end of the First World War the deep chasm, which before 1914 separated the workers from the ruling classes and the proponents of international socialism from the adherents of national states, seemed bridged. The workers had supported their governments during the war, and in acknowledgment of this show of willingness to recognize the value of the national state, the governments had extended the political rights of the masses. The lowering of the voting age, suffrage for women, elimination of property qualifications, proportional representation—some, or all, of these measures had been adopted in every state of western and central Europe after the war. Most of the demands for political democratization raised by radicals before the war were fulfilled.

But while political democratization had lowered the temperature of the class conflict between workers and bourgeoisie, this did not mean that divergent economic interests had been reconciled. In this area too the war opened new perspectives. The socialists had lost some of their enthusiasm for revolution—partly because they rejected vigorously the theories and actions of the leftist radicals who had come to power in Russia, partly because the introduction of economic controls and regulations by the various governments during the war had demonstrated that the change from a free economy to a controlled and planned economy could be obtained within the existing system. Correspondingly, the members of the bourgeoisie had become aware during the war of beneficial consequences of smooth collaboration with the workers, and they were frightened by the specter of the Russian Revolution, which seemed to show what might happen if the workers were driven to desperation. Moreover, the economic decline following the war hit both workers and employers, two groups that were interested in giving impetus to economic life.

Hence the socialists and the bourgeoisie were willing to take some steps to meet each other. It was acknowledged that workers were entitled to such concessions as the eight-hour day, increased unemployment benefits, recognition of the right to strike, and the establishment of the closed shop, which made trade unions the only legitimate representatives of the workers in the factories. In exchange, the socialists toned down their revolutionary propaganda, emphasized the possibility of achieving their aims by democratic means, accepted some arbitration machinery in labor disputes, and acknowledged the need for the maintenance of national armed forces until disarmament was achieved.

Details varied about the advances achieved in the social legislation of the various European countries after the war; in Germany, where a revolution had taken place, the rights of the workers and trade unions were better secured than in France. Yet an improvement in labor conditions and in the relations between employers and workers had undoubtedly taken place.

However, the period of compromise was short-lived. The economic crisis again widened the gap between the classes. With governments drafting budgets to save money, meaning that unemployment benefits were cut, and with industrial enterprises dismissing workers ruthlessly, the hope of achieving socialist goals through a gradual transformation of the capitalist system appeared increasingly illusory. There was a renewed trend toward revolutionary radicalism. At the same time, industrial entrepreneurs tended to become more antilabor, regarding the trade unions as obstacles to retrenchment through lower wages and a reduced labor force. Reactionary and authoritarian notions received new impetus, and their resurgence was accompanied by a revival of nationalism. In the grim climate of depression, each government thought first of its own people and introduced measures of economic protection to fend off foreign competition. Concessions to other nations were condemned as signs of weakness.

Two areas of the European scene were particularly affected by intensified nationalist attitudes. In the Balkans, hostilities among the various states sharpened, and the exhortations of the greater powers for cooperation and toleration were no longer heeded, especially since they were no longer reinforced by loans.

The French influence, which had been predominant in this area, lost ground, and Italian and German influence increased. But tension also became more acute among the great powers of Western Europe. Because the economic crisis had left Great Britain too weak to exert the role of intermediary and arbiter, which it had assumed in the Locarno agreements, the resurgence of Franco-German hostility was almost unavoidable.

Thus, all over Europe the economic crisis awakened and strengthened extremist tendencies on the left and on the right and undermined the moderate center, which clung to the ideals of democracy.

To understand the events of the 1930s, however, one must go beyond the effects of the economic crisis on the development of party politics. The entire political climate of the 1930s was different from that of the 1920s. One might say that only during the depression years did the full consequences of the shock represented by the First World War come to the surface. In large part this shock resulted from the collapse of assumptions once taken for granted. Before 1914, the steady progress of civilization had seemed assured, and the general principles of European morality were spread and accepted in widening areas of the world. The experience of the war, in which men ruthlessly attempted to create the most efficient machinery of death and destruction and to apply it against whole nations, disregarding conventions and morality when they stood in the way of national victory, could not easily be reconciled with the old principles, which with the return of peace were again proclaimed to be the acknowledged forms of civilized existence. Moreover, the young men who had been thrown straight from school into the conflict had learned that they had instincts and powers that the world of their parents seemed to have suppressed and which found no fulfillment or expression in the pattern of life to which their parents wished them to conform. The moving book by Paul Fussell *The Great War and Modern Memory* registers well the intensity in emotional and ethical consciousness that the experience of the war had produced. It is no accident that after the war Lytton Strachey revealed the concealed hypocrisy of the Victorian age, that Sigmund Freud's theories of repression and of the strength of the unconscious permeated art and literature. Nevertheless, in the period just after the coming of peace, the belief that the postwar years provided a chance for building a new and better democratic world prevailed over the mood whose essence was rejection of historical values and traditions. But when in the 1930s the disillusionment of the postwar world was combined with the miseries of the depression, it became much more difficult to deny the voices of those who preached that the forces revealed by the experiences of the war—violence, ruthlessness, the drive for power—were the truly effective factors in society. In social and political life the use of war and warlike weapons seemed possible and permissible. With the strength of a delayed effect, the shock administered by the experiences of the First World War transformed the psychological approach to politics and social life.

This change in the European climate helps explain a surprising and shocking development. Not much more than ten years after Great Britain and France had completed the arrangements meant to establish them safely as leaders of a democratic Europe, these two powers were in retreat; initiative had devolved to antidemocratic powers.

THE FIRST STIRRINGS OF REVOLT AGAINST EUROPEAN CONTROL OF THE GLOBE

Although developments within the European state system were decisive for the events of the thirties and ultimately for the outbreak of the Second World War, events outside Europe played their role in shifting the balance of power to the dictators. We have mentioned the decline of European economic power through the rise of industries outside Europe, through the sale of foreign assets to pay for the expenses of war. But the position of Great Britain and France, and therefore their influence on the balance within Europe, also was weakened by the rise of nationalist movements aimed at ending the period of colonial rule and exploitation. The war, in which all races had fought side by side, had given impetus to movements for emancipation from colonial rule. By the beginning of the thirties these movements had become factors of considerable political relevance. The areas in which antagonism between the European ruler and settler and the native population began to play an increasingly important role were Africa and southern Asia.

Africa

In Africa one must distinguish between the northern arc, which the Arabs had conquered many centuries ago, and central and southern Africa. In central and southern Africa the British and French governments tried to establish in their colonies advisory councils that would gradually give the native population some part in government. These measures had to be taken because British and French control over the former German colonies in Africa (Tanganyika, Togo, the Cameroons) was exercised in the form of a mandate, carried out under supervision of the League of Nations, with the purpose of educating the indigenous peoples for self-government. Naturally, the concessions made in the former German colonies had to be extended to other areas as well. But in these parts, self-government or even independence was a very distant goal.

In North Africa and the Near East the movement against European imperialism had much deeper roots. Since the Egyptian Jamal-ud-Din al-Afghani (1838–1897) had raised national and liberal claims for the Muslims in the nineteenth century, nationalist movements had taken hold in North Africa and the Near East. Even before the First World War the Arabs had begun to react against Ottoman rule. When the Turks entered the First World War, this Arab nationalism received support from the British and the French, and with the encouragement of agents like T. E. Lawrence (1888–1935), the famous Lawrence of Arabia, hopes were high for the establishment of a larger Arab kingdom reaching from Arabia to Damascus and Baghdad. But these hopes were crushed in 1920—the year the Arabs called *âm an-nakba* ("the year of the catastrophe"). The French drove the Arabs out of Damascus and took control in Lebanon and Syria, which were assigned to them as mandates. Anti-Jewish riots were crushed in Palestine, which the British government in the so-called Balfour Declaration (1917) had promised as a national home for the Jewish people and which the British administered as a mandate. The British tried to reconcile the Arabs by creating a number of Arab states—Transjordania, Iraq, and Hejaz— but Arab hostility to European imperialism remained alive, and the British and French could maintain their control in this area only by playing on religious and racial antagonisms, like those of the Christian Arabs and the Druzes toward the Muslims, or by using force. Nationalism also reached the westernmost of the Arab settlements. Starting in the 1920s, the young Tunisians, as the Tunisian nationalists called themselves, exerted increasing pressure, and in the 1930s a nationalist movement became active in Morocco as well. Nevertheless, only slowly and gradually, during the 1920s and 1930s, did these anti-imperialist movements become a serious threat to the control of this part of Africa by Great Britain and France; there was only one—Egypt—where Arab nationalism became politically significant immediately after the war.

Anti-British feeling in Egypt had intensified during the war, when the British entirely took over Egyptian rule and interfered in Egyptian life, requisitioning cattle and foodstuffs and forcing Egyptians to work on railroads and other installations needed for the campaign in the Near East. The resentment created by these harsh measures promoted the emergence of the Wafd, a well-organized movement whose goal was complete Egyptian independence. Disorders were frequent from March 1919, when Britain refused the demands of the Wafd, until 1922, and under the impact of these revolts the British were forced in 1921 to release the organizer and leader of the Wafd, Saad Zaghlul Pasha (c. 1860–1927), whom they had exiled to Malta. After his triumphal return a certain stabilization was finally achieved. The British recognized Egyptian sovereignty but retained the right to intervene in Egyptian affairs. They kept the Sudan under their control and assumed responsibility for the defense of Egypt and the protection of foreigners living there. Even after this compromise the situation remained precarious. Zaghlul continued to press for the abolition of all the special rights the British had preserved, and the Wafd was regularly victorious in elections. The British, however, had the support of the Egyptian king, who disliked the democratic tendencies of the Wafd. Although the British were forced to make further concessions, their retreat was slow. Nevertheless, throughout the interwar years Egypt remained a serious political concern for Britain, and the maintenance of a position there absorbed part of Britain's military strength.

India

While Arab nationalism was gaining ground only slowly, a most serious challenge to the rule of the white man arose in India at just about the time the First World War came to an end. The events in India provided the most striking example of the mounting strength gained by the movements of non-European peoples for liberation from European rule. More than half a million Indians fought in the First World War, and both princes and commoners distinguished themselves by their bravery. Even before the war ended, the British government realized that this active participation in battle gave justification to the Indians' claims for participation in the government of their country. In August 1917, Edwin Montagu, secretary of state for India, announced in the House of Commons that the British government planned "not only the increasing association of Indians in every branch of the administration but also the granting of self-governing institutions with a view to the progressive realization of a responsible government in India as an integral part of the British Empire."

The British believed that in effecting changes in the status of India, they would be dealing chiefly with the British-educated upper classes and with the rulers of the princely states. They felt sure that they could proceed slowly and cautiously. But the movement toward Indian independence assumed a quick tempo and became a dramatic conflict because of the inspiring personality of its leader, Mohandas Gandhi (1869–1948).

For twenty years Gandhi had lived in South Africa, where he had been the acknowledged leader of the large number of Indian workers who had gone there as indentured laborers. Gandhi had brought about remarkable improvements in their legal and economic position. The methods he had employed in achieving these gains had involved strikes, demonstrations, and hunger marches; but he had kept his followers from committing any violence, and when the police took action, he and his followers had gone to prison willingly, without offering resistance. Gandhi's struggle for the Indians in South Africa had made him a well-known and highly respected figure, and when he returned to India in 1916, leadership in the nationalist movement devolved upon him almost automatically.

Gandhi infused two crucial new ideas into the movement for independence. First, its basis had to be broadened. It was not to be limited to the educated upper classes but was to include members of all social classes, particularly the poor agricultural and industrial workers. Second, the method to be employed in obtaining independence was to be the one he had successfully used in South Africa: nonviolence.

Broadening the social basis required a revolutionary step: breaking down the barriers between caste members and untouchables. When Gandhi began to live among untouchables and adopted an untouchable girl as his daughter, his people were deeply shocked. But gradually his moral courage aroused admiration and reinforced his political leadership. His insistence on nonviolence gave the movement a strong moral basis. Gandhi himself stated that his campaign constituted "an attempt to revolutionize politics and restore moral force to its organic station. We hope by our action to show that physical force is nothing compared to moral force and that moral force never fails." The instrument through which Gandhi hoped to obtain a withdrawal of the British without using violence was noncooperation. Again, this idea was powerful because it contained a strong moral element. As Gandhi said, "Non-cooperation with evil is as much a duty as is cooperation with good."

Noncooperation also implied practical measures that greatly weakened the British hold over India. Lawyers, among them future leaders such as Nehru (1889–1964) and Patel (1875–1950), left the courts; students left the universities; and like the *narodniki* in Russia in the nineteenth century, professional men and intellectuals went into the villages, to educate the people and to preach noncooperation. For the success of noncooperation, the rejection of all imported goods was essential, and the symbol of autarky became the wearing of homespun cloth. Gandhi admonished every Indian to spin daily. He attributed particular value to this work because while spinning, one had time for religious contemplation.

Organization of the movement for Indian independence was in the hands of the All-India Home Rule League, of which Gandhi became president in 1920. Under him a democratic mass organization was created, with village units, city districts, and provincial sections, all culminating in the All-Indian Congress Committee. The fight for Indian independence became a struggle between the congress and the British. The congress adopted a policy of noncooperation, declaring that "it is the duty of every Indian soldier and civilian to sever his connections with the government and find some other means of livelihood." Noncooperation, however, developed into civil disobedience, and the latter was frequently accompanied by riots and violence. Gandhi's response to the outbreaks of violence was a fast, which he ended only when the disturbances had stopped. Indicative of the religious veneration in which the Indians held Gandhi, he could almost always control them by means of a fast; the people accepted Gandhi's demands because a prolonged fast might endanger his life.

The British were rather insecure in their handling of Gandhi. In 1922, they arrested him as the author of a number of seditious articles and condemned him to six years in prison, but they released him after two years to quiet the resentment his imprisonment had caused.

A crisis occurred in 1930. Because the British government had refused to give a definite promise of independence, a new campaign of civil disobedience was started, and Gandhi, after some years of withdrawal from politics, agreed to lead it. He decided to dramatize this campaign by an action breaking the government's salt monopoly, and accordingly he organized and led a march to the sea, covering two hundred miles in twenty-four days. At the shore he picked up and ate some salt the waves had left, as a demonstration that he did not feel bound by the regulations concerning it. Again, Gandhi was arrested. But the British government realized that some agreement had to be reached and released him. In appreciation of this gesture, Gandhi expressed the wish to see the viceroy, Lord Irwin, later earl of Halifax (1881–1959). In the course of this famous visit, the viceroy offered Gandhi a cup of tea, and Gandhi, taking a paper bag out of his shawl, answered: "Thank you. I will put some salt into my tea to remind us of the famous Boston Tea Party." Gandhi's meeting with Lord Irwin resulted in the cessation of civil disobedience, the release of all political prisoners, the abandonment of the British salt monopoly, and the agreement of the Congress Party to participate in a roundtable conference in London. Gandhi himself went to London as a Congress representative. In London, the immense difficulties the internal situation of India put in the way of independence became strikingly apparent. The conference produced a dramatic split between Hindus and Muslims; the Muslims, a minority in India, demanded separate electorates, an arrangement that would prevent them from being outvoted; the Hindus insisted on a single electorate. The British government's decision for separate electorates inflamed the struggle anew, and it moved in a quickened tempo through the 1930s: campaigns of civil disobedience, arrests, fasts by Gandhi, British concessions followed one upon the other. The solution—independence accompanied by the division of India into two states, one largely Hindu, the other largely

Gandhi's march to the sea in defiance of Britain's salt monopoly in India.

Muslim, within the British Commonwealth of Nations—was achieved only after the Second World War.

The Change in the Far East: Japan and China

As a consequence of the First World War, two non-European powers—the United States and Japan—became equal in strength and importance to the European great powers; without their participation the affairs of the globe could no longer be decided. Indeed, developments in the Far East showed the extent to which in this particular area the United States and Japan now not only equaled the European great powers but even overshadowed them.

The involvement of the European nations and the United States in the European theater of war had given Japan opportunities it knew how to make full use of. Japan was particularly anxious to strengthen its hold over China. China was forced to recognize Japan as the heir of Germany's rights in China and to give Japan extended economic privileges in Manchuria. Moreover, having taken over Germany's island possessions in the Pacific, Japan intended to keep them.

But Japanese policy ran counter to the interests of the United States. The occupied islands, particularly Yap, were so situated that control of them implied control of communications in the Pacific, and the Japanese hold over China nullified the American open-door policy. A naval armament race seemed unavoidable. But in the difficult economic circumstances after the First World War this aggravation of financial burdens seemed so senseless that the great naval powers were willing to make a serious attempt to settle their differences by negotiations. Accordingly, on December 12, 1921, they met in Washington, D.C., to discuss naval armament and the situation in the Pacific. In the opening speech, the American secretary of state, Charles Evans Hughes, made a number of concrete proposals for the limitation of naval armaments. On February 4, 1922, the conference ended with a settlement that in essence embodied these proposals in a series of complicated arrangements. One was the establishment of a definite ratio controlling the tonnage of the battleships of the great naval powers. Great Britain abandoned its claim to having the strongest navy in the world and agreed to an American navy equal to its own. Britain and the United States were each allowed five hundred twenty-five thousand tons of capital ships, Japan three hundred fifty thousand tons, and France and Italy one hundred seventy-five thousand tons each. Moreover, during the next ten years no new capital ships—that is, ships of ten thousand or more tons—were to be built. This naval agreement was supplemented by the Nine Power Treaty, signed by the United States, Great Britain, France, Italy, Japan, Belgium, the Netherlands, Portugal, and China, guaranteeing the integrity and sovereignty of China and promising maintenance of the open door. In consequence of this treaty, Japan returned the former German colony of Kiaochow to China. Finally, in another treaty—the Four Power Treaty—the United States, Great Britain, France, and Japan acknowledged one another's insular possessions in the Pacific and agreed to mutual consultation if their possessions were threatened. The Four Power Treaty is usually regarded as the most important diplomatic achievement of the Washington Conference. At the time of the conference the old alliance between Japan and Great Britain was due for renewal. The United States looked with distrust on this special bond between Great Britain and Japan, and the British were reluctant to retain a commitment that might place them in opposition to the United States. The Four Power Treaty was to replace the British-Japanese alliance and initiate an era of cooperation among all the powers interested in the Far East, preventing Japan from taking isolated action.

Taken together, these agreements reveal a remarkable shift of power in the Pacific. In that area, Great Britain clearly had become secondary to the United States. It had bowed to American wishes in abandoning its old alliance with Japan, and because it could keep only a part of its navy in the Far East, the arrangements about naval strength made any unilateral involvement of Britain in a Far Eastern war an impossibility. Britain's efforts now had to be directed toward gaining cooperation and, if necessary, common action among all the powers interested in the Far East. But it is very doubtful whether the policy worked out at the Washington conference was suited to this goal and whether the consequences of the replacement of a British-Japanese alliance by the Four Power Treaty were beneficial.

The Japanese withdrew from China and for a number of years adhered scrupulously to the Washington agreements. But feeling became strong in Japan that the nation had gained little from its participation in the First World War, and the moderate Japanese statesmen anxious to cooperate with Great Britain, the European powers, and the United States lost influence, while a militaristic group bent on imperialist expansion and opposed to the parliamentary regime gained in appeal.

These developments were furthered by events in China itself. The Revolution of 1911, brought about by the Chinese resentment against foreigners and indignation about the impotence of the imperial regime, was followed by a confused period of civil war, with the various provincial governors, the so-called warlords, fighting one another. The First World War gave events a new turn.

The handing over of the former German colonies in China to the Japanese aroused national resentment in China, especially among intellectuals and students. On the other hand, the end of tsarism and the seizure of power in Russia by the Bolsheviks meant that China was no longer faced by a united front of powerful foreign states; on the contrary, China now had a defender among them, since the Communist International made the cause of colonial peoples and exploited races one of its main concerns. The Russians also gave proof of their interest in China by giving up the privileges granted to tsarist Russia by the imperial Chinese governments. The intellectual leader of the Chinese Revolution and protagonist of a united and socially reformed and modernized China, was Sun Yat-sen (1866–1925), who had been proclaimed president of the Chinese republic. But in 1922, China was divided by the feuds of warlords who ruled in the various provinces, and Sun Yat-sen was almost powerless. He then turned to Russia and admitted Communists into his party, the Kuomintang. The alliance was not purely opportunistic: Sun Yat-sen saw in various measures of the Bolsheviks, mostly in their agrarian policy, models for what ought to be done in China. For a short time the Russians, since the chance for a revolution in central and western Europe seemed hopeless, believed that through the conquest of China by Communism a new impetus could be given to a forward march of the world revolution. With the help of Russian advisers, among whom Mikhail Borodin was the outstanding figure, the Kuomintang was organized in a more effective way and the army was reformed. Sun Yat-sen died in 1925, but his successor, Chiang Kai-shek (1887–1975), succeeded in establishing Kuomintang rule over the principal parts of China. This consolidation, accomplished by another wave of anticapitalist strikes and demonstrations, induced the Western powers to follow the Russian example, to give up their privileges and evacuate the harbors they had occupied in imperialist days; in this way they hoped to maintain trade with China and realize what was the officially proclaimed aim of their policy: open door and independence of China. Encouraged by the support of the West, Chiang Kai-shek, who, more than Sun Yat-sen, considered cooperation with the Communists an emergency measure, broke with them. The Communists were driven out of the Kuomintang and of the government, although under the leadership of

Mao Zedong in 1933, when he was the leader of the radical left opposition to the Kuomintang under Chiang Kai-shek.

Mao Zedong (1893–1976) and Zhu De (1886–1976) they remained in control of some agrarian areas in northern China. The national government under Chiang Kai-shek proclaimed as its aim the establishment of a constitutional democracy but announced that this goal could only be reached after a transitional period in which all power was in the hands of the Kuomintang. Nationalist China became a one-party state. It was a period of centralization and organizational improvement: the currency was unified, the introduction of a budget brought some order into government financing, and the building of railroads and highways furthered economic development and strengthened administrative control.

In contrast to the Western powers, the Japanese did not consider consolidation of the Chinese government in their interest. They feared that a politically strengthened China, pursuing a nationalistic economic policy, might exclude Japanese industrial goods from the Chinese market and make the Japanese economic situation critical. The Chinese, on the other hand, regarded the Japanese economic penetration into Manchuria with increasing distrust, and Japan became the chief target of anti-imperialist movements and demonstrations; a boycott of Japanese goods was started. In September 1931, the so-called Mukden incident, a railway explosion for which the Japanese blamed the Chinese, brought about a break. Japan invaded Manchuria, and a war began, which ended only with the end of World War II. The European powers were unable to prevent the outbreak of this conflict, nor could the machinery of the League of Nations resolve it. Japan refused to accept the recommendations of the League and withdrew from it in March 1933.

The failure of the League during this crisis was one visible sign of the weakening of the system that had been established by the Paris Peace Conference; as such, it represented a serious blow to the authority of those powers considered the founders and chief defenders of the system, Britain and France. It became clear that suffering from the effects of the economic crisis, they were unable to mobilize the necessary forces to stop the Japanese advance and impose a settlement. Those in Europe who were opposed to the political establishment also believed that the time had come for a change. Thus did the revolt against the settlement of Paris extend into Europe.

THE RISE OF NAZISM IN GERMANY

The event that decisively brought an end to the system established in Paris and also to the era of political stabilization was the rise of Nazism in Germany. The reasons for this rise were of course manifold. The economic crisis gave strong impetus to the Nazi movement, but this was not the only—and perhaps not even the most important—reason for its spread. To a large extent, Nazism was an inner German phenomenon, one that revived old political attitudes dominant in imperial Germany: authoritarianism and nationalism.

Adolf Hitler and the Foundation of the Nazi Party

As students of the Nazi and Soviet dictatorships have often noted, Adolf Hitler (1889–1945), the man who led the Nazi movement to prominence in Germany, had certain biographical elements in common with his later rival, Joseph Stalin. Like Stalin, Hitler was an "outsider"—not a German by birth but an Austrian. He and Stalin both had abusive fathers and doting mothers. Both began their careers as revolutionary terrorists against established state authority, and both landed in prison as a result of their insurrectionary activities. The political careers of both would have been impossible without the radicalizing effects of World War I. Yet at bottom Hitler's political style proved to be quite different from Stalin's. While the Soviet leader loved the details of political intrigue and tried to micromanage even the most humdrum matters of state, the German Führer was given to grand flights of ideological fantasy and generally showed indifference to the tedium of day-to-day policy making (except in matters of culture). There being no such thing as a generic path to dictatorship, Hitler's rise from provincial obscurity to the leadership of Germany is best understood within the context of the unique set of circumstances that made this singular man appear, in the eyes of millions of Germans, to be the right man for the times. As with Stalin, or for that matter Mussolini, Hitler's political success depended not just on opportunism and genuine talent but also on the complicity of vast flocks of eager followers.

Hitler, who did not become a German citizen until 1932, was born in the little town of Braunau, on the Austrian-German border, on April 20, 1889, and spent his earliest years in the Upper Austrian town of Linz. His father, who had been a customs official, died when his son was fourteen. His mother spoiled him, allowing him to lead a lazy and undisciplined existence. He did poorly in school and dropped out when he was sixteen. Imagining himself to be an artist, he moved to Vienna in 1907 to study painting but failed to gain admission to the local Academy of Arts. After his mother's death in 1908 he lived for a time as a young dandy on the money his parents had left him, but he soon exhausted these resources and drifted through various menial jobs without ever settling on a definite career. He slept in flophouses and wore shabby clothes. On the advice of a friend, he began to paint postcards of local buildings, which his friend peddled around. With his human contact limited mainly to other vagabonds, Hitler did not learn the art of conversation. His way of expressing himself was to engage in monologues, a habit he never lost. In these monologues, which often focused on the "evils of Jewry," Hitler showed that he had already become caught up in the extreme anti-Semitic ideology that was so pervasive in early twentieth-century Vienna. As an outsider with no special training, he could not find a regular job, though in truth he did not really want one. He seemed content to drift aimlessly through life, painting his pathetic little pictures and haranguing his fellow tramps.

What saved Hitler from this fate—though it would have been far better for the world had it not done so—was the First World War. Hitler had moved to Munich in 1913 because he believed that he might have better luck as an artist in that city, which was then Germany's art capital. Moreover, as he said later, he preferred a real German city to Vienna with its "promiscuous swarm of foreign people." But in Munich his existence was just as shiftless and miserable as it had been in Vienna. Thus, when the war broke out in 1914, he leaped at the chance to join a Bavarian regiment in the German Army, for which as an Austrian citizen, he needed special permission from the Bavarian king. Hitler proved to be a good soldier, winning the Iron Cross First and Second Class. In the trenches of the western front, where he served as a message runner, he felt himself for the first time to be a valued member of a community. There he met men who later became his most devoted friends and followers: Rudolf Hess, his secretary, and Max Amann, the press chief in Nazi Germany. The war experience made Hitler an admirer of all things military, especially the hierarchical order and strict chain of command.

The German defeat in 1918 was a personal catastrophe for the young Hitler. He could not admit that the loss had been caused by his beloved military leaders; in his view, it was the result of a "stab in the back" by the dark forces he had come to hate in Vienna and Munich: Marxists and Jews. During the revolution of 1918–1919 he returned to Munich as an intelligence operative for the army, employed to investigate the welter of small parties sprouting up in the chaos of the postwar environment. He also gave speeches at demobilization centers designed to keep the military spirit alive. In the course of this activity he came into contact with a small group calling itself the German Workers' Party, which had been founded in January 1919. Hitler was not very impressed by the group, but he soon joined it with the idea of putting his personal stamp on it. This he quickly did, largely by using his speaking ability to attract new members. Within a few months he established himself as the leader of the party, whose name he changed to National Socialist German Workers' Party Nazis, for short.

As its name suggests, the Nazi Party aimed to combine nationalist elements with socialist ones, the "socialism" in question deriving not from Marxist internationalism but from the wartime fellowship of frontline soldiers and patriotic workers. To protect their rallies and break up the meetings of their opponents, the Nazis established their own political army, the Sturmabteilung (SA, or Storm Troopers). Exploiting the political and economic chaos of postwar Munich, the party soon became a force to be reckoned with on the local scene. By late 1923, as ruinous inflation engulfed Germany, Hitler believed that he might be strong enough to seize power in Munich and then launch a march on Berlin, similar to Mussolini's March on Rome in the previous year. On the night of November 8–9, 1923, Hitler staged his now-famous Beer Hall Putsch, during which after having crashed a political meeting at a local beer hall, he led his followers to the center of Munich in hopes of taking over the city. Bavaria's police and army, however, were not prepared to place themselves under Hitler's control, despite the presence at his side of General Ludendorff. Hitler's first grab for power ended in a hail of gunfire at Munich's Feldherrnhalle. The future Führer survived the gunfire but was arrested soon after the putsch and put on trial for treason; his party was outlawed. By all rights Hitler should have been deported to Austria or imprisoned for life, but instead he was given the extraordinarily light sentence of five years' fortress arrest. The conservative Munich judges, it seems, bought his argument that he had acted for patriotic motives. After less than a year he was released from prison and allowed to return to Munich and his political career. An excellent chance to put him away for good had been missed.

While in prison, Hitler dictated his memoir *Mein Kampf.* Here he spelled out his guiding principles and political ideas. His worldview represented a strange amalgam of Social Darwinism, Wagnerian romanticism, Nietzschean philosophy, and Machiavellian realpolitik—all simplified and vulgarized. "The whole work of nature is a mighty struggle between strength and weakness—an eternal victory of the strong over the weak," he said. Politics was to Hitler a struggle among races, but in his opinion, the races were not equal; the "Aryan race" was superior to all others. Hitler believed in the importance of elites. Among the "Aryans," the Germans were the elite, with the right and duty to lead and to rule. Because struggle was the law of life, war was a necessity, and the main task of a national leader was to make his state militarily strong so that it could win in battle and expand. The primary area in which Hitler hoped to gain added *Lebensraum* ("living space") for the German people was in the east. He envisaged wars with Poland and Russia that would bring Germany this space. Fighting Russia was also necessary, he thought, because Soviet Communism was Nazism's most dangerous foe. Not only was it backed by a virile dictatorship, but it was also tied to the international Jewish conspiracy that was bent on keeping Germany weak.

Of course, Hitler's claim that the Germans had an intrinsic right to rule based on their supposed racial superiority made the Nazis' ideology fundamentally different from that of their Soviet-Communist rivals: Communism at least *claimed* to stand for human progress and proletarian brotherhood across national and ethnic boundaries. As the historian Richard Overy has noted, this crucial divergence in ideology helped set the stage for the "hegemonic war" between the two dictatorships.

The anti-Semitic nostrums that informed Hitler's hatred of Bolshevism remained central to his political thought and proved to be an effective propaganda tool in Germany. The Jew could be blamed for those incomprehensible economic forces that destroyed the independence of small entrepreneurs and shop owners. But the usefulness of anti-Semitism was secondary for Hitler; he was a convinced, passionate hater of the Jews. An admirer of Wagner's operas, Hitler was obsessed by the drama of Teutonic heroes, caught in a net by the dark dwarfs with their hoards of gold. There is no possibility of finding a rational explanation for such notions, nor did Hitler himself really try to do so. As his whole career was to show, and as he himself frequently bragged, in his crucial decisions he followed his intuition.

Yet, whatever Hitler's claims regarding his intuitive powers, the future Führer's rapid transformation from a down-and-out ex-soldier to a power on the Bavarian (and later German) scene cannot be understood in terms of some sixth sense for political decision making. Indeed, one of the challenges for students of the Hitler phenomenon is to explain how this awkward, generally introverted character could command any significant following among reasonably sophisticated people. Here again, it seems to have been primarily Hitler's oratorical ability that allowed him to expand the Nazi movement into a credible force, at least in Munich. Contrary to a myth that Hitler himself advanced, this oratorical ability did not come out of the blue—a "gift of Providence"—but was the product of assiduous practice in front of the mirror. Like Stalin, then, Hitler was at once a practitioner of self-help and a good exploiter of others.

Decline of Parliamentary Government in the Weimar Republic

When Hitler returned to political action in Munich in 1925, his first order of business was to get the Nazi Party legalized, and this he was quickly able to do because the authorities no longer considered it a serious threat. In addition to reestablishing his control over the party, Hitler set up another paramilitary group, the elite Schutzstaffel, or SS, which served as the leader's personal bodyguard. Later, under its chief Heinrich Himmler, the black-uniformed SS became one of the most powerful institutions in the Nazi state, a rival even to the army. In the mid-twenties, however, the prospects for the Nazis did not look good. The Weimar order, having narrowly survived the chaos of the great inflation, putsch attempts from right and left, and the humiliation of the Versailles Treaty, seemed finally to be gaining a measure of acceptance. During the three or four years of increasing prosperity that followed acceptance of the Dawes Plan and conclusion of the Locarno agreements, the republican regime gained some ground, and a slight swing to the republican left took place in the elections of 1928. It was a sign of the change in the political climate that the monarchist German People's Party entered a coalition with the three republican parties. However, the situation changed quickly. One year after the elections, the economic depression began to make itself felt. In September 1929 Germany had 1,320,000 unemployed; one year later, 3 million; in September 1931, 4,350,000; and in 1932 the peak was reached with over 6 million. In Germany the widespread poverty and wretched conditions caused by the depression had an especially devastating psychological effect because they came so soon after the hardships of the inflation. Republican governments seemed unable to create a secure economic foundation for society. Left-wing and right-wing radicalism increased, with a resultant sharpening of tension between the left and right wings of the ruling coalition. The socialists, fearful that their adherents would go over to the Communists, became increasingly unwilling to agree to economic measures that might increase unemployment, and the German People's Party tried to strengthen its appeal by adopting a more nationalist line in foreign policy. Particularly unfortunate was the death in October 1929 of Gustav Stresemann, who had exerted a moderating influence in the German People's Party. Shortly before his death he had achieved an important success: the acceptance of the Young Plan, which reduced the amount of the annual German reparations payments, eliminated the international controls over German economy, and brought to an immediate end the military occupation of the Rhineland. But because this agreement had been preceded by bitter diplomatic struggles, its acceptance aroused nationalist passions and resentment and weakened rather than helped the advocates of a policy of international understanding.

With Stresemann gone, the gap between the right and the left in the government widened steadily, and in March 1930 the coalition disintegrated. The parties were unable to agree upon measures to overcome the accelerating economic crisis. The particular issue that led to the resignation of the government was very similar to one that brought about the fall of the Labor government in Great Britain a year later: payments to the unemployed. The socialists wanted to maintain unemployment benefits, but to minimize the budget deficit, they proposed raising the contributions. On the other hand, this seemed to the industrialists a unique opportunity to reduce the rights of the trade unions to participate in decisions on wages and dismissals and to become again masters in their own house.

During the elections to the Reichstag in 1932, parties distribute propaganda before a polling place.

Although never concealing his monarchist convictions, Hindenburg carried out his duties in accordance with the constitution during his first years as president. But he was surrounded by monarchist officers and friends who believed that the collapse of the coalition government might afford an opportunity for a change to a more authoritarian system, paving the way for a new monarchy. In 1930, they picked a rather nationalist member of the Center Party, Heinrich Brüning (1885–1970), as chancellor. A strict Catholic, Brüning lived ascetically and tended toward obstinacy and self-righteousness. He was an administrator rather than a politician, an authoritarian rather than a democrat. He had made his career in the Center Party as an expert in financial affairs and was a strict adherent of orthodox views on economics. He believed that the crisis could be overcome only by deflation and strict economies, including cuts in unemployment insurance. Fully aware that such a policy would never be approved by the socialists, he expected to draw his support from the center and the right; he was willing to woo the right by effecting a constitutional change that would result in a more authoritarian form of government. When the Reichstag refused to approve his financial proposals, Brüning dissolved that body and put his financial proposals into effect by emergency decrees.

The elections that took place on September 14, 1930, showed the expected shift to the right, but not to the German People's Party and the German Nationalist Party, which might have cooperated with Brüning; instead, gains were made by the Nazis, who increased their seats from 15 to 107.

The outcome of the elections did not deter Brüning from his course: he rejected all suggestions that he resume cooperation with the socialists. He also began to rely on a clause in the Weimar constitution (Paragraph 48) that allowed the chancellor, with the consent of the president, to rule by emergency decree. Although this provision by its very nature was meant to be used sparingly and for short periods, Brüning received backing from President Hindenburg to employ it on a regular basis. The rightist parties in the Reichstag also backed this approach, though it undercut their own influence as well as that of the socialists. In effect, Brüning had killed Weimar democracy even before Hitler came to power.

Brüning further ingratiated himself with the forces of the right by giving a nationalist turn to German foreign policy. In June 1930, when the last French troops evacuated the Rhineland, official speeches celebrating this event expressed no appreciation of the French concessions but instead raised demands for further revisions of the peace treaty. The British ambassador in Berlin wrote: "It is an unattractive feature of the German character to display little gratitude for favors received but when the receipt of favors is followed up by fresh demands there are grounds for feeling impatient." If the British government had followed the advice of its ambassador and had stood with France, the Germans might have become more cautious in making complaints and raising new demands. But Great Britain just tried to smooth things over without taking any definite stand, and Germany went ahead with its policy of seeking revision.

The most disastrous German step in this campaign was the conclusion of a customs reunion with Austria in March 1931. Such an agreement was hardly compatible with the 1919 prohibition against Anschluss, and it was in direct contradiction to stipulations Austria had accepted in 1922 to receive financial support from France, Great Britain, and Italy. France brought the issue before the Permanent Court of International Justice in The Hague, and the customs union was declared invalid. The political uncertainty created by the conflict over the customs union triggered in the summer of 1931 the dramatic explosion of the financial crisis that began in Vienna, then moved to Germany, and finally extended to London.

During that summer Brüning and the president of the Reichsbank were forced to make desperate trips to London and Paris to plead for financial relief, and these appeals to former enemies damaged the prestige of the government in the eyes of the nationalists. In the winter of 1931–1932 the nationalist opposition was still gaining in strength, and unemployment reached frightening proportions.

Brüning was further handicapped by the fact that he could rule by emergency decrees only as long as he had the confidence of the president, to whom the power to issue the decrees actually belonged. In March 1932, Hindenburg's first presidential term ended. In the subsequent election he received 53 percent of the votes; Hitler received 36.8 percent. Despite Hindenburg's imposing majority, the result was a disappointment to him. The figures showed that right-wing radicalism had continued to grow. Brüning had failed to gain the cooperation of the rightist groups, and at the end of May 1932 he was curtly dismissed by Hindenburg.

The details of what happened in Germany between Brüning's dismissal and Hitler's assumption of power in January 1933 are intricate. But the general pattern was constant. The continuing increase in popularity of nationalist extremism on the right made moderate conservatives less than ever inclined to resume cooperation with the socialists. Moreover, Hindenburg, getting old and dependent, decided against a return to parliamentarism. These authoritarian tendencies were strongly supported by the generals of the Reichswehr. They were sympathetic, if not to the National Socialist leaders, at least to the revival of nationalism and militarism that National Socialism preached. In their eyes, the Nazis would be valuable material to be incorporated into the army when the hour arrived to break the chains of the disarmament clauses of Versailles. They were not willing to risk a serious political conflict in which the Reichswehr might have to fight the National Socialists with their paramilitary organizations. Indeed, they were not even sure that officers ordered to attack the Nazis would obey the command. Thus, all the men around the president wanted to cooperate with the National Socialists.

The only stumbling block was the demand of their leader, Hitler, that he must be chancellor of any government supported by his party. Hindenburg's advisers wanted to use the National Socialists for their own purpose, but they did not want to get into a position in which the National Socialists might be able to call the tune. Brüning's successor, Franz von Papen, an ambitious and elegant former officer who through his great wealth had acquired newspapers and political influence, tried unsuccessfully to cooperate with Hitler. His successor, von Schleicher, was equally unsuccessful. By December 1932, however, the situation had begun to change. Elections in November showed for the first time a slight decrease in the National Socialist vote; it became clear that the economic crisis had reached its peak. The conservatives and nationalists feared that if these trends continued, the occasion for the establishment of an authoritarian government and for a restoration of the monarchy might be missed. Likewise, the National Socialist leaders began to feel that they might have waited too long. The masses might defect, having become convinced the National Socialism would never come to power. Under these circumstances Papen attempted once again to form a coalition with the National Socialists. He conceded to their leaders that Hitler should become chancellor, but only two other Nazis, Wilhelm Frick (1877–1946) and Hermann Göring (1893–1946), would become members of the cabinet, and

Adolf Hitler before the conquest of power. With Hitler are his then most prominent lieutenants, from left to right, G. Strasser, Röhm, Hitler, Göring, Brückner.

Göring was to be minister without portfolio. The other members were to be either conservative politicians like Alfred Hugenberg (1865–1951), leader of the German Nationalist Party, or experts. Papen himself, as vice chancellor, would be present at all Hitler's audiences with the president. In such a government, Papen and his friends believed, Hitler's chancellorship would be of no danger. Completely surrounded by sound conservatives, Hitler would have no freedom of action. With these arguments Papen, supported by Hindenburg's son and by his secretary, overcame the president's resistance. On January 30, 1933, Hitler was appointed chancellor.

The Implementation of the Nazi Program

On the evening of January 30, the Nazis celebrated Hitler's appointment with a gigantic torchlight parade, in which they marched, along with organizations of military veterans, through the government quarter of Berlin. This demonstration was meant to emphasize that the formation of the Hitler government signified a new beginning and represented a revolution. The parallel with the rise of Fascism in Italy is striking. The formation of the government by Mussolini had been preceded by negotiations with other parties and by court intrigues; the outcome was a coalition. The traditional nature of the methods employed by Mussolini to gain office was concealed by the March on Rome, which made the seizure of power a conquest by force—a revolution. The torchlight parade on the evening of January 30 in Berlin was Hitler's March on Rome. The people around Hindenburg and the reactionary non-Nazi members of Hitler's government expected to control Hitler and to use the Nazis for their own purposes, indicating that they had no understanding of Hitler's personality or of the reasons so many people had been attracted to the National Socialist Party. Though their final rise to power was due to the intrigues and subtle calculations of the military and the reactionaries, the Nazis had become a force in German politics because large masses of the German people approved of their radical demands for a new departure and saw in Hitler a messiah.

Hitler's aim was to obtain full power and then to launch Germany on a course of expansion, thereby fulfilling what he regarded as the natural law of politics. When he became chancellor, such an aim seemed far beyond his grasp. His government was a coalition in which the National Socialists were a minority. In foreign policy, Germany's freedom of action was still restricted by the treaties of Versailles and Locarno. The size of the German Army was limited, and the Rhineland was demilitarized. One may reject Hitler's aims and detest his brutal methods but still find remarkable the technical virtuosity with which he quickly freed himself from these internal and external restraints. A year and a half after he became chancellor, Hitler was the all-powerful dictator of Germany, and less than two years after that, in March 1936, he made the treaties of Versailles and Locarno valueless pieces of paper.

The Nazi Party Congress in Nuremberg in 1934. In the middle, Hitler, between Himmler, the leader of the SS (*left*) and Lutze, leader of the SA.

At first Hitler made use of the coalition with the German Nationalist Party to stress the moderate and conservative character of his "national revolution." The black, white, and red of the German Empire replaced the black, red, and gold of the national flag of the Weimar Republic; carefully staged celebrations emphasized the continuity between the old imperial Germany and the new National Socialist state.

Hitler and the National Socialists had several reasons for the temporary adoption of a conservative line. First, Hitler had to win the confidence of old Hindenburg, who, by refusing to sign emergency decrees, could still bring about the fall of the government. Also, the new chancellor was anxious to avoid any obstruction by the bureaucracy and to make sure that the military leadership would not turn against him. Moreover, popular support of National Socialism would be strengthened if the members of the various conservative and nationalist parties and organizations, who had stayed away from the Nazis, could be lured into enrolling in the Nazi Party. The conservative line also helped secure the continuation of financial support for the Nazi Party from the leaders of industrial trusts and banks, such as the Krupp steelworks and the I. G. Farben chemical works.

When the government was formed, Hitler insisted that the Reichstag be dissolved and new elections take place. The National Socialists entered the election campaign with immense advantages. They enjoyed the prestige of having their leader as head of the government. They could use the government machinery for propaganda, and on the basis of Paragraph 48 of the constitution they issued emergency decrees that limited the right of assembly of opposition parties and suppressed their newspapers and political publications. However, the decisive turn in the election campaign was brought about on the night of February 27, 1933, when the building in which the Reichstag met went up in flames. Though Marinus van der Lubbe, the young Dutchman who was caught in the building, never denied the deed, it was assumed that he alone could not have caused the immense fire. Many people, then and since, suspected that the Nazis themselves had set the fire, though recent research suggests that this was not the case and that van der Lubbe was the lone culprit after all. In any event, the Nazis were quick to blame the fire on the Communists, who they said had simply used the poor Dutchman as a front man.

On February 28, the day after the burning of the Reichstag, the government issued a number of emergency decrees that were not rescinded until the end of Hitler's Third Reich in 1945. As a "defensive measure against Communist acts of violence," the government rescinded the guarantees of such basic rights as personal freedom, the free expression of opinion, the freedom of assembly and association, the privacy of postal and telephone communications, and the inviolability of property. In addition, the number of crimes to which the death penalty could be applied was increased, and the spreading of rumors or false news was

An illustration of the anti-Semitic policy of the Nazis. The sign reads, JEWS ARE NOT WELCOME IN THIS TOWN.

The burning of the Reichstag on February 28, 1933.

classified as treason. Finally, the Reich government was empowered to take over the government of the various federal states if necessary.

The elections, a week after the Reichstag fire, gave the National Socialists 43.9 percent of the vote. It has been argued in favor of the political maturity of the German people that although the elections took place under severe pressure and restrictions, the National Socialists did not receive a clear majority. It is perhaps more significant that even after the dictatorial character of the Hitler regime had revealed itself, almost 44 percent of the German people voted for the Nazis. Together with the German Nationalist Party, with 8 percent of the vote, the National Socialist Party had the majority.

But application of the emergency decrees soon made this alliance unnecessary. The Communist deputies, representing 12.2 percent of the vote, were arrested and not permitted to enter the Reichstag. Now even without the German Nationalist Party the Nazis had a majority.

For Hitler this was only a first step. He wanted to eliminate entirely both parliament and elections. His government therefore proposed an enabling law, that would transfer the legislative power from the Reichstag to the government for four years; as a change in the constitution, such a law had to be approved by two-thirds of the Reichstag. Hitler obtained the support of the Catholic Center Party by threatening to use the emergency decrees against this party as he had used them against the Communists. The members of the Center Party reasoned that by agreeing to the Enabling Law, they might save their party and retain some influence. The Enabling Law was accepted on March 23; only the Social Democrats voted against it, while outside the hall storm troopers shouted, "We want the bill or fire and murder."

With the emergency decrees of February 28 and the Enabling Law of March 23, all legislative and executive power was concentrated in the hands of the Hitler government, and all guarantees against transgressions by the executive had been removed. This was the "legal" framework for Hitler's dictatorship from 1933 to 1945.

However, the possession of the legal instruments for establishing a dictatorship did not overcome all obstacles to Hitler's unlimited control. Although his party now constituted a majority in the Reichstag, he was committed to retaining the coalition government. The prestige of the president, Hindenburg, was superior to his. Opposition parties and newspapers, though hampered, continued to exist. The traditional spokesmen for educated public opinion—civil servants, professors, clergymen—could still make themselves heard. Hitler's technique for weakening and finally eliminating these remaining centers of independence was masterly. His approach was always the same. Instead of moving against all his opponents at once, he attacked one at a time, in each case proceeding gradually.

Characteristic was the way in which he ended the multiparty system. After the Communist Party had been eliminated, Hitler's first target was the Social Democratic Party. In this effort his coalition partners were willing helpers, and few objections were raised by the other bourgeois parties. The strength of the Social Democrats lay in their close relation to the trade unions, whose strikes could severely handicap the work of the government. Hence Hitler's first move was to separate the trade unions from the Social Democrats; he did so by promising the unions undisturbed, continued existence if they abandoned political activities and concentrated exclusively on economic goals. Timid and bureaucratic, the union leaders fell into this trap and accepted the restrictions. Next, the Nazis declared that independent trade unions were unnecessary. The unions ought to become part of a great comprehensive organization that would include employers as well as workers. With a great celebration on May 1, which was declared a national holiday, a German labor front was founded. The next day the buildings of the unions were occupied, their funds were confiscated, and some of their leaders were arrested. With the elimination of the trade unions the Social Democrats lost all their remaining power to exert pressure. When some important socialists, threatened by imprisonment, left Germany and attacked the regime from the outside, the Nazis used their conduct as an excuse to declare Social Democratic activities treasonous; they prohibited the party and imprisoned many of its leaders.

Next, Hitler proceeded against the bourgeois parties outside his government. Most important among them was the Catholic Center Party. Hitler again applied the tactics he had used against the socialists: he destroyed his antagonist's source of power. A basic reason for the existence of the Center Party was the need to maintain and protect the position of the Roman Catholic Church and its members. Hitler sent Papen to Rome to negotiate a concordat; for many years the Vatican had been eager for such an agreement, which would secure the legal status of the Catholic Church in Germany and would guarantee the bishops freedom of communication with the Vatican. But no previous federal government had been willing to conclude a concordat. The Vatican accepted Hitler's offer, probably as a result of the authoritarian inclinations of Pope Pius XI and the pro-German bias of his secretary of state, Eugenio Pacelli, later Pope Pius XII. It was a fatal mistake. The concordat gave the first international approval to the Nazi regime and raised its prestige. It did not secure the position of Roman Catholicism in Germany, which Hitler went on to attack and undermine as soon as his immediate aim, the dissolution of the Center Party, had been achieved. At the time, however, German Catholics, assured by the concordat that their religion would not suffer under the Nazi regime, abandoned membership in the Center Party, and under pressure from the Vatican the party's leaders on July 8 agreed to its dissolution.

Hitler still had to dispose of his coalition partner, the German Nationalist Party. When he became chancellor, he had promised not to change the composition of the government, which was to include, besides himself, only two National Socialists. However, he managed to increase the influence of his own party in the coalition by creating new departments headed by Nazis: Göring, who had distinguished himself in the war as a pilot and was the most respectable of Hitler's close collaborators, became air minister; Joseph Goebbels (1897–1945), who had been head of the Nazi Party in Berlin and was the most intellectual and also the most cynical of the Nazi leaders, became minister of propaganda. Moreover, members of the German Nationalist Party who went over to the National Socialists were rewarded with advantageous positions in the administration and in the party. Those who refused encountered endless difficulties. Therefore, strong pressure developed within the German Nationalist Party to assure its members of continued influence in the government and administration by amalgamating with the Nazi Party. Thus, the party began to disintegrate and was finally dissolved. On July 14 a government enactment proclaimed that "the National Socialist German Workers' Party constitutes the only political party in Germany"; to attempt to maintain or organize any other political party became a crime. Germany was a one-party state. The elimination of the multiparty system was certainly Germany's most decisive step toward totalitarianism. But it was only one among many. Nazi commissars were placed at the head of the various federal states and they appointed state governments dominated by Nazis. The press and the publishing houses were coordinated by the formation of a comprehensive Nazi-controlled association. Only members of this association were permitted to own, edit, or work on newspapers. A similar takeover occurred in the universities. New chairs were created for fields like racial science, and these were filled by National Socialists. The politically

Goebbels addressing a Nazi mass meeting. To the right are the standard-bearers of the Berlin Hitler Youth.

oriented newcomers were supported by the rectors of the universities, now not elected but appointed by the Nazi minister of education. The expression of pronounced Nazi views became the prerequisite for obtaining tenure and promotion. No excuse is possible for the lack of resistance shown by the German intellectual community to the abolition of academic freedom. But because the Nazi infiltration of the universities happened gradually, many professors became aware of the systematic destruction of their independence only after it had been lost.

Similarly, the full aims of Hitler's anti-Semitic policy were only gradually apparent. It is likely that from the outset his mind was set on what during the Second World War became the "final solution"—the annihilation of the Jews. But at the beginning of the Nazi regime, Hitler created the impression that Jews would be permitted to continue their activities in economic life and in the professions; they were to be excluded from government service except for those who had done military service during the First World War. Soon, however, the screws were tightened. The exemption of war veterans from dismissal was rescinded. Doctors, lawyers, journalists, writers were organized in associations from which Jews were excluded; those who did not belong to these associations met increasing difficulties in the exercise of their professions. Admission to schools and universities was denied to Jewish youth. Gradually the same method was applied to business and economic life. Such activities required

Kristallnacht: Smashed windows of a Jewish shop on the morning after November 9, 1938.

membership in organizations from which Jews were excluded. At the same time currency regulations and export restrictions made immigration a way of escape only for those who were still at the beginning of their careers, for middle-aged and older persons immigration seemed hardly feasible; most hesitated until it was too late.

The anti-Semitic policy reached a climax in the Nuremberg Laws of September 15, 1935, which deprived Jews and people with Jewish blood of German citizenship, prohibited marriage and sexual intercourse between people with Jewish blood and non-Jewish Germans, and denied Jews the right to employ non-Jewish female servants. Jews were forced to wear a yellow Star of David on their clothing whenever they went into the streets. They were pushed back into the ghetto. Protests against these measures were to no avail. As a matter of fact, few dared to endanger themselves by indicating disapproval.

All these changes were accompanied by a systematic policy of terror. Yet the Nazis themselves, of course, did not see themselves as "terrorists;" rather, they believed that their policies of repression were necessary weapons against those who opposed the regime—these opponents, in their view, were the true "terrorists." It must also be stressed that most of the policies and actions that became integral to Nazi "terror" enjoyed wide support among the general populace in Germany. As with Stalin's system of state terror, millions of ordinary citizens chose to interpret the regime's brutal repression—along with the gutting of civil liberties that this entailed—as vital to the "war on terror" the regime claimed to be waging. Moreover, again as in Russia, thousands of ordinary citizens who did not belong to the official terror apparatus willingly assisted the state in its policy of repression. As for the victims of that repression, their alleged deviousness, secret foreign connections, and supposed determination to commit their own acts of terror against the German people enabled the regime to speak ominously of a "permanent enemy" and the necessity of eternal vigilance. When the Nazis came to power, one of their first moves was to obtain control of the police. Since the ministers of the interior in the federal states were in command of the police, the Nazis made sure that these posts were filled by reliable party members. Nazis also were appointed as police presidents in the larger urban centers. These officials arranged for the storm troopers to serve as an auxiliary police force. The emergency decrees passed after the Reichstag fire gave the police the right to arrest and keep in custody anyone suspected of disloyalty to the state. Nobody was secure; an incautious remark or the personal hostility of a storm trooper might result in imprisonment. People disappeared and were never heard of again. The police refused to interfere with Nazi demonstrations, as on April 1, 1933, when the Nazis marched unhindered through the streets of the center of Berlin, throwing stones into the windows of department stores and shops owned by Jews. Similar outbreaks by Nazi students in the universities forced professors regarded as unfriendly to the new regime to abandon their courses. In the atmosphere of terror, made more nightmarish by the official silence about these dark happenings, people gave up asking questions and closed their eyes and ears to what was going on around them. Moreover, the terror did not recede after the first few months; instead, it was embodied in an organization—the Secret State Police, or Gestapo—that developed into a large institution with headquarters in Berlin and offices all over Germany. The Gestapo devoted itself to the task of ferreting out the enemies of Nazism, who were arrested, interrogated, tortured, and placed in detention camps, without any legal recourse.

Under these circumstances the only serious threat to Hitler's leadership came from within—from the Nazi Party itself. Many of those prominent in the party, like the fanatic but colorless Heinrich Himmler (1900–1945), the leader of the SS (Schutzstaffel, Security Force), and the intelligent but generally despised Goebbels, the minister of propaganda, were aware that they had little personal following and were entirely dependent on Hitler. Göring, whose primitive enjoyment of luxury and power gave him a certain human appeal, was entirely satisfied with the power and riches he obtained as second-in-command and as Hitler's designated heir. But many of the early party members sincerely believed that the Nazi assumption of power would bring about a social revolution and that they would be the leaders of a new society very different from the old. A center of such aspirations was the SA (Sturmabteilung, Storm Troopers), and the main advocate of these ideas was the leader of the SA, Ernst Röhm (1887–1934). His concrete aim was to have the SA become part of the army, with the SA leaders receiving officers' ranks. Such demands disquieted the generals of the Reichswehr, who did not want to see their control of the training and organization of the army disturbed by the "wild men" of the SA. Hitler was anxious not to arouse the distrust of the military leaders because he anticipated needing army support for his plan to combine the position of president with that of chancellor after the death of Hindenburg, which in 1934 was imminent. The situation was further complicated by the activities of the conservatives, who were fully aware that without Hindenburg they would lack the power to halt a second revolution and were therefore trying to put a stop to Nazi radicalism before Hindenburg's death.

Out of this tangle of motives arose the bloodbath of June 30, 1934. Hitler himself led the action against Röhm and the other leaders of the SA, whom he surprised in a small summer resort in Bavaria. Röhm and his associates were executed without trial; in his speech of justification Hitler emphasized his having discovered them in bed with young SA men. Actually he had known for a long time of the prevalence of homosexuality within the SA. In Berlin, Göring proceeded not only against the leaders of the SA but also against other adversaries of the Nazis, like Schleicher, the former chancellor; he also arranged the execution of two of Vice Chancellor von Papen's secretaries, who had acted as spokesmen of the conservatives. Papen himself was placed under house arrest. Thus, Hitler shook off the radical wing of his party and earned the gratitude of the military leaders; he also demonstrated that he had not become a prisoner of the conservatives. The events of June 30 were both an expression of Hitler's utter disregard for law and morality and a sign of the omnipotence he had reached. When Hindenburg died on August 2, Hitler combined the offices of president and chancellor without encountering objections.

In two sectors of social life—economic affairs and military affairs—the changes brought about by the Nazi dictatorship were less pronounced than in others. From the beginning, the interests of the economic and military leaders harmonized with Hitler's aims. Economic life became strictly organized and controlled; industrial and commercial activities were coordinated by the trade associations to which all the entrepreneurs had to belong and from which, as we have seen, Jews—and also Freemasons—were excluded. The intermediary between the government and business was Hjalmar Schacht, who served Hitler as president of the Reichsbank and as minister of economics. Schacht abandoned the deflationary policy of previous governments; he pumped new money into the economy by initiating public works, such as the construction of the system of autobahns, and by providing industry with armament contracts. The inflationary consequences of this policy were kept to a minimum by strict currency controls and import restrictions. Moreover, the secrecy with which German rearmament was surrounded kept the public in the dark about the extent of government expenditures and pump priming.

As the entire world has now learned, government support of economic activity—pump priming—can prove an effective means of overcoming economic depression. However, there are limits to the successful pursuit of an inflationary policy. Schacht himself believed that they had been reached by 1938, and he left the government because Hitler insisted on continuing this course. The damaging consequences did not come out into the open before the outbreak of the war in 1939. By then, Germany was faced by the alternative of either a recession or a war and the Nazi leaders were entirely aware of this problem.

Once the danger of SA interference had been removed, the military leaders were quite content with Hitler's rule. In Hitler, Germany had a head of state who not only approved of rearmament but was anxious to accelerate the process. Thus, the military leaders no longer encountered government opposition to their desire for rearmament. However, their independence of Nazi control was more apparent than real. The air force, created only after 1933, was under the command of Göring, and its officers were enthusiastic Nazis. Moreover, the quick promotions resulting from the expansion of the army made the younger officers favorably inclined toward the Nazi regime. In 1938, when the old army leaders began to fear that Hitler's foreign policy might be too risky, Hitler had no difficulty in replacing those he regarded as obstructionists with more subservient generals.

By 1936, Hitler could claim with justification that he had established a totalitarian state; with the exception of some pockets of resistance by small groups in the Roman Catholic and Protestant churches, all activities, organizations, and institutions had been adjusted (*gleichgeschaltet*) to the Nazi regime and were subject to the direction by the Nazi leader. But was there equal justification for the claim—which Hitler and the party chiefs made with still greater emphasis—that the Nazi conquest of power represented a revolution? "Revolution" may be understood as the overthrow of a ruling class and its replacement by another; in what respects, and to what extent, did the Nazi regime transform the basic structure of German social life?

The Nazi movement cannot be identified with a particular class or stratum of German society. Farmers and members of the lower middle class formed its backbone. But in the period of economic misery, the unemployed swelled the Nazi ranks, and civil servants and white-collar workers joined them. Within these groups, the younger generation in particular became Nazis; in 1930, the year of the party's first great electoral victory, more than two-thirds of its members were under forty, and more than one-third under thirty years of age. Those who saw before them only a hard and bleak future were enticed by the Nazi promise of a complete change; the varied membership of the party was united only by common disaffection with the present.

Consequently, when the Nazis came to power, they had no economic or social program aimed at changing the German social structure. They had promised their middle-class adherents protection against the absorption of small businesses by department and chain stores, and indeed, they issued decrees that restricted the kinds of merchandise these stores might sell and subjected them to a special tax. But the opposition of banks and other credit institutions that had invested in these enterprises led gradually to mitigation of the measures against chain and department stores. Beyond this somewhat ephemeral concession to the small middle-class businessman, the Nazis had no concrete economic or social plans when they came to power. Their "revolution" consisted in infusing a new "spirit" into the entire social body. Their apparently revolutionary actions were primarily propagandistic. They aimed at showing that a new nation had arisen in which all groups and classes harmoniously cooperated for the common good. The first of May became a national holiday intended to recognize the importance of the workers; this was only one of the many holidays created to emphasize the solidarity of the German nation. With the establishment of comradeship among the classes, "German Socialism," it was proclaimed, would become a reality. Organizations like the Hitler Youth and the Labor Service were meant to serve this purpose. The Hitler Youth consisted of boys and girls in their early years. The Labor Service was obligatory for students, voluntary for others; its disciplinary and educational effects were more highly appreciated by visiting foreigners than by those who had to undergo this training.

Scene from a Nazi book-burning in Berlin, May 1933. SA leaders threw copies of "anti-German literature" on the bonfire to the cheers of young Germans.

For Hitler the dividing lines in modern society were created not by differing education, differing professions, differing economic status, but by race. However, even within a superior race like the Germans there was an elite that alone had the right to rule. Those few who came from the right stock and had excelled in their activities in the Hitler Youth were prepared for their tasks of leadership in special training schools, housed in buildings modeled after the castles of the knightly orders of the Middle Ages; the training—and these surroundings—were intended to awaken in the trainees the qualities of obedience, physical prowess, instinctivity, and willpower.

The mixture of propaganda and racial romanticism in the social policy of the Nazis reflected the absence of concrete ideas about desirable changes in the German social structure. But this lack had its advantages for the Nazi regime. Since no revolution had occurred that changed the German class structure and no ruling class had been toppled and replaced, each group of society seemed to have kept the position it had held before the Nazis obtained power. Except for the obvious victims of the change of regime—Jews and politicians who had fought the Nazis—the individual did not experience an immediate diminution of status; the tenor of his life was not perceptibly changed, and this apparent stability was one reason for the lack of resistance to the Nazi regime in all levels of society.

The emphasis that Nazi propaganda placed on the establishment of a new national community was to a large extent directed toward mitigating the resentment arising from the realization of political powerlessness. The Nazi rulers took particular care to keep the industrial workers content. The labor front gave much attention to conditions in the factories, secured regular vacations for the workers, and through a special organization, called Strength through Joy, subsidized travel for the workers and their families during these vacations.

Nevertheless, it might be doubted whether propagandistic flattery and handouts would have been effective if employers and employees had not been consoled for their loss of political influence by economic prosperity. At the time the Nazis took over, recovery from the depression was beginning, and this trend the Nazis aided by their policy of military rearmament. In 1938, the federal budget was seven times as large as it had been before the Nazis came to power, and 74 percent of this budget was used for military purposes. Enterprises carrying out government contracts were given credit or were assured of orders for a fixed number of years. For example, in December 1933 the government contracted to buy motor fuel from the large German chemical concern of I. G. Farben for ten years at fixed prices. By such arrangements, industry gradually surrendered its independence and granted the government control over production and prices. But as a collaborator with the regime, industry—and particularly the large companies—began to flourish.

The spurt in economic life that resulted from rearmament also transformed the situation on the labor market. In 1936–1937 the number of employed was greater than the number of employed and unemployed together had been in 1933. Soon there was a labor shortage in Germany. Although on the average, wages were even lower than they had been in the 1920s, the unskilled worker in Nazi Germany in the 1930s had the advantage of being sure of finding a job, and the skilled worker was so much sought after that his wages were kept high. After the haunting experiences of the depression, economic security seemed to both employers and employees a benefit worth paying for.

In 1936, Nazi Germany hosted the Olympic Games in Garmisch-Partenkirchen and Berlin. By putting on successful shows, during which anti-Semitic displays were temporarily suspended and athletes from all over the world, including America's sensational black sprinter, Jesse Owens, competed without incident, Nazi Germany conveyed the impression of having transcended the violent excesses of its early years.

Nazi Policies toward Women

How did the Nazis' assumption of total power in the German state affect the status of the nation's female population? The National Socialists' policies toward women represented an extension, and radicalization, of the traditional conservative perspective. In essence, the Nazis argued that a woman's place was in the home with her family, not in an office or university. They insisted that female "emancipation" had led to widespread disorientation and misery for the women themselves (not to mention for German men). Accordingly, they promised to return women to their "true" roles and to recognize and celebrate the female contribution to the state as mothers and wives.

In their rise to power, the Nazis did not make any concerted effort to draw on the services of women. National Socialism was an overwhelmingly male movement that explicitly rejected a female role in leadership or policy making. Hitler himself claimed to take no political counsel from women, insisting that a female influence had been the ruin of many a great male leader. In one of his more revealing comments he stated that "a woman must be a cute, cuddly, naïve little thing—tender, sweet, and stupid." (The Führer resisted getting married until such an alliance could presumably do him no harm; it was on the very day of his suicide that he finally married his longtime mistress, Eva Braun.) While in the Weimar era Nazism attracted a certain following among female antifeminists, who did their part to strengthen the movement's appeal by preaching on street corners and running soup kitchens, German women for the most part kept their distance politically from the party. In most of the elections women voted in greater numbers for the established conservative parties or, if they were working class, for the socialists and Communists. As the depression deepened, however, more and more women supported the Nazis because they saw Hitler's party as the best solution to the economic catastrophe.

Once in power, the Nazis sought to turn their views on women into law. True to their concept of females as broodmares above all, they passed legislation designed to coerce women to have more children. A marriage loan became available to the couple whose female partner promised to stay home and make babies; every baby the couple produced canceled a portion of their loan obligation. In another measure to increase the birthrate, the government granted awards and decorations to women who bore large broods for the fatherland. The Honor Cross of the German Mother came in three classes: gold, for more than eight children; silver, for more than six; and bronze for five. Those models of fecundity who produced nine kids (or seven sons, if that came first) received, in addition to their gold badges, a chance to meet Hitler. Although these policies encouraged legitimate births, the regime was so desperate for future cannon fodder that it also set up an institution called Lebensborn, in which "racially suitable" unmarried women coupled with SS men and then had their offspring raised by the state. Not surprisingly, couples that chose to have no children were condemned as selfish slackers—virtual enemies of the state. Measures that actively impeded the production of children, such as contraception and abortion, were outlawed. Soon after coming to power, the Nazi government shut down sexual counseling centers that provided information on contraception, and over the years it prosecuted thousands of women for obtaining illegal abortions. On the other hand, women belonging to "inferior races," like Jews and Gypsies, were encouraged to get abortions, while mentally ill women (and men) were often sterilized. To ensure that there would be no organized resistance by women to these and other policies, the regime dissolved all independent women's groups into the German Women's Association, which was headed by a fanatical Nazi named Gertrud Scholtz-Klink. Careful never to try to define policy herself, Scholtz-Klink encouraged German women to follow their Führer in all his commands and to support the Reich in their roles as mothers, wives, and consumers (remembering, for example, never to shop in Jewish-owned establishments).

Committed as they undoubtedly were to their vision of returning women to their "rightful" place, the Nazis honored this ideal more in rhetoric than in reality because it turned out to conflict sharply with their more pressing goal of refashioning Germany as a major military and economic power. The regime soon discovered that it could not build a modern economy and revive the army without bringing women into the workforce in large numbers. There simply were not enough men to fill the expanding ranks of the military and factory workforce at the same time. In 1937, two years before the onset of World War II, the government reversed the marriage loan program; now women were given loans to work outside the home. By the time the war broke out Germany had a record 14.6 million women in its labor force. However, because of its traditionalist ideology regarding women, the regime did not think that it could force women to do "volunteer" labor, as it did men. Even during the war the Nazis preferred to rely on foreign slave labor (some of whom, of course, were women) rather than on native women to fill the gaps in their workforce.

Mention of the war should remind us that virtually all of Hitler's policies, including those toward women, were designed to prepare the nation for the great military conflict the Führer considered necessary and inevitable. Thus, it is not surprising that when it came to Germany's relations with other nations, Hitler's aim was to gain as much ground as he could through diplomacy and then to gain the rest through war.

The Beginning of Nazi Foreign Policy

Hitler began his conduct of foreign policy with loud protestations of peaceful intentions: he was willing to disarm if Germany received equal treatment. Nevertheless, in October 1933, he declared that the plans for disarmament discussed in the Disarmament Conference, which had been meeting at Geneva since 1932, discriminated against Germany; Germany withdrew from the conference and the League of Nations. This was the first step toward a new foreign policy. Hitler softened this blow by declaring that his nation would be willing to reenter if its claims to equality in armament were recognized. The British government, occupied with the pursuit of economic recovery, refused to participate in any strong counteraction and began to explore the possibility of coming to some agreement on armament limitations. The British felt encouraged in these attempts to bring Germany back to international cooperation when on January 26, 1934, in a sudden reversal of foreign policy, Hitler concluded a nonaggression pact with Poland. The German demands for a return of Danzig and the Polish Corridor had always been regarded as a serious danger to European peace. In coming to an agreement with Poland, the new ruler of Germany, however brutal his domestic policy might be, seemed to show that he was aware that methods of violence were inappropriate in international relations. The first year of Hitler's conduct of foreign policy ended with a great plus for the Reich. Germany had indicated that it no longer felt bound by the military clauses of the Treaty of Versailles and yet was still courted as a participant in international negotiations.

In 1934, the skies darkened for Germany. Himself an Austrian, Hitler felt emotional about the Anschluss. He reacted sharply to measures of the Austrian chancellor, Engelbert Dollfuss, who established a Catholic authoritarian regime with the purpose of keeping Austria independent. By prohibiting Germans from traveling to Austria, Hitler ruined the Austrian tourist industry, and he gave active support to the Austrian Nazi Party, which Dollfuss had outlawed. Austrian Nazis who fled to Germany were organized into a military legion stationed near the border. On July 25, 1934, the Austrian Nazis tried to seize power by force. They succeeded in assassinating Dollfuss, but the putsch failed. Another Catholic chancellor took over and continued Dollfuss's anti-Nazi policy. The German government tried to shake off responsibility for the putsch and dissolved the Austrian legion, but the disclaimers were not believed, and the image of Hitler as a man of peace was severely damaged.

The revelation of Hitler's aggressiveness had two important consequences. France strengthened its bonds with the eastern neighbors of Germany and began to cooperate with Soviet Russia, which was thoroughly alarmed by Hitler's vehement anti-Communism and suspected that his pact with Poland might mean the preparation of a Polish-German war against Russia. Sponsored by the French, the Russians entered the League of Nations in September 1934, and eight months later a Franco-Russian alliance was concluded in which each promised to come to the other's aid against unprovoked aggression.

Hitler's Austrian policy also brought about a change in Italy's attitude. Mussolini had regarded the rise of Hitler with satisfaction and in the first months of 1933 had done his best to calm the fears the Nazi seizure of power had raised in Europe and to dissuade France and Great Britain from taking action. Mussolini, with his antagonism against democracy and pacifism, his contempt for disarmament and the League of Nations, sympathized with Hitler's very similar attitude toward foreign policy. Mussolini saw definite advantages in a strengthened Germany, envisaging Italy as a balance wheel between Britain and France on one side and Germany on the other, and hoping that by acting as a broker, Italy would gain increased power. But he recognized that the absorption of Austria by Germany would be counter to Italy's interests. Germany might then interfere in Italy's sphere of interest in the Danube Valley and the Balkans. Moreover, with a greater Germany on the other side of the Brenner Pass, the Germans under Italian rule in South Tyrol would become entirely intractable. Mussolini therefore helped Dollfuss to establish his anti-Nazi dictatorship, and when the news of Dollfuss's assassination came, he sent troops to the Brenner frontier to show that he would not permit the Anschluss. From cautious support of Hitler, Mussolini had moved into the anti-Nazi camp. In January 1935, negotiations in Rome with the French foreign minister, Pierre Laval (1883–1945), led to an agreement that even envisaged conversations between the French and Italian military staffs with the purpose of arranging for concerted action in case of war with Germany. The deterioration of the German position became evident when Hitler made his next move. In March 1935, he declared the disarmament clauses of the Treaty of Versailles abolished and announced a great augmentation of the German Army and the introduction of general conscription. In a conference at Stresa, Great Britain, France, and Italy agreed to a sharp condemnation of this unilateral violation of an international treaty, declared their interest in the maintenance of Austrian independence, and threatened that further aggressive actions would evoke not only protests but counteraction. At this time Germany, except for the understanding with Poland, was isolated and seemed unable to move.

But the situation changed rapidly. Two months later, in June, Great Britain and Germany signed a naval agreement that defined the relative strength of their navies. Germany was permitted to have as many submarines as Britain, while the strength of the rest of the German fleet was to be restricted to one-third that of the British fleet. Among the many mistakes of British foreign policy with respect to Nazi Germany, the conclusion of the Anglo-German naval agreement is the most incomprehensible. The practical advantages for Britain were slight, for Germany was more interested in building a strong force of submarines than in creating a high-seas navy. The political disadvantages were immense, since by recognizing this departure from the military provisions of the Treaty of Versailles, Britain undermined the basis on which the Stresa front had been formed. Strangely enough, the British government seems not to have foreseen the implications of this naval agreement with Germany and was apparently guided by purely technical considerations, notably the belief that the fixed strength of the German Navy would facilitate negotiations with other powers about naval limitations.

The Italian Conquest of Ethiopia

Hitler, however, was encouraged to continue an aggressive foreign policy, and Mussolini felt himself confirmed in his view that democracies were unable to act vigorously; therefore, cooperation with Hitler could produce more concrete results than cooperation with Britain and France. Military conversations between the French and Italian staffs were postponed. Moreover, although Mussolini had found cooperation with France and Great Britain useful for the preservation of Austrian independence, he expected to be paid for his support, and he decided to cash in as quickly as possible. The result was the Italo-Ethiopian War. The Italian conquest of Ethiopia, completed in May 1936, in a sense constituted revenge for the old defeat at Adua, a visible demonstration that Fascist Italy had become a great imperial power, stronger and more influential than democratic and parliamentary Italy had been. Also, Mussolini hoped to settle some of Italy's surplus population in Ethiopia In his negotiations with Mussolini in January 1935, Laval had indicated that France would have no objection to extension of the Italian influence over Ethiopia, and Mussolini expected a similar attitude from Great Britain. But strangely enough, while Hitler's actions had always found defenders in Britain, Mussolini's invasion of Ethiopia met vehement indignation. To the British people, this seemed the occasion to set in motion the machinery of the League of Nations against aggression. When, in December 1935, it appeared that the British foreign secretary, Sir Samuel Hoare (1880–1959), was willing to make a bargain with Mussolini, popular excitement in Britain was so great that Hoare was dismissed and replaced by Anthony Eden (1897–1977), a strong advocate of the League of Nations and of collective security. But this did not mean that after the rejection of the bargain with Mussolini by the British public the government had now decided to carry out a policy of collective security even if it should result in war. The British continued to pursue an ineffectual middle course; they were not too

German troops advance to occupy the Rhineland, March 7, 1936.

unhappy when the French tried to slow down their attempts to use sanctions against Italy, and they hesitated to insist on the application of the one effective sanction—the cutting off of Italy's oil supplies. The result was that in the League of Nations the British demanded only halfhearted measures, which embittered the Italians against Great Britain and France without preventing their advance in Ethiopia.

The Remilitarization of the Rhineland

It was in this situation, on March 7, 1936, that Hitler ended the demilitarization of the Rhineland by ordering his troops to march into the region, thus violating not only the Treaty of Versailles but also the Locarno pact. Hitler counted on the disarray into which the Ethiopian war had put the Stresa front to prevent action by the Western powers. Nevertheless, he was aware that he was gambling. As he later stated, the twenty-four hours while he was waiting for the reaction of the French were the most exciting and nerve-racking of his life. If the French had answered by sending troops into the Rhineland, the German forces would have been withdrawn to the right bank of the Rhine. This was the condition the German military leaders had forced on Hitler before agreeing to this move. But there was no French military response. Hitler's gamble had come off, and the political balance in Europe was entirely altered. As long as the Rhineland had been demilitarized and the important industrial areas of the Ruhr had remained unprotected, France had held the military advantage and had been in no real danger of attack. Now, with German troops near the French border and the Ruhr area in the hinterland, a conflict with Germany would mean bitter and serious war. Germany was again the strongest military power on the European continent.

CHAPTER 7

Toward the Inevitable Conflict

THE YEARS OF APPEASEMENT

How DID the Western powers, Great Britain and France, react to the threat which the rise of Nazi Germany represented to the system established after the First World War? Or, as we might ask with the wisdom of hindsight, why for almost a decade was their response so very weak? The obvious answer is of course that they too were hard hit by the economic crisis and that their forces and resources were absorbed in the struggle to overcome their economic difficulties. But although this answer is correct, it does not go far below the surface. The economic crisis had such a powerful effect in Great Britain and in France because after the First World War, neither had adjusted their economic activities and institutional structures to the new developments and the new constellation of forces that had arisen during the war or whose emergence the First World War had accelerated. To understand the hesitation of the British and French governments to take up the challenge represented by the rise of Nazism, we have to go back beyond the thirties to the economic situation and the social problems Great Britain and France had faced ever since the end of the First World War.

Great Britain

The economic world crisis did not create Great Britain's economic vulnerability; it only made people aware of it. During the First World War the diminution of foreign assets as a result of the overseas procurement of war materials had sapped the strength of an economy in which imports exceeded exports. Furthermore, after the war, the British government adopted two courses of action which, though they seemed safe and appropriate in the relatively prosperous period of the middle 1920s, turned out in the subsequent depression to severely aggravate the economic crisis and retard recovery: one was the industrial policy that centered in the handling of the general strike in 1926; the other was the return to the gold standard in 1925.

THE GENERAL STRIKE

The general strike of 1926 developed out of a crisis in the British coal industry, which had been lagging behind its German and American competitors even before the First World War and was now also hit severely by the increasing use of oil. During the war, coal mining had been controlled by the government; the return of the mines to private ownership led, unavoidably, to a crisis. The miners' trade union demanded guarantees that a general wage level would be maintained. The owners were not willing to give these guarantees because some of the mines were considerably less profitable than others and many were not profitable at all. Three-fourths of all British coal was produced at a loss. With the help of government subsidies a showdown was postponed, and the French occupation of the Ruhr, which temporarily eliminated the competition of German coal, gave relief to the British coal industry. But in 1923, after the German passive resistance in the Ruhr had ended, a crisis could no longer be avoided. When wage contracts had to be renegotiated, the owners and the miners' trade unions were at loggerheads about a reduction of wages, an extension of working hours, and so on. A commission established by the government sided with the workers rather than the owners in its report and recommended a thorough reorganization of the coal-mining industry. But though in its general tenor the report was favorable to the workers, it did suggest that they accept wage reductions pending reorganization. On this issue negotiations broke down. The miners were backed by all the British trade unions, and the consequence was a general strike lasting ten days, in May 1926. Prime Minister Baldwin had probably been anxious to avoid this gigantic industrial conflict. But some members of his government, eager to put labor in its place, considered a showdown desirable.

The government was well prepared for a general strike. A state of emergency was declared, the country was divided into districts under civil commissioners supported by civil servants, and a force of volunteers trained for such an emergency was mobilized. The most urgently needed services were maintained, and food supplies reached the cities. Thus, the government gradually neutralized the major effects of the work stoppage, and some members of the cabinet, among them Neville Chamberlain and Winston Churchill, urged that the strike be declared illegal, its instigators imprisoned, and the funds of the trade unions confiscated. The union leaders feared that when the financial reserves of the unions were depleted, either the strike would peter out or the workers in their desperation would resort to force, perhaps causing civil war. Therefore, relying on a compromise formula that envisaged wage reductions only after measures of reorganization in the coal industry had been effectively adopted, they called off the general strike. It was a defeat for the workers, all the more humiliating because the miners, infuriated by the suggestion of wage reductions in the compromise formula, continued to strike throughout the summer. But then their powers of resistance were exhausted. Increasingly discouraged, they returned to work. They had no national contract, only local and regional contracts; the overall result was that they had to work longer hours for lower wages.

In the prosperity of the second part of the 1920s English life took on something of the glamour of the prewar years, and the general strike soon seemed a thing of the past. But its consequences were far-reaching. The opportunity for a thorough overhauling of the coal industry had been missed; it continued to ail, and the mining regions remained centers of low wages and unemployment. The bleakness, hardships, and dangers of life among British coal miners have found literary expression in George Orwell's realistic and moving *Road to Wigan Pier* (1937).

Moreover, the general strike increased distrust between the working class and the rest of the population. The failure of the government to force concessions on the employers that would have prevented the stoppage raised suspicions about the intentions of the ruling group, and they were reinforced by the intransigent and vehement pronouncements of some of its members while the strike was in progress. After its collapse, Baldwin took a conciliatory attitude, urging that industry reinstate the workers without reducing wages. But he lacked energy in the pursuit of this policy and was not able to restrain his anti-labor colleagues. In 1927, the Conservative majority in Parliament struck a blow against the trade unions by passing a bill that limited the right to strike to trade disputes; sympathy strikes became illegal. Furthermore, the unions were no longer allowed to collect money for political purposes. The intransigence of the government stiffened the resistance of the workers against all measures that might involve a temporary reduction in wages or a temporary increase in unemployment through the closing of unprofitable enterprises. To compete effectively on the world market, British industry required modernization, but this was not feasible without the workers' cooperation, which was unobtainable after the general strike.

Equally fatal for Britain's economy was the return to the gold standard that Winston Churchill, Conservative chancellor of the exchequer, announced in his first budget speech in April 1925. At this time nobody questioned the principle that the basic unit in a currency must be defined as equivalent to a stated quantity of gold. The mistake of Churchill's measure was not so much that the pound was tied again to a fixed weight of gold as that the ratio chosen—namely, the prewar parity—was too high. Churchill was acting on the advice of the governor of the Bank of England, who hoped that by returning to the prewar standard, London would regain the dominating position in the money market it had lost to New York during the First World War. However, the result of this step was an increase in the price of British goods on the world market and hence a weakening of Britain's position in international trade. This effect was the more dangerous because of Great Britain's adverse balance of trade. Financiers would now view every further widening of the gap between exports and imports as seriously endangering British economic life. Furthermore,

British unemployment during the Great Depression. Workers wait for news of job possibilities at the labor exchange at Wigan Pier.

lulled into false security by the prosperity of the nineteenth century, British industrialists had been remiss in renewing and modernizing their equipment; now the decline in profits made investments for these purposes impossible. John Maynard Keynes was one of the few who realized that the return to prewar parity represented a further "competitive handicap." In general, these difficulties were fully recognized only after it was too late, when the prosperity of the later 1920s had ended in depression.

From 1924 to 1929 a Conservative government was in power, headed by Stanley Baldwin. He had risen to a leading position in the Conservative Party only after the war. He was very different from the great aristocrats Salisbury and Balfour, who had been Conservative prime ministers earlier in the century and who might have had a sharper understanding of the change in the distribution of political and economic power brought about by the war. Baldwin was a rich industrialist, and his assumption of the Conservative leadership indicates the importance businessmen had gained in the party. However, he was not the conventional businessman: unsentimental, purposeful and efficient. He was lazy and had no clear program or plans. He acted only when action was unavoidable, and then his conduct was determined by intuition rather than cold reason. In his expressions of longing for a quiet and peaceful life, remote from the turbulence of industrial society, he reflected perfectly the nostalgic mood of the middle classes, which were frightened by the size of the problems of the postwar world and constructed an idealized picture of the stability and prosperity of Victorian and Edwardian England. Thus, Baldwin was content to see some of the splendor of prewar England return in the later 1920s without questioning how firm and deep-rooted the prosperity of this period was. Moreover, Baldwin's easygoing attitude permitted his cabinet a free hand; energetic ministers were able to make their own policy. The tenure of Austen Chamberlain as foreign secretary was a success. His half brother Neville Chamberlain (1869–1940), minister of health, enlarged the system of social security by gaining passage of an old-age pension bill. Churchill, chancellor of the exchequer, tried to stimulate industry by lowering income taxes and increasing death duties. But the manner in which, against Baldwin's expressed desire, Churchill and Chamberlain insisted on making use of the defeat of the general strike to obtain passage of legislation curtailing the power of labor showed the tension that existed below the surface during these few fat years.

When signs of an incipient depression appeared, the popularity of the Conservatives was immediately reduced, and as a result of elections held in June 1929, another Labor government under Ramsay MacDonald came into power. Actually, the Conservatives still remained the strongest in the popular vote, but the boundaries of the electoral districts were drawn in such a way that Labor received 280 seats in the House of Commons and the Conservatives only 261; the 59 Liberal members turned the scales. Because, as in 1924, the Labor government relied on Liberal support, radical measures involving socialization were precluded, but Labor had no real program for solving the unemployment problem within the existing economic system. The government's freedom of action was further limited because MacDonald had given the chancellorship of the exchequer to Philip Snowden (1864–1937), an old member of the Labor Party and a convinced adherent of free trade and economic orthodoxy. Meanwhile, with the spread of the depression unemployment increased until in December 1930 it reached 2.5 million, about 1.5 million more than when Labor had come into power eighteen months previously. With income from taxation declining and payments to the unemployed rising, the budget became unbalanced. A committee that investigated the economic situation took a very gloomy view. Its report recommended economies in government and particularly a reduction in unemployment benefits. This pessimistic evaluation of the British economy coincided with the financial crisis in Germany, in which British banking interests were deeply involved. A panic followed, and the consequence was that those who owned pounds transformed them into other currencies: a flight from the pound set in; a currency crisis was added to the budget crisis. Because Labor had no majority in the House of Commons, negotiations with the leaders of the other parties became necessary; urged on by British and American bankers, these leaders made their further support contingent upon a reduction in unemployment benefits. This was a bitter pill, hard to swallow for members of a Labor government. When the members of the government could come to no agreement on whether to accept such a cut, resignation seemed inevitable; a coalition of Conservatives and Liberals was expected to take over. But instead of submitting his resignation, MacDonald astonished his party with the announcement that he had agreed to remain as prime minister, heading a national government that would include the leaders of all three parties. Most members of the Labor Party refused to follow him; only two Labor politicians of reputation—Snowden and J. H. Thomas (1874–1949)—accepted positions in the new government. A national Labor Party that MacDonald founded remained insignificant. Nevertheless, MacDonald's "treason"—as his action was regarded by his former party associates—was a blow from which the Labor Party began to recover only at the end of the 1930s.

MacDonald's behavior in this crisis is a puzzle. Many ascribe it to defects in his character, particularly to his vanity and social snobbery. When after the formation of the national government MacDonald was told that he would find himself popular in unfamiliar circles, he is reported to have exclaimed, "Yes, tomorrow every duchess in London will be wanting to kiss me." But it should not be forgotten that his socialist beliefs arose from a vague political idealism. He had never been a Marxist and had never concerned himself with economic analysis. In economic questions he was accustomed to following the views of experts, and he was probably honestly persuaded that he was placing country before party.

FROM RAMSAY MACDONALD TO NEVILLE CHAMBERLAIN

The new government began by introducing severe measures of economy: a reduction in the salaries of civil servants and a cut in unemployment benefits, which were now limited to twenty-six weeks a year and given only after a means test. Wage reductions in the armed services led to a mutiny in the British Navy at Invergordon, Scotland, and although the mutiny ended quickly, it triggered a new financial panic. The government reacted with a step that a few months before would have been considered out of the question: taking the pound off the gold standard. As a result, the share of British exports in world trade remained relatively stable. Elections held on October 27, 1931, to provide a popular mandate for the government resulted in its overwhelming triumph; Labor received 46 seats, while the parties in the national government now had 556, of which 472 were Conservative. Although the label of national government was retained and MacDonald ended his tenure only in 1935, actually the Conservative Party ruled in Britain until the Second World War.

Stanley Baldwin remained leader of the Conservative Party and as such was the most powerful figure in the national government, even while MacDonald was prime minister. After MacDonald's withdrawal, Baldwin took over the prime ministership. He resigned two years later, in 1937, at the height of his influence and fame. These had been immensely increased by his skillful handling of the crisis brought about by Edward VIII's insistence on marrying a divorcée, a matter that ended with his abdication as king. Baldwin's successor as prime minister was Neville Chamberlain, a son of Joseph Chamberlain. In his family, Neville had been regarded as inferior in political talent to his older brother Austen; Neville therefore had been destined for a business career. When he finally entered political life, he became concerned primarily with affairs of economic policy. After he had been minister of health in the Conservative government of the 1920s, he served as chancellor of the exchequer in the national government; as such he was chiefly responsible for the manner in which the national government tried to lift Great Britain out of the depression.

The economic policy of the national government was strictly orthodox. The main aim was to keep the budget balanced and, as far as was compatible with this aim, to stimulate industry by keeping taxes low. Under the shield of a national government, the Conservatives were able to carry through a measure that symbolized the death of the liberal England of the nineteenth century: they introduced protective tariffs. For the party of Joseph Chamberlain, and especially for his son, this was a unique opportunity to establish closer economic ties between Great Britain and its empire by means of preferential tariffs. To do so seemed the more desirable because in the course of the twentieth century the cohesion of the British Empire had steadily weakened. The bond between Great Britain and the dominions (Australia, Canada, New Zealand, the Union of South Africa, and the Irish Free State) had become tenuous, sentimental rather than legal. A formula accepted by Great Britain and the dominions at a conference in 1926 stated that the dominions were "autonomous communities within the British Empire, equal in status, in no way subordinate one to another in any aspect of their domestic or external affairs, though united by a common allegiance to the Crown, and freely associated as members of the British Commonwealth of Nations." In 1931, the Statute of Westminster defined this new notion of a British Commonwealth of Nations in contractual constitutional terms. Because the dominions regarded themselves as fully independent in domestic and foreign policy, they gave a cool reception to the British government's suggestion to improve the economic situation by preferential tariffs among the members of the empire. The negotiations in Ottawa during the summer of 1932 were difficult, and the results fell far short of Joseph Chamberlain's dream of free trade within the empire; essentially, it was agreed that the dominions would retain their existing duties on industrial products from Great Britain but would raise duties on industrial products from other countries.

Thus, the economic policy of the British government remained cautious. Neville Chamberlain himself called the course he pursued a "pegging away." Indeed, a gradual but slow economic recovery, assisted by a general improvement in the world economic situation, took place in Britain. But the industrial apparatus was never thoroughly overhauled, and in the severely depressed areas, people continued to live close to starvation. Unemployment never went below a million.

The issues the British government had to handle in the 1930s—independence of the dominions, unrest in India, shocks like the abdication crisis, and, most important, the economic difficulties of Great Britain—were diverse and complex. Since a balanced budget was the cornerstone of British economic policy, the government shied away from new, additional burdens that could easily unbalance the budget and might halt the march toward recovery. There was great reluctance therefore to embark on a policy of rearmament or to pursue a foreign policy that demanded a strengthening of Britain's military forces. To justify this reluctance, most members of the ruling Conservative Party tended to minimize the dangers that threatened from the dictators, particularly from the rise of Hitler, and to take an overly optimistic view of the possibility of coming to peaceful terms with them. Churchill, almost alone among the Conservatives, raised a warning voice against Hitler's aggressive tendencies. But at this time his political influence was at its lowest. While Labor's opposition to the dictators was clear and definite, the pacifist tradition in the party made the Laborites unwilling to accept the necessity of military rearmament; their recommendation of relying on collective security was rather unrealistic.

There was an influential group in the British ruling class, however, that regarded the rise of Nazism with a favorable eye. To this group belonged Geoffrey Dawson, the influential editor of the London *Times*, who since the early 1920s had been fighting a pretended pro-French orientation of British foreign policy; and empire-minded politicians like Lord Lothian, who wanted to free England from bonds to the Continent; and Germanophile aristocrats like the Astors, who saw Hitler as a restorer of the good German society of imperial days. The benevolent attitude of this group toward Hitler arose from a variety of sources. The members of the group accepted the revisionist thesis that Germany had been unfairly treated in the Treaty of Versailles and that Germany would be a satisfied and peaceful power if these injustices were removed. They had a certain admiration for the disciplined and orderly German ways that Hitler was supposed to have reintroduced; moreover, because Germany was the strongest nation in Europe, they believed that Germany was entitled to hegemony on the European continent and would then keep that restless continent orderly and quiet. They were inclined to believe the Nazi propaganda thesis, that before the Nazi seizure of power, Germany had been in danger of becoming Communist, and they were anxious to have on the European continent a powerful force that would form a dam against the spread of Communism. The importance of this group—the Cliveden set, as it has been called after the country place of the Astors—lies in the fact that it influenced and almost prescribed the policy Neville Chamberlain followed after he became prime minister in 1937.

Neville Chamberlain turned his particular attention to foreign policy because he was impatient with the disturbances of economic life by political crises. He possessed a naïve arrogance that considered all other peoples inferior to the British, so that there was not much difference whether they were democracies or dictatorships. He saw no reason therefore why Britain should not come to an understanding with the dictators, and lacking in imagination, he had no inkling of the dynamic expansionism inherent in Nazism. Chamberlain approached the negotiations with Hitler as a businessman approaches a deal with other businessmen, trusting that among men of property and common sense a bargain to reciprocal advantage should always be possible. If Great Britain showed Hitler goodwill by a number of concessions, he assumed, Hitler would be willing to cooperate with Great Britain in maintaining peace. With such misconceptions, Neville Chamberlain embarked hopefully on a policy of appeasement. The original view of the Chamberlain family that Neville lacked political talents proved fully justified.

France
Although the French reaction to Nazi expansion was as weak as that of Great Britain, the weakness of French foreign policy had very different origins. In the 1930s a net drop in population and a shift in the French economic structure contributed to a sense of national decline, unrest, and tension.

Although France had acquired Alsace-Lorraine as a result of the war, its losses had been so heavy that in 1921, when the first postwar census was taken, its population—39,210,000 people—was smaller than in 1914. During the First World War, and for many years after, the French government never dared make an official statement about the number of men killed in the war. More than a quarter of the 1.4 million dead or missing would have been between twenty and twenty-five years of age by the end of the war; this necessarily resulted in a decline in births, and in the middle of the 1930s the number of births became smaller than the number of deaths. The following year the population began to increase again, but only because of the immigration of foreigners into France. The lack of manpower and the need for using the available manpower in economic life led the French to reduce conscription to one year; France was less formidable than it might have appeared after the victory in the First World War.

While the demographic statistics presented a somber picture, the tension that accompanied the shift in the French economic structure might be regarded as a kind of growing pain. At the beginning of the decade, in 1931, 45.1 percent of the labor force was employed in industry, in contrast to 36.1 percent twenty-five years before; clearly there had been a shift from agriculture to industry. Particularly noticeable was the growth of heavy industry, such as mining, iron and steel production, and the manufacture of machinery; for instance, in 1931 the iron and steel industry employed over a hundred thousand more men than in 1906. Accompanying this development, during the interwar years, was a trend toward industrial concentration. The increasing importance of the workers led to demands for an active social policy, while the French bourgeoisie, frightened by the Russian Revolution, the loss of Russian investments, and the inflation of the early 1920s, tended to regard labor's claims as the beginning of a dangerous revolutionary development.

During the 1930s these tensions were sharpened by a deterioration of the economic and financial situation. Throughout the preceding decade French economic development had been favorable. Reconstruction of the destroyed areas, completed by 1926, had resulted in a modernization of industrial installations. Poincaré, who in 1926 had returned as prime minister, though without influence on foreign policy, had quickly ended the inflation by drastic economies that balanced the budget. The nation entered the depression period in an economically strong position, and because France was more self-sufficient than other highly industrialized powers, it remained, at least at first, relatively immune to the effects of the depression. The French government made use of this economic strength in the critical political and financial negotiations about the Anschluss and the Hoover moratorium during the hectic summer of 1931. In the following years, however, the general weakness of the international markets had repercussions on France. Exports declined rapidly. If those of 1912 are taken as a base and represented by 100, they had risen to 125 in 1929 but declined to 59 in 1936. The decrease in exports resulted in a steadily widening deficit in the balance of trade, reaching 64 percent in 1936, and was accompanied by a lower rate of industrial production, which in 1935 was back at the prewar level. Because of the demographic situation, unemployment was a less serious problem in France than in Germany or Great Britain; nevertheless, in 1935 the number of unemployed had reached half a million. A degree of waste in government spending, of slight consequence in the days of prosperity, now resulted in budget deficits. Fear of inflation led to a flight from the franc. The parties of the left regarded these problems chiefly as the result of the selfish attempts of the rich to save their own fortunes; economic difficulties would end if the flight from the franc could be stopped. Thus, it was difficult, if not impossible, for the government to get parliament to accept measures of economy and tax increases. Because only stopgap actions were taken, the situation continued to deteriorate, and the politicians were accused of incompetence and corruption. By the end of 1934, both Poincaré and Briand were dead, and the political leaders of this period—Édouard Herriot, Édouard Daladier, André Tardieu— lacked the prestige and the authority enjoyed by their predecessors—the heroes of the Dreyfus Affair and the French victory.

A striking indication of the tension developing in French society was the Stavisky Affair of 1934. In comparison to the Dreyfus Affair, which had involved great questions of principle, this was a murky business, a small financial swindle revealing some corruption. But the Stavisky scandal has its place in history because it showed that the old conflict between right and left—existing since the French Revolution, surfacing in the Dreyfus Affair but seemingly overcome by the national revival brought on by the First World War—had broken out again, in renewed strength. The eagerness with which the scandal was blown up into a crisis of republican and democratic institutions was an expression of the desperate feeling of the French middle classes that they were losing out against the forces of big business and labor. The explosion caused by the Stavisky Affair must also be regarded as a sign of the malaise arising from the impression that the successive French governments had wasted the brilliant position France had gained with its victory in the First World War.

Serge Alexander Stavisky was a financial swindler of tremendous charm and ingenuity. He had managed to make many acquaintances among politicians, and because he had served as an informer, his relations with the police were good. If not for these contacts the fraudulence of his financial dealings would have been discovered earlier. When finally his enterprise collapsed, puzzling things happened. The police surrounded his house but reached Stavisky only after he had shot himself. One of the judges investigating the scandal was found dead on the railroad tracks. Rumors spread that Stavisky had not committed suicide but had been shot by the police because he knew too much and that the investigating judge had been eliminated for the same reason. A high official, a brother-in-law of one of the most influential leaders of the Radical Socialists, was suspected of responsibility for silencing the scandal. The rightists boiled over in indignation about the corruption among the parliamentary leaders of the left. When the prime minister, Daladier, dismissed the president of the Paris police, who with little justification was regarded as an embodiment of energy and integrity, war veterans and other organizations of the right arranged demonstrations, marched to the parliament building, and tried to storm it. The police fired, but one of France's most distinguished military leaders announced that on the following day he would march at the head of the demonstrators. Unable or unwilling to face this outburst, Daladier resigned, and a new government of national unity was formed.

The head of the new government was Gaston Doumergue (1863–1937), who had been president of the republic from 1924 to 1931, and it included all the surviving former prime ministers as well as military heroes, such as Marshal Pétain. It was a last—rather ephemeral—attempt to hold together the divergent forces of French society by an appeal to national solidarity and to infuse new life into French foreign policy. Louis Barthou (1862–1934), the foreign minister under Doumergue, tried to make full use of the decline in Hitler's prestige in the summer of 1934 resulting from the purge of the SA and the murder by Nazis of the Austrian chancellor Engelbert Dollfuss. Barthou cold-shouldered British attempts to resume negotiations about armament limitations with Germany and visited the capitals of Czechoslovakia, Yugoslavia, and Romania, which were allied in the so-called Little Entente, and of Russia in order to forge a firm alliance between these powers and France. An "eastern" Locarno, which would prevent German expansion toward the east, was to supplement the "western" Locarno, with its guarantee of the permanence of the Franco-German frontier. But on October 9, 1934, King Alexander of Yugoslavia, on a visit to strengthen his nation's ties with France, was assassinated in Marseilles by a Macedonian nationalist; another victim was Barthou himself, who was seated in the car next to the king. With Barthou's death French foreign policy returned quickly to a dependence on Great Britain.

The Doumergue government made an attempt to overcome the most evident weaknesses of French political life. It concentrated on plans to strengthen the executive at the expense of the legislative, chiefly by facilitating the dissolution of parliament and by depriving deputies of the right to augment suggested financial legislation. But Doumergue overplayed his hand; he tried to overcome resistance by appealing through radio addresses directly to the people. This authoritarian technique went against all republican tradition, and the parliamentarians gained broad support as defenders of democracy against the penetration of "Fascist" ideas into French political life. The Doumergue government fell, and the succeeding governments mainly marked time until the elections scheduled for the spring of 1936. In this period of weak transitional governments Hitler marched into the Rhineland. The French government in power was not strong enough to make a decision which would have demanded an abandonment of the dogma that France could not march alone, that it had to keep in line with England. So instead of ordering its troops into the Rhineland the French government acceded to the urging of England that the issue ought to be solved by negotiations.

The election campaign of 1936 was entirely a struggle between the right and the left. The left fought the election as a Popular Front that reached from the middle-class Radical Socialists to the Communists. The Popular Front won an impressive victory. While the Communists agreed to support the government without actively participating in it, the Socialists, for the first time in French history, entered the government as a party, and their leader, Léon Blum (1872–1950), became prime minister. Blum was a strange figure to be leader of the Socialist Party. He was neither a tough politician nor a Marxist. He was an intellectual, a man of wide culture, and a humanitarian. His sympathies with the underprivileged had brought him into the Socialist camp. His human qualities would shine brilliantly in his courageous stand against the Nazis during the German occupation of France. After the Second World War he would be prime minister again, and at the end of his life he was recognized as a major national figure. But when Blum became prime minister for the first time in June 1936, his particular qualities were little suited to the situation. He was a pacifist, an internationalist, with little interest in the details of foreign policy. His main concern was social reform; he expected to improve the situation of the poorer classes by modernizing French life. A wave of strikes underlining the urgent need for social reform accompanied the formation of the Popular Front government. These strikes were of a new type, the sit-down; the workers refused to work but remained in the factories, making the use of strikebreakers impossible. Removal of the strikers would have required force, which the Popular Front government did not want to employ against its own supporters. Hence the industrialists were forced to make a number of concessions, granting the workers rights their counterparts in

Léon Blum, French prime minister, addressing a meeting.

most other European industrial countries already possessed—compulsory collective bargaining, the forty-hour week, paid holidays—and also wage increases of from 12 percent to 15 percent. These arrangements were negotiated under government auspices and were supplemented by legislative measures intended to restrict the influence of high finance and big business on French policy. The Bank of France was brought under government control; its credit policy could no longer obstruct the financial measures of the government. The armament industry was nationalized, and the government inaugurated a series of public works to fight unemployment. Such reforms were long overdue. Thus, if France was to develop a strong air force, the nationalization of the armament industry was necessary, since it would make possible concentration on a few types of mass-produced airplanes. Even so, because time was needed to harvest the advantages of the change, airplane production in France remained dangerously weak for some years.

Meanwhile, the direct consequences of the measures taken by the Blum government were a sharpening of internal conflicts and then also a weakening of the coherence of the Popular Front. Industrialists and bankers, deeply resentful of the concessions to which they had been forced, continued the flight from the franc and sharply attacked the government policy of spending freely without attempting to balance the budget. The government had promised to maintain the value of the franc but was soon forced to devaluate. This measure spurred fear of inflation among the middle classes, and the Radical Socialists, their representatives in the government, became doubtful about continued cooperation with the parties on the left. First Blum had to declare a "breathing spell" in social reforms to restore confidence among the bourgeois partners in his coalition. Then he was replaced as prime minister by a Radical Socialist, although the Socialists still remained members of the government. Then the Socialists left the government, although they continued to support it in parliament. But in 1938 Daladier, the Radical Socialist prime minister, turned to the right, and the Communists and the Socialists resumed their old roles as members of the opposition.

One reason for the formation of the Popular Front, and the main motive underlying the Communist participation in it, had been to establish a firm stand against the advance of Nazism and Fascism. Unavoidably, many of those who resisted the social program of the Popular Front also opposed its ideas on foreign policy; they complained that both the domestic reforms and the international action against Fascism served the aims of international Communism rather than the national interests of France. "Better Hitler than Blum" was a slogan that spread among the rightists. Only a few organizations, although rather noisy ones, favored a Fascist regime in France, but many adherents of the right believed that because of its terrible losses in the First World War, their nation should avoid involvement in another conflict at almost any cost; they saw no reason that France should obstruct Germany's ambitions in the east. France had built along the German frontier a strong defense line, called the Maginot Line after the politician responsible for its construction. Its conception shows clearly the dilemma that faced French policy. In case of a war against Germany the French troops under arms would not be strong enough to embark immediately on offensive action. This would become possible only after full mobilization and would take time; the Maginot Line was intended to provide the shield behind which the mobilization would take place. On the other hand, the fortified region was limited to the area opposite the German border, from Switzerland to Luxembourg; the more northern part of the frontier was hardly fortified. This was meant to show that the French were able and willing to act energetically in case of a crisis, that they were able to take the offensive, to advance into Germany through Belgium. It was to indicate that they were not willing to give Germany a free hand in eastern Europe. But this concession to the political concepts of the past began to become doubtful in the face of the military realities of the present.

Officially no French government ever admitted that it was willing to write off the alliances with the Eastern European states. But the governments of the right that succeeded the Popular Front were inclined to minimize French commitments rather than to reinforce them. French foreign policy remained strong in words but timid in deeds. Its only serious concern was to avoid separation from Great Britain.

THE DEMOCRACIES IN RETREAT

The militarization of the Rhineland upset the assumptions on which European statesmen had based their foreign policy. Germany was no longer open to French attack, and the great industrial area of the Ruhr was no longer exposed to the fire of French guns. The weakening of the French position had immediate repercussions in eastern and southeastern Europe. Except for Czechoslovakia, which continued to rely on the support of Great Britain and France, the states of this region began to drift into the German orbit; this development was assisted by the German economic policy under the clever direction of Hjalmar Schacht. The eastern European countries, suffering acutely from the slump in agricultural prices, welcomed the opportunity offered by Germany to conclude barter agreements by which they could exchange agricultural products for German manufactured goods. Moreover, the German success in the Rhineland and the Italian triumph in Ethiopia had increased the prestige and appeal of the totalitarian systems. Mussolini, who in the 1920s had declared that Fascism was not an export article, was now proudly proclaiming that the democracies were obsolete and decaying and that Fascism represented the wave of the future. The various dictatorial regimes in Poland, Yugoslavia, Hungary, Romania, and Bulgaria now began to imitate Fascist or National Socialist forms and methods and claimed that their systems of government embodied a new political spirit, appropriate to the twentieth century.

Mussolini's praise of Fascism as a young international force that would triumph over the dying world of the democracies indicated that he had moved into the German camp. Close cooperation between Italy and Nazi Germany was established by October 1936, after the trip to Germany of Count Galeazzo Ciano (1903–1944), Mussolini's foreign minister and son-in-law. The so-called Rome-Berlin Axis was then confirmed by an exchange of visits, with Mussolini going to Berlin in September 1937 and Hitler to Rome in May 1938. The meetings of the two dictators were accompanied by immense military reviews, which were recorded on film so that the world would be impressed with the might of the Fascist powers. The Western democracies were confronted by the alternatives of opposition by force and negotiations ending in concessions. Appeasement began.

The Spanish Civil War
The event in which the Axis powers first tested the democracies' will to resist was the Spanish Civil War. The contest in Spain was bitter, vehement, and long because it represented the clash of forces deeply rooted in Spanish social and intellectual life. Essentially a struggle of modern industrial and democratic forces against the continued existence of agrarian feudalism, it became enmeshed with the traditional movements for regional independence against Castilian centralism and with the age-old dispute about the position of the church in Spanish social life.

In 1931, the inability of the Spanish Army to put down a Moroccan uprising compromised the monarchy and the ruling group; revolt followed, and a republic was established in which full power was held by a democratically elected parliament. From the beginning, the republican regime led a precarious existence. The new constitution separated church and state, but attempts to remove the church from all activities that were not strictly religious aroused the resistance of the Catholic hierarchy and of many Catholics among the population. The workers, by tradition radical and anarchist, were dissatisfied by the failure of the republican government to put through anticapitalist measures. Riots, strikes, and burnings of churches occurred in various parts of the country; violence led to a resurgence of rightist parties, and the counterrevolutionaries organized themselves into a movement on the Fascist pattern, the Falange. To fight reaction, all the parties from the center to the extreme left joined together in a Popular Front, which triumphed in the elections of February 1936, more than two months before the victory of the French Popular Front.

The victors regarded their success as a mandate to purge the administration of reactionaries and to go ahead with a program of modernization and social reform. The Popular Front government took steps to divide the great estates, it forced industrialists to take back workers who had been dismissed because of participation in strikes, and it closed Catholic schools. But the far-reaching nature of these measures spurred the rightist opposition to action. The military had been considering a coup d'état for a long time; now the Spanish antirepublicans received encouragement from Mussolini, who promised money and weapons. A putsch was planned for the middle of July 1936. On July 12, 1936, the murder of the monarchist leader by a republican who was captain of the police played right into the hands of the conspirators. This crime seemed to show that the government was unable to guarantee order and security and gave

Nationalist troops in Madrid, 1936.

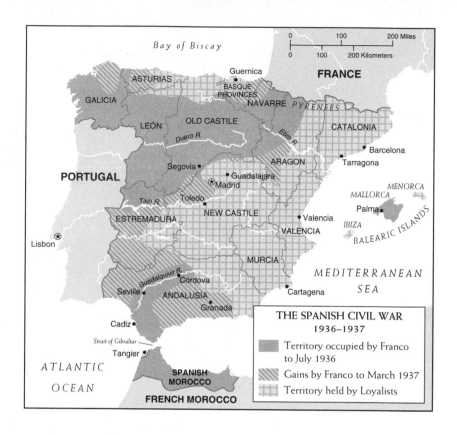

Bay of Biscay

0   100   200 Miles

0   100   200 Kilometers

FRANCE

Guernica

ASTURIAS

BASQUE PROVINCES

GALICIA

NAVARRE *PYRENEES*

OLD CASTILE

LEÓN

Duero R.

CATALONIA

Ebro R.

Barcelona

Segovia

ARAGON

Tarragona

PORTUGAL

Guadalajara

⊕Madrid

MENORCA

MALLORCA

Tajo R. Toledo

Palma

ESTREMADURA

NEW CASTILE

Valencia

IBIZA

VALENCIA

BALEARIC ISLANDS

Lisbon ⊛

MURCIA

MEDITERRANEAN

Guadalquivir R. Cordova

Seville

ANDALUSIA

Cartagena

SEA

Granada

THE SPANISH CIVIL WAR

Cadiz

1936–1937

Strait of Gibraltar

Tangier

Territory occupied by Franco to July 1936

ATLANTIC

OCEAN

SPANISH MOROCCO

Gains by Franco to March 1937

Territory held by Loyalists

FRENCH MOROCCO

some justification for the rebellion, which erupted on July 17. Although the revolt was popular among upper- and middle-class groups and had the active support of organizations like the Falange, it began primarily as an officers' conspiracy. The officers ordered their troops to occupy government buildings and took over the administrations of various towns or entrusted them to rightist political leaders.

The course of the Spanish Civil War was long and confused. Originally the military coup was not a success. The generals seized power in extended areas of northern and northwestern Spain and in North Africa, where the best-trained units of the army were stationed under General Francisco Franco (1892–1975). But the entire southwest (except for a few small isolated areas), the center of Spain, and the Basque coast in the north remained loyal to the republic. By the end of July the ground forces of the two opposing camps were numerically roughly equal. To strengthen their forces, the republican leaders, after some hesitation, distributed weapons to the workers. The resulting dependence on the masses led to a government shift toward the left, with the socialists, Communists, and anarchists becoming increasingly influential.

After the incomplete success of the military putsch both sides appealed for foreign aid: the republicans to France and Russia, the military to Italy and Germany. The Fascist powers were quick to respond. Mussolini sent bombing planes; Hitler authorized the immediate dispatch of some twenty transport planes. The acquisition of these airplanes was crucial; the Spanish Navy had remained loyal to the republican government, and air transport was the only means for bringing the well-disciplined Moroccan troops from Africa into Spain. Hitler said correctly, some years later: "Franco ought to erect a monument to the glory of the German transport aircraft. The Spanish Revolution of Franco has to thank this aircraft for its victory." By means of the Moroccan troops led by Franco, the Spanish Fascists succeeded in extending their rule over the south of Spain and in establishing a bridge to the territory they controlled in the north. By the end of September the republicans no longer had a common frontier with Portugal. But even though the Fascists advanced in four columns into the suburbs of Madrid and had a "fifth column" of adherents within the city, their attempt to take the capital failed as the Spanish republicans rose heroically to its defense in the winter of 1936–1937. The Fascists halted outside Madrid and from there extended their rule toward the west. Only three regions remained under republican control. One of these stretched from Madrid to southeastern Spain. It was connected by a small coastal strip with the second center of republican power, Catalonia. Finally, the Basque country in the north, along the Atlantic coast, remained republican. Isolated as they were, these centers of republican strength were no match for the Fascists, who conquered one after the other. The anti-Fascist regime in the Basque area fell in the summer of 1937. Then the war dragged on. Barcelona, the chief city of Catalonia, was taken in January 1939, and thousands of freezing and starving Spanish republicans along with the remaining republican troops—altogether almost four hundred thousand people—crossed the frontiers to France, where on open land, fenced in by wires, lacking shelter and food, they dragged on their lives. Two months later, in March 1939, Madrid surrendered. By then Spain was no longer a center of international politics.

The Spanish Civil War and European Diplomacy
The war was not just an internal Spanish affair. It was a struggle in which directly or indirectly the whole of Europe was involved. If the dispatch of German and Italian planes had been crucial in revitalizing the military revolt after its initial setback, the arrival of Russian tanks and aircraft in the fall of 1936 decisively helped the republican defense of Madrid against the renewed attack of the Fascists; moreover, Russian advisers gave coherence to the somewhat disorganized military effort of the republicans. Germany and Italy responded by boosting the Spanish Fascist regime with diplomatic recognition. But they also gave concrete assistance. The Germans sent more aircraft, and pilots as well—bomber squadrons of the so-called Condor Legion. The most famous—or infamous—

exploit of the German fliers was the attack on Guernica during Franco's campaign against the Basque country (April 1937). First they bombed the small rural town; then they machine-gunned the streets, killing and wounding about twenty-five hundred of the seven thousand inhabitants. Later the Germans would admit that this assault had been an experiment to test the effects of terror bombing.

Mussolini concluded a secret treaty with Franco in November 1936 that secured Italy against the possibility of French-Spanish cooperation, promised Spanish benevolent neutrality in case of a war, and if necessary, the establishment of Italian bases on Majorca and Spanish territory. Mussolini now ordered the transportation of volunteer Blackshirt brigades, under the command of Italian officers, to Spain; by February 1937 forty-eight thousand Italians were fighting there. But they were badly trained and disciplined; driven into an offensive by Mussolini's expectation that Italian help would quickly end the war in Franco's favor, they received a severe setback at Guadalajara, near Madrid (March 1937). This loss of prestige impelled Mussolini to continue sending troops and now, most important, airplanes to Spain.

Undoubtedly the German and the Italian assistance to the Fascists was more effective than the Russian aid to the republicans, especially since the long route through the Mediterranean from the Black Sea was threatened by German and Italian submarines and warships. A balance could have been struck if the republicans had received airplanes, tanks, and supplies from the north, from France. But though Léon Blum, the French prime minister, was willing to send assistance, he was opposed by the British leaders and the non-Socialist members of his own government, who feared international complications, particularly the strengthening of Communism. Blum yielded to these pressures despite the indignation of the Communists and of many members of his own Socialist Party.

Disagreement concerning the Spanish Civil War was an important factor in breaking up the French Popular Front. Hoping to localize the conflict, France and Great Britain suggested to the other powers a policy of nonintervention. The negotiations to implement this policy were long and drawn out, and even after Russia, Germany, and Italy had been won over and a committee entrusted with the supervision of nonintervention had been established, Germany and Italy raised endless difficulties; they finally withdrew their troops only when they felt sure that doing so would not endanger the victory of Fascism in Spain.

For Hitler and Mussolini the Spanish Civil War was heartening proof of the weakness of their adversaries; they learned that although Russia, France, and Great Britain might be opposed to any disturbance of the status quo, they did not agree about how to control Fascist aggression. Evidently the main concern of the Western powers was to avoid war.

But the Spanish Civil War did more than reveal the immense strength the Fascist powers had gained. With the failure of the democracies, the opposition to

Francisco Franco enjoys
dinner at the front during
the Spanish Civil War.

Fascism lost its drive. When the Spanish Civil War began, it had seemed evident that the democratic forces had right on their side and that democracy and Fascism met in Spain in a situation of equality—not prejudiced in favor of Fascism. It had appeared that if Fascism received a check in Spain, the myth of its inevitable progress would be destroyed. After this one great effort the Fascist nightmare under which Europe lived might disappear.

> Tomorrow for the young the poets exploding like bombs,
> The walks by the lake, the weeks of perfect communion;
> Tomorrow the bicycle races
> Through the suburbs on summer evenings. But today the struggle.[1]

Men from all over the globe volunteered to fight for the Spanish republic. One of the most efficient of the republican military units was the International Brigade, in which Communists, socialists, and liberals served. Writers of many nationalities—George Orwell, who was British; Ernest Hemingway, an American; André Malraux, of France; Arthur Koestler, a Hungarian—came to Spain, fought with the republicans, and advocated their cause in their writings. Their hour of triumph was the heroic defense of Madrid. But they also experienced the dissension that broke out with the approach of defeat—particularly a bitter struggle between Communists and anarchists in which many sincere fighters against Fascism were brutally killed.

[1] W. H. Auden, "Spain 1937," quoted by Hugh Thomas, *The Spanish Civil War* (New York, 1961), p. 221.

In the years of appeasement that followed, those who had served in defense of the Spanish republic had a hard time. The governments of the Western democracies looked with disfavor on these freedom fighters—"premature anti-Fascists," they were later termed by American officials. In Russia, after Stalin had turned away from the idea of a Communist-democratic alliance against Fascism, many of the participants in the Spanish Civil War were treated as criminals. However, some of the fighters for the Spanish republic survived and were able to begin new political careers after the Second World War. But in the years immediately following the Spanish Civil War the spirit of the fight against Fascism in Spain seemed to remain alive only in works of art; the painting *Guernica* (1937) by Pablo Picasso and Ernest Hemingway's novel *For Whom the Bell Tolls* (1940) expressed the tragic hopelessness of man's struggle against inhuman forces.

Anschluss and the Invasion of Czechoslovakia
The weakness the Western democracies had shown—first in the Rhineland crisis and then in the Spanish Civil War—gave Hitler the green light to proceed with his aggressive and expansionist foreign policy. In a meeting with his chief military and civilian advisers in November 1937, he announced that Germany needed more living space, which could be secured only through war; such a war ought to take place in the early 1940s because German rearmament would then reach its peak. Preconditions for a successful war were the elimination of Czechoslovakia and the achievement of the Anschluss. Hitler also intimated that the situation that had developed in the Mediterranean as a result of the Spanish Civil War might afford an opportunity for quick action. Although subsequently he adjusted his tactics to changing circumstances, and the actual sequence of events was different from the one envisaged at this meeting, this speech did reveal his fundamental aims. When his chief military advisers expressed some reservations and doubts, they paid for their hesitation with loss of their positions. The dismissal of these generals demonstrated that the army had lost its independence. At the same time the foreign minister, Konstantin von Neurath (1873–1956), a professional diplomat who had been a compliant servant of the Nazis but was somewhat too cautious in Hitler's views, was replaced by a Nazi, Joachim von Ribbentrop (1893–1946). All obstacles to action had been removed.

Hitler's first victim was Austria. Stepped-up Nazi propaganda in Austria for Anschluss with Germany had led to increased measures of suppression by the Austrian government. In an interview with Chancellor Kurt von Schuschnigg on February 4, 1938, Hitler demanded that these measures be lifted and that some of the Austrian Nazis be included in the government. Intimidated by Hitler's vehemence and by the threat of German troop movements toward the Austrian border, Schuschnigg gave in. But he soon realized that once the Nazis had entered the government they would take complete control. On

Anschluss: Hitler announces the incorporation of Austria into greater Germany at a mass meeting in the center of Vienna.

March 9, in desperation, he announced a plebiscite in which the people were asked to vote on whether they wanted to keep Austrian independence. On March 11, Hitler sent an ultimatum demanding postponement of the plebiscite, and on March 12 he dispatched his troops into Austria under the pretext that Schuschnigg's government was unable to maintain order. On March 14, 1938, Vienna, where Hitler in his youth had lived in utter misery, saw him return in triumph; the Anschluss creating a greater Germany had been achieved. The Western powers did nothing except protest feebly on paper; Mussolini, who in 1934, when the first Nazi putsch took place in Austria, had moved his troops to the Brenner frontier, now declared that he was uninterested in the fate of Austria; he had gone too far to deviate from his pro-German course. Overjoyed, Hitler told Mussolini that he would never forget what he had done for him.

The next victim was Czechoslovakia. Hitler wanted the incorporation into Germany of the Sudeten region, a broad stretch of northern Czechoslovakia populated chiefly by Germans. Because this area was south of the mountains separating Germany from Czechoslovakia and included the Czechoslovakian line of fortifications, its loss would mean the end of Czechoslovakia as an independent factor in European power politics. Here again, the Western powers put up only weak resistance against Hitler's expansionist policy. The crisis first erupted in the spring of 1938, and several times in the months that followed Europe seemed to be on the brink of war. Although the British government of Neville Chamberlain was little concerned about the fate of the Sudeten Germans and of Czechoslovakia—the affair being, in Chamberlain's words, "a quarrel in a faraway country between people of whom we know nothing"—the British were aware that they could not remain on the sidelines of a European conflict developing from Hitler's demands on Czechoslovakia. This danger was great, for since 1924 France had been tied to Czechoslovakia through a clear and definite defensive alliance, and Soviet Russia was obligated to support France and Czechoslovakia if they had to defend themselves against German aggression. Hence the British government's main concern was to prevent a clash by force that would make fulfillment of the alliance commitments by France and Russia an automatic consequence. The British tried to persuade Hitler to be content with autonomy for the Sudeten Germans within the Czechoslovak state, and pressed Czechoslovakia to agree to this concession. But Hitler spurred the Nazis in the Sudeten area to demonstrations that led to clashes with the police; he then declared that Czechoslovakian brutality made further existence of the Sudeten Germans under Czechoslovak rule impossible and demanded complete separation of this region from Czechoslovakia, threatening to back his demand by military action.

At this critical moment Chamberlain decided to fly to Berchtesgaden, where he met Hitler on September 15, 1938. There Chamberlain gave Hitler what he wanted, the Sudeten area, in return for a promise that Germany would refrain from immediate military action. The British and French governments forced the Czechs to accept this solution by threatening to withdraw all support if they refused. But Hitler was still not satisfied; in a second meeting between Hitler and Chamberlain, in Bad Godesberg on September 22, Hitler declared that the procedure envisaged at Berchtesgaden for the German takeover was too slow. The transfer would have to be completed by October 1—if necessary, by military invasion. The deadlock seemed complete, and Chamberlain returned to London with little hope that peace could be maintained. But Mussolini, anxious to avoid war and eager to increase his prestige by appearing as Europe's arbiter, intervened, persuading Hitler to convene a conference at Munich on September 29.

The Munich Conference was a shocking demonstration of the extent to which the methods of international politics had deviated from those envisioned for the new world order at the end of the First World War. Then the expectation had been that the great and the small nations would have an equal voice. But at Munich, the leaders of the four great European powers—Hitler, Mussolini, Daladier, and Chamberlain—conferred alone; only after all decisions had been made were the representatives of Czechoslovakia, the state most concerned, informed of the agreement by a yawning Chamberlain and a nervous Daladier.

Neville Chamberlain and Hitler after the Munich Conference, 1938.

Hitler had made one concession. The deadline for the complete occupation of the Sudeten area was postponed to October 10. One may wonder what would have happened if the Czechoslovaks had rejected the Munich agreement and fought, whether then public opinion in Britain and France might have forced these powers to come to the rescue. But the Czechoslovaks and their president, Beneš, exhausted from endless negotiations and broken promises, felt that they could not risk such a gamble. They gave in; Beneš abdicated, leaving the government of the country to men he believed might get along better with the triumphant Nazis.

In an eloquent attack on British foreign policy in the House of Commons, Winston Churchill characterized the Munich Conference as "a disaster of the first magnitude." But his was a lonely voice. Returning from Munich, Chamberlain was received like a victorious conquerer. To the enthusiastic crowds he said, "This is the second time in our history that there has come back from Germany to Downing Street, peace with honour. I believe it is peace for our time." Perhaps no remark shows more clearly the erroneous assumptions of Chamberlain's appeasement policy. Later he tried to defend the Munich agreement by explaining that it gave Great Britain and France time to rearm. But this justification was palpably false. In the year between Munich and the outbreak of the Second World War the gap in armed strength between Germany and the Western powers did not narrow; it widened. The elimination of Czechoslovakia freed numerous German forces for service elsewhere, and the substantial military equipment installed in the fortifications of the Sudeten area now fell into German hands. Chamberlain did not put enough energy into the drive for

British rearmament to compensate for this increase in German military strength. He regarded Hitler as a great German patriot who wanted only to complete Bismarck's work by uniting all Germans in one national state and would then rule happily and peacefully ever after. Defending the Munich settlement in the House of Commons, Chamberlain said, "There is sincerity and goodwill on both sides."

During the winter of 1938–1939 European politicians were in a euphoric mood. The French signed a pact that provided for consultation in all questions of dispute with Germany and indicated that the Germans could have a free hand in southeastern Europe. The British also expressed their willingness to regard southeastern Europe as a German sphere of interest. The harmony between the Western democracies and the Axis powers was somewhat disturbed by Mussolini, who suddenly made loud claims for Nice, Savoy, and Tunisia, but the British recognized the Italian conquest of Ethiopia and hoped to act as mediators between the French and the Italians.

None of the men in control in France and Great Britain was very much bothered by events in Germany showing that Nazi brutality had not abated. In one night all the synagogues were burned and destroyed; the Jews were eliminated from German economic life and deprived of their property. At the beginning of 1939 the British government was convinced that political appeasement could now be strengthened by close economic cooperation between Germany and Great Britain. Chamberlain stated on March 10 that Europe was settling down to a period of tranquillity. Six months later Great Britain and France were at war with Germany.

The End of Appeasement

The event that changed British policy from appeasement to resistance was the incorporation of what had been left of Czechoslovakia into Greater Germany. The Nazis stimulated agitation for independence of the Slovakian region of the Czechoslovak state, and when the Czechoslovakian government took measures to suppress this movement, Hitler ordered Emil Hácha (1872–1945), Beneš's successor as president of the republic, to Berlin and forced him to recognize a German protectorate over Czechoslovakia. The next morning, on March 16, 1939, German troops poured over the borders and Hitler entered Prague.

Suddenly British public opinion turned against Germany. This abrupt explosion of British anger—after so many retreats—is difficult to understand. It has been said that British indignation was aroused because with this action Hitler demonstrated that he was not content with uniting Germans under his rule, and showed that his previous appeals for national self-determination had been hollow pretense disguising a brutal policy of expansion. It is true that the occupation of Czechoslovakia showed up the misconception of those who had presented Hitler as a great German patriot. It is more likely, however, that many

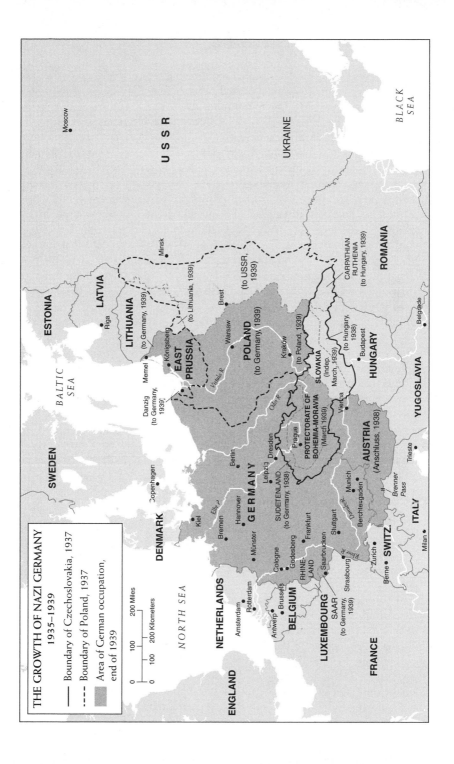

THE GROWTH OF NAZI GERMANY
1935–1939

——— Boundary of Czechoslovakia, 1937

----- Boundary of Poland, 1937

▓ Area of German occupation,
end of 1939

0   100   200 Miles

0   100   200 Kilometers

people in Great Britain were simply tired of being faced by one crisis after the other, of being bullied. And it appeared unlikely that a Hitler dominating Europe would leave the British Empire undisturbed.

Chamberlain now reversed his policy, but because of the pressure of public opinion rather than because he had changed his mind. Indeed, he tried until the last moment to renew contacts with Hitler. Publicly, however, he gave the impression of having abandoned appeasement and dramatized this shift with a spectacular diplomatic move. His government gave guarantees to the two states that were now most directly in the way of further German expansion and therefore most immediately threatened, Poland and Romania. Many Frenchmen might have preferred to evade their obligations to Poland, behaving as they had toward Czechoslovakia, but the British support of Poland meant that French retreat was impossible. When Hitler marched his troops into Poland, on the pretext that the Poles had not accepted his demands for restoration to the Reich of Danzig and the Polish Corridor, Great Britain and then France declared war on Germany, on September 3, 1939.

Hitler does not seem to have expected that his action against Poland would result in war with Great Britain and France. Lacking all sense of moral values, he had no appreciation of the revulsion his march into Prague had aroused, nor did he understand why powers that had refused to fight for strategically important and relatively accessible Czechoslovakia would undertake war for distant and indefensible Poland. On the other hand, it appears that in his quarrel with Poland, Hitler was not willing to agree to another peaceful settlement. He was convinced that to restore German prestige, damaged by the defeat in the First World War, a successful military campaign was needed. Instead of being exhilarated by the results of the Munich Conference, he had been depressed. He had felt that in yielding to Mussolini's demands for a conference, he had let slip the opportunity for a victorious war. Nevertheless, although he did not fear war if his actions against Poland involved him in a conflict with Great Britain and France, he would have preferred these powers to remain neutral, so that the campaign against Poland could be kept localized. He had a trump card that in his opinion would secure British and French neutrality. On August 23, 1939, a week before the attack on Poland, Germany had signed a nonaggression pact with Soviet Russia.

The surprise was great because in all the calculations of the policy makers the insuperability of the contrast between Nazi Germany and Communist Russia had been taken for granted. When after the German march into Prague, Great Britain gave guarantees to Poland and Romania, the British and French governments felt sure that they would also be able to gain Soviet Russia's help in stemming further German expansion. British and French missions were sent to Moscow, but after a period of fruitless negotiations they heard the news that instead of tying Russia to the Western powers, Stalin had made a pact with Nazi Germany.

SOVIET RUSSIA DURING THE INTERWAR YEARS

It is a strange reversal of fortunes that in the weeks preceding the outbreak of the Second World War, Soviet Russia's friendship and assistance were eagerly sought by the great European powers. History seemed to have turned full circle. Twenty years before, the statesmen arranging in Paris the future of Europe and of the world had been anxious to move Russia out of Europe. Indeed, during most of the interwar years Russia had remained on the periphery of international events. In the 1930s, with Hitler gaining increasing power, Russia gradually took a more active role in European affairs, but still, in 1938, it had been allowed no voice in the arrangements for settling the Czech crisis.

If now, in 1939, Russia's support was eagerly sought by both of the antagonistic groups, this was proof of the breakdown of the principles on which the settlements reached at the Paris Peace Conference had been based: the notion that the exercise of democracy and obedience to international law were requisites for acceptance as an equal partner in international life. With the return to power politics implied in the breakdown of the international system established at Versailles, it became increasingly obvious that in the eventuality of war, Russia's wealth in natural resources, foodstuffs, and minerals and Russia's military strength would be important.

During the interwar years, European intellectual and scholarly circles had never lacked an interest in the developments in Russia, and the chances of success or failure of the Soviet experiment had been the object of vehement, rather partisan discussion. But the answer to the puzzling question of the extent to which industrialization had created a new modern society in Russia was made immensely more complex and difficult by the violent methods with which the Bolsheviks had established themselves and had carried through the policy of collectivization and industrialization. How strong was Soviet Russia, and to what degree could it be relied on? These uncertainties, which had contributed to make Russia an outsider for so long during the interwar years, had deepened as a result of events in Russia in the second part of the thirties.

Stalinism and the Purge Trials

The publication in June 1936 of the draft of a constitution had raised the hopes that Russia was now entering a period of liberalization, but these hopes were soon destroyed by Stalin's purges, which made him a dreaded absolute ruler, with the secret police his most important and most feared instrument of government. The number of people who became victims of these purges—who were imprisoned, exiled, or executed—runs into the millions. The most prominent among them were condemned in "show trials," the first of which took place in August 1936, two months after the publication of the new constitution. Best known among the sixteen defendants in this trial were Grigori Zinoviev and Lev B. Kamenev, both former members of the Politburo. The second great trial was staged in 1937. Among the seventeen defendants was Karl Radek, Soviet Russia's leading political writer. Between the second and the third trials there occurred a secret purge of the Russian general staff; its victims included Mikhail Tukhachevsky, a hero of the civil war and the Russo-Polish War, and a number of generals. The third and last trial, in March 1938, was the most sensational; among its twenty-one defendants were Nikolai Bukharin, who had edited the newspaper *Izvestia* ("News") and was recognized as a leading Bolshevik theoretician; Aleksei Rykov, who had been chairman of the Council of People's Commissars; H. G. Yagoda, a former head of the secret police; N. M. Krestinsky, a deputy commissar for foreign affairs; and a number of high diplomats. At all these trials the defendants made "confessions," perhaps obtained through pressure. Most of the defendants were condemned to death and executed, and even those, like Radek, who received only prison sentences never reappeared in public life.

In the light of revelations made after the death of Stalin, the purges have usually been ascribed to his abnormal psychology. Undoubtedly Stalin's pathological distrust and suspicion did play a role in the organization of these trials and the cruelty of the punishments meted out to the defendants. Before 1936 and then again after Stalin's death, Bolshevik leaders who recommended a line of policy the majority rejected were demoted or removed from power, but they were not killed. The use of the death penalty for political opposition was limited to the time of Stalin's reign. Although the manner of procedure against the defendants in the purge trials was determined by Stalin's abnormal mentality, he did have rational cause to fear the influence of these men.

Some of them, like Bukharin, had opposed Stalin's agrarian policy and maintained that agricultural production could have been increased more effectively by working with the kulaks than by eliminating them. These men were probably more popular than the strict bureaucrats and experts—Stalin's loyal followers—who imposed the hardships of the five-year plans.

Most of those who doubted or opposed Stalin's economic policy recommended a change toward greater production of consumer goods, and the occurrence of such a change might have been expected to promote their chances for a successful political comeback. Stalin was unwilling to permit any loosening of controls or any alterations in economic policy, anticipating that the result would be a threat to his position.

But there was still another element in Stalin's campaign. Those against whom the purges were particularly directed were the old Bolsheviks. In the purges, the old leadership of the Bolshevik party from top to bottom was destroyed. Having been trained in discussions of Marxist theory, the old Bolsheviks were not willing to accept orders from above without question, and it has been reliably reported that behind the closed doors of the Politburo and of party committees, vehement debates took place. Moreover, many of the old Bolsheviks were internationalists, with a strong belief in the common interest of workers all over the world; in the years of rising Fascism and Nazism they wanted to transform the Communist International into an organization comprising all workers' parties and operating independently from dictates by Moscow. The old Bolsheviks expected a more liberal course, which would realize some of the old socialist ideals of a free and progressive way of life; for example, they were anxious to see a slowdown of the policy of forced collectivization that had begun in 1932 and 1933. The main representative of this liberalism was the leader of the Bolshevik party in Leningrad, Sergei Kirov; he was assassinated in 1934, as we now know, by Stalin's orders, although at the purge trials one of the main accusations against the defendants was that they had been responsible for Kirov's death.

Stalin undoubtedly saw a threat to his power in the attitude of the old Bolsheviks working for relaxation in the drive toward industrialization and for an improvement of economic and social life of the masses. But with the rise of the Nazis in Germany the possibility of international war had been greatly increased. Armament production had to be augmented and accelerated, not slowed down: a continued emphasis on heavy industry, not a shift toward consumer goods, was needed.

On the diplomatic front, prudence indicated that all options ought to be held open and no premature decision made in favor of the democracies against the Axis powers. Every possible obstacle to a uniform direction of policy appropriate to the dangerous situation had to be removed. This consideration was probably a motive in one of the most astounding purges: the execution of Tukhachevsky

Stalin in his office in the Kremlin; note portrait of Karl Marx.

and other military leaders. Under Tukhachevsky the army had developed into an almost independent power factor, and Stalin may have wondered to what extent he would be able to rely on the army if his policy was contradictory to the views of the military leaders. Stalin's distrust of Tukhachevsky seems to have been fomented by the Nazis, who expected that Tukhachevsky's fall would weaken the Russian military organization. Through Eduard Beneš, the president of Czechoslovakia, they succeeded in placing before Stalin cleverly falsified documents compromising Tukhachevsky. Significantly, the elimination of Tukhachevsky and his followers was accompanied by the reintroduction of political commissars into the army.

The ruthlessness with which Stalin pursued a policy of continued economic austerity and tightened the reins of government may have been a means of giving Russia greater strength in the critical years of the thirties, but these explanations for the purges do not mean that anyone who was not as suspicious and brutal, not as jealous of power and autocratic as Stalin was would have found it necessary to proceed in this inhuman manner.

Stalin's Foreign Policy

In the threatening atmosphere of the middle 1930s, continued economic austerity and a tightening of the reins of government seemed appropriate. But the ruthlessness with which these policies were pursued had a dubious effect on Russia's relations with other powers.

When the Russian leaders had embarked on a policy of socialism in one country, they were naturally anxious to remain undisturbed by the outside world. They had normalized diplomatic relations with their neighbors in the West and participated in international efforts toward securing peace, including the Kellogg-Briand pact and the Disarmament Conference. Because of Hitler's emphatically pronounced anti-Communism, his rise to power was disquieting to the rulers of Soviet Russia, and they began to seek closer ties with countries that might be equally interested in checking Nazi expansionism. After Russia joined the League of Nations in September 1934, the Soviet foreign minister, Maksim Litvinov (1876–1952), became a chief advocate of strict sanctions against aggressors. In 1935 Soviet Russia concluded with France and Czechoslovakia agreements promising mutual assistance in case of unprovoked aggression. Correspondingly, on orders from Moscow the policies of the Communist parties in Western Europe began to change. At the Seventh Congress of the Comintern, in the summer of 1935, the formula was proclaimed that initiated the new policy of the Popular Front: Communists were now willing to cooperate with the leaders of any group—socialist or rightist—that took a line of resistance to the Nazis.

Just when these broad movements of opposition to Nazism and Fascism seemed to be gaining impetus and the Popular Front obtained electoral victories in Spain and France, the occurrence of the Russian purges resulted in renewed doubts among the democratic forces about the possibility of cooperation with the Bolsheviks. The Russians even extended the purges to the various Communist parties outside the Soviet Union, attempting to eliminate from power those whom they considered allies of the purge victims and to establish as leaders of the Communist parties men of proven loyalty to Stalin. Russia intervened in the Spanish Civil War not only to defeat Franco but also to eliminate the leaders of the left who were not Stalinists. Such developments strengthened the hands of those politicians in Great Britain and France who from the outset—for ideological and economic reasons—had opposed cooperation with the Soviet Union. It was said that a regime that had to take recourse to terroristic measures could hardly be regarded as a stable and reliable ally, and the question was raised of whether the Russian government was any more humane or civilized than the Nazi and Fascist dictatorships. In the negotiations on the Czechoslovakian crisis during the summer of 1938, Great Britain and France cold-shouldered Russia as they steered openly toward appeasement with Nazi Germany.

We do not know whether Stalin ever had much interest or confidence in an alliance with the Western democracies. It is certain, however, that the Munich Conference and the appeasement policy of the Western powers increased his fear that these states might come to an agreement with Germany at the expense of the Soviet Union, perhaps giving Hitler a free hand to attack Russia. Moreover, Stalin was enough of a Marxist to regard as negligible the difference between capitalist Nazi Germany and the capitalist democracies of the West. Thus, when in the summer of 1939 British and French missions appeared in Moscow, and at the same time the Nazis expressed eager interest in a pact with Russia, Stalin's main interest was to make sure that these various powers did not unite against the Soviet Union. An agreement with Nazi Germany had the advantage that the Nazis were willing to hand over to Russia the Baltic states and parts of Poland, which Britain and France refused to do. Stalin may also have found the single-minded, ruthless Hitler more attractive than the vacillating Western statesmen, who until recently had embraced appeasement. Everything points to the conclusion that Stalin favored an agreement with Hitler. If he continued the negotiations with Great Britain and France, the chief reason was that otherwise the Western powers, despairing of Russian support, might drop Poland; Russia would then be faced alone by a Nazi Germany strengthened by victory over Poland. In short, the purpose of Stalin's diplomacy was to bring about war between Germany and the West.

Like all the other statesmen of the time, Stalin miscalculated. If Great Britain and France were slow and not very forthright in their approach to Russia, the reason was that they believed erroneously that Soviet Russia and Nazi Germany could never come to an understanding. Meanwhile Hitler had been persuaded by his foreign minister, Ribbentrop, that a German agreement with Russia would intimidate Great Britain and France into abandoning Poland so that his forces would have a quick and easy victory. And Stalin believed that the Western

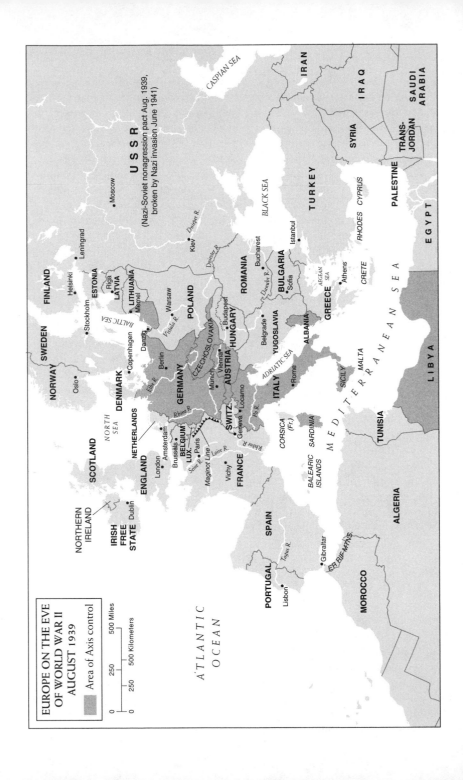

EUROPE ON THE EVE
OF WORLD WAR II
AUGUST 1939

Area of Axis control

0   250   500 Miles
0   250   500 Kilometers

ATLANTIC
OCEAN

NORTHERN
IRELAND

IRISH
FREE
STATE • Dublin

SCOTLAND

ENGLAND
• London

NORTH
SEA

NETHERLANDS
• Amsterdam
• Brussels
BELGIUM
LUX.
• Paris
Maginot Line
Seine R.   Loire R.
Vichy
FRANCE
Rhône R.

NORWAY
• Oslo

DENMARK
• Copenhagen

SWEDEN
• Stockholm

BALTIC SEA

FINLAND
• Helsinki

Leningrad •

• Moscow

U S S R

(Nazi-Soviet nonagression pact Aug. 1939,
broken by Nazi invasion June 1941)

CASPIAN SEA

ESTONIA
Riga •
LATVIA
LITHUANIA
Memel •

• Warsaw

POLAND

Danzig •
Vistula R.
Berlin •
Elbe R.
GERMANY
• Munich
Rhine R.
SWITZ.
Geneva • • Locarno
Po R.

Vienna •
AUSTRIA
Budapest •
CZECHOSLOVAKIA
HUNGARY

• Kiev
Dnieper R.
Dniester R.

ROMANIA
• Bucharest
Danube R.

BLACK SEA

BULGARIA
• Sofia

Belgrade •
YUGOSLAVIA

ADRIATIC SEA

ITALY
• Rome

CORSICA
(Fr.)

SARDINIA

MALTA

SICILY

ALBANIA

GREECE

AEGEAN
SEA

• Athens

CRETE

RHODES   CYPRUS

TURKEY

IRAN

IRAQ

SYRIA

TRANS-
JORDAN

SAUDI
ARABIA

PALESTINE

EGYPT

M E D I T E R R A N E A N   S E A

TUNISIA

LIBYA

ALGERIA

MOROCCO

ER RIF MTNS.

Gibraltar •

SPAIN

PORTUGAL
• Lisbon

Tagus R.

BALEARIC
ISLANDS

• Istanbul

democracies and Nazi Germany were almost equal in strength and would exhaust themselves in a long and bitter war; Russia—remaining at peace—would emerge as the strongest power on the European continent. The tragedy of the Second World War began with a comedy of errors.

If the war had not broken out over Poland in the summer of 1939, it probably would have been triggered by some other issue. Hitler was straining for control of the Continent, and from 1933 on, Europe had been disturbed by crisis after crisis, each more serious than the one before. With everyone living under the threat of an imminent war, the situation had become almost unbearable. Yet when hostilities finally erupted over the German invasion of Poland on September 1, 1939, the public reaction was very different from what it had been at the outbreak of the First World War twenty-five years before. In 1939 there was no enthusiasm, no feeling of liberation. The dreary procession of democratic retreats and defeats, the demonstrated inability to subordinate social conflicts and divergent class interests to the common aim of preserving the basis of freedom had weakened confidence in the strength of the Western powers. There seemed validity in the claim of the totalitarian states that they were the wave of the future. Behind the acceptance of the necessity of the war by the people in democratic countries there was a feeling of doom. In the face of terrible defeats, it would require the awakening of a primitive feeling of national pride to shake off this fatalism and to restore hope and confidence.

CHAPTER 8

The Second World War

THE SECOND World War began as a war of Poland, Great Britain, and France against Nazi Germany and for the next two years remained primarily a European war. It became a global conflict in December 1941, when the Japanese attacked Pearl Harbor and provoked the United States into the war. The fifteen months following the entry of the United States were decisive. Winston Churchill, in the fourth volume of his history of the Second World War, saw this period as "the turning point" of the war.[1] Until the end of the summer of 1942, Germany attacked and advanced. Thereafter the initiative was held by the opponents of Fascism.

Holding the initiative, however, did not bring with it the assurance of final victory. As the British historian Richard Overy has persuasively argued, there was nothing inevitable about the Allied victory, even after the great turning points of 1942. The Allies' economic superiority was certainly important, but it alone could not have guaranteed victory. Of crucial importance was the Allies' ability to learn from their initial mistakes, to make the organizational, logistical, and managerial reforms that allowed them to collaborate more effectively and to bring the full force of their superior numbers and firepower to bear against the enemy. Yet even this achievement might not have been decisive had not the Allied soldiers and peoples shown that they were every bit as determined, resourceful, and courageous as their Axis foes.

THE EUROPEAN WAR
Germany in Command
Until the autumn of 1940 the Germans marched from triumph to triumph. Poland, whose resistance to Hitler's demands had ended the period of

---

[1] Winston S. Churchill, *The Second World War*, vol. IV, *The Hinge of Fate* (Boston, 1950), p. 830.

appeasement, was eliminated in a campaign of just one month, which provided the first glimpse of the military weapons and tactics that would dominate the conduct of the war. The Germans used their tremendous air superiority to destroy the Polish Air Force on the ground and then to bomb roads and railroads and interrupt communications so that the Polish troops lost any possibility of movement. There was no such thing as a relatively safe rear. By concentrating an overwhelming force of tanks at certain points, the Germans broke through the Polish lines; they then secured their flanks at the breakthrough points and sent the tanks, followed by motorized infantry, streaming into the open countryside, where they turned to the right or left, dividing the enemy forces into isolated segments, which were encircled and annihilated one after the other. In the confusion created by this lightning attack, or blitzkrieg, only the big cities maintained organized resistance. Warsaw was heroically defended; the German answer was a bombardment from the air that reduced it to ruins—the first example of the destruction of a large city by air attack.

On September 27, hardly four weeks after the outbreak of the war, Polish resistance was at an end, and Poland was partitioned between Germany and Soviet Russia. The Russians quickly occupied the eastern half of Poland, which had been promised to them in the German-Soviet treaty, and they also advanced into the Baltic states—Lithuania, Estonia, and Latvia. Thus, they gained control of a long stretch of the southern coast of the Baltic Sea. The Germans annexed a large part of Poland and for the remainder created a Polish protectorate ruled by a German government. The delimination of the German and Russian spheres was settled in Moscow on September 28 in what was called the German-Soviet Boundary and Friendship Treaty.

The "Phony War"

French and British military leaders were slow to learn the lessons of the Polish campaign. They believed that the blitzkrieg tactics had been effective only because of Poland's military weakness and could not be applied against armies of greater power. Although German strength in the west was limited, the British and French had not supported the Poles by an attack on Germany, being satisfied to gain time for building up their forces.

What followed was the period of the "phony war." In the west the enemies confronted each other without engaging in serious fighting. German inactivity lulled the French and British into false security. They placed unjustifiably high hopes on the effects of economic warfare; from the outset they set up a tight blockade to prevent Germany from getting goods from abroad. Because they doubted that the Germans would dare to attack in the west, their measures for strengthening the defenses in France lacked the necessary energy. The Maginot Line was not extended along the Belgian frontier to the coast. The French and British governments felt so secure in the west that their attention focused on

The beginning of the Second World War. German motorized troops driving into Poland. Note the boundary sign with the Polish eagle, which the Germans removed and took along.

other areas. When the Russians invaded Finland in November 1939, to improve their military defense line in the north, the French and British decided to assemble an expeditionary force to aid the Finns. But before this assistance could be sent, the war ended, in March 1940, with the Finns conceding to the Russians the demanded frontier revision.

Concerned by the British and French interest in this northern area, Hitler decided to eliminate the possibility of military action by the Western Allies from the north. On April 9, German troops drove over the Danish frontier and occupied Denmark; at the same time they attacked Norway. The Norwegians resisted but were overwhelmed. The German success was due to a brilliantly executed combination of action by naval and air forces and paratroops. The British and French countermeasures were fumbling; troops were thrown in without antiaircraft protection and artillery and were quickly destroyed by the Germans.

From the British point of view, the Norwegian defeat had one favorable consequence. A dramatic session of the House of Commons showed that Neville Chamberlain had lost the confidence of his countrymen. He resigned on May 10 and was succeeded by Winston Churchill, who formed a government in which all three parties—Conservative, Liberal, and Labor—participated. Churchill writes that he went to bed that night with "a profound sense of relief. At last I had the authority to give directions over the whole scene. I felt as if I

View of communications trench, floored with saplings and walled with chicken wire and stakes, on the Maginot Line.

were walking with Destiny, and that all my past life had been but a preparation for this hour and for this trial."[2]

The Opening of the Western Offensive

On the very day this change of government took place, the German offensive in the west began. While the Maginot Line remained quiet, the northern wing of the German armies advanced on a broad front, invading the Netherlands and Belgium. German paratroops seized the Dutch airfields and bridges and made an orderly defense of the country impossible. An air raid on Rotterdam obliterated the center of the city, and on May 14 the Dutch army capitulated after Queen Wilhelmina (ruled 1890–1948) and the government had succeeded in escaping to England. Belgian resistance lasted longer, thanks to British and French support. But the Germans, utilizing the same tactics as in Poland, achieved a breakthrough in the Ardennes, and their tanks raced ahead into France, toward Amiens and Abbeville, splitting the defending forces into two parts. The northern part, including the entire Belgian Army, most of the British troops in France, and a portion of the French Army, was then enclosed in a steadily contracting ring. On May 27 the Belgian king Leopold III (ruled 1934–1951) capitulated with his army. British and French troops were pushed back to the beaches of Dunkirk and evacuated from there. Waiting on the beaches, the Allied forces were subjected to

[2] Ibid, vol. I, *The Gathering Storm* (Boston, 1948), p. 667.

steady bombing from the air. A German tank attack probably would have been disastrous, but Hitler evidently believed that the destruction of the exposed troops could be left to the air force and kept his tanks back. Nevertheless, saving these forces required an immense effort; the miracle of Dunkirk was made possible by the strength of the British Navy, under whose protection an endless number of small craft brought the soldiers over the Channel. Between May 27 and June 4, 338,226 men reached England.

The tanks Hitler did not employ at Dunkirk were used in the attack against the other half of the Allied forces, consisting of the bulk of the French Army, which had formed a front along the Somme. Again, the German tanks succeeded in breaking through the defenders' lines. Roads were clogged with refugees; German airplanes strafed people scurrying along, creating panic and confusion. The collapse of communications prevented French airplanes and antitank guns from reaching the front, and the enemy was able to advance rapidly.

On June 14, the Germans entered Paris. The French government had fled southward. In hurried visits, Churchill tried to persuade the French to remain in the war. Prime Minister Paul Reynaud (1878–1966) was willing to do so. But with Germans advancing over the Loire and attacking from the rear the Maginot Line, where the last well-organized French military force was stationed, the military leaders declared all further resistance useless and demanded that the government end the war. Reynaud resigned and was succeeded by Marshal Pétain, who on June 17 asked for an armistice. Most of the country was occupied by the Germans; only southeastern France and North Africa remained under French control. In the unoccupied part of France, with Vichy as capital, a French government under Pétain as head of state was established; in the later periods of the war, starting in April 1942, the directing spirit of this government was Pierre Laval, who expected a German victory and regarded close cooperation with the Nazis as the only possible French policy.

North Africa's freedom from German occupation subsequently proved of great value to the Allied forces, but in the spring and summer of 1940 the French surrender appeared an unmitigated disaster. This impression was reinforced by the establishment under Pétain of a new authoritarian government in Vichy, so that even unoccupied France was absorbed into the antidemocratic camp. There is no doubt that in the shock of defeat many Frenchmen shared Pétain's belief that an abandonment of the ideas of the Third Republic and a new hierarchical organization of society were desirable. Few remained convinced, with Charles de Gaulle, that France had lost a battle but not the war. "The outcome of the struggle has not been decided by the Battle of France. This is a world war."[3] This statement was part of de Gaulle's first appeal from London, in June 1940, to form a movement for the liberation of France. De Gaulle had

---

[3] Quoted in *The Complete War Memoirs of Charles de Gaulle*, vol. I, *The Call to Honour*, trans. by Jonathan Griffins (New York, 1955), p. 84.

made a name for himself through writings in which he had stressed the importance of tanks and motorized forces in future wars. In the campaign of 1940 he had proved himself as a tank commander against the Germans; he was named undersecretary of war by Reynaud on June 6 because he could be relied on to support the prime minister's efforts to keep France in the war. When those proved abortive, de Gaulle escaped in a British plane to London. There he organized the Free French movement, insisting that he alone spoke for France and that France was still a great power. He kept a proud distance from the various governments-in-exile that, after the German occupation of their countries, were set up in London.

The Battle of Britain

On June 10, before the French campaign had ended, Italy entered the war. The Italians had been resentful that Hitler had gone ahead even though they had told him that Italy was not ready for war in 1939. As long as the "phony war" lasted, neutrality seemed appropriate, since it might give Italy a chance to act as a mediator. But as Germany progressed unchecked, Mussolini became increasingly restless. His proud claims of having created a new disciplined and powerful state would seem idle boasts if Italy remained outside the war. For the outcome of the campaign in France, Italy's entry into the conflict was irrelevant. But it

Victorious German troops arriving in Paris, June 1940.

presented a serious threat to British communication through the Mediterranean and to the British position in the Near East.

Great Britain was dangerously alone. The German high command was sure that "the final German victory over England is only a question of time,"[4] and plans were made for invading England. But German strategy had always centered on land warfare, and the military leaders, including Hitler, felt insecure in planning for a campaign combining naval and land operations. According to the German military leaders, a successful invasion first required air attacks to eliminate all serious British resistance. And Göring, the commander of the German Air Force, gave assurances that his bombers and fighter planes could force Great Britain to its knees.

The German air fleet was superior to the British, although antiaircraft artillery and the concentration of air squadrons in southern England compensated somewhat for the difference in numbers. The Germans began in July with an attack on airfields and military installations, forcing the British into air battles in order to destroy the Royal Air Force. Indeed, the RAF did lose continuously in strength. Then, at the beginning of September—in a change generally considered to have been a crucial mistake—the Germans switched to bombing attacks on London. The decisive days of the Battle of Britain were in the middle of September, when the British had to put their reserves into the defense of London. The British inflicted heavy losses on the German air fleet. These blows made the Germans aware that full air protection for a landing operation was unobtainable, and they abandoned their invasion plans. However, they continued night raids on London until November, averaging two hundred bombers on each mission. These had no direct strategic purpose; they were intended to weaken British morale and will to resist. The blitz on London was followed by attacks on other cities, the most devastating being the raid on Coventry on November 14, in which four hundred people were killed and the center of the city, including its historic cathedral, was completely destroyed. At the end of the year, London again became the target of an air attack; incendiary bombs were used, and many of the city's most ancient monuments, including Guildhall and numerous churches designed by Sir Christopher Wren, were badly damaged or destroyed. But the morale of the people was not broken, nor was the production of war materials interrupted. Britain actually managed to produce more airplanes than Germany in 1940. In the Battle of Britain, Hitler had received his first check; he was forced to abandon the plan to achieve quick victory through a direct attack on Great Britain. As Churchill said of the British pilots who were instrumental in this triumph, "Never in the field of human conflict was so much owed by so many to so few."

---

[4] From entry dated June 30, 1940, "War Diary of General Jodl."

THE SHIFT OF THE THEATER OF WAR FROM
THE WEST TO THE EAST

England's Chances of Survival

The victory in the Battle of Britain gave an immense lift to the morale of the opponents of the Nazis because after the almost clocklike precision of the campaigns in Poland, Norway, and France, it demonstrated that even Nazi plans could go awry. Still, the British situation seemed hopeless. Churchill himself later confessed that whereas "normally I wake up buoyant to face the new day," in 1940 "I woke with dread in my heart."

Churchill saw little chance that England could win the war alone but believed that if England could hold out long enough, the United States would enter the war against the Nazis. When Churchill became a member of the government on the outbreak of the war, he began a correspondence with President Roosevelt, informing the president about the developing war scene. Roosevelt's antagonism to Nazi despotism was well known. Moreover, it was his basic axiom, which he had held since the First World War, that it was of vital importance for the security of the United States to have the command over the Atlantic in friendly hands. He fully sympathized with the English, whom he was

After the air raids in London. Tumbling ruins with St. Paul's Cathedral in the background.

most eager to help. But he certainly preferred that the Nazis be held in check without the United States's taking an active part in the war. Roosevelt also felt that the United States could enter the war only with the full backing of Congress and the American people and that they had not yet been awakened to the dangers democracy and their way of life would face if the Nazis ruled Europe. Organizations like the America First Committee, which included such influential figures as Charles Lindbergh and William Randolph Hearst, argued that world Communism was a greater danger to America than Nazism. Roosevelt knew that before the United States took any action that might lead to war, it had to be better prepared militarily; only in 1940 was the military budget increased and conscription introduced.

Churchill's demands for concrete support became urgent in the summer of 1940; Britain's losses in small ships and destroyers during the evacuation at Dunkirk were so great that Britain's shipping lanes had become extremely vulnerable to attack by German submarines. The maintenance of the shipping lanes not only for the provision of food but for import of raw materials needed to manufacture war equipment and airplanes was vital. Thus, Churchill wrote to Roosevelt: "We must ask, therefore, as a matter of life or death, to be reinforced with these [American] destroyers." On the American side, the difficulties—constitutional as well as practical—of such a move were very great, but after long and complicated negotiations, on September 2, 1940, an agreement was reached that helped to increase the security of both countries. Britain would receive fifty overage destroyers from the United States; in exchange, it would lease naval and air bases in the West Indies for ninety-nine years to the United States. This deal did not represent a violation of American neutrality, but it certainly gave strong public expression to the community of interests between the United States and Britain. Churchill was not wrong in thinking that after this first step was made, other steps would follow, which would bring American participation in the war nearer and nearer. Indeed, in a broadcast on December 29, 1940, Roosevelt declared formally that it was the task of the United States to serve as "the arsenal of democracy," and Congress responded by passing in March 1941 the Lend-Lease Act, which permitted the president to provide war materials to those states whose survival was vital to the security of the United States; after the Nazi invasion of Russia this act was applied also to Soviet Russia. The identity of American and British interests was publicly announced in the Atlantic Charter, a document issued after a meeting between Roosevelt and Churchill on a warship off the coast of Newfoundland in August 1941. In the Atlantic Charter, the two leaders emphasized that the war must result in freedom, independence, and an improvement in living standards for all people. Thus, although Churchill remained impatient for the United States to become a full participant in the war, his expectation that this would happen—which in the summer of 1940 seemed a wild gamble—appeared more and more a correct calculation.

Hopeful signs for Britain could be found not just in the diplomatic field. In modern military operations information and intelligence, an area that in previous times held only a rather subordinate role in comparison to strategy and tactics, had become vitally important. It was in this field that the English had a great asset. They had been able to get hold of a "complete, new, electrically operated" cipher machine, fabricated in Germany under the manufacturing name of Enigma; it was by means of this machine that Hitler and the German high command exchanged signals with the various chiefs of the army, air, and navy staffs and with the army group commanders. It was possible therefore to receive these signals in England. Of course, they were given in code, and the decoding required mathematical skill of the highest order. But by means of Ultra—the code name for this intelligence operation—the British gained a good amount of advance information about military movements planned by the Germans. Ultra proved its value first in the Battle of Britain: information about the areas the Luftwaffe was to attack and knowledge of the direction from which the planes came made it possible to intercept them before they reached their goal or to concentrate planes from various regions in the threatened areas. Ultra, together with radar—which, in contrast to the Germans, the British had fully developed—contributed importantly to the outcome of the Battle of Britain. Ultra played its role in all further campaigns in which British and American troops were involved: in the earlier years, when the Germans were superior and on the offensive, frequently by indicating where and when the attack would come, so that retreat from untenable positions could be arranged in time—this happened in North Africa when Rommel opened his general offensive—and later, in revealing the distribution of German tank divisions in France—information that had great importance for the success of the Normandy invasion in June 1944.

The British had also broken the code of the Abwehr, the German secret service. In consequence, they knew about the spies the Germans had in England and began to "control" them, offering them the alternative either to disappear in prison or to continue their activities but to tell their employers in Germany what the English wanted them to know. This double cross system had few risks for the English, because they were in possession of the code of the Abwehr, they knew exactly what these agents reported to Germany. The result was the establishment of an elaborate system of deception, which had some success in keeping the German troops dispersed—either by threatening landings in France long before it was feasible or by giving the Germans incorrect information about where the invasions on the Continent would take place.

During the winter of 1940–1941, British scientists also determined that the rapid development of an atomic bomb was possible, although continuation of work on this project was then transferred to Canada and the United States.

However, even if Britain could hold out, would there be any chance to regain a foothold on the Continent from which a counteroffensive could be started? The struggle that took place in the Mediterranean area in the winter of

1940–1941 and the spring of 1941 was England's attempt to keep the door open for a later invasion of Europe; for Hitler, it was a campaign to ensure complete control of the European continent.

The Mediterranean Campaign

After the triumphant French campaign, the Germans had forced Hungary and Romania into the German orbit; they had even sent troops into Romania to guard the oil fields against possible attacks by enemies. Mussolini had always considered the Balkans his own domain and was not pleased to see the Germans extending into this area. Moreover, he was dissatisfied with the minor role his country was playing in the European conflict and decided to gain military laurels by attacking Greece. But the Italian troops that moved from Albania toward Greece were not prepared for the valiant resistance they encountered. Instead of the Italians' occupying Greece, the Greeks conquered a fourth of Italian-controlled Albania.

The Italian plight in the winter of 1940–1941 was made even worse by defeats inflicted by the British in North Africa, where Hitler finally felt that he had to come to the assistance of his fellow dictator by sending German tanks, under one of the best German tank commanders, Erwin Rommel. But Hitler's main attention was directed toward the Balkans. The Italian difficulties gave him the opportunity to establish firmly the German hegemony over this area. While Hungary, Romania, and Bulgaria accepted close ties with the Axis, assuming the role of satellites, Yugoslavia refused a similar arrangement; Hitler overwhelmed the country in a quick campaign, which he continued into Greece. The Greeks were unable to hold off the Germans, and their country was occupied in a few weeks. Finally, through the daring use of paratroops, even Crete was conquered and in German hands by May 31, 1941. In vain had the British sent support to Greece from Africa.

It had been a rather desperate move by the British since the chances of resisting the German onslaught were small. But Churchill and Anthony Eden, who had again become secretary of foreign affairs, were convinced that they would have no possibility of mobilizing the European peoples against the Nazis at a later, more favorable time, if they could not show that they had tried to help the one country that had been willing to take up arms against the Fascist powers.

The resultant weakening of their forces in Africa left the British unable to resist Rommel, who drove them back to the Egyptian frontier. The entire area seemed helpless and open to a German onslaught, and it is difficult to imagine what would have happened if Hitler had moved into Egypt, Turkey, and other states of the Near East. But Hitler's target was the Soviet Union. Although the Balkan campaign had caused delays in his plans for an attack against Russia, Hitler now ordered them carried out; on June 22, 1941, German troops marched over the borders of Russia. At the same time the Finns resumed military operations against Russia.

The Eastern Offensive

After the failure to achieve a quick decision against Great Britain, Hitler seems to have been somewhat uncertain what his next move ought to be. It was then that the plan of a campaign against Russia began to take definite form. German expansion toward the east had always been Hitler's aim, but he had intended to postpone this enterprise until the western nations had been defeated. However, after the victory in France, Great Britain's aggressive potential seemed negligible, and Hitler concluded that the subjection of Russia could be achieved while the war against Great Britain continued. His hostility toward Russia had been reinforced by the energy with which the Bolshevik leaders had acted after the defeat of Poland, taking immediate possession of those areas that had been defined in the German-Soviet treaty as belonging to the Russian sphere of interest. In a visit to Berlin in November 1940, the Soviet foreign minister, Vyacheslav Molotov (1890–1986), showed that the Russians were by no means willing to give the Germans a free hand in the Balkans. Even earlier Hitler had ordered the German general staff to work out plans for an attack against Russia; after Molotov's visit he decided to carry out these plans in 1941.

The Soviet rulers had received warnings of what was coming, but up to the last moment they made desperate attempts to avoid a break with Germany. They had no illusions about how precarious their situation would be in case of war with Germany.

From the outset, Hitler envisaged the eastern offensive as a "purely ideological war" and a "war of extermination." Special SS units called *Einstatzgruppen* followed the Wehrmacht into Russia, where they systematically murdered targeted civilian groups, including Bolshevik political commissars, Soviet intellectuals, and Jews. Although various SS units did most of the actual killing of civilians, Wehrmacht officers were fully informed of the extermination plans and largely concurred in their implementation. Indeed, Wehrmacht commanders such as Erich Hoepner, Erich von Manstein, and Walter von Reichenau gave speeches and orders to their troops that echoed Hitler's racist propaganda. As Manstein stated in an order dated November 20, 1941: "Soldiers must show understanding for the necessity of harsh measures against Jews, who have been a moving force behind Bolshevist terror and must pay the penalty for it. These measures are also necessary to suppress uprisings, which in most cases are instigated by Jews, at the first sign of unrest."

At first, the campaign against Russia seemed to lead to a quick and complete triumph, even discounting Nazi exaggeration of the number of Russian prisoners of war taken in the early weeks of the campaign. The Russians conceded after the war that "Soviet strategic theory as propounded by the Draft Field Regulations of 1939 and other documents did not prove to be entirely realistic. For one thing, they denied the effectiveness of the blitzkrieg which tended to be dismissed as a lopsided bourgeois theory."[5] The Russians were surprised by the German use of tank formations for breakthroughs and encirclement. The Germans' air superiority enabled their air force to attack Russian airfields and destroy Russian planes on the ground. The Russian debacle was magnified by orders ascribed to Stalin to hold out in advance positions, causing the troops to miss opportunities to retreat before the ring of encirclement was closed. At Kiev, in one such encirclement of Russian forces, the Germans took one hundred seventy-five thousand prisoners of war.

Recent research has shown that the German army committed many atrocities against Russian civilians during its eastern offensive. The Wehrmacht systematically murdered Jews and burned settlements to the ground under the pretext of suppressing partisan resistance. Thus, contrary to the claims made by many German officers after the war that the Wehrmacht had always maintained "clean hands," Hitler's army was a full participant in the crimes of the Third Reich.

By October the Germans were before Moscow and Leningrad, and in a speech on October 2 Hitler announced a "final drive" against Moscow. People began to flee the city. Trains were packed, officials set out in their cars, and although some factories worked day and night to produce antitank defenses, or hedgehogs, that were immediately placed in the roads around Moscow, other factories were evacuated. Doubts grew that the capital could be held.

The official will to defend the city was underlined by an announcement that Stalin was in Moscow. In the first weeks of the war he seems to have been near a nervous collapse and to have almost lost control. But his firmness in the desperate situation when the Germans were beleaguering Leningrad and approaching Moscow muted all criticism and established him in undisputed authority as the supreme military leader. He began to be presented as a second Peter the Great. In newspapers and literature there was a deliberate stimulation of interest in the Russian past, even in tsarist history, and the war came to be called the Great Patriotic War. The Bolshevik leaders wanted the struggle to be seen as an event that concerned not only Communists but all the Russian people. At the beginning of November, in two great speeches, Stalin invoked Russian nationalism as the inspiration for resistance to the hordes of invading barbarians. By then, the German offensive had lost its impetus, probably less because of the strength of the Russian stand than because of logistical difficulties: the necessary supplies for the tanks, artillery, and men had not kept up with the rapid advance. When the Germans started a second push in November, the Russians were prepared; their embittered resistance, together with an early onset of winter, which severely hurt the insufficiently clad German troops, caused this second offensive against Moscow to fail.

Nevertheless, the Russian situation remained serious. By the end of the campaign of 1941, the Germans had conquered most of Ukraine, were close to

[5] This citation is from the Russian official *History of the War* (1960). Quoted by Alexander Werth, *Russia at War, 1941–1945* (New York, 1964), p. 133.

AXIS EXPANSION
IN THE WEST
1942

Greatest extent of Axis
occupation or control

Areas controlled by
Vichy France

0   250   500 Miles

0   250   500 Kilometers

Moscow, and had surrounded Leningrad, which remained under siege for eighteen months. These advances had been bought with very heavy losses—between seven and eight hundred thousand men. The Russian losses were far greater. By December 1941, the Red Army had lost 4.5 million men. The severed heads of Russian soldiers littered the battlefields like potatoes turned up in the newbroken ground. Lacking personnel adequately to guard the thousands of prisoners they captured, the Germans simply herded them into barbed-wire pens and left them to starve to death. And yet, resilient and tough, the Russians were quick to learn from their defeats. Generals who had been promoted because of their political merits were replaced by brilliant professionals. The Russians showed great ingenuity in transporting factories from threatened areas into the safe hinterland of the Urals and Siberia. They were able to accelerate the production of tanks, airplanes, and artillery, and the Russian heavy artillery proved to be superior to that of the Germans. Moreover, supplies from Great Britain and the United States began to arrive in convoys that traveled on hazardous sea lanes to Murmansk. These supplies filled the gaps in production that occurred while factories were being moved to safe areas. In contrast to what had happened in Poland, France, and the Balkans, victory in one quick campaign escaped the Germans in Russia.

THE WAR AT ITS HEIGHT

The Global War

At the beginning of 1942, the entire war changed in character. It ceased to be a purely European conflict and became global. To Japanese advocates of expansionism, the European struggle seemed to offer a unique opportunity for establishing a Japanese Empire in the Far East. Great Britain was unable to intervene, and the German occupation of the Netherlands and France made the Far Eastern possessions of these countries an easy prey. From French Indochina, which they occupied in 1940, the Japanese prepared to move against Burma, the East Indies, and Singapore. The United States, which wanted to help Britain and in addition had a vital interest in preventing the domination of this area by a single power, opposed these Japanese moves by diplomatic representations and economic pressures. Negotiations conducted in Washington between the two states were unsuccessful, however, and were near collapse when, on December 7, 1941, the Japanese made a surprise attack on the U.S. fleet in Pearl Harbor, sinking three battleships and severely damaging five others. The next day the United States formally declared war on Japan.

The outbreak of hostilities between Japan and the United States was followed on December 11 by declarations of war on the United States by Germany and Italy. The Axis powers were bound by a treaty concluded in 1940 to assist Japan in case of attack by a state not involved in the European war; it remains strange, however, that Hitler, who had few inclinations to honor treaty obligations, believed that he had to fulfill this one. To declare war on the United States was his personal decision, and his hatred of President Roosevelt, the protagonist of the democratic world, was probably a prime motive. Most of all, Hitler's decision showed that despite the setbacks in Russia, he felt supremely confident. His lack of knowledge of American politics also played its role. He seems never to have considered that without this declaration of war, American military action might have focused on the Far East rather than Europe.

There can be no doubt also that the German declaration of war on the United States solved the dilemma Roosevelt had faced in the preceding months. The United States and Great Britain had moved closer and closer together, and American protection of a neutrality zone far into the Atlantic Ocean had considerably diminished the effects of the German submarine war. Yet Roosevelt and his advisers had become increasingly convinced that direct participation of the United States in the war was needed for defeating Nazi Germany. Roosevelt also believed that although the American people approved a policy of giving strong support to Great Britain, they would still have to be shown that they were directly threatened to accept the necessity of participation in the war unhesitatingly, but so far the Germans had avoided all direct provocation. After the German declaration of war it was now possible to coordinate British and American war efforts in a much more systematic and effective fashion.

On December 22, Churchill and a number of his military advisers arrived in Washington, and except for a trip to Canada he stayed in the United States until January 14, 1942. In the meetings in Washington, two important decisions were made, one strategical, the other organizational. It was agreed that a defeat of Hitler was the first goal; the European theater of war was given precedence over the Far East. In addition, a unified command was created; within each of the various theaters of war the British and American troops were placed under a single commander, either British or American. The direction of the strategy of the war was entrusted to a committee, the Combined Chiefs of Staff, in which the outstanding figures were General George C. Marshall (1880–1959), the chief of staff of the army on the American side, and Sir John Dill (1881–1944), on the British side.

There was never close cooperation in military planning between the Combined Chiefs of Staff and the Russian general staff. On the contrary, the Russians were most reluctant to give information to the British and American military representatives in Moscow. The organizational unification of British

FDR and Churchill conferring at the Atlantic Conference, off the coast of Newfoundland, August 10, 1941. The conference produced the Atlantic Charter, which set the stage for the Anglo-American alliance of World War II.

and American military effort helped prevent the delays, frictions, and disorders that usually occur in the conduct of a coalition war; even so, some decisions were reached only after long debates. It was the bond of friendship and respect that existed between Roosevelt and Churchill—together with their interest in and understanding of military affairs—that served to smooth out the difficulties that arose from differences among the generals.

The main issue under dispute throughout the war years was the timing of the invasion of France. The Americans were eager to embark on this enterprise in 1942; the British were probably right in considering such an undertaking premature at a time when the Germans were at the height of their power and the American troops were inexperienced. The British idea of abandoning the plan of a continental invasion in 1942 and substituting a landing in North Africa was appropriate, just as at a later stage the Americans were probably justified in opposing British plans to extend operations in the Mediterranean area by an attack through the Balkan Peninsula—the "soft underbelly" of the Axis"—and in insisting instead on invasion of France across the English Channel.

Total War

In becoming global, the war also had become total, at least in the sense that in all countries the needs of war were accepted as controlling all spheres and activities of life, although, according to geography, wealth, and closeness to war, the degree of control and regulation varied.

Britain's insular position and its dependence on other countries for food had quickly led to controls of imports and exports, allocation of raw material, and, to prevent a lowering of morale, limitations on profits. Rationing of food and clothes was efficiently organized. The main problem for Britain as well as for all the European belligerents was manpower; the British National Service Act of December 1941 established that men and women—men from eighteen to fifty, women from twenty to thirty—were subject to either military or essential civilian war service. The manpower needs became so great that in the final year of the war a "grandmother category" had to be added: The conscription of women was extended to age fifty.

The most severe manpower regulations, however, were those in Russia. There all men from sixteen to fifty-five and all women from sixteen to forty-five were mobilized. The reason for the almost unbelievable extent of this mobilization was the catastrophic effect of the German victories in the early months of the war: the occupation of Russia's industrially most advanced regions; the loss of about 2.5 million men and immense amounts of equipment, most important fourteen thousand tanks, more than 90 percent of what the Russians had originally possessed. Industries now had to be constructed in the security of the remote Ural region to which workers had to be transported, and more than 50 percent of the labor force employed in these factories were women. By 1943, the

Russians were producing two thousand tanks and three thousand airplanes per month.

The greatest change brought about by the transformation of the European war into a global war took place in Germany. This may seem astounding because the expansionist and aggressive policy the Nazis had conducted could be expected to have prepared from the outset for total war. But Nazi leaders were thinking in terms of blitzkrieg. Their aim was to have a limited military production that provided a supply of weapons and equipment adequate for a blitzkrieg. A material reservoir of this size would be maintained; after a blitzkrieg campaign was over, the loss of material would soon be replaced, especially since the material taken from the enemy would compensate for part of the losses. This approach to military production had the advantage of flexibility so that changes could be easily made, suited to the particularities of a planned campaign. Moreover, this method left the working of a great part of the German industrial machine undisturbed. The continuation of a peace economy in wartime was also secured by partial demobilization after each campaign.

The failure of the blitzkrieg in the east changed this situation. Supplies of equipment and weapons lasting for a limited number of months would no longer suffice. An increase in armaments and an expansion of the army were necessary, meaning that Germany had to convert to total mobilization, with allocation of war materials, standardization of weapons, and reduction of plane production to a few types. A Ministry of Armaments and Production provided centralized direction; indeed, under its minister, Albert Speer, it tripled German armaments production within two years. In handling its manpower mobilization, Germany did not rely on its female population as much as did the Allied countries. Although the Nazis did exploit female labor during the war, their traditionalist view of gender roles induced them to keep German women at home as much as possible while filling vacancies in the work force with imported foreign labor and Jews.

Europe under the Nazis

The adjustment of economic and civil life to the needs of total war not only affected Germany but also had repercussions in all the countries occupied by the Nazis—that is, throughout Europe. Soon after the conquest, the occupied areas were organized according to Nazi aims. In the occupied territories of the east the Germans acted as if they were permanent rulers. Many of the inhabitants were removed and resettled, and large landed estates were given to German generals and Nazi leaders. Yugoslavia was divided, with one part forming the kingdom of Croatia, ruled by an Italian prince, and the rest remaining under direct German administration. Bulgaria, Romania, and Hungary, being Nazi allies, retained their old rulers but were dominated by German-supported parties patterned after the Nazis. Norway, the Netherlands, Belgium, and part of France were under German occupation. The Germans used puppet governments as instruments for their rule, which came to be known as Quisling governments, after the Norwegian Nazi leader Vidkun Quisling.

Of all of these collaborationist regimes, the one with perhaps the most shameful record was Vichy France, in principle an independent state, though in reality a puppet of Berlin. In an effort to retain as much of its sham sovereignty as possible, the Vichy regime of Pétain and Laval diligently did the Germans' bidding, including helping it solve the "Jewish problem." Indeed, as historians Robert Paxton and Michael Marrus have shown, in this domain Vichy sometimes tried to out-Nazi the Nazis—for example, by beginning to deport Jewish children when this was not yet the policy of the Germans. In the end, Vichy deported some seventy-six thousand Jews from France, most of whom died in the camps.

One of the chief aims of German occupation policy was economic exploitation. All the occupied countries had to pay for the costs of German occupation, and these costs were set extremely high. A good part of business profits were swallowed up in taxes, which went to Germany, mostly in form of deliveries of raw material and food. Moreover, rationing was introduced in the occupied countries but on levels very different from those in Germany. An industrial worker in Germany received twice as much bread, three times as much meat, seven times as many fats as an industrial worker in France. And although the difference in rations that the general consumer received was not quite as striking, it was considerable. Almost until the last year of the war it was possible to maintain a fairly high standard of living in Germany; meanwhile, people in many occupied areas were starving. Regular economic activities and personal lives were further interrupted by the conscription and transportation of men of captive countries to Germany to work there in factories and labor battalions. The propaganda intended to justify these measures emphasized that German arms were defending Europe against Communism and that German domination would usher in a new period in which Europe would be unified. In all the subject countries, the Germans organized parties in the pattern of the German Nazi Party and military units were formed to join in the fight against Communism. Thus, in the campaign against Russia, Romanian, Hungarian, and Italian armies, as well as legions of volunteers from all over Europe—even from Spain—fought under the German command.

With the tightening of German controls over Europe, resistance movements arose in almost all the occupied countries. Originally these movements consisted of isolated groups, such as the remnants of the former political parties, among which the socialists and Communists had particularly kept some cohesion, or of groups of nationalists, Catholics, and Protestants, who felt that they dishonored themselves if they allowed the brutal and un-Christian behavior of the Nazis to go on without taking some action. In time these various units began to cooperate with one another and combine into coordinated resistance organizations. All these movements worked underground.

AXIS EXPANSION IN THE EAST
1942

Greatest extent of Axis control

For several years their activities consisted mainly of giving help and protection to those who, for political or racial reasons, were persecuted by the Nazis; *Anne Frank: The Diary of a Young Girl* (1947) gives a moving portrayal of the existence of a Jewish family hidden by Dutch friends, but in the end found by the Nazis.

Another function of the resistance was the transmission of intelligence, particularly about German military movements; the French were able to maintain secret contacts with Great Britain, and the headquarters of de Gaulle's Free French movement in London were extremely well informed about developments in France. The various resistance groups kept in contact through secretly printed newspapers, many of a very high intellectual level. They contained not only uncensored news but also lively debates on what the political structure of the occupied countries should be after liberation. The generally accepted aim was a thorough reorganization of political and social life. This demand for radical changes was only partly the result of the importance of socialists and Communists in the resistance; repudiation of the prewar ruling groups, whose policies had led to defeat and occupation, was general, and contempt for the men of the former ruling circles was intensified by the willingness of many financial and industrial leaders to collaborate with the Germans.

Throughout the occupation, the men of the resistance undertook single acts of sabotage, but the introduction of more elaborate guerrilla operations depended on circumstances. The Germans never succeeded in completely controlling the wild and inaccessible mountain regions of Yugoslavia; Yugoslav military organizations—the Communists under Marshal Tito (1892–1980), the royalists under Draža Mihajlović—remained active, usually fighting the Germans but sometimes fighting each other. In the wide forests and swamps of Russia, units composed of peasants and of soldiers who had escaped German encirclements operated behind the front, substantially damaging the German lines of communication. Resistance armies in Italy and France went into action when the invasion by American and British forces was imminent, contributing considerably to the collapse of German rule in the occupied areas.

Those participating in the resistance constituted a relatively small part of the populations, and they were exposed to great danger up to the end. The German secret police ruthlessly tortured people believed to possess information about underground activities, and the German troops, particularly the fanatic members of the SS, tried to stamp out sabotage and resistance by brute force. They made arrests in the middle of the night, took hostages and killed them on the smallest provocation, and shot people for the slightest suspicious moves.

The names of Lidice and Oradour are testimonies of Nazi terrorism. In revenge for the assassination of the Gestapo leader Reinhard Heydrich in 1942, the Czech village of Lidice was destroyed; its entire adult male population was killed, the women were placed in camps, and the children, separated from their families and nameless, were dispersed. In the French town of Oradour, in punishment for presumed support of partisans, the men were shot, and the women and the children were herded into the church and burned. (The fact that the Waffen-SS company that carried out this atrocity included fourteen native Frenchmen from Alsace came back to haunt the French when, after the war, they set out to use the Oradour massacre as a symbol to unify the nation in the contemplation of Nazi barbarism.) Because the conqueror's controls were so thorough and brutal, the resistance movement could exert effective pressure on the Nazis only when the Germans' reserves became strained and their grip started to loosen.

German soldiers arresting Jews in Budapest for deportation to concentration camps.

It is frequently said of the Germans that they are a systematic people. In confirmation of what admittedly is a somewhat doubtful generalization, it can be pointed out that when the Germans systematized the war effort by total mobilization, the Nazis thought the time had also come for what they called "the final solution" to the Jewish question. On January 20, 1942, in Wannsee, near Berlin, a conference was held under the chairmanship of Reinhard Heydrich, then the chief of the dreaded Security Service of the SS. Along with delegates of the chief organizations of the Nazi Party, representatives of the ministries of the Interior and of Justice and of the Foreign Office took part; other participants were high officials of the civil administrations of all the occupied territories. The presence of this last category was particularly important because as Heydrich stated in presenting the agenda of the conference, the main purpose was to arrange for the particular measures needed so that Europe could "be combed through from west to east" for Jews, who would be evacuated "group by group, into so-called transit ghettos, to be transported from there farther to the east." An exception was made for Jews over sixty-five or those wounded or decorated in the First World War; they would be herded into a ghetto in Theresienstadt in Bohemia. All others would be transported to the east; indeed, now began the tragic spectacle of long trains coming from all parts of Europe, even as far as Rome, carrying Jews packed in cattle cars to the east. The east meant the extermination camps of Chelmno, Belsek, Majdanek, Treblinka, and Auschwitz, where gradually, often after having been forced to labor for the Nazis, nearly six million Jews were annihilated in the gas chambers.

What did the average German citizen back in the Reich know about this industrialized mass murder in the east? We shall never be able to say with any precision how many Germans were aware of the details of the "final solution," but the sheer ambitiousness and thoroughness of the enterprise, the rounding up and transport of masses of people out of Germany to the east, certainly presupposed the knowledge and indeed complicity of thousands of "ordinary Germans." Recent research has shown that much of the organizational work and even some of the killing were handled by civilians and military personnel who were not members of the Nazi Party. The Nazi terror in general depended for its implementation and effectiveness on the cooperation of the broad mass of the German people; it was not simply the work of a small "elite." On the other hand, it overstates the case to argue, as has the political scientist Daniel Goldhagen in his controversial book *Hitler's Willing Executioners: Ordinary Germans and the Holocaust* (1997), that the Holocaust derived from a deep-seated and long-standing ambition on the part of the German people as a whole to eliminate the Jews from the face of the earth. German Gentiles' complicated attitude toward the Jews and things Jewish cannot be reduced to such a tendentious generalization, nor can the evil of the Holocaust be comprehended—if it can be comprehended at all—by locating it in the supposed national psyche and culture of a particular population. Accusations of collective guilt err not only by obscuring variations of opinion and practice within an allegedly uniform group but also by letting other complicit parties all too easily off the hook.

THE HINGE OF FATE

After the setback the Germans had received before Moscow in the winter of 1941, it was evident that the war would last long and that superiority in resources and materials would become increasingly decisive for victory. The entry of the United States into the war provided the Allies with a productive capacity that assured them material superiority. But it required time until American industrial potential was fully realized and American troops could effectively intervene in the war. The situation in the year 1942, therefore, was still precarious for the opponents of the Axis powers, which still possessed the initiative. It seemed by no means impossible that the Japanese might gain full control in the Far East and that the Axis in Europe might drive the British from the Mediterranean and knock Russia out of the war, thereby attaining an almost invincible position before the United States could make its weight felt.

In the first months of 1942, the advance of the Japanese in the Far East was awesome. They took the Philippines from the Americans; they conquered British forces on the Malay Peninsula and by February 15 were in Singapore, where they took sixty thousand prisoners. In combined land and sea operations they overran the Netherlands East Indies, reaching Batavia in March. They occupied Burma

German concentration camp at Sachsenhausen, near Berlin. In 10°F weather, the thinly clad inmates of the camp were forced to stand at attention for over six hours as guards searched outside the camp for an escaped prisoner. This was usual procedure in case of an escape and often lasted much longer; many died from the cruel exposure, and others dropped from exhaustion.

and took Mandalay on May 2. The road to India seemed open to them, and the barriers against their advance into Australia appeared to have fallen.

In Europe, the campaigns of 1942 were of crucial importance. A German offensive in the east was undertaken at a time when, despite the failure before Moscow, German power was still at its peak. Hitler counted on accomplishing in a second Russian campaign what he had not succeeded in doing in 1941. The offensive began in June. It was mainly directed toward the southern half of the Russian front, its purpose being to deprive the Russians of the agricultural areas of Ukraine, the industrial areas of the Donets Basin, and the oil fields of the Caucasus. The Nazis expected that Moscow and Leningrad, cut off from supplies, would be taken from the rear by encircling movements. The German armies succeeded in penetrating into the Caucasus, but their advance to the Volga was stopped at Stalingrad, and the battle for Stalingrad developed into one of the decisive battles of the war. Stalingrad was strategically important because its conquest would have cut communications between Moscow and the south. Moreover, the name had great symbolic value to both Germans and Russians.

At the beginning of the winter, except for a few buildings on the right bank of the Volga, all Stalingrad had been taken, and Hitler announced on November 9 that the city was "firmly in German hands." But the Russians resisted obstinately, using heavy artillery from the other side of the river. Then they succeeded in breaking through the front north and south of Stalingrad, and by the end of November the Germans, led by General Friedrich Paulus, were no longer attacking the Russians but defending themselves; the army before Stalingrad, three hundred thousand men strong, was encircled. Hitler forbade any attempt at withdrawal by a breakthrough toward the west, assuring Paulus of provisions by air. But this proved impossible, and slowly but steadily the ring around Paulus's army was drawn closer, until the German forces were reduced to a few isolated groups. On January 31, 1943, Paulus surrendered, with the one hundred twenty-three thousand men left of his army. Hitler's reaction was an emotional outburst of reproach that Paulus had not committed suicide.

The hole torn in the German front through the encirclement of the army before Stalingrad made the Germans' situation in southern Russia untenable and forced them to draw back. The Russian soldiers took tremendous pride in this decisive victory and now pressed their counterattack with a grim determination animated by a bitter hatred of an enemy that had visited so many atrocities on their land. The Red Army soldiers, much more than their Western counterparts, were motivated by thirst for revenge. By the spring of 1943, the lines on the eastern front were roughly the same as they had been one year earlier.

The battle for Stalingrad. One of the last German airplanes to take off from Paulus's encircled army.

In the fall of 1942, while the German military situation was deteriorating in Russia, there was a reversal of fortune in the Mediterranean area as well. In the winter of 1941–1942 the British had succeeded in forcing their opponents back from the Egyptian frontier, but in 1942 Rommel, commander of the German-Italian forces, had pushed the British back into Egypt, where overextended supply lines forced him to a halt. A lull permitted the British to strengthen their position through reinforcements sent by sea around Africa; at the end of October, the British Eighth Army under a new commander, Bernard Montgomery, was able to take the offensive. The Battle of El Alamein became the first victory of British troops over a German army in the Second World War. The fighting began on October 23, 1942, with a heavy artillery barrage that opened some holes in the German lines; British tanks penetrated these gaps and forced the Germans to withdraw. The front was small, consisting of hardly forty miles between sea and desert; because of British air superiority and control of the sea, the German supply lines, which ran along this narrow stretch between sea and desert, became unusable, and Rommel's troops were forced back from one position to another, finally from Libya into Tunisia.

While the British were exploiting their victory at El Alamein, a combined force of British and American troops under General Dwight D. Eisenhower landed in French North Africa on November 8. The Americans had yielded to the British insistence that an invasion of the European continent was not feasible in 1942, but some action that would divert German forces from the Russian front seemed necessary, and North Africa was chosen as the site for a surprise invasion. The operation was entirely successful. The French in Morocco offered only token resistance and then transferred their support to the British and Americans. The Germans in Tunisia had to fight not only Montgomery's Eighth Army coming from the south but also the British-American forces coming from the west. Encircled, the German beachhead in Tunisia was eliminated by the middle of May 1943.

During this same period, the summer of 1942, the Allies were also beginning to make gains in the Pacific theater. In three great sea and air battles—of the Coral Sea in May, of Midway in June, and of the Solomon Islands in August—the Japanese fleet was crippled, and further advances toward the south were checked. The British succeeded in bolstering the defenses of India, and Chinese resistance on the Asian mainland remained alive. Despite amazing conquests, Japan was still enclosed in a ring of hostile forces. By the end of the summer the offensives of Japan and the Axis forces had been halted and the initiative was held by the anti-Fascist coalition.

Germany before Surrender

Having come close to conquering all of Europe, Germany was now in danger of being conquered itself. The American industrial machine was in full gear and was producing planes, ships, and tanks at a rate that would have seemed

Wernher von Braun among German officers at Peenemünde, center of construction of German V weapons.

impossible at the beginning of the war. The Russian factories that had been transported into the Urals and Siberia were working to capacity. British war production increased steadily because air superiority gained with American help meant protection from sustained German air attacks. Now it was Germany that suffered from steady bombings; by the end of the war most of the larger German cities were in ruins. Clearly the decisive factor in warfare had become superiority in weapons and equipment, based on industrial mass production. Even Hitler recognized this fact and in the final stages of the war expected a favorable outcome only from new miracle weapons. But the guided missiles, the V-1 and the V-2 rockets that Germany was able to put into use in 1944, were of limited effectiveness, and work on jet engines had not been completed when the war ended. Nor had the Nazis made significant progress toward the development of an atomic bomb. Hitler distrusted nuclear science as "Jewish physics," and his top theoretical physicist, Werner Heisenberg, may have secretly undercut the limited atomic program that did exist to prevent nuclear weapons from falling into Hitler's hands. In any event, the Nazis' botched atomic bomb project pointed up the ingrained distrust among party officials, military officers, and civilian experts that increasingly undermined the German war effort.

For the Germans, the sole rational hope for victory lay in the possibility of breaking up the coalition closing in on them from all sides. The relations of the United States and Great Britain with their Russian ally had been troubled from the start. When the Germans invaded Russia in 1941, Britain and the United States promised to give the Soviet Union all possible support, and indeed, the supplies sent there were of crucial importance in maintaining Russian resistance in the critical first years of the German-Russian struggle. But the Russian leaders did little to publicize this outside help among their people; in their public statements about their allies they blew hot and cold. Their main interest was to promote a "second front," an Allied invasion of western Europe. Sometimes the Russians accused Britain and the United States of timidity and lack of energy in their pursuit of the anti-Fascist war; sometimes they praised them—depending on what approach seemed more likely at the moment to accelerate the opening of this second front.

Relations were further troubled because the Russians were unwilling to recognize the governments-in-exile, particularly the Polish government. They wanted to avoid any commitments that might affect the settlement of frontiers after the war. In Eastern Europe they supported only the resistance movements led by Communists. When in January 1943, after the successful landing in North Africa, Churchill and Roosevelt met in Casablanca, one of their purposes in demanding from Germany "unconditional surrender" was to dispel Russian fears that the Western powers might make a "deal" with Nazi Germany at the expense of the Soviet Union. At the meetings of Roosevelt and Churchill with Stalin in December 1943 in Teheran and in February 1945 in Yalta, in the Crimea, military questions stood in the foreground. But at Yalta the approaching end of the war made the consideration of the postwar settlement a necessity, although the decisions remained vague and general. The liberated and the defeated countries were to become democracies. Germany and Austria were to be occupied, with each of the victorious powers receiving a zone of occupation, although in the capitals—Berlin and Vienna—a central administration assuring uniformity of occupation policies was to be established. With regard to postwar boundaries and compensation for war damages, general principles were laid down rather than settled in detail. There was no real reason for the Nazis to hope that the anti-Fascist coalition could be broken up before Germany was completely defeated. Neither the Russians nor the Western powers were willing to negotiate as long as Hitler was in power. Germans with political insight believed that better peace terms or a separate settlement with either the West or the East might be obtained if Hitler was removed. The result was a conspiracy by socialists and liberals, high civil servants and generals, which culminated on July 20, 1944, in an attempt on Hitler's life. But the attempt failed; just a moment too soon, Hitler moved away from the place where a bomb exploded. The war was thus destined to last for almost another year.

Although the decline of the German fortunes after 1942 weakened the hold of Hitler and of Nazism over the minds of the German people, a corps of loyal Nazis survived until the end. Members of the SS particularly stayed firmly tied to the Nazi regime, and their military units remained a valuable fighting force, which was thrown into combat at critical points until the final weeks of the war. Moreover, many of the teenage members of the Nazi youth organization, who were conscripted in the last winter of the war, continued to regard Hitler as a man of destiny. The fanaticism of the SS guaranteed to the Nazi rulers an instrument for control by terror, and toward the end it was primarily fear and terror that kept the German people in the war. Himmler and his police imprisoned and tortured everyone suspected of holding anti-Nazi opinions or defeatist views. Such crimes—judged in Nazi-staffed People's Courts, from which there was no appeal—were punished by death. The ruthlessness of the SS police increased after the attempt on Hitler's life. Entire families of persons suspected of political crimes were placed in custody. There was a grisly report in the last days of the war about corpses of soldiers by the hundreds dangling from the trees of one of Berlin's streets because they had absented themselves from their military units.

Organization of resistance to the Nazi rule was impeded not only by the thoroughness and the terror methods of the police but ironically also by Allied bombing attacks. The saturation bombing of German cities disrupted communications and thereby strengthened the control of the Nazi rulers, who had priority use of roads, railroads, telegraph, and telephone. In coping with civil disasters, the Nazis made certain that water and food were given only to those who had appropriate identification papers. The Nazis were in charge of evacuating people from bombed quarters, and for weeks the whereabouts of the evacuees might be unknown even to close relatives and friends. The Nazi leaders and the Nazi apparatus alone maintained awareness of the situation as a whole; for the rest of the population life became atomized.

Even though the end seemed in sight in the spring of 1943, after the victories at Stalingrad and in North Africa, the military operations of the last two years of the Second World War were bitterly fought. Severely mauled, the German war machine was still formidable, and the Japanese still controlled a vast area of great natural resources and great defensive strength. A serious Allied defeat might have raised a cry for negotiations with the enemy, which would inevitably have been accompanied by all the difficulties involved in gaining cooperation among members of a coalition.

The Overthrow of Mussolini

The first of the Axis powers to collapse was Italy. After the defeat of the Germans in Tunisia, the American-British forces, now in control of air and sea in the Mediterranean, landed in Sicily and soon conquered the island. During the Sicilian invasion, on July 25, 1943, Mussolini was overthrown by a group that included leaders of the anti-Fascist underground, some prominent Fascists, and the military high command. Although the new government officially declared it would continue the war, secret negotiations for an armistice were started immediately. The Nazi leaders were prepared for such an event. When the armistice was announced on September 8, German tank divisions closed in on Rome, and plans for an Allied landing on the beaches near Rome had to be abandoned as too risky. During the winter the fronts stabilized between Rome and Naples; even the landing of Allied troops in Anzio did not lead beyond the formation of a beachhead. Central and northern Italy remained under Axis control.

After being overthrown, Mussolini had been imprisoned, but German paratroopers succeeded in liberating him. He was induced by the Germans to establish a Fascist government in northern Italy, where he proclaimed that free from conservative and monarchist restraints, he could now pursue the original Fascist ideas of social reform. But actually his government was controlled by the Germans. It was the Germans who insisted on holding trials for six Fascist leaders who had participated in the overthrow of Mussolini. They were condemned to death and executed.

The End of the War in Europe

The collapse of Fascism did not end the fighting in Italy, but it had a great moral effect, spurring anti-German activities all over Europe and, in addition, was of military significance for all the theaters of war. The Allies could give more effective support to the partisans fighting in Yugoslavia; German manpower resources became severely strained because the Italian occupation troops in the

D-Day. In preparation for the invasion, artillery is loaded aboard American transport ships on the southern coast of England.

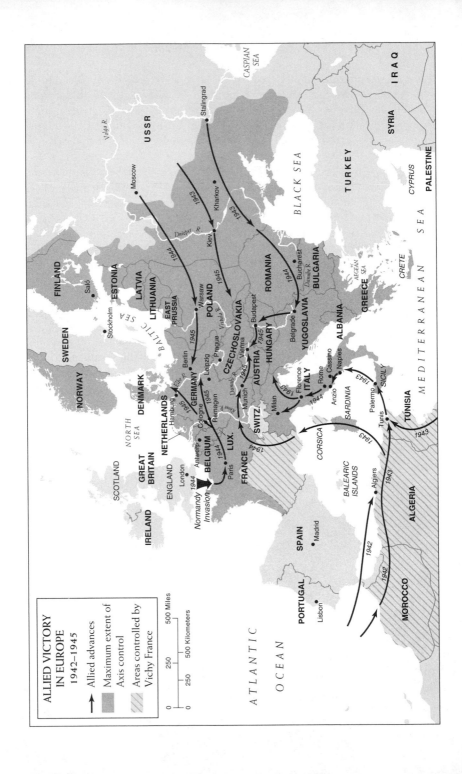

ALLIED VICTORY
IN EUROPE
1942–1945

→ Allied advances

Maximum extent of
Axis control

Areas controlled by
Vichy France

0   250   500 Miles

0   250   500 Kilometers

Balkans now had to be replaced by German forces. Moreover, the necessity of sending German tank divisions from the Russian front to Italy in July, at the time of the overthrow of the Fascist regime, had its impact on the eastern theater. The Germans were then undertaking another offensive, their last in the east, in the center of the Russian front. But the Russians, in a counteroffensive, forced them back on a broad front, reaching the Dnieper and reconquering Kiev in November 1943.

From this time on, the Allies held the initiative entirely, and in 1944 they advanced everywhere. The Russians continued to attack throughout the winter and by the beginning of the summer of 1944 were driving on to the borders of Poland and Romania. By the end of the summer they had reached East Prussia, forced Finland out of the war, and shifted the chief weight of their attack to the southern part of the front, where they brought about the surrender of Romania and Bulgaria. The Russian armies thus were approaching the frontiers of Nazi Germany from the southeast as well as from the east, their advances facilitated by the increasing pressure Great Britain and the United States were able to exert.

The stalemate on the Italian front was broken; Rome and Florence were taken, so only northern Italy remained in German hands. Greece was liberated.

The decisive accomplishment, however, of the United States and Great Britain in 1944 was the invasion of western Europe. On June 6, 1944, American and British forces crossed the English Channel and established beachheads on the Normandy coast. The success of this daring operation was primarily due to the complete Allied domination of the air, which frustrated German efforts to reinforce and supply their front lines. Moreover, the landings were protected by the heavy guns of the British and American ships, their fire directed in accordance with the excellent information about the German positions provided by the French underground. Artificial harbors brought over from England solved the problem of establishing a continuous stream of supplies for the invading troops, a problem that had appeared to stand in the way of any landing on a great scale. Nevertheless, it was a difficult operation, which had been meticulously planned and brilliantly executed under the supreme command of General Dwight D. Eisenhower, with the British general Bernard Montgomery and the American general Omar Bradley as field commanders.

The hours after the initial waves of American and British troops had landed on the beaches were critical. But the German military leadership proved to be uncertain and faulty. The German generals could not agree on whether to defend the entire coastline or to permit the Allies to move into the interior and draw them into a battle while they were still relatively weak. Moreover, at the crucial moment, Hitler refused to allow the employment of the German tank reserves because he was convinced that the landing on Normandy was a feint and that a stronger force would attack elsewhere on the coast. Once landed in strength, the Allies were able to effect a breakthrough with their tanks and to fan out in the rear, driving the Germans to retreat. By September, the liberation of France and Belgium was nearing completion, and the Allied armies were establishing themselves along the former German frontiers, where they were forced to stop because supplies were running short. A question that has been raised but can never be answered is whether the war might have been ended in 1944 if the Allies, instead of advancing on a broad front, had kept their northern wing back and given all their supplies to the advancing tank forces of General George Patton on their southern wing, which then might have crossed the Rhine and penetrated into southern Germany.

As it was, a further campaign in 1945 was needed. Before the Allies could resume their advance in the west, Hitler ordered a last German offensive, with troops and tanks brought together from all parts of the front. In December 1944, the Germans attempted to break through the center of the American-British line in the Ardennes. This last German offensive was so secretly prepared that even Ultra had given no indication to the Allies of what was coming. On the first two

A Russian soldier raises the Soviet flag on the Reichstag after the conquest of Berlin, May 1945.

days of their attack the Germans advanced quickly and inflicted heavy losses on the Americans. Moreover, the initial German success shook Anglo-American morale because it seemed to demonstrate the illusory nature of the assumption that the war was almost over; the alliance with Russia rose in value. But after moving forward two days, the Germans were halted; the Western Allies were able to regain the initiative, and in two weeks of fighting the German armies were pushed back to the line from which they had started. German losses in men and particularly in tanks were so severe that probably the effect of the Battle of the Bulge was to shorten the war. To relieve the pressure on the Allies on the western front, the Russians resumed the offensive in Poland early in January, and by the end of February they had driven the Germans out of Poland and were within fifty miles of Berlin. The British and American forces were able to mount an offensive in February, and on March 8 the American First Army crossed the Rhine at Remagen, south of Bonn. While the Germans were still fighting desperately in the east, the Allies in the west were mainly conducting mopping-up operations. On April 26, Russians and Allied forces met at the Elbe River. Three days later the German troops in Italy surrendered. On April 30, with Russian troops converging on Berlin from all sides, Hitler committed suicide in his bunker in the center of the city. With Hitler's death, German resistance ended. The German military commanders surrendered unconditionally on May 7 in Rheims to Eisenhower and one day later in Berlin to Zhukov, the Russian conqueror of Berlin.

The complete defeat of the German military forces after their series of stunning victories has raised many questions about the nature of Hitler's military talents and leadership. German generals, anxious to maintain the prestige of the German general staff, have claimed for themselves the credit for all the successes while putting the blame for the defeats on Hitler. Their explanation is too simple. Hitler rightly emphasized, contrary to traditional military thought, the importance of tanks and airplanes in modern warfare. He made certain that due attention was given to the construction of these weapons and to training in their use. Unlike many of his generals, Hitler was aware of the daring ways these new weapons could be employed, and he took an active part in planning the successful Norwegian and French campaigns of 1940, which showed the possibilities of the modern blitzkrieg. And Hitler's strategic judgment was not much worse than that of his generals. He was undoubtedly right when, against their advice, he insisted on defending an advanced front line in Russia during the winter of 1941–1942; retreat would have brought certain disaster. But Hitler lacked technical training and the patience for logistic details; he was inclined to plan and order operations without taking such factors as supplies and communications fully into account. He relied on his intuition, particularly after the early successes of the German Army had confirmed his own and his followers' faith in his supreme military talents. His intuition, however, played him false at two critical moments: in 1940, when he refused to use his tanks

The bodies of Mussolini (*third from left*) and his mistress Clara Petacci (*third from right*), placed on show in the Piazza Loreto in Milan, where in August 1944 Italian hostages had been shot by German military orders.

against the encircled British Army at Dunkirk, and in 1944, when he believed that the invasion in Normandy was a feint and reserves had to be kept back to repulse a landing elsewhere. There were other signs of deterioration in Hitler's military leadership during the last three years of the war. Confident of his intuition and unable to grasp fully the technical difficulties involved in fighting in Russia or in the desert, he regarded each reverse as the fault of cowardly or treasonous subordinates; he denied his generals any freedom of action and reserved all decisions, even at the local level, for himself. By prohibiting withdrawals, he sacrificed troops that could have been saved. He lived shut off in his headquarters, avoiding all encounters that might deter him from indulging in his strategic daydreams. Because he seldom visited the front and bombed German cities, he lost contact with the crude reality of totalitarian war. In the final months he gave orders to armies that did not exist or existed only on paper. It seems that not until April 22, when he was informed of the failure of SS troops to attack the Russians, did he realize the hopelessness of the situation and decide to stay in Berlin to the end.

One of the last scraps of news Hitler received was of the end of his fellow dictator Mussolini on April 28. When the German Army in Italy surrendered, Mussolini and his mistress had tried to escape to Switzerland, but at Lake Como, near the Swiss border, Italian resistance fighters caught and shot them. Then their bodies were brought to Milan and hung head downward in the Piazza

Loreto. The news of Mussolini's death confirmed Hitler in his decision to commit suicide. At this last moment he married his mistress, Eva Braun, and then dictated a long verbose testament that repeated the usual accusations against "international Jewry"; having poisoned his favorite dog so that it would not have to live with another master, he shot himself and, together with Eva Braun, who had taken poison, was burned. The facts of Hitler's melodramatic end are well proved.

The Fall of Japan

The German surrender made it possible for the British and Americans to concentrate their final effort on the Far East. In May 1945, when the war in Europe ended, Japan found itself in roughly the same position of Germany five months before; the initiative was in the hands of the Allies. By the beginning of May, just before the monsoon season would have forced a halt in military operations, British, Indian, and Chinese troops under the command of Lord Louis Mountbatten, reconquered Burma in a difficult and risky operation; most of the supplies had to be brought in by air, and more than two hundred thousand engineers and laborers were employed in building the airfields and roads needed to maintain the impetus of the advance.

A similar success was registered by the Americans in the Philippines. Their operations to recover these islands had started in October 1944. In a brilliant strategic stroke the Americans passed up the most southern Philippine island, Mindanao, and began their offensive with an operation against the central Philippine island of Leyte. The landing there on October 20 was made possible by a naval victory in Leyte Gulf, which severely crippled the Japanese Air Force and eliminated the Japanese fleet as a factor of military importance. The battle was of great significance for naval history, demonstrating that the time had passed when victory at sea could be decided by encounters among heavy battleships. At Leyte Gulf, aircraft carriers, airplanes, destroyers, and torpedo boats were the chief instruments of destruction. The defeat of their navy prevented the Japanese from getting supplies to their troops in the Philippines, and the American forces under General Douglas MacArthur (1880–1964) proceeded without setback to victory in the islands.

Having gained control of the Philippines, the Americans could advance to Iwo Jima and Okinawa, islands closer to Japan that might serve as bases for a direct attack on the Japanese mainland. Well aware of the strategic importance of these two islands, which formed their homeland's outer line of defense, the Japanese resisted tenaciously, and the fighting was sharp and bloody. However, in the middle of March, Iwo Jima was conquered, and on May 21, two weeks after the surrender of Germany, Sugar Loaf Hill, the key to the Japanese position on Okinawa, was taken.

Japan was now subjected to continuous intensive bombing by American planes. The loss of shipping resulting from these air attacks was fatal to the Japanese war effort, for Japan was dependent on imported coal, oil, and food. Recognizing that their situation was hopeless, the Japanese were ready to surrender; their decision was accelerated on August 6 and 8 when two atomic bombs were dropped, one on Hiroshima and one on Nagasaki. The resulting explosions, fires, and radiation burned out more than half of these cities, killed one hundred thirty thousand people, and injured an equal number. Japan accepted the Allied terms of surrender on August 14. On September 2, 1945, the Second World War officially came to an end on the deck of the battleship *Missouri* in Tokyo Bay, as the Japanese signed the articles of surrender in the presence of General MacArthur.

The decision to drop the atomic bomb aroused a dispute that is still going on. Scientists had counseled against its use because of its terrifying destructive power. An initial explosion of the bomb on a deserted island, which would have demonstrated its efficacy to the Japanese, would have been more in line with American ideas about morality and law in international relations. Yet when the decision was made, American leaders were not aware of how near Japan was to surrender and believed that heavy fighting was still ahead. It is perhaps instructive that the last military action in the Second World War demonstrated that as devastating as the war had been, the limits of destruction that modern technology could achieve had not yet been reached.

Japan itself of course offered ample evidence of the horrific power of modern atomic weaponry, but it also became in the postwar era a kind of laboratory for the implantation of Western democratic ideals in heretofore alien soil. Under General MacArthur the American occupation government set out to graft American political principles onto ancient Japanese traditions. Crucially, MacArthur decided against deposing Emperor Hirohito and charging him with war crimes. Instead, General Hideki Tojo and the other wartime leaders were made to take full responsibility for Japan's aggressive actions and abuses of human rights. This decision undoubtedly helped maintain social order in the immediate postwar period, but it had highly problematical consequences in terms of the Japanese people's understanding of their nation's role in the war. Because the emperor in whose name the war was fought was not held responsible, Japan as a whole began to think that it should not be held responsible. The emperor himself continued to be seen as a passive tool of the militarists when as recent research reveals, he played a fairly active role in strategic planning and decision making. With its "guiltless" emperor sitting safely on the throne, Japan embarked on its remarkable march toward economic revival partly at the cost of a rigorous denial or repression of its actual contribution to the horrors of the twentieth century.

PART III

REBUILDING EUROPE

CHAPTER 9

Postwar Uncertainties

FROM WARTIME COOPERATION TO CONFLICTS OVER THE PEACE SETTLEMENT

Europe at the End of Hostilities

THE MOST visible imprint left by the Second World War was physical destruction. Except for the university towns of Oxford, Cambridge, and Heidelberg, which out of consideration for their historic value had been left intact, all the larger towns of England and Germany had suffered extensive damage, with many areas, particularly in their centers, completely razed. Warsaw, Vienna, Budapest, and Rotterdam were in ruins. In France, most of the harbors along the Channel coast had been hit severely.

In contrast, the European countryside, except where it had been the site of military operations, was untouched. But communication between rural and urban areas had been severed, and the various parts of a country existed almost in isolation. Roads, bridges, and railroad lines had been demolished or damaged. Locomotives and railroad equipment had been broken or stalled at the military fronts or had so deteriorated that they were almost unusable. The factories that produced the equipment needed for reconstruction had been wrecked, and manpower was not immediately available. Roads were clogged with people trying either to return to their own countries or to find new homes. To those who saw the European continent in the spring and early summer of 1945, it seemed incredible that within a few years life might again become normal.

The Germans had been adequately fed during most of the war, but they had been supplied at the expense of the Nazi-occupied countries. Hence in most of Europe people were near starvation, and their capacity for work was small. The inhabitants of the Nazi-occupied countries, having served as forced laborers, were dispersed in labor camps all over Europe. Civilians who had been imprisoned and tortured because of participation in the resistance or because they had been held as hostages came back from their prison camps. A reporter described the arrival of a train with such women prisoners in Paris: "All the women looked

De Gaulle marching through the Arc de Triomphe in Paris after the German retreat. To the left of de Gaulle, in the center of the picture, is Georges Bidault, influential French politician of the 1950s.

alike; their faces were gray-green, with reddish-brown circles around their eyes, which seemed to see but not to take in. They were dressed like scarecrows, in what had been given them at camp, clothes taken from the dead of all nationalities."[1]

During the war, the populations of entire regions had been moved; thus, the Nazis had transferred the inhabitants out of parts of Poland and Ukraine so that Germans could be settled there. At the end of the war, an analogous policy was carried out by Hungarians, Yugoslavs, and Czechs who were unwilling to tolerate troublesome German minorities within their borders. In addition, Germans of East Prussia and Silesia, in fear of the approaching Russian armies, fled toward the west.

Impoverishment, scarcity, physical destruction, and social disintegration were not confined to Germany, Austria, and Italy; all Europe, not only the defeated

[1] Janet Flanner (Genêt), *Paris Journal: 1945–1965* (New York, 1965), p. 26.

countries, was undergoing suffering and privation. The most urgent need was to bring back some order and stability; initially this task fell upon the victors, whose troops were stationed all over Europe, since occupation of the defeated countries required secure lines of communication. Only the victors—mainly the Americans—could supply food and the basic resources needed for rebuilding roads and houses. It was in the victors' own interest to restore tolerable conditions of life; the morale and discipline of the occupying troops would suffer if they were surrounded by a starving, desperate population. But economic help could not be separated from the reorganization of an administrative apparatus, and this in turn was clearly tied to the reestablishment of some political order and authority. In most of the liberated countries, the political situation was tense, almost revolutionary. The leading politicians of the prewar era, who had withdrawn or gone into exile during the period of Nazi rule, came forward in the expectation that they would again play a leading role. Their aim was restoration of the prewar situation in their respective states. But new ideas had been developed in the resistance movements, which envisaged a united Europe and a society in which the powers of big business would be curtailed and opportunities would be more equally distributed. Thus, the returning politicians were confronted by new leaders who had come to prominence through their activities in the resistance movements and now wanted social and political changes that would weaken the influence of the previously ruling circles. Because of the omnipresence of their military forces, it was inevitable that the victors would exert a certain amount of political influence even in areas over which they had less than complete control. All over Europe the Americans, the British, and the Russians became involved in the revival of political and social life.

Wartime Preparations for Postwar Europe

During World War II, both the Western allies and the Soviets had praised each others' virtues in order to bolster the common martial effort. But behind the picture painted in wartime there remained the image formed in previous decades. For the Americans, Russia remained the country of Communism and the protagonist of world revolution. For the Russians, the United States and Great Britain, but chiefly the United States, were the prototypes of capitalism and the advocates of Russian encirclement. It must be added that on both sides the notions about the nature of the other country were hardly based on concrete knowledge. The Russians certainly had no clear idea about the working of the American Constitution and the limitations on the power of the American president; the Americans— partly because even in wartime the Soviets had prevented foreigners' access to information and severely limited their travel within Russia—had no concrete notion of the staggering losses in manpower and industrial installations Russia had suffered and they probably overestimated Russian strength.

The leaders of the various Allied countries were certainly aware of the difficulties of cooperation among powers so differently constituted and expected that fundamental divergences might emerge in discussions about the organization of postwar Europe. As long as the war against the Nazis was being fought, the appearance of tensions and conflict was undesirable, and wartime conferences among the Big Three—Churchill, Stalin, and Roosevelt—at Teheran and Yalta were chiefly concerned with plans of military strategy. The issue of a peace settlement had been agreed on only in very general terms. Russian agreement to the foundation of a United Nations Organization was taken as a sign, particularly in the American delegation, of Soviet willingness to cooperate in the postwar era. It was accepted that Russian national security required friendly governments along Russia's western borders; in this context an expansion of Russian territory toward the west into Poland was envisaged, while Poland was to receive compensation from German territory. The main principle on which the German settlement was to be based was "to ensure that Germany would never again be able to disturb the peace of the world." Hence the powers agreed that leading Nazis were to be punished and Germany was to be demilitarized. The question of reparations created great difficulties at Yalta. The Russians were firmly determined to get compensation from the Germans for the immense damages they had suffered. The British were adamantly opposed to reparations. Roosevelt finally agreed to a figure of $20 billion of which one-half would go to the Russians, but in order to avoid the economic disorder and disruption that had occurred after the First World War, reparations would be made in goods, production, and equipment, not in gold. This would have to be arranged by a central administration, the assumption being that Germany would remain united.

There was one concrete question about which agreement was reached during wartime: the question of occupation. In general the armies of Russia and the Western powers occupied those areas into which they had advanced, but in Germany and in Austria, specified zones were assigned to each of them. Thus, at the end of the war the following picture emerged.

Russian troops were stationed in the Balkans, with the exception of Greece and Yugoslavia, where the partisans, under Tito, had succeeded in driving out the Germans without any Russian military support. The Russians also occupied Poland, Czechoslovakia, and an eastern section of Austria; in Germany, American troops had advanced to the Elbe but were withdrawn in accordance with an agreement to give the Russians an occupation zone that extended beyond the Elbe into central Germany, including Thuringia. The western parts of Austria were divided into three zones—American, British, and French—and the same was done with the non-Russian occupied area of Germany. The American zone in Germany was the largest of the three, and it had about 17 million inhabitants. The British zone was smaller but had 5 million more people because it included the densely populated Ruhr area. The French zone was the smallest in size and population (5 million). The line drawn between the Russian zone, on the one hand, and the three zones of the Western powers, on the other, remained the boundary that separated East Germany, the German Democratic Republic,

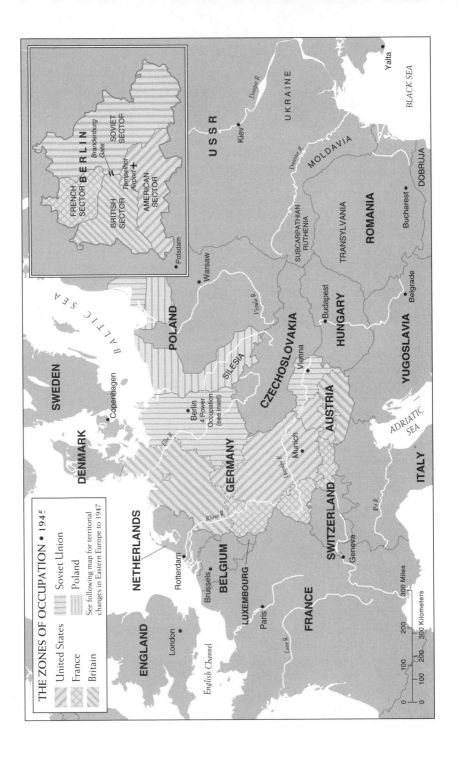

THE ZONES OF OCCUPATION • 1945

- United States
- France
- Britain
- Soviet Union
- Poland

See following map for territorial changes in Eastern Europe to 1947

Inset (Berlin):
FRENCH SECTOR
BRITISH SECTOR
SOVIET SECTOR
AMERICAN SECTOR
BERLIN
Brandenburg Gate
Tempelhof Airport
Potsdam

ENGLAND
London
English Channel
NETHERLANDS
Rotterdam
BELGIUM
Brussels
LUXEMBOURG
Paris
FRANCE
Loire R.
SWITZERLAND
Geneva
DENMARK
Copenhagen
SWEDEN
BALTIC SEA
GERMANY
Berlin 4 Power Occupation (see inset)
Elbe R.
Rhine R.
Munich
Danube R.
Po R.
ITALY
ADRIATIC SEA
POLAND
Warsaw
SILESIA
CZECHOSLOVAKIA
Vistula R.
AUSTRIA
Vienna
HUNGARY
Budapest
YUGOSLAVIA
Belgrade
SUBCARPATHIAN RUTHENIA
TRANSYLVANIA
MOLDAVIA
ROMANIA
Bucharest
DOBRUJA
Dniester R.
U S S R
Kiev
UKRAINE
Dnieper R.
Yalta
BLACK SEA

0 100 200 300 Miles
0 100 200 300 Kilometers

from West Germany, the Federal Republic of Germany. But when the zones were established, no long-term political division of Germany was foreseen. A sign of this was that Berlin, the German capital, was intended to be occupied and administered by the United States, Britain, France, and Russia in common.

It is evident that the issues over which agreement had been reached during the war—basic principles and division of occupation zones—were either so general or so technical that all practical questions were left open. They were to be decided at a postwar conference of the Big Three in Potsdam. France's exclusion from the conference was a reminder that the Big Three did not consider France a full and equal partner in the occupation of defeated Germany. In retaliation for this humiliation, France later refused to acknowledge the decisions made at Potsdam and tended to go its own way in handling occupation policy.

The Potsdam Conference

For the meeting to take place in Potsdam emphasized the equality in status among the three powers. If the conference had taken place in the United States, Great Britain, or the Soviet Union, this might have implied superiority of the power acting as host. Thus, Berlin—which, by agreement, was to be ruled by the United States, Great Britain, France, and Russia in common—was a natural choice. However, air attacks, and at the end fighting, had wreaked such destruction in the city that it seemed simpler to go into the suburbs and accommodate the statesmen and the accompanying diplomats and military personnel among the palaces and villas around the lakes of Potsdam. But undoubtedly a consideration of historical nature also played its part. It seemed appropriate to seal the end of Prussianism and militarism at Potsdam, which, since the eighteenth century, had been considered the embodiment of the Prussian militaristic spirit.

When the Big Three assembled in Potsdam, they approached the settlement with widely different ideas. Churchill and Stalin were inclined to divide the globe into spheres of influence; insofar as they had concrete areas in mind, such a division would have meant that Russia would have had eastern Europe and the Balkans in its sphere, Great Britain the Mediterranean with Italy and Greece. In the American delegation, such spheres of influence were unpopular because the term smacked of *ancien régime* diplomacy. The view about the postwar world held by the great majority of the American people and strongly represented in the American delegation was less power-conscious, more idealistic. This view was that the best, almost the only possible guarantees of peace, would be the spread of democracy and self-determination all over the world and the establishment of basic human rights and freedom of economic exchange underpinned by international cooperation and the easing of inequalities in the economic and social sphere. Although Roosevelt himself was tinged by this idealistic globalism to which their eighteenth-century tradition made the American people strongly inclined, he had also been very much aware of the importance of the power factor and had made no commitment that would have made impossible any adjust-

The Allied "Big Three":
Churchill, Truman, and
Stalin at the Potsdam
Conference, July, 1945.

ment to a settlement based on the principle of balance of power. His successor, Harry S. Truman, had not been clearly informed about the diplomatic negotiations and approached his task with the view generally held by the American public: an idealistic, one world view. Actually, at Potsdam the weight of the United States and Soviet Russia was greater than that of an exhausted and financially weak Great Britain. Moreover, during the conference, elections took place in Great Britain, and Churchill, who was in Potsdam at the opening of the conference, and who, despite the losses of the war, was firmly decided to maintain Britain's imperial position, was replaced as prime minister and British representative by the leader of the Labor Party, Clement Attlee, who was convinced that only a reorganization of political, economic, and social institutions could secure a continued influential position in the world for Britain. Thus, the main contrast at the conference was between Truman, representing an idealistic, global view, and Stalin, aiming at concrete gains and hardly enamored of a spread of parliamentary democracy.

The chairman of the Potsdam Conference was Truman. Truman's conduct of his chairmanship has been praised because of his decisiveness, but there is some question of whether this attitude did not arise from a certain insecurity and whether his eagerness for quick results meant that the really knotty problems were not thoroughly discussed and solved. Truman had some reason in rushing the conference because while at Potsdam, he received news that the atomic bomb had been successfully tested. In the American delegation the view was widely held that when American possession of the atomic bomb became generally known, many of the questions now under dispute would be decided in ways the United States wanted. Briefly, it was to the American advantage to establish methods of procedure but to postpone decisions of substance. At the conference, Truman informed Stalin of the existence of the atomic bomb, but the offhand manner in which he offered this information might have increased Stalin's distrust of the United States, since it could be taken to indicate that the United States wanted to keep possession of this weapon for itself. (In fact, Stalin was well aware of America's work on the atomic bomb because the Soviets had a spy in the Manhattan Project, Washington's top-secret atomic weapons program in New Mexico.)

The Potsdam Conference ended with a communiqué that seemed to indicate success, but the agreements arrived at referred to principles and methods rather than substance. The one concrete result, Russian assurance to enter the war against Japan, was really futile since the atomic bomb eliminated the need for Russian support. There was some agreement over the reparations question: the Russians would take their reparations out of their zone and would receive 25 percent of the industrial equipment removed from western zones; 15 percent would be counted as payment for food brought from the agricultural eastern zone to the industrial western zone. These provisions were in contradiction to the principle of treating Germany as an economic unit, which was again proclaimed to be fundamental. It was also stated that peace treaties should be prepared with "recognized democratic governments" of former enemy states—that is, Italy, Romania, Bulgaria, Hungary. But since one of the disputed issues was whether the governments Russia had established in the eastern countries were democratic governments, this formulation concealed the continued existence of divergences. There was agreement about the mechanism to which the solution of these questions ought to be entrusted. A Council of Foreign Ministers, in which France and China should also be members, would handle the peace treaties and general political questions. A Four-Power Allied Control Council, composed of the United States, Great Britain, Russia, and France, would handle the German questions.

There were some areas in which final decisions were made and successfully carried out. One was the punishment of major war crimes. A trial before an international tribunal at Nuremberg between November 1945 and October 1946 resulted in the death sentences and subsequent hangings of ten Nazi leaders, among them Foreign Minister Joachim von Ribbentrop, Hitler's military advisers Wilhelm Keitel and Alfred Jodl, Minister of the Interior Wilhelm Frick, and the Jew baiter Julius Streicher. Göring committed suicide in prison. Himmler had killed himself after capture.

Also, the issue that traditionally formed a main center of dispute in peace negotiations—the question of drawing new boundaries—caused no great diffi-

The Nuremberg Trials. Among the Nazi leaders in the front row are Göring (*at the extreme left*), Hess (*second from left*), Ribbentrop (*third from left*), and Schacht (*at the extreme right*). In the second row Papen is third from left and Speer third from right.

culties. Readjustments were relatively minor, and the victorious powers took care that serious conflicts did not arise in the areas they controlled. In the east, Romania had to cede northern Bukovina and Bessarabia to Soviet Russia, and part of Dobruja to Bulgaria. But Romania received northern Transylvania from Hungary, which also had to relinquish some land to Czechoslovakia. Finland lost to Russia the territory of Petsamo in the north and the Karelian Isthmus in the south. Russia kept the Baltic states and extended its dominance southward along the Baltic Sea by annexing the northern part of what had been East Prussia; Poland recognized the frontiers Russia had established in 1939 as a result of the Nazi-Soviet pact but was promised extension of its frontiers in the west as compensation.

When the two councils established for the conclusion of peace treaties and for the problems arising out of the occupation of Germany began their work, they were immediately faced by two issues that eventually would cause the wartime alliances to break down: the stumbling block in the negotiations about the conclusion of the peace treaties was the composition of the governments of countries under Russian occupation; the one relating to the occupation of Germany was the question of German reparations.

THE UNITED STATES AND SOVIET RUSSIA
CONFRONT EACH OTHER IN EUROPE

The Problem of the Peace Treaties and the Development
of East-West Conflict

Ostensibly, the efforts of the Council of Foreign Ministers to draft peace treaties were successful. After negotiations extending over almost one and a half years, peace treaties with Italy, Bulgaria, Romania, Hungary, and Finland were signed in February 1947. But the negotiations—conducted in a number of meetings of the Council of Foreign Ministers in London, Moscow, and Paris—had revealed the Russian unwillingness to accept the formula proposed by the United States that these states ought to have a "government broadly representative of all democratic elements in the population and pledged to the earliest possible establishment through free elections of government responsive to the will of the people." The discussions were sharp, and breakdowns sometimes seemed unavoidable. By the end, some compromise was obtained by allowing some representatives of non-Communist parties into the governments of the Eastern states. But this was only a token, avoiding the impression of capitulation to Russian demands rather than a real loosening of the Communist grasp over this area. The result of these meetings was a deterioration of the political atmosphere. America and Britain were aware that they had failed to open up Eastern Europe to Western influence. Winston Churchill put a name to the new European division when he coined the term *iron curtain* in a speech in Fulton, Missouri, on March 5, 1946.

In the United States, the conviction now grew that Russian resistance to the demand of allowing truly democratic forms of government in these countries

Winston Churchill delivers a famous address. On March 5, 1946, in a speech delivered in Fulton, Missouri, the former British prime minister warned that an "iron curtain" separated Eastern Europe from the rest of the Continent. The phrase "iron curtain" was to be often repeated during the Cold War years.

was an indication that after having been saved from defeat, the Russians had returned to the idea of world revolution and were planning Communist expansion all over Europe. The emergence of difficulties and friction had a strongly disillusioning effect. The Russians seemed to have been deceptive. The dictatorial character of their regime and the brutality of Stalinism had been somewhat underplayed during wartime. It came now almost as a revelation that Russia was not a democracy. An incitement of public opinion against Russia to increase the armament budget and to maintain a strong military posture also played a role in producing anti-Soviet feeling.

The interpretation that Russia planned an aggressive policy seemed confirmed by events in several areas. Early in 1947, it had become clear that the Soviet Union was not willing to accept the American plan for the control of atomic energy, which would have secured an American monopoly in atomic weapons for a number of years and which called for an international inspection system that the Russians felt encroached on their sovereignty. At the time, Russian obstructionism was considered a further indication of their unwillingness to subordinate themselves to an international order. At the same time it was believed that Russia was expanding by aggressive action in the Balkans. In Greece, the government seemed unable to defeat Communist guerrillas operating in the north of the country. The guerrillas were able to continue the fight because of the support they received from their Communist neighbors in the north. Great Britain, which had assisted the non-Communist forces in Greece since the war, no longer felt able to do so, and the United States decided to take Britain's place. The American government acted in the belief that only by direct participation could it prevent Russian domination over Greece and Turkey. This was the occasion of the announcement of the Truman Doctrine in March 1947, in which the president stated "that it must be the policy of the United States to support free people who are resisting attempted subjugation by armed minorities or by outside pressures." The Truman Doctrine became crucial in European politics during the following decade.

In the American view, it was necessary to build a dam against further Russian advances. It was assumed that the Russians had been encouraged to embark on their aggressive and expansionist course because they believed it would be easy to establish Communist regimes all over Europe: economic misery had created great dissatisfaction, and Communist parties of great strength had been formed. In France and Italy, elections had taken place soon after the war, and within a somewhat changed and modernized constitutional framework—Italy, for instance, had become a republic—parliamentary regimes were functioning again. The great role the Communists had played in the resistance movements in both countries had given them a strong popular appeal. They had become mass parties whose leaders participated in the government. The American leaders decided that preventing Europe from falling into Russian hands required measures of two kinds: in the political field and in the economic field. In the spring

Scene from the Greek civil war. Mules carrying munitions into the mountains.

of 1947, under discreet prompting by the United States, the Communist ministers were removed from the governments in France and Italy. The United States had indicated that the elimination of the Communists from the governments would smooth the way for economic help from the United States, and indeed, on June 5, 1947, General George Marshall, then American secretary of state, announced that if the European nations would work out a comprehensive plan describing the requirements for their economic recovery, the United States would respond with loans and technical assistance. Ten months later, in April 1948, the Marshall Plan began to function.

The Problem of German Reparations and the Break between
Russia and the West
    In 1947, American and Russian policies were so much set on a course of confrontation that there was probably little chance for returning to any kind of cooperation. But if there had been such a possibility, a conflict on German reparations extinguished all such chances. The American government was convinced that attempts to make Western Europe secure against Communist penetration or domination could be successful only if Germany could revive economically and if its economic resources could be used for the needs of Western Europe. In a foreign ministers' conference in Moscow in the spring of 1947 that was meant to prepare the draft for a peace treaty with Germany, the Russians insisted on receiving $10 billion in reparations from current German industrial production. The United States and Great Britain saw in this insistence more than an emphatic bid for compensation for war damages; it appeared to them an attempt to prolong misery and chaos in Germany, also damaging the economic life in western Europe. The Russian reparations policy seemed a clear sign that the Russians were preparing the ground for a spread of Communism all over the West. Thus, the American and British governments not only refused the Russian

demand but took measures in the later part of 1947 and the early part of 1948 to rebuild the economic life of West Germany and to prepare for Germany's participation in the European Recovery Plan. The British and American occupation zones became economically united, and one German administration for the two zones was established. Right after the war only a very limited amount of German industrial production had been allowed to prevent the possibility of future German rearmament; in the summer of 1947 the level was raised to prewar heights. These economic measures were sustained by a currency reform that extended to all three western zones of occupation; the Russians had to respond with a currency reform of their own. Then German political life was revived; local elections had taken place in the various provinces and federal states in all three zones. Obviously the next step was the establishment of a parliament and a government for the whole of West Germany. The Russians could have no illusions that West Germany, which was much more powerful in population and mineral resources than the Russian-occupied East Germany, was being constituted as an independent power and slipping out of their grasp.

The Beginning of the Cold War: The Berlin Blockade

There can be no doubt that most of those who made American policy were seriously convinced that they faced a dangerous threat that might at any time lead to war. This was a misconception, for the Soviets had no serious plans to take over Western Europe, nor were they ready to wage war with the West in order to build their new "empire" in Eastern Europe. This does not mean, however, that there were not some ticklish moments when because of misunderstandings or just plain accident, a new conflict might have broken out. The long-term avoidance of a new world conflagration amid the tensions of the Cold War was no more inevitable than the victory of the Allies in World War II. Only now is it clear, on the basis of declassified Soviet documents, that Moscow's main reason for imposing its control over Eastern Europe was to ensure its survival as a major power, not to promote "world revolution." As one Soviet spymaster recalled, "For the Kremlin, the mission of Communism was primarily to consolidate the might of the Soviet state. Only military strength and domination of the countries on our borders could ensure us a superpower role."

On the other hand it must also be said that the Russians were no less guided by misconceptions about American policy than the Americans about Russian policy. As Andrei Zhdanov (1896–1948), one of Stalin's most trusted lieutenants, said about the Truman Doctrine in 1947: "The United States proclaimed a new, frankly predatory and expansionist course. The purpose of this new, frankly expansionist course is to establish the world supremacy of American imperialism." This view of the world situation clearly had its usefulness for Stalin because it justified continued emphasis on heavy industry and a rigidly disciplined life. Dictatorial measures could be presented as national necessity. This view also hit a responsive chord, however, because it agreed with what the

TERRITORIAL CHANGES IN EASTERN EUROPE TO 1947

——— 1947 boundaries

– – – – 1939 boundaries

·········· Nazi-Soviet boundary, 1939

Territorial changes resulting from pre- and postwar settlements

0   100   200   300 Miles

0   100 200 300 Kilometers

Petsamo

Murmansk

(to USSR)

(to USSR)

FINLAND

NORWAY   SWEDEN

Oslo

KARELIAN ISTHMUS (to USSR)

Helsinki

Leningrad

Stockholm

NORTH SEA

DENMARK

ESTONIA (to USSR)

Riga   LATVIA (to USSR)

Moscow

Copenhagen
(to USSR)

LITHUANIA (to USSR)

NETHERLANDS

Königsberg   EAST PRUSSIA (to Poland)

USSR

BALTIC SEA

Minsk

(to Poland)

Danzig (to Poland)

Berlin

Warsaw

EASTERN POLAND (to USSR)

BELGIUM   GERMANY

POLAND

Kiev

Prague

Kraków

LUXEMBOURG

NORTHERN BUKOVINA (to USSR)

CZECHOSLOVAKIA

Vienna   Bratislava

(to USSR)

BESSARABIA

SWITZERLAND   AUSTRIA

Budapest

SUB-CARPATHIAN RUTHENIA (to USSR)

Odessa

HUNGARY

Trieste (Free City)

(to Yugoslavia)

ROMANIA

Belgrade

Bucharest

BLACK SEA

ADRIATIC SEA

ITALY

YUGOSLAVIA

DUBRUJA (to Bulgaria)

CORSICA

BULGARIA

Rome

Sofia

Istanbul

ALBANIA

SARDINIA

Tirana

AEGEAN SEA

TURKEY

GREECE

MEDITERRANEAN SEA

SICILY

Russians had been told in theoretical writings and had experienced in the first years of the regime. That is, the Russians saw themselves still threatened by the same danger they had feared throughout the interwar years: a capitalist encirclement aiming at the overthrow of their regime. They were unable to conceive that American interest in truly representative regimes in Poland, Hungary, and Czechoslovakia had no ulterior motive; they believed it would be an attempt to move the jumping-off place from which operations could be launched as close as possible to the center of Russia. On the basis of this misconception of American intentions they acted in these countries with a ruthlessness that seemed only to confirm the American view of the dangerous character of Russian policy. When Communists were eliminated from the governments in Italy and France, the Russians forced leaders of non-Communist parties in the Eastern satellites out of the government. Some were also put on trial with trumped-up charges of treason. Maniu, the revered leader of the Romanian Peasant Party, ended his life in solitary confinement. Purges and trials were accompanied by loud accusations against the aggressive intentions of the capitalist world and further poisoned the atmosphere. The last and also the most brutal coup to eliminate possible political opposition took place in Czechoslovakia in February 1948. By clever use of an opportunity given by a government crisis, the Communists established themselves as sole rulers. This event was the more shocking because during the interwar years Czechoslovakia had stood out as a democratic Western-oriented country, and its leaders had enjoyed a high reputation in the West. Now Beneš, the president, resigned and the foreign minister, Jan Masaryk (1886–1948), the son of the founder of the state, died in circumstances that were suspicious enough to raise serious doubts about the official explanation of suicide.

These purges coincided with the reconstruction of an international Communist organization in September 1947. The Communist International had been dissolved during the war as a concession to the Western Allies. The new organization was called the Cominform because its center was an "information bureau" charged "with the organization of interchange of experience and, if need be, coordination of the activities of the Communist parties on the basis of mutual agreement." The latter task soon became paramount. The Cominform determined the line the various Communist parties were to follow. Thus the USSR was able to force all the members of the Cominform to reject any funds from the Marshall Plan, which initially had been offered to Eastern as well as Western European countries. While this decision helped protect the emerging Soviet bloc from Western influences, it also guaranteed that the East would remain substantially poorer than the West. In retrospect, it can be seen as a strategic blunder on the part of Stalin.

While the Russian goal was clearly to create a wide glacis on their western front as protection against attacks by enemies, their policy concerning Germany was more complex. Considering the thorough devastation of Russian industrial installations in the war, there is no reason to doubt that the Russians were passionately concerned with receiving reparations from Germany. Such demands were presented to their allies by the Russians from the earliest wartime conferences on, and they placed great value on Roosevelt's agreement with the figure of $10 billion for Russia. But it must also be said that the Russians—with some justification, as two world wars had shown—had great fears of Germany and believed that a recovered and remilitarized Germany would be the natural spearhead of an attack against Russia. The Russians were undoubtedly aware that reparations from current production would postpone German economic recovery and also retain for Russia a voice in the handling of German affairs. They saw therefore in America's plan for putting Germany on its feet again proof of American aggressive plans against Russia, and they resented the creation of a western Germany, the development of which they were unable to influence.

The Russians now decided on a drastic measure, the full purposes of which have been clarified by documents from recently opened Soviet archives. On June 18, they halted road and rail traffic between western Berlin and the West, and on June 24 they stopped barge traffic as well, along with deliveries of electrical power and coal from the eastern sectors to the West. The Soviets hoped to use their stranglehold over Berlin to force the Allies to rescind their plans for a separate West German state; they also wanted to regain the right to extract reparations from the western zones. These were the immediate goals; down the line they hoped to show the Western powers that it made no sense for them to stay in Berlin at all, deep within the lair of the Bear.

The Soviets believed that the West would be reluctant to risk a full-scale war over Berlin; they expected a negotiated settlement to their satisfaction. Actually, however, war was a greater possibility than the Russians realized; their blockade of Berlin almost resulted in the Cold War's turning hot. General Lucius Clay, who headed the American occupation of Germany, proposed that a convoy of American troops should force its way into Berlin with orders to shoot in the event of resistance. General Curtis LeMay, commander of the U.S. Air Force in Europe, offered air support, suggesting that this was a fine opportunity to launch a preemptive strike on all Russian airfields in Germany. The Pentagon and State Department considered Clay's plan far too risky, however, and decided instead to try to break the Berlin blockade by supplying the city from the air. Thus began the famous Berlin airlift, during which Western Allied planes flew around the clock to bring the western Berliners the food, coal, medicines, and even baby formula they needed to survive. The Soviets knew that if they shot down the transport planes, World War III would likely result, so they desisted. When it became clear that they could not force the Western Allies to alter their policies in Germany via their squeeze on Berlin, the Soviets lifted the blockade. On May 12, 1949, traffic resumed between western Germany and the western sectors of Berlin.

Berlin was to remain a ticklish spot. Nikita Khrushchev, who took over control of the USSR after Stalin's death, called Berlin the "testicles of the West," a

The Berlin blockade. An American airplane arrives with supplies.

tender place he had only to "squeeze" to make the Western leaders scream. He was to find his own opportunity to put on the squeeze and thereby to provoke another dangerous confrontation in the Cold War when he authorized construction of the Berlin Wall in 1961. Western and eastern Berlin had entirely separate administrations, and to make economic life in western Berlin possible, it received financial support from western Germany. West Berlin became a western showcase in Russian-dominated Eastern Europe. In contrast to gloomy and bleak East Berlin, life in West Berlin appeared rather splendid.

The blockade was over, but the Cold War continued. The importance of Europe as a central theater of the Cold War soon waned. The Far East became the main theater of this strange war.

EXTENSION OF THE COLD WAR
TO THE FAR EAST

Asia at the End of Hostilities

The Second World War had been a global war. It is somewhat misleading therefore to focus solely on European issues in discussing the problems of the postwar world. The tensions that arose in Europe were closely connected with the developments that had taken place in the Far East, and the Cold War was as much an event in the Far East as in Europe.

When Japan surrendered on August 14, 1945, friction between Russia and the West in this area seemed unlikely. During the war, Russia had been anxious to concentrate all its military efforts on Germany and had carefully avoided embroilment with Japan. However, at the Yalta Conference, Stalin had promised that his nation would enter the war against Japan after the termination of military operations in Europe. Accordingly, Russian forces were assembled near the Manchurian border, and Russia declared war on Japan on August 8. Since the Japanese military situation had become hopeless by then and the atomic bomb dropped on Hiroshima on August 6 had broken the Japanese will to resist, Russia's entry into the war played no part in the Japanese defeat. The procedures followed by the Americans in negotiating and accepting the Japanese surrender showed clearly that they regarded the settlement with Japan exclusively their own. During the following years, the United States remained the only outside force to exert control and influence over the reconstruction of Japan as a political power.

But Japanese troops had penetrated far into China and had occupied most of Southeast Asia. The Japanese surrender had wide repercussions in these regions. In these areas not only the United States but also China and Great Britain had fought, and America's allies were unprepared for Japan's sudden collapse.

The size of the area, the number of inhabitants, and the variety of peoples made handling the problems of Southeast Asia a complex task. These inherent difficulties were aggravated by revolutionary ferment resulting from Japanese rule and occupation.

Japan had treated the nations of Southeast Asia in various ways. For instance, Thailand had been considered an ally and had been permitted to enlarge its frontiers at the expense of its neighbor French Indochina. In other areas, in Malaya and in the islands of Indonesia—Java, Sumatra, Borneo, Celebes—the Japanese had ruled through military administrations. In China, in the Philippines, and in Burma they had established puppet governments. French Indochina was a special case. As long as France was in the Nazi orbit, the French administrators of Indochina had collaborated with Japan. But after the liberation of France, the French turned against Japan, and the Japanese established a puppet government.

Japan exploited all these areas brutally. Yet the Japanese occupation had revolutionary and lasting consequences. The Japanese invasion of this area demonstrated that Asian people were able to shake off the yoke of European rulers; nationalism had received a powerful impetus. The attitude of the nationalist leaders of these peoples to Japanese rule was ambiguous. Some regarded the formation of a national government, even if limited in its freedom of action by Japanese power, as a first step toward independence and were willing to cooperate with the Japanese in setting up the puppet regimes. Others considered Japanese rule to be quite as oppressive as that of the Western powers and organized resistance movements. In the course of these developments indigenous leaders gained a strong hold over the masses. The nationalist leader in Indochina, Ho Chi Minh (1890–1969), fought against the Japanese; in Indonesia, Achmed Sukarno (1901–1970) cooperated with the Japanese but held out against their plans to divide the region into independent units, championing a united Indonesia.

The Retreat from Colonialism

Since the Allied forces in Southeast Asia were under British command during the war, the British took charge of the area after hostilities ended. The first task of the British was to organize the surrender of the Japanese forces that were stationed in this area and burdened its economy. The presence of large armies, the disturbances of war, the flight of people from their homes, and the interruption of communications had restricted cultivation of the land, and in many regions people were starving. Therefore, a foremost concern of the British authorities was to increase the production of food, particularly rice, and to arrange for its distribution. In attempting to accomplish this task, the British were confronted with an unpleasant political dilemma. Undoubtedly cooperation with the indigenous governments and forces would have been most effective. But this would have strengthened the governments that the French and the Dutch, who had formerly been the rulers in these regions and were anxious to resume control, wanted to eliminate. The French and the Dutch were Britain's allies, and Britain itself had colonies in Southeast Asia. This contradiction between short-range and long-range interests prevented the development of a uniform policy for the entire area. Settlements were difficult to arrive at, and they varied from one region to the other. The Dutch were unable to reinstate themselves and were forced to recognize the independent republic of Indonesia in 1946. The French reestablished their rule in Indochina, but fighting against them never ceased, and after long and costly campaigns, climaxed by the defeat at Dien Bien Phu in 1954, the French withdrew and left three independent states: Laos, Cambodia, and Vietnam. The British returned to Malaya and Singapore and promoted a political evolution through which Malaya became independent but remained part of the British Empire. In Southeast Asia, the Japanese defeat started a process of revolution that has not yet been completed.

The first manifestos of the Communist International had stated that the liberation of the peoples of Asia and Africa from colonial rule formed an integral part of the Communist fight against capitalism. Thus, the Russians, although not directly involved in the struggle in Southeast Asia, clearly favored nationalist movements in this region, and they had close contacts with some of the nationalist leaders. For instance, Ho Chi Minh was trained in Moscow and worked in Communist movements in Europe before returning to his native Indochina.

Since American foreign policy too had an anticolonial tradition, the rise of nationalist movements in Southeast Asia did not necessarily place Russia and America on opposite sides. However, the United States acted in close cooperation with Great Britain and France in Europe, and there was danger therefore that the United States would be stamped as an ally of traditional European imperialism and that because the United States was more powerful, American imperialism would appear as the most sinister force. This actually did happen in China, the nation that presented the most difficult problems of the Asian postwar situation.

A Chain of Open Conflicts

THE STRUGGLE IN CHINA

That China would be a source of conflict between Russia and the United States was not apparent at the end of the war. Here again the most urgent task was to effect the disarmament and withdrawal of the Japanese armies, stationed in the vast regions along the Yangtze and the Yellow rivers. Much time had to be spent arranging the removal of these troops, and this proved to be a disadvantage to the Chinese Nationalist government under Chiang Kai-shek. In the interim period the Communist armies of Mao Zedong in the north had the opportunity to expand their power. In August 1945, Russia had recognized Chiang Kai-shek's regime as the central government of China, so it seemed justifiable to assume that the Russians were anxious to establish cooperation between the Communists in the north and Chiang's government in the south. The United States had a similar aim. The Chiang Kai-shek government had been frequently criticized in the United States for its lack of energy in pursuing the war against the Japanese, and many Americans hoped and believed that cooperation with the Communists would stimulate the Nationalists and provide an impetus to social and agricultural reform that would be highly desirable for China. But protracted negotiations failed to settle the differences between the Nationalist government of Chiang Kai-shek and Mao Zedong's Communist forces. Instead, a sharp contest developed between the two opposing Chinese governments for the control of Manchuria, and in this conflict the Russians decided to back Mao. At the time of the Japanese surrender, the Russians had occupied Manchuria—temporarily, they declared. In the next months they made no effort to evacuate the area, but in April 1946, when the struggle over German reparations became critical, they removed their troops from Manchuria very suddenly, and the rapidity of their retreat gave the Chinese Communists the opportunity to move in.

The American government continued its efforts to establish peace in China, but neither of the warring factions really wanted an agreement because each believed that it could win over the entire country. When General Marshall, who had been sent to China in December 1945, abandoned his peace efforts in January 1947, he assigned responsibility for the failure of his mission to both sides:

the "dominant group of reactionaries" in Chiang Kai-shek's government and the "dyed in the wool"[2] Communists in the other camp. The final result was an open confrontation and civil war between Chiang Kai-shek's forces, somewhat reluctantly and halfheartedly backed by the United States, and Mao's Communists, supported by Russia.

THE KOREAN WAR

By the beginning of 1949, the victory of the Chinese Communists under Mao Zedong was a certainty, and by the end of the year the Nationalist government under Chiang Kai-shek had withdrawn to Formosa (Taiwan). The United States refused to recognize the Communists as the legitimate rulers of China and continued to give recognition and protection to the Nationalist government. The tension between the United States and Communist China became the crucial element in the next dangerous crisis of the Cold War, that of Korea.

After the Second World War, the area of Korea north of the thirty-eighth parallel had been occupied by the Russians, that south of it by the Americans. As in Germany, agreement on a single government for the entire country had been impossible to reach. Eventually the occupying forces were withdrawn, the Russians leaving a Communist regime in North Korea, the Americans a Western-oriented democracy in South Korea. On June 25, 1950, North Korean troops began to invade South Korea, attempting to unify their divided nation. American military leaders had gradually become convinced that a non-Communist South Korea was indispensable for the defense of Japan, and the U.S. government ordered its troops into South Korea to support the faltering South Korean government. The matter was brought before the United Nations at a time when the Russians were boycotting the Security Council, and a resolution was passed condemning the North Korean aggression. A United Nations command, headed by General Douglas MacArthur, was set up, and although most of the troops were American, they were supported by contingents from many other countries. The UN military operations were conducted with wavering success. Having succeeded in driving the North Koreans out of the south, the Americans advanced beyond the thirty-eighth parallel, but there they encountered opposition by strong North Korean forces aided by Communist Chinese armies and were driven back into South Korea. Finally a front along the thirty-eighth parallel was established, and armistice negotiations were initiated. In July 1953, after almost two years of negotiations, an armistice was concluded that ended the war and virtually restored the status quo ante. Korea remained divided along the thirty-eighth parallel.

THE FRENCH DEFEAT IN INDOCHINA AND THE END OF THE COLD WAR

While the Korean War slowly petered out, another dangerous military clash developed on the southern frontier of China. There a nationalist and

---

[2] These phrases are from General Marshall's statement on China on February 7, 1947.

Communist-led movement known as the Vietminh, under the leadership of Ho Chi Minh, was fighting the French for greater autonomy in that part of Indochina which, after the separation of Laos and Cambodia, was called Vietnam.

The Vietminh received recognition and aid from Communist China and Soviet Russia, while France and the puppet regime it had established were supported by Great Britain and the United States. Modern weapons and bombing from the air were unable to destroy the guerrilla forces fighting in millet fields and rice paddies, and when the French advanced into the north, a part of their forces were cut off and finally forced to surrender at Dien Bien Phu in May 1954; ten thousand French soldiers became prisoners. At this point mediation by Russia, the United States, and Great Britain resulted in an armistice; among its terms were provisions for an election to be held in 1956 to unify Vietnam. Until then, Vietnam was to be divided along the seventeenth parallel, with the northern half Communist-controlled and the southern half Western-oriented. This was not a solution that would last. Tensions smoldered on until the explosion happened, but this was in a different situation. With the agreement on Vietnam the most acute phase of the Cold War had ended.

CHAPTER 10

Reconstruction and Revolt: The 1950s

THE BASIC TASKS OF RECONSTRUCTION

SIMULTANEOUSLY WITH the struggle between the superpowers, the rebuilding of a political order had begun in the various European countries. Because their revival and continued existence depended on the protection of either the United States or Soviet Russia, these nations could not develop exclusively according to their own inherent tendencies; rather, they had to follow the leadership and, to a certain extent, the prescriptions of Soviet Russia in the East and of the United States in the West. Unavoidably the forms that reconstruction took in the West and in the East were widely different. In the countries in the Soviet sphere—East Germany, Poland, Czechoslovakia, Hungary, Romania, Bulgaria—the organization of government that existed in the Soviet Union became the model: an executive elected and controlled by the Communist Party or its leadership. In the Western bloc no direct imitation of the Constitution of the United States took place, but all the states of the Western bloc became parliamentary democracies, a constitutional form considered the European equivalent of American democracy. Despite these fundamental differences in form and principles, the foremost task of reconstruction was the same in all European countries, both of the West and of the East, which meant that frequently they encountered rather similar difficulties.

Of necessity, all governmental activities centered on the revival of economic life; thus, economic issues shaped and dominated political reconstruction. This order of priorities was taken for granted in the Eastern bloc, since Marxist philosophy has always viewed the organization of economic life as controlling the political and social order. Of course, the importance of economic prosperity for political stability was also recognized in the non-Marxian world, especially since the economic crisis of 1929, which had opened the door to Nazism and to the catastrophe of the Second World War. Nevertheless, it may be doubted whether before the war concern with the economic situation would have been considered the almost all-absorbing task of government. Assigning government an active role in economic reconstruction blurred the lines between politics and economics in Western-oriented nations; governments had not only the right but the duty to play an active role in the reorganization of economic life and to exert a directing and controlling influence on economics.

The paramount importance of the economic issue for the reconstruction of Europe encouraged the tendency to enter into plans and actions beyond national boundaries and to organize on supranational regional levels. This approach was strongly supported by the superpowers not only because it seemed more practical and efficient but also because it solidified the bloc under their leadership. Cooperative procedure was also favored by various individual governments because it might make possible projects that went beyond the financial means of an individual state. Such cooperation led, for example, to the establishment of CERN, the European Research Center for High-Energy Particle Physics, in northern Italy, and of ESRO, the European Center for Space Research, in Paris.

It would be wrong, however, to see at work in these efforts for supranational cooperation and integration only motives of a practical, political, and financial nature. They corresponded to feelings that had developed among the European peoples during the war, to a subtle shift that had taken place in the attitude toward nationalism. During the war a reaction had set in against the strident nationalism embodied in Hitler's doctrine of the superiority of the German race. This did not mean that nationalism was replaced by cosmopolitanism. The individual heroics of a young Yugoslav partisan shouting defiance at German soldiers as they executed him or of a French resistance leader who took poison to avoid betraying his comrades under torture were certainly inspired by deep national feeling. It would seem, however, that the nationalism that emerged from the Second World War was no longer the nationalism of the early twentieth century, which had been intensely competitive and had placed one's own nation above all others. The nationalism of the Second World War was inspired by the belief that in the nation and through that nation higher, more general eternal values could be realized. Catholics, socialists, and Communists all were convinced that their ideas drew strength from being rooted in the requirements of a national existence. The two greatest poets of the French resistance, Louis Aragon and Paul Éluard, were Communists, protagonists of a new social order and devoted internationalists, but in their poems these themes were interwoven with a passionate praise of French life and customs, landscape and history. The manner in which nationalism as a reaction to Hitlerian tyranny had become tied to and permeated by supranational values is reflected in the fact that in the postwar years the political parties that had the widest political appeal were the Catholic Party and the Communist Party, both wedded to supranational ideologies.

THE CONTEXT OF RECONSTRUCTION: SCIENCE, TECHNOLOGY, AND ECONOMICS

Notions of European unity or of organization on a regional basis could hardly have been put into practice if, after the Second World War, science and technology had not created conditions that facilitated cooperation and integration. The impetus military needs had given to scientific and technical developments continued into the period following the war, and it gained in strength and speed. The application of new discoveries and inventions to economic life had an impact on the forms of economic organization and on both public and individual life. It is important to be aware that the context in which reconstruction of Europe took place was a steadily progressing and accelerating transformation extending into all spheres of human activity.

The explosion of atomic bombs over Hiroshima and Nagasaki is usually viewed as the beginning of the nuclear age. The harnessing of atomic energy was so dramatic an event that it often obscured the powerful impetus the war gave to scientific discoveries and technological inventions in a variety of other fields. Transport planes used in the war opened the way for mass air transportation, which brought the continents closer together; the jet engine, invented during the war, accelerated air travel over large spaces. The motorization of the military forces created the basis for a rapid development of the automobile industry, for business firms as well as private individuals.

Whereas before 1939 only the most affluent had traveled abroad, the revolution in transportation gave the middle classes the possibility of moving easily beyond the frontiers that separated one country from another.

Widened horizons were also provided by radio and television. Radio had already been in use before the war. In wartime it had become the main source of information about the state of the world, the approach of enemy airplanes, or, as in occupied countries, a secret source of moral support. With improved instruments and enlarged programs, radio almost took on the aspect of a necessity of life. Television was first displayed to large audiences at the Berlin Olympics of 1936 but remained expensive for several years after the war, with extremely limited programming. It became lower priced in the fifties; by 1975 every fourth person in Western Europe, every tenth person in Eastern Europe, and every fifth person in Russia had a television set.

Reconstruction was not limited to the restoration of previously existing industrial installations; the exploitation of scientific and technological innovations made in wartime meant that certain industries expanded and that for some new products new industrial enterprises had to be established. Previously existing enterprises like Fiat in Italy or Volkswagen in Germany became new industrial giants; on the other hand, a small tool manufacturer like Max Grundig, recognizing the possibilities of radio and television, built up the largest radio factory in

Europe. Of the industries that had stimulated the Second Industrial Revolution, the chemical industry retained a leading role after the Second World War. In the fifties its output tripled. This expansion was due partly to a remarkable increase in synthetic products, which replaced metals, wood, and glass, and partly to the marketing of numerous new pharmaceutical products, the result of medical research stimulated by the war. However, competition in the chemical industry was keen, and much capital investment was needed, with the result that only large enterprises could work profitably. The largest chemical firm on the continent was the Italian Montecatini; another giant was the West German Bayer. Bayer had been part of I. G. Farben but had become independent after the war when Farben, because of its monopolistic character, had been dissolved by order of the Allies. Of equal, if not greater, importance were developments in the electrical industry, which widely expanded because of the manufacture of products using electronics. The age of the computer had begun; radio began to be superseded by television; movies and television became color movies and color television. After the Marshall Plan had provided a spark, the rise in industrial productivity was astounding. By 1956, industrial production in Germany and Italy was more than double what it had been in the last normal peace year of 1937. In France and Great Britain, production had also advanced by more than 50 percent.

Industrial growth was an interconnected process advancing on a broad front over a wide area for a variety of reasons. The influence of the superpowers stimulated planning for the entire region, many wartime patents were of an international character, and advances in transportation and communication facilitated marketing across national borders so that production of one good in various factories was frequently uneconomical.

A further crucial factor in overcoming national separation and isolation was the employment situation. In the later part of the fifties, when the industrial machine was again in full swing, neither Germany nor France had enough workers to keep it going, so both added workers from other countries to their labor forces; in the middle of the sixties the number of foreign workers in Germany amounted to 1.3 million, in France to 1.8 million. Most came from the Mediterranean area, a great number from Italy, where, in the agrarian south, unemployment was very high. Although in the late sixties the effects of a population increase and a beginning recession made the employment of foreign workers less desirable, Europe had begun to become more integrated through internal migration.

RECONSTRUCTION IN THE EASTERN BLOC

Reconstruction in Soviet Russia

A peculiar and unique feature of the situation in Eastern Europe was that Soviet Russia, which dominated the states in the East and gave them leadership, was itself one of the countries in need of reconstruction. Actually, Russian reconstruction presented more extended, more serious, more difficult problems than reconstruction in any other part of the world. The Soviet Union is estimated to have lost 16 to 20 million citizens in the Second World War, more than Central and Western Europe together. Other statistics are equally startling: seventeen hundred towns and cities and seventy thousand villages were devastated, primarily in western Russia, which in prewar times had been the Soviet Union's most highly developed area. Russian industrial installations and transportation facilities in this area had been entirely destroyed, and masses of human beings had been forced to move elsewhere.

Russian reluctance to finance the rebuilding of its economic life by American loans was probably equaled by American hesitancy to grant them. But the financing of reconstruction by means of the labors of the Soviet people meant that the Iron Age of the first Five-Year Plan was now followed by another Iron Age. The production of consumer goods remained rigidly curtailed, and a housing shortage forced large families, often consisting of several adults, to live in a single room. The losses suffered in the war also produced a shortage of labor; to exploit fully all available resources, labor camps were formed in which prisoners of war, displaced persons, and all those whom the regime mistrusted were assembled and put to work.

Concentration on heavy industry and expansion of the collective farm system remained the economic program. Moreover, the prospects for an increase in production of consumer goods diminished because the rising tension with the United States led to an expenditure on military weapons greater than ever before. It was unavoidable that after the immense efforts of the war, the imposition of continued hardships and the reinforcement of controls were hard to accept and aroused a certain degree of discontent. Perhaps such dissatisfaction could not be entirely disregarded because the victory in war had given the army and its leaders a reputation and prestige not unequal to that enjoyed by the leaders of the Communist Party. There was danger that the army might become a state within the state, that with resentment against the government's repressive measures growing, the military might try to influence policy decisions.

Stalin, deeply suspicious by nature, regarded it necessary to reassert the authority of the Communist Party and, still more, his own dictatorship by taking brutal action against all possible opposition. The outward sign of Stalin's policy to reduce the prestige of the army was to remove its most famous general, Marshal Zhukov, from his prominent position as commander of the Russian forces in Berlin to an obscure command post in Russia. Soviet writers and scientists had gained some freedom during the war and showed in their writings some knowledge of Western literature and even a certain admiration for it. Andrei Zhdanov, the Communist Party leader in the successful defense of Leningrad and, till his death in 1948, Stalin's greatest collaborator, reminded writers and scholars in a famous speech in August 1946 that despite being "outwardly beautiful," bourgeois

The Confrontation Between the Superpowers • 1950

"culture is putrid and baneful in its moral foundations"; writers ought to be "engineers of human souls" and had "an enormous responsibility for the education of the people and for the education of Soviet youth." Zhdanov reorganized the literary and scientific organizations by excluding those who had shown signs of admiration for the West and laid down the correct line the organizations ought to follow.

The weapon, however, that Stalin most thoroughly and most effectively used to eradicate opposition and to enforce absolute obedience was the police; he was particularly close to the people's commissar for state security—-that is, the head of the secret police, Lavrenty Beria. Whenever Stalin found, or only suspected, opposition to his authority, or even a possibility of opposition, Beria would act as if a conspiracy had taken place and would execute the conspirators. There is no doubt that in the last years of Stalin's life the pathological aspects of his character—his paranoia that he was surrounded by rivals and enemies, his constant fear of losing power, his megalomania and ruthlessness, his complete disregard for human life—dominated him so completely that even those who ruled with him lived in terror of him and felt freed when he died on March 9, 1953. There were bitter fights for the succession until, three years later, Nikita Khrushchev emerged as the leading figure, and in a closed session of the Twentieth Congress of the Communist Party ended the Stalinist era by revealing the criminal features of Stalin's regime.

Stalin left to his successors no easy legacy. Although he had succeeded in organizing the various states of Eastern Europe according to the Soviet pattern, the brutal repressiveness of his procedure and his unwillingness to accept any adjustments to special circumstances had created tensions which endangered the coherence of the Eastern bloc.

Reconstruction in the Satellite Countries

TREATY BONDS BETWEEN SOVIET RUSSIA AND THE SATELLITES

The fundamental basis for the pursuit of a common line by the Communist powers was provided by the Cominform. In addition, Soviet Russia created particular ties with all the Communist-controlled states. During the war Russia had concluded mutual assistance treaties with the governments-in-exile of Yugoslavia, Czechoslovakia, and Poland that guaranteed help in case of future German aggression and provided for close economic, cultural, and political cooperation. Similar pacts were negotiated in 1948 with Bulgaria, Romania, Hungary, and Finland, the former Axis satellites. A comparable treaty, assuring assistance against attack by Japan or by powers allied to Japan, was signed with China in 1950. Chinese agreements with North Korea and North Vietnam tied these countries to the Russian bloc. Finally, in 1955 the relation of the Communist states in Europe to one another and to Soviet Russia was redefined by a pact concluded in Warsaw; in addition to the partners of previous mutual assistance agreements—Soviet Russia, Albania, Bulgaria, Hungary, Poland, Romania, Czechoslovakia—the treaty included East Germany, which now advanced to full membership in the Soviet alliance system. The Warsaw Pact precluded participation of its members in any other coalition or alliance and assured members of immediate assistance, including the use of armed force, in the event of armed aggression, establishing for this purpose a joint command for the armed forces of the members as well as a consultative committee to harmonize political action. The stationing of Russian troops in Eastern European countries, notably in Romania, Hungary, Poland, and East Germany, had formerly been justified by the need to maintain communications with the Russian occupation zones in Germany and Austria; now it was guaranteed by bilateral treaties.

THE ESTABLISHMENT OF A NEW ORDER IN THE SATELLITE COUNTRIES

The precondition of the establishment of a Communist political and social order in Eastern Europe was the elimination of all bourgeois and non-Communist parties and elements from political power. Socialists, members of the middle classes, and peasants had participated in the last phases of the struggle against the Fascist regimes in Hungary, Czechoslovakia, and the Balkans, and the demand of the United States and Great Britain for the formation of democratic governments in these countries had assured representatives of these groups of some hold in the governments. We have discussed that in 1947–1948, in connection with the increase in tension between Russia and the United States, the Communists in all the Eastern European countries became the sole possessors of power. In towns, villages, factories, and business enterprises, committees of the Communist Party were established and acquired undisputed authority, which guaranteed that all aspects of life would be handled in accordance with the principles of the Communist Party and the orders of the state; the hold of these party committees over the organizations they supervised was also secured by the favors they could distribute.

With the ending of the influence of any bourgeois, non-Communist elements in the government, the construction of a new economic order was to begin. Bulgaria and Czechoslovakia were the first to act, drafting four-year plans in 1949; in 1950 Hungary followed with a five-year plan and Poland with a six-year plan; the last countries were Romania and East Germany, both issuing five-year plans in 1951. The primary aims of all these plans were identical. The Soviet model— that is, industrialization that placed emphasis on heavy industry and collectivization of agriculture—was to be introduced in all these countries. It has been said that the adoption of the Soviet model was hardly suited for these areas; their real strength lay in agriculture, and in some of these states—Czechoslovakia, Romania, Bulgaria—agricultural reforms, which broke up great landed estates and created small peasant holdings, had taken place after the First World War. However, the adoption of a policy of industrialization and collectivization in the satellite countries was not solely a blind imitation of the Russian model. In the past these areas had been oriented toward the West; they exported agricultural products to the West and received from the West machinery and industrial products. The economic reorganization of these states after the Second World War was therefore aimed at breaking their ties with the West—that is, making them industrially independent and orienting their trade toward Russia.

If one takes an overall view, these goals were attained. By 1951, 92 percent of Bulgaria's trade was with Soviet Russia. Even Poland's trade with Russia, which before the war amounted to only 7 percent of the country's foreign trade, had reached 58 percent by 1951. At the same time, industrial production increased remarkably. By 1952, annual production in Poland and Czechoslovakia, the two most industrialized countries of the bloc, was double its prewar level, and the total steel production in Eastern Europe was then roughly equal to that of West

Germany and twice what it had been before the war. The labor force employed in industry in Eastern Europe increased about 33 percent by the early 1950s.

This immense transformation—the creation of a new social and economic order, the change from a primarily agrarian to a strongly industrial society— naturally created tensions and aroused criticism, opposition, and also obstructionism. Moreover, in addition to the unrest such a social revolution must generate, there were particular reasons for dissatisfaction. The Soviet leaders, regarding the economic recovery of their own country as their foremost target, pursued a policy of direct exploitation in these areas. Hungary and Romania, even after the Communists were in full power, were forced to continue to pay reparations to Russia. Moreover, the Russians seized all German property in these countries and dismantled all German industrial installations, which they then transferred to Russia. The Russians also participated in a number of joint companies controlling such enterprises as the Romanian merchant marine and the Hungarian bauxite mines. Thus, a portion of the earnings of these companies went directly to Russia. Moreover, the Russians imposed upon these countries agreements to deliver certain goods, such as coal, at extremely low prices. Having lived for decades under bourgeois or Fascist regimes, these countries were ideologically unprepared for Communist rule. Thus, after the Communist seizure of power, measures of indoctrination were pursued with ruthless energy. The Communist youth organizations, backed by the power of the ministers of education, promoted an educational system propagating a strictly Marxist ideology. In many countries in the East, however—Poland, Czechoslovakia, and Hungary—the Catholic Church had a stronghold, and a clash with the church was therefore unavoidable. Indeed, in every satellite country with a strong Roman Catholic population, Church leaders were subjected to sensational trials in which they were accused of conspiring against the government. Most notably, in 1949 József Cardinal Mindszenty of Hungary was imprisoned and relentlessly tortured to coerce a confession of "crimes against the state."

These factors—Russian exploitation and antichurch action—exacerbated tensions over the most unpopular and most hotly resisted part of the Sovietization of this area: the collectivization of agriculture. By tradition and also by the more recent agrarian reforms mentioned above, small peasant farms were numerous; collectivization meant loss of cherished values without any visible advantage. Some of the Communist leaders of these countries had doubts that collectivization was appropriate to their areas or at least were in favor of a slow and cautious procedure. This issue brought about the first big crisis in the Eastern bloc.

THE DEFECTION OF TITO AND THE STALINIST PURGES

Immediately after the war, Yugoslavia appeared to become more quickly and more thoroughly a replica of the Soviet model than any other of the Eastern European states. Because the Yugoslavs themselves, rather than foreign armies, had thrown off the Nazi rule, and because this liberation was chiefly the work of the

Josip Broz Tito, the World War II Communist partisan leader who ruled Yugoslavia with an iron hand from 1945 until his death in 1980.

Yugoslav Communist Party under Tito, no bourgeois or socialist elements had to be taken into the Yugoslav postwar government. It was therefore a purely Communist government and, in accordance with the Soviet model, began immediately a program of industrialization and collectivization.

But because it was composed of different nationalities, and because of the old rivalries and conflicts among these nationalities—Serbs, Croats, Slovenes— circumspection had to be used in proceeding toward the new socialist society so as not to provoke friction and endanger the unity of Yugoslavia. Since Yugoslavia lay on the borders between the East and the West, Stalin regarded delays and deviation with particular distrust; he wanted to keep the situation there under sharp control. But Russia had no strong lever with Yugoslavia, for Yugoslavia was the only country of Eastern Europe that had not been liberated by Russian armies. When Stalin demanded that Russia be given control over the Yugoslavian army and the secret police, Tito refused. Thus, in June 1948, in reaction to Tito's disobedience, at a Cominform meeting that Yugoslav representatives did not attend, Yugoslavia was excluded from the Cominform.

The Russians evidently expected that this measure would force Tito to submit, but as the military leader of the partisans during the war Tito had become a national hero with a very strong hold over the people. His popularity, together with some economic help from the West, made it possible for him to retain power, and the Russians resigned themselves to this situation although they continued vehement vocal attacks against him and maintained an economic blockade of Yugoslavia. Under Tito, Yugoslavia developed a special form of Communism, a mixed economy. There was no overall economic planning for the entire country. In agriculture, collective farms coexisted with privately owned farms. Industry was nationalized, but control was exercised by the workers in the individual factories, and there was a free market for the sale of many consumer goods.

Tito's defection aroused fears in Stalin and the Russian leaders that other Eastern European countries might follow the Yugoslav example, with each country forging its own individual type of Communism. Consequently, under pressure from the Russians, widespread purges took place in the Eastern states. Whereas the purges of 1947–1948 had been chiefly directed against politicians from the bourgeois camp, this new wave of purges was directed against Communists.

One aim of the purges was to make the Communist Party an absolutely reliable instrument for execution of directives given from above. In every Eastern European country the size of the Communist Party had increased considerably since many former members of the dissolved and suppressed non-Communist parties thought it useful to enter the Communist ranks. This influx of incompletely trained and untested members was considered especially dangerous for the efficiency of the party because even the upper strata contained discordant elements: on the one hand, those who had taken refuge in Moscow during the war and, on the other hand, those who had remained at home working in the underground. These two groups now competed for control of the party. In danger of becoming unwieldy and divided, the Communist parties in Eastern Europe instituted mass purges. Hundreds of thousands were deprived of membership in the party as "alien" or "hostile" elements. Another aim of the purges was to eliminate those Communist leaders who might be inclined to follow the example of Tito, and the consequence was a substantial change in the composition of the central committees of the Communist parties in the various states. Leaders who might be inclined toward Titoist deviations were brought before tribunals in sensational procedures patterned after the Russian purge trials of the 1930s, complete with accusations of treason, confessions, and finally the imposition of the death penalty. The most outstanding victims of these trials, starting in 1949, were the vice premier of the Bulgarian government; the minister of the interior in Hungary; and in Czechoslovakia, the foreign minister and the general secretary of the Communist Party and deputy prime minister. Władysław Gomułka (1905–1982), the general secretary of the Polish Communist Party, was deposed and later imprisoned, but he escaped execution.

The purges and trials of the leadership in the Russian satellite countries continued until 1953, and in time their purposes went beyond those of party discipline and the elimination of Titoists. The motives for the persecution of individuals are frequently obscure. These were the years when Stalin's suspiciousness had clearly become pathological and when anticipation of his approaching death sharpened the conflicts among Russian Communist leaders anxious to eliminate possible rivals. The trials in the satellite countries appear to have been repercussions of the struggles in the Russian leadership group, as is suggested by the fact that some of these trials, like some of those in Russia, had anti-Semitic overtones. In his dealings with the various Eastern European nations Stalin preferred to work through one person entirely devoted and obedient to him. The purges served to concentrate power in each country in the hands of one entirely pro-Stalin Communist leader: Mátyás Rákosi in Hungary; Walter Ulbricht in East Germany; Klement Gottwald in Czechoslovakia; Boleslav Bierut in Poland. Like Stalin himself, though to a slighter extent, each of these leaders became the center of a cult of personality. By the time Stalin died in 1953, the various means that had been applied to unify the Russian-controlled areas of Europe—ideological uniformity, institutional identity, economic integration, force—appeared to have transformed them into a monolithic bloc ruled and directed by Russia.

The price that had been paid was high; dissatisfaction and tension were pushed below the surface only by means of force. How tense the situation was became clear in the summer of 1953, after Stalin's death, when the introduction of a new wage policy led to a revolt of workers in East Berlin, suppressed only by intervention of Russian military forces. All over the Eastern bloc this was taken as a sign that a danger point had been reached and that a change of course in economic policy was urgent and had to be undertaken as quickly as possible. The state that embarked on the changes with greatest energy was Hungary; Rákosi, who had risen to the prime ministership of Hungary as a loyal Stalinist, remained general secretary of the party but lost the prime ministership to Imre Nagy, an advocate of the new course. In other Eastern European countries the shift in direction was more moderate. In Poland the all-powerful Stalinist Bierut prevented any radical change.

Obviously, the establishment of a new leadership and a new political line could proceed more easily in an atmosphere of lowered international tension. This was one reason the Russians were in favor of ending the acute phase of the Cold War by a compromise over Indochina and why in the spring of 1955, to almost everyone's surprise, they agreed to a treaty that terminated the occupation of Austria and restored Austrian sovereignty, thus removing one of the sources of friction along the line where American and Russian spheres of interest touched. The various facets of the new Russian policy were clearly indicated by Khrushchev in his speech to the Twentieth Congress of the Communist Party. He admitted the possibility of different "forms of transition of various countries to socialism," and he revised the traditional Marxist thesis that "war is inevitable so long as imperialism exists."

The Russian leaders were not unaware that the relaxation of tensions between East and West, combined with an economic policy that permitted the Eastern European states considerable variation within the prescribed general framework, might endanger Russian domination. Not only had the Warsaw Pact of 1955 had the purpose of strengthening military cooperation against the West, but the Russians were anxious to counteract the dangers of a lessening of tension and the centrifugal consequences of greater economic autonomy in the satellite countries by reinforcing political and military bonds. The formation early in 1956 of a Joint Nuclear Research Institute including all the Communist states reflected this trend. There can be little doubt that the uniformity Stalin had pressed upon the European Communist world had brought things almost to a breaking point; the attempt of the new Russian leaders to modify his policy was almost unavoidable, but because of the explosive tensions that had accumulated under Stalin, "controlled transition" proved to be a complicated process full of dangers for the coherence of the Russian alliance system.

RECONSTRUCTION IN THE WEST

Treaty Bonds in the Western Bloc

Originally when the war ended, there was a great difference between the situation in the East and the situation in the West. Russia, the superpower in the East, was a European power. It had contiguous frontiers with the states of Eastern Europe. The United States, the superpower in the West, was far removed from Europe, and it was generally expected, although this soon proved to be erroneous, that it would withdraw from Europe after hostilities had ended. The peoples in Western Europe living under the threatening shadow of Russia were naturally anxious to acquire greater strength by forming a bloc; moreover, in Western Europe the tendency to supranational corporation, which had developed during the war, had found a particularly strong echo. The first step toward a closer tie among the nations of Western Europe was the Pact of Brussels, concluded on March 17, 1948. Great Britain, France, and the so-called Benelux countries (Belgium, the Netherlands, and Luxembourg) promised to come to one another's help in the case of a military attack and agreed to the formation of a permanent council that would advise on common interests and common action. Simultaneously delegates from most of the non-Communist European countries met in Brussels to make plans for European cooperation and integration of a more comprehensive character. From this initiative developed both a regularly meeting council, of which the foreign ministers of all the Western European states were members, and a Council of Europe, which included delegates from Western European parliaments. An unwillingness to have their sovereignty limited, strongly emphasized by Great Britain and later also by France and other powers, restricted the practical efficacy of these institutions and enthusiasm for them declined. But they

Bombed-out Berlin
being rebuilt in the
postwar era with the
help of Marshall
Plan funds.

continued to exist and were significant in keeping the trend toward European integration alive.

It was also obvious that as important as the Pact of Brussels was as an expression of European willingness to resist Russian pressure, even the combined forces of the states that had concluded the pact were not strong enough to resist the Russians in case of war. Thus, almost immediately after the conclusion of the Pact of Brussels, attempts were made to include the Americans in military arrangements to defend western Europe. The outcome was the North Atlantic Treaty Organization (NATO). It comprised—next to the members of the Pact of Brussels—the United States, Canada, and five other European powers: Italy, Portugal, Denmark, Iceland, and Norway. The most important practical consequence of this agreement lay in the military field: the military forces of the European partners of the treaty and the American-Canadian forces stationed in Europe were integrated and placed under an international command. But NATO was also a political alliance, with the participating powers promising to defend one another against any attack on "the freedom, common heritage, and civilization of their people." Thus, by 1950 most of Western Europe was tied together with the United States by close military and economic bonds.

Closer cooperation in the West had a problem, however, which Soviet Russia had not encountered. The Russians had been able to integrate their German occupation zone by establishing a Communist regime in East Germany. Reliability and obedience were guaranteed by the complete dependence of this regime on Soviet Russia. But the establishment of parliamentary democracy in West Germany did not exclude the possibility of political changes that might bring nationalistic forces back into power. Moreover, the German mineral riches might make a resurrection of German military power possible. Thus, the defeat of Nazism did not end all fear of German aggressiveness among Germany's Western neighbors. It was clear that German partnership in the Western bloc implied that in the course of time Germany would again become a fully sovereign power, but the problem was to make sure that this freedom of action would not result in another German attempt to gain hegemony and domination.

These difficulties were removed by a number of further agreements reached after long and difficult negotiations. The issue that was first resolved concerned an economic question: After eliminating the danger that Germany might use its mineral resources for rearmament, how could German steel and coal be made available to European economic reconstruction? This problem was solved by the creation of the European Coal and Steel Community (ECSC) in 1951. The French foreign minister, Robert Schuman, made a courageous proposal to place the coal and steel production of Germany, France, and the Benelux countries under common administration. This agency, the so-called High Authority, composed of experts from the various participating countries, had the right to set and regulate prices, to increase or limit production, and to levy fees that would finance the organization. Great Britain did not participate in the belief that this organization would hamper the English coal industry and was incompatible with its relations to the countries of the commonwealth; thus began a long-lasting separation of Great Britain from economic cooperation with the countries of the Western European continent, since the coal and steel community proved to be the first step in the gradual process of European economic integration.

One of the aims of the Second World War had been the eradication of German militarism; to persuade Germany's neighbors to revise this policy and allow German rearmament was much more difficult than agreement on economic collaboration with Germany. The proposal for a revision of policy came from the United States. Because of the outbreak of the Korean War, the American government feared that its military resources might become overstrained, and it demanded that Germany be permitted to rearm to strengthen the Western military posture in Europe. For some time a positive outcome seemed to be lost in a maze of negotiations. America's allies, particularly the French, responded with an understandable lack of enthusiasm to this American eagerness to forget the past. But unable to resist the request of their powerful ally, the French suggested an integrated European army, in which they hoped the German contribution would be kept to a minimum. After lengthy negotiations, a treaty for a European Defense Community was concluded in May 1952. But most of the signatory powers felt doubtful about the abandonment of sovereignty over their military forces implied in an integrated army. The French themselves in August 1954 rejected ratification of the treaty, and suddenly a different and much simpler solution was obtained. West Germany became a member of NATO; foreign troops stationed on German soil could now be regarded not as occupation forces but as allies, present on the basis of NATO membership. The French were reconciled to German rearmament by a British promise to leave several divisions on the Continent; and by Germany's agreement to keep its new army, the Bundeswehr, relatively small and devoid of atomic, chemical, and bacteriological weapons.

In contrast to the situation in the Eastern bloc, integration in the western part of Europe could not be attained exclusively by pressure from above. The feeling for common values above national interests that had developed during resistance against the Nazis was an important factor in fomenting an impetus for integration. But also, the threat to security and military needs played a decisive role in bringing about closer cooperation. This had its influence on the course of the rebuilding or political order in the different countries of Western Europe. The war had ended with the expectation among the great mass of peoples of Europe that a new era was beginning. It was commonly held that in view of the extreme sufferings people had undergone, they deserved to have full employment, full protection in the case of illness, and pensions that provided them with material security in their old age. As the interests of private entrepreneurs, large banks, and big industrial enterprises were contradictory to such aims and placed obstacles in their way, the government should take them over and exercise all the power necessary to ensure that economic affairs would be conducted in the interest of all citizens and not of a wealthy elite. In the postwar situation, all the European governments moved somewhat in this direction. But it turned out that a quick reconstitution of industrial activity, which could allow the buildup of a strong military apparatus, and long-range economic and social reforms were difficult to pursue simultaneously. Moreover, the American inclination to identify democracy with a free enterprise system lent support to the opponents of fundamental structural changes. The demands and needs of military security took much wind out of the sails of reformism, which had been very strong in the immediate postwar period.

Internal Developments in Western Bloc Nations

During the first decade after the end of the Second World War, parties of very similar political aims and outlook were in power—namely, political parties that emphasized Christianity and Roman Catholicism as a common feature. In Italy the party was called Democrazia Cristiana (Christian Democracy), and from 1948 to 1953 it had the absolute majority in parliament. In West Germany the name of the party was Christlich-Demokratische Union (Christian Democratic Union), and it became the largest German political party in the parliamentary elections of 1949, the first elections held after the war; the Christian Democratic Union obtained an absolute majority in 1953. In France the MRP (for Mouvement Républicain Populaire), as the Catholic party was called, had its greatest

Konrad Adenauer taking the oath as West Germany's first chancellor on September 20, 1949.

strength immediately after the war and then declined, first slowly, later rather rapidly. Nevertheless, no government in France was formed in this period without the participation of the MRP. Among members of these parties the idea of a unified Europe, of building a Christian fortress against the attack of barbarians, had strong historical roots, and the leaders of these parties enthusiastically pursued a policy of European collaboration. The men chiefly responsible for the European direction of French, Italian, and West German foreign policy in these critical years were Robert Schuman, between 1947 and 1953, French prime minister and later foreign minister, who initiated the creation of the Coal and Steel Community; Alcide de Gasperi, Italian prime minister from 1945 to 1953; and Konrad Adenauer, German chancellor from 1949 to 1963.

The Recovery of the Defeated Powers

De Gasperi and Adenauer impressed themselves upon the history of their countries by charting the political course of postwar Italy and Germany. Both leaders were very different from the idealistic statesmen of the early years of the twentieth century, with their passionate commitment to the great causes of social reform or national expansion. Their speeches emphasized concrete points and justified their policies with practical, commonsense reasons. What they wrote or said tended to be monotonous and pedestrian; Adenauer's chief saving grace was a dry wit that revealed his sharp eye for the weaknesses of his fellow men. De Gasperi and Adenauer appeared disinclined to embark on a discussion of broad principles and seemed to consider a good style and beautiful phrases as unnecessary embroidery. They gave the impression of being always in a rush, always exclusively concerned with settling the business at hand. The matter-of-factness of these two may have been rooted in their feeling that they no longer had much time to accomplish what they felt destined to do. De Gasperi had been at the beginning of a promising political career when Fascism came to power in Italy; he spent the next twenty years partly in prison, partly as an employee in the library of the Vatican. He was in his sixties when he reentered politics as a leader of the Italian resistance. Adenauer was close to seventy when, after twelve years in a political wilderness during the Nazi regime, he was reinstituted as lord mayor of Cologne by the occupying American forces and could resume a political career.

The situation in Italy and Germany when De Gasperi and Adenauer took over was hardly suited for men of great plans and imagination. For the leaders of the two defeated nations, the targets were prescribed: setting economic life in motion and achieving membership in the society of sovereign states.

ITALY

These prosaic aims somewhat contradicted the political atmosphere of Italy after the defeat of Fascism; the experiences in the resistance in the final phase of the war seemed to have broken down barriers between classes. It was widely expected that Italy after Fascism would be a new, more democratic, and more equalitarian state. This explains why socialists and Communists emerged in great strength, but the Christian Democratic Party, an amalgam of Catholicism and political moderation, emerged as the strongest party in the elections of 1946. As a result of the work of this constituent assembly, Italy changed from a monarchy to a republic; in other respects, however, the constitution adopted by the assembly was very similar to the one that had existed before Fascism. Only the anticlerical emphasis of the nineteenth-century liberal constitution was eliminated: Mussolini's concordat with the pope became an integral part of the new constitution, and Roman Catholicism remained in Italy "the sole religion of the state."

The Italian economic situation was so miserable that, inevitably, wider claims for reform had to take a backseat to the problems of economic recovery. In this area De Gasperi had an extremely capable helper. Luigi Einaudi, Italy's leading economist, first as director of the Bank of Italy and then as minister of the budget, balanced the Italian budget by rigorous means; in 1948 he became the first president of the Italian republic.

Thanks to the rapid progress of the Allied armies into the Italian industrial north, and thanks to the activities of the partisans, the damage done by the war to industrial installations was a relatively low 15 percent. Italy therefore was able quickly to restore industrial production and to export consumer goods to the rest of Europe. But as other countries set their own industrial machinery in motion, the demand for Italian goods decreased. Then the Marshall Plan provided a new stimulus, and the Italian government used the industrial and financial holdings inherited from the Fascist government to provide capital for industrial modernization. The results were startling indeed. The index of industrial production in 1954 was 71 percent above that of 1938, the last prewar year. And electric power production—because of Italy's lack of coal, probably the most important of the country's industries—had increased in 1953 by more than 100 percent over 1938. By 1954, real wages were more than five times what they had been at the end of the war and almost 50 percent higher than they had been in 1938. Nevertheless, the Italian economic situation still had great weaknesses. The domestic market remained rather undeveloped because of the poverty of the agrarian south. Although in 1954, 40 percent of the national income came from industrial activities and only 26 percent from agriculture, 42.4 percent of the working population was engaged in agriculture. These figures show that the rural population had remained utterly poor, unable to buy any manufactured goods.

In 1951, 5 million Italians were still illiterate. Many of these people tried to leave the land and to find work in the industrial centers of the north, where they swelled the labor market; some made use of opportunities, which by then had opened up, to work in Germany and France. Although unemployment had decreased, Italy still had more than 4 million jobless in 1954. This problem could be solved only by land reform in the agrarian south, which would give more land to the peasants but would also bring industry into this region. In dealing with this issue, the De Gasperi regime failed because the old ruling group opposed any changes that would fundamentally alter the social structure.

Alcide De Gasperi addresses a crowd before the 1948 elections.

The pressure of the poor and unemployed from the south coming to the industrial north in the hope of finding work kept radicalism among the workers alive; the Communists and their left socialist allies continued to exercise strong appeal among the workers and made gains among the peasants and rural workers in the south. The trade unions in Italy were, and remained, Communist-controlled. The Christian Democrats themselves split into a right wing, which was willing to cooperate even with monarchists and former Fascists to prevent any change in the social structure, and a left wing, which believed in the necessity of cooperation with the leftists to effect thorough social reforms. This split, together with discontent about the inertia of the government, resulted in elections in 1953 that denied De Gasperi his desired absolute majority, and he was forced to retire. But the hopes that his withdrawal would give a new impetus to structural reforms were deceived.

WEST GERMANY

In many respects the task Adenauer had in West Germany was easier than that of De Gasperi. In West Germany, the break with the past, not only with Nazism but also with the pre-Nazi past, was more thorough than in Italy. The severance of eastern Germany meant the disappearance of the Junkers, the owners of large estates east of the Elbe, who had continuously pressed for protective tariffs and government subsidies and opposed democratic reform. The creation of the Coal and Steel Community kept the industrial barons of the Ruhr in check. Thus, the German ruling group was freed of its socially most reactionary and politically most aggressive elements. One result was a change in the composition of the German civil service, since the classes from which its members had been recruited no longer existed; although still a power within the state, the civil service became less authoritarian.

Germany's situation also differed from Italy's in that its cities and industries had been thoroughly destroyed. The huge task of reconstruction required the cooperation of all strata of the population—of government, employers, and employees, of capitalists and workers. At the same time, the scarcity of goods of all kinds made production, once begun, highly profitable; in the first years the Germans themselves eagerly bought all they could produce. Workers were therefore in great demand, and unemployment disappeared almost completely. The economy of West Germany was able to absorb the refugees from the eastern part of Germany and even benefited from their presence.

They turned out to be less of a discontented nationalist pressure group than had been expected and feared. The shortage of workers made employers willing to accept improvements in the status of labor. Maintenance of full employment was recognized as a legitimate government function; an extended social security system that provided pensions in adjustment to changes in standard of living was adopted; and codetermination, which gave the workers a share in the management of industry, was established by law. After the dictatorial handling of social questions by the Nazis, such government intervention in labor relations was considered entirely compatible with the principles of the "free market policy" advocated by the Adenauer government. If employers shared a willingness to improve the status of labor, the workers too were in a cooperative mood. They were anxious to work so that with their earnings they could begin to obtain the necessities of life. Thus, although wages at the outset were low, the attitude of the trade unions in wage negotiations was conciliatory, and no strikes of significance occurred in Germany in the first years after the war. Consequently, German goods quickly reconquered a position on foreign markets.

The prevailing eagerness to prevent conflicts that might delay reconstruction and economic recovery goes far to explain the popularity of the majority party, the Christian Democratic Union, in Germany. Another reason, of course, was that the loss of the eastern part of Germany meant a great increase in the percentage of Catholics in the population, since the south and west of Germany had always been predominantly Catholic (in 1933 Catholics constituted 32.5 percent of the German population; in West Germany in 1950 the figure was 43.8 percent). However, the Christian Democratic Union was strong even in the northern, predominantly Protestant areas. The predecessor of the Christian Democratic Union, the old Center Party, had always included a variety of social groups, ranging from the workers in the Catholic trade unions to industrialists and landowners. After the Nazi collapse, when external circumstances as well as emotional needs required a new beginning through common action, the appeal of a party that could be regarded as a microcosm of the entire population was obviously great; the German Christian Democratic Union could be characterized as an organized consensus.

The position of Chancellor Adenauer, the leader of the Christian Democratic Union, was strong also for constitutional reasons. In an effort to avoid the instability characteristic of the Weimar Republic, the constitution of West Germany had sharply restricted the rights of parliament. Once a chancellor had been appointed and had received a vote of confidence, the vote of a majority against him could force him to resign only if his opponents had agreed on who would replace him. The only other parties of significance were the Free Democratic Party, a small bourgeois party, which, although it later changed course, was then on the right of the Christian Democratic Union, and a Socialist Party, the SPD, on the left. It seemed most unlikely that these two extremes would come together and agree on a candidate for the chancellorship.

The opposition was also ineffective because it had no clear alternative policy to offer. The Socialist demand for socialization of key industries aroused little enthusiasm even among the workers because the trade unions were concentrating on the immediate problem of getting the economy moving again and were not bothering about an ideal society in a distant future; moreover, the social security system and codetermination protected the basic interests of the workers. Party rivalry also took a less bitter form because West Germany had retained a federal structure, and in some of the states a coalition between Socialists and Christian Democrats was in power.

Most West Germans were so focused on economic recovery that they had little time or inclination to reflect seriously on the evils that Germany had visited upon the world during the Third Reich. There was little public discussion of the Holocaust in the first postwar decade. To some degree, the de-Nazification trials conducted by the Allies helped ordinary Germans avoid contemplating their own complicity because they tended to off-load responsibility onto the shoulders of the top Nazi leaders. Still, if West Germany hoped to be readmitted to the community of civilized nations, it had to take some practical steps to atone for the Nazi crimes. In 1953, the Bundestag passed the first in a series of measures offering financial restitution to victims of the Holocaust. Moreover, between 1953 and 1965, Bonn delivered ships, machine tools, trains, medical equipment, and telephone technology to the state of Israel. Unfortunately, Adenauer's government did not match its conscientiousness in material matters with similar efforts in the arena of justice. It elected not to prosecute thousands of former Nazis, including some known to have committed serious crimes, on the ground that these people's talents were needed in the national revival. This policy was certainly morally questionable, and it may not even have been necessary. As Jeffrey Herf has asked in his study on the Nazi past in the two Germanys, "Were the skills of those who had served the Third Reich so indispensable and irreplaceable that a democratic state and a market economy could not be built without them?" By neglecting the dark past in the name of a bright present and future, West Germany in the fifties managed only to postpone, not to escape, a wrenching national debate about the Nazi crimes. That discussion would transpire in the late sixties and seventies, prompted by the angry and accusatory questions of the younger generation.

POSTWAR STRAINS IN FRANCE AND BRITAIN

France

France was deeply divided. Geographically the nation had been separated into German-occupied France and Vichy France; ideologically into resisters and resistance sympathizers versus collaborators and those who had tolerated collaboration. These divisions were not class divisions. The resistance movements had included men and women from the entire political spectrum—from nationalists on the right to Communists on the extreme left. The members of the resistance believed that the reorganization of French political life was their right and their duty. They wanted something better than what had existed before, but they had not worked out how this new world should look. They were united in their hatred of Nazi collaborators and in their rejection of the prewar political system.

It was not difficult to settle accounts with individual traitors; in all the formerly occupied countries, trials against Nazi collaborators and war criminals took place. In France, the pro-Nazi writer Robert Brasillach was tried and executed in early 1945; his case was extremely controversial since he was condemned for his ideology, not for any specific actions. Members of the Vichy government were also brought to account. Laval was executed; Pétain was sentenced to prison and died there. In the first year after the war, some forty thousand out of one hundred twenty-five thousand defendants brought to trial for collaboration received punishment of varying degrees. Significantly, however, none of these trials focused on Vichy's role in the persecution and deportation of Jews from France; treason was the charge. When it came to complicity in the Holocaust, France was in deep denial, deeper than Germany. It was not until the 1980s and 1990s that France began to reckon with this shameful dimension of its recent past. Trials involving Klaus Barbie, the head of the Gestapo in Lyons; Paul Touvier, a leader in the Vichy militia; and Maurice Papon, a lawyer in charge of Jewish affairs in Bordeaux, brought the ugly details of Vichy's contribution to the Holocaust to the surface.

The men of the resistance, or at least most of them, attributed responsibility for the surrender to Fascism and Nazism not only to individuals but to a system that had allowed a determining political influence to industrialists and bankers. Democracy, it was believed, could not flourish where economic power was concentrated in the hands of a few big capitalists. The successful functioning of a parliamentary democracy was thought to be predicated upon social and economic reforms that would strengthen the position of the great masses of the population against the rich upper group. In the last months of the war and in the liberation period, resistance groups tried in many areas to assume executive power and constitute themselves as governments. They were balked by the military leaders of the victorious American and British armies, who were primarily interested in smoothly functioning supply and communication lines and feared disorder and chaos. Furthermore, de Gaulle, the acknowledged head of the French resistance, opposed the encroachment of individual groups on what he considered the paramount authority of the state.

Yet despite the failure of the resistance to effect changes and reforms during the fluid situation at the war's end, it was generally recognized that France could not just reactivate its former constitution. A plebiscite determined that it was necessary, as de Gaulle declared in a broadcast in September 1945, "to adopt a different system in order to revive the spirit of clarity, justice and efficiency which is the true spirit of the republic." Most of the members of the constituent assembly elected in 1945 to draft a new constitution agreed that government instability had been the chief weakness of the Third Republic. De Gaulle, who returned to France with immense prestige, emphasized the necessity of strengthening the power and independence of the executive branch. But the left wing (the Communists and Socialists), which dominated the constituent assembly, attempted to ensure stability in the government by means of a complete subordination of the executive to the legislative branch; the National Assembly became all-powerful. De Gaulle saw in this arrangement a disturbing sign that the period of party squabbles was returning, and he resigned as head of the Provisional Government in January 1946.

He was right, in that government stability turned out to be no greater in the Fourth Republic than it had been in the Third. There were prolonged government crises and an endless succession of ministries. In 1946 the Communists had emerged as the strongest political party. But after they had been eliminated from the government in May 1947, they never received much more than 25 percent of the vote. The majority was formed by a left-center coalition of Catholic Democrats, the MRP, Socialists, and left-liberal groups; almost every French government under the Fourth Republic obtained its support from these parties. Frequent changes in administration were caused less by political conflicts and disagreement over issues than by the maneuverings of ambitious politicians eager to become ministers and inclined to intrigue against one another. In the 1950s, French political life found itself in a depressing rut. When the same men or groups remain in power for a very long time, opposition tends to increase in strength and shrillness. Majorities for the existing government became increasingly precarious, but no alternative was in sight. Extremists, particularly of the right, were gaining in popular appeal. The left and right wings of the coalition began to pull in opposite directions in their efforts to pacify the radicals on their fringes.

Yet the troubles of the Fourth Republic cannot be blamed just on the resentment of the outs against the ins or on the bickering of the politicians, who in truth did not quite deserve the harsh criticism they received. Obviously, it was very difficult to work simultaneously for two different goals: to achieve transition from a wartime to a peacetime economy and to fulfill demands for social change. In actuality, important measures of social reform were carried through. Work committees in all establishments with more than one hundred workers were introduced to give the employees some part in the organization of work in factories, and a number of key industries—fuel and power, insurance and large financial concerns, air transport and the merchant marine—were nationalized. But with a drift of the parties away from the center to the right and to the left, the reform impetus waned. Moreover, the problem was really more fundamental: it was how to renew the outmoded French industrial apparatus that, with its numerous small family enterprises, was resistant to modern technology. The Fourth Republic did handle this matter well. It set up a special office under Jean Monnet (1888–1979) to draw up a comprehensive scheme of economic modernization. The Monnet plan established voluntary programs for updating the basic industries, improving farming methods, and furthering reconstruction and new building. The government was to provide advice by experts, facilitate the procurement of the necessary labor, and make available the capital needed for investments. Marshall Plan aid, coming at a very opportune moment, was used to help carry out this policy of modernization. Nevertheless, time was needed for the results to become evident, since as in the Russian five-year plans, the emphasis was placed on heavy industry and the production of machinery. The plan gave priority to coal, electricity, transport, steel, cement, and agricultural machinery. And it would be the Fifth Republic of Charles de Gaulle that would harvest much of what the Fourth Republic planted in the field of economic improvement and modernization.

By 1956, French industrial production was 50 percent higher than it had been in 1929, France's best year during the interwar period, and 87 percent higher than in 1938, the last year before the war. But this progress in modernizing industry went relatively unnoticed, while the failure of the French government to handle urgent pocketbook issues was all too obvious. The development that hurt the French people most was inflation, produced by the scarcity of goods after the war, by large government loans to industry, and by a series of budgetary deficits. The rapid course of inflation was marked by a steep rise in prices. Wages, although rising, did not keep step, and the purchasing power of both the workers and the middle classes was low; in 1951, the average working-class family spent a third of its weekly budget on meat. Attempts to stem the inflation were futile because the government was unable to get along without a rising deficit. The nationalized industries were unprofitable at this time. The introduction of new forms of management had been costly, the government lacked the courage to brave the indignation that would be aroused by dismissal of superfluous personnel, and in view of the inflation, the government felt unable to burden the populace further by increases in the costs of railroads and electricity. The social security system also showed a high deficit because its funds came from a percentage of the workers' wages, but the size of its benefits was determined in relation to prices. In addition, the French system of taxation was unsatisfactory, and the left and right wings of the government were unable to agree on reform.

But even without these many difficulties, it is unlikely that the budget could have been balanced, for funds spent in the effort to preserve French colonial power seemed to pour into a bottomless hole. During the war, the French Empire had been thrown into confusion. The colonial administrators, possessing a freedom of action that had been lost by the inhabitants of Axis-controlled Europe, were torn between Vichy France and the Free France of de Gaulle. Some segments of the empire, such as Indochina, were taken by the Japanese; others, such as Madagascar, Syria, and North Africa, were occupied by British and American forces. The loosening of ties with France during the war revealed widespread dissatisfaction with the French colonial system; the chief targets were the authoritarianism with which the colonies were ruled from Paris and the economic exploitation that had cut off the colonies from trade with all countries but France. In all the colonies, dissatisfaction was fed by the nationalist movements that had been active since the First World War and received new impetus during the Second World War.

The members of the French constituent assembly realized the necessity of redefining the relationship between France and its overseas possessions. But the arrangements that resulted were a compromise and lacked clarity: The new constitution provided for a French Union, to consist of metropolitan France, its overseas departments (that is, the administrative units of Algeria, which was regarded as part of France proper), its protectorates (Tunisia and Morocco), its colonies (primarily in West Africa), and its associate states (Vietnam, Cambodia, Laos, together constituting Indochina). The president of the French republic was also to be the president of this French Union, and he was assisted by an assembly. But the assembly had only advisory functions, and half its members represented metropolitan France, so real power remained with the Paris government. A promise for elected assemblies in each of the overseas territories was also deceptive, since the composition and the powers of these assemblies were to be determined by the French parliament. Certainly the influence of the natives remained carefully hedged in, and the very limited concessions to the desire for self-rule could not stem the colonial movements toward nationalism and independence.

Yet preservation of the empire bore not only upon French financial interests and economic power but upon the most sensitive nerve of the French political body, the army. Postwar developments strengthened the ties between the officer corps and the French colonial empire. In 1940, the military had suffered a crushing loss of prestige, and at the end of the Second World War cadres of the French resistance demanded a place in the army; for the regular officers they were intruders, an alien and unpalatable element. The entire atmosphere of postwar France was antagonistic to the traditions of the army. Contrary to the ideas in which French officers were trained were the political climate in which Socialists were regarded as a moderating force and the intellectual climate in which the value of revolution was accepted by the most prominent intellectual leaders of postwar France whatever their political views might be—by the Communist Jean-Paul Sartre (1905–1980) or the anti-Communist Albert Camus (1913–1960). The close military collaboration in Europe with officers of other nationalities, particularly with Americans, resulted in an emphasis on new weapons and the technological aspects of warfare and a tendency to overlook the values of the past, while the joint European military organization did not grant French officers that prominent place to which they felt entitled by the great military history of France. But in the colonies the army could be what it had always been; it could maintain, or regain, its identity.

Thus, the army embarked with enthusiasm on the task of asserting France's claim to regain its former possessions in Indochina. Many civilian politicians also supported the army, since they perceived that a gain in French international prestige might earn them the popular appeal they had lost by their handling of domestic affairs. After this enterprise ended in the ignominious defeat at Dien Bien Phu and in bitter recriminations between civilian and military leaders, the latter tried to regain prestige for the army by eager support of other enterprises that would show that France was still an imperial power—for example, the cooperation with Great Britain and Israel against Egypt in the Suez Affair (to be treated below).

BRITAIN

The people of Great Britain, under siege since 1940, also expected the end of the war to usher in a better world. Their longing for an escape from the dark and anxious years of the war and for a new life revealed itself almost immediately. Even before Japan's surrender, the British electorate overthrew Churchill. The Labor Party received just one hundred thousand more votes than the other parties, but they were so distributed that Labor emerged with a majority of 146 over the Conservatives and Liberals in the House of Commons. There were several reasons for this change in government. The Conservatives had been in power since 1931, and if elections had not been postponed because of the war, the usual swing away from the party in power would probably have occurred five years earlier. The credit that Churchill's war leadership had gained could not be transferred to the Conservative Party. The slowness with which the Conservatives had enacted measures to overcome the depression before the war; the failure of Chamberlain's appeasement policy; the lack of energy in pursuing rearmament, which had left Great Britain open to Nazi aggression—all these were still in the minds of the people. Greater enthusiasm and greater effort for social reform could be expected from Labor than from the Conservatives. An important factor was that Labor had been a coalition partner in the Churchill government, and some of Labor's leaders—Clement Attlee, Ernest Bevin, Sir Stafford Cripps—had played distinguished roles in the war.

The government now formed by Clement Attlee (1883–1967) became one of Britain's great reform ministries. Building on the foundation laid by Asquith's Liberal government before the First World War, Labor established the "welfare state." The National Insurance Act, which became law in 1946, provided for almost complete coverage in cases of sickness, old age, and unemployment. It is characteristic of the connection between Labor and the pre-1914 Liberals that this act grew out of a report by the Liberal economist William Beveridge. The National Insurance Act was complemented by a National Health Service Act, which assured complete medical care to all residents of Britain; it aroused the bitter resistance of physicians and was carried through by the energy of Aneurin Bevan (1897–1960), probably the one Labor leader who somewhat resembled Churchill in imagination, charm, and rhetorical power. Like the Liberals before the First World War, the Labor Party encountered resistance in the House of Lords. The result was further curtailment of the power of the upper chamber with respect to legislation; henceforth it could only impose a veto effecting a brief delay.

In economic policy, Labor went far beyond anything the Liberals had ever envisaged, undertaking to create a socialist society, although the term used was "nationalization" rather than "socialization." The Bank of England, the road transport system, coal mines, civil aviation, canals and docks, the electrical supply industry, and the iron industry were placed under state control and managed by government-appointed boards. The previous owners received compensation.

Through such measures Labor expected to provide a new impetus to British economic life and increased opportunity to the masses. However, these reforms did not provide the expected stimulus to society because the British people were exhausted after the tensions of the long war. Moreover, the beneficial effects of these reforms were counteracted by their coincidence with a severe economic crisis.

The developments of the Second World War had aggravated the long-standing difficulties of British economic life, particularly the problem of its unfavorable balance of trade. British foreign assets had disappeared, and foreign debts had increased. Some temporary relief and some improvement in the competitive position of British goods on foreign markets was achieved through loans from the United States and a devaluation of the currency in September 1949. But a lasting remedy could come only from a limitation of imports and an increase in exports—restriction of the production of consumer goods for the home market and forced production of goods for foreign markets. The Labor government, whose socialist ideology justified a controlled economy, continued rationing of food, fuel, clothing, and restricted the amount of currency a traveler might take out of the country. The architect of this austerity policy was Sir Stafford Cripps (1889–1952), a brilliantly gifted technocrat, also an ascetic, who was little inclined to acknowledge the need for human amenities. The time of labor rule was constraining rather than liberating, gloomy rather than exhilarating.

The economic situation was further aggravated by the expense involved in maintaining Britain's empire. Colonies facilitated access to such raw materials as oil, rubber, and cotton and to such foodstuffs as coffee, tea, and rice. But they also burdened the mother country with the need to maintain a strong military posture all over the globe. Indeed, of the many justifications for colonial rule produced by the Victorians, the one that still had some validity was that only a modern industrial power could adequately defend a colony against attack. The preservation of an empire required an extended military establishment, with all the expenses necessary for the equipment of a modern army, navy, and air force. In a time of shrinking distances, successful military protection also involved participation in the politics of the entire area in which the colonial territory was situated. Indeed, at the end of the war, British troops were distributed all over the world. They were to be found in Germany, Italy, and Greece; in the Near East, Egypt, and Africa; and in the extended regions of Southeast Asia. There was no conflict on the globe in which Britain was not involved. Unquestionably the occupation forces in Germany, expensive as they were, had to be maintained if Great Britain was to continue to play a role in Europe. But in the

Fuel shortage in Great Britain. During the bitterly cold winter of 1946–1947, the British people stood in long queues to draw their meager coal rations.

nation's straitened economic circumstances, an increase in the working force at home and a reduction in military expenses were evidently desirable, and the Labor government became anxious to decrease non-European military obligations as far as possible.

Abandonment of Britain's colonies was entirely compatible with Labor's fundamental principles. The party had always opposed imperialism and its concomitant, power politics. Although in the wartime conferences Churchill had emphasized the special interest of Great Britain in the eastern Mediterranean, the Labor government in 1947 declared itself unable to defend Greece and Turkey against Communism and left this task to the United States. The result was the Truman Doctrine. Moreover, the Labor government was anxious to give independence to those British colonies and dependencies that had fully developed political institutions and to introduce self-government for those still ruled by British governors because they were believed to be unready for independence. The most spectacular result of this policy was the granting of independence to India. The Labor government offered full freedom to India in March 1946, but implementation was delayed by difficulties chiefly of an internal nature, caused by the differences between Hindus and Muslims. After long negotiations, the only feasible solution appeared to be the establishment of two states, one Hindu and one Muslim. The creation of India and Pakistan involved an exchange of population, the moving of millions of refugees, accompanied by terrible hardships. Moreover, the delineation of the frontiers did not cleanly separate Hindus from Muslims, and some controversies, such as the dispute over the control of Kashmir, led to bitter and long-lasting tension between the two states. The most distinguished victim of the hatred aroused by the division of India was Gandhi, the founder of the modern Indian nationalist movement; in 1948 he was assassinated by a fanatic Hindu who resented his agreement to the establishment of two states. Nevertheless, the creation of an independent India and Pakistan ended an explosive situation that had troubled the British Empire for decades, and Labor had the added satisfaction that India decided to remain a member of the British Commonwealth. The granting of independence to India led unavoidably to the same change in status for the other states of this area, Burma and Ceylon (now known as Myanmar and Sri Lanka), with Burma leaving and Ceylon remaining in the commonwealth.

However, the continued restrictions on economic life at home were diminishing the government's popularity, and Labor began to lose ground. Elections in 1950 resulted in a Labor majority so small that it was almost unmanageable. In October 1951, the Conservatives were returned to power, and Churchill again became prime minister. The Conservatives remained in power for the next thirteen years, from 1951 to 1964.

THE GROWTH OF TENSIONS WITHIN
THE EASTERN AND WESTERN BLOCS

It is a strange coincidence that in the fall of 1956 in the East and West the leading powers of the two blocs, the United States and Soviet Russia, took action against members of their own alliance, Russia against Hungary, the United States against France and Britain. The strangeness of this coincidence, however, consists less in the fact itself than in the simultaneity of the events. It was not unnatural that the bonds of the two alliances, which had been very tightly knit under the pressure of postwar events, began to loosen, especially when, as after the settlement in Indochina, the world situation looked less threatening. We have mentioned that the Russians had become aware that their demands for rapid industrialization and collectivization created dangerous social tensions in the satellite countries. Thus, they were modifying their policy; the Hungarian Revolt of 1956 arose out of the ticklish situation that such a change in policy can create. In the West, political and economic bonds had been forged simultaneously, but although their effects were long-lasting, the active phase of the European Recovery Program had ended by 1952. The weight of the alliance shifted to diplomatic and military cooperation. As a result the ideological bond—the notion of defending the traditions and values of Western civilization—which had helped cement the Western alliance, began to lose its significance. The alliance seemed more and more an instrument of American power politics, a development that emerged strongly in the question of the treatment of the Spanish dictatorship of Francisco Franco.

During the Second World War, Spanish volunteers had fought on the side of the Axis against Russia, although Franco, emphasizing the poverty of his country, avoided direct participation; after the war, the victorious governments seriously considered taking steps to overthrow the Franco regime. But in 1953, after vainly trying to overcome the resistance of its European allies to the admission of Spain to NATO, the United States made agreements with Spain by which in return for assistance to the Spanish army, navy, and air force, it obtained military bases in Spain. This was a decisive step in stimulating industrial activity in Spain, which in the following years gained increasing power and speed. When in 1955, after a visit to Spain, the American secretary of state, John Foster Dulles, joined Franco to issue a communiqué stating that they "found themselves in mutual understanding" with regard to "the principal problems that affected the peace and security of free nations," the term *free world*, which Western statesmen liked to apply to the American alliance system, acquired a somewhat hollow sound. If the United States could act in this way on its own, the Western European leaders felt they had the right to do likewise.

CRISIS IN THE EAST

Unrest in Poland and Hungary

Although the basic reason for discontent—forced and rapid collectivization—was the same in Hungary as in other satellite countries, the Hungarian situation had its peculiar complicating features. The possibility of a revolt arose from a struggle between Stalinists and the adherents of the new Communist line. When Nagy became prime minister, his Stalinist predecessor, Rákosi, remained party secretary. In the first year of Nagy's regime, 51 percent of the collective farm members left the collective system, and 12 percent of the collective farms had to be dissolved; Nagy intended to continue the policy of abandoning concentration on heavy industry and instead strengthening the development of the other sectors of the economy. Since the war, the working classes in Hungary had increased by almost 50 percent, and a thorough training of these masses in Communist doctrine had not been possible. With the slowing down of collectivization in agriculture, Communist control of the rural population also became weakened. Accordingly, the Communist Party regarded the measures introduced by Nagy with suspicion and feared that it might be losing its grip over the workers and peasants.

When Khrushchev accused Georgi Malenkov, his rival for Stalin's succession, of mistakes in the direction of industrial and agricultural policy, Rákosi, who controlled the Central Committee of the Hungarian Communist Party, incriminated Nagy as a follower of Malenkov. Taking advantage of Nagy's temporary illness, he succeeded in deposing him as prime minister and expelling him from the party. Rákosi returned to power as prime minister in the spring of 1955. But the clock could not be turned back. In the meetings of clubs named for the poet Sándor Petöfi, which had been set up by the government for intellectual improvement, students and intellectuals debated political issues; both industrial workers and the rural population remained critical and suspicious of the Rákosi government. When in the summer of 1956 Rákosi moved to arrest Nagy and four hundred of his associates, he encountered opposition in the Central Committee, and some members of this opposition turned to the Soviet embassy for help. Perturbed by the revolutionary ferment in Hungary, the Russians decided to drop Rákosi and install a new prime minister, Ernö Gerö, who was expected to steer a middle line between Rákosi's Stalinism and Nagy's new course.

That this attempt at "controlled transition" failed was to a large extent the result of external events. Just at this time Khrushchev moved to improve relations with Yugoslavia. The rejection of Stalin's policy, which early in 1956 had been publicly proclaimed at the Twentieth Congress of the Communist Party, included a condemnation of Stalin's treatment of Tito. In consequence, meetings between the Russian and Yugoslav leaders took place, resulting on June 20, 1956, in a communiqué declaring "that the ways of socialist development vary in different countries and conditions" and "that the wealth of the forms of socialist development contributes to its strength." Naturally, the Russian satellites in Eastern Europe asked why they should not have that freedom of choice in the form of socialist development that had been granted to Yugoslavia.

The first country in which demands for autonomy in domestic affairs were raised was Poland. There the changed Russian attitude after Stalin's death had not resulted in any great shift in leadership or any dramatic reversal in economic policy; it had largely meant a general relaxation, which curtailed the power of the secret police and permitted greater freedom in intellectual expression. In March 1956, the sudden death of Bierut, who had dominated the Polish Communist Party since the war, gave new impetus to the liberalizing trend. In April, amnesty was granted to thirty thousand prisoners, among them nine thousand political offenders. It also became evident that demands for a change had spread widely among the workers. In June, a strike in Poznán had to be suppressed by military forces. Impressed by the amount of dissatisfaction that had come to the fore in the Poznán strike, the majority of the government, including Bierut's successor as party secretary, accepted the need to accelerate liberalization. Władysław Gomułka, who had been released from prison, was permitted to participate in the deliberations of the Central Committee and became a member of the

Polish Politburo, while Marshal Konstantin Rokossovsky, the commander of the Russian troops in Poland, was relieved of his membership in the Polish Politburo. The great question was whether the Soviet leaders would regard these actions as provocative. However, in negotiations with the Russians, Gomułka was able to overcome their distrust. Though he had always been critical of the precipitate collectivization of agriculture that the Russians had imposed on the satellites, he was a loyal Marxist-Leninist, convinced of the need for the Communist Party to keep control and exert leadership and persuaded that Russia and Poland had to stand together. Briefly, he assured the Russians that Poland would remain a reliable member of the Warsaw Pact. Assured of Polish loyalty in foreign policy, the Russian leaders were willing to permit Poland autonomy in seeking its "ways of socialist development." On October 21, 1956, Gomułka was elected general secretary of the Polish Communist Party.

The Revolt in Hungary

The Russian concessions to Yugoslavia and Poland provided the spark for events in Hungary. When the Hungarians heard of the success of the Polish move, they felt that they too should try to gain greater independence. At the universities of Budapest, Pécs, and Szeged, in the Budapest technical college, and in other public buildings, heated debates took place about the means to force the government into greater activity; it was agreed to hold a "silent sympathy demonstration" before the Polish embassy on October 23. It is estimated that more than fifty thousand people participated in this demonstration. In the evening Prime Minister Gerö made a broadcast. He had been expected to accept the need for a more independent and liberal policy but instead, surprisingly, he took a hard Stalinist line in his speech. In response, the public demonstrations assumed a sharply antigovernment character. The gigantic statue of Stalin in the city park was demolished, and students attempted to take over the radio station to broadcast the demands of the opposition. To protect the building, the police began to shoot. Troops were sent against the crowds surrounding the station, but instead of dispersing the demonstrators, they fraternized with them. The government proved powerless to control the opposition.

The distinguishing feature of the Hungarian Revolution was that in contrast to the Polish events of the same month, it did not remain limited to a struggle within the party between the Stalinists and the adherents of a new course but developed into a movement against Communist rule in general. Encouraging broadcasts from the West, which seemed to promise outside support, played their role in transforming the intraparty conflict into an anti-Communist revolt. But the reasons for the broadening impact of the revolt were manifold. On the night of October 23, the government, in panicky desperation, appealed to the Russian troops for help and announced at the same time that Imre Nagy had become prime minister. Nagy's appointment was expected to appease the demonstrators, but he was also expected to share the powers of government with Gerö

The Hungarian Revolution. The Stalin statue is pulled down and destroyed.

and other Stalinists. The Russian military forces in Hungary were weak, and their advance into Budapest resulted in bitter, indecisive fighting, while in the countryside, now free of troops, revolutionary committees were formed. The frontier between Hungary and Austria was opened.

Nagy, whose appointment had been announced without his own approval, was in a thoroughly untenable position. Because of the government appeal for help to Russian troops and Nagy's presumed cooperation with Gerö, the opposition leaders regarded Nagy with the greatest distrust. They believed that his assumption of office could not be considered a guarantee of the beginning of a new course and that therefore, this was not the time to relax pressure on the government. Complying with the demands of the anti-Stalinists, Nagy got rid of Gerö and formed a government composed chiefly of members of the Communist opposition; György Lukács, the famous Marxist scholar, became minister of education. But by then many non-Communists had joined the opposition movement, and they were not content to abandon the struggle without further liberation measures. For instance, Cardinal Mindszenty, who was freed from prison and whose courageous stand against the government gave him great authority, demanded the formation of a Christian Democratic Party similar to Adenauer's party in Germany. He stated that he "rejected en bloc everything Hungary had done since 1945, not only since 1949, and the establishment of dictatorship." He also came out in favor of "private ownership."

Nagy was rightly afraid that the Russians might interfere if order were not quickly reestablished. He tried to appease the non-Communist opposition by taking into the government leaders of the former Social Democratic, Small Holder, and National Peasant parties. But they were willing to cooperate with him and the Communists only if he made further concessions. On October 30, Nagy announced the restoration of a multiparty system, and on October 31, he declared that Hungary proposed to withdraw from the Warsaw Pact.

The Russians could not permit a break in their bloc. "Budapest," declared Khrushchev later, "was like a nail in my head." After some dithering he decided to extract the nail through a strategy of shock and awe, sending five hundred thousand troops into Budapest on the morning of November 4. Encouraged to resist by the CIA-funded Radio Free Europe, hundreds of Budapest citizens tried to stand up to the Russian tanks, hoping that aid from the West might come at any moment. But of course the aid never came, and the revolt was over by nightfall. Cardinal Mindszenty, who had been freed from prison during the uprising, found asylum in the American embassy. Nagy sought refuge in the Yugoslav embassy but was handed over to the Hungarians, and he and other leaders of the liberating movement were executed. Some of the participants managed to escape over the Austrian frontier, and there, as along the Franco-Spanish border seventeen years before, camps were established to house the disillusioned and impoverished refugees whose desperate stand for freedom had been crushed by the pitilessly functioning machines of totalitarian dictatorship.

THE SUEZ AFFAIR

An underlying motive of the British Conservative government in taking action in Suez was its concern with the decline of British imperial power; it was an attempt to restore British authority in the Near East. But the occasion for action arose out of long, involved negotiations about the independence of Egypt that had started immediately after the war. The Labor ministry had not been able to resolve the issues in dispute between Great Britain and Egypt. Labor had declared its readiness to withdraw British forces from Egypt, as desired by the Egyptian government, but had refused to let the Sudan come under Egyptian rule against the wishes of the Sudanese people. Egypt's pride had been further hurt by the failure of its army to crush the state of Israel, which had arisen after the British mandate ended in 1948. The United States and Soviet Russia granted immediate recognition to Israel, and after a successful defense against the surrounding Arab states, Israel was taken into the United Nations. The withdrawal of British troops from Palestine weakened Britain's military posture in the Near East, and this stimulated Egyptian nationalist demands. Nationalist students and an aroused populace engaged in fierce demonstrations against foreigners and put the Egyptian government under pressure to force the withdrawal of British troops from Egypt, the Sudan, and Suez. Clashes between British troops and Egyptian volunteers, the looting and burning of buildings and shops in Cairo by the excited masses, and the power struggle between a discredited government and a luxury-loving king brought Egypt to the brink of chaos. In 1952, a revolution by nationalist army officers deposed the king, ended the rule of the old party politicians, and established an authoritarian republic. The new regime was anxious for a success in foreign relations; the Conservatives now in power in Britain used this opportunity to arrive at a settlement. They agreed to a complete withdrawal of British forces from Egypt and the Suez Canal in exchange for guarantees that free passage through the canal and its control through the international Suez Canal Company would be maintained. Moreover, in case of war the British received the right to reenter the canal area with their troops. The Sudan became an independent state. Opposition to this agreement came from Conservative diehards, who regarded the treaty as a British defeat. But the government explained that with the growing importance of air transport and air warfare, the Suez Canal had lost its strategic significance.

It is evident, however, that the British policy makers had still other reasons for seeking an understanding with the new Egyptian rulers. No longer burdened with the mandate over Palestine, which had poisoned British relations with the Arab states, Britain's Conservative rulers were anxious again to establish Great Britain as the great ally of the Arab nations and the leading power in the Near East. The wealth of this area—notably in oil, with pipelines running to the Mediterranean—and its geographical situation as a link between the Mediterranean and India meant that the power controlling it was an important force in world politics. Gamal Abdel Nasser (1918–1970), who had emerged as a leader of the new Egypt, was trying to combine the Arab nations in a unified bloc, and the British regarded their agreement with him as a step toward strengthening their nation's hold in the entire region. But they seem to have been too confident of Arab backing. When in 1955 Britain made a defense pact with Turkey and Iraq, the so-called Baghdad Pact, Egypt reacted sharply against this Western interference in Near Eastern policy, particularly in the plans for a common Arab defense league. Nasser showed his independence from the West by recognizing Communist China and ordering armaments from Czechoslovakia. This Egyptian flirtation with the East was taken amiss by the United States, which on July 19, 1956, withdrew its offer to help finance the building of a dam at Aswan. A week later, on July 26, Nasser declared that Egypt was nationalizing the Suez Canal Company and would use the revenue for the building of the Aswan Dam.

The Suez Affair of October 1956 must be seen against this background. The Conservative government wanted to maintain a strong British position in the Near East and had agreed to a troop withdrawal from Egypt and the Suez area because it expected to gain Arab cooperation. When Nasser showed more independence than had been expected, the British saw in his breach of the agreement on the Suez Canal an opportunity to crush him. Anthony Eden, who had followed Churchill as prime minister in 1955, joined the leaders of Israel and France in secretly preparing a military operation that would begin with a clash between Israel and Egypt and then lead to the intervention of French and

British troops, which would occupy the Suez Canal to separate the Egyptian and Israeli forces. Militarily the operation was executed as planned, but diplomatically the plot failed. The British miscalculated the American attitude. President Eisenhower feared that Britain's and France's bullying of Egypt would alienate the Arabs, pushing them into the Communist camp. Thus the United States, cooperating in the UN with the Soviet Union, forced the British and French to accept a cease-fire on November 3, 1956, and to evacuate the canal area. Instead of restoring Britain's old influence in the Near East, the affair marked the end of a chapter in British imperial history. This episode also launched the start of a new era in the politics of Europe, the Middle East, and America. Smarting from their humiliation at the hands of Washington, European leaders started down the path that would lead to the creation of the European Union. Suez spurred pan-Arab nationalism and helped turn the Israeli-Palestinian dispute into a broader Israeli-Arab one. It confirmed the United States, for good or for ill, as the dominant outside power in the Middle East, setting the stage for its many later interventions in the region, most of them not so peaceful.

In 1958 a coup d'état overthrew the pro-British regime in Iraq, killing King Faisal II, his heir, and the prime minister, Nuri as-Said. Britain had lost its most reliable ally in the Near East. When the pro-Western president of Lebanon felt threatened, his position was upheld by the landing not of British but of American troops. In 1959, Britain conceded independence to Cyprus, thereby abandoning its last important military stronghold in this region. Henceforth, if outside powers played a role in the rivalries and maneuverings of the Arab countries, they were Soviet Russia and the United States; they no longer included Great Britain.

PART IV

RESURGENT EUROPE

CHAPTER 11

Europe's Abundant Decade: The 1960s

THE YEAR 1956, the year of the Hungarian Revolt and Suez, proved to be a turning point in European and world history in the second half of the twentieth century. In retrospect, we can see that the postwar era as such had ended, and a new era had begun.

The Hungarian Revolt made it clear that the Western powers were not willing to risk war to liberate the countries of Eastern and Central Europe from Soviet domination. Those who revolted against Communist rule in Hungary announced both their willingness to withdraw from the Eastern alliance system and their expectation of support from the West. Many Hungarians—one estimate is 180,000—crossed the border into Austria, a good number in the hope of forming a military force to help free their country. But the Western powers did not intervene, and though their view was never formally stated, their inactivity indicated that they recognized the area from the Baltic Sea to the Black Sea, which Russian troops had occupied by the end of the Second World War, as within the Russian sphere of interest. This, at least, was the Russian interpretation. Consequently, in 1968 the Russians felt free to suppress ruthlessly the attempt by Czechs to "liberalize" the Communist dictatorship in their country. On the other hand, when in 1962 the United States reacted vigorously to the installation of Russian missiles in Cuba and demanded Russian respect for the American sphere of interest, the Russians quickly withdrew.

The tacit acceptance of Europe's division into two spheres of interest did not mean, however, that the competition between the two superpowers, the United States and Soviet Russia, had ended in other parts of the world; tension grew in Southeast Asia until it exploded into war in Vietnam. But this shift in focus of the East-West conflict presented the European powers with the possibility for fresh initiatives in domestic and foreign policy.

The Suez Affair confirmed and reinforced the trend toward a change in the relationship between the United States and Western Europe. By turning against France and Britain, the United States intimated that it no longer intended to support attempts by the European powers to maintain control over their

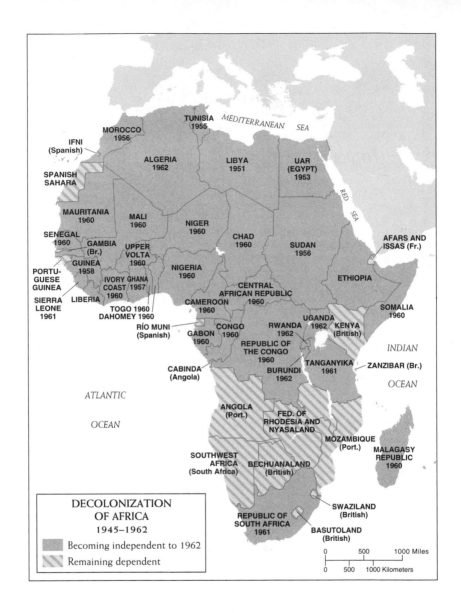

DECOLONIZATION
OF AFRICA
1945–1962

Becoming independent to 1962

Remaining dependent

colonies. This added impetus to the process of ending colonial rule, especially in Africa, where France and Britain entered on a new course in their colonial policies after Suez. The devolution of colonial rule, however, created tragic situations that resisted quick and simple solutions. The question of whether independence for Africa meant independence for Algeria, where generations of Frenchmen had settled, shook France deeply and kept its political life in turmoil for several years. Though Great Britain proceeded quickly in granting its

African colonies independence, it took more than a decade to end the fighting between blacks and whites in Rhodesia and to establish a basis for transforming Rhodesia into the independent states of Zimbabwe and Zambia in 1980.

The transformation of Africa from a colonial area into a group of independent states also changed the character of the United Nations. In 1980, of the UN's 154 members, 80, or more than one-half, had been admitted after 1956. With this increase in numbers, decisions of the UN were no longer determined by the United States, Russia, and their respective allies. The votes of the newly formed states of Africa became objects of competition by the two great superpowers, and this gave greater political weight to the powers of Western Europe that still exercised influence in their former colonies.

Still, Europe remained a region of major importance. With the exception of the United States it was the most industrialized and technologically the most advanced area of the world. Europe's industrial and technical apparatus contributed significantly to the rapid change in military organization and strategy that marked this period. The usefulness of conventional military forces began to decline, while the Russians' acquisition of the atomic bomb and the development of the hydrogen bomb set off a nuclear race in which only the industrial powers could participate. Also, next to the United States and Soviet Russia, the Western European powers alone had the requisite capacity for the development of nuclear power.

THE PURSUIT OF STABILITY AND PROSPERITY IN THE WEST

Conservative Government in Great Britain, 1956–1964

As the arena of competition between the superpowers shifted from Europe onto the global scene, the Western European powers enjoyed a greater freedom of action. This had as its first result closer collaboration among the countries on the Continent. Great Britain remained somewhat distant, however. Winston Churchill once declared that three concerns determined British foreign policy. The first and most important concern was the maintenance of close relations with the countries of the commonwealth; the second was Britain's special relationship with the United States; its relationship to continental Europe came only in third place.

When the Suez Affair strikingly demonstrated the decline of British imperial power, close relations with the United States became particularly important for Britain. Some of the commonwealth countries could now be better protected by the United States than by Great Britain, and other commonwealth nations had become more closely tied economically to the United States than to Great Britain. Thus, although the Suez Affair forced Great Britain and the United States into opposition, good relations were soon reestablished. An important role in the restoration of British-American friendship was played by the British prime minister Harold Macmillan, who had succeeded his fellow Conservative Anthony Eden after the failure of the Suez enterprise, Eden's brainchild and personal concern. The Conservatives, first under Macmillan and then under Douglas Home, remained in power until 1964.

It seems astounding that despite their resounding defeat in the Suez Affair, the Conservatives continued to govern for another seven years. But the first parliamentary elections after Suez were held in 1959, by which time the event's significance had faded. Moreover, Macmillan, who enjoyed the prestige of having been one of Churchill's most loyal political friends, towered over the other politicians of this period as a man of great flair, experience, and weight. The chief reason for the continued rule of the Conservatives, however, was the general disenchantment with Labor's plans for socialization that had set in after the great reform period under Attlee's Labor government following the Second World War. The Conservatives also avoided hostility by not embarking on a sharply reactionary course.

The Conservatives agreed with Labor about the crucial importance of maintaining full employment; in the following decade, unemployment hardly existed in Great Britain. Moreover, the Conservatives shunned a frontal attack against the reforms of the Attlee government. Certainly they preferred private enterprise to a state-run economy, but they proceeded cautiously. In a government paper issued in 1961, it was recommended "that sound economic management take precedent over social service considerations and that each nationalized industry should earn both a return on capital employment and over the year surpluses to constitute a fund for development and investment." Thus, the Conservatives pitched their opposition to nationalization on the basis of economic practicability rather than ideology.

Nevertheless, the Conservatives attempted to introduce a new direction in economic policy. Labor had placed the entire British transportation system—rail, road, internal waterways—under the British Transport Commission, a large combine that had soon run into deficits. The Conservative government tried to solve this problem by returning the road services to private hands; however, this measure only increased the difficulties of the railroads, which now had to compete with privately owned bus services and haulage companies. As a result, subsidies for the railroads had to be steadily increased.

The Conservatives had no more luck in their attempt to revoke the nationalization of steel and iron by allowing the previous owners to buy back those companies, which had been placed under the government's Iron and Steel Combine. The return to private ownership went ahead slowly, and one of the largest steel companies was still under government control when Labor came to power again in 1964 and began to reverse the course.

The Conservative government also had difficulties in handling the coal-mining industry, once the basis of British prosperity but in the twentieth century an industry with an incurable problem. Because of its inadequacies and backwardness, this industry had been nationalized in 1946 with general public approval, but European competition and the increasing use of oil further weakened its position. Various plans were made to restrict the production of coal and to increase efficiency with new machinery for mining, but the results were disappointing.

Since the lifting of duties on the import of grain during the first half of the nineteenth century, Britain had had to import foodstuffs, thus creating a large foreign debt. The Second World War had further increased Britain's external debts. In order to maintain British industry at full capacity, with full employment and high wages, the government subsidized the shipbuilding and coal-mining industries. These subsidies precluded competition, allowing prices to rise and the unfavorable balance of payments to grow steadily worse. The Conservative government looked again at a remedy it had originally rejected. The coal and steel union of Germany, France, and the Benelux countries established in 1951 had been transformed six years later by the treaties of Rome into a Common Market, the European Economic Community (EEC), with ambitious plans for an amalgamation of the economies of the participating countries. Britain refused to participate because it did not want to subordinate control of its economic policy to other powers. The Conservative government reversed this policy, beginning negotiations on Britain's entry into the EEC in the hope that the opening of the European market would give a spurt to British industry. But in the 1960s, opposition from Charles de Gaulle, who saw Britain as a stalking horse for America, prevented these negotiations from going anywhere.

Defense was another area in which Britain hoped to alleviate the burden of taxes and spur capital investment. The Conservative government had expeditiously, in a cooperative manner, caused the emancipation of the British colonies in Africa. In 1957, Ghana, the former Gold Coast, became independent; at the celebration the duchess of Kent, the queen's cousin, danced the foxtrot with President Kwame Nkrumah under the admiring gaze of the American vice president, Richard Nixon. Nigeria gained independence in 1960; Sierra Leone and Tanganyika, in 1961; Uganda, in 1962; Kenya, in 1963. All these new republics remained members of the commonwealth. Only British Somaliland, which in 1960 united with Italian Somaliland, became an independent state outside the commonwealth.

Britain was no longer obligated to defend these former colonies, and the Conservative government set out to reduce the size of the army and the defense budget. The draft was abolished in 1960. Still, the hope for considerable savings in defense spending went unfulfilled because the expense of acquiring nuclear weapons and upgrading military technology more than balanced the savings gained by reducing the size of the army.

LABOR'S RETURN TO POWER

Thus, the initiatives of the Conservative government failed to improve Britain's economic situation. Moreover, they created strong opposition among many Labor politicians, who, for reasons of principle, opposed the building of nuclear weapons, and among the trade unions, which resisted Britain's entry into the EEC. The Labor Party and the unions feared that subordination to EEC regulations might nullify some of the advantages they had gained, particularly protections against layoffs, and might make further nationalization of industry difficult, if not impossible.

Finally, the prestige of the Conservative government suffered from security scandals revealing that John Profumo, the minister of defense, had met with the Russian military attaché in the apartment of a prostitute. These problems combined to bring Labor to power in 1964. The new Labor government was less impressive than Attlee's of 1945, which had assembled able leaders with experience gained in the opposition of the 1930s and in the governing coalition during the war. By 1964, most of these leaders were dead, as were the most brilliant Labor politicians of the postwar generation, Hugh Gaitskell and Aneurin Bevan. The new prime minister, Harold Wilson, was a former Oxford don; he and the members of his government belonged to a younger generation that was more concerned with administrative efficiency than with ideology and more anxious to make things work than to extend socialism into wider spheres of life.

Wilson's government did not, however, entirely disregard the principles on which the Labor Party program was based. It revoked the measures by which the Conservative government had returned the iron and steel industries to private hands, and it increased payments to the unemployed, sick workers, and widows, raising the contributions made by employers and employees. The Labor government also made sure that excessive profits from North Sea oil would not fall into private hands; it placed the exploitation of this oil under public control by establishing the British National Oil Corporation.

The Labor government continued the policy of diminishing inequalities. In an Equal Pay Act it established that wages for women should not be lower than wages for men in equivalent positions. The government worked hard also to stimulate the organization of comprehensive schools that would eliminate the difference in social prestige between the exclusive, expensive private schools and modern secondary schools. The effort to reduce class differences in education was important because the number of schoolchildren between the end of the war and the 1970s rose from 5 to 8 million.

But the primary goal of the Labor government was to get the British economy into better shape. Since the 1920s the value of the pound in relation to other currencies had been too high. This helped England import more foodstuffs, a necessity for the small island, but brought the disadvantage of making English goods very expensive. Moreover, the effort to enforce regulations favorable to labor provoked bickering between management and workers that slowed production and impeded innovation. English products could no longer compete with the goods of other countries, especially after the economy of continental Europe revived. Britain's balance of payments problem grew worse each year, and unemployment again began to grow. In 1967 it rose to over half a million for the first time, and it reached 1 million in 1975. The government did not want to respond to its cash shortage by raising the price of foodstuffs, and for reasons of prestige, it was very hesitant to devalue the pound.

Nevertheless, in 1967 it was forced to do so. The dollar equivalent of a pound was reduced from $2.80 to $2.40. In general, a currency devaluation increases a nation's competitiveness on foreign markets, but it also leads to rising prices. Moreover, when wages rise along with prices, the advantages of devaluation are soon lost. The Labor government therefore tried to impose a policy of austerity and introduced, after difficult negotiations with employers and trade union leaders, government control over wage increases. The workers and trade unions opposed this, and strikes broke out. Wilson hoped to hold the situation stable until Britain's entry into the EEC could spur the economy. But in 1970, before the results of Labor's policies had become clear, the time for new elections had come around, and predictably, in light of Britain's grim economic condition, the Labor government did not pass the test.

France: The Return of de Gaulle

After the crisis year of 1956, Great Britain's first move in foreign policy had been to repair its ties with the United States, and only then did it move closer to the Continent and make use of the somewhat greater freedom of action the new constellation of world politics allowed. Quicker to take advantage of this new political world was France, which became the protagonist of European independence and nationalism.

In many respects France was in an excellent position to play a greater role in world politics. Before the world wars, one of France's worst problems had been its declining population. This was now reversed: between 1946 and 1960 the French population increased by 5 million while national income shot up by 85 percent. Agriculture was transformed as the number of small peasant holdings steadily declined and mechanization spread. The number of tractors in use rose from forty-six thousand in 1946 to eight hundred sixty thousand in 1963. Moreover, France developed into a leading power in electronics and airplane construction under the guidance of an *aristocratie de la compétence technique*, or elite group of technical experts.

France's weakness was political. Twenty-five percent of the population regularly voted Communist. Many other Frenchmen supported a rightist group in which contradictory trends, such as opposition to modernization and dissatisfaction with the loss of national purpose, were combined. The third force, the middle, was weak. It consisted of Socialists, Radical Socialists, and the Catholic Democrats (MRP), and they were unable to act together or to solve the financial problems created by the colonial wars in which France was entangled.

Prime Minister Pierre Mendès-France (1907–1982) had reached a settlement of the hostilities in Indochina in November 1954, and in March 1956 France granted Morocco and Tunisia their independence. The French hoped that these two Arab countries would withhold their support from the Muslims who had risen in revolt in Algeria two years earlier. The French Army had responded to this revolt with an obstinate defense of colonial rule. After France's defeat in Indochina and the Suez debacle, many French officers were anxious to prove their value and to show that their great military traditions were still alive.

The French government also had a different attitude toward the Algerian Revolt than toward problems in Indochina or even Tunisia and Morocco. Algeria had been a French possession for more than a hundred years. Many Frenchmen had settled there, and administratively Algeria, which was divided into the departments of Algiers, Oran, and Constantine, formed part of continental France. Dissatisfaction with French rule in Algeria arose from the fact that the role of the Muslims was subordinate to that of the *colons*, or European settlers. There were two electoral colleges, each choosing the same number of deputies, but the electorate of one consisted of 1.2 million settlers, that of the other of 8.5 million Muslims. Because Algeria essentially formed part of France, the granting of independence was vehemently opposed not only by the army and the extreme right but also by many adherents of the parties supporting the French government. The government therefore jogged a weary course. When the Suez Affair ended in a fiasco, the movement for Algerian independence grew in strength. Guerrilla warfare, which the Muslims conducted with great skill, absorbed more than four hundred thousand French soldiers, who were unable to put an end to terroristic acts or to restore safety in the hinterland. The mounting costs of the war increased the French budgetary deficit and accelerated inflation.

The barbaric cruelty with which the war was pursued aroused sharp criticism among French intellectuals and men of the church. A left-wing opposition to the war began to develop. Various French governments tried to restore peace by offering the Muslims greater political influence, but fearing the strength of those opposed to surrender, they did not go very far in their concessions, and the French in Algiers, with the full backing of the military in command there, were adamant in refusing to accept any diminution of their power. It came to the point that orders of the French government that ran against the wishes of the *colons* and the army were barely obeyed.

In the spring of 1958 the crisis came to a head. Weak and frequently changing governments slowly moved in the direction of further concessions to the Muslim majority. On May 13, 1958, during a government crisis in Paris, a demonstration by the *colons* against the vacillations of Paris led to the occupation of a government building in Algiers, prompting the army to agree to spearhead the move against further concessions. A new government quickly established in Paris was

Charles de Gaulle in a
characteristic pose during a
campaign rally.

unable to assert its authority over the military in Algiers. On the contrary, the rebelling French officers in Algeria were in direct contact with officers and deputies in European France; to prove the helplessness of the government, troops under order of the generals in Algiers occupied Corsica. Without means to suppress the rebellion, the parliamentary politicians gave in and voted to put in office the one general who could end the chaos. On May 29, 1958, Charles de Gaulle was installed as prime minister.

Those who brought de Gaulle into power—army officers in Algiers and European France; *colons* in North Africa; politicians of the right and center—later had reason to regret what they had done. But in 1958 de Gaulle, who was both an officer and the leader of a popular movement, seemed the only person who might be able to inspire the French people to the efforts required to bring the Algerian War to a victorious end. Much psychological insight would have been needed to realize that he was not the man to serve a movement, that he was accustomed to stand for himself and to chart his own course.

In his first measures as prime minister in 1958, de Gaulle acted according to expectations. He accepted office on condition that he be permitted to rule by decree for the first six months and to draft a new constitution, which would be submitted to the people for approval in a referendum. As could be foreseen, the constitution, adopted by a clear majority in September 1958, strengthened the executive branch of the government. The president was to be elected for seven years by the members of the parliament (consisting of a Senate and a National Assembly) and by representatives of the local and regional councils. But a few years later, in 1962, this law was changed, and by a referendum popular election was introduced. The president was a powerful figure. He had the right to appoint the prime minister and to dissolve the National Assembly. The powers of parliament were weakened in that a vote to overthrow the government required a majority of the total membership of the National Assembly, not just of the members present. Moreover, with the approval of the assembly the government could, for a limited time, rule by decree; only after this period had ended, which would frequently be after the decrees had fulfilled their purposes, did they have to be ratified by parliament. Assured of being able to carry out what he had in mind, de Gaulle, in January 1959, assumed the presidency of the Fifth Republic, to which he had been elected late in December.

Independence for Algeria

De Gaulle's constitution also provided a settlement of the colonial question, and this aspect of his constitution showed an unexpected adventurousness. It envisioned a French community in which the various colonies would be autonomous, although in matters of defense, foreign affairs, and overall economic policy, they would act jointly. Actually this plan for a French community was never completely realized. De Gaulle permitted the colonies to vote on whether they wanted to become members of the community or to enjoy complete independence. In 1960 the French colonies (Dahomey, Cameroun, Ubangi-Shari, Chad, Gabon, Ivory Coast, Mali, Niger, Senegal, Upper Volta) achieved full independence, but cultural and economic ties with France remained close.

Algeria, however, was excluded from these arrangements, and the war there dragged on. While de Gaulle continued to insist that Algeria had to remain French, he cautiously and gradually moved into a more flexible position and on September 16, 1959, announced that self-determination for Algeria was the only dignified method by which France could discharge its obligations toward North Africa. In a referendum, the Algerians were to be given the choice of assimilation, full independence or—as a middle way—close association with France. De Gaulle tried to placate the opposition by stating that such a referendum could be held only after the region had been pacified. Nevertheless, his acceptance of

French soldiers manning barricades during the Algerian War, January 1960.

self-determination opened the floodgates. The movement toward the separation of Algeria from France became irresistible.

On July 8, 1961, the French people approved in a referendum the principle of self-determination for Algeria. The army officers there, in a last desperate move, tried to repeat the game they had played in 1958. But now they received no support from France, and their own soldiers began to refuse to obey them. The insurrection collapsed; prominent generals who had led the rebellion and politicians who were passionate protagonists of a French Algeria fled and were condemned in absentia. Negotiations with Algerian nationalist leaders now began, and although they were interrupted by recurrent crises, a settlement was reached in March 1962. Algeria was officially named independent on July 3, 1962.

In terminating the Algerian War, de Gaulle succeeded in doing what no other French government had been able to do. He did it by turning the eyes of the French Army away from the past and toward the future. He proclaimed that the real opportunities for French greatness were in Europe. The loss of the empire was both a definite end and a new beginning.

De Gaulle's Vision for France

De Gaulle was a fierce patriot. He wanted to see France become great, the leader of Europe. His patriotism had an almost mystical source. In his *Memoirs* de Gaulle wrote that he imagined France "like the princess in the fairy stories or the Madonna in the frescoes, as dedicated to an exalted and exceptional destiny. . . . Providence had created her either for complete successes or for exemplary misfortunes. If, in spite of this, mediocrity shows in her acts," this is "an absurd anomaly. . . . France is not really herself unless in the front rank. . . . In short, to my mind, France cannot be France without greatness."

This romantic patriotism was quite different from the aggressive nationalism of the nineteenth century, which aimed at elevating one nation at the cost of all others. De Gaulle's concern was with preserving the integrity of France: the inviolability of its territory, the uniqueness of its spirit. Because de Gaulle viewed France as an individual, he also had an understanding of the individuality of other nations. While rejecting a united Europe that would submerge individual nations, he favored a closer connection among all the countries on the Continent so that Europe would become the "Europe of the Fatherlands."

The course of de Gaulle's foreign policy was based on these concepts. He steered France away from the Anglo-Saxon powers. In his antagonism to the United States and Great Britain there may have been a residue of personal resentment at the coolness he had experienced from Roosevelt and Churchill during the war. But there were more basic reasons. De Gaulle saw in the cooperation of the United States and Great Britain the danger of Anglo-American rule over the globe or over wide parts of the globe, a Pax Americana; he feared in particular the ideological and institutional uniformity that these Anglo-Saxon protagonists of democracy and world government might want to impose.

He felt that such internationalism might suffocate the individual character of a nation.

De Gaulle's eagerness to restrict and diminish Anglo-Saxon influence showed itself in many ways. For example, he made a strong stand to secure the maintenance of French as a language of diplomacy. More important was his resistance to the attempts of England to enter the Common Market. When, after lengthy negotiations, the way seemed free for Great Britain to enter the European Common Market, de Gaulle vetoed this move, first in 1963 and then again in 1967. He used every opportunity to regain independence for France by emancipating it from bonds the Western alliance had placed on French freedom of action. In gradual steps de Gaulle withdrew French forces from the NATO command: in 1959 he withdrew the Mediterranean fleet, and in 1963 the Atlantic fleet, and in 1966 he ended all French participation in NATO. Its headquarters were transferred from Paris to Brussels.

Whereas de Gaulle evidently feared that the French might be seduced by the Anglo-Saxon ideology, he did not think that Soviet Russia represented a similar threat. Soviet Russia was for him a traditional great power rather than the center and protagonist of a world-encompassing international movement. During the war de Gaulle had concluded a treaty with Soviet Russia. In 1964 he negotiated a commercial agreement with Soviet Russia, and in June 1963, three months after France left NATO, de Gaulle visited Moscow, where he received the welcome of a hero. But the fact that de Gaulle regarded Communism as less dangerous than Anglo-Saxon imperialism did not mean that he was not suspicious of further increases in Russian power and anxious to prevent the possibility of Russian expansion into the heart of Europe. In this context it is significant that although de Gaulle had withdrawn the French forces from NATO command, France still remained a member of the Atlantic alliance. Moreover, his opposition to Russian expansion was a crucial reason for his policy of Franco-German cooperation.

Although de Gaulle had fought the Nazis in their attempt to dominate Europe, he saw Germany as similar to France, as a "fatherland," a country with its own culture, one of the constituent elements of the Europe of independent nations he wanted to re-create. Moreover, Germany could serve as a dam against Russian expansion. Thus, de Gaulle backed West Germany against the Russian attempts to drive the West out of Berlin, he established close contacts with German Chancellor Adenauer, and in 1962 he made a successful tour through West Germany, initiating a new era in the relations between the two countries.

The basis for de Gaulle's policy had been laid in the ten years preceding his rise to power, when France's transformation into a modern industrial society had begun. De Gaulle's government was eager to accelerate this development, and some think this complicated the problems of the coming decade by creating two economies that coexisted uneasily: a modern one, implanted mostly since the war, consisting of a few big state and private firms; and beneath it a traditional infrastructure based on artisanship, high profit on a modest income, and the ideal of the small family business.

One aspect of France's economic modernization was crucial for de Gaulle: he felt that no nation could be independent and strong without building a modern mechanized army. It was this aspect of his policy that helped heal the wounds of the Algerian War and reconcile the officer corps with the government he had created, the Fifth French Republic. The officers knew that an army equipped and trained to fight colonial wars would be of little value under European battle conditions. Moreover, modernization of the army provided the officers with new and exciting tasks. In his resolve to make France again one of the great powers, de Gaulle decided to provide his country with the *force de frappe*, as nuclear armament was called. The French governments before de Gaulle had already initiated nuclear research, somewhat resentfully because of America's lack of support in this enterprise. De Gaulle extended the work, and in 1960 the first French atomic bomb was exploded. In 1966, the French exploded a hydrogen bomb, and two years later they tried out a variety of nuclear weapons in the Pacific. These were powerful indications of de Gaulle's success in making France again one of the world's leading powers.

Italy's Opening toward the Left

While not directly involved in the critical events of 1956, Italy was deeply influenced by these events. They changed the party constellation in Italy and so changed the character of the Italian government. Since Italy had seventeen governments between 1945 and 1970, some might argue that governmental changes are not events of great significance in Italian politics. But the importance of these frequent governmental changes should be neither underestimated nor overestimated.

As was true of France, Italy's officials both in Rome and in the various provinces were highly competent civil servants who maintained administrative continuity regardless of the minister in charge. Italy preserved political stability despite frequent changes in government also because these changes often brought only a reshuffling of ministers or the return of those from a previous government. In short, Italy's various governments were composed of the same relatively small group of experienced politicians. The crisis of 1956 affected Italy politically because it brought a change in the composition of this ruling group.

Since 1945, Italy had been governed by the Christian Democratic Party, and from 1945 to 1953, Prime Minister Alcide de Gasperi headed the government; in 1947, he ousted the Communists from his government and led Italy into the American camp. For their parliamentary majority the Christian Democrats needed the support of small, bourgeois splinter parties on their left since their pro-American policy had created what appeared to be an unbridgeable gap between their party and the other two large mass parties, the Socialists and the Communists. In 1953, de Gasperi tried to gain a clear majority for the Christian

Democratic Party through new elections, but the attempt failed. The Christian Democrats then began to look for more stable support, and the crisis of 1956 created the opening they needed. Russia's ruthless suppression of the Hungarian Revolt disappointed and antagonized many Socialists and Communists. In the following year, 1957, Pietro Nenni, the leader of the Socialists, obtained the approval of his party to end the action agreement (*patto d'azione*) in which the Socialists and Communists had promised to enter the government only together, never separately. The adoption of an autonomous policy by the Socialists created the possibility for cooperation between Nenni's party and the Christian Democrats. This made the question of the opening toward the left a principal issue in Italian politics.

Both the Socialists and the Christian Democrats were willing to cooperate in addressing Italy's troubled economy. While the economies of Germany and France had taken off sooner than the Italian economy, Italy's takeoff had been more rapid. During the 1950s the annual growth rate of the Italian economy, 6 percent, was 1.5 percent higher than in the rest of Europe, and in the same decade Italian exports tripled. The success of such great northern Italian enterprises as Fiat and Olivetti was remarkable in a country so lacking in essential raw materials. The takeoff of Italy's industrial economy was powered by two public corporations: ENI, which had a monopoly on the production of gas and oil, and IRI, composed both of enterprises fully owned by the state, such as the airline Alitalia and the national television network, and of enterprises partially owned by the state, such as the shipbuilding industry.

Despite its great economic takeoff, Italy did not become a prosperous country. Industrial progress had not overcome the traditional weaknesses in the Italian economy. Widespread resistance to taxes had created huge budget deficits and rising inflation. Much of the peasantry, particularly in Italy's south, continued to live in misery. A plan to redistribute land in the south to quiet peasant unrest was initiated but soon halted. Age-old tenancy laws prevented the peasants of central Italy from owning the land on which they lived and required that they hand over a fixed part of the harvest to the legal owner. The steady growth of the population, particularly in the south, worsened the situation; in the decade of the 1960s, the Italian population rose by more than 4 million, or 9.1 percent.

The peasant's way to escape the misery in the south was to seek work in the industrialized north; in 1963, for instance, three hundred thousand southerners moved to the north, and similar figures hold for the other years of this decade. But even northern Italy's rapidly growing industry could not absorb such numbers, and unemployment remained high. Those lucky enough to find work encountered wretched living conditions because there had been no systematic attempt at building housing for the industrial workers. In addition, the immigrants from the south, many of whom were illiterate and spoke a dialect that northern Italians found almost impossible to understand, were treated as unwel-

Pope John XXIII. The pope records a speech calling for world peace, September 11, 1962.

come aliens. A significant indication of the misery existing below Italy's rather brilliant economic surface was the fact that throughout these decades the Communists consistently received 25 percent of the vote.

The question facing the Italian economy in the late 1950s was whether development ought to be focused in the public or private sector. Certainly the industrial entrepreneurs composing the Confindustria, an extremely powerful pressure group, wanted the great state-controlled enterprises placed in the service of private industry, and a wing of the Christian Democrats supported them. But the Christian Democratic Party was a mass party; it had a history of strong opposition to Fascism before the rule of Mussolini, who suppressed the party, and it was vital enough to reemerge after the fall of Fascism. Understandably, then, its left wing strongly embraced the goal of general social reform.

The left wing of the Christian Democrats knew that to succeed with such a policy, they needed the support of the Socialists to overcome right-wing opposition in their own party. The possibility of cooperation was opened not only by the Soviet intervention in Hungary but also by the new policies of Pope John XXIII. His 1961 encyclical *Mater et Magistra* called for a social policy to improve the economic situation of the lower classes. His 1963 encyclical *Pacem in Terris* emphasized the paramount importance of peace, which might require collaboration with all forces of the left, including non-Christians not pronouncedly "Godless." These encyclicals made it easier for the Christian Democrats to cooperate with the Socialists, who themselves knew that without progress toward reform they would lose their adherents to the Communists. The Soviet action in Hungary left the Socialists less inclined to ally themselves with the Communists. But the Socialists had their own reservations about cooperation with the Christian Democrats, and this prevented the establishment of a coalition government until 1963, when under the Christian Democratic prime minister Aldo Moro, the leader of the Socialists, Pietro Nenni, became deputy prime minister.

The formation of this coalition was a slow, gradual process that led the Socialists from a position of political abstention to direct participation. But the coalition government did not last long. Discontent with the slow tempo of reform split the Socialists, leaving only a small group in continued support of Moro's government. Nevertheless, some progressive reforms were achieved: the electrical industry was nationalized, and attendance at middle schools was required, an effort to eliminate remaining pockets of illiteracy and the class distinctions inherent in the existence of various school types. Despite the failure of his coalition government, Aldo Moro remained a leading figure in the Christian Democratic Party and a force for progressive reform.

Germany: A Western Power

Unlike Britain, France, and Italy, Germany was little affected by the Suez Affair and the Hungarian Revolt. The end of Germany's postwar period was marked by its admission to NATO in 1955. In the same year, the Allied High Commission was dissolved, and American, French, and British troops were in Germany no longer as occupying forces but with German consent as allies.

Chancellor Adenauer's steady support of American foreign policy during the Cold War was largely responsible for Germany's return to the circle of important European powers. But this policy exposed Adenauer's government to attack by both the socialists on the left and the nationalists on the right because of his alleged subservience to American policy and his willingness to rearm Germany within the framework of NATO. His opponents thought Adenauer's posture precluded the neutralization of Central Europe and the reunification of West and East Germany. But Adenauer was convinced that after the horrors of the Nazi regime, Germany had to show that it belonged to the Western world. He also believed that only full cooperation with the United States could protect West Berlin from the pressure exerted by the East. Throughout Adenauer's chancellorship the Russians had impeded the connection between West Germany and West Berlin in a continuous effort, it seemed, to make life in West Berlin impossible and force its surrender to East Germany. This policy took concrete form in the wall East Germany built between West and East Berlin in August 1961, partly as an attempt to stop a hole through which East Germans escaped to the West. Only by showing that the cause of West Berlin was the cause of the entire West, Adenauer reasoned, could the position of Berlin be maintained. When President Kennedy proclaimed in his famous 1963 speech in Berlin, "*Ich bin*

Part of the Berlin Wall.

ein Berliner ['I am a Berliner']," he justified Adenauer's pro-American policy by displaying America's interest in the defense of West Germany's existence and rights.

France's president, Charles de Gaulle, also strengthened Adenauer's foreign policy. De Gaulle and Adenauer got along very well, and de Gaulle's view of Europe as a coherent combination of independent nations, each with its own individuality, suggested that cooperation among the nations of the West would not compromise national identity. But the most powerful source of Adenauer's political strength lay in Germany's flourishing economy. With the help of the Marshall Plan at the end of the 1940s, Germany began to rebuild its industrial base, and the results were astounding. Industrial productivity tripled between 1949 and 1962, and since all wages were low, exports also tripled during this time. Germany enjoyed a consistently favorable balance of payments and full employment. Only 0.5 percent of the workers were unemployed in 1960, despite the absorption of 2.5 million refugees from the East. Government subventions and loans provided housing for the immigrants.

Under these economic circumstances extreme parties of the right and left remained small. The Communist Party was declared unconstitutional by the courts in 1956, but it had always received only a small percentage of the vote.

Similarly, a rightist party of refugees gained a remarkable number of votes at the beginning of the 1950s only to melt away quickly and disappear. Just three political parties of importance remained into the 1960s: Adenauer's Christian Democratic Union; the Free Democratic Party, which participated in the government; and, finally, the chief opposition party, the Social Democrats. But in the Godesberg program, which the socialists adopted in 1959, they distanced themselves from Marxism by proclaiming that economic planning should take place only insofar as it was necessary and that there should be as much freedom left in economic development as possible. The Godesberg program represented an abandonment of the notion of class struggle. It was emphatically a program of reform, not revolution, and was directed toward cooperation in economic life among all those who had a stake in it.

The trade unions had always been a strong influence on the Social Democrats. After their first successful attempt to achieve codetermination, or worker participation, in the management of the iron and steel industries and mining, they began to encounter increasing resistance and changed their course. The unions began to concentrate on securing better wages for the workers, and their efforts found favor among employers, who in times of rising economic prosperity were interested in avoiding labor conflicts and strikes. In fact, most Germans at this time were not eager to engage in political and social conflict; they were willing to compromise.

Western Europe: Coherence and Tension

The events of the mid-1950s allowed the European states a greater amount of initiative and autonomy, but this could not restore the prewar Europe of independent sovereign states. Pressure from the Communist bloc kept Western Europe tied closely to the United States, especially in military matters. After the attempt at forming an integrated European army had failed, the delicate question of using German manpower and industrial resources for the defense of Western Europe was solved by making Germany a member of NATO. Within NATO, American and European military leaders coordinated organization and strategic planning. These military bonds were reinforced by stationing American troops in West Berlin and elsewhere in Germany and by maintenance of American air bases in Great Britain and naval bases in the Mediterranean. Even the French, despite de Gaulle's removal of NATO bases from France, continued to cooperate with NATO in military planning. The connection between the European and American military was a guarantee, stronger than any alliance treaty, that in the case of an attack from the East, Western Europe would receive American support. None of the European states would have wanted to act in such a way as to jeopardize American support.

Pressure from the Communist bloc caused the European powers to cooperate not only militarily but also economically. European economic cooperation began soon after the Second World War with the formation of a Council of

Europe, a consultative assembly composed of delegates from the national parliaments, and of the European Coal and Steel Community. After some years of stagnation and the crises of 1956, progress toward European economic integration resumed with the establishment in 1957 of scientific institutions combining the various national research programs: EURATOM, working in the area of nuclear research, and ESRO, active in the field of space research.

The most important step toward economic cooperation and integration was taken with the Treaty of Rome of March 25, 1957. The signers were the same six countries that had formed the European Coal and Steel Community: France, Germany, Italy, Belgium, Holland, and Luxembourg. They agreed on the establishment of a Common Market (European Economic Community; hereafter EEC or Common Market). Its aims were to abolish all trade barriers among the six, to establish a common external tariff, to permit the free movement of labor and capital among the member states, and—by equalizing wage rates and social security systems—to bring about uniform working conditions in the Common Market area without creating unemployment. Clearly, these goals could not be achieved in a single stroke. The Rome agreement therefore envisioned a development in stages, to be completed within fifteen years. A European Commission with headquarters in Brussels, acting under the instructions of a regularly convened council of ministers, was entrusted with the administration of the Common Market and the guidance of its development. On January 1, 1959, the Common Market began to function by lowering tariffs 10 percent among the member countries, and thereafter, despite difficult negotiations and crises, progress was made in realizing its program.

The lowering of tariffs proceeded even more quickly than had been thought possible. Customs among the member states were abolished by 1968, and a common tariff for trade with nonmember states was simultaneously introduced. This acceleration of the original plans was made possible by the striking economic results of the integration: between 1957, when the Common Market was established, and the end of the 1960s, trade among member states increased by 720 percent, and trade with nonmember countries by 305 percent.

For Europe, the 1960s were the abundant decade; prosperity changed the face of the Continent. The growth of industrial activity gave a new aspect to Europe's urban centers. Steel and glass office buildings and high-rise hotels rose in the main streets and squares. Modern apartments to house the middle and working classes were built outside the towns. London and Paris emerged in new splendor. The houses in the older parts of London, many of them damaged or destroyed during the war, were rebuilt and repainted. In Paris the Louvre and surrounding buildings, which generations had known only as dirty gray, emerged with clean, gilded façades.

But the cooperation joining the industrial policies of the European nations was less successful in the field of agriculture. While France, owing to efficient planning by the government, enjoyed great agricultural surpluses, West Germany,

POSTWAR ALLIANCES

ICELAND,
CANADA,
U.S.

Military Alliances:

NATO, 1949–1955

Warsaw Pact

▲ Brussels Pact, 1948

NORWAY
SWEDEN
FINLAND

NORTH SEA

IRISH REPUBLIC
UNITED KINGDOM ▲
NETHERLANDS ▲
DENMARK

BALTIC SEA

BELGIUM ▲
WEST GERMANY ▲
EAST GERMANY
POLAND
SOVIET UNION

LUXEMBOURG ▲
GERMANY
CZECHOSLOVAKIA

FRANCE ▲
SWITZ.
AUSTRIA
HUNGARY

PORTUGAL
SPAIN

ITALY
ADRIATIC SEA
YUGOSLAVIA
ROMANIA
BULGARIA

ALBANIA
GREECE
TURKEY
AEGEAN SEA

MEDITERRANEAN SEA

| 0 | 250 | 500 Miles |
| 0 | 250 | 500 Kilometers |

ATLANTIC

OCEAN

Economic Blocs:

European Economic
Community (EEC)

Benelux Customs Union,
since 1947 (also EEC)

Council for Mutual Economic
Assistance, since 1949

European Free Trade
Association, since 1960

NORWAY
SWEDEN
FINLAND

NORTH SEA

IRISH REPUBLIC
UNITED KINGDOM
NETHERLANDS
DENMARK

BALTIC SEA

BELGIUM
WEST GERMANY
EAST GERMANY
POLAND
SOVIET UNION

LUXEMBOURG
GERMANY
CZECHOSLOVAKIA

FRANCE
SWITZ.
AUSTRIA
HUNGARY

PORTUGAL
SPAIN

ITALY
ADRIATIC SEA
YUGOSLAVIA
ROMANIA
BULGARIA

ALBANIA
GREECE
TURKEY
AEGEAN SEA

MEDITERRANEAN SEA

| 0 | 250 | 500 Miles |
| 0 | 250 | 500 Kilometers |

deprived of its rich agricultural areas in the East, remained a country of relatively small and unproductive peasant farms. The French wanted few restrictions impeding the trade of their surpluses, but the Germans insisted on maintaining government support and protection for agricultural production. This gap in agricultural policy was difficult to bridge, and negotiations brought only temporary compromises. European cooperation was weakened also by the tension between urban and rural areas that spread through much of the Continent in the wake of industrial expansion. Even small countries like Denmark and the Netherlands, which in previous years had shown no signs of governmental instability, now began to flounder between right and left.

De Gaulle presented another obstacle to rapid progress in unification. Although he recognized the usefulness of the Treaty of Rome, he opposed economic measures that might encroach on French sovereignty. He also wished to preclude any potential challenge to French-German hegemony over Europe. This was one reason for his opposition to Great Britain's entry into the Common Market.

But the reluctance to include Great Britain and the Scandinavian countries in the Common Market went deeper than de Gaulle's French imperialism. Unlike the Common Market countries, whose mixed economies combined private and public elements, Great Britain and the Scandinavian countries worked toward the realization of the welfare state. Of these, Sweden went furthest in this direction. Social insurance covered all spheres of life; pensions, amounting to 65 percent of the highest salary earned during a person's working years, gave financial security after retirement. Within this framework, free enterprise continued to prevail, even though the government set wages and entered into intensive consultation, particularly with the trade unions, before any new legislation was brought before parliament; the trade unions had almost a veto power. High taxes were the basis for the functioning of this system. Representing 40 percent of the gross national income, Swedish taxes were the highest in the world. As long as the European economy flourished, Sweden's wealth in timber and iron ore and its long experience in industries like shipbuilding and car manufacturing made it one of the wealthiest countries of Europe. The economic regulation characterizing the welfare states did not combine easily with the largely unregulated conditions that prevailed among the nations in the Common Market.

DE-STALINIZATION IN EASTERN EUROPE

Khruschev's Domestic Policies

The revolt in Hungary affected Eastern Europe differently from the West, where it opened possibilities for new political and economic initiatives. In Eastern Europe, Stalin's death in 1953 had set a new course into motion *before* the Hungarian Revolution, which itself then forced a reconsideration of the correctness, tempo, and direction of the new, post-Stalinist course.

Stalin's death, a watershed in Soviet history, began a decisive shift in Soviet policy. After a few years of uncertain, collective leadership, the first secretary of the Communist Party, Nikita Khrushchev, emerged as the dominant figure in the Soviet government. A native of Ukraine, Khrushchev distinguished himself in its defense during World War II and rose through the party ranks with the help of Stalin's favor. But by February 1956, Khrushchev was powerful enough to launch a posthumous attack in a closed session of the Twentieth Congress of the Communist Party on Stalin's rule. Stalin, Khrushchev charged, "used extreme methods and mass repression at the time when the Revolution was already victorious. . . . Instead of proving his political correctness and mobilizing the masses, he often chose the path of repression and physical annihilation, not only against actual enemies, but also against individuals who had not committed any crimes against the party and the Soviet government." Khrushchev's "secret" speech officially introduced the policy of de-Stalinization, the central issue in the Eastern bloc during the ensuing decade.

De-Stalinization in the Soviet Union meant first of all the abandonment of the police state's most brutal techniques. Of the political leaders whom Khrushchev had defeated and ousted, only Beria, the feared head of the KGB, was executed. The others lived in retirement with a pension, as Khrushchev himself would after his own ouster in 1964. Some of the wretched Siberian prison camps—immortalized by Aleksandr Solzhenitsyn in his *Gulag Archipelago*— were dissolved. Solzhenitsyn's early works, particularly his novel *A Day in the Life of Ivan Denisovich*, were approved by Khrushchev, who showed some cautious interest in the promotion of intellectual life, and were for the first time

Soviet Premier Nikita Khrushchev. In domestic and foreign policy, Khrushchev initiated the period of de-Stalinization in the Eastern bloc.

published in the author's native land in 1962. Other literary works assisted de-Stalinization by satirizing bureaucratic slowness, corruption, and insensibility. The loosening of the reins in the 1950s was temporary, however, and Soviet intellectual and cultural life continued to be racked by alternate waves of liberalization and restriction.

De-Stalinization also brought decisive and in many respects irrevocable changes in Soviet economic policy. Under Stalin, the Soviets were committed to the development of heavy industry to the exclusion of almost everything else; their aim was to ensure national security by creating a modern army with sophisticated rocketry and weaponry. Khrushchev promised to modify this policy by giving more attention to the needs of the consumer. He initiated a drive to increase agricultural production by promoting the production and use of farm machinery, especially tractors. For political as well as economic reasons Khrushchev also sought to increase the production of household goods and clothing.

During the postwar years, the difficulties of imposing centralized industrial planning had steadily increased for the Soviets. The difficulties encountered by the Soviets were evident in the Baltic countries of Lithuania, Estonia, and Latvia, all of which had lost their independence as a result of the German-Soviet Treaty of 1939. During the German occupation of this area many of its inhabitants collaborated with the Germans in the hope of regaining their independence. When the Soviets took over these areas after the war, they saw no reason to treat these countries with benevolence or to proceed gradually with their Sovietization.

The Soviets industrialized the area with brutal energy, making the water-power of these countries the most important source of energy for the whole northern area of Soviet Russia, including Leningrad. By 1966, industry had become the largest sector of the economy in these formerly agricultural areas. In that year, industrial production accounted for 60 percent of Latvia's gross national product (GNP) and 80 percent of Estonia's. In 1945, two-thirds of the Baltic population lived on and farmed the land; by the middle 1960s, two-thirds of the population required by industrialization came to a large extent from Russia. The influx of Russians soon eroded the ethnic and cultural distinctiveness of these countries, but even while subject to such pervasive change, the peoples of this area, used to centuries of foreign rule, adapted. They managed to boost industrial and agricultural production to a level higher than that of any other region in Russia.

Still, it was increasingly difficult to apply to areas of widely different resources, traditions, and work habits the same means of economic development. So a central element in de-Stalinization was Khrushchev's decision to decentralize the Soviet Union's industrial organization by creating a large number of regions and tailoring economic goals to the resources, conditions, and potential of each region. This benefited the lower echelons of the economic bureaucracy, which were capable now of exercising an initiative they had not possessed under Stalin.

Khrushchev's Foreign Policies and the Sino-Soviet Split

Soviet foreign policy in the late 1950s and the 1960s seemed to follow a zigzag course from the bellicose to the moderate. But throughout, the Soviets were careful not to enter upon any action in foreign policy that might endanger their control over the satellite countries. Khrushchev and his colleagues realized that the domestic goals of de-Stalinization required a generally peaceful atmosphere that would allow Russia to be less preoccupied with questions of security and armament. Khrushchev proclaimed that "peaceful coexistence" between capitalist and noncapitalist powers was possible, and his first actions were meant to lend substance to the slogan.

In May 1955, after long negotiations, Russia signed the Austrian State Treaty with the United States, France, and Great Britain. The treaty provided for the withdrawal of all occupying troops from Austria; five months later the foreign troops had indeed left Austrian soil, and Austria had become a sovereign, neutral state. Also in the spring of 1955, Khrushchev marked the end of Russia's conflict with Yugoslavia by visiting Tito and assuring him of Yugoslavia's complete independence, territorial integrity, and political autonomy. Economic collaboration and cultural relations between Russia and Yugoslavia were reestablished. But this reconciliation with Yugoslavia had consequences that sharpened the differences between East and West. Russia's concessions to Yugoslavia stimulated hopes for similar actions in Poland and Hungary and contributed to the 1956 revolts in these countries. The sympathy displayed in the Western world for the leaders of the revolt and for those who had succeeded in fleeing Hungary after the Russians had marched in raised the level of East-West tension again.

Khrushchev responded to the events of 1956 by emphasizing with brutal frankness that he would tolerate no interference with the Russian bloc in Eastern Europe and that its future was with the Soviet, not the Western, system. Although he showed some willingness to cooperate by appearing at United Nations meetings in New York in 1959 and 1960, the tone of his speeches there was aggressive, and shortly thereafter he used the capture of an American U-2 spy plane over Russia as a pretext to cancel a planned summit conference with President Eisenhower. By then the situation in Berlin had become the most critical issue in East-West and particularly in American-Soviet relations. The Russians continually harassed traffic on the roads between West and East Berlin, and in 1961 the Berlin Wall rose as a means of preventing East German migration and as a symbol of Soviet determination to maintain its supremacy in Eastern Europe.

It is not clear why Khrushchev then extended his aggressive policy into the Western Hemisphere, but the resulting event, the Cuban missile crisis, ended in a Russian defeat. Khrushchev may have wanted a diplomatic victory to assert in Russia's contest with the Chinese, with whom the Soviets were struggling for world leadership of the Communist Party.

The Sino-Soviet split had its origins in the late 1950s, when Mao and his colleagues concluded that the Soviets were not willing to help them win control of

Taiwan, the seat of the rival Nationalist Chinese government under Chiang Kai-shek. The Communist Chinese were angry too over the Soviets' tendency to meddle in internal Chinese politics. The Russians, seeing Mao as too independent from Moscow's tutelage, had tried to build up rival leaders in the Chinese Communist Party who seemed to favor closer ties with the Soviet Union. Against this background, Soviet offers of military cooperation on the mainland struck Mao and his advisers as pretexts, at best, for the use of Chinese territory and, at worst, for exercising outright control as in Eastern Europe. Mao told Khrushchev: "We've had the British and other foreigners on our territory for years now, and we're not ever going to let anyone use our land for their own purposes again."

In Chinese eyes the Russians had also become ideological bullies. The Chinese leaders were indignant that Khrushchev would launch his attack on Stalin's legacy in 1956—a major shift in Communist orthodoxy—without even consulting them. The Soviets, for their part, were equally appalled by China's Great Leap Forward, which deviated sharply from the Soviet pattern of development and seemed to constitute an effort to dispense with Soviet economic assistance and even to vault past the sluggish Russian economy. No wonder the Soviets, having promised to help the Chinese develop an atomic bomb in 1957, reneged on this promise in 1960. Indeed, they went on to sign in 1963 the Limited Test Ban Treaty with the United States, one purpose of which was to complicate the task of developing atomic weapons for those countries (including China) that had yet to acquire them. The Chinese refused to sign the treaty and denounced the Soviet Union along with the United States, accusing both superpowers of conspiring against China. Thereafter the Chinese strengthened their ties with the part of the world that belonged to neither camp, a constellation that embraced many of the poorer nations of Asia, Africa, and Latin America, as well as the Eastern European states of Romania and Albania, which were also feuding with the Soviets.

Poland and Hungary

Post-Stalin reform in the satellite countries had two dimensions. The first was the effort to remove those among Stalin's henchmen and confidants who would not have been able or willing to change their former policies. The second was the effort to alter the economic organization and improve living standards without abandoning the tenets of a Communist society. Poland and Hungary were the two satellite countries in which the de-Stalinization period was marked by serious unrest. Simmering discontent with an oppressive regime, combined with the personnel changes of de-Stalinization, sparked trouble first in Poland and then, following a "silent sympathy demonstration" for the Poles, in Hungary. But once the Communist regimes in these two countries had regained full control, Poland and Hungary took very different paths.

Władysław Gomułka, the Polish Communist leader who had been overthrown and imprisoned in 1949 by the Stalinists, was carried back to power in

1956 by the discontent in Poland. Gomułka remained a committed Communist; he strongly pushed Poland's industrial development, which was aided by a remarkable increase in population from 25 million in 1950 to 30 million in 1960. The number of workers increased, and the weight of the population shifted now from rural to urban areas. However, this increase in the urban population worsened the shortage of food in the cities. Gomułka increasingly became the target of criticism from intellectuals and radicals who objected to his control of intellectual movements, maintained in part to ensure ideological purity and in part to discourage Russian interference. Continued material hardships and intellectual discontent marred Gomułka's attempt at reconciling Communism with Polish traditions and needs. To most Poles, the government remained an oppressive force.

The Russians responded to the Hungarian Revolution by deposing its leader, Imre Nagy, and installing the János Kádár government, which at first promised an entirely ruthless return to Stalinism. But in the following years Kádár pursued a somewhat surprising course. He was indeed pitiless in punishing the leaders of what he called the counterrevolutionary movement, including Nagy, who was seduced into leaving his asylum in the Yugoslav embassy, captured, and then executed. Under Kádár two thousand Hungarians were executed, and twenty thousand imprisoned.

Kádár showed his adherence to party doctrine by collectivizing agriculture with ruthless energy. Before the outbreak of the revolt in 1956, not even 16 percent of Hungary's agricultural area was collectivized (next to Poland, Hungary had the largest number of peasant owners in the Soviet bloc); by 1961, 96 percent of the agrarian sector had been collectivized. At the same time, however, Kádár decentralized the administration of agriculture and industry, and this mitigated the oppressive features of the regime and encouraged a limited degree of free enterprise.

After three or four years of higher agricultural production and the mining and sale of rich raw materials like bauxite and uranium, Hungary began to enjoy a certain prosperity, and the government began to feel secure. It released political prisoners and, at the end of 1960, issued a broad amnesty. The government relaxed its control of literary and intellectual life, allowing Hungary to develop closer intellectual connections with the West than any other satellite country. Foreign books appeared in the bookshops, travel in the West became more common, and in the 1970s the government was able to announce with some pride that over 90 percent of the Hungarians who had visited the West during the summer had not defected but returned to Hungary.

Romania and East Germany

Though geographically very distant from each other, Romania and East Germany (the Deutsche Demokratische Republik or DDR) had this in common: among the Russian satellites, they were the least affected by the end of Stalinism.

Romania turned away from Germany in the fall of 1944, and into power came democratic parties willing to accept the armistice offered by the Allied anti-Nazi coalition. Russian troops then occupied Romania, and the Russians threw their support behind the Communist Party and its leaders, most of whom had either been in Russia or imprisoned during the war. For a number of years after the war non-Communist parties were permitted to exist and were represented in the Romanian parliament. Peter Groza, an agrarian leader who was friendly toward the Communists but not a Communist himself, remained prime minister until 1952. It was only in the early 1950s, therefore, that Romania fully adjusted to the Soviet system. But Soviet power had not advanced far in dominating Romania when Stalin died. As a result, de-Stalinization in Romania did not bring decisive policy changes.

The continuity marking Romanian Communist leadership throughout the 1950s and 1960s did not result in coherent policy. The government pushed ahead quickly with the collectivization of agriculture by confiscating not only the great estates but also the larger peasant properties, and this led frequently to bloody clashes. The government was hesitant to impose comprehensive industrial planning and concentrated primarily on electrification. The revolt in Hungary caused Romanian officials to slow the tempo of industrialization, increase wages, and supply the larger towns with foodstuffs by forced deliveries.

The pace of collectivization in Romania again accelerated in 1958, when the Russians agreed to withdraw their troops from the country. By 1962 collectivization was declared complete; only 5 percent of the land remained in private hands. On the other hand, Romania was able to pursue its own course in industry and trade because it possessed oil, the raw material that other countries, especially the European countries, needed. Romania accepted Western financial and technical support for the development of its industries, some of which were owned in part by Western Europeans. Romania's economic independence was made plain at the 1963 meeting of COMECON (Council for Mutual Economic Assistance), where Ceauşescu successfully opposed all attempts to impose on member nations comprehensive economic plans that did not give appropriate weight to the unique economic conditions of each of the principal countries.

In its cultural policy, Romania also maintained a stance of cautious independence. In 1963, Russian was dropped as the first foreign language to be taught in the schools; the Latinity of the Romanian people was again emphasized. Romania also maintained relations with China and Yugoslavia even when hostility between these two countries and Russia grew. Nevertheless, the Romanian Communist regime continued to proclaim its adherence to the Warsaw Pact and emphasized that Romania was a socialist state. Despite its ties to Soviet Russia, Romania was able to sustain a measure of autonomy because of its strong awareness of its unique history and culture. Even if the independent attitudes in foreign policy were not much more than gestures, the recognition given to the importance of Romanian nationality broadened the basis of the regime and formed a counterweight to the resentments that develop in a strictly controlled society.

In contrast to Romania, East Germany was ruled by a strong Communist regime undeterred by any viable strain of national independence. Nationalism in East Germany would have meant unification or compromise with the Federal Republic of Germany, and this would have threatened the Communist regime in the East. The leaders of East Germany therefore were the most loyal and obedient followers of Russia; on the other hand, the Russians treated the German Communist leaders with great care because any division within the Communist party might open the possibility of West German influence and endanger the continued existence of an independent East Germany.

Walter Ulbricht, the decisive figure in East Germany and a close adherent of Stalin's, was able to remain in power from 1946 to 1971, when illness forced him to retire; he died in 1973. He pursued an orthodox line, pushing for a planned economy, industrial development with an emphasis on heavy industry, and collectivization of agriculture. During the first decade of its existence, the government of East Germany focused its attention on the economy. The state took over and directed such large industrial enterprises as coal and chemicals and acted as a partner in smaller industrial enterprises. By 1962, only 2.7 percent of East Germany's industrial production was still in private hands. Through

Walter Ulbricht, chairman of the Council of State of East Germany, at the microphones, surrounded by Communist leaders.

its ruthless construction of a large-scale chemical and electrical industry and its energetic promotion of coal and steel factories, East Germany became industrially the most important country in the Eastern bloc.

The focus on heavy industry led to a slower and more cautious approach to changes in agriculture. Eastern Germany had historically been the country of the Junkers and great landed estates. The partition of these estates among peasants and agricultural workers created at the outset a popular basis for the Communist regime. From 1959 on, however, collectivization accelerated, and while in the 1950s still more than half the cultivated land was in the hands of independent peasants, their share declined below 10 percent in the early 1960s. Popular support for the regime diminished.

The most difficult problem facing the Communist regime was manpower. Industrial development required heavy migration from rural to urban areas, but the resulting depopulation of the land made it difficult to supply the cities with food. In addition, wages were low in the first stages of industrialization. Consequently, emigration from the East to the West was considered highly desirable, and in the twelve years between 1950 and 1962 an estimated 2.6 million East Germans fled to the West, primarily through the gap opened by the division of Berlin into an eastern and western sector. Since East Germany's population was only 17.2 million, such a large migration represented a damaging loss of labor power. In the summer of 1961, the East German government decided to stop this migration by building a wall between East Berlin and West Berlin, making escape from the East at best very dangerous.

Czechoslovakia

De-Stalinization and the Hungarian Revolt had little immediate effect in Czechoslovakia, where the timing of events was quite different from in the other satellite states. During the war Czechoslovakia had been the first Eastern European nation to come under the grip of the Nazis; the Czech government-in-exile had early on concluded an alliance with Soviet Russia. The first postwar regime in Czechoslovakia tried to imitate Western democratic forms, although from the outset the Communists were more strongly represented in the government than was justified by the votes they received. The regime was led by Eduard Beneš, one of the founders of Czechoslovakia, who had resigned under Nazi pressure and returned after the war's end. The events of 1948 gave the Communists complete political control and led to a period of moderation that ended in the early 1950s, when the Stalinist faction of the Communist Party purged the more moderate group. Several of the moderates were executed.

Thus, before Stalin's death the wing of the Communist Party that might have furthered de-Stalinization had been made powerless. The Stalinists had gone ahead with their economic program, which emphasized the production of machines, tractors, and motorcars and ignored a traditional Czechoslovakian industrial specialty, textiles. Collectivization of agriculture had become a high priority. By the middle of the 1950s, power was so firmly in the hands of a small coherent group that de-Stalinization could have no immediate impact on Czechoslovakia. While the monuments to Stalin in the other satellite countries were falling, the statue above Prague remained in place.

Still, Khrushchev's secret speech and the de-Stalinization movement elsewhere in Eastern Europe caused some corrosion in the power of Czechoslovakia's Communist leaders. Many in Czechoslovakia believed that the Slansky group had been unjustly condemned and that the men in power were tainted with the crimes of the Stalin period. Demands for political change, to be expected when the same group holds power for a long time, were strongly imbued with feelings of moral disapproval and condemnation, which did undermine the hold of the Czech Communist leadership.

A Shift in Theory

In Eastern Europe the years after 1956 saw the strengthening of individual national interests and traditions. Since theoretical assumptions and prescriptions play such a fundamental role in the Communist world, a theoretical justification for this development was soon forthcoming. Palmiro Togliatti, the Italian Communist leader, used the word "polycentre" to analyze the situation in the 1950s. "The Soviet model cannot and must not any longer be obligatory . . . even in the Communist movement we cannot speak of a single guide." Although the leaders of Soviet Russia hardly agreed fully with Togliatti, Khrushchev recognized the new forces that had developed in the "socialist camp" by accepting the validity of a "multiplicity of forms of socialist development."

CHAPTER 12

The Years of Disillusionment: 1967—1973

EUROPE'S ABUNDANT decade ended in 1967 when a variety of disturbances undermined the prevailing feeling of security and steady economic progress. During the late 1960s and 1970s, the superpowers became entangled in Asia and the Middle East. America became embroiled in a guerrilla war in Vietnam that escalated in 1965 and involved, by 1967, four hundred thousand American troops. The Vietcong's 1968 Tet offensive, although a military failure, suggested that a quick American victory was not forthcoming. In the Middle East, the Israelis won the so-called Six-Day War of June 1967 and conquered the West Bank of the Jordan River, the Sinai Peninsula in the south, and the Golan Heights to the north. While Israel's great ally and protector, the United States, remained preoccupied in Vietnam, Syria and Egypt saw the opportunity to regain their lost territories and, encouraged by Soviet Russia, undertook a surprise attack that launched the so-called Yom Kippur War in 1973. Their offensive failed, however, and the complete defeat of Egypt and Syria was prevented only by a United Nations cease-fire. The Arab nations resented the support the United States and its allies had given Israel and this sparked the 1973 Arab oil boycott, which had far-reaching economic consequences around the world.

These events had important effects in Europe. Because of their heavy commitment of men and supplies in Vietnam, the Americans called for increased European contributions of manpower and money to NATO to secure Europe against the threat of Russian aggression. American policies in Vietnam and the Middle East also created doubts in the minds of the Western European allies about their relations with the United States. Their alliance with America increasingly entangled Western Europe in actions and commitments that conformed neither to the ideological principles on which the alliance had been formed nor to European economic interests. In Vietnam, the United States seemed to defend the position of a small and corrupt ruling group. It seemed as eager as any other power to pursue its strategic and economic interests, which called into question its claim to be the selfless defender of freedom and democracy. In the Near East the United States revealed a contemptuous attitude toward Western

Europe. With its rich oil reserves, America was in a better position to withstand the threat of an Arab oil boycott, but for Europe, whose industrial life depended on the availability of Arab oil, the consequences of a boycott promised to be catastrophic. The political atmosphere in Western Europe became somber as the numbing feeling grew that events were beyond its control.

PRAGUE SPRING

The unrest that followed the 1960s was primarily a Western European phenomenon. Yet the first intense struggle for a change of the existing order occurred in Eastern Europe, in Czechoslovakia; it was the Prague Spring that first revealed a widespread social discontent.

In the late 1960s, the situation in Czechoslovakia was determined by two factors. The de-Stalinization that had changed the composition of the rulership in most countries of the Eastern bloc had not extended to the Czech Communist rulers. Still tainted with Stalinist vices, they were held in low esteem even by fellow Communists and considered unnecessarily brutal. Moreover, the ruling group's emphasis on developing heavy industry, a Stalinist policy, had led to a centralization deeply resented by the Slovaks, one of the formerly autonomous national groups composing Czechoslovakia. Meetings of intellectuals and writers gave passionate expression to these feelings of discontent, and student demonstrations echoed their criticisms. Pressure for concessions by the ruling

A Czech youth taunts Soviet soldiers with a bloodstained flag as Russian tanks roll in to crush the Prague Spring in 1968.

group grew, and in January 1968 Antonín Novotný, the first secretary of the Czech party, was replaced by a Slovak, Alexander Dubček.

The seven months from January to August 1968 marked the Prague Spring during which Dubček sought to introduce comprehensive reforms while maintaining Czechoslovakia's position in the Eastern camp. "Prague Spring" refers to both the sense of rebirth occasioned by the Dubček reforms and the season in which they were instituted. Dubček advocated introducing democratic procedures in the organization of the Communist Party to allow a larger part of the population to participate in policy decisions, a concession particularly important in allaying Slovak resentments. He also tried to remove some of the oppressive features of Czechoslovakia's socialist society by lifting many of the regulations inhibiting free movement and free expression. The demand for intellectual freedom had been particularly insistent from Czechoslovakia's large and vocal intellectual middle class. Academics, writers, and students began now to participate in vital and brilliant intellectual discussions that were described in newspapers, periodicals, and books and were reported in detail all over Western Europe.

Dubček tried to assure the Russians that this outburst of enthusiasm for intellectual freedom was not a first step on the road out of the socialist camp and that the Czech Communist Party remained in firm control. But the Russians, with some justification, were not convinced by these assurances, and Dubček was forced to prove his reliability by making far-reaching concessions, which included the promise that reform would go no further. This alienated Dubček from a good part of the reformist movement and only weakened his position. Under these circumstances the Russians saw the opportunity to end a movement on which they looked with considerable anxiety: Czechoslovakia was of great strategic importance to the Soviets because of its proximity to the West. On August 21, Russian tanks and troops, which had been poised at the Russian border with Czechoslovakia, moved in and occupied Prague. A Czech student set himself on fire in a central square to protest the reinstitution of Russian control, but of course the Soviets did not let this act of self-sacrifice deter them from their course.

Slowly but inexorably the Russians eased the leaders of Czechoslovakia's reform movement out of power. In so doing, they were supported by the Communist rulers of Hungary, Poland, and East Germany. Whatever sympathies these leaders might have had for Dubček's attempt to chart his own way to socialism, they were moved more by concern for the stability of their own regimes and by the fear that leaving the Czechoslovak reform movement in power might allow the West a foothold in the Eastern bloc.

The Prague Spring did not undermine the regimes of other satellite countries, but it did mean the definitive end of de-Stalinization in Eastern Europe. Leonid Brezhnev, Khrushchev's successor as first secretary of the Soviet Communist Party, was mainly responsible for the decision to intervene in Czechoslovakia.

With confrontation with the United States a possibility in many parts of the globe, security had become Russia's main concern. The hope that de-Stalinization had kindled for a freer, more relaxed, less bureaucratically centralized Communist system was extinguished.

In Western Europe, however, the Czech movement had aroused great sympathy, and Russia's suppression of the movement aroused strong indignation. Just as after the Hungarian Revolt of 1956, the period following the Prague Spring was marked by a number of defections from the Communist Party, particularly of prominent intellectuals. Jean-Paul Sartre, the French existentialist philosopher and a member of the Communist Party since the Second World War, called the Russian action "pure aggression, such as is defined in terms of international law as a war crime." Among Europe's Communists the view gained ground that if the Communist movement should have any future in Western Europe, they must gain some independence from Moscow.

The Prague Spring also excited discussion because of the prominent role played by students; Dubček's ascent to power had been the result of student demonstrations. To many this raised the probably fallacious hope that even in the face of modern armaments students might play a creative revolutionary role. Prague Spring sparked the movements that in the following years held the center of the political stage in Western Europe: student revolt, Eurocommunism, and terrorism.

STUDENT REVOLT

Discontent seethed among European students in the late 1960s, culminating in upheavals in Paris in April–May 1968. Problems began at Nanterre, one of the schools in the University of Paris system, where for some time students had discussed proposals to modernize the university. When Daniel Cohn-Bendit, one of the advocates of the most radical reforms, was expelled from the university, younger members of the faculty united with the students in vehement protests that forced the dean to close the university. The center of the student movement then shifted to the Latin Quarter of Paris, seat of the Sorbonne, where Cohn-Bendit and other student leaders were to appear before a disciplinary council of the University of Paris early in May. The students called a meeting to determine how they ought to react, and the rector of the Sorbonne, fearing violence, called in the police.

When the police started throwing students into waiting vans, the movement spread beyond the small group of radicals to the great majority of students, who felt that the police did not belong on university grounds. In fact, this was the first time since 1791 that the police had entered university property, where students traditionally felt they had asylum from outside intervention. A bitter struggle ensued in which students marched down the Boulevard St. Michel and, when

The events of May 1968 in Paris. Students throwing pavement stones at the police on the Boulevard St. Michel.

halted by the police, began erecting barricades and throwing cobblestones. Many demonstrators and more than four hundred policemen were injured, and four hundred sixty students were arrested. The police, infuriated by the resistance they met at every corner, reacted wildly, beating the captured students in police vans and police stations. The sympathy of witnesses to these events turned toward the students, transforming their revolt into a general movement of protest against the government. A general strike was launched on May 13, and by late in the month 10 million French workers were on strike. Ironically it was the participation of the workers in the protest movement that broke the back of the student revolt. The government succeeded in satisfying the workers by raising their wages, which isolated the students again and gradually restored quiet to university life.

The events in Paris were the most spectacular example of the widespread discontent among students in Europe. Explosions had occurred in Germany and Italy even before the revolt in Paris. In 1967, Berlin students protested the visit of the shah of Iran, causing riots that brought the death of a student. An attempted assassination of one of the student leaders triggered attacks against the headquarters of newspapers that had taken a strong stand against the students, interrupting their sale. Student strikes in Italy were frequent, and some were long-lasting, but they were aimed largely against overcrowding in the universities. As a result, they lacked broad popular support.

Unrest at the universities was only a more sharply focused version of the discontent that permeated wide strata of European society. A generation gap had been created when the wartime decline in population was followed by a rapid rise in the birthrate from the late 1940s on. By the late 1960s a new generation, whose outlook was formed by experiences in many respects very different from those of their elders, had appeared on the scene. Advances in technology had transformed the lives of many. Crossing the ocean had taken at least four to five days by ship in the 1950s; now it could be done by airplane in one day. The impact of the automobile was even more significant in Europe. Before the outbreak of the war in 1939, 3,600,000 cars were in private use in Europe. After the war the number had come down to 2,750,000, but it then began to increase, and it did so very rapidly from the middle of the 1950s on. By 1970, 10,478,000 cars were in private use. The creation of a unified European tariff system and the almost complete elimination of passport controls on the frontiers meant that travel in Western Europe and the Mediterranean—whether by airplane, railroad, bus, car, bicycle, or foot—no longer had to undergo delays at national frontiers.

People's image of the world began to be formed less by what they read in books than by what they saw on the movie or television screen. The cinema had become, like the theater, a subject of serious critical discussion and, at the same time, more popular. From the 1960s on television enjoyed a booming success, reinforcing this trend away from books, newspapers, and magazines. Reading helps establish a bond with the national past, while reliance on cinema, television, and travel focuses attention on the contemporary global scene. As a result, new artistic movements such as pop art, which ironically treated the symbols of consumer society as art forms, spread quickly from the United States to Europe and back, arousing enthusiasm among the young on both sides of the ocean.

The intellectual atmosphere of the 1970s, however, was characterized not only by the emergence of a new generation attuned to the new media but also by a pervasive feeling of oppression and powerlessness. Both the state and private industry were now run by great bureaucratic machines consisting of separate, specialized compartments, each of which fitted the individual into a definite place in a hierarchical order. The lives of individuals seemed to follow predetermined patterns, independent of choice.

The new postwar generation was impatient with received values. In the years immediately following the war, material values had received the highest priority because of the need to reconstruct the external conditions of life. The prosperity of the 1960s reinforced this emphasis on the importance of material goods. But to a generation just starting out, the focus on material values seemed contemptuous, especially since prosperity, or at least economic security, seemed a certainty. Perhaps this generation underestimated the fundamental role played in life by the struggle for achieving satisfactory material conditions.

Samuel Beckett's *Waiting for Godot*, a play written in 1952, continued to be widely discussed and frequently performed during the following decade. In it people eagerly compete to placate a power they are not sure exists. The play offered an indictment of a world in which life had lost its sense. The younger generation was attracted to the writings of Herbert Marcuse, particularly to the book *One-Dimensional Man*, in which he argues that the overwhelming emphasis of Western culture on science and the accumulation of wealth have stunted man's aesthetic and intellectual capabilities. Such marginal groups as students and minorities, Marcuse claimed, were better fitted to become leaders of the future revolution than workers, who were increasingly inclined to a bourgeois life. Pierre Mendès-France, the eminent French statesman, expressed the deeper motives of the student revolts: "This dispute is not simply over personalities or institutions. It also dramatizes the determination of Frenchmen no longer to be considered impotent subjects in a harsh, inhuman, conservative society but rather to perform their own role freely in a society they can look upon as their own."

Still, it was political events that brought this discontent and restlessness to the surface in Western Europe at the end of the 1960s. In both the Russian suppression of Prague Spring and the American intervention in Vietnam, the ideology that bound the superpowers to their allies and formed the source of their claim to leadership was easily abandoned when national interests came into play. The conflicts into which the rivalry of the superpowers threatened to draw their allies seemed to have little to do with the ideas and aims that originally forged these alliances.

Within the framework of Western European politics there was one other lesson to be drawn from the student revolts. The events of the late 1960s, especially in Paris, made it obvious that student revolts had little hope for success without the support of other political forces. Only when the French workers intervened and proclaimed a general strike did the student actions become a threat to the government. Those who opposed the existing political system had now to take a new look at their position and to assess the tactics to be used in their attempt to gain power.

REACTIONS TO THE REVOLUTION THAT FAILED

Terrorism and Eurocommunism were the leftist political movements in Western Europe that sprang—directly and indirectly—from the suppression of reform in Czechoslovakia and the student protests in Western Europe. Both terrorists and advocates of Eurocommunism aimed to change the existing European social system in favor of the "suppressed classes," but the methods they advocated were diametrically opposed. The terrorists were convinced that Europe's ruling groups were so firmly entrenched that only violent acts could instill fear in them and induce them to respond with cruel and despotic countermeasures. These would intensify latent social tensions sufficiently to provoke open conflict and rekindle the fire of revolution. The advocates of Eurocommunism were also convinced that the ruling classes were firmly entrenched in power, but they concluded that reform was feasible only by gaining a role in the government and working within the system. They preferred to use the handles of the parliamentary system to attain power.

Terrorism and Eurocommunism each saw the other as confirmation of the correctness of its views. The advocates of terrorism regarded the Eurocommunists' willingness to cooperate in the parliamentary system as a betrayal of the suppressed classes and as an acknowledgment of the failure of the Communist parties. They believed that new tactics had to be adopted. On the other hand, the disgust and fear that the violent acts of the terrorists aroused gave renewed strength to the idea of law and order and seemed to justify the conviction of the Eurocommunists that only by working within the system, by legal means, did Communists have a chance to come to power.

Terrorism

In the late 1960s and early 1970s, terrorism was an international movement only in a very limited sense. Terrorist acts certainly generated imitation. The detonation of an explosive in a department store in one country set off similar attempts in other countries, and terrorists of one country helped those of other countries by providing hideouts or furnishing weapons. German terrorists fleeing from the police, for instance, found refuge with the Palestinians, and the rich Italian publisher Feltrinelli, originally an idealistic supporter of noble left-wing causes rather than a political activist, supported West German terrorists with money and weapons. So did the East German secret police (Stasi). Moreover, even terrorists with nationalist aims did not hesitate to bomb embassies or assassinate diplomats in other countries if this helped their cause. In this period, however, there was no evidence of an international terrorist network with central direction or a unified plan of action.

The terrorists engaged in the struggles of national liberation movements, such as the Palestine Liberation Organization (PLO) or the Irish Republican Army (IRA), have different roots from the terrorists of the extreme left in Western Europe. After the failure of the student revolts of the late 1960s, radicals began to use terrorist tactics to spur the overthrow of the existing order. That nationalist and revolutionary terrorist activities reached a high point more or less simultaneously in the late 1960s and early 1970s was coincidental, not coordinated. The IRA was moved to violence when British troops entered Northern Ireland in 1969 in response to popular demonstrations by the Catholic working class. PLO terrorism was sparked by Israel's victory in the 1967 Six-Day War.

In Western Europe it was the fatal shooting by the Berlin police of a student protesting the visit of the Iranian shah and the attempt on the life of the student leader Rudi Dutschke that aroused not only young students but many others to indignation against police brutality and provided fertile ground for extremism. Shortly after these events the so-called Baader-Meinhof Gang, which called itself the Red Army Faction, began to set fires in department stores, commit bank robberies, and explode bombs in American military headquarters in an attempt to arouse revolutionary sympathies. In 1972, the leaders of the German gang were captured, but they managed with the help of their lawyers to escape to Jordan and then return clandestinely to Germany to resume their terrorist activities with increased ruthlessness. They were again caught, but the preparation of their trial took three years, during which time they tried to arouse sympathy with a hunger strike.

Now an even more desperately driven terrorist group was formed. The Movement of June 2nd (named for the day on which a Berlin student had been shot) undertook a number of spectacularly violent acts. They attacked the German embassy in Stockholm and killed some prominent Germans, including judges and heads of business enterprises. They made an attempt to attain release of the Baader-Meinhof Gang by hijacking a Lufthansa plane and holding its passengers hostage. However, the German police responded by flying a rescue team to the airport in Somalia where the hijacked plane had landed, freeing the hostages, and killing the hijackers. On receiving news of this failure, the imprisoned leaders of the Baader-Meinhof Gang committed suicide, and the wave of terrorism in Germany quickly receded. Instead of arousing popular discontent, the terrorists had alienated even those writers and educators who at the outset had shown some sympathy for the young revolutionaries.

In Italy, the other Western European country troubled by terrorism, extremists hoped to create a revolutionary atmosphere through acts of violence—a "strategy of tension"—that extended over the entire decade of the 1970s and continued into the 1980s. This began on December 12, 1969, when a bomb exploded in front of the Bank of Agriculture on the Piazza Fontana in Milan, killing sixteen and wounding many others. The terrorism soon spread as bombs were placed on railroad tracks, thrown into political meetings, and used to kill policemen. Responsibility for these terrorist acts is not easy to disentangle from the complexities of Italian domestic politics. Many of the early terrorist acts, although said to be inspired by the Communist Party, were actually committed by neo-Fascists, who, in magnifying the Communist danger, hoped to re-create the fear that had brought Mussolini to power. Italy's military was clearly unhappy with the parliamentary regime and appeared ready to stage a rightist coup. When the Red Brigades was formed in 1971, it presented itself as a defense against the threat of a rightist coup.

Support for the Red Brigades was strengthened by certain developments in the Italian universities during the 1970s, when the number of students doubled from a half million to a million. As a result of this increase, many students had great difficulty in finding employment after receiving their university degrees. Each year during the decade of the 1970s left another hundred thousand university graduates unemployed. The combination of the steady increase in Italy's population (in 1971, Italy counted 50 million inhabitants, an increase of 8 million

Former Italian Prime Minister Aldo Moro. Moro was murdered by the terrorist Red Brigades on May 9, 1978.

over the preceding twenty years) with the onset of an economic depression created a situation that unavoidably fostered radicalism, particularly among students who had been raised with great expectations but were now without prospects.

The Red Brigades thrived on this situation. It developed as an organized force with members in most of Italy's cities, and although the number of full-time members did not go much beyond one thousand, the Red Brigades had a large number of part-time members willing to support particular actions or help in hiding activists. The Red Brigades committed many violent crimes in which the perpetrators were neither discovered nor caught. In 1978 it committed its most sensational crime: it captured Aldo Moro, a former prime minister and an influential leader of the Italian Christian Democratic Party, held him hostage, and, when the government refused to negotiate, killed him and left his body in an abandoned car near the headquarters of the Christian Democratic Party. Slowly, the police succeeded in infiltrating the Red Brigades, and although some acts such as the kidnapping of an American military officer still took place, the high point of terrorist activities in Italy had passed.

The two terrorist organizations responsible for the most fearsome violence in the 1970s were nationalist groups: the IRA and the PLO, or its more radical associate, the Black September. In 1973 and 1974, the IRA exploded bombs before renowned historical buildings in London (the Old Bailey and the Tower), in Guildford and Birmingham, and at various military installations, killing and injuring a number of bystanders. These acts created an atmosphere of such tension that even the stately British Museum was forced to place guards before its entrance to examine briefcases, raincoats, and umbrellas for explosives. At the Olympic Games in Munich in 1972, the PLO attacked the quarters of the Israeli athletes and killed eleven of them. The PLO specialized in hijacking airplanes and holding passengers hostage until the Israelis, in their audacious July 1976 raid on the Entebbe airport in Uganda, dramatically battled PLO and Ugandan forces and freed the passengers of a hijacked Israeli airplane, ending this form of terrorist action for a time.

The members of the IRA and the PLO saw themselves as engaged in wars of national liberation aimed at achieving autonomy for their homelands, Northern Ireland and Palestine. They believed that the absence of international recognition and the weakness of their standing forces made covert and illegal acts most effective for them. They claimed to have specific purposes when they extended terrorist acts beyond Northern Ireland and Palestine to other countries. The IRA bombings in London were aimed at changing the attitude of the House of Commons and the policy of the British government; the PLO hijacked airplanes in order to liberate Palestinians who had been imprisoned for terrorist acts. They also wanted to punish the leaders of countries that defended Israel.

Thus, terrorist movements in this period, as similar as they were in the means they used, had different aims. Some aimed to achieve national independence while others sought to spark revolution. These revolutionaries used terrorist means because they believed that the traditional protagonists of revolution, the Communist parties, had abandoned their revolutionary aims and deserted the cause. Indeed, a change in the aims and tactics of the Western European Communist parties *was* taking place, a change encompassed in the term "Eurocommunism."

Eurocommunism

Eurocommunism was mentioned for the first time in a June 1975 newspaper article and then quickly entered the political vocabulary. The Communist leaders of France, Italy, and Spain claimed that the term implied only that the three great Communist parties of these countries shared common concerns peculiar to their existence in capitalist societies with parliamentary constitutions. But this explanation of Eurocommunism was meant to conceal its larger meaning with regard to Communist Party politics. Eurocommunism evolved as an extension of the Italian Communist leader Togliatti's pronouncement that Communism must be polycentric. This notion was openly acknowledged and eloquently expressed by the Spanish Communist leader, Santiago Carillo:

In former years Moscow, where dream began to take on reality, was our Rome. We talked of the great socialist October Revolution as the day of our birth. Those were the times of our childhood. . . . The existence of new problems has made our differences apparent, has made us realize the divergent opinions among us that could not be solved otherwise but through discussion, in a spirit of criticism and self-criticism, in the recognition of the diversity of views and of national forms of socialism and of socialist politics. . . . We, the Communists of today, have no center that gives us directives, have no international discipline imposed upon us. What unites us today are the bonds of affinity based on the theory of scientific socialism.

Eurocommunism implied decisive changes in the Communist line. It meant that the Communist parties of France, Italy, and Spain would no longer be directed by Moscow but would respond to the particular problems they faced in autonomous fashion. Eurocommunism meant also that the Communist parties in Western Europe no longer considered the violent overthrow of existing governments the only avenue to power. They were now willing to participate in government as members of parliamentary coalitions. This in turn allowed the Communists more flexibility in foreign policy. They no longer had to agitate within their countries for a neutral foreign policy; they were now willing to concede the maintenance of the Western alliance and also, if necessary, to fulfill the commitments required by membership in NATO.

Eurocommunism was adopted by the great Communist parties of Western Europe in response to the decline of Soviet prestige after the events in Hungary and Czechoslovakia; had they not distanced themselves from Russia, the European Communists feared, they would have risked losing votes to their closest competitors, the socialists. Moreover, many leading Communists were severely shocked by Russia's ruthless actions. The advocates of Eurocommunism also made the point that in a society characterized by a mixed economy, where large industrial enterprises belong to the government and where much of the economy is directed by the government, it makes no sense to overthrow the regime. Europe in the 1970s was quite different from the society Marx had analyzed and from the society encountered by the Bolsheviks in 1917 Russia. In contemporary Europe it made more sense to join the government and extend its sphere of control until a socialist society evolved. Beyond these shared ideas the motives for adopting Eurocommunism varied according to the conditions characterizing each country.

The reasons for the Spanish Communist leader Carillo's forceful advocacy of Eurocommunism were largely internal. Between 1950 and 1970 Spain entered a period of rapid industrialization in which the number of Spaniards working in industry doubled while the number of those active in agriculture declined by 50 percent. This was also a period of remarkable population growth, which magnifies the significance of these figures. Industrialization increased the size of the middle and working classes and spread dissatisfaction with Franco's autocratic regime. Strikes, student revolts, and antigovernment demonstrations broke out, and when Franco died at the age of eighty-three in 1975, his regime was in crisis. What the Spaniards feared most was another civil war. Thus, they willingly accepted the restoration of the monarchy under Franco's chosen heir, King Juan Carlos, who initiated a gradual but steady return to democracy. But this process evoked the opposition of Franco's adherents, some of whom were still powerful. Spain's democratic forces had to maintain their unity and strength to avoid another civil war. Had the Communist Party raised the threat of renewed political disorder by continuing to advocate revolution in Spain, it would have risked losing most of its support.

In France and Italy, the Communists also steered their own course. For the French, Sartre's abandonment of the Communist Party was characteristic. The Soviets' ruthless suppression of the Eastern satellites brought about a serious rift in the alliance between French intellectuals and the Communist Party, an alliance forged in the resistance movement during the Second World War. In Italy the Communists had attained control of municipal administration in almost all the large northern cities. They succeeded in establishing less corrupt, more efficient municipal government but lacked sufficient power to improve the economic situation in the localities. Local Communist officials needed a foot in the central government, and Italian Eurocommunism was intended to achieve this by pursuing a coalition with the ruling Christian Democrats.

Eurocommunism without question offered one great advantage to the Communist parties of Western Europe: greater political flexibility in a situation that, as the crisis in the Near East and the worsening economic depression showed, was full of new dangers, most clearly manifested in the oil crisis of 1973.

THE OIL CRISIS

The oil crisis was triggered by the Yom Kippur War of October 1973. After Egypt and Syria failed in their attack against Israel, the Arab nations imposed restrictions on the output and the distribution of their oil. These restrictions were especially directed against the powers that had supported Israel, particularly the United States and the Netherlands, but the Arab oil embargo had far-reaching repercussions throughout Western Europe. In contrast to the United States, which, though a heavy buyer of Arab oil, could draw on oil resources other than those of the Arab countries, the nations of Western Europe were entirely dependent on Arab oil. Their economies suffered immediately from the Arabs' reduction of the oil supply and from the consequent increase in oil prices.

All the European countries introduced measures for saving oil: Driving cars on Sundays and holidays was forbidden; replacing oil with coal in industry and home heating was encouraged. Many European states established ministries or departments of energy. The Arab oil embargo effectively ended in March 1974, when the Arab nations decided that they had made their political point and that it was time to reestablish normal trade relations with Western Europe. (The sanctions against the Netherlands lasted somewhat longer.) But the embargo itself was only the most public episode in a crisis that had begun long before the Yom Kippur War and that continued to have its effects long after the embargo ended.

For some time the oil-rich countries of the Middle East and North Africa had been anxious to take full advantage of the riches buried within their borders. Because they lacked the necessary technology for exploiting, refining, and marketing their oil, they needed the services of the large American oil companies— Exxon, Socal, Gulf, Mobil, and Texaco—that had acquired concessions for exploiting the oil fields in this area. Negotiations began about the kind of partnership the companies holding the oil leases should concede to the Arab governments and about the taxes the oil companies would have to pay for permission to export the oil they tapped. An agreement reached in April 1971 permitted a considerable rise in oil prices but also pleased the oil companies by pledging that no further price increase would take place during the next five years.

However, hardly had this understanding been reached when it proved to be unworkable. The agreement had set the price of oil in dollars, and in August 1971, four months after the negotiations had been concluded, the United States ended the convertibility of the dollar into gold. A devaluation of the dollar quickly followed, and the agreement was renegotiated to establish a higher price for oil.

The embargo of 1973 was spurred largely by political motives. The Arabs were angered by America's support of Israel and by President Nixon's announcement of a new energy policy in April 1973. The United States would now encourage competition in the oil trade and lift the quota system, which until then had provided Arab oil with a larger share of the American market. The embargo therefore was also intended to give the American government clear notice that the Arab countries and the Organization of Petroleum-Exporting Countries (OPEC), which they led, were a powerful economic and political force. By March 1974 both the embargo and OPEC's ability to control oil prices seemed to have demonstrated the new power of the Arab world. Western European and American newspapers wrote of "our"—meaning the Western world's—dependence on the Arabs. Actually the Arab victory proved temporary. The demand for oil was reduced by economy measures as well as by the increasing substitution of less costly sources of power, such as coal and electricity. At the same time the supply of non-Arab oil increased with the discovery of oil in the North Sea, most of which went to Britain and Norway, and the opening of previously neglected oil fields in Alaska. In addition, divergent interests within OPEC somewhat weakened its negotiating power.

The oil crisis was an important cause of the economic recession that gripped the Western world in the late 1970s. From the end of the 1960s on, the price of oil rose steadily. By January 1975, oil cost $10.46 per barrel, more than six times as high as it had been in 1973, before the boycott, when the average price of a barrel of oil was $1.73. Rising oil prices spurred an inflationary spiral that boosted interest rates and, consequently, the price of almost everything else. Moreover, European goods now met stiff competition from industry in Asia and Africa, where economic development had been enthusiastically promoted by the Western countries during the postwar years. Japan emerged as an especially dynamic economic force, challenging the old industrial powers with its exports of electronics and automobiles. By 1980, Japanese-made automobiles had taken 10 percent of the West German market and 25 percent of the Belgian market.

The Organization of Petroleum-Exporting Countries (OPEC). Composed of oil-rich Arab nations, OPEC became a major economic and political force in the early 1970s.

The rising price of oil combined with these developments to endanger European economic prosperity; postwar reconstruction, which had given impetus to Europe's economic life, had ended. From the mid-1970s to 1984, unemployment in Europe rose to about 19 million. A serious economic recession had taken hold.

WOMEN IN REVOLT

Against this backdrop of international political upheaval and economic turmoil, Western Europe's women were making their first concentrated push for improvements in their status since the suffragette campaigns of the pre-World War I era. Obtaining the vote had preoccupied female activists in much of Europe even after World War I, since the Catholic European countries of France, Italy, Portugal, and Belgium did not grant women the franchise until the years 1944 to 1948. In France, de Gaulle granted the vote to women as a "prize" for their role in the resistance; ironically, this prize coincided with the brutal shaving and parading through the streets of women accused of "horizontal collaboration" with German occupants during the war. Finally gaining the suffrage did not radically transform women's social and economic position, however, partly because women themselves tended to vote for conservative parties that perpetuated traditional policies. (It was just this calculation that had prompted right-of-center governments, like de Gaulle's, to grant women the vote and motivated liberal parties to resist the change.) Female activists realized that they had to change the consciousness of their sisters as well as that of men to achieve major breakthroughs at the social and cultural level.

In certain vital areas, women's lot had certainly improved in the decades following World War II. Life expectancy for women in Western Europe increased dramatically, reaching seventy-five by the early 1970s, about five years longer than men. Death during childbirth was no longer a common occurrence. The number of years that women typically devoted to child rearing also shrank significantly: at the beginning of the twentieth century, women could expect to devote over one-half their lives to child rearing; by 1970 that figure was about one-quarter. Advances in contraception—especially the birth control pill, which, in contrast to condoms, was a *female* method of contraception—made it possible for women to control their fertility better. This led to lower birthrates and more time away from the birthing and child-rearing process. By 1970 the average birthrate in Western Europe was sixteen per one thousand, so low that almost all the industrialized European nations were obliged to import foreign workers to keep their economies functioning. Interestingly, even women in Catholic countries like Italy and France flocked to the pill despite impediments to its distribution and injunctions from the church against "artificial" methods of birth control. In hopes of countering the plunge in birthrates, all the European countries sought to make motherhood more attractive by instituting prenatal care programs and generous maternity allowances. In general, however, freedom from the burden of raising small armies of children was more enticing than the maternal benefits offered by the state, and birthrates continued to fall.

If Western European women lived longer and were better off materially in the post-World War II era than ever before, their lives as workers outside the home and as political citizens of their respective states did not change so significantly. Although more and more women worked outside the home, the types of jobs available to them remained for the most part traditional "female" labor, such as stenography and typing, nursing and midwifery, schoolteaching, dressmaking, house and office cleaning, semiskilled factory work, and service positions. Such work was often boring and repetitive, and it paid on average from one-third to one-half less than typical "male labor." Perhaps even worse, these jobs generally offered little hope for advancement. In the decade between 1975 and 1985, women's share of employment growth in Western Europe rose 100 percent faster than men's, but 60 percent of the increase was in relatively low-paying part-time jobs. Moreover, even if women were typically bearing fewer children than before, those who worked outside the home still had to combine their wage-earning labor with the burdens of raising their families and maintaining their households. True, some men, inspired (or intimidated) by the new assertiveness of "women's liberation," shared household duties with their wives, but women continued to do the lion's share of this work. A European Community survey of

1973 revealed that almost one-half the married men in Italy, one-third of the Germans and French, and one-quarter of the men of the Low Countries did no housework whatsoever (and were undoubtedly proud of that fact).

As busy as women were in their homes and workplaces, they were not yet very conspicuous in the halls of politics. In the first decades of the postwar era, Western European women were grossly underrepresented in political leadership positions and in parliamentary bodies. Britain did not have a female prime minister until Margaret Thatcher in 1979; France was female-free at the highest levels of government until 1993, when Edith Cresson, a protégée of François Mitterrand, assumed the prime ministership and held it (alas, rather ineptly) for one year. Germany was not to have a woman on top until Angela Merkel won the chancellorship in 2005, while Italy continued to reserve its highest political posts for men, preferably old (and corrupt) ones. Sweden boasted a 20 percent female representation in its national assembly in the mid-1970s, but in the three decades following World War II Britain and France averaged only 4 percent or 5 percent female representation in their lower houses of parliament. Women in the United States liked to say that a woman's place was "in the House—and in the Senate," but Western European women, at least until the 1980s, tended to stick to their usual places in the kitchen, nursery, shop, and typing pool.

French writer and noted feminist Simone de Beauvoir, 1967.

Starting in the late 1960s and early 1970s, however, various female emancipation campaigns, modeled on America's women's liberation movement, pushed hard to promote social, political, and economic equality between the sexes, along with a new sense of gender identity, a women-centered view of the world. The feminist activists started from the proposition that European women were socially and culturally oppressed, whether or not their male oppressors, or the women themselves, chose to recognize this fact. To achieve gender equality, the activists knew that they would have to overturn deep-seated conventions about sexuality and family life. Their bible was Simone de Beauvoir's *The Second Sex*, which argued that women's "nature" derived from male-dominated culture rather than from biology. The book had been published in France way back in 1949, but it did not gain much influence until the late 1960s, after it had been adopted by American feminists and relayed back to Europe. Many of the leading Western European feminists had socialist backgrounds, but they realized that the socialist and progressive rhetoric about liberation and equality differed greatly from the reality of their own lives. As one French feminist wrote in a socialist journal in 1969, "I was struck by the great words: liberation of peoples, liberation of women. [But] *my* liberation consists of serving him after my work while he reads or 'thinks.' While I peel the vegetables, he can read at leisure— either *Le Monde* or works on Marxist economy. Freedom only exists for the well-off ones in the real world, and the well-off one is the man."

Although feminists in France and other Western European countries were energized by the political upheavals of 1968, they soon discovered that their male colleagues on the barricades were not particularly interested in sexual equality; most of them seemed to agree with their conservative counterparts that the best place for women was in bed. If women wanted to call attention to their continued oppression, they would have to take matters into their own hands. In a now-famous gesture in 1970, a dozen French women placed a wreath at the Tomb of the Unknown Soldier dedicated to "the unknown wife of the unknown soldier." As they were led away by police, the women shouted, "We're the mothers of future veterans!" In reality, however, motherhood was hardly the primary goal of most of these women, who believed that having children was often another source of oppression and that unless the decision to bear a child (whether or not conception had occurred) was entrusted to those who had to do the bearing, motherhood would remain a way to keep women "in their place." As abortions were still illegal in France in the early 1970s, in April 1971 some 343 women, including de Beauvoir, signed a manifesto stating that they had had illegal abortions, which, given the need for secrecy, had often been conducted under dangerous conditions. "Just as we demand free access to birth-control methods," the manifesto concluded, "we demand freedom to have abortions." Four years later the French parliament, over objections from the church, passed a law permitting abortion on medical grounds in the first ten weeks of pregnancy. Not surprisingly, this did not satisfy the nation's feminists, who continued to push for more liberal regulations. Although abortion rights were indeed expanded in subsequent years, they remained more limited in France and in most other Western European countries than in Eastern Europe, where abortion became the primary mode of controlling family size.

In the 1970s, the French and British women's movements diverged in significant ways. French feminists identified male-dominated cultural institutions and the family as the primary agents of female subjugation and looked to the welfare state for support in their struggle for socioeconomic betterment. They expected the state to acknowledge women's special needs by encouraging companies to provide flexible schedules and part-time labor for working women with families. Ironically, this approach damaged women economically when France went into recession in the mid-seventies, and companies began to cut costs by employing women on a part-time basis with no social benefits; feminist arguments regarding women's "uniqueness" were used to justify this policy. In Britain, by contrast, feminists took the state as their primary target from the outset, and they insisted on equality rather than on special treatment. They demanded that women receive the same wages and social benefits as men regardless of marital status. This resulted in lower levels of female employment in Britain than in France, but the jobs were higher paying. Having little trust in the state, British feminists were not surprised when Thatcher, the country's first female prime minister, closed social programs and shifted their functions to private charities and families, thereby increasing the burden on women.

Frustrated by their inability to achieve full equality and complete freedom over their own bodies, some European women renounced alliances with progressive male groups altogether and denounced men *tout court* as oppressors. As the symbol of their militant sexual sectarianism, they made a vulvalike form with their hands by lifting the fingers and lowering the thumbs of both hands, while turning the palms outward. This was radical feminism's version of the omnipresent peace sign. At the same time, however, feminism increasingly became part of the mainstream culture, as universities across Europe inaugurated women's studies programs, established presses published countless books on women's issues, and feminist-oriented magazines and journals flooded the newsstands. France and Germany established cabinet posts dealing with women's affairs, which of course were headed by women.

CONTRADICTORY IMPULSES

The events of the late 1960s and 1970s brought to the forefront two contradictory tendencies in European society. Although the public generally disapproved of student unrest, demanded severe punishment of terrorist activity, and harbored reservations about radical feminism, many people considered these movements reflections of Europe's increasingly rigid social structure. Bureaucracies had become obstacles to, rather than avenues of, social ascent. The wealth the abundant decade had created contributed to the formation of a social stratum composed of internationally oriented businessmen that was out of reach to most people. The expectations raised by the postwar reconstruction for economic security and a broadening and enhancement of cultural life had not been fulfilled.

The rebellions and upheavals of 1968—like 1956, a watershed year in the history of postwar Europe—reflected the pervasiveness of popular discontent. The student revolts in Western Europe (particularly in Paris) and the anti-Soviet upheaval in Prague were thoroughly beaten down, but they pointed up an explosive impatience in both West and East with the sociopolitical order that had emerged from the Second World War. While the Prague rebellion challenged the authority of Soviet hegemony in Eastern Europe and the legitimacy of orthodox Communism, the student revolts in the West questioned the sanctity of material prosperity, consumerism, and the gospel of growth, all values associated with the American economic and cultural domination of Western Europe since the war. France's prime minister Georges Pompidou captured the meaning of the revolt in France when he said at the height of the crisis: "The events which we have just experienced are not just a flash of fire. Our civilization is being questioned, not the government, not the institutions, not even France, but the materialist and soulless modern society."

Pompidou was right. Though neither the student revolts in the West nor still less the anti-Soviet rebellion in Prague succeeded in their immediate aims, the malaise they reflected did not die with their physical suppression. After 1968 the political culture of Europe would be characterized by continuous protests on many fronts. In the West, both terrorism and Eurocommunism, for all their differences in goals and methods, were responses to the events of 1968. So, less directly, were the environmental and feminist movements that sprang up in most Western nations in the 1970s. In the East the torch of Prague Spring was passed to human rights organizations like Charter 77 (Czechoslovakia) and KOR (Poland) and eventually from them to the group that would do the most to undermine Soviet control in Eastern Europe, Poland's Solidarity. Out of these diverse expressions of protest would emerge a new and more confident (though no less troubled) Europe, one whose peoples were increasingly anxious to end the division of their continent and to emancipate themselves from the tutelage of the superpowers.

CHAPTER 13

The Decade of Détente: 1969–1979

IN THE SUMMER OF 1973 Leonid Brezhnev declared: "The Cold War as far as we are concerned is over." This statement was somewhat premature, since renewed tensions between the superpowers at the end of the 1970s and in the first years of the 1980s led some commentators to speak of a "new Cold War." Yet Brezhnev was correct in pointing toward a new willingness on the parts of both superpowers to find ways out of the old bipolar standoff. Through a series of pathbreaking treaties and arms control agreements, they substantially eased the menacing atmosphere of East-West confrontation that had prevailed for most of the postwar era. This change in direction stemmed not from any single conscious decision but from both superpowers' growing preoccupation with issues other than those that had produced the Cold War. Détente, in other words, arose essentially from a new constellation of diplomatic priorities and domestic economic needs in the Soviet Union and the United States.

East Asia had become the main concern of both the United States and Soviet Russia. American troops began to withdraw from Vietnam in June 1969 but were still involved in heavy fighting through 1971 and 1972. The last American troops left Vietnam in February 1973, and fighting between South Vietnamese forces and the North Vietnamese Army finally ended in 1975, when the Communists took Saigon. Out of fear that the Russians, who had backed North Vietnam, would now spread their influence throughout Southeast Asia, the United States began cautiously to loosen its ties with Taiwan and to establish relations with the Soviets' primary rival in East Asia, mainland China.

The Chinese Communists were for their part willing to pursue a gradual rapprochement with the United States because their rift with the Soviet Union had grown more intense in the late 1960s. One source of friction was the Soviet invasion of Czechoslovakia in 1968, which Moscow justified with the so-called Brezhnev doctrine, the claim that the Soviets had the right forcibly to restore orthodoxy in Communist countries that had taken a "deviant" line. The Chinese leadership, fractured by the ongoing Cultural Revolution, feared that this might presage a Soviet attempt to install a compliant pro-Moscow faction in

China. Indeed, Soviet Russia's extensive support of North Vietnam in its war with America was seen by the Chinese less as a friendly gesture toward a beleaguered fellow Communist regime than as an effort to gain a base in Southeast Asia from which Russia could threaten China. Moreover, Soviet Russia's role in Vietnam seemed especially ominous to the Chinese because it was combined with a Soviet military buildup along the Russo-Chinese borders in Manchuria and Siberia. This led to a series of sharp border clashes between Russian and Chinese troops in 1969 and 1970.

Just as the intensifying Sino-Soviet rift helped persuade the Chinese to work for better relations with the United States, it pushed the Soviets in the same direction. Wishing not to be caught between a hostile China and a hostile America, Moscow hoped to dilute the dangers to Soviet interests inherent in a possible Sino-American rapprochement by reducing the chances of conflict with the United States. Domestic considerations also moved the Soviets toward détente. After Stalin's death, Soviet leaders became anxious to apply Russia's economic resources to a broad program of industrial production rather than to a continued concentration on heavy industry and the military. They hoped too to secure financial and technical aid from Western Europe and the United States.

The United States was also anxious to restrain the arms race with the Soviet Union. The Vietnam War had aroused such opposition to military expenditures that an attempt to scale them down seemed politically appropriate and economically necessary. America's widening trade deficit and a weakening dollar exerted similar pressures.

SUPERPOWER DÉTENTE AND ARMS CONTROL

The SALT I Negotiations

Arms reductions talks between the United States and Soviet Russia had been proceeding slowly for two years when in 1971 they agreed their first aim should be to limit the deployment of antiballistic missile systems (ABMs), which were designed to shoot down incoming enemy missiles before they could hit their targets. Such an agreement was reached in the spring of 1972, but its content was meager. Each country was allowed only two sites for antiballistic missiles, one to cover their respective capitals, the other to shield one complex of ICBM launch silos. The accord also forbade the transfer of ABM systems to another country. When it became evident, however, that ABM systems were expensive and of little military value, both countries abandoned deployment.

More significant was the broader arms reduction package now known as SALT (Strategic Arms Limitation Talks) I. This accord, signed in Moscow by Nixon and Brezhnev in May 1972, obliged the superpowers to maintain approximate parity in numbers of offensive land and sea launchers. Satellite photo reconnaissance was to guarantee verification of the agreement, which was limited to five years. Despite the surveillance provision, the accord had some signif-

The architect of détente. U.S. Secretary of State Henry Kissinger (*left*) meets with Soviet Premier Leonid Brezhnev.

icant loopholes. It did not adequately regulate the upgrading of existing missile systems or even forbid their replacement with entirely new ones. Though it barred the replacement of "light" by "heavy" missiles, it did not define "heavy." Both sides soon took advantage of these loopholes. The Soviets began deploying a new generation of MIRVs (Multiple Independently Targetable Reentry Vehicles), including the formidable SS-19, an intercontinental missile with six warheads, twice as many as the MIRVed Minutemen. The United States, for its part, started development of the radar-evading Cruise missile system, which it claimed was not covered by the SALT agreement. SALT was also compromised in spirit, if not in letter, by the Soviets' new Backfire bomber, which could reach targets in the United States, and by the Americans' plans for a new intercontinental bomber (the B-1) and the Trident submarine, which replaced the aging Polaris.

The Helsinki Accords

Ongoing disagreements over the interpretation of SALT I did not prevent the superpowers from committing themselves to negotiations regarding European security and international cooperation between the two blocs. In 1973, the Conference on Security and Cooperation in Europe began meeting in Helsinki, Finland; it culminated in August 1975 with the signing by thirty-five nations of a nonbinding agreement called the Final Act. This agreement confirmed the legitimacy of Europe's postwar borders and called for closer technological and cultural cooperation among the signatory states. The clause for which the act became best known, however, was a promise to "respect human rights."

The Helsinki agreement, particularly its human rights provision, had its share of critics from the outset. Could one, it was asked in the West, really expect the

Russians to abide by an agreement that had no teeth in it? Although President Jimmy Carter, who took office in January 1977, was committed to making the protection of human rights around the world a foundation of American foreign policy, his administration was plagued by dissension over just how far America should carry this crusade. Should it, for example, pursue this agenda even to the possible detriment of "national security," or to its ability to maintain leverage over "friendly" states, or when sanctions for violations hurt the poor and innocent more than the wielders of power? Though America found many opportunities to remind the Soviet Union and its satellites of the Helsinki agreement, citing in particular Russia's mistreatment of dissidents like Andrei Sakharov and Czechoslovakia's persecution of a domestic human rights organization called Charter 77, it said little or nothing about abuses by pro-U.S. dictatorships, such as Iran under the shah, South Korea, and the Philippines under Ferdinand Marcos.

The signatories of the Helsinki Final Act had agreed to a follow-up meeting in Belgrade in 1977. But with Brezhnev condemning Western accusations of Soviet human rights abuses as "interference" in Soviet internal affairs, and some Western leaders dismissing the entire enterprise as counterproductive, it is not surprising that the Belgrade Conference produced little of substance. Nevertheless, despite continuing violations of human rights around the world, the original Helsinki agreement was a milestone in postwar diplomacy. As one commentator noted, it brought the issue of human rights, first addressed in the United Nations Charter of 1945, "to the attention of a new generation." Groups like Amnesty International and Americas Watch, founded in the 1960s, made the defense of human rights their primary concern. In the long run, this development could not help but work against Moscow, which now had to contend with demand after demand from various quarters across the sprawling Soviet Union that the Kremlin respect these claimants' "human rights." Brezhnev had thought that Helsinki, by confirming existing borders and discouraging intervention by signatory states in the internal and external affairs of other signatory states, had finally guaranteed the sanctity of Moscow's doddering empire, but in fact it sowed the seeds of the empire's demise.

SALT II

SALT I, designed to be an interim agreement, contained a provision for continuing negotiations aimed at a more comprehensive regulation of nuclear weapons. But progress toward the agreement now known as SALT II was impeded by a number of factors, political and technical. In August 1974 the Watergate scandal forced the resignation of President Richard M. Nixon, who was a known quantity to the Russians and enjoyed Brezhnev's confidence. When Nixon's successor, Gerald Ford, went to Vladivostok in November 1974 to assess progress on SALT I and to discuss a new ceiling on MIRV launchers, he had reason to proceed cautiously. Continuing Russian violations of human rights, along with their support for leftist rebellions in Angola and Mozambique, generated increasing doubts in the United States about the USSR's reliability as a partner in the preservation of world peace. A congressional resolution of 1974 making trade concessions to the Soviets contingent on improvements in their human rights record reflected the American Congress's determination to take a firmer line in U.S.-Soviet relations. The Soviets responded to this economic "blackmail" by suspending their existing trade agreement with the United States. Arms control talks continued despite this worsening diplomatic climate, however, because both powers considered this issue too important to be held hostage to failures or crises on other fronts. As Carter put it, "It is precisely because we have fundamental differences with the Soviet Union that we are determined to bring this dangerous element of our military competition under control."

Determined as the negotiators were, however, the talks were slowed by formidable technical difficulties, not the least of which was estimating the effectiveness of the many different types of weapons in each country's nuclear arsenal. The Carter administration, convinced that both SALT I and the 1974 Vladivostok accord, which set equal ceilings for both powers on numbers of missiles, launchers, and MIRVs, had left the Soviets with too great an advantage in missile throw-weight (the size of warhead a missile could loft into space), put forth a so-called Comprehensive Proposal in March 1977 that offered to cancel development of the MX (missile experimental), a ten-warhead MIRV that could be moved about in tunnels or on huge trucks to reduce its vulnerability to a nuclear strike, if the Soviets would cut their heavy ICBM force in half. The Soviets, disinclined to trade half their existing land-based nuclear capacity for an as-yet-undeveloped American weapons system, said *nyet*, adding that they resented having to start from scratch on arms control every time a new president came to Washington. To the dismay of hard-liners in the Senate and in his own administration, Carter then softened the American position sufficiently to allow the talks (in Brezhnev's words) "to take a turn for the better." They finally resulted in a new accord, SALT II, signed by Carter and Brezhnev at their Vienna summit in June 1979.

In SALT II the Soviets accepted a lower ceiling on ICBM launchers and a freeze on the number of warheads per type of ICBM; the United States agreed not to develop the MX. Both sides agreed to new limits on sea-launched ballistic missiles and strategic bombers. Still, the SALT II agreement left each superpower with enough nuclear weaponry to destroy the world several times over.

The SALT II treaty aroused considerable opposition in the United States on both the left and right. Liberals objected that the pact did not stop the arms race, much less reverse it. Conservatives noted that its constraints on missile launchers and its freeze on warheads left the USSR with an approximately five-to-two lead in ICBMs and throw-weight. The American general who represented the Joint Chiefs of Staff on the SALT delegation warned ominously of a "window of vulnerability." This seemed particularly disquieting in light of a new round of threatening Soviet actions around the world: their support of Vietnam's invasion of Cambodia and of the Sandinista rebellion in Nicaragua and, above all, their own invasion of Afghanistan in December 1979. Aware that the Senate would not ratify the SALT II treaty in this atmosphere, Carter withdrew it from consideration on January 3, 1980. And to punish the Soviets for their invasion of Afghanistan, Carter ordered an American boycott of the Moscow Olympics of 1980 (to which Moscow later responded with a boycott of the Los Angeles Olympics of 1984). Détente, at least for the moment, seemed to be dead.

WEST EUROPEAN POLITICS IN THE DECADE OF DÉTENTE

The superpowers were not alone in the pursuit of détente in the 1970s. The governments of West Germany, France, and Britain made concerted efforts to improve their relations with the Soviet Union and its Eastern European satellites. While the Western European governments hoped to remain on cordial relations with the United States, they wished not simply to echo American policy but to forge their own identities as players in the international arena. On the domestic front, these governments launched ambitious social reform programs designed to improve the lot of the least fortunate groups in their societies. These initiatives generated a great deal of opposition, however, and were undermined further by the international economic recession sparked by the oil crisis. In domestic affairs the Decade of Détente proved for many to be the Decade of Disillusionment.

West Germany

The key to reducing East-West tensions in Central Europe, the epicenter of Cold War conflict, was the inauguration in October 1969 of a new socialist-dominated government in West Germany. Unlike its conservative predecessor, whose motto was "No experimentation," the incoming Social-Liberal coalition (SPD and Free Democrats, or FDP) pledged itself to experimentation in all domains, including foreign policy.

West Germany's new chancellor was the SPD leader Willy Brandt. Born Karl Herbert Frahm into a working-class family in 1913, he took the name Willy Brandt after fleeing to Norway following Hitler's seizure of power in 1933. While in Norway he graduated from Oslo University and began working as a journalist. With the German occupation of Norway in 1940, Brandt escaped to neutral Sweden, where he served as a link between the Norwegian and German anti-Nazi resistance movements. Returning to Germany in 1945, he helped build up democratic socialism in the western sectors of Berlin, where he served as mayor from 1957 to 1966, when he became West German foreign minister. Throughout his career Brandt showed himself to be a highly pragmatic politician, but one with an exceptionally warm and engaging personality.

Upon assuming the chancellorship, Brandt set his sights on opening a new era in West Germany's relations with the East—with the USSR, Poland, and the German Democratic Republic (GDR). In launching his Eastern policy (*Ostpolitik*), Brandt was motivated by a number of considerations. His implacable opposition to all that the Nazis stood for and his recognition that the Third Reich's collapse had hardly wiped the German slate clean made him anxious to mend fences with the nations that Germany had brutalized in the war. His experience as mayor of West Berlin had convinced him that the hard lot of those millions of Germans locked behind the iron curtain in the GDR could be eased only by improved relations with the East. He believed it was time to put the day-to-day interests of the German people on both sides of the border above abstract commitments to German reunification, which had only antagonized the Soviet and GDR governments, hardening their opposition to contacts between the citizens of the two German states.

Bonn's initial attempts to improve relations with the GDR met with little success, because that state was still under the control of the hard-line Stalinist Walter Ulbricht. In a meeting between Brandt and Willi Stoph, head of the GDR's Council of Ministers, Stoph effectively scuttled possibilities for understanding between the two German states by demanding that West Germany pay "reparations" for the human productivity lost by the GDR through the flight of its citizens to the West. Nor was Ulbricht pleased by the wildly enthusiastic reception Brandt received in the East German town of Erfurt when he paid a state visit there in March 1970.

Turning their attention to East Germany's "protector," the Soviet Union, West German diplomats met a friendlier reception. The Russians realized that their recent invasion of Czechoslovakia had heightened their unpopularity in Eastern Europe, making it all the more important that the West, especially West Germany, recognize the legitimacy of Europe's postwar boundaries. The Soviets were also anxious to expand trade with the economically robust Federal Republic. Nevertheless, the West German-Soviet negotiations that opened in Moscow in January 1970 proved difficult. They showed some elements of classical eighteenth-century diplomacy: memoranda with interpretations of treaty articles on which one power insisted but the other wished not to acknowledge were given to the porter at the Russian Foreign Ministry, allowing the German delegation to say they had been delivered and the Russian representative to say they had never reached him. When an agreement was finally reached at the end of July 1970, Brandt and his foreign minister traveled to the Soviet capital to initial the accord, the Treaty of Moscow. Both governments renounced the use of force and any claims to each other's territory or that of other states. They formally recognized as "inviolable" the postwar boundaries, including the border between the two Germanys and that between Poland and East Germany (the so-called Oder-Neisse line). However, West Germany managed to avoid granting East Germany full recognition as a separate state, while the Soviet Union, for its part, refused to mention the possibility of German reunification.

The Treaty of Moscow opened the way to negotiations between the Federal Republic and the country that had suffered most from German aggression in World War II, Poland. In preparation for its normalization of relations with Poland, Bonn finally abandoned that relic of the Cold War, the Hallstein Doctrine (1955), under which it had refused to maintain normal diplomatic relations with any nation (other than the USSR) that recognized the GDR. After long and complicated discussions, West Germany and Poland signed the Treaty of Warsaw in December 1970. As in its treaty with the USSR, Bonn formally accepted the Oder-Neisse border, while the Poles agreed to allow ethnic Germans residing in Poland to move to one of the German states, a concession that brought thousands of them to the West. Brandt himself traveled to Warsaw to sign the treaty. During his visit he laid a wreath at the Tomb of the Unknown Soldier and wrote in the visitors' book: "In memory of the dead of the Second World War and the victims of violence and betrayal, in the hope of an enduring peace and solidarity between the nations of Europe." At the Warsaw Ghetto, where in 1943 some seventy thousand Jews had been massacred by the German occupation forces, Brandt suddenly dropped to his knees and wept. This totally

Chancellor Willy Brandt, during a visit to Poland in 1970, kneels before a memorial to the victims of the Warsaw Ghetto. Brandt's trip culminated with the signing of a German-Polish treaty, part of his policy of *Ostpolitik*.

unrehearsed gesture, which Brandt later described as "an attempt, through the expression of fellow-feeling, to build a bridge to the history of our nation and its victims," was much criticized by conservative Germans, who considered it inappropriate or unnecessary. But the Poles understood Brandt's intentions, and his moving gestures of conciliation did as much as the Treaty of Warsaw itself to improve Polish-German relations.

Improved relations between the two Germanys, on the other hand, still faced significant obstacles. One of the most important was the continuing dispute regarding the status of divided Berlin, which the four former Allied powers had jointly administered since the war. In an accord signed in September 1971, the Americans, Soviets, British, and French established new regulations for the governing of Berlin. The three Western powers conceded that West Berlin was not a fully sovereign state of the Federal Republic: the West German parliament could no longer meet there, West Berlin could not send delegates with voting privileges to the federal parliament in Bonn, and the city's citizens would not be eligible for conscription into the Bundeswehr, the West German Army. The Soviet Union, for its part, abandoned its traditional insistence that West Berlin lay within GDR territory and therefore under Russian jurisdiction. The Russians also conceded that the Federal Republic might represent West Berlin in the international sphere and maintain a number of governmental agencies in the city. Most important for the citizens of both German states, the new accord allowed West Berliners, who had been largely forbidden access to East Berlin and the GDR since the building of the Berlin Wall in 1961, the right (albeit limited) to cross the border and visit friends and relatives in the East. By conceding all this, the Soviet Union was implicitly declaring that it did not wish the Berlin question to stand in the way of improved relations with the West.

Since the former Allied powers made the implementation of this accord contingent upon the two German states' working out the practical details of its execution, the Berlin agreement served as an effective prod to intra-German negotiations, whose progress was also facilitated by the ouster of Ulbricht in May 1971. In early 1972, Bonn and East Berlin embarked on a sustained effort to normalize relations between the two Germanys, and by December 1972 the historic Basic Treaty was ready to be signed. The two states renounced the use of force and accepted each other's borders as inviolable. The Federal Republic formally abandoned its oft-repeated claim to be the only legitimate representative of the entire German people. The two states acknowledged each other's sovereign existence, though at the insistence of West Germany they did not extend each other full diplomatic recognition. Instead of embassies, they established permanent missions in each other's capitals. Still, this was a significant step forward for the GDR. In response it agreed to permit its citizens to visit relatives in the West in times of family emergency. (Later it allowed aged pensioners the right to move permanently to West Germany, a concession that unburdened its own economy at the expense of the Federal Republic's.)

Completion and ratification of the Basic Treaty enabled both German states to become members of the United Nations in September 1973. But this was not the end of Brandt's *Ostpolitik*. Bonn rounded out its "opening to the East" by signing a treaty (similar to that with Poland and the USSR) with Czechoslovakia and by exchanging ambassadors with Bulgaria and Hungary (Romania had violated Communist orthodoxy by establishing ties with Bonn in 1967). Now West Germany had formal diplomatic relations with all the East bloc states save the "hermit state" Albania, not thought to be a significant exception. Clearly, Bonn, long content to take its foreign policy marching orders from the Western powers, especially from the United States, was showing that it could seize the diplomatic initiative and define its own interests in world affairs.

The independence exhibited by the West German government in launching its *Ostpolitik* was not wholeheartedly welcomed by the West, certainly not by Washington. Secretary of State Henry Kissinger wrote a number of memoranda to President Nixon stating that while he had no doubts about the "basic Western orientation" of the German political leaders, he believed that the West German *Ostpolitik* had "worrisome aspects." He feared that the Federal Republic might try to act as mediator between East and West, impairing America's leadership over Western Europe and therefore also its strength vis-à-vis the East. He feared also that an aggressive West German *Ostpolitik* might weaken the coherence of the NATO alliance. Kissinger therefore aimed to defuse the possible consequences of the German initiative by placing the German *Ostpolitik* into the more general framework of superpower détente. This would, he believed, allow America to maintain influence over the evolution of West German foreign policy and prevent Bonn from drifting too far from its Western moorings.

Important as Brandt's *Ostpolitik* was, the Social-Liberal coalition in West Germany was elected not so much because of its foreign policy promises as because of the strength of its commitment to domestic sociopolitical change. Shortly after taking office, Chancellor Brandt increased social security payments and government spending on education. He also began to liberalize Germany's antiquated legal codes governing women's rights, abortion, divorce, and pornography. Most important, he announced plans to expand the system of "economic codetermination," whereby workers received representation in factory boardrooms.

Like Brandt's bold foreign policy initiatives, these reforms met with strong opposition from the conservative Christian Democratic Union and Christian Social Union (CDU/CSU), and even from elements in the liberal Free Democratic Party (FDP), Brandt's coalition partner. Indeed, defections from the FDP emboldened the CDU to try in April 1972 to bring down Brandt's government through a vote of "constructive no confidence" in the Bundestag. Preparatory to this vote, the CDU condemned Brandt's domestic reforms as a threat to order and prosperity and his foreign policy as an abandonment of West Germany's duty to free East Germany from Communism. Brandt won the showdown in the Bundestag, but his margin of victory was so thin that he decided to hold federal elections in hopes of gaining a more solid mandate. The new election, held in September 1972, proved to be a vindication of his policies. Winning 45.9 percent of the vote, the SPD outpolled the CDU for the first time in the history of the Federal Republic.

Despite this victory, however, Brandt was unable to carry through some of his more costly and ambitious social reform plans. The oil crisis of 1973 suddenly disrupted Germany's economic growth, bringing a decline in tax revenues. At the same time, higher rates of unemployment led to resentment in some quarters toward the 2.5 million foreign workers that West Germany had imported (largely from Turkey and southern Europe) when it desperately needed additional labor in the 1960s. Brandt was barely able to resist demands that these "guest workers" be summarily expelled and their jobs turned over to native Germans.

In the spring of 1974, Brandt learned that one of his most trusted aides was an East German spy who had long been passing intelligence information to the East. Humiliated by the scandal, Brandt quickly resigned. This decision delighted his enemies at both ends of the political spectrum: conservative business interests who feared that his reforms would erode their privileges and radical young socialists who believed that the chancellor's appeal to the "new center" betrayed the SPD's Marxist traditions.

Brandt's departure marked the end of a remarkable chancellorship. Through the force of his actions and convictions, he had helped build a new, more positive image of the Germans in the rest of the world. Though resentment of Germany did not die out, the Germany represented by Brandt could be seen as more willing to come to terms with the crimes of the Nazi past. It was also more willing to jettison ideological dogmas with no practical application in favor of policies leading to a demonstrable easing of tensions between East and West. Finally, Brandt personified postwar Germany's commitment to peace. "We are condemned to peace for life," he once said. "There are worse things in life than that." It was thoroughly appropriate that Brandt was awarded the Nobel Peace Prize in 1971.

Brandt's fall from power allowed a more conservative faction within the SPD to gain control over the party. Helmut Schmidt, the leader of this faction, became West Germany's next chancellor in May 1974. Schmidt was a different sort of man from Brandt. Though he affected an Elbe bargeman's cap, he came from a middle-class background in Hamburg and lacked his predecessor's warm personality. One of his rivals quipped that he had learned his socialism at the officers' casino (he had, in fact, been a lieutenant in the Second World War and remained a reserve officer in West Germany's new army, the Bundeswehr). From 1969 to 1972 he headed the Defense Ministry, then served as finance minister. During his rise to prominence he developed a reputation for cool pragmatism

West German Chancellor
Helmut Schmidt.

punctuated by acerbic wit and a certain condescending arrogance, qualities that did not necessarily endear him to his colleagues.

Schmidt began his eight-year tenure as chancellor at a difficult time in Germany's postwar history. The economic dislocations that had bedeviled Brandt's last year in office turned into a deep recession marked by zero or low GNP growth and high unemployment. Pragmatist that he was, Schmidt responded by cutting public spending and raising taxes, policies that earned him the lasting enmity of the more radical factions in his own party. Nevertheless, he did manage to push through one important socioeconomic reform: the enactment of a new codetermination law (originally promised by Brandt) that gave workers equal representation with executives on the supervisory boards of companies employing two thousand or more people.

Enjoying relatively peaceful labor relations, West Germany began in the late 1970s to recover from the international recession that continued to plague the rest of Western Europe and increasingly to assert its influence on the international stage as one of the world's strongest economies. It became a world leader in the production of automobiles, chemicals, machine tools, and communications equipment. The Federal Republic's achievement was acknowledged by the West's leading industrial nations, whose heads of state chose to hold their economic summit in 1978 in Bonn. On this and other occasions Schmidt took it upon himself to explain to his counterparts—particularly to Jimmy Carter—how modern economies ought to be run. He was equally forthright in defending West Germany's decision to help build a pipeline that would bring natural gas from Siberia to Germany, a step the United States feared would make West Germany an "energy hostage" to Soviet policy. Schmidt, in effect, told the Americans to mind their own business. More quietly, West Germany used its economic clout to extend credits to the GDR and to pay "ransom" for East German dissidents who wished to emigrate to the Federal Republic.

Yet West Germany, for all its prosperity, continued to produce its own dissidents. In addition to the radical Red Army Faction, whose terrorist actions in the mid-seventies have been described earlier, a more long-lasting protest movement grew up in response to ecological and nuclear energy issues. West Germany's heightened reliance on nuclear power, partly a reaction to the Arab oil embargo, led thousands of young people to take to the streets in antinuclear demonstrations. Related protests focused on the industrial pollution of Germany's rivers and the decimation of its cherished forests through acid rain (*Waldsterben*). Out of this ecological protest movement emerged a new political party, the Greens, which gained representation in two state parliaments in 1979. In the coming years the Greens increased their parliamentary representation and assumed cabinet posts in some state governments. Although other European countries, including Britain, France, and Sweden, also produced Green parties in the 1970s, at that time only the West German Greens managed to gain real political clout.

In foreign policy, Schmidt sought to preserve Brandt's *Ostpolitik*, and at the same time he continued the buildup of West Germany's armed forces that had begun when West Germany joined NATO in 1955 and on which the Federal Republic now spent more than any other European NATO power. The German defense buildup proceeded against a background of rising tensions with the Soviet Union, which, despite the ongoing SALT II negotiations, began deployment in 1977 of a new medium-range nuclear missile, the SS-20, aimed at targets in Western Europe, including West Germany. From Schmidt's point of view, these weapons were especially pernicious because they added a tactical nuclear superiority to the Soviets' advantage in conventional weapons. Schmidt therefore acquiesced in an American plan to develop and deploy in Europe the neutron bomb, a tactical enhanced-radiation weapon designed to kill invading troops without destroying material property (a feature that led one critic to label it a "symbol of mental perversion"). When, much to Schmidt's dismay, President Carter changed his mind on the neutron bomb, the German chancellor encouraged NATO to adopt a so-called two-track policy involving the deployment in Europe of American medium-range missiles (Pershing IIs and Cruise) while at the same time offering to cancel such deployment if the Soviets dismantled their SS-20s. Since West Germany, with a territory the size of Oregon, already had thousands of nuclear weapons on its soil, this plan, which NATO formally adopted in 1979, did not sit well with the country's large and growing antinuclear community. Moreover, since many of the most vocal protesters were in the SPD, Schmidt, like Brandt before him, increasingly lost the support of his own party. By the end of the decade some pundits were predicting the imminent demise of his government (though in fact it lasted until September 1982).

France

In 1969, the year Willy Brandt assumed the chancellorship in West Germany, a new government also came to power in France. De Gaulle's domination of French policy had been shaken by the student revolt and the general strike of May 1968. Although he had won a great majority in the elections of June 1968, it was general knowledge that the man who had ended the revolt had been not de Gaulle but his prime minister, Georges Pompidou. De Gaulle, who did not like to be overshadowed by anyone, dismissed Pompidou in July 1968. This did not halt the decline in de Gaulle's prestige, however, since his government seemed unable to handle the economic problems associated with the developing recession. When he submitted a proposal of administrative reforms to a referendum in April 1969, it was rejected, and the seventy-nine-year-old president resigned. "I have had a contract with France . . . this contract has been broken . . . the French have no national ambition any longer." With these bitter words, according to the writer André Malraux, de Gaulle explained his resignation.

De Gaulle's successor, Pompidou, was two years older than Brandt and, unlike his German counterpart, was a member of the academic and financial bourgeoisie that had ruled France in the period before the Nazi conquest. In the 1950s Pompidou as director of the Rothschild Bank had become convinced of the need for international economic and political cooperation. As France's leader, he modified the sharply nationalistic tone of de Gaulle's foreign policy. He supported, for instance, Britain's entry into the European Economic Community and moved France closer to NATO. While supporting Brandt's opening to the East, Pompidou urged the Americans to keep their troops in Germany as a guarantee against the "neutralization of Central Europe." His relationship with Nixon's America, however, was not harmonious. On a trip to the United States in 1970, he and his wife were heckled and spit upon by Jewish American demonstrators protesting France's refusal to sell arms to Israel while supplying the Arabs. Pompidou vowed never again to set foot on American soil.

Pompidou's domestic course also differed from de Gaulle's. His policies reflected the belief that not only *grandeur* ("greatness") but also *bonheur* ("prosperity") had to be a government's concern. Trade unions received the right to representation in industrial enterprises, a national minimum wage was introduced, and student complaints about overcrowding were relieved when the number of universities was increased from twenty-two to sixty-five. Yet as a practical ex-banker, Pompidou understood the need to combine social welfare with economic prowess. He opened the state banks to various promoters and industrial developers, who were given easy credit. He relaxed the height limitations on Parisian buildings, with the result that architectural disasters like La Tour

Maine–Montparnasse were allowed to blight the capital's skyline. He devalued the franc to make French exports more competitive and scaled back some costly public works projects. He did not, however, cut back government subsidies in the cultural field. An avid connoisseur of the arts, he frequently expressed the view that France ought to be not only powerful but also a leader in world culture. It was appropriate that in Pompidou's honor a museum of modern and contemporary art was erected in the Beaubourg district of Paris.

When Pompidou, who had been in failing health for some time, died in 1974, the Gaullists put up Valéry Giscard d'Estaing as their candidate for president. As Pompidou's finance minister Giscard had won the support of conservative Gaullists who had opposed the president's domestic reforms. Running on the slogan "Change Without Risk," Giscard managed narrowly to defeat the Socialist-Communist bloc's candidate, François Mitterrand.

The new French president was a wealthy and elegant man with an aristocratic title appropriated from a defunct line of distant relatives. A graduate of the École Polytechnique, one of the *grandes écoles* that emerged after the war as the major training ground for the French governmental elite, Giscard was determined to "rationalize" France's economy and bureaucracy. He spoke of creating an "advanced liberal society" dominated by technocratic managers drawn from industry, banking, and the universities. Yet his own understanding of high technology was not always what it might have been. When France was faced, like the other European powers, with the loss of cheap Arab oil in 1973–1974, he invested a billion francs in a scheme devised by a Belgian con man to "sniff" offshore oil from the air. When the scheme failed to turn up any oil, he launched the most ambitious nuclear energy program in Europe. While this policy enraged some environmentally conscious citizens (of whom France had fewer than West

Georges Pompidou.

Germany or Britain), Giscard's initiatives in the sociocultural field—which included lowering the voting age to eighteen, liberalizing abortion and divorce laws, imposing a capital gains tax on the wealthy, and appointing women to high office—shocked many conservatives. Thus, like his German counterpart, Giscard ended up alienating many of his original supporters.

In foreign policy, Giscard showed more caution, though here too he could be innovative. While convinced that Europe had a larger role to play in the wake of America's growing economic troubles and foreign policy failures (most notably in Vietnam and Iran), he did not pursue European supranationalism, except to advance, along with Helmut Schmidt, a common European monetary policy (European Monetary System) that helped reduce violent currency fluctuations. In security affairs he further modified de Gaulle's policy toward the Atlantic alliance by ordering French officers to join a NATO planning group and by hinting that France would participate in the defense of Europe even if not directly attacked. The cornerstone of his foreign policy, however, was the establishment of a cordial relationship with West Germany, France's "hereditary enemy." Giscard and Schmidt, who played chess together and traded confidences in fluent English, worked to improve industrial and political cooperation between their two countries, which together had an economy about half the size of America's and considerably larger than the Soviet Union's. Giscard's goal of making France's economy even larger than West Germany's was impeded, however, by a backward agricultural sector, a weak currency, gross inequities in the distribution of income, and an inadequate technical infrastructure. These failings notwithstanding, France under Giscard continued to play a leading role in world affairs, a place that its European neighbors, not to mention the United States, were not entirely convinced it deserved.

Great Britain

In 1970, Edward Heath, a carpenter's son who had become a Tory during his student days at Oxford, became Britain's new prime minister. Like his continental counterparts, Heath was determined to forge a new identity for his nation by becoming less dependent on the United States, whose "betrayal" of Britain and France in the Suez crisis of 1956 he never forgot. Though Heath welcomed the steps toward détente between America and Soviet Russia, he resented Britain's exclusion from the superpower negotiations, just as he resented the fact that President Nixon gave him just one hour's notice before reversing U.S. policy toward China. Instead of focusing on Britain's traditional "special relationship" with America, therefore, Heath sought closer ties with Europe. In his maiden speech to the House of Commons in 1950 he had stressed the urgency of Britain's "joining Europe"; now, in 1973, he presided over Britain's entry into the EEC, a step made possible by de Gaulle's exit from power in France. In cementing this European connection, Heath finally reversed (albeit only partially) a dominant postwar trend in British politics, of combining nostalgia for

England's imperial role with an unfounded belief that the nation could prosper outside the European framework.

EEC membership, however, did not solve Britain's economic problems; indeed, opening the British market to greater competition in heavy industry dramatically exposed long-standing structural weaknesses while tying the country into the community's expensive agricultural price support policies. Britain also suffered because it joined the EEC precisely at the onset of a general world recession. Convinced, no doubt correctly, that higher labor costs and inefficiency were major factors in Britain's economic malaise, Heath pledged to "put the unions in their place." The result was a series of devastating strikes. The government was obliged to settle a long and bitter coal miners' strike by increasing the miners' wages by 27 percent. Settlements like this helped push up Britain's inflation rate, which in 1974 was running at 13 percent. Hoping for a stronger mandate to deal with the country's economic woes, Heath called an election in February 1974. In his campaign he aggressively asked, "Who runs Britain?" His challenge backfired, for the Tories lost and the Labor Party returned to power.

The new head of state was Harold Wilson, who had been prime minister during the abundant period of the 1960s. In the mid-seventies, however, the economic index that rose most dramatically was the inflation rate, which soared to 27 percent in the wake of new and ever more generous wage settlements. Wilson called his relationship with Labor a "social contract" in which the unions would curb wage demands in exchange for food subsidies and rent controls granted by the government. But as one commentator put it, the only "give and take" in this contract "was that the government gave and the unions took."

Though Wilson won a slender victory in a new election called in October 1974, he became increasingly frustrated over his inability to rein in the unions. He took his sixtieth birthday, in April 1976, as an opportunity to resign, turning over the prime ministership to James Callaghan. Mr. Callaghan, unlike Wilson, was actually of the laboring class. The son of a seaman and a domestic servant, he had not attended Oxford or Cambridge, indeed had not attended any university at all, instead having "gone to school" in the labor movement, in which he had held various official posts. Later he had served as chancellor of the exchequer, home secretary, and foreign secretary.

Despite his old ties to the unions, Callaghan was prepared to try to discipline labor in the interest of restoring Britain's competitiveness. Unlike Wilson, he did not believe that the country could spend its way out of its troubles. In a policy reminiscent of Heath's, he introduced austerity measures and called for a wage freeze. But as before, this brought the unions out in a new series of highly disruptive strikes. The most crippling of these was a truckers' walkout, which the government eventually settled with a 20 percent wage hike.

By the end of the decade, many Britons were complaining that the nation was being "held hostage" by the unions, a state of affairs that they (not entirely fairly) blamed on Callaghan. After the "winter of discontent" (1978–1979), which featured news stories about pickets holding up medical supplies and preventing burials, the nation turned Callaghan out in favor of Margaret Thatcher, who, many apparently believed, was the only politician in the country capable of curtailing the unions' power.

Democracy Comes to Portugal and Greece

Portugal is the country in which the frontal-lobe lobotomy was invented. This accomplishment, for which the surgeon-inventor won the Nobel Prize for Medicine in 1949, has since been described by many progressive-minded Portuguese as symbolically fitting for their nation: had the place not been virtually brain-dead for most of its modern history? Under the long dictatorship (1932–1968) of Antonio Salazar, Portugal remained in a state of suspended animation, its elites looking back nostalgically to the glorious days of empire, its subjugated masses fatalistically looking only to the next world; even the public clocks in Lisbon stood still because nobody bothered to wind them.

In 1968, that year of rebellion for so much of the Western world, Salazar's reign came to an end, but only because the aging dictator was too sick to go on. His successor vowed to keep the regime intact, to continue to hold the twentieth century at bay.

He might have managed to do so for a long time to come had he not also tried to hold on to all of Portugal's African colonies—Angola, Mozambique, and Guinea. In the face of bitter black nationalist rebellions, this put the impoverished

A soldier restrains a Lisbon crowd during Portugal's Carnation Revolution, April 1974.

mother country under intolerable strain. By the early 1970s, Portugal was spending roughly half its annual budgets on its colonial wars. In April 1974, a group of junior officers, tired of seeing the army decimated and the national treasury depleted in what seemed a hopeless and anachronistic cause, and strongly influenced by radical Portuguese university students who had been forced to serve in the African colonies, turned against the government. Showing its decrepitude, the old regime collapsed overnight in the face of this Carnation Revolution, so named because the victorious rebel soldiers paraded about with red flowers protruding from the barrels of their rifles.

The euphoria of revolutionary victory, however, wilted like the soldiers' carnations as the rebel leaders discovered that it was one thing to topple an antiquated regime, quite another to construct a viable political system in its place. For two years following the revolution, some fifty different military factions, most of them radical leftist, sought to impose their rival utopias on Portugal. In 1975, the Communist Party, which had managed to penetrate the government, made an unsuccessful bid for full power. The Communists were opposed by the Socialist Party under Mario Soares, which had the support of some moderate senior officers and the socialist movements of Western Europe. Soares could also count on financial help from the United States, since Portugal was important to American interests as a charter NATO member and supporter (albeit shaky) of Henry Kissinger's anti-Soviet policy in Africa.

The failure of the Communist coup and that party's subsequent decline opened the way for the Socialists to institutionalize democracy in Portugal. In 1976, the country adopted a new constitution, which counterbalanced a strong presidency with an independent judiciary and multiparty legislature. Though Portugal continued to suffer from economic anemia relative to most of Europe and saw nine different governments hold power between 1976 and 1983, it avoided relapsing into either revolutionary chaos or reactionary slumber. Indeed, the nation seemed to be well established as Europe's westernmost outpost of democracy.

Greece, the world's "cradle of democracy," had not shown much more aptitude or inclination for this form of government in the postwar era than had Salazar's Portugal. Saved from a possible Communist takeover by the Truman Doctrine aid program in the late 1940s, it had fallen in the 1950s under the control of various rightist governments backed by the monarchy, the military, and the CIA. After a left-center coalition managed to gain ascendance through the electoral process in the early 1960s, a group of right-wing army colonels staged a coup in 1967 and established a military dictatorship. The junta was notoriously repressive and brutal, its police forces killing or torturing political opponents, banning "subversive" books (including Plato's *Republic*), and jailing young people who had the effrontery to wear long hair. The king, who had initially supported the colonels, tried to overturn their rule, only to be forced to flee into exile. The junta's policies also irritated the Johnson administration in the United

States, for Greece was a member of NATO, an organization pledged to "protect democracy." The colonels' undoing was their unwise decision to try to annex the island of Cyprus over the objections of Greece's old rival, Turkey, another NATO power with questionable democratic credentials. When Turkey responded by militarily humiliating Greece in 1974, the junta lost all legitimacy and collapsed.

The next half decade saw the inventor of democracy reacquaint itself with this governmental system. Presiding over a generally smooth transition to democracy was Constantine Karamanlis, a moderate conservative who had held power in the late 1950s. One of his first actions was to hold a referendum on the monarchy, which resulted in its clear rejection. In foreign policy Karamanlis was obliged to distance himself somewhat from the United States in view of lingering Greek resentment over America's support of the junta. Greece also withdrew from NATO after the Turkish war, but rejoined in 1980. On January 1, 1981, Greece was allowed to join the EEC, even though its economic situation was quite shaky and its relationship with democracy was still in the getting-to-know-you stage. As one scholar of postwar Europe has noted, many in Brussels would come to regard Greece's admission to the EEC as "a regrettable triumph of hope over wisdom."

In the same year Greece elected a new prime minister, Andreas Papandreou, who as the left-leaning son of a prejunta prime minister had spent much of his life in exile, including a stint as professor of economics at Berkeley. As prime minister through most of the 1980s, Papandreou introduced a form of socialist populism that claimed to be more genuinely leftist than the Social Democratic regimes of northern Europe. Yet by the mid-1980s he was forced to adopt austerity measures that alienated radical leftists and the unions. Despite much talk about Greece's going its own way economically, Papandreou did not pull out of the EEC, a wise move given Greece's perennial need for subsidies from Brussels.

A TIME OF UNCERTAINTY

The triumph of democracy in southern Europe notwithstanding, for most Western Europeans the 1970s were a decade of jolting contradictions, one that began in a spirit of confidence and ended on a note of uncertainty and disillusionment.

Détente between the superpowers brought hopes in Europe that the Cold War tensions that had sharply divided the Continent since World War II were finally coming to an end. Western Europeans, especially West Germans, took advantage of the new atmosphere to pursue their own policies of conciliation with the East. In addition to signing diplomatic accords that improved political relations, they opened new and lucrative trade ties with Moscow and Eastern Europe. Though these initiatives harmonized in general with American foreign policy, they signaled a determination on the part of the European governments to reduce their economic and diplomatic dependence on America. When the superpowers returned to a policy of confrontation in the late 1970s, Western Europe hesitated to jeopardize the gains of détente by loyally toeing the American line. Many Europeans, moreover, were increasingly alarmed by what they considered a decline in the quality of U.S. leadership. Nixon's fall in the wake of the Watergate affair (a scandal that bewildered most Europeans) ushered in the brief and (in European eyes) ineffective administration of Gerald Ford. President Carter's sudden abandonment of détente for a renewed emphasis on anti-Communism and counterinsurgency inspired serious doubts in Europe regarding the coherence of Washington's foreign policy.

The consistency that European governments were searching for in foreign affairs was hardly evident in their domestic policies during the 1970s. Western Europe began the decade more or less committed to a continuation of high government spending, easy credit, and generous social programs. The energy crisis of the early 1970s, combined with increased industrial competition from low-cost, high-technology Pacific Rim countries, brought a quick end to the abundance that seemed to make such policies affordable. By the mid- to late-1970s inflation was running high and unemployment levels had reached 1930s proportions. Now no government, including the Social Democratic and Labor governments that ruled West Germany and Britain, harbored any hope that the old Keynesian recipe would still work. Instead of trying to spend their way out of the recession, they cut public works expenditures, curtailed or ended subsidies to inefficient industries, reduced welfare programs, tightened money supplies, devalued currencies, and increased taxes. These measures did not immediately produce salutary results, however, and by the end of the decade the governments in power in all the larger Western European states were in political trouble. Between 1979 and 1982, a changing of the guard would sweep out the Gaullists in France and the left-of-center governments in Britain and West Germany.

The general failure of Western European governments to realize the hopes of the 1960s brought about the emergence of several alternative or nonmainstream forms of political activity. In the first place, there was an upsurge of single-interest groups focusing on ecological or feminist issues that the established parties had largely neglected. One of the most important developments in this period was the rise of the Green movement in Western Europe. Its attraction was based not only on fears for the environment but on a growing dissatisfaction with urban life, commercialism, and relentless industrial growth. Another response to the perceived inadequacies of the conventional party system was an increasing recourse to "direct action" by disgruntled or thoroughly alienated citizens. Trade unions resorted to the political strike in Britain, France, and Italy. More frightening but less effective, political terrorists waged guerrilla war against "the system" by "kneecapping" or assassinating politicians and businessmen, torching department stores, and bombing or robbing banks. Terrorism was also employed by some of the regionalist parties and movements that for a brief period in the 1970s seriously challenged the democratic system. The Basques in northern Spain and the Catholics in Northern Ireland launched violent separatist campaigns. Less violent, but hardly less impassioned, crusades for cultural autonomy or self-government were waged by Scots and Welsh in Britain and by Corsicans, French Catalans and Basques, Provençals, and Bretons in France. In Belgium, Flemings fought ethnic battles with the Walloons. All such efforts reflected a new consciousness of ethnicity, a search for roots that had younger people turning to their elders to preserve what they could of regional folklore and fast-disappearing languages. They also bespoke a dawning discontent with the anonymous rule of distant bureaucrats and rigidly centralized government—a discontent that would only increase over the coming years with yet more centralization of power in Brussels and the added pressures of "globalization."

CHAPTER 14

Western Europe in the Troubled 1980s

FORTUNATELY FOR the people of Western Europe, the collapse of détente in the late 1970s and early 1980s did not make their part of the world a focal point of new confrontations between the superpowers. On the contrary, the superpowers' preoccupation with non-European trouble spots—Afghanistan for the Soviets, Iran and Central America for the Americans—allowed the West European nations to recover some of the international influence they had lost with the advent of the Cold War and the bipolar division of Europe. Their efforts to emancipate themselves from American tutelage gained impetus from the continuing inconsistencies in U.S. foreign policy: Washington's lurches from détente to containment and back again; its oscillation between Atlanticist internationalism and "Fortress America" isolationism. Though not all European leaders were equally discontented with America's international role, most were convinced that Europe had to do more to develop common policies of its own.

One important step in this direction was the decision in 1985 to institute by the year 1992 a "single European market" that would not only eliminate all internal trade barriers within the twelve-member European Economic Community but also provide the basis for closer political cooperation among the Western European nations.

On the domestic front in Western Europe, the main development of the 1980s was a conservative retrenchment considerably more thorough than the partial retreat from the welfare state noted in the late 1970s. New conservative governments in Britain and West Germany and even socialist regimes in France and southern Europe sought to revive ailing economies by curtailing public spending and encouraging private initiative. In this domain, if not so much in foreign policy, Western Europe and Reagan's America operated on the same frequency.

THATCHER'S BRITAIN

"I am not a consensus politician, I'm a conviction politician." With this famous statement, Margaret Thatcher summed up her political credo. Unlike many of her predecessors, who downplayed ideological commitments (if they had any) in favor of finding an elusive middle ground, Thatcher prided herself on the resoluteness with which she followed the course she considered to be right. That course involved, above all, a return to the individual self-reliance that she believed had made Britain great but that had been sorely lacking since the end of the war, when Britons had begun relying all too heavily on the state. In a speech in 1976, she lamented that "a man is now enabled to choose between earning his living and depending on the bounty of the state." She saw it as her mission to eliminate this "morally debilitating" choice.

Thatcher came to these views naturally. Born in 1925 to the family of a prosperous provincial grocer, she had absorbed the instinctive conservatism of "shopkeeper's England." Her formative memories were of ration books, queues outside the butcher's, and strikes—all products, she believed, of the misguided policies of postwar socialist governments. A hardworking and precocious student, she studied chemistry, then law, at Oxford, where she also served as president of the University Conservative Club. After graduating from the university in 1947, she married a wealthy businessman and started a family but, determined to be her own woman, also launched a successful law practice. Soon thereafter she entered politics, securing election to Parliament in 1959. Prime Minister Edward Heath, recognizing her considerable talents and industrious-

British Prime Minister
Margaret Thatcher.

ness, made her his secretary of state for education and science in 1970. By 1975 she had taken advantage of disarray in the Conservative top ranks to seize the leadership of the party from Heath, her former patron. Through this coup she became the first woman to lead a major political party in Britain. Four years later she entered Number 10 Downing Street as Britain's first female prime minister.

As prime minister Thatcher embarked on a deflationary monetary policy and introduced budget cuts in education, national health, and public housing. Her policies in this regard were part of an international return to market capitalism, which sought to overcome the global malaise of recession and inflation chiefly through reduced taxation and encouragement of private economic initiative. Thatcher's government sold off state-run industries, lowered inheritance taxes, and increased exemptions from the capital gains tax. It also discouraged private enterprises from granting wage increases and urged the closing of factories in which higher wages would have eliminated profits.

The new economic strategy significantly reduced inflation and helped make British industry more profitable and competitive in the international marketplace.

Thatcher's economic policies pitted her government against striking miners and other trade unionists.

On the other hand, it also produced high levels of unemployment. When Labor left power in 1979, unemployment had stood at 5.6 percent of the work force; two years later the rate had doubled. By 1982, 2,910,000 workers, or 12.2 percent of the work force, were unemployed; in the following year, the rate surpassed 3 million. The Trades Union Congress erected a giant billboard above its headquarters in London to display unemployment statistics while jobless demonstrators paraded down Whitehall carrying hostile signs calling for Thatcher's ouster.

The dissatisfaction created by Thatcher's economic policy apparently needed a more violent outlet, and in April 1981, riots extending over several days broke out in London, Liverpool, and other industrial cities. Some of the riots, including those in London, had an ugly racial aspect, pitting native English against recent immigrants from the Caribbean, India, and Africa. Worse riots erupted in the summer of 1981 and extended into Scotland, where unemployment was especially severe.

Economic discontent was not the only cause of violent upheaval in Thatcher's Britain. The "troubles" in Northern Ireland heated up once again as imprisoned members of the IRA began a series of hunger strikes in 1981 to dramatize their claim that they ought to be treated as war prisoners and not as criminals. When Thatcher refused to yield, Bobby Sands and nine other hunger strikers starved themselves to death. A new wave of sectarian shootings and terrorist bombings required London to send more military forces to Northern Ireland. The troops' presence there became an added source of tension, as IRA members and their supporters waged a bloody war against the British "army of occupation."

In response to what many Laborites considered the reactionary policies of the Thatcher government, the left wing of the Labor Party came to the fore. Ironically, the leader of this radical wing, Tony Benn, had much in common with Thatcher. Like her, he was an ideologue who distrusted moderation and saw consensus politics as conspiracy. While Thatcher found her "conspirators" among the liberal Tories (whom she labeled "Wets"), Benn and his ideological allies attacked the moderates in the Labor Party, accusing them of selling out the interests of the working class by embracing capitalism. The Labor left demanded that the party place itself solidly behind the most militant trade unions, push for the full nationalization of the economy, and take Britain out of the Common Market and NATO.

The ascendancy of the left wing in the Labor Party, combined with Margaret Thatcher's domination of the Conservatives, polarized British politics to a degree that concerned moderates in both parties. While some thirty Conservatives, uneasy over Thatcher's spending cuts, voted against her budget in 1982, a number of Labor moderates denounced Benn's policy as "Fascism of the left." It seemed the opportunity had arrived to unify the middle against the extremes on right and left by reviving a policy of consensus. A group of moderate Laborites therefore split off to found the Social Democratic Party and simultaneously entered an alliance with the small Liberal Party, the remnant of a once-great political power. Their goal was to emulate the success of the Social Democratic Party in West Germany, though ironically, they got organized just as their German model was faltering.

At first, however, it looked as if the new alliance might soon put Margaret Thatcher out of office. A poll in December 1981 suggested that in a general election the alliance would win 50 percent of the vote, compared to 23 percent each for the Labor and Conservative parties. Thatcher's own popularity was at low ebb, as many Britons, even Conservatives, became convinced that the socioeconomic policies of the "Iron Lady" were tearing the nation apart.

Yet eighteen months later, with unemployment still rising, Thatcher was swept back into office in a landslide victory. This astounding development can be explained primarily by the Falklands factor, the wave of patriotic excitement that accompanied Britain's war with Argentina over control of the Falkland Islands, an outpost of the British Empire some three hundred miles off the coast of Argentina. When Argentine troops invaded the Falklands in April 1982, Thatcher determined to drive them off and reassert British dominion. This crusade became popular in Britain because it came at a time when everything appeared to be going wrong for England. As one commentator noted, there was a strong "psychological need . . . for a success, a success of some kind, an end to failure and humiliation, to do something well, to win." Thatcher took full advantage of this climate of opinion. Rejecting all attempts at a negotiated settlement, she sent the Royal Navy to the South Atlantic. In less than two months the Falkland Islands—complete with their eighteen hundred islanders and six hundred thousand sheep—were back in British hands.

While the Falklands War certainly contributed to Thatcher's election victory in 1983, it also helped that the Conservatives' traditional opponent, Labor, was isolating itself as the party of "declining Britain," its base of support increasingly confined to the decaying inner cities and depressed industrial regions of the north. The Social Democratic-Liberal Alliance, for its part, was not catching on with the electorate as many pundits had predicted it would. In 1983, the voters seemed bewildered by the dual leadership of the "two Davids"—David Owen of the SDP and David Steel of the Liberals. In subsequent years, Owen's attempts to dominate the movement led to quarrels that pulled the organization apart.

In the wake of her victory in 1983, Thatcher seemed as firmly in control as ever, her constituency growing as the Conservatives siphoned off skilled and prosperous workers from the Labor ranks. Her policy of selling publicly owned houses to their tenants and shares in newly privatized firms (like British Gas and British Telecom) to individual buyers also attracted new supporters. These successes vastly outweighed Tory losses among the university-educated intelligentsia, many of whom feared that Thatcher would permanently cripple Britain's institutions of higher culture and learning through her austerity budgets. The 1987 election, which Thatcher won handily, showed that the majority of voters had accepted her campaign claim to have saved the nation from socialism, reversed its economic decline, and made it confident once again. "It's great to be great again" was the successful Tory slogan.

Yet it should be noted that while much of England prospered (the result in part of the timely discovery and exploitation of North Sea oil), significant sections of the nation, particularly in the north, continued to founder. The gap between rich and poor yawned ever more widely as government taxation policies favored the better off. In the opinion of Thatcher's critics, British society became dominated by a mean-spirited selfishness. For many, this was the other side, the dark side, of the "Thatcher Revolution."

In January 1988, Margaret Thatcher surpassed Herbert Asquith (governed 1908–1916) as the longest-serving prime minister in twentieth-century Britain. Like Ronald Reagan in the United States, she had orchestrated an economic turnaround aimed at replacing the interventionist and redistributive ethos of the welfare state with a revival of private initiative and individual enterprise. Yet as the decade came to an end, she again found herself in political trouble. Economic setbacks—most notably dramatic increases in the national budget and foreign trade deficits, a return to high inflation and interest rates, and continued high unemployment—shook confidence in her government. There was discontent too with the growing influx of immigrants from Britain's former Asian and African colonies, to whose presence an increase in urban crime was attributed. Against this background, Thatcher's offer of the right of abode in Britain to fifty thousand citizens from Hong Kong (population 5.7 million), the British crown colony scheduled for incorporation into China in 1997, raised cries of outrage. While some conservatives thought this figure was too high, critics on the left complained that Thatcher's plan to accept only Hong Kong's wealthier and better-educated citizens was narrowly elitist. The prime minister was also held responsible for the continued decline of Britain's transportation system, especially its railroads, whose deterioration threatened London's role as gateway to Europe. Following the resignation of her finance minister in October 1989, Thatcher's popularity rating dropped to the lowest level recorded for a prime minister in the fifty years the polls had been taken. Seeing her as a possible political liability, some Conservatives suggested that she should hand over power to a less controversial colleague before the next elections. But Thatcher made clear that she had no intention of stepping down until she had accomplished her "mission" and ensured that her legacy was sufficiently entrenched to keep Britain on the "right track" well into the twenty-first century.

WEST GERMANY TURNS RIGHT

The party that the British Labor moderates admired most, the West German Social Democratic Party (SPD), was experiencing severe difficulties as the 1970s drew to a close. It and its coalition partner, the Free Democratic Party (FDP), had emerged from the 1976 Bundestag elections with only ten more seats than the conservative Christian Democratic Union/Christian Social Union (CDU/CSU), and the CDU had again become West Germany's largest single party. Helmut Schmidt's decision in 1979 to back the stationing of new American medium-range missiles in Germany, combined with his failure to fulfill a campaign pledge to raise senior citizens' government pensions, alienated the SPD left wing and severely divided the party.

The social-liberal coalition might well have been turned out of office in the 1980 Bundestag elections had their conservative opponents not chosen Franz Josef Strauss as their candidate for chancellor. Strauss, a brilliant but mercurial and demagogical right-winger from Bavaria, frightened many moderate voters outside his native state. But no sooner had Schmidt won the election than he was faced with a second "oil shock" that plunged the German economy into a new recession, complete with rapidly rising unemployment. When Schmidt proved unwilling to combat the economic downturn by curtailing the welfare state (he believed he had already overantagonized the SPD left wing), his more conservative partner, the FDP, abandoned ship. In September 1982, the FDP leader and foreign minister, Hans-Dietrich Genscher, engineered Schmidt's downfall through a "constructive vote of no confidence" in the Bundestag. The parliament then chose the CDU leader Helmut Kohl as chancellor, and Kohl promptly put together a new government coalition with the FDP. West Germany, like Britain two years before, had taken a turn to the right.

German Chancellor Helmut Khol.

Germany's new chancellor, however, was in personality and political style rather different from Margaret Thatcher. Amiable and folksy, Kohl was often lampooned as a provincial bumpkin who knew little of the wider world. Unlike the cosmopolitan Schmidt, who could joke with some credibility that he had taught Henry Kissinger how to speak English, Kohl knew no foreign languages and (at least at the beginning of his chancellorship) seemed out of his depth in foreign affairs. On the other hand, he was unquestionably a talented political infighter and party manager, having swiftly risen through the CDU ranks in his native Rhineland/Palatinate, then assumed leadership of his party in 1976, and finally helped engineer the crucial FDP switch in October 1982 that toppled Schmidt.

In March 1983, Kohl called a federal election in the hope of securing a firmer mandate for his chancellorship. To do this, he had to arrange for the fall of his own cabinet through another—this time a sham—constructive no-confidence vote, for the West German constitution had no provision for the dissolution of parliament at the whim of a chancellor. Nevertheless, Kohl did secure his broader mandate, winning an additional eighteen seats by campaigning on a Thatcheresque promise to open the German economic system to more free market enterprise and individual initiative.

Having secured his mandate, Kohl made good on his campaign promise to cut taxes and government spending to spur growth in the private sector. While these measures resulted in moderate gains for the economy as a whole, they also (as in Britain) generated increasing unemployment. Jobless rates were especially high in the old-industrial Ruhr Valley (where they reached almost 25 percent) and among recent university graduates. In an ominous sign of the times, some West German youth began wearing jackets with the slogan "No Future!" stenciled across them.

Though it proved unable to reduce unemployment rates, the Kohl government could take credit for a slow but steady economic recovery that substantially enhanced the prosperity of most West Germans. Indeed, by the mid-1980s West Germany had emerged as Europe's best example of a postindustrial society, one in which heavy industrial workers were outnumbered by white-collar and service industry employees, and traditional class distinctions lost much of their significance in the face of rising prosperity for all workers. Higher wages brought demands for more leisure time in which to spend surplus income. By mid-decade many West Germans were working less than forty hours a week, and almost all were enjoying six weeks of annual paid vacation. Though some German employers (and envious workers elsewhere) wondered what had happened to the fabled German work ethic, productivity per manhour remained so high that West Germany's foreign trade was second in volume only to that of the United States, with which Germany enjoyed a significant trade surplus.

Prosperous and stable as the West German state had become, the conservative-liberal coalition that governed it in the 1980s was on precarious ground.

Chancellor Kohl could maintain power only with the support of the Bavarian CSU and the liberal FDP, whose leaders, Franz Josef Strauss and Hans-Dietrich Genscher, openly attacked each other. At issue in particular was Genscher's pursuit of accommodation with the East, a policy that Strauss, though he brokered loans to the GDR, found dangerously one-sided. Fortunately for Kohl, the opposition SPD also remained in disarray as contending factions fought to define the party's position on divisive issues like nuclear power and NATO missile deployment. The Greens too were sharply divided between a "realistic" faction prepared to work within the existing political system and a "fundamentalist" wing determined to avoid doctrinal compromises or the taint of association with the traditional parties.

The 1987 Bundestag elections, held against this fragmented and confusing background, resulted in embarrassing setbacks for the CDU/CSU, but the conservative-liberal coalition managed to retain power because the SPD also suffered losses, while the FDP did well. The most surprising winner was the Green Party, which, despite its internal divisions, added fifteen seats to its parliamentary delegation. The success of the Greens showed that a significant segment of the population continued to be dissatisfied with the way in which the mainstream parties addressed (or failed to address) environmental issues and social questions important to women and younger people.

While Kohl and other conservatives understandably made much of West Germany's economic and political successes, there was one aspect of the German condition about which they increasingly expressed concern—namely, postwar Germany's alleged failure to generate a sense of pride and firm national identity in the wake of the National Socialist trauma. Kohl often spoke of the need for the Germans to "overcome" the debilitating effects of the Nazi past, about which he considered himself free of guilt by virtue of his being "the first Federal Chancellor of the post-Hitler generation." On this point, Strauss agreed with Kohl. Confessing himself unable "with the best of will to drum up a guilt-complex" over the Nazi crimes, he insisted that it was time for the Germans to get off their knees and to "walk tall" again.

While many other Europeans were not terribly anxious to see the Germans walk tall again—they had been trampled by German forces too recently—Kohl's most important foreign ally, the United States, encouraged this process. The Federal Republic, after all, had emerged as America's most loyal ally on the Continent, and it contributed more men to NATO than any other European power. Thus, the American ambassador maintained that the time had come for the Germans to free themselves from the "tragedy of the period 1933-1945" and to concentrate on the positive aspects of their history. On the occasion of the fortieth anniversary of Germany's defeat in World War II, President Ronald Reagan paid a ceremonial visit to the small West German town of Bitburg, at whose military cemetery he laid a wreath "in a spirit of reconciliation, in a spirit of forty years of peace, in a spirit of economic and military compatibility." In response to widespread protests that the cemetery he so honored contained the graves of some Waffen-SS soldiers, Reagan insisted that the young SS men had also been Hitler's victims.

In addition to American encouragement, the Kohl government received assistance in its efforts to throw off the shadow of the Nazi past from some members of the West German historical profession. A number of conservative historians began arguing that the Nazi crimes, while lamentable, were not terribly different from other atrocities committed in the twentieth century, such as the Turkish mass murder of Armenians during World War I, the firebombing of Dresden and the nuclear attacks on Hiroshima and Nagasaki in World War II, and Pol Pot's genocidal policies in Cambodia. This and other revisionist contentions occasioned spirited rebuttals from other West German historians. Indeed, the historical community soon became embroiled in a heated internal debate—the so-called *Historikerstreit*—that gained international publicity and focused the world's attention on Germany's agonized search for a "usable past."

MITTERRAND'S FRANCE

Like West Germany, Britain, and the United States, France experienced a significant change in political direction in the early 1980s, but here the move was to the left rather than to the right. Plagued by discord in his center-right coalition, Giscard d'Estaing lost to the Socialist-Communist bloc candidate, François Mitterrand, in the elections of April-May 1981. Together with Callaghan's fall in Britain and Schmidt's ouster in West Germany, Giscard's exit signaled the eclipse of a political style that sought consensus through the application of technocratic socioeconomic policies.

Giscard's successor, Mitterrand, had been on the political scene in France for almost forty years. Emerging a hero from the war (his actions in the resistance earned him the Croix de Guerre), he was elected as a Socialist deputy to the Assembly in 1946, and apart from three years in the Senate he held that position until 1980. During this period he ran twice for the presidency, both times unsuccessfully. Though tenacity was obviously one of his strong points, he had other virtues as well. Like de Gaulle, he seemed to identify completely with France and its historic culture. In the manner of the departed general, he was given to talking grandiloquently about France's "civilizing mission in the world," clearly resenting the fact that America and Soviet Russia had divided most of the world between them without even consulting France. He combined a sincere determination to reduce class inequalities and injustices with a pragmatic sense of politics as the art of the possible. His Socialist credentials notwithstanding, he had a feel for political ceremony that was reminiscent of the Bourbons or (again) of de Gaulle. In his inauguration, which he called *La Cérémonie à la mémoire*, he went to the Pantheon to deposit single red roses on the tombs of the resistance

French President François Mitterrand. At his inauguration, Mitterrand lays a single red rose, symbol of the Socialist Party, on the tomb of the French Socialist Jean Jaurès.

martyr Jean Moulin, the slavery abolitionist Victor Schoelcher, and the pre-World War I Socialist leader Jean Jaurès. In the background, the Orchestre de Paris played Beethoven's Ninth Symphony and Placido Domingo sang the "Marseillaise." Foreign guests at the grand event included many prominent writers and intellectuals; their presence was meant to symbolize France's leadership in international culture.

Mitterrand's inauguration perhaps merited such elaborate pomp, for his assumption of the presidency was indeed a historic occasion, the first real political change France had experienced after twenty-three years of rule by various right-of-center coalitions. After the Socialists and Communists won a large majority in the Assembly elections held in June 1981, Mitterrand appointed four Communists to minor ministerial posts. His Socialist-Communist coalition was only the second instance of such collaboration in French history, the first being the Popular Front government of 1936. Once constituted, this new coalition proceeded to nationalize five major industries, including electronics and telecommunications, and those banks still in private hands. Among these was the Rothschild bank, which had been in business for more than 150 years in Paris; its disappearance aroused the most comment.

Mitterrand's nationalization measures led to a flight from the franc, which many Frenchmen exchanged for sounder currencies. The government's financial difficulties were exacerbated by its obligations to pay the owners of the nationalized enterprises 9 billion dollars in compensation and to carry out a general increase in wages. High government spending often leads to job creation, but in France's case unemployment, not employment, increased. During Mitterrand's first year in office the numbers of jobless climbed from about 1.7 million to over 2 million.

The obvious failures of Mitterrand's economic policies forced the government to reverse itself: in June 1982 it devalued the franc and declared a freeze on prices and wages. This dramatic shift created tensions between the Socialist and Communist members of Mitterrand's coalition. In any case, the Communists had long been uneasy about their cooperation with a "bourgeois" government, which they feared might damage their radical credibility and undermine party unity. In 1984 they left the government and returned to the "purity" of opposition.

The Communist departure made a kind of doctrinal sense because the Mitterrand government had always appeared more radical than it really was. Many of the firms the government took over were already heavily mortgaged to the state. As one contemporary observer acidly noted, Mitterrand "substituted for an unwieldy state capitalism an equally unwieldy state socialism, and called it change." Nor did the new government significantly redistribute wealth or alter in any fundamental way the social composition or mentality of the ruling elites.

The government's economic reversal in 1982 soon succeeded in bringing down inflation and in rehabilitating competition and the entrepreneurial spirit. Mitterrand's minister of research managed to reconnect French universities and the research community with industry, a policy that stimulated technological growth and innovation. On the other hand, the government was unable to bring down France's huge state budget deficit or foreign trade imbalance. The country's economic growth remained below that of its major trading partners while the unemployment rate remained higher than the average in the European Community. Competition for scarce jobs fueled animosities toward foreign workers and black immigrants from northern Africa who had established significant enclaves in most of France's larger cities. The foreigners and immigrants were accused not only of "stealing French jobs" but also of spreading crime and disease, especially AIDS. As in West Germany, these animosities created a racist backlash and spurred the growth of extreme nationalist parties, most notably the National Front, led by Jean-Marie Le Pen.

France's pressing economic and social problems hurt the Socialists in the legislative elections of March 1986, which saw a new shift to the right, the two main conservative parties winning 55 percent of the vote. This presented a problem for President Mitterrand, for according to the constitution of the Fifth Republic, the president had to appoint a prime minister supported by (or at least not opposed by) a majority in the Assembly. Forced to select one of the conservative candidates as prime minister, Mitterrand chose Jacques Chirac, the mayor of Paris and former prime minister under Giscard.

Chirac's appointment opened a brief era in French politics called cohabitation, governance by a president and a prime minister from opposing parties. As one might expect in such an arrangement, there were many quarrels. Chirac's government, which had the primary power to shape domestic policy, embarked on an attempt to revitalize the French economy by reprivatizing some of the industries nationalized by Mitterrand's first prime minister, Pierre Mauroy. Borrowing a leaf from Thatcher's book, it also gave entrepreneurs greater "flexibility" by removing administrative obstacles to the dismissal of - workers. Its social policy was dominated by anticrime legislation that allowed a significant enhancement of police powers. It dealt with the "immigration problem" by making it easier for the bureaucracy to deny entry to foreigners or to expel them. Mitterrand often objected to these policies but lacked the power to prevent their enactment. He therefore focused his attention on the next elections, when he expected the French people not only to reelect him as president but also to give his party sufficient votes to recapture the prime ministership.

This opportunity came in the spring of 1988 when France voted for both the presidency and a new National Assembly. In the presidential balloting, Mitterrand was opposed by Chirac, another conservative named Raymond Barre, and Le Pen, the National Front leader, who organized his campaign around attacks against black immigrants. Though Mitterrand managed to retain the presidency, the legislative elections gave the leftist parties only a very slight edge, which meant that the Socialists could rule only with the support of some centrist deputies. Hemmed in by the Communists on the left and the conservative bloc on the right, Mitterrand's new prime minister, the Socialist Michel Rocard, was in no position to deal decisively with France's economic and social problems or to prepare coherently for the country's role in the single European market planned to be in place by 1992.

Indeed, the government was unable even to plan effectively for the celebration of republican France's two hundredth birthday in July 1989; preparations for the bicentennial of the Great Revolution were severely hampered by political infighting among various factions. Yet when the big event finally did occur, Mitterrand displayed his usual talent for political pageantry. Not only did he loftily preside over a plethora of bicentennial festivities—including the inauguration of the Bastille Opera and of the Louvre's new glass pyramid entrance designed by I. M. Pei—but he concurrently hosted the Western economic summit, bringing to Paris the leaders of the West's six strongest economies. The logic of such showmanship, which Mitterrand inherited from de Gaulle, would have been well appreciated by the old general, who knew, as indeed did most Frenchmen, that being important in the world depended a lot on acting as if you were.

SOUTHERN EUROPE

Spain

Like France, Spain moved left in the early 1980s. In the October 1982 parliamentary elections the Socialist Workers Party, led by Felipe González, won a landslide victory. González, a Social Democratic pragmatist in the tradition of Germany's Helmut Schmidt, set about completing Spain's relatively smooth transition to democracy from the rigid authoritarianism of the Franco years. He took over from a center-right politician, Adolfo Suarez, who together with King Juan Carlos had gradually but decisively dismantled the Francoist state. This had prompted two attempts by right-wing military groups to turn back the tide, but the poorly organized coups quickly crumbled in the face of Juan Carlos's condemnation. The election of González in 1982 could be seen as another litmus test for Spanish democracy, for Socialist victories before—most notably that of the Popular Front in 1936—had been bloodily contested by the self-appointed guardians of Old Spain.

This time Spain's conservative business classes joined with González to turn the nation into Europe's most striking economic success story of the 1980s. Throughout the second half of the decade Spain enjoyed the highest economic growth rate in the Common Market, which it joined in 1986. A boom in consumption created 1.5 million new jobs, mainly in manufacturing. Foreign investors began pouring more than 10 billion a year into Spain. These accomplishments were achieved by policies that seemed more Thatcheresque than Socialist. González, whose party had officially abandoned Marxism in 1979, pursued a course of industrial reconversion that forced uncompetitive businesses into bankruptcy while opening the manufacturing economy to entrepreneurial initiative.

As in Thatcher's Britain, these policies had their costs for those Spaniards who could not keep up. Despite the expanding workforce, there remained 17 million unemployed (Europe's highest count), and unskilled workers and pensioners could barely survive at income levels that took little account of Spain's galloping inflation. The spending spree of the middle and upper classes sharpened contrasts between the "new Spain" of rich young professionals flashing their Rolex watches and another, seemingly abandoned Spain of struggling blue-collar workers, impoverished farmers, and homeless people sleeping on benches in Madrid's Retiro park.

Not surprisingly, many workers believed that "Felipe" (as González was known in Spain) had abandoned them. "Felipe is looking after businessmen more than workers" and "Felipe has forgotten the fundamental values of the left" were often-heard complaints. By the end of the decade many dissident Socialists had joined a Communist-led United Left Coalition to try to unseat González in the October 1989 elections. González ended up winning this election, though his party secured a majority of only one vote in the Spanish parliament.

In any event, the very fact that the campaign against González was purely electoral showed that Spain had indeed been transformed, that democracy was taken for granted by the left as well as the right. There could be no doubt that Spanish society had also irrevocably changed, with divorce and abortion legalized, emancipated women joining the workforce in droves, and church attendance so low that the once-powerful Catholic hierarchy was obliged to give up its traditional place at the center of Spanish life.

González's Spain was also afflicted with regionalist tensions, though these were hardly new. The aspirations of the Basques and Catalans for autonomy (or outright independence) dated back to the nineteenth century and had played an important role in the Spanish Civil War of 1936–1939. The new Spanish constitution of 1979 defined Spain as a multicultural country and granted far-reaching self-government to the Catalans, the Basques, and other "national minorities." Though these measures appeased some of the minorities, many members of the Basque community remained dissatisfied that the new arrangement had stopped short of granting full independence. Separatist aspirations were voiced by radical Basque groups like the Herri Batasuna (Unity of the People) party and the ETA (Euskadi ta Askatasuna, Basque Homeland and Liberty). Frequently the campaign became violent, as militant Basque separatists bombed central govern-

Basque separatists demonstrate before a copy of the painting *Guernica*, Picasso's rendering of the horrible bombing of the Basque town during the Spanish Civil War.

ment buildings and shot Spanish soldiers and police. Clearly these Basques did not feel significantly more at home in the "new Spain" of Felipe González than they had in the authoritarian Old Spain of Francisco Franco.

Italy

Like Spain, Italy experienced considerable political, economic, and social ferment in the late 1970s and early 1980s. Limited cooperation between the Communist Party (PCI) and the Christian Democratic government was brought to a brutal end by the Red Brigades' kidnapping and murder of Premier Aldo Moro in 1978. Although the economy was booming, the lira became so inflated that the government stopped minting coins or printing bills in small denominations; people were reduced to making change in caramels and chewing gum. Measures legalizing abortion and divorce were successfully introduced despite the spirited opposition of the Catholic Church and the Christian Democrats (DC), the main political representative of Catholicism in Italy. Conservatives received further shocks when in the elections of 1981 and 1983 the Christian Democrats steadily lost ground. In 1981, they had to concede the prime ministership to Giovanni Spadolini of the Republican Party, the first non-DC politician in Italy's postwar history to hold that position.

Two years later a Socialist, Bettino Craxi, became prime minister, a development that led some Christian Democrats to predict the imminent collapse of civilization as Italians had known it since the war. In fact, however, Craxi, like his Spanish counterpart, was a pragmatist who was more interested in promoting economic growth and political stability than in conforming to Marxist principles, which he had never seriously harbored anyway. Calling his socioeconomic policy *decisionismo* (to distinguish it from the Christian Democrats' corrupt old *clientelismo*), he reduced the salaries of state employees and tried to rein in the powerful unions. This led to numerous strikes, but strikes had always been as ubiquitous as pasta on the Italian scene.

Craxi stayed in power for roughly three years, almost a record in postwar Italy, which had seen forty-five governments come and go since the end of the war. These governments, however, tended to be drawn from the same small circle of veteran politicians who traded positions like players in a game of musical chairs. In 1986, the Christian Democrats recaptured the prime ministership, but their margin of victory was so thin that they had to rule in coalition with the Socialists, just as Craxi had been obliged to rule with the DC. As if to underscore the underlying continuity of modern Italian politics, Giulio Andreotti, a veteran DC politician who took over the prime ministership in July 1989, assumed this office for the *sixth* time.

But continuity at the top should not obscure the fact that there *had* been significant changes on the Italian political scene. The Christian Democrats and their allies in the Catholic hierarchy were no longer so clearly dominant. Their main rivals, the Communists, had also lost ground, because their efforts at a "historic compromise" with the Christian Democrats had alienated the hard-line left without convincing the center and the right that the Communists deserved a place in the national government. Though the PCI continued to maintain influence at the municipal level, particularly in the north, it no longer seemed capable of making a breakthrough to national power. Its decline, combined with the isolation of the once-powerful French, Spanish, and Portuguese Communist parties, signaled the atrophy of Marxism as a viable political ideology in Western Europe.

While the most significant trends in European domestic politics during the late 1970s and early 1980s were increased economic prosperity for most working people and the extension or stabilization of democracy, developments in foreign affairs, particularly the growing spirit of confrontation between the superpowers, fostered a climate of insecurity in Europe. The peoples of Western Europe feared being pulled into conflicts over which they had little control. Though America and the USSR were working to restore détente by mid-decade and indeed achieved historic new arms control agreements in the late 1980s, the very fluctuations in the superpower relationship imposed new pressures on the Atlantic alliance. Disagreements between the United States and its Western European allies deepened to the point that some observers began speaking of a "post-Atlantic world," a "Europe without America," and "Continental drift."

EUROPEAN-AMERICAN RELATIONS IN THE REAGAN ERA

The Collapse of Détente

Détente collapsed in the same way it had begun: not all at once or as the result of policy but generally through the convergence of a number of disputes. The Middle East continued to be the focus of a bitter struggle for influence between the United States and the Soviet Union. The hostility between Israel and the Arab states led the latter, since Israel was backed by the United States, to turn to Russia for support. The upheavals provoked by the dictatorships in South Yemen and Ethiopia also brought official requests for Soviet help, and the Russians responded with either direct aid or indirect assistance to these governments through Cuba. The spread of Soviet influence in the Middle East and eastern Africa, viewed by the Western powers as within their own sphere of interest, angered the United States.

The most shocking development from the American perspective, however, occurred right on the border of the Soviet Union. In late December 1979, the Soviets sent thousands of troops into Afghanistan, claiming that they had been asked to do so by the pro-Soviet government in Kabul, which was under attack from Islamic-nationalist rebels. The Carter administration, already frustrated by the Soviets' deployment of SS-20 missiles in their western territories, worried

An Afghan woman walks past a Russian tank following the Soviet invasion in December 1979.

that this move might foreshadow a grab for the Persian Gulf. To "punish" the Soviets for what he hyperbolically called "the greatest threat to peace since the Second World War," Carter immediately announced a number of sanctions, including a ban on licensing technology to the Soviet Union, a partial embargo on U.S. grain sales to Russia, and a curtailment of Soviet fishing rights in American waters; he also threatened to prohibit U.S. citizens from competing in the summer Olympic Games in Moscow (a threat he later carried out).

Although the Western European governments were also appalled by the Soviets' Afghan invasion, most of them interpreted it differently from the Americans. They saw it as a hastily improvised effort to rescue a government whose fall would promote the entrenchment of anti-Soviet Islamic fundamentalism in Afghanistan and possibly spread it to Russia itself, whose southern republics, most notably Azerbaijan, contained large populations of Muslims. This differing interpretation of the Afghan situation was emblematic of the Europeans' tendency to see the Soviet Union primarily as a defensive power, while the Americans were returning to Cold War dogmas that postulated the Soviets' world hegemonial ambitions.

If the European leaders worried that President Carter's foreign policy had become dangerously ideological and inflexible, they could take little comfort in his replacement by Ronald Reagan in January 1981. Reagan had campaigned on a militant anti-Communist line, promising at one point to get the Russians out of Afghanistan by blockading Cuba. As president he immediately embarked on a massive arms buildup that included some previously canceled systems, including the B-1 bomber, the MX missile, and the neutron bomb. This program drew criticism in Europe because it seemed designed to build a Fortress America that could operate independently of NATO, an organization for which many American neoconservatives indeed had very little respect. The Europeans were also alarmed over the huge financial costs of the American arms buildup, since they would actually be more immediately affected by these costs than would the Americans. This was attributable to Washington's policy of paying for the weapons through borrowing rather than taxes, which dramatically increased the budget deficit, forced up American interest rates, and encouraged an outflow of European capital to the United States and a stagnation of investment at home. "How can we defend our alliance with the United States," asked French Finance Minister Jacques Delors, "when critics say American policy is making us bankrupt?"

There was much concern in Europe too about Reagan's attitude toward the arms control talks that had dragged on despite increasing international tension. The American arms control negotiation team was led by men who believed that we were "living in a prewar and not a postwar world." In their conviction that war might be imminent, Reagan's security advisers began working on strategies for the United States to fight and survive a nuclear conflict by confining it to tactical operations in the European theater. They also spoke enthusiastically of "decapitating" nuclear strikes aimed precisely at Soviet centers of political control. These strategists were called Nuclear Use Theorists (NUTs)—to distinguish them from the traditional apostles of deterrence through Mutual Assured Destruction (MAD). Reagan put himself firmly in the camp of the NUTs when he told a group of editors that he "could see where you could have the exchange of tactical [nuclear] weapons against troops in the field without it bringing either one of the major powers to push the [strategic nuclear] button."

Such talk alarmed the Western European powers, for a "limited" nuclear war would hardly be limited from their point of view; their countries would be the theater in which the contending power blocs staged their horrendously destructive drama. The Germans, sitting at the foot of the iron curtain, were particularly apprehensive at this turn of events; it seemed to confirm their fear that the superpowers intended to fight World War III "to the last German."

These fears might not have been so pressing had relations between the superpowers not continued to deteriorate. In December 1981, the Polish government arrested the leaders of the independent trade union Solidarity and declared martial law. Since it was evident that Moscow stood behind this move, the Reagan administration quickly announced a new list of sanctions, including a ban on technology relating to the transport of oil and gas. The United States also made it clear that it expected its European allies to suspend their oil pipeline construction contracts with the Soviets. While the European governments joined in condemning the crackdown in Poland, they were unwilling to let this new crisis disrupt the pipeline project, on which a great deal of money and thousands of jobs depended. Moreover, they regarded Reagan's insistence on their compliance with U.S. policy as an invasion of their sovereign rights.

The worsening relations between the superpowers, in other words, were also straining relations between America and Western Europe. *Le Monde* editorialized that America's attempt to disrupt the pipeline project "had in fact done more damage to what [Reagan] wanted to strengthen—the cohesion of the Atlantic alliance—than to the Soviet Union which he wanted to punish." Helmut Schmidt declared that American policy had assumed a form that suggested "an end to friendship and partnership." Even Margaret Thatcher, whose government generally supported Reagan's hard line vis-à-vis the Soviets, declared herself "deeply wounded" by America's stance on the pipeline.

The Euromissile Controversy

Against this backdrop of East-West tension and squabbling between America and Western Europe, NATO continued with preparations for its two-track program to deploy Pershing II and Cruise missiles in Europe unless the Soviets eliminated their growing arsenal of SS-20s by the end of 1983. The Western European governments had approved this decision because they genuinely believed that their security was compromised by the Soviet missiles and hoped the threat of new NATO intermediate-range missiles would persuade the Russians to pull back their SS-20s. The governments in whose countries the missiles would be stationed (Britain, Holland, Belgium, Italy, and West Germany) hoped actual deployment would never take place, for they knew that many of their citizens were vehemently opposed to such a move.

Within months of the announcement of the NATO decision to go ahead with missile deployment, West European leaders were learning just how controversial this policy was. At the end of 1981, demonstrators took to the streets in London, Amsterdam, Bonn, Rome, and Madrid by the hundreds of thousands. They carried banners saying "We Are Not America's Guinea Pigs" and "Reagan's Peace Is Our Death." The only important Western European capital not to see such huge demonstrations was Paris, no doubt because no American missiles were to be stationed in France and also because the French had always been proud of their own nuclear weapons, which they saw as a symbol of sovereignty and independence from the United States. But even without significant French participation, the domestic campaign against the Euromissiles was, in the words of one commentator, "the most impressive display of populist muscle in the postwar era." The Reagan administration sought to dismiss the demonstrations as KGB-inspired, but while the Soviets certainly did everything to fan the flames of anti-Euromissile sentiment, there was no evidence that they had ignited them.

Two hundred thousand marchers protest the threat of nuclear war. This October 1983 demonstration in London was sparked by the plan to install American Cruise missiles in Western Europe.

Massive as they were, however, the populist protests did not prevent the deployment of the Pershing II and Cruise missiles, which went ahead as scheduled beginning in 1983. The actual installation of the missiles, moreover, yielded much smaller demonstrations than had the announcement of the decision to deploy them. Most significantly, the anti-Euromissile groups failed in their promise to bring down any government that went ahead with deployment. On the contrary, Kohl and Thatcher, both proponents of the NATO policy, won in the elections of 1983 (and again in 1987), while the Euromissile opponents remained in the political wilderness. In Italy, the Socialist Craxi government came to power as a firm advocate of the NATO buildup, and Mitterrand lost no popularity in France for insisting that the new missiles "restored the balance" in nuclear potency between East and West.

How does one explain the discrepancy between the European peace movement's impressive campaign in the streets and its anemic performance at the ballot box? In the first place, large popular demonstrations do not necessarily translate into majorities in elections; even when their impressive size captures headlines, their numbers are small compared to the voting public. The majority of Western Europeans clearly thought differently from the demonstrators when it came to security policy. Though generally not enthusiastic about the Cruise and Pershing II missiles, most Europeans were sufficiently alarmed by the "imbalance" in intermediate-range nuclear force (INF) weapons between East and West to see the new missiles as necessary if the Soviets did not scale back their own forces. The anti-Euromissile cause, moreover, had become associated in many people's minds with neutralism and opposition to NATO per se. Only a minority of Europeans wanted to see the breakup of NATO or the exodus of U.S. forces from the Continent. Important as the missile issue was, finally, it was not the key question for most voters in the elections of the mid-1980s. Poll after poll showed that economic issues were decisive, and the parties or politicians that seemed most able to promote prosperity enjoyed electoral success.

Return to Détente

In response to NATO's installation of Pershing II and Cruise missiles in Europe, the Soviets walked out of the arms control talks in Geneva in November 1983, vowing not to return unless the West stopped the missile deployment. NATO, in turn, vowed to continue the deployment process unless the Soviets dismantled their SS-20s. Yet this tough talk notwithstanding, both sides were under pressure to return to the bargaining table. Congress, complaining about the high cost of Reagan's arms buildup and sensing the American public's nervousness over the breakdown of détente, urged the administration to search for ways to resume negotiations. For their part, the Soviets gradually realized that their boycott of the negotiations had not, as they had hoped, either effectively mobilized the European peace movement against deployment or jeopardized Reagan's chances for reelection in 1984. They were also anxious to open discussions aimed at preventing further development of the American Strategic Defense Initiative (SDI, or "Star Wars"), President Reagan's high-tech program aimed at rendering offensive nuclear weapons "impotent and obsolete." Realizing that what Reagan had in mind was rendering Soviet weapons impotent and obsolete, the Russians faced the choice of either spending vast sums to counter this project or seeking to negotiate a stop to the "militarization of space." In spring 1984, Soviet Premier Konstantin Chernenko proposed new arms talks to begin in the fall. The United States accepted the proposal but insisted that the negotiations embrace strategic and intermediate-range weapons as well as space-based systems.

The superpowers did not resume arms control negotiations until March 1985, and then the negotiations did not go smoothly because the Soviets focused primarily on limiting space-based antimissile systems, while the Americans aimed at getting rid of intermediate-range missiles, including the Soviet SS-20s. In mid-1985, the Americans reacted unenthusiastically to a proposal by the new Soviet chief, Mikhail Gorbachev, to freeze intermediate-range missile systems at their existing level: NATO's Pershing II and Cruise deployment was only about 20 percent completed. Each side accused the other of not negotiating seriously and of violating existing treaties.

In October 1986, Reagan and Gorbachev met at Reykjavik, Iceland, for their first summit conference. In the course of this meeting Reagan suddenly declared his willingness to negotiate not only the removal of all INF missiles from Europe but also the elimination of all strategic nuclear weapons from the face of the earth. This proposal was not carried out because Reagan was unwilling to include SDI in the negotiations and Gorbachev was unwilling to leave it out.

Though the Reykjavik meeting produced no important agreements, roughly two months later the Soviets changed their position and indicated a willingness to accept the American agenda: they would concentrate on INF weapons independent of other systems, including SDI. In February 1987, Gorbachev announced that the Soviets would negotiate on the basis of America's zero solution, which foresaw the total elimination of medium-range nuclear weapons in Europe. At their summit in Washington in December 1987, Reagan and Gorbachev were able to sign the INF treaty providing for the dismantling of both classes of medium-range missiles (those with a range of one thousand to five thousand kilometers, and those with a five-hundred- to one-thousand-kilometer range). This double-zero solution also provided for extensive on-site verification procedures. Removal of the missiles was completed in 1988.

As soon as the INF treaty was announced, the NATO military leadership, which had opposed the double-zero solution on the ground that it would reduce the West's deterrent capacity, began pushing for the beefing up of NATO's short-range nuclear weapons to compensate for the loss of the Pershing IIs and Cruise missiles. They stressed in particular the need to replace aging Lance short-range missiles with weapons having a longer range and greater accuracy. While the

U.S. President Ronald Reagan greets Soviet leader Mikhail Gorbachev at the start of their talks in Reykjavik, Iceland.

American and British governments stood solidly behind this program, the West Germans, on whose territory most of the Lances were stationed, balked. They had never liked these weapons because if ever used, they would fall primarily on German territory. As one West German politician succinctly put it, "The shorter the range of the weapon, the deader the Germans." Though the proposed upgrading of the Lance system would extend the weapons' range beyond German territory—indeed would allow them to hit targets in the Soviet Union—that very fact made them a more likely magnet for Soviet weapons in the event of war.

Aware of his people's strong antipathy toward Lance modernization, Chancellor Kohl insisted on a postponement of this program, a demand that the Americans reluctantly accommodated for fear of undermining his position at home. The controversy, however, did not lose significance, for the West German foreign minister, Hans-Dietrich Genscher, broadened the German attack against short-range missile modernization to include the strategic argument used to justify it—namely, the proposition that the Soviet forces stationed in Eastern Europe continued to pose a significant threat to Western security. In taking the stance he did, Genscher transformed a technical debate within NATO into a deeper dispute about how the West should respond to the dramatic "peace offensive" being launched by Mikhail Gorbachev.

More specifically, NATO and the West were obliged to interpret and respond to such dramatic developments in early 1989 as the Soviet retreat from Afghanistan, the unilateral withdrawal of six Russian tank divisions from Eastern Europe, and Gorbachev's call for the total "denuclearization" of the Continent. While some in the Western camp—particularly in America, Britain, and France—remained suspicious of Gorbachev's motives and sincerity, others, especially in West Germany, believed that the Soviet turnabout offered an unprecedented diplomatic opportunity that must not be squandered. Arguing that the Russians' military retreats were the result of a fundamental shift to domestic priorities, Genscher insisted that NATO could and should scale back its own forces; it no longer needed to intimidate the Soviets with ever more elaborate armaments.

While neither Genscher nor any other Western leader questioned the legitimacy of NATO, the alliance faced a kind of mid-life crisis in the late 1980s as it approached the fortieth anniversary of its establishment (April 1949). At the very least, it would have to work harder to justify itself before a Western public that, like its Russian and Eastern European counterparts, was anxious to make fewer sacrifices for defense. It would have to be flexible enough to respond both to the challenge of Gorbachev and to growing pressures in the United States and in Western Europe to scale back commitments to the alliance. In essence, the question NATO faced at forty was, Could an organization created by the Cold War survive the Cold War's demise?

THE EUROPEAN ECONOMIC COMMUNITY: PLANNING FOR 1992

As NATO wrestled with its mid-life crisis, another postwar international organization, the European Economic Community (EEC), seemed on the ascendance. As the historian Paul Kennedy has pointed out, in the mid-1980s the EEC could be considered potentially the world's "fifth great power." With its new members, Spain and Portugal, the twelve-nation body now had a population totaling around 320 million, or 50 million more than the USSR and almost half again as many as the United States. This population was for the most part well educated and highly skilled. Many of the community's member states had higher per capita incomes than the United States, not to mention the USSR. With a combined GNP about equal to that of the United States and controlling more than a quarter of total world trade, the EEC constituted the world's largest trading block and richest consumer market.

Yet the EEC bloc could be considered only a potential great power because persisting internal disunity hampered its effectiveness. Disunity was particularly evident in the military realm, where diversity of languages, training, and equipment bedeviled attempts at coordinated planning and operations among some of the member states. At a joint Franco-German military exercise in 1987, for example, tank officers from the two nations had such difficulty understanding each other that they needed more than twenty minutes to agree on a single map reading. Maneuvers involving several nations' forces often seemed like a latter-day effort to build the Tower of Babel. The task of evolving common defense strategies was even more difficult, for the twelve members had different military traditions and strategic priorities: Ireland was neutral, France was an independent nuclear power (outside the NATO joint command), Britain was closely tied to the United States, and West Germany was required by international treaty to forgo the possession of strategic nuclear weapons and was prohibited (by one of its own constitutional provisions) from deploying troops outside Europe.

In the area of economic integration, the original and still-primary aim of the community, considerable progress had been made since the Common Market had been formed in 1957, but the EEC remained much less unified than sovereign states like the United States or Japan, its major competitors in world trade. Each member state had its own banking and fiscal system, credit regulations, taxation policies and currency. In the early to mid-1980s the so-called common frontiers inside the community still had many customs posts that inhibited the rapid passage of people and goods.

Persisting disunity within the EEC was particularly troubling because it was accompanied by a growing perception that Western Europe, still suffering in the early 1980s from high unemployment, relatively slow GNP growth (compared to America and Japan), and tardy development of new high-tech industries, was stagnating, perhaps even beginning to decline. There was much alarmist talk of "Eurosclerosis."

Widespread fears in the EEC that Western Europe might fall permanently behind the United States and Japan led to a movement at mid-decade to arrest the "rot" before it was too late. At the forefront of this movement was Jacques Delors, Mitterrand's former finance minister and president of the European Economic Community's Executive Commission. Arguing that it was a "question of survival or decline" for Europe, Delors lobbied his colleagues in the commission for the creation of a true "common market," a single economic entity fully free of the frontiers and hidden trade barriers that continued to impede the free passage of people, goods, services, and ideas within the community. Though not all EEC officials or political leaders in Western Europe were as enthusiastic as Delors about a "united Europe," the member states signed in 1985, and ratified in 1987, the Single European Act, which provided for the institutionalization of an internal European market by 1992.

Specifically, this act embraced three broad goals, only the first two of which were to be realized by 1992. First, it envisaged the end of frontier barriers impeding the flow of people and goods among member states; second, it called for the elimination of national rules and subsidies that allowed states to keep certain imports out of their domestic markets; and third, it contained a set of grand accompanying visions, including a common social policy designed to help the poorer peoples, the creation of a monetary union with a common currency and a central bank, and expanded cooperation in foreign and defense policy, a true "European Union."

Planning for the first phases of the 1992 program was extremely complicated since hundreds of new trade laws and tax regulations had to be written. But it was the Executive Commission's pursuit of the more far-reaching goals of monetary union, common social and environmental policies, and increased political cooperation that truly brought out second thoughts among some of the member states regarding the value of European unity. Though all Western European leaders had reservations of one sort or another (Germany's Kohl, for example, opposed a central bank because the West German Bundesbank might thereby lose the dominant role it played in the European monetary system), Britain's Thatcher soon made herself known as the most determined "reluctant European" in the community. She protested that the commission's plans would extend the community's competence into many areas that she believed were the proper prerogative of the national states. In particular she resisted the idea of a common currency since this would eliminate the autonomy of the pound. She also expressed concerns that a common European social policy might force Britain to reintroduce "through the back door" paternalist and welfare state policies she had worked so hard to eliminate. Nor did she welcome a common labor policy that would allow the commission in Brussels, rather than the national governments, to establish guidelines for wages and working conditions. As for the abolition of border controls, Thatcher protested that this would impede her nation's fight against drugs and terrorism as well as complicate its attempt to enforce immigration regulations that sharply limited the inflow of refugees.

If some EEC insiders like Margaret Thatcher had reservations about the move toward a united Europe, countries outside the community, notably Japan and the United States, had their concerns about this momentous step as well. Japan welcomed the prospect of another great market to conquer but feared that 1992 might make Europe less conquerable. America could hardly protest the movement toward a stronger and more unified Europe since this ideal had been its professed goal since the end of World War II. Yet the prospect of a less malleable Western partner—more self-interested in its economic policies and more self-willed in its attitude to foreign policy and defense—heightened existing worries in Washington regarding America's loss of leverage over its old allies. America's business community, meanwhile, wrung its hands over the possibility that the new single European market might erect high external tariffs to keep out foreign imports. A phobia concerning Fortress Europe took hold in the U.S. Trade Commission. Though the community's planners had not yet worked out an external trade policy by the late 1980s, they promised that the overall level of protection would not go up. The reassuring slogan was "Not fortress Europe, but partnership Europe." Belatedly Americans began to plan for the new era—for example, by enrolling in seminars on the economic and business implications of 1992. It was clear that with the rapid approach of that crucial date, a year in which Europe would celebrate both its new single market and the five-hundredth anniversary of Columbus's discovery of the New World, America could only hope that the New World and the Old would continue to work together as partners.

CHAPTER 15

A New Order in Eastern Europe

IF THE NATIONS of Western Europe betrayed a measure of restlessness with American tutelage in the 1980s, those of Eastern Europe rose up one after another at the end of the decade to throw off forty years of domination by Soviet-sponsored Communist regimes. The pent-up demand for thoroughgoing change was so strong that even significant concessions by backpedaling Communist governments only stimulated more radical demands. Reforms that would have seemed unbelievably generous as recently as 1988 were being dismissed as too little too late. The Soviet Union, which tolerated the reforms in hopes that they might make the Soviet bloc better able to compete with the West, became itself a victim of the dynamic of the reform process, which proved impossible to control or channel from above. Yet the transition to pluralistic democracy and market-based economics following the collapse of Communism also turned out to be difficult to manage, leaving many disillusioned citizens wondering whether the Western road was the right route to follow after all.

THE SOVIET UNION

Among the many ironies that attended the collapse of the Soviet Empire in Eastern Europe, perhaps the most striking was that the process started in the Soviet Union itself, with the startling reform campaign of President Mikhail Gorbachev. Yet sudden as Gorbachev's reforms seemed to many, there were certain precedents in previous Soviet regimes. At least in the immediate context, the proper beginning point for an understanding of Gorbachev's innovative administration is the reign of Leonid Brezhnev.

The Brezhnev Era

Brezhnev's eighteen-year rule (1964–1982) was the longest in Soviet history except for Stalin's. A burly Ukrainian of peasant stock, Brezhnev differed from Stalin in that he was not a tyrant who brutally imposed his personality and will on the Soviet people. He was a team player, a politician who sought to build consensus and continuity. Taking power after helping to oust the brash and impulsive Khrushchev, he was given a mandate to reimpose discipline, conformity, and stability in the Soviet system. Because he and his colleagues believed that Khrushchev's anti-Stalin campaign had generated a potentially dangerous critical spirit, the new regime undertook to rehabilitate Stalin's political legacy, although not his harshest policies. Brezhnev strengthened the Communist Party bureaucracy and the KGB and launched more systematic campaigns against political dissent and social nonconformity.

Though unimaginative, Brezhnev's rule registered some important successes. Soviet citizens enjoyed higher levels of education and health care than ever before. The government was able to combine slow but steady improvement in these areas with a dramatic military buildup and expansion of Russian strength around the world. Unlike Khrushchev, Brezhnev did not threaten brashly to "bury" the West, but his methodical arms buildup represented the most significant challenge to Western security since the Korean War.

Brezhnev's military expansion, however, was hardly an unmixed blessing for the Soviet Union. It required that the country allocate about twice as much of its GNP to defense purposes as did the United States, and this meant draining off money, manpower, and machinery from the civilian economy. So while Russia grew substantially in military stature, its civilian economy continued to lag well behind Western standards. Consumer goods taken for granted in the West, such as automobiles and refrigerators, were often almost impossible to obtain, and those goods that were available generally were shoddily made.

Soviet agriculture remained so weak that in the early 1970s the nation was obliged to import millions of tons of wheat and corn, much of it from America. (A century earlier Russia was one of the largest grain exporters in the world.) Agricultural production stagnated largely because Brezhnev continued to pursue the old Stalinist policies of collectivization and centralized planning. Soviet farmers neither owned the fields they worked nor decided what crops to plant or fertilizers to use; all decisions were made by distant bureaucrats struggling to meet centrally fixed five-year plans. Lack of flexibility also hampered progress in the industrial sector, especially in the high-technology fields that were so crucial to modern industrial expansion. Russia failed to develop a sophisticated computer industry, for example, largely because the government feared the free exchange of ideas and information that lay at the heart of the computer revolution. (Home computers and personal copying machines were illegal in the Brezhnev era.)

A regime that outlawed the personal ownership of copying machines and computers could not be expected to pursue a liberal cultural policy, and in this domain Brezhnev adhered to the old Stalinist approach. The relative openness of the Khrushchev era gave way to the reimposition of cultural orthodoxy and the repression (though not the mass liquidation) of dissenters of all stripes. Artists, scientists, and intellectuals whose works or ideas were deemed "anti-Soviet" found themselves in jail, confined to psychiatric hospitals, shipped off to the provinces, or forced into exile. The physicist Andrei Sakharov, father of Russia's hydrogen bomb and indefatigable campaigner for human rights, was sent away for six years to the provincial town of Gorky. Among the critics of the regime who were forced into exile were some of the country's most creative figures: the cellist Mstislav Rostropovich, the poet Josef Brodsky, the novelist Aleksandr Solzhenitsyn. Despite the regime's oppressive vigilance, however, dissenters continued to express their "subversive" views, sometimes openly in small demonstrations, more often clandestinely via *samizdat* ("self-published") books, magazines, and broadsheets that circulated underground. Sakharov's denunciations of the regime's abuses of human rights first appeared in this form.

As in the Stalinist period, Brezhnev's repression of dissent went hand in hand with government campaigns to promote public patriotism and reverence for Soviet institutions. The regime did all it could to keep alive memories of Russia's victory over Nazi Germany in World War II (and to warn the people that "Hitler's heirs," the West Germans, again posed a threat to Soviet security). Lenin, his mummified body perpetually on display in his tomb in Red Square, continued to be venerated as an almost holy figure. A new theme from the mid-1970s on was the cult of Brezhnev himself, who began to be celebrated in Stalinist fashion as "the Great Helmsman," a "great military leader," even a "great writer."

Yet all the glorification of Brezhnev and his supposed achievements could hardly disguise the fact that under the Great Helmsman the Soviet ship of state had drifted into a stagnant backwater from which it seemed incapable of extricating itself. By the end of the 1970s the economic situation had worsened significantly. Basic foodstuffs were in short supply, consumer goods were scarcer than ever, life expectancy declined, and infant mortality rose; still, the party leaders and state bureaucrats seemed concerned only with avoiding any changes that might threaten their own privileges. Little in the way of fresh thinking could be expected from members of the ruling Politburo, whose average age in 1980 was seventy. In Khrushchev's day there had been a strong measure of idealism, many Soviet citizens apparently believing both in the inherent superiority of Communism and in the prospects for "surpassing the West" in everything from military power to material comforts. In Brezhnev's last years this confidence was replaced by a widespread cynicism and hopelessness. Nobody believed the optimistic government statistics regularly printed in the state-run press. "*Pravda*," it was knowingly said, "lies in such a devious way that even the opposite isn't true." The one state-made item that did seem honest and true was vodka; its sales tripled between 1979 and 1982, the year Brezhnev finally died.

The Andropov-Chernenko Interregnum

The problems confronting the Soviet Union in the last years of Brezhnev's reign convinced many Soviet citizens of the need for a strong leader who was prepared to make fundamental changes in the prevailing system. Brezhnev had had considerable power, but he shrank from using it except to protect the status quo. When he died in November 1982, he was succeeded as general secretary of the party by the sixty-eight-year-old Yuri Andropov, a man who many believed was capable of at least beginning the process of social and political renovation. Though he had spent most of his career running the KGB and had served as ambassador to Hungary during the suppression of the uprising there in 1956, he was thought to be a flexible pragmatist who understood the need to reverse the stagnation and decline of the last Brezhnev years. His previous KGB career was considered an advantage in this regard because he owed few political favors to party bureaucrats and knew well where party skeletons were buried.

Shortly after coming to power, Andropov outlined his political agenda. He called for a partial decentralization of economic policy making, increased popular participation in economic decisions, improved managerial accountability, and a more disciplined work ethic.

To place himself in a position to pursue his agenda effectively, Andropov rapidly seized the main levers of power, becoming, in addition to general secretary of the party, chairman of the Supreme Soviet, chairman of the Defense Council, and commander in chief of the armed forces. He quickly cleared some of the Brezhnev-era deadwood from party and state offices, though the majority of bosses, from the Politburo on down, remained Brezhnev appointees. According to one Soviet expert, Andropov had amassed more real power after seven months in office than either of his predecessors had ever wielded. But at this point he suffered a heart attack, and for the remaining eight months of his life he was too sick to play an active role in the affairs of state, though he continued to hold titular power until he died in February 1984.

Andropov was succeeded by Konstantin Chernenko, a lackluster functionary who had never held a position of major responsibility. An expert in agitation and propaganda, he had slowly risen through the party ranks as an aide to Brezhnev, to whom he had clung like a barnacle. At the time of Andropov's death, Chernenko was seventy-three and suffering from a wide assortment of maladies, including emphysema. He wheezed through speeches that were vacuous even by the unexacting standards of traditional Soviet rhetoric. His appointment to the highest office in the land pointed up the shortcomings in the Soviet system of political succession. Apparently the older members of the Politburo pushed for his selection because he was "safe," while the younger members (that is, those under seventy) accepted him because they could not agree on an alternative from among their own ranks. Thus, Chernenko was picked as a stopgap figure, a lame-duck ruler who, it was hoped, might hold on just long enough for a capable successor to be groomed.

As it turned out, Chernenko proved to be an even lamer duck than his colleagues had imagined. He spent almost his entire time as chief of state either hospitalized in Moscow or resting in the Crimea. In foreign policy his major contribution was a push for new arms limitation talks with the United States, talks that he did not live to conduct himself. On the domestic front he tried to push the clock back a bit by throwing out some of Andropov's appointees and rehabilitating Molotov, Stalin's old foreign minister and obedient collaborator in the dictator's purges of the 1930s. Those Soviet citizens anxious for progressive change could only hope that Chernenko's many diseases would rapidly do their work. This they did in March 1985, hardly more than a year after he had taken office.

Gorbachev: Glasnost and Perestroika

In October 1985, seven months after Gorbachev had succeeded Chernenko as general secretary, the noted Sovietologist Peter Reddaway suggested that a "turning point" in Soviet history might be impending. But he asked cautiously, "Will the change, if it comes, be in the direction of reform, as present hints suggest, or of reaction?"

It was soon to become clear that the main direction under Gorbachev was reformist, but as the new leader began his herculean effort to transform Soviet society, questions remained whether he could effect deep and lasting changes and whether the very attempt to do so might not bring his abrupt fall from power. Certainly his task was daunting, for no Soviet leader since Stalin had managed to bend the unwielding state bureaucracy to his will, let alone transform it into an efficient instrument of social and economic modernization.

Yet if anyone had the potential to succeed in this effort, Gorbachev seemed to be that person. Born in 1931 of peasant parents in the northern Caucasus, he had won the Order of the Red Banner while still a teenager for his work on a mechanized tractor station, studied law at the University of Moscow, joined the Communist Party at age twenty, then climbed the party ladder faster than any Soviet leader of the post-Stalinist era. In 1978, he was brought from his home province to Moscow to become secretary of the Central Committee in charge of agriculture, one of the regime's most demanding assignments. Two years later, at age forty-nine, he became the youngest full member of that political geriatrics ward the Politburo. Within a few months after becoming party general secretary in March 1985, he was fully displaying those traits for which he became famous: vision, forceful personality, flexible mind, great energy, mastery of maneuver, and above all the ability—so rare in Soviet politicians—to speak persuasively to ordinary people, both at home and abroad.

The message that this young and dynamic man conveyed to the Soviet people was, however, by no means entirely new. Like Khrushchev thirty years before, and like Andropov more recently, he spoke of the need to get Soviet society moving, to improve economic performance, to end corruption high and low, to get ordinary people involved in the political process. The terms that he most frequently employed for his reformist agenda—glasnost (openness) and perestroika (restructuring)—had been used before by Soviet leaders.

Nevertheless, Gorbachev brought an intensity and seriousness to this undertaking that had not been seen since Khrushchev, and perhaps not even then. Most important, he showed he meant business by quickly getting rid of some of the more corrupt or incompetent regional party bosses; these men were not "honorably retired," as some miscreants had been under Andropov, but fired with full public disclosure of their misdoings. Though he was slow to move against aging conservatives in the Politburo, he managed to remove that symbol of the old era Andrei Gromyko from the foreign ministry and to bring in his own man, Eduard Shevardnadze. He also forced the archconservative chairman of the State Planning Commission (Gosplan) to retire.

Aside from these important personnel changes, Gorbachev quickly showed his commitment to reform by attacking one of the most stubborn and debilitating problems in Soviet society, alcoholism. This was no small undertaking, since drinking, *serious* drinking, had long been as important to the Russians as borscht and bathhouses. With drinking so common, the Russian state began to monopolize the production of vodka, a highly lucrative enterprise that continued in the Soviet era. The high rate of alcohol consumption severely undermined public health and economic efficiency, however. Earlier Soviet governments, including Stalin's and Khrushchev's, had halfheartedly tried to curb the Russian drinking habit, but with predictably little effect. Gorbachev mounted a more comprehensive attack, banning drinking on the job, limiting the number of state stores that sold alcohol and the hours in which they sold it, and significantly increasing the price of spirits. To set a sober example for his people, he even replaced vodka at state functions with mineral water, a policy that won him the not entirely complimentary epithet "Mineral Secretary."

Though the regime at first hailed the antialcohol campaign as a great success, it soon became apparent that it was anything but that. The reduced availability of state-produced vodka led to a massive increase in illegal home brewing of spirits. Alcohol-starved Russians also turned to various vodka surrogates, including liquid shoe polish, eau de cologne, glue, nail varnish, brake fluid, anti-freeze, cockroach poison, and a cattle growth stimulator called verosin. In 1987, some forty thousand Russians poisoned themselves (eleven thousand fatally) by drinking these surrogates. At the same time, the loss of tax revenues (some 49 billion rubles from 1985 to 1989) exacerbated the budget deficit. In 1989, though not formally conceding failure, the government reopened shuttered vodka stores, expanded hours of sale, and raised state production of alcoholic drinks. It seemed that the regime had belatedly realized that it could not effectively combat alcohol consumption through restrictive measures, a lesson it might have more easily learned by examining the Prohibition-era history of its Yankee rival.

Gorbachev's abortive antialcohol crusade was the first major social campaign launched under glasnost. The general secretary defined this term as follows: "The new atmosphere is perhaps most vividly manifested in *glasnost*. We want

In many ways, Gorbachey's leadership represented a break with the Soviet past.

more openness about public affairs in every sphere of life. Truth is the main thing. Lenin had said: More light! Let the party know everything. As never before, we need no dark corners where mold can reappear."

One moldy corner in which Gorbachev was determined to shine the light of revelation was the Stalinist past, whose abuses he believed must be openly confronted if the Soviet Union was to move forward. He therefore reopened the critical investigation of the Stalinist era that Khrushchev had begun and Brezhnev had closed. In a much-anticipated speech commemorating the seventieth anniversary of the Bolshevik Revolution, Gorbachev spoke of Stalin's "enormous and unforgivable crimes . . . for which our people paid a heavy price and which had grave consequences for the life of our society." At the same time, however, he said that "historical truth" required the recognition of Stalin's "incontestable contribution to the struggle for socialism, to the defense of its gains." Gorbachev was, in other words, willing to criticize Stalin's "excesses" but not the system of Communist control that he had built up.

Tentative and cautious though it was, Gorbachev's anniversary speech was interpreted by some of his countrymen as an invitation to denounce Stalin and his system in clearer terms. Journalists, historians, novelists, playwrights, and filmmakers began openly attacking the Stalinist heritage. "Everyone is sick of silence," says the narrator of the anti-Stalinist film *More Light*. "We are going to try to talk about the past with more honesty, more light."

But not everyone wanted more light. Conservative party leaders who had made their careers in the Brezhnev era were understandably reluctant to see Brezhnev's patron Stalin vilified as a betrayer of the Bolshevik Revolution. For such stalwarts of the old order, criticism of Stalin amounted to "playing into the hands of bourgeois historiography." More ominously from their point of view, it might also encourage attacks on present authority and on the "traditional values" and social norms they held dear. This threat seemed all the more genuine because Gorbachev indeed encouraged critical discussion of present problems in the Soviet system. Intellectual groups were allowed to organize and bring forth new ideas. Dissidents like Sakharov were released from prison and encouraged to take part in the debate. The regime stopped jamming foreign radio stations, tolerated street demonstrations, and even allowed a small counterculture, replete with long-haired kids and rock music, to develop in an old Moscow district called the Arbat.

Glasnost might have generated less controversy in the Soviet Union if it had inspired only intellectuals, artists, and long-haired kids to challenge the traditional order. By the late 1980s, however, non-Russian ethnic groups along the country's borders were taking the new policy as an invitation to express, often with extreme violence, long-repressed nationalist and religious resentments. Christian Armenians, for example, fought pitched battles with Islamic Azerbaijanis in a vain effort to force the assimilation into Armenia of Nagorno-Karabach, an Armenian enclave in Azerbaijan, a Soviet republic bordering the Caspian Sea and Iran. In Uzbekistan, Crimean Tatars whose ancestors had been deported to that Central Asian republic by Stalin during World War II were fighting for their lives against the Uzbekis, who had never accepted the Tatars' presence in their homeland. These conflicts were unnerving to Soviet authorities because they showed that old ethnic, religious, and semitribal loyalties and traditions had hardly been touched by decades of "rationalistic Communism." What made matters worse, in the eyes of the traditionally dominant ethnic Russians, was that the Asian and Islamic populations were growing much faster than their own; Russian demographers were speaking ominously of a "yellowing" of the Soviet Union.

Equally threatening to the internal viability of the Soviet Union were the nationalist aspirations of the Baltic states, Georgia, and Ukraine. In the Baltic provinces (Estonia, Latvia, and Lithuania), local nationalists looked back nostalgically to these states' brief independence between the wars. Far from welcoming their inclusion in the Soviet state, they deeply resented Russian control, particularly in the economic and cultural spheres. In the late 1980s, the Baltic provinces demanded, and received, considerable autonomy in these areas. Matters did not end there, however, for the most militant nationalists wanted complete independence. The Estonian parliament passed laws aimed at disenfranchising the ethnic Russian workers who lived in that state; the Russian workers responded by going on strike. In Lithuania, where 80 percent of the population was Catholic and Lithuanian-speaking, the local Communist Party separated itself from the Soviet Party, and nationalist leaders announced their intention to take Lithuania out of the Soviet Union. On March 11, 1990, the republic formally declared its independence. In Stalin's native province, nationalists gathered in the streets of the capital and waved the red, black, and white flag of the short-lived independent republic of Georgia. When Soviet troops intervened, killing some twenty civilians, the people shouted, "Invaders, go home," and called for the breakup of the Russian Empire.

Though conservative critics of glasnost in the Soviet Union complained that this policy was fostering dangerous liberal-democratic attitudes and threatening centralized control, the new "openness" also allowed extreme antiliberal, anti-Semitic, and antidemocratic forces to come to the fore and make their voices heard. Neo-Stalinists associated with the magazine *Sovyetskaya Rossiya* attacked Gorbachev and his reformist allies for undermining respect for the party and encouraging a heretical belief in "the intrinsic value of the individual." Extreme Russian nationalists, who found their historic models in the anti-Western Slavophiles and proto-Fascist Black Hundreds of the late nineteenth century, revived old campaigns against "foreign forces" allegedly plotting the destruction of traditional Russian culture. They included among these "alien" forces native Jews, who after decades of discrimination and persecution were finally receiving important new freedoms under Gorbachev, including the right to open Jewish cultural centers and rabbinical schools and to teach Jewish history. Deeply resenting this official liberalization and complaining that the Jews were "over-represented" in Soviet culture, a right-wing Russian group called Pamyat ("Memory") demanded that Jews be excluded from Soviet universities, scientific academies, and cultural institutions. Fearing that the upsurge of grassroots anti-Semitism, which included anti-Jewish pogroms in some Soviet cities, was a more significant sign of the times than the government's official policy of toleration, an ever-larger number of Soviet Jews began to leave the country. In the first eleven months of 1989, 62,504 Jews had emigrated, breaking the previous annual record of 51,333 set in 1979. Some five hundred thousand more applied for permission to emigrate. This was hardly welcome news for Gorbachev, since many of the departing Jews were trained professionals whose skills would have been invaluable in reforming the economy.

Although Gorbachev, an ethnic Russian himself, hardly envisaged the destruction of all things Russian, his glasnost policy *was* meant to make the hidebound Soviet society, economy, and political system more amenable to "restructuring," the second dimension of his reformist agenda. The ambitiousness and complexity of this perestroika program were such that Gorbachev embarked on

Anti-Soviet rally outside the Catholic cathedral in Vilnius, Lithuania, January 1990.

it only after considerable preparation. But like a twentieth-century Peter the Great, he was determined to revamp the Russian state as quickly as possible so that it might effectively compete with the West, as well as with Japan and China, the latter another Communist state increasingly committed to private initiatives in the economy. What was at stake, he said, was nothing short of the "ability of the Soviet Union to enter the new millennium in a manner worthy of a great and prosperous power." The chief impediment to this goal, Gorbachev believed, was his country's hypercentralized system of economic management and planning. In early 1987, he announced plans to scale back the control over the economy wielded by top-heavy state corporations, or ministries. Their functions would be delegated in part to smaller "socialist-market" cooperatives and private family businesses. Gorbachev also began to open the Soviet economy more extensively to foreign investment, joint ventures, and Western consumer goods.

Like glasnost, these efforts at economic restructuring occasioned bitter resistance from conservative elements in the party and bureaucratic elite, who understandably saw in them a threat to their traditional powers and privileges. One of the leaders of the anti-Gorbachev resistance, Yegor Ligachev, attacked Gorbachev's radical reform aspirations as irresponsible and unsocialist. The party and bureaucratic cadres that Ligachev represented strove to thwart Gorbachev's restructuring by doing what bureaucracies always do best: digging in their heels and strangling innovation in red tape.

Substantial economic modernization was also thwarted by the resistance of millions of average Soviet workers to the challenges of perestroika. Though virtually everyone wanted more and better consumer goods and services, they also wanted full employment, state subsidies, controlled prices, and the benefits of the welfare state. Many citizens, moreover, were deeply suspicious of an "incentive" or "risk" economy that allowed some people to fare much better than others. Nor were the employees and managers in most state-run industries oriented toward "quality" production, profitability, and a disciplined work ethic. "They pretend to pay me, and I pretend to work" was the Soviet adage with which all too many remained comfortable. No wonder, then, that the state industries and agricultural collectives continued to founder while the much smaller "second economy," the black-market and moonlighting economy, produced those goods and services that people actually wanted to buy. But such goods and services—for example, well-made suits or competent repair work—remained in painfully short supply, and the problem of shortages was aggravated by the government's partial curtailment of subsidies to state industries and agriculture. Thus, under Gorbachev the Soviet consumer economy actually got worse rather than better. This presented great dangers to the government since the normally patient Soviet people had come to expect rapid improvements under their dynamic new leader. Gorbachev himself well understood this, declaring that "people will judge our policies . . . by tomorrow's tangible results." By the late 1980s, the lack of tangible results was already leading to widespread strikes in the Soviet coal industry, which the government had to settle with massive wage increases it could ill afford. Some observers, both Soviet and Western, were beginning to ask how many "tomorrows" Gorbachev would have.

Impatience with the rate of change in the Soviet Union was also evident at the political level. As part of his "restructuring" of the Soviet system, Gorbachev liberalized the process by which delegates were elected to the Congress of People's Deputies, the Soviet parliament. In the elections of March 1989, many voters took advantage of the new rules to elect Communist dissidents or even non-Communists to the congress. When the new parliament assembled in May, hundreds of delegates attacked the government for moving too slowly (or in some cases too quickly) with its reforms. Boris Yeltsin, the maverick boss of the Moscow party apparatus, became a popular hero through his attacks on party privilege and corruption. Roughly a year later, in March 1990, the Congress of People's Deputies voted to end the constitutional guarantee of the Communist Party's monopoly of power. Responding to the party's growing enfeeblement, Gorbachev shifted his power base to the new office of president, to which he was elected by the congress, not by the people. Some observers believed that Gorbachev could not have won a popular election to this office. It seemed, in other words, that Gorbachev's "revolution from above" might be turning willy-nilly into a "revolution from below." Gorbachev, it was suggested, resembled the proverbial "sorcerer's apprentice" who could not control the wild forces he had set in motion.

EXIT GORBACHEV, ENTER YELTSIN

In terms of the Soviet Union's viability, the devastating implications of Gorbachev's revolution became dramatically evident over the course of 1991. The rambling structure that Lenin and Stalin had built crumbled like a house of cards as one republic after another defected from the union and declared itself independent. The Baltic states—Latvia, Lithuania, and Estonia—were the first to bolt, not surprisingly given their long-standing resentment over having been forcefully absorbed into the Russian Empire in the first place. In a brutal effort to reverse the defection, pro-Moscow Communists, backed by Soviet tanks, attacked the main communications center in Vilnius, Lithuania, whose parliament had declared independence as early as March 1970. Lithuania's parliament building emerged as a vibrant symbol of national resistance when ordinary citizens barricaded themselves in the compound and constructed antitank barriers around it. On the wall they painted such slogans as "Gorby, hell is waiting for you!" and "The Red Army is Red Fascism."

The Baltic republics' example was soon followed by other Soviet states, including Byelorussia (which took the name Belarus), Georgia, Moldavia (which became Moldova), Ukraine, Armenia, Azerbaijan, and the Central Asian republics of Uzbekistan, Kirghizia, and Tadzhikistan. In each case, declarations of independence were accompanied by outpourings of popular enthusiasm. The speed with which the Soviet structure collapsed pointed up its weak foundations and lack of ideological mortar. As the distinguished Sovietologist Dimitri K. Simes noted, "Despite a seventy-year effort by the Soviet propaganda machine, the people of the USSR were never successfully socialized to believe themselves to be citizens of one great multiethnic country. The USSR was able to create Homo Sovieticus only to the extent that the inhabitants of the territory of the Soviet Union were raised as obedient subjects of a repressive totalitarian state."

Russia itself, the backbone of the Soviet Empire, played a crucial role in dismantling the system. In June 1991, Boris Yeltsin was elected to the newly created office of president of the Russian Federation. He was the first leader in Soviet history to come to power by a popular vote. His burly physique, autocratic style, and weakness for vodka made him seem at first glance like a throwback to Brezhnev, but in reality he was as radical as Gorbachev, indeed more so. Gorbachev, after all, remained a believer in the Soviet Union and Communism even as his reforms undermined them; Yeltsin, while loyal enough to the system in his early career as an apparatchik in the Urals region, gradually came to see both the party and the union as lost causes. Having resigned from the Central Committee in October 1987, he worked his way back to political prominence by pursuing a Russia first agenda within the union. Gorbachev's weak leadership had created a political vacuum that Yeltsin was more than happy to fill. In June 1990, the parliament of the Russian Federation, at Yeltsin's instigation, voted to suspend "acts of the USSR which contradict the sovereign rights of the RSFSR [Russian Federation]." One year later Yeltsin's government banned the Communist Party throughout the Russian Federation. Gorbachev fumed that Yeltsin was "acting like a tsar," but he was unable to reassert his authority over his Russian rival.

Not surprisingly, Gorbachev's inability to prevent Russia and other republics from going their own way alarmed hard-line Communists, who believed he was in league with Yeltsin to destroy the Soviet system. When Gorbachev flew down to his retreat in the Crimea for a much-needed vacation in August 1991, a cabal of hard-liners back in Moscow staged a coup in hope of restoring the territorial and ideological integrity of the Soviet Union. To prevent Gorbachev from acting against the coup, the rebels dispatched emissaries to the Crimea to hold him incommunicado in his vacation hideaway. However, while the coup leaders were successful in keeping Gorbachev out of the picture, they could not similarly isolate Yeltsin. Alerted to the coup while playing tennis at his dacha outside Moscow, Yeltsin immediately rushed into town and broadcast an appeal for popular resistance to the coup. As his call for help went out, he took up position in the "White House" (the popular name for the Russian parliament building), which was soon surrounded by volunteer defenders from

Boris Yeltsin delivering a speech against the abortive anti-Gorbachev coup attempt of August 1991.

the populace. In a famous gesture that greatly strengthened the spirit of the defenders, Yeltsin boldly emerged from his parliamentary bunker to confront personally a column of tanks that the putschists had ordered to attack the building. While members of the crowd argued with the tank crews, Yeltsin climbed up on one of the tanks and waved the white, blue, and red tricolor that had been Russia's flag before the 1917 revolution. Faced now with the choice of trying to recruit new troops to support their cause or backing down, the rebels chose the latter alternative. Savoring his victory, Yeltsin sent a plane to the Crimea to bring Gorbachev back to Moscow. As the plane took off for the capital, Gorbachev observed, "We are flying into a new era." He had no idea how right he was.

The August 1991 coup turned out to be the last gasp of the old Soviet system. In trying to oust Gorbachev, the putschists succeeded only in ensuring the final victory of Yeltsin and the other dissident republican leaders, who were determined to bring down the Soviet Union once and for all. The Soviet president watched helplessly as the republics drifted away. On the day Ukraine declared its independence, August 24, Gorbachev resigned as head of the Communist party and disbanded its executive body, the infamous Central Committee. Upon vacating their headquarters in central Moscow, members of the committee were jeered by citizens shouting, "Shame, shame." It was an ignominious end for an institution that had ruthlessly ruled for almost three-quarters of a century. The oppressive severity of that rule of course was the main reason the system died with hardly a whimper of regret from the masses in whose name the party had exercised its iron control. Only later, when the new order proved fraught with horrors of its own, did some wax nostalgic for the "good old days" of Communist rule.

By the end of 1991, the USSR was in a state of such rapid decomposition that the only reasonable course of action was to bury it. Gorbachev, who clung tenaciously to his position of Soviet president, was not given the role of undertaker because he refused to recognize that the body was dead. Without so much as consulting him, Yeltsin, along with the leaders of Ukraine and Belarus, met near Minsk (in Belarus) on December 8, 1991, to draw up the USSR's death certificate and to draft the birth document for the Commonwealth of Independent States (CIS), the loose federation of autonomous entities that was supposed to fill the vacuum left by the defunct Soviet Union. Shortly thereafter, on Christmas Day, Gorbachev resigned as president of the USSR. That evening the Soviet flag was hauled down from the Kremlin for the last time and the tricolor of Yeltsin's Russia was hoisted up in its place.

THE RETURN TO DIVERSITY
IN EASTERN EUROPE

Well before the Soviet Union itself collapsed, the USSR's Eastern European empire had begun to fall apart as the various satellite states threw off the control of Communist regimes that Moscow was no longer willing to defend against growing domestic opposition. This opposition was inspired in part by Gorbachev's own reform program in the Soviet Union. Moreover, by abandoning the Brezhnev doctrine, which strictly limited the sovereignty of the satellite states, and emphasizing instead the right of the various countries to find "their own paths to socialism," Gorbachev encouraged Eastern European reformers to believe that their efforts would not be crushed by Soviet tanks. This meant that the various countries could and would respond differently to the new possibilities opened up by Gorbachev and that the responses would reflect national differences and strategies that preceded the Gorbachev reign. In short, the new era allowed a return to diversity in Eastern Europe, a development that was both exciting and full of challenges.

High Noon in Poland

The breathtaking changes that occurred in Poland in 1989—the legalization of the free trade union movement Solidarity, the overwhelming victory of non-Communists in the country's first semifree elections of the postwar era, the installation of the East bloc's first non-Communist government—were made

ATLANTIC
OCEAN

THE FALL OF COMMUNISM
IN EUROPE 1989–1991

Communist governments fall

SWEDEN
FINLAND
NORWAY
RUSSIA
NORTH SEA
ESTONIA
EAST GERMANY
LATVIA
DENMARK
LITHUANIA
Moscow
BALTIC SEA
NETHERLANDS
RUSSIA
Berlin Gdansk Warsaw BERLARUS
POLAND
Bonn Leipzig Prague
WEST GERMANY CZECHOSLOVAKIA
UKRAINE
KAZAKHSTAN
Vienna Budapest
MOLDOVA
SWITZ. AUSTRIA HUNGARY
ROMANIA
ITALY YUGOSLAVIA Timisoara
ADRIATIC SEA Belgrade Bucharest
BULGARIA BLACK SEA
Sofia
Rome ALBANIA GEORGIA ARMENIA
CASPIAN SEA
TURKEY
GREECE AEGEAN SEA AZERBAIJAN
MEDITERRANEAN SEA
SYRIA IRAN
IRAQ

possible by Gorbachev's new dispensation in East European affairs, but they
were set in motion by the unrest that gripped Poland at the beginning of the decade. Frustrated by decades of repression and economic stagnation under corrupt, incompetent, arrogant Communist functionaries, Polish workers launched
a series of nonviolent strikes in the summer of 1980. The center of the strike
movement was the huge Lenin shipyard in Gdańsk (formerly Danzig), which
was taken over by workers under the leadership of an electrician named Lech
Wałęsa. The workers demanded that the government permit the establishment
of independent trade unions with officials elected by the members. The actions
of the Gdańsk workers were received with great enthusiasm by all social strata.
Academics began to work as advisers to Solidarity, and many members of the
Catholic Church openly showed their sympathy. Church support was especially
significant, for the church enjoyed tremendous influence in Poland. Catholicism was closely intertwined with Polish nationalism, a tie reawakened and reinforced by Pope John Paul II, the first Polish pope in Vatican history, who paid an
emotional visit to his homeland in 1979. Among the results of the cooperation

between the church and workers in 1980–1981 were live radio broadcasts of Catholic masses, until then forbidden.

The support for Solidarity's demands was so overwhelming that the government gave in and on August 31, 1980, reached an agreement with the workers. The chief provision of the agreement was permission to "create new union organizations which will run themselves and which will be authentic expressions of the working class". The agreement stipulated that the new independent unions would not "play the role of a political party" and that they would "recognize the leading role of the Polish United Workers Party [the Communist Party] in the state and will not oppose the existing system of international alliances." The distinction between economic and political functions insisted upon by the government was, to say the least, ambiguous in a socialist state where the direction of economic life was a central function of government.

Strife over the meaning of this agreement kept Poland in turmoil during the following year, which was marked by frequent changes in the government and the party and by numerous local strikes. The workers demanded a five-day week and better pay, whereas the government insisted that workers intensify their efforts by working Saturdays and suspending strikes throughout the winter. In the course of this continuing debate, Solidarity's demands went beyond economics into politics. Among them were calls for free elections and a relaxation of restrictions on foreign travel. The government, which from February 1981 was led by a former defense minister, General Wojciech Jaruzelski, also stiffened in its attitude and began using troops to break up local strikes. In December 1981, the crisis reached its high point when Solidarity's leadership demanded a part in running the economy. The government responded by declaring martial law, suspending civil rights, forbidding union activity, imprisoning union leaders, and giving full power to a military council. The strikes that broke out spontaneously in protest against the declaration of martial law were quickly crushed by military force. Though no Soviet tanks were involved in this repression, it was clear to all that the Soviets stood solidly behind the Polish government's brutal crackdown.

For the next eight years Poland stagnated economically and politically. In 1988 the national product per capita was 13 percent lower than in 1978. Inflation ran close to 100 percent a year. Poland's indebtedness to Western banks reached such heights that the government could not meet its annual interest obligations and had to request deferrals of payment. These were granted because the banks had no real choice; they had lent Poland so much money that they could not afford to let the country go under. But such debtor's leverage was about the only leverage the Polish government had. It was attacked by Western governments and the majority of its own citizens for toeing the Soviet line, yet it was not really trusted by Brezhnev and his immediate successors, who believed it was not repressive enough vis-à-vis "anti-Soviet" and "antisocialist" elements. Indeed, the Polish government was not a very effective censor, succeeding only in pushing Solidarity and other dissident voices underground, where they continued

Lech Wałęsa speaking to fellow strikers at the Lenin Shipyards, Gdańsk, August 1980.

to speak out almost as loudly as during the brief "opening" in 1980 and 1981. The church, which the government could hardly ban or even effectively muzzle, became more than ever a focus of oppositionist culture and (to a lesser degree) dissident politics.

A prominent historian of Eastern Europe suggested in the mid-1980s that the Polish situation resembled a stalemate in chess: the regime could not obtain legitimacy from the downtrodden but still defiant people, while the huge dissident community could not translate its considerable potential into actual power. A chance to break the stalemate arose when Gorbachev appeared on the scene in the Soviet Union and urged reform not only in his own country but in other East bloc states as well. He seemed particularly anxious to foment change in Poland, sensing in Jaruzelski a possible ally against the old-line Stalinists in East Germany, Czechoslovakia, Romania, and Bulgaria. This assessment proved well founded. The Polish government was fairly quick to follow the Soviet leader's example; in November 1987 it held a referendum asking Poles to approve a series of radical economic reforms, including price increases. When the voters, showing their continuing contempt for the government, roundly rejected the referendum, the government proceeded to institute the price increases by fiat. This brought a wave of strikes, centered in Nova Huta and Gdańsk, in spring 1988. The government broke the strikes with military force, but it was clear that the workers, who were demanding above all the relegalization of Solidarity, would not stay down for long. They went out on strike again in August, forcing the government this time to invite Solidarity leader Lech Wałęsa to Warsaw for "peace talks."

Though this was a hopeful sign, no one could have predicted that these so-called round-table negotiations would within two months produce agreements to legalize Solidarity and hold free elections. But for these government concessions the opposition paid a price: the elections would be held immediately, giving Solidarity's political wing little time to prepare for them, and 65 percent of the seats in the lower house of parliament would be reserved for the Communists and their allies regardless of the election results. Many in Solidarity thought this was too high a price for official acceptance of the union.

Nevertheless, Solidarity threw itself wholeheartedly into the campaign, staging dozens of rallies and plastering the larger cities with posters showing (oddly enough) Gary Cooper striding resolutely forward, ballot in hand, the Solidarity emblem affixed to his vest above his sheriff's star, and underneath the slogan, "High Noon in Poland, 4 June 1989." Solidarity's electoral slogan, "With us you're safer," was perhaps less inspired, but it probably would not have mattered what slogans Solidarity employed, for most Poles were as anxious to vote against the government as for the opposition. The results showed that Solidarity won ninety-nine out of one hundred seats in the new Senate and all but one of the seats it was allowed to contest in the lower house.

The same day the Polish people were voting so decisively against their Communist government, China's Communist bosses were brutally crushing the vast prodemocracy demonstrations in Beijing. The Poles, who had seen their earlier bids for freedom snuffed out by either the Soviets or their own government, could not help wondering if Warsaw's Victory Square, where Solidarity supporters gathered to celebrate their triumph, might not soon resemble Beijing's Tiananmen Square. But instead of resorting to repression, the Polish government, unable to put together a new cabinet acceptable to Solidarity, simply turned the reins over to the opposition forces. The new prime minister, Tadeusz Mazowiecki, was the personal selection of Lech Wałęsa. General Jaruzelski was appointed president by the lower house of parliament, but much of the power had passed to Solidarity and its allies.

The significance of the moment was perhaps best captured by a magazine cartoon that showed two Solidarity officials in the cockpit of an airliner handing the plane's steering wheel over to Wałęsa. "It took some doing," one says, "but she's all yours." The "plane" that Solidarity took over in August 1989 may not have been entirely bereft of controls, but its passengers were certainly in for some rough flying. The economy, weak for decades, was in worse shape than ever. The zloty declined dramatically in value as the government desperately tried to cover its debts by printing more currency. Curtailment of government price subsidies and regulations led to a huge jump in commodity prices, though in many cases this was irrelevant because the goods simply were not available. Increasingly, Polish workers took time off from work to hustle around for hard (Western) currency and to trade on the black market. Of course the decline in productivity resulting from this behavior worsened the shortages of essential goods and services. It became not unusual to see well-dressed Poles rooting in Dumpsters for food. No wonder Poles began to leave their country in droves. In 1988, more doctors emigrated than were trained in all the country's medical schools that year. The only factor that kept the exodus from becoming truly massive was the unwillingness of Western countries to grant more visas to Poles (the so-called golden curtain).

Poland's new non-Communist leaders hoped to turn the economy around by throwing off the socialist straitjacket in favor of a competitive free market. This would hardly be easy, given Poland's lack of a convertible currency, investment banks, credit analysts, and a stock exchange. Though some entrepreneurs might profit from the transition phase, millions of other Poles would find themselves out of work when their decrepit factories, some of which resembled museums of the Industrial Revolution, had to close because they could not compete. Would the unemployed workers, comparing their own lot with that of the nouveau riche minority, remain enthusiastic about Solidarity, or would they turn to Solidarity's chief rival, the populist, anticapitalist union called the OPZZ?

As it happened, neither Solidarity nor its chief rival prevailed in the post-Communist era. The dissidents who led the resistance to Communist control themselves became victims of the travails attending the difficult transition to democracy and capitalism. Solidarity lost the parliamentary elections of October 27, 1991, the first truly democratic elections in Poland since before World War II. Solidarity's charismatic leader, Lech Wałęsa, retained the Polish presidency he had assumed in late 1990, but he became increasingly isolated, in part the result of his own megalomania and conceit. As Solidarity dissolved into a welter of feuding factions, its symbolic home, the Gdańsk shipyard, proved unable to compete in the capitalist marketplace and had to be liquidated in 1996. Meanwhile an institution that in the late 1980s seemed headed for the historical museum—namely, Polish Communism—reasserted itself in the 1990s to the degree that a reformed version of the old Communist Party could capture control of the presidency (ousting Wałęsa) in 1995. Deeply disillusioned, Wałęsa blamed the West for his own fall and for Poland's difficulties. "The West encouraged us to abolish the old system, but they had nothing to replace it with," he complained. "We're left with Communist rubble, the shipyards, mines and steelworks. We were failed by Western politicians. They are responsible for our misfortunes."

The New Hungarian Revolution

At the beginning of 1989 Poland and Hungary stood more or less alone among the Eastern and Central European states as apostles and practitioners of radical reform. Developments in the two countries were in many respects similar. Beginning in the late 1980s, both combined attacks on their Communist heritage with efforts to revive older nationalistic traditions. Both joined praise for Gorbachev's reforms in the Soviet Union with campaigns to throw off the "Russian yoke" once and for all. Both hoped to cure severe economic ills with strong doses of free market capitalism and infusions of Western investment. Both embarked on rapid, though peaceful, transitions from one-party rule to multiparty democracy—or something close to it. But there was one big difference between the Hungarian and the Polish cases: Hungary had no Solidarity; the initiatives to transform (or to abandon) Communism there came primarily from the Hungarian Communist Party itself.

Under János Kádár, who had assumed control over Hungary after the Soviets crushed the rebellion of 1956, the nation enjoyed a measure of economic prosperity and cultural freedom. During the 1970s it was more open to the West than any of the other Soviet satellite states. But by the late 1980s Kádár, now in his seventies, was not keeping up with demands for political change and economic liberalization. Like his counterparts in East Germany, Czechoslovakia, Romania, and Bulgaria, who were all of the same vintage, Kádár tried to keep Hungary from emulating Gorbachev's reformist example. In May 1988, a group of young "liberals" within the Socialist Workers (or Communist) Party called a special party conference and managed to kick Kádár upstairs to the newly created and largely ceremonial post of party chairman. His entire inner circle was also expelled. The old guard was replaced first with a single leader, the centrist Károly Grósz, and then, in June 1989, with a four-man presidium including two radical reformers. This so-called Gang of Four agreed to lead the party until the next regular party congress was held in October 1989.

Its new leadership launched Hungary into the vanguard of Communist "reform from above." In May 1989, Grósz had ordered the dismantling of the barbed wire and detection devices along Hungary's border with Austria, a move that inspired hundreds of East Germans vacationing in Hungary to flee to the West. In another, more symbolic dismantling operation, the Hungarian government cleared away the old Communist dogma that the uprising of 1956 had been a "counterrevolution" inspired by the West. Instead, the government admitted that it had been a "popular uprising" against Soviet control, an admission similar in import to the new Polish government's official declaration that the thousands of Polish officers killed during World War II at the Katyn Forest had been murdered by the Russians, not the Germans. To reinforce its rehabilitation of the 1956 uprising, the Hungarian government retrieved the body of the executed rebel leader Imre Nagy from an unmarked grave near Budapest and reinterred it in a stately tomb during an emotional public funeral. Shortly thereafter, on the anniversary of the uprising, a hundred thousand Hungarians assembled outside the parliament building (atop which the huge red star was no longer illuminated) to chant, "Russians go home!" and (somewhat inconsistently) "Gorby! Gorby!"

In fact, however, Gorbachev was already passé as a model for Hungarian reform. In spring 1989, the government started permitting independent opposition parties to form and announced free parliamentary elections for the following year. The Communist Party's leadership well understood that it might totally lose power in these elections if it did not undergo an internal transformation. Poland, after all, had shown what could happen to a Communist party that did not change with the times. The Hungarian party hoped to avoid the fate of its Polish counterpart and stay aloft after the first free elections by unloading as much Communist ballast as possible. At their historic congress in October 1989 the Communists changed their name to the Hungarian Socialist Party and spent much of the time denouncing their old organization as a "state party" that would have to become thoroughly "democratic" to survive. Not "Soviet brotherhood" but "Europe" was the party's new code word.

Nevertheless, many Hungarians remained skeptical about the genuineness of their leaders' conversion to democracy. Remembering that prewar Budapest had boasted clinics that promised to restore women's virginity, the Hungarian people wondered if the party was not touting an equally credible operation. Yet partially burdened with the ballast of the past as they remained, Hungary's Communists did have one advantage over their Polish counterparts: They faced a non-Communist opposition that was fragmented into a number of rival parties. Many of these opposition parties pushed the revival of Hungarian nationalism, an enterprise often no more liberal or democratic than similar nativist campaigns in Poland and Russia. In their effort to reclaim their national culture, they distinguished between "real Hungarians" and "cosmopolitans" (i.e., Jews). They found another outlet for pent-up nationalism in mass protests against neighboring Romania's oppression of ethnic Hungarians living in that state. Once freed from the constraints of "socialist brotherhood" imposed by the Soviet Union, Hungarians could let their true feelings toward their neighbors come to the fore. In this they were not alone, for other East bloc peoples were also discovering that freedom to express their national identities could also mean freedom to reassert old national hatreds.

If there were problematical aspects to the reemergence of nationalism in Eastern Europe, there was also a darker side to the Hungarians' (and the Poles') efforts to revive their ailing economies with free market capitalism and Western investment. To the degree that the transition was possible at all, the local people most likely to profit from the conversion to private enterprise were the very ones who had mismanaged the old socialist system. This was because conversion regulations gave the initiative for private buyouts of state firms to top managers. These procedures might have the salutary effect of pacifying disgruntled and potentially rebellious nomenklatura (Communist elites) but at the risk of alienating the majority of average citizens who were again left out in the cold. Western investment and development, pursued with particular vigor by Hungary, represented a potential source of much-needed capital, jobs, and hitherto unavailable goods and services. Yet Western companies' aspiration to produce, as well as to sell, their goods in Hungary carried dangers along with potential rewards. The Western firms were attracted to Hungary (and, again, also to Poland) largely because these Eastern European countries had an abundance of well-trained but very cheap labor. They would continue to be attractive only so long as wages and benefits remained substantially below norms in Western Europe.

East Germany: The Wall Comes Down

Writing of the events that shook East Germany in the summer and fall of 1989, the historian Fritz Stern observed: "Not since 1848 have Germans appeared on the stage of history so spontaneously, so daringly, and—to all appearances—so successfully." What made the transformation of the GDR so astounding was the East German people's reputation for obedient, if not necessarily enthusiastic, acceptance of state authority. With the exception of the brief workers' rebellion in East Berlin in June 1953, the people had offered no concerted challenge to the country's highly orthodox and repressive Communist leadership. Unlike Hungary and Poland, East Germany had no tradition of violent struggle against pro-Soviet dictatorship. The majority of citizens who were dissatisfied with their lot in the "Socialist Garden State" east of the Elbe tended either to emigrate to the West (up until the building of the Berlin Wall in August 1961 this was relatively easy to do) or to go into "inner emigration"— that is, to conform outwardly to the demands of the state but to retreat as much as possible into private worlds of artistic, intellectual, and social activity unconnected to their public roles as citizens. This kind of dual existence prevailed in all East bloc countries, but nowhere more strongly than in East Germany, where the Lutheran tradition of inwardness had held inner "spiritual" freedom more important than the exercise of political and social rights. Though the Communist regime made constant claims on the inner life as well, these were generally confounded by what one observer called the "counterrevolution of reality," the unwillingness of most people to give their hearts and minds to the system.

The small minority of East German citizens who refused to confine their protests to private grumbling and "inner emigration"—highly vocal critics of the regime like the satirical balladeer Wolf Biermann, the physicist Robert Havermann, the dissident Communist politician Rudolf Bahro—found themselves either expelled from the country or jailed. Hundreds of lesser-known dissidents, many of them connected to the Protestant church-backed peace movement, were also jailed. The regime of Erich Honecker (governed from 1971 to 1989) eventually allowed West German authorities to buy some of these prisoners' free passage to the West, a tactic that both earned the state hard currency and undermined the development of a stronger opposition in the GDR.

Still, the limited opposition with which the GDR government had to deal might have blossomed into a full-scale protest movement much earlier than it did had not East Germany enjoyed a level of economic prosperity that, while lower than in the West, was the highest in the East bloc. Despite dependence on Soviet oil and financial credits from West Germany, East Germany managed in the 1970s and early 1980s to register significant increases in economic growth each year, particularly in heavy industry. While there were periodic shortages of consumer goods and long waiting periods to purchase major items like automobiles, East Germans at least did not suffer from genuine want, as did many of their East bloc neighbors.

East Germany's version of the *Wirtschaftswunder* ("economic miracle") did not, however, last through the 1980s. Like the other East bloc states, the GDR proved unable to keep up with rapid changes in high technology. Increasingly it could export manufactured items only to its allies in the East, which did not earn it precious hard currency. As long as the GDR remained wedded to the inflexible, centralized economic system created by Walter Ulbricht and perpetuated by Honecker, there seemed little hope that East Germany would ever emulate its Western counterpart in producing high-quality items that could be sold all over the world.

It is impossible to say how long the East German people would have put up with this situation had not Gorbachev's dramatic reforms in the Soviet Union and the new developments in Poland and Hungary stimulated demands for similar changes in the GDR. Young people began openly demonstrating for reform, shouting, "Gorby! Gorby!" as the police dispersed them. Honecker insisted that the GDR did not need perestroika or glasnost because it was already a "progressive and enlightened society." But it became increasingly difficult to maintain this position when in the summer and fall of 1989 thousands of East Germans began fleeing their country over the Hungarian border or crowding into West German embassies in Budapest, Warsaw, and Prague in the hope of gaining passage to the West. The situation became even more volatile when young East Germans in Dresden stormed the railway station in an attempt to clamber aboard sealed trains carrying refugees across the GDR to West Germany.

Gorbachev's visit to East Berlin to mark the fortieth anniversary of the founding of the GDR in October 1989 was the occasion of huge demonstrations against the Honecker government. Similar mass demonstrations in Leipzig apparently persuaded Honecker that it was time to attempt a "Chinese solution"—that is, to order police and soldiers to shoot down the demonstrators as the Chinese had done at Tiananmen Square in June. But before this order could be executed, Egon Krenz, the former head of state security and the youngest member of the East German Politburo, is said to have unilaterally squelched the crackdown. A week later, on October 18, Krenz and his allies in the Politburo succeeded in forcing Honecker to resign "for reasons of health." Krenz became his successor as party chief and head of state. The new leader immediately made a number of public appearances promising reform; he even flew to Moscow and formally endorsed perestroika for East Germany.

These dramatic developments did nothing to calm the situation because most East Germans simply did not trust their government. "How can we have faith in a regime that has lied to us for forty years?" people asked. When Krenz announced on November 4 that East Germans could freely emigrate to West Germany through Czechoslovakia, roughly ten thousand a day began surging across the border. Those who preferred to stay in the GDR realized that only continued pressure from the streets would bring meaningful change. Thus, on the same day that Krenz opened the Czech border, five hundred thousand people demonstrated for democracy in East Berlin. Three days later, in a desperate attempt to win credibility, Krenz announced the resignation of the entire Council of Ministers; on the following day the whole Politburo followed suit and was replaced by a smaller group, including Hans Modrow, a popular reformer from Dresden. Yet the demonstrations persisted.

In the early evening of November 9, an East German official casually announced that the government had just drafted a new law giving citizens the right to leave the country through any border crossing. This meant that the Berlin Wall, already rendered partly obsolete by the free passage through Czechoslovakia, was now little more than an ugly remnant of the Cold War. Later that evening West and East Berliners met atop the wall near the

Fifty thousand East Germans demonstrate in Leipzig against the Honecker government, November 1989.

East German border guards
look on as a demonstrator
helps bring down the Berlin
Wall, November 11, 1989.

Brandenburg Gate and threw a huge spontaneous party. During the next few days millions of East Germans passed through new checkpoints in the wall (eventually including one at the Brandenburg Gate) to visit the West. To the relief of the government, which hoped that if people could leave at will, they would not leave for good, most returned. Amid all the euphoria, it was easy to miss the irony that the East German government had built the wall in 1961 to keep its people from fleeing to the West and was now punching holes in it for exactly the same reason.

The crumbling of the Berlin Wall and the other dramatic changes in East Germany may have relieved some problems, but they brought many more to the fore. They put tremendous new pressures on East Germany's anti-Communist opposition, which, unlike Poland's and Hungary's, was poorly organized and almost completely inexperienced. The main opposition group, the New Forum, was not a political party and initially did not intend to become one. The opposition could boast no leaders with a wide popular following. Figures connected to the opposition understandably worried that if the free elections Krenz promised were held soon, the anti-Communist forces would not have time to prepare for them. Krenz, for his part, clearly hoped that his promise to surrender the Communists' constitutional monopoly on political power would win the party enough support to stay firmly on top.

This did not happen, however, for on December 3, less than a month after the wall's collapse, Krenz's reform Communist government also collapsed. It was first replaced by a group of ad hoc committees that were expected somehow to hold things together until the promised elections in May (later moved up to March) 1990. Soon it was announced that Hans Modrow would be the new premier, and Gregor Gysi, a young lawyer who had defended the rights of the opposition, would head the beleaguered Communist Party. Meanwhile, Honecker and some of his cronies were placed under house arrest for using their offices to salt away huge private fortunes. "They acted like this was Haiti," exclaimed indignant citizens. Yet even these desperate measures did not restore confidence in the government. The Communist Party headquarters in East Berlin became the target of almost daily protest demonstrations, and angry citizens, fearful that the Modrow government planned to retain the hated Stasi (secret police), ransacked that agency's offices. The GDR, once considered a bastion of old Germanic order, was coming apart at the seams.

The most momentous issue raised by the new developments in East Germany (and more broadly in Eastern Europe) was the question of German reunification. For the first time in forty years there seemed to be a genuine possibility—and indeed within weeks of the wall's fall the probability—that the two Germanys would merge into one nation. Yet if reunification meant the creation of a single sovereign state (as opposed to, say, a loose confederation between the FRG and GDR), certain obstacles remained to be cleared. The GDR government at first opposed full reunification, believing that the Communists could hope to continue their rule only in a sovereign Eastern state. Opinion polls showed that the majority of East German citizens favored some form of reunification, and the "united fatherland" theme became increasingly prominent in East German popular demonstrations. On the other hand, many of the best-educated people were more anxious to reform their socialist homeland than to plunge headlong into the capitalist West. With the ongoing erosion of popular confidence in a separate East German state, however, this constituency became increasingly irrelevant. When East Germany's first free elections were held on March 18, 1990, a conservative alliance favoring rapid unification won a decisive victory over the Social Democratic Party and the party of Democratic Socialism (former Communists), who preferred a more gradual approach. The majority of East Germans clearly believed that the sooner Germany was reunified, the sooner they would share in the prosperity long enjoyed by their Western cousins.

Polls taken in West Germany in late 1989 and early 1990 also recorded strong support for the principle of reunification. Reflecting a growing spirit of German national assertiveness, in November 1989 Chancellor Kohl announced, without consulting the other Western powers, a ten-point program on German unity. Yet as compelling as the principle of reunification was for most West Germans, many were concerned that their half of Germany would be made to shoulder most of the economic sacrifices attending reunification, at least in its early stages. They feared that a currency conversion rate of one to one, which the East Germans demanded, would significantly inflate the German mark, traditionally one of the world's soundest currencies. Some of the opposition parties also expressed political reservations. The Greens, for example, feared reunification might foment a rebirth of extreme nationalism. They, along with some Social Democrats, insisted that this step must not be taken to mean an attempted restoration of the German borders of 1937 (which included areas now in Poland and the Soviet Union).

But German reunification was not strictly a German question. Since no peace treaty had ever been signed with defeated Germany after World War II, the four Allied powers retained responsibility for Berlin and the ultimate delimitation of Germany's borders; at the very least, they would have to be consulted before reunification could occur. And what was their policy on this issue? The U.S. government said it would welcome German unity but hoped that it would be achieved slowly and carefully. The Russians initially stated that they opposed it for the time being. No doubt Gorbachev feared that a precipitate move toward German unity would weaken his position at home, where memories of German aggression in World War II were still very much alive. But Gorbachev was no more able than Modrow to arrest the growing popular demand in Germany for reunification. Bowing to the pressure of events, he announced in February 1990 that he too favored reunification, though he also expressed his opposition to a united Germany's remaining in NATO and called for the removal of all foreign troops from German territory. As for France and Britain, they no longer worried quite so much about the military potential of a united Germany, but they feared that a single German state might possess inordinate economic power. They spoke of the need to secure European economic unity before German reunification. It was talk like this that inspired Willy Brandt to declare at an SPD congress in December 1989: "Nowhere is it written that the Germans have to stay stuck in a siding until the all-European train has reached the station." Brandt was right. On September 12, 1990, the four wartime allies signed a final settlement with Germany, relinquishing their occupation rights and opening the way for East and West Germany to reunite on October 3.

Czechoslovakia: From Velvet Revolution to Velvet Divorce

Poland, Hungary, East Germany, then Czechoslovakia. The domino theory, invented to describe the supposedly inevitable serial collapse of non-Communist regimes in Asia if South Vietnam fell to Communism, ironically now seemed applicable to the disintegration of Soviet Russia's Eastern European empire in the wake of Gorbachev's reforms. Yet before the dramatic events of November 1989, most observers of Eastern Europe believed that the Czech regime would not soon topple. Even more than East Germany, Czechoslovakia seemed to be an impregnable bastion of old-line Communist orthodoxy. Its government, which had been put into power by the Soviets following their brutal crushing of Prague Spring in 1968, was one of the most efficiently repressive in Eastern Europe. President Gustav Husák and his chief aide, Miloš Jakeš, had conducted a sweeping purge of the liberal Communists around reformist leader Alexander Dubček; one in every three party members, or roughly five hundred thousand people, had been expelled. Dubček himself was exiled to a job as director of forestry in Bratislava (a place where many of the trees were dead or dying from acid rain). The regime also culled the universities, cultural organizations, and economic institutions of "subversives," who thereafter were allowed to take only the most menial jobs. The new party and bureaucratic elites were chosen for their servile willingness to toe the party line. They collaborated with Husák and Jakeš in "normalizing" the situation after 1968, which meant above all enforcing a collective amnesia regarding the ideals that were trampled upon in the suppression of Prague Spring. When Czech citizens began laying wreaths and signs saying WE REMEMBER at the grave of Jan Palach, a young man who had burned himself to death in protest against the Soviet invasion, police removed Palach's body to an unknown place and buried another body in his former gravesite.

Although Husák and Jakeš were not hesitant to use force to maintain "normality," they could also rely on economic incentives to keep the majority of Czechs obedient. Until the late 1980s, Czechoslovakia's economy, like East Germany's, was able to provide a certain measure of prosperity to most citizens. Though consumer durables were shabby and often in short supply, Prague's stores were generally better supplied even than East Berlin's. Apparently convinced that they had too much to lose by making trouble, Czechoslovakia's workers, unlike their Polish and Hungarian counterparts, did not join with local intellectuals to form significant opposition movements. Czechoslovakia's main dissident group, Charter 77, remained a small coterie of outcast artists, writers, and musicians whose constant persecution by the state occasioned more foreign than domestic protest. When the group's most outspoken member, playwright Václav Havel, was jailed in 1979, only a few fellow writers bothered to demonstrate.

On the other hand, the Soviets' decision in 1983 to station nuclear missiles in Czechoslovakia aroused the anger not just of intellectuals but also of workers. Mass protests against the missiles pointed up the existence of a largely untapped reservoir of hostility toward Soviet overlordship in this country. Czechoslovakia had, moreover, proud nationalist traditions dating back to the early nineteenth century and memories of democratic government between the wars. As Poles and Hungarians began rebelling in the name of democracy and national independence, some Czechs—at first primarily students from Prague's Charles University—began protesting in the name of *their* nation's democratic past. On November 17, 1989, for example, a group of students marched to Prague's St. Wenceslas Square, waving Czechoslovakia's pre-Communist national flag and shouting the names of Tomáš Masaryk (Czech president in the interwar period) and Alexander Dubček. Acknowledging the exciting changes all around them, they screamed, "We don't want to be last!" and "Dinosaurs, resign!"

Husák and Jakeš (who had become head of the party in 1987) responded predictably: they ordered police and paramilitary forces to disperse the students, which they did with sickening brutality. More than a hundred students were injured, fourteen seriously. This tactic was an error, for it radicalized previously apathetic workers and even many middle-level employees, who now joined the students in demonstrations of ever-increasing size. On the first Sunday after the November 17 "massacre," fifty thousand people demonstrated against the government in St. Wenceslas Square. By the following Friday the number had swelled to half a million. The protests spread from Prague across the country to Bratislava, prompting that province's most famous forester, Dubček, to return to the capital and publicly demand the resignation of the government. Here, as in East Germany, the regime was thus confronted with the choice of crushing the huge protest movement with force or resigning. On November 23, party boss Jakeš and the entire Politburo chose the latter alternative; the Czech domino had finally fallen.

Yet here, again as in East Germany and Hungary, people remained skeptical. Jakeš and his colleagues were at first replaced by another group of Communists, who seemed willing to make some cosmetic reforms but not to give up power. Increasingly, however, the Czech people were demanding full democracy and not just partial democratization; they wanted a free economy and not just "socialism with a human face," the slogan of 1968. Dubček himself seemed somewhat outdated in the rapidly evolving Czech scene, almost as much a relic of the past as the hard-line Communists he was attacking. A new opposition group, Civic Forum, a successor to Charter 77, called for the immediate installation of a coalition government including non-Communists, to be followed by free elections that might end the Communists' forty-year hold on power. In the face of continuing massive demonstrations and threats of a general strike, the government caved in; on December 9, President Husák resigned, and opposition leaders formed a cabinet dominated by non-Communists. The entire revolution had taken about three weeks, and it had been achieved without a single act of serious violence on the part of the government's opponents. Havel, who now became Czechoslovakia's new president, called the events of November–December 1989 "a velvet revolution."

Like their neighbors in Poland, Hungary, and East Germany, the Czechs wanted to turn away from Soviet Russia and embrace "Europe"—the prosperous Western Europe of the EEC and the impending single European market. Emulating Hungary, the new Czech government began pulling down the barbed-wire fences along Czechoslovakia's border with Austria. It seemed, in short, that

A demonstrator carrying the Czech flag marches on Prague's St. Wenceslas Square, November 23, 1989.

in Czechoslovakia as elsewhere, hopes for the future blended with potent memories of the past.

It soon became apparent, however, that one dimension of Czechoslovakia's past—namely, lingering hostilities between the Czech and Slovak populations—would make it difficult for the unified state to weather the resurgence of ethnic nationalism in the post-Communist era. The Slovaks, who had long felt themselves to be second-class citizens in the Czech state, wanted a loose confederation that would give them considerable autonomy. The Czechs insisted on a more tightly integrated federation. The Slovak part of the newly renamed Czech and Slovak Federation was also more wedded to the old socialist economic system and therefore reluctant to accept the radical market reforms embraced by the Czech leadership. The Slovak prime minister, Vladimir Meciar, a former Communist who had turned virulent Slovak nationalist, advocated the division of the federation into two states. The Czechs were at first reluctant to accept this solution, but their premier, Václav Klaus, eventually concluded that separation was preferable to continued partnership with Slovakia, whose commitment to retaining its aging state-run heavy industry would, he feared, hinder Prague's transition to market capitalism. On November 25, 1992, the Federal Assembly approved the division of Czechoslovakia into two independent republics. Fortunately, the separation process was nonviolent, the velvet revolution giving way to a velvet divorce.

Changing Guard in Bulgaria

Unlike Czechoslovakia, which as an essentially westward-looking nation had never enthusiastically accepted Russian control, Bulgaria remained a model

Czechoslovakia's new president, former dissident Václav Havel.

Soviet client state when its Balkan neighbors were periodically trying to go their own way. There was no such thing as a Sofia Spring. The lack of significant anti-Soviet activity in Bulgaria reflected, according to one authority, "a real complementarity of economic interests and developmental strategies." After Stalin's death, Bulgaria was allowed to concentrate not on heavy industry, which it could not do well, but on light manufacturing and agriculture, both strengths. It found a constant market for its fruits and vegetables and wine in the Soviet Union.

From March 1954 to November 1989, Todor Zhivkov served as general secretary of the Bulgarian Communist Party; after 1962 he became sole ruler of the state. Such longevity would be impressive in any country, but it was especially so in Bulgaria, where frequent clan feuds and military putsches had traditionally made rulership rather like Thomas Hobbes's description of life: "nasty, brutish, and short." Zhivkov was obviously a gifted political infighter, but he owed his staying power even more to his political style, which was autocratic yet populist and accessible.

At the same time, however, Zhivkov was also pursuing policies that brought discredit on his regime and his nation. His tightly controlled security forces were involved in an abortive assassination attempt on the pope in 1981. He was also known to have supplemented his modest official salary with hard currency earned from international drug and arms smuggling. In 1984, he inaugurated a campaign to "Bulgarize" the country's ethnic Turks by forcing them to adopt Bulgarian names and forbidding them from practicing their Muslim faith. When this met spirited resistance, he began expelling them en masse from the country.

This last move turned out to be his undoing, for the loss of so many skilled people raised havoc with the previously stable Bulgarian economy. The country's foreign minister, Petar Mladenov, who had worked hard to restore Bulgaria's international reputation after the papal assassination attempt, decided that it was time for the seventy-eight-year-old Zhivkov to go. He orchestrated a peaceful coup in the Politburo that ended with Zhivkov's resignation on November 9, the day on which that other aging East bloc monument the Berlin Wall also toppled. Zhivkov, like East Germany's Honecker, was soon charged with corruption and placed under house arrest.

After the ouster and arrest of Zhivkov, Bulgaria's Communist Party emulated its counterparts in East Germany and Czechoslovakia by abandoning its claim to a leading role in national politics and announcing free elections for the coming year. Perhaps even more boldly, Mladenov reversed Zhivkov's brutal policy of forced assimilation of Bulgaria's Turks. In late December, he announced that the Turks could take back their old names, practice the Islamic religion, and speak Turkish in public. Thousands of Turks who had been expelled under Zhivkov returned to Bulgaria. While this policy was applauded in the West, it produced a violent backlash at home. Most Bulgarians had no love for the Turks, who had occupied their country for some five hundred years. Those Bulgarians who had bought up the homes and household possessions of the expelled Turks at bargain prices feared that they would have to return these items to their original owners. Hard-line Communists who resented Mladenov's partial dismantling of the old political system capitalized on this nationalist fervor in their efforts to slow or reverse the reform process. These developments showed that in Bulgaria, as elsewhere in Eastern Europe, old nationalistic and ethnic rivalries were reasserting themselves with a vengeance as the postwar order fell apart.

Such tendencies persisted as Bulgaria struggled to replace Communist institutions with viable democratic ones. Here, in contrast to the northern tier of Eastern and Central European states, former Communists remained from the outset formidable players in the transition process. It was not until 1991 that an anti-Communist coalition government could gain power and begin a push for de-Communization and free market reform. Bulgaria's new leaders also launched a prosecution of former Communists, including Zhivkov, who was sentenced to seven years in prison. However, economic stagnation and rising crime soon soured many Bulgarians on their new rulers, and in January 1995 the Bulgarian Socialist Party, as the old Communist Party was now called, returned to the helm. Its policies, which aimed at slowing market-oriented reforms and protecting old state-run companies, generated massive inflation and resulted in a devaluation of the currency. Retread socialism proving so disastrous, Bulgarians brought back a reformist regime in 1997. But however the leaders defined themselves, Bulgaria's experiment with democracy and market capitalism remained tenuous well after the collapse of the old system.

Romania: Ceauşescu's Bloody End
    While no one would have described Bulgaria as an open or a liberal society, it almost seemed so in comparison with Romania, its Balkan neighbor to the north. Under President Nicolae Ceauşescu, absolute *conducator* (führer or duce) since 1965, Romania developed a political and social order of which Stalin might have been proud. Huge portraits of Ceauşescu, always depicting him as a young man, hung on billboards and building façades across the country. Romanian citizens were forbidden to talk to foreigners; members of the Securitate (security police) seemed to be omnipresent. The slightest hints of dissidence were immediately repressed. No doubt the regime believed it needed to be especially vigilant because the Romanian people had no reason but fear to remain obedient to it. Rich in oil deposits and fertile lands, Romania exported so much of its natural wealth that by the 1970s there were constant energy shortages and little food on market shelves. Romanians joked grimly that their economy was ruled by the "duke of Kent" because Kent cigarettes were the prevailing currency in the black market, virtually the only market that had anything of value to sell. Believing that Romania would be militarily stronger with a larger population, Ceauşescu banned contraceptives and made abortion punishable by up to five years in prison (fetuses, he said, were the "property of the state"). The result was the deaths of thousands of women who tried to abort themselves or got unsafe illegal abortions. This policy also filled the nation's orphanages with unwanted children.
    For years Ceauşescu sought to distract attention from domestic repression by pursuing a foreign policy that featured rudeness to the Russians (whom most Romanians despised). Instead of supporting the Soviet Union in its quarrel with China, Romania stayed neutral. It also reduced its participation in the Warsaw Pact, allowing no pact maneuvers on its territory and forcing the removal of Soviet troops from its soil. As his isolated country slipped ever deeper into poverty and despair, Ceauşescu tried to legitimize his regime by holding himself up as the embodiment of the historical virtues of the Romanian nation, whose "Latin" civilization he said was under attack from Slavs to the east and Hungarians to the west. He appealed to crude nationalistic sentiments by repressing the cultural traditions of the ethnic Hungarians living in Transylvania.
    Given Ceauşescu's exploitation of Romanian nationalism, it is ironic that one of his most notorious policies, the "systemization" of the country's architectural landscape through the replacement of traditional single-family houses with uniform concrete apartment blocks, aimed to destroy a vital dimension of Romania's cultural heritage. Announced in 1974, this program had by the late 1980s obliterated nearly all the handsome and distinctive old villages around Bucharest and moved their occupants into prefabricated concrete housing. In the capital itself ancient churches and art nouveau buildings were razed to make way for more faceless blocks.
    Grotesque as his rule was, Ceauşescu at first seemed invulnerable to the cataclysmic changes that were transforming the rest of Eastern Europe. His very iso-

lation was clearly an advantage here: Gorbachev had no leverage on him, and neither did the West. (He had managed to pay off virtually all Romania's foreign debt with his obsessive export policy.) The collapse of Communist dictatorships all around him seemed only to harden Ceauşescu's determination to hang on. This was abundantly demonstrated at the Romanian Communist Party Congress held on November 20, 1989. While handpicked delegates rose repeatedly like marionettes to applaud their leader, Ceauşescu promised in a five-hour speech to keep Romania free of the evils of capitalism and bourgeois liberalism.

But time was running out for the self-proclaimed "genius of the Carpathians." Less than a month after the party congress, on December 15–16, Ceauşescu's regime suddenly encountered open public opposition when it attempted to evict a dissident Protestant pastor from his church in the town of Timisoara. Hundreds of people formed a human chain around the pastor's church, while others burned copies of the dictator's books. Security forces rushed to the scene and began firing point-blank into the crowd. Army officers who refused to shoot their countrymen were summarily executed by the security police. As news of the massacre at Timisoara spread, popular hatred for Ceauşescu, always simmering below the surface of Romanian life, rapidly came to a boil. Anti-Ceauşescu riots and demonstrations erupted across the country. The final moment of truth came, ironically enough, on December 21 at an official rally in Bucharest, which Ceauşescu organized to show support for his regime. After a few ritual choruses of praise from government cheerleaders, groups of students began shouting antigovernment slogans. Soon the entire crowd joined in; defiant

Citizens of Bucharest take cover during fighting between the army and pro-Ceauşescu troops, December 24, 1989.

cries of "Down with Ceauşescu" filled the Palace Square. Shocked and frightened by this turn of events, Ceauşescu left the palace balcony where he had been speaking and fled the city (along with his equally hated wife) by helicopter. Before departing, however, he gave orders to his security police to crush the popular opposition as the Chinese had done in Tiananmen Square.

Ceauşescu's attempt brutally to repress the growing rebellion, combined with the Romanian people's desire for revenge after twenty-five years of humiliation and misery, ensured a bloody end to Eastern Europe's most repressive regime. He and his wife were captured on December 21 by army units that had turned against the dictator. On Christmas Day, after a hasty "trial," the Ceauşescus were executed by firing squad. Three hundred soldiers volunteered to participate in the killing of the man who had declared himself "the most loved son of the people."

The end of the Ceauşescu regime did not bring genuine stability, ethnic harmony, or much economic progress to Romania. Like Bulgaria, but even more so, Romania found that its first steps toward market capitalism generated widespread resistance from some occupational groups, such as the miners, whose livelihoods were tied to the old system. The old Communist elite feared that economic liberalism would bring greater political freedom—and with it the opening of secret police files that told the true story about Ceauşescu's rule and their role in it. Ion Iliescu, an authoritarian former Communist, exploited the fears and social dislocations of the post-Communist era to install himself as a virtual dictator, a new Ceauşescu in pseudodemocratic dress. Like the *conducator*, he fanned ethnic hatreds, especially against the Hungarian minority, to solidify his hold on power. He drew support in these campaigns from a number of radical right parties, which also attacked the nation's Gypsies and tiny Jewish population. By the mid-nineties Romania was slowly Westernizing, but its leaders' unwillingness to throw off the old ways prevented it from receiving much Western aid or investment.

Yugoslavia: Ethnic Turmoil in the Balkans

The bloody events attending Ceauşescu's end in Romania served as a catalyst for new outbreaks of political and ethnic turmoil in Yugoslavia, an independent Communist nation whose emancipation from Soviet control in the late 1940s had led local Communist leaders to believe that their regime was less vulnerable than the other Eastern European states to pressures for democratic change. But as one party leader put it, Romania "suddenly made the possibility of violence and revenge [against Communist officials] very real." Hoping to prevent a Romanian-style anti-Communist upheaval, some Yugoslav Communists openly embraced popular calls for a multiparty system and a full market economy. At a party congress in Belgrade on January 21, 1990, reformist Communists from Slovenia, one of the country's six semiautonomous republics, called for an end to the party's constitutional monopoly on power, the creation of non-Communist parties, free elections, and the transformation of the Yugoslav Communist Party into a federation of six independent parties, one for each republic. Hard-line leaders from Serbia, the country's largest and traditionally dominant republic, resisted these demands, and the party virtually fell apart.

Serbia's Communists had good reason to fear for the continued domination both of the party and of their republic within the state. As the Communists were meeting in Belgrade, a large number of anti-Communist organizations were springing up to demand the legalization of opposition parties, new environmental protection laws, and enhanced regional liberties. The press, which had long been obedient to Communist directives, began printing dozens of interviews with dissidents, accounts of terrible prison conditions, and stories of official corruption. Even Tito, long above reproach as the hero of postwar Yugoslavia, was increasingly the target of critical analyses as the tenth anniversary of his death approached.

Questions of Communist control and unity, however, were increasingly overshadowed by challenges to the unity of the nation itself. In March 1989, ethnic Albanians living in Kosovo, an autonomous province within Serbia, revolted against limits on their self-rule imposed by the government of the Serbian republic. Twenty-eight people died in battles among the ethnic Albanians, Christian Serbs, and Muslim Montenegrins living nearby. The Kosovo fighting ignited an upsurge of Serbian nationalism and new attempts to reassert centralized control from Belgrade. This in turn produced a second round of ethnic violence in Kosovo in January 1990. Thousands of Serbs fled the area, while Macedonians, also caught up in the fighting, appealed to neighboring Bulgaria for help. Serbia insisted that it could not allow Kosovo to become an independent republic in the Yugoslav state because it was historically important as the place where the Serbs had fought a sacred battle in their war of independence against the Turks. "Kosovo is the mythical heart of Serbia," said the republic's minister of foreign affairs. "It is our Jerusalem."

WOMEN IN POST-COMMUNIST
EASTERN EUROPE

If the transition from state socialist regimes to multiparty governments based on capitalist market economies was often difficult for the peoples of Eastern Europe, this passage was particularly trying for the female component of the population. The advantages for women under Communism have often been exaggerated, but it is undeniably true that women enjoyed a more elaborate, or at least more easily obtained, array of state-sponsored rights and privileges under the old order than under the new. The Communist governments, including that of the Soviet Union, provided women with extensive educational opportunities at state expense, free day care for their children, maternity benefits, and job guarantees for those who took leave during their pregnancies. Most Communist states—Romania being a notable exception—provided free abortions to women who chose not to carry their pregnancies to term. The Communist states ordained that women were equal to men. Accordingly, women often performed jobs that were typically done by men in non-Communist societies. On the whole, however, Eastern European women still tended to do less remunerative and prestigious work than men, and they were underrepresented at the managerial level. The female doctors and technicians in the USSR earned less than their male counterparts, despite Soviet laws guaranteeing equality in the workplace. Of Polish women, it was said that they were like the sediment of good wine: "They sank to the bottom." In the end, when it came to female labor, the primary goal of the Communist states was to exploit their womenfolk, not to make them equal. Thus, the regimes did little or nothing to encourage equality in the home, where men reigned as supreme as ever. (The Western "new male," who shared household and child-rearing duties with his wife, was nearly unheard of in the East bloc.) Western-style feminism was decried as "bourgeois," its advocates denounced as violent, bra-burning lesbians.

On the political front, the Communist states set quotas for female participation in national and local legislative bodies, typically granting them one-quarter to one-third of the seats. It must be noted, however, that such representation rarely brought real power. Aside from some assertive political wives, such as Elena Ceaușescu, Mira Milošević, Margo Honecker, and Raisa Gorbachev, women rarely exercised significant influence over policy. With only a few women in the central committees and politburos, government at the top remained essentially a male preserve, replete with the hunting, drinking, whoring, poker-playing, and locker-room bravado typical of male leadership circles in most parts of the world.

The collapse of Communism tended to bring a reduction (though rarely an end) to the extensive social benefits that women had enjoyed under the old regimes. The day care programs sponsored by the newly democratized governments offered shorter hours, and in some cases they were no longer free. In Russia, for example, the Yeltsin government substantially reduced child and family benefits, including state-subsidized day care centers. Easy access to abortion was no longer nearly universal, as in the days of Communism. Female citizens of the former East Germany had to conform to the more restrictive abortion policies that had prevailed in West Germany once the two Germanys became unified in 1990, in Hungary abortion was restricted to "crisis situations," and in Poland the revitalized Catholic Church managed to secure legislation that outlawed abortion except in cases of rape or incest. At the same time, Eastern European women were hit especially hard by the economic dislocations accompanying the transition to market capitalism. By 1993, over 70 percent of Russian women were unemployed, according to the Ministry of Labor. Their high unemployment derived in part from layoffs in industries traditionally dominated by women, such as textiles. Yeltsin's government justified the layoffs on the ground that it was time for women to return to their "natural predestination," meaning home and motherhood. In Poland, the percentage of women who worked for wages fell from 79.9 in 1987 to 71.3 in 1991. In December 1991, for every hundred Polish women who held jobs, thirteen were unemployed. In the former GDR, where under Communist rule nearly 90 percent of all women eligible for employment were either studying or in the labor force, some 63.6 percent were unemployed by 1992. By 1998, women constituted about 60 percent of the unemployed across Eastern Europe. Women's loss of employment not only compromised their families' economic viability but also undercut their self-esteem.

This was all the more the case when for want of socially acceptable employment, women were forced to turn to the Mafia-controlled prostitution and pornography industries that expanded across Europe in the 1990s. Such work was highly dangerous as well as degrading, since the criminal gangs that smuggled young women from East to West thought nothing of beating or even killing anyone who tried to break free of their control. By the late 1990s, the corpses of several hundred young women—strangled, shot, or beaten to a pulp—were fetching up all around Europe each year.

In the political domain, the demise of the Communist practice of automatically granting women a percentage of seats in state and local government led to lower rates of female participation in politics. Overall, women's parliamentary representation dropped by about one-third in the first years of the new order. Symbolic or token as much of the females' political work might have been under Communism, loss of such activity often meant another blow to self-esteem. On the other hand, the new system offered women opportunities for genuine advancement and power, a welcome change from the old days. Frustrated by the Yeltsin government's cuts in social and family programs, a group of female activists in Russia formed an all-woman party called Women of Russia, which campaigned for the restoration of benefits to women and support for the industrial sectors dominated by women workers. Women of Russia won 8 percent of the vote in the 1993 legislative elections, which entitled it to name twenty-one deputies. In 1992, the Polish parliament elected Hanna Suchocka as the country's first female prime minister. In the Czech Republic, Rita Klimova became her nation's ambassador to Washington; Dagmar Burešová chaired the Czech National Council. In Hungary, a woman became vice president of the Christian Democratic Party. A group of female politicians belonging to Hungary's Alliance of Free Democrats created the Foundation of the Women of Hungary, which promoted women's participation in the formation of policy on gender issues. Angela Merkel, a politician hailing from the defunct GDR, became head of Germany's conservative CDU in the wake of Helmut Kohl's fall from power, a position she could never have held in East Germany.

Interestingly, few of the female political activists in the former East bloc wanted to be associated with Western-style feminism, though at the same time they greatly resented the lack of interest in women's problems shown by their male colleagues. In their efforts to improve conditions for women, they had to fight not only against uninterest or opposition from men—the resurgence of ethnic and religious-based politics, after all, encouraged a revival of patriarchal notions concerning the proper role of women—but against passivity and resignation among their sisters. The social and political dislocations of the new era led many women to pine for the sureties of the old days. "You hear women saying that things are worse now, but it just isn't true," said Jirina Siklova, head of Gender Studies at Prague's Charles University in 1997. Unfounded as this perception might have been, however, its pervasiveness was one of the more pressing challenges faced by all the societies of Eastern Europe as they sought to adjust to the demands of pluralistic democracy and market capitalism.

CHAPTER 16

Continental Drift

As THE LAST DECADE of the twentieth century dawned and the new millennium beckoned, most Europeans looked to the future with more confidence than they had mustered in previous years. After all, Communism was in retreat, the old political divisions between East and West seemed to be collapsing, and the Continent was largely at peace. Over the course of the next decade and a half, however, much of this confidence faded, and prognostications of smooth sailing gave way to anxieties over all manner of tempests, dangerous currents, and frustrating drift. In France, Britain, Italy, and Germany, changes in national leadership did not result in significant alterations of policy or dramatic improvements in governmental performance. Reunified Germany experienced great difficulty in revitalizing the former East German state, where chronic high unemployment, social malaise, and political disaffection persisted despite huge infusions of money from the federal government. In Russia, the new regime of Boris Yeltsin seemed to offer some hope that parliamentary institutions and liberal values might eventually take hold, but Yeltsin's hand-picked successor, Vladimir Putin, soon dashed those hopes through a campaign of authoritarian backsliding aimed at the restoration of all power in the Kremlin. On the Continent's southeastern edge, open warfare of an intensity not seen since World War II erupted, and to contend with that violence Europeans found themselves once again dependent on the United States, now the world's sole remaining superpower.

MILLENNIAL BLUES: FRANCE, BRITAIN, AND ITALY

For France, the last decade of the twentieth century was not particularly happy or glorious—except, of course, in the world of soccer. German reunification came as a rude shock, threatening France's claim to being the dominant power on the Continent. President François Mitterrand made some awkward attempts to stall the German unification process, but in the end he managed only to damage Paris's relations with Bonn. France's futile efforts to assert itself

French President Jacques Chirac.

in Francophone Africa, NATO, and the Balkans also highlighted its decline as a world power.

France's fin-de-siècle woes were hardly confined to foreign affairs. At home there was political ineptitude and widening social crisis. Between 1990 and 1997, France endured six different prime ministers and a major change at the presidential level, when the Gaullist Jacques Chirac replaced the Socialist Mitterrand in 1995. For all the political shuffling, however, the national leadership seemed largely incapable of coming to grips with such nagging socioeconomic problems as high unemployment, a bloated civil service, labor unrest, urban violence, declining family farms, and rising xenophobia.

On the cultural front, France was not the influential force that it had been through much of the twentieth century, not to mention in the nineteenth. Even in the realm of haute couture Paris had to share center stage with New York, London, and Milan. Signs of the Americanization of French culture and society were everywhere, from a plethora of McDonald's restaurants to an outpost of Disneyland right outside Paris. Although France still made significant contributions in scientific research and technology, it was on the wrong side of the barricades when it came to the crucial high-tech information revolution. As late as 1997, fewer than 15 percent of French households had personal computers and fewer than 1 percent were connected to the Internet, figures much lower than France's European neighbors. (In this domain, Chirac himself set an unfortunate example, dismissing the Web as "an Anglo-Saxon network.") Behind such parochialism was the fear that France's social and cultural institutions had become too fragile, too debilitated by corrosive outside influences, to accommodate radical change. As the political scientist Pierre Birnbaum put it, "Our problem is that we have not found the way to modernize while preserving our imagined community."

Chirac's insular view of the Net notwithstanding, the new president considered himself a social-economic modernizer, and upon taking office, he launched a campaign to reduce France's high public debt and onerous tax burden by trimming the national civil service, whose pampered employees enjoyed near-total job security and shorter work hours, more pay, longer holidays, larger pensions, and wider health coverage than their counterparts in the private sector. Led by university students, the public servants responded by staging massive strikes that essentially shut down the country. Chirac, showing that though he was a Gaullist, he was no de Gaulle, quickly caved in and rescinded the cuts. His government backed down also when France's truckers went on strike in 1996 to win a reduction of their workweek from thirty-nine to thirty-five hours (with no loss in pay) and a lowering of their retirement age from sixty to fifty-five, conditions that then became the model for much of the private sector. Next to strike were the farmers, who in protest against planned cuts in their state subsidies drove to Paris in their tractors and blockaded the major roads into the city. The farm subsidies were not reduced.

The new face of Paris: a burka-clad Muslim woman reading *Le Monde*.

In 1997, President Chirac called parliamentary elections a year early in hope of gaining enough leverage to make another try at trimming some of the fat from France's bloated social midsection. Aware of his intention, the voters turned back to the left, forcing Chirac to "cohabit" with a new Socialist prime minister, Lionel Jospin. As in the mid-1980s, when President Mitterrand had been forced to share power with Prime Minister Chirac, the president now had to live with a premier from the opposition party, a situation that never makes for a happy household.

At the time of his election, Jospin promised to create seven hundred thousand new jobs, half of them in the public sector. This obviously conflicted with Chirac's desire to shrink the civil service and to cut the budget deficit. Jospin, however, proved unable to create very many new jobs, and in time he adopted a more pragmatic line. Instead of excoriating the "excesses" of the market-oriented economics favored in America and Britain, as he had during his election campaign, he began to speak of the need to balance social justice with economic efficiency and the "realities of today's capitalism." He even lectured his countrymen that they "should not expect everything from the state and the government," sounding an awful lot like Chirac—or, for that matter, like Jospin's British counterpart, Tony Blair. Putting policy where his mouth was, in 1999 Jospin announced plans to trim public spending from 54 percent of GDP to around 51 percent and to reduce the budget deficit from 3 percent of GDP to 1 percent by 2002. As soon as he actually made some cuts, however, the public service unions went on strike, and his coalition partners in the Communist and Green parties warned him not to depart too far from the Socialist principles that had gotten him elected. Jospin got the message and backed away from his heretical flirtation with "Anglo-Saxon" socioeconomic policies.

In 2003 this pattern repeated itself when a new conservative prime minister, Jean-Pierre Raffarin, tried and failed to make public and private sector workers contribute a greater share to their pension plans. Three years later, yet another conservative premier, Dominique de Villepin, sought to encourage job creation with a reform called the "first job contract," which reduced job protection for young workers during their first two years of employment. In response, union-backed protestors marched in cities across the country while students shut down their universities with disruptive sit-ins. Buckling under the pressure, Villepin reluctantly dropped his plan. Thus, as Jacques Chirac approached the end of his long tenure as president, he and a parade of prime ministers serving under him had proven themselves unable to do very much to curb the *acquis sociaux* ("acquired social privileges") that many French workers apparently considered essential to their very identity as Frenchmen.

Chirac's tenure was also beset by tension over immigration, an issue that had been bedeviling France since the 1960s. Despite various efforts to stem the foreign tide, waves of immigrants, mainly from Northern Africa and Southeast Asia, kept streaming into France, fueling native resentment. In the presidential elections of 1995, the far-right, anti-immigrant candidate Jean-Marie Le Pen received 15 percent of the vote, and in the legislative elections of 1997 his National Front emerged almost as strong as the two mainstream parties, the Socialists and the Gaullists. Even more astounding, in the presidential poll of 2002, Le Pen won 18 percent of the vote, putting him in second place behind Chirac. Defending Le Pen's program of "France for the French," a National Front spokesman declared: "If we want to send the Arabs and Asians back to where they came from, it's not because we hate them: it's because they pollute our national identity and take our jobs."

As in the Mitterand era, resentment of immigrants was also fueled by a rising crime rate among the so-called *jeunes des banlieues*, the heavily immigrant suburban youth clustered in the bleak tenement districts ringing the nation's major cities. Juvenile crime doubled in the last half of the 1990s, with youths under eighteen committing nearly a quarter of the reported crimes. Worries over youth violence in the seething suburbs turned into panic in fall 2005 when clusters of rioters, mostly young men of immigrant stock, burned cars and torched businesses around Paris's periphery and in the suburbs of several other large cities. It was the worst social turmoil France had seen since the student-led protests of 1968. For almost two weeks, as hooded vandals ran amok in the streets, French authorities showed themselves powerless to contain the mayhem. Finally, a desperate Premier de Villepin, backed by President Chirac, gained control of the situation by imposing a blanket curfew on the troubled areas; the legal underpinning for this measure was a state-of-emergency law dating back to France's brutal war in Algeria in the 1950s. In the soul-searching that followed the riots, governmental officials seemed to realize that the immediate trigger for the upheaval—the accidental self-electrification of two immigrant teenagers in a suburban Paris power station—was not the real issue here. Behind the rioting lay a deep sense of alienation among thousands of young people of Arab and Asian stock who saw little future for themselves in a country that, while professing to be color-blind and animated by social cohesion, kept its "visible minorities" massively underemployed and clustered together in bleak high-rise suburban ghettos. Various governmental officials promised new measures to integrate disaffected immigrant youth, but (as we shall see in the following chapter), an upsurge of Islamic fundamentalism in France's large Muslim community complicated any hopes of assimilating the growing multitudes existing on the margins of French society.

The decade of the 1990s began no better for Britain than for France. Britain too agonized over German unification, which was all the harder to take since it coincided with Germany's victory over England in World Cup soccer. Speaking for many of his countrymen, Nicolas Ridley, Margaret Thatcher's secretary of trade and industry, warned in July 1990 that the Germans were getting "uppity" and might try once again to take over the world. (Ridley's views on this matter resembled Thatcher's, but because he spoke too openly, he had to be fired.)

Thatcher herself was gone four months later. Her autocratic style made her a divisive figure in the nation and even in her own party. Seeing her as a political liability, a majority of her colleagues in the Conservative Party turned against her, causing her to step down in November 1990. "I do not believe that we will see her like again," said the Conservative Party chairman, perhaps as much out of relief as regret.

Britain certainly did not see Thatcher's like in her successor, John Major, who had served as trade secretary, foreign secretary, and chancellor of the exchequer before taking on the premiership. At forty-seven, Major was the youngest British prime minister in almost one hundred years. His background was considerably more plebeian than that of his middle-class predecessor. Major's father was a music hall performer, who with his first wife, Kitty Drum, had an act called Drum and Major. Young John left high school at sixteen and never attended a university, much less Oxbridge. Having failed the examination to become a bus conductor, Major spent some time on the dole. Eventually he found work in the insurance and banking industries before entering politics at the local level in South London. His rapid rise in the Conservative Party was due to hard work, diligence, tenacity, and the favor of his domineering patron, Mrs. Thatcher, who claimed to have invented him. What he lacked was flair or charisma, his personal style being about as galvanizing as the cricket matches he loved to watch.

Major's primary departure from the Thatcher line involved his stance on Europe. Unlike her, he was not viscerally opposed to closer ties with the Continent, even insisting that he wanted to see Britain "in the heart of Europe." His vaguely pro-Europe posture, however, ran into stiff resistance from the Thatcherites in his own party, and in the end his government embraced European unity only partially, keeping its distance from the union's single currency initiative (about which more below.)

Major's tenure in office continued to be bedeviled by the Conservative Party's internal battles over Europe, which became especially vicious when Thatcher led the "Euroskeptics" in condemning any plans to emulate continental social policies as "socialism through the back Delors," a reference to the president of the European Commission, Jacques Delors. Major also suffered from his inability to convince his European Union (EU) partners to rescind their ban on the importation of British beef, which had been imposed because "mad cow disease" was detected in some of the local herds. Roast beef being as essential to the British way of life as warm beer, many Britons saw the EU ban as an attack on John Bull himself. Finally, Major's government, which talked a great deal about family values and high moral principles, was buffeted by repeated scandals, many of them deliciously sexual. Sixteen of Major's ministers and senior members of Parliament had to leave office in disgrace, nine of them for sexual peccadilloes.

John Major's government could not be held responsible for the bizarre family values of the House of Windsor, but the royals' unseemly antics further

The funeral of Princess Diana.

tarnished the ruling establishment and, along with a tenacious economic recession, helped generate a mood of doubt and gloom in Britain in the mid-1990s. By 1992 the fairy-tale marriage of Prince Charles and Lady Diana Spencer was openly on the rocks, with Charles carrying on a much-publicized affair with Mrs. Camilla Parker-Bowles and Lady Di falling victim to bulimia and episodes of suicidal depression. Charles and Diana's mutual disillusionment came in the immediate wake of the bustup of two other royal family marriages, those of Princess Anne and Captain Mark Phillips and Prince Andrew and Sarah Ferguson, the duchess of York (aka Fergic). Reprehensible behavior on the part of the British royal house was nothing new—one need merely recall the adulterous affairs of Edward VII and the scandalous romance between Edward VIII and his American divorcée, Wallis Simpson— but the Windsors had been a pretty staid lot for the past half century. Now the royal family was beginning to look almost as dysfunctional as those dole-supported, council flat–dwelling menageries regularly pilloried in the conservative press. The only consolation for Major in all this was that the tragic conclusion to the Lady Di saga in a Paris underpass in August 1997 did not come on his watch.

By early 1997, Britain had had enough of Major and his Tories, and when the prime minister called an election in May of that year, his government was turned out by the Laborites under Tony Blair. At forty-one, Blair was even younger than Major when he had taken office; indeed, he was Britain's youngest prime minister since Pitt the Younger. Although he came from an academic family and had an Oxford education, Blair was consciously unstuffy, carefully letting it be known that at college he had played guitar in a rock band called Ugly Rumours (but also letting it be known that he had never touched drugs, making him unique in the annals of rock band guitarists of the seventies). After the university, he became a lawyer in London, married another London lawyer, joined the Labor Party, and rose quickly through the ranks from fledgling Member of Parliament (MP) in the early eighties to party leader in the early nineties. He owed his meteoric rise, and for that matter his victory in the general election of 1997, to his ability to appeal to the skilled working classes and middle-management types that had deserted Labor for Thatcher and Major.

As prime minister, Blair promised a new and revitalized politics "free from outdated dogma and doctrine" and fully in tune with the demands of the modern global market. Although he also promised to remain mindful of the needs of the poor and insisted that he would "not leave all to the market," his "New Labor" policies hardly looked like Labor policies at all—at least not to the stalwarts of Old Labor. Despite some carping on the left, however, Blair rapidly emerged as a wildly popular leader, blessed with a mandate to effect genuine political change.

The new prime minister began to exploit that mandate right away. In the realm of constitutional politics, he launched a program of devolution, whereby long-held central powers were partly ceded to regional and local bodies. He reestablished the Scottish Parliament for the first time since the Act of Union in

British Prime Minister Tony Blair.

1707, and he introduced the first-ever regional assembly in Wales. The Bank of England was granted the authority to set monetary policy. London would be allowed, also for the first time, to elect its mayor directly. By contrast, the House of Lords, or at least its hereditary component, would lose some power because Blair's government eliminated most of the hereditary seats. Only 91 of the 750-odd hereditary peerages survived this blue-blood letting, which was effected by making all the peers submit brief essays explaining why they should be spared the ax. Needless to say, the peers were not pleased with this arrangement.

Unhappy peers constituted a minor problem for the British government compared to the apparently endless "troubles" in Northern Ireland. Shortly after taking office, Blair paid a personal visit to Belfast to try to bring peace, at long last, between the feuding Protestant and Catholic factions. Encouragingly, he managed to convince the Catholic IRA to commit to a cease-fire in July 1997, and in the fall of that year Sinn Fein, the IRA's political wing, joined peace talks with its Protestant counterparts held under the auspices of America's Senator George Mitchell. Blair himself attended the talks, becoming the first British prime minister to have contact with Sinn Fein since 1921. With the signing of the so-called Good Friday Agreement in 1998, the contending parties committed themselves to solving their disagreements by "peaceful means," but low-level sectarian violence continued until the IRA decommissioned its arsenal in September 2005.

In another, much farther distant corner of the once globe-girdling British Empire, Blair's government presided over the formal return of Hong Kong to China. (The transfer had been agreed upon when Margaret Thatcher was prime minister.) Beijing promised to respect democratic rights in the former British crown colony, and Blair warned that Hong Kong would be "destroyed" as a bastion of freedom and prosperity if the Chinese reneged on this pledge.

Blair's assumption of Britain's top office brought another change as well: the unprecedented election of 120 women to Parliament, most of them first-time members representing the Labor Party. The press immediately dubbed them Blair's Babes. Inevitably, a few of the babes began having babes themselves and, being modern women, demanded that the crusty old Parliament accommodate their needs as busy working moms. Specifically, they asked for a day care center on the premises, high chairs in the Commons dining room, and the right to breast-feed their babies in committee rooms. Noting that Blair's government had promised to make things easier for women in the workplace, they fully expected to be accommodated. But they were rebuffed in all their demands. Whereas Scandinavia's parliaments had been filled with nursing mothers for years, Westminster retained the atmosphere of a gentlemen's club.

In the late 1990s, Britain's economy was among the most dynamic in the European Union, and most ordinary Britons seemed to have recovered from the malaise of the Major years. If, as American Secretary of State Dean Acheson famously said in 1962, the British had "lost an empire but never found a role," they had, it seemed, largely gotten over that problem by century's end. Observing the atmosphere of happy hedonism in London in 1999, a visiting American journalist reported that the Britons had "finally stopped seeking a role and started getting a life." On the other hand, if one turned from the man in the pub to the country's conservative pundits for a reading on the state of the national soul, one encountered a litany of woe. Books with titles like *The Death of Britain*, *The Abolition of Britain*, and *Who Do We Think We Are?* suggested that there was at least one faction on the British scene as morose and confused as the French.

Tony Blair, fully sharing (and helping promote) the dominant mood of optimism, moved farther away from the Conservative Party's Euroskepticism by signing on to the EU's social program, which sought to harmonize living and working standards among the member states. Yet he did not adopt fully the Continental perspective in this area. On the contrary, his government, like those of Thatcher's and Major's, took delight in lecturing the Europeans on the need for less regulation and more private initiative. Under New Labor, Britain achieved a more flexible and nimble economy than did its EU partners. On the other hand, it also had the longest working hours in the EU and the highest rates of divorce and teenage pregnancy. Moreover, despite the best efforts of "Blair's Babes," women's wages on average remained significantly lower than men's, partly because a high percentage of women continued to work in the relatively low-paying service sector.

Not surprisingly, Blair continued to receive criticism from the old left that he had deserted Labor's core constituency and forgotten his pledge to protect the less fortunate. His critics enjoyed a moment of partial revenge in the municipal elections of May 4, 2000, which saw Labor lose nearly six hundred council seats across the country, including, most humiliatingly, the first-ever mayoral race in London. The winner there, "Red" Ken Livingston, was a former Laborite who had become profoundly disillusioned with the centrist policies of Tony Blair. He won London on an avowedly populist, feminist, egalitarian, beer-for-the-blokes and damn-the-cappuccino ticket.

Fortunately for Blair, Labor's primary rivals, the Tories, remained too divided and rudderless to take advantage of his government's failings, and it was largely for want of attractive alternatives that Blair secured a comfortable victory in the general elections of June 8, 2001. He hoped to use that victory to address some of the chronic domestic problems that he had been accused of neglecting in his first term, such as Britain's crumbling public services and transportation system. Instead, he found himself fully preoccupied by foreign policy issues, most notably his decision to participate in the American-led military operations in Afghanistan and Iraq. Like America's Lyndon Johnson in the 1960s, Blair expended so much political capital on his military commitments that he lost his effectiveness at home. Although he managed to win one more national election, in May 2005, his victory was exceedingly narrow, and in September 2006, yielding to pressure from his own party, he announced he would step down within one year. However one judged Blair's idiosyncratic mixture of pragmatism and missionary zeal, his passing was likely to constitute another watershed in the history of postwar Britain and the Western world.

In the months before he announced his intention to leave office prematurely, Tony Blair was caught up in a corruption scandal involving the sale of peerages to Labor Party donors, but this practice seemed a mere peccadillo compared to the illicit wheeling and dealing carried out on a regular basis by the top politicians of Italy. For most of the Cold War era Italy had been run by the conservative Christian Democratic (DC) Party, which, though infamously corrupt and often inefficient, stayed in power by exploiting Italians' fears of the rival Communist Party (PCI), the next most influential force on the Italian political scene. "Hold your nose and vote DC" was the word of the day. With the fall of the Berlin Wall and the rollback of Communism, however, the stink of the DC's corruption became too much for Italians to bear, and they gave themselves over to a frenzy of political fumigation known as the *Mani Pulite* (Clean Hands) campaign. Nationwide investigations exposed hundreds of dirty politicians and revealed extensive ties between the political establishment in Rome and the Mafia. As the campaign progressed, one-third of the national parliament and one-half the Sicilian parliament came under some form of investigation. The two most powerful figures in Italian politics, the DC leader Mario Andreotti and the Socialist chief Bettino Craxi, underwent trials for corruption and were driven into political exile.

The Clean Hands campaign, combined with the collapse of Communism, brought major changes to the Italian political scene, at least on the surface. In the 1992 parliamentary elections the DC lost significant ground for the first time. The Communists, weakened by the fall of Communism in Russia and Eastern Europe, were not strong enough to form a viable alternative to the DC. The parliamentary elections two years later, which were held under new rules, finally brought an end to the long DC domination at the national level. (The DC subsequently split into seven different smaller parties.) The DC-dominated coalition gave way to a new center-right coalition headed by Silvio Berlusconi, a charismatic media mogul who promised to modernize Italy and to turn it into a mecca for entrepreneurs like himself. The name of Berlusconi's party, Forza Italia (Go Italy), sounded like a football cheer, not surprising as the new prime minister owned Italy's premier soccer club, A. C. Milan. He also owned private TV networks, newspapers, and a huge financial services company. His primary coalition partner was the Milan-based Lombard League, whose leader, Umberto Bossi, trafficked in anti-immigrant sentiment and northern resentment against the more backward, tax-eating south. While Berlusconi advertised himself as a go-getter businessman of impeccable character, it turned out that he had used many of the old methods, including kickbacks to governmental officials, to build his business empire. There were also rumors of ties to the Mafia. "I'm forced to

Italy's Silvio Berlusconi.

enter politics, otherwise they'll put me in prison," admitted Berlusconi, alluding to the promise of parliamentary immunity if he won office. Moreover, it soon became apparent that Berlusconi could not get along with his chief coalition partner, Bossi. In December 1995, Bossi brought down the government, leading to Berlusconi's replacement by a colorless technocrat named Lamberto Dini.

The parliamentary elections of 1996 brought what seemed to be a cleaner break with the past—namely, a center-left government headed by a liberal economics professor named Romano Prodi, who for once had no dirt (or blood) on his hands. Under Prodi, Italy underwent just enough economic belt tightening to meet the requirements for joining the European Union's single currency scheme. Yet even Prodi found it difficult to put Italy on a clear course of economic and political modernization. Like other leaders who had tried to transform the Italian way of life, most notably Mussolini, Prodi encountered a deep-seated resistance to fundamental change that could absorb and defeat all sorts of superficial movement. "If we want things to stay as they are, then things will have to change," says a character in *The Leopard*, Giuseppe Lampedusa's seminal novel about Sicily and Italian unification. Prodi found that most of his countrymen were more satisfied to drift in quiet but trusted waters than to strike out boldly for new shores. Despite some economic gains and rising prosperity, growth was hampered (as in France) by high taxes and stifling regulations, which would have been even more crippling had Italians followed them to the letter. The nation continued to be convulsed by frequent strikes, reminding Italians that when all was said and done, the powerful unions had a greater impact on their daily lives than did the government. Fearing the unions, Prodi made no effort to cut pensions, health benefits, or the welfare system. His government made extensive investments in the southern provinces, but in the end it could not do much to overcome the huge gap in productivity and living standards between north and south.

In October 1998, Prodi resigned as prime minister and was replaced by Massimo d'Alema, the head of the party of the Democratic Left, which is what the main branch of the old PSI now called itself. D'Alema was the first ex-Communist to lead a Western European country. This might have been more significant news had d'Alema ever been much of a Communist, but his politics were essentially centrist. He envisaged himself as an Italian Tony Blair, yet another prophet of a Third Way between the traditionalist left and the unreconstructed right. He spoke of carving out a larger role for Italy in foreign affairs and of making Italy more competitive by reducing taxes, reforming the welfare system, and bringing the unions to heel. But in the end d'Alma proved as ineffectual as Prodi, and just as colorless. Throughout this period Berlusconi exploited his TV stations and newspapers to push his own political comeback.

Berlusconi duly returned to power in spring 2001 with the promise that this time he really would turn Italy on its head. And, as it turned out, this time he was granted some five years to prove that he was the miracle worker he claimed to be. But once again his government was shaken by repeated political scandals. Although Berlusconi himself managed through political and legal skulduggery to avoid being convicted of any crimes, his closest adviser was found guilty in 2004 of aiding and abetting the Mafia. Meanwhile, Berlusconi became so preoccupied with the protection of his own business interests that he had little time or energy to reform the Italian economy, which continued to stagnate. Moreover, like Tony Blair, he deeply damaged himself at home by sending a military contingent to Iraq in 2003.

When Berlusconi ran for reelection in early 2006 his prospects did not look good, and his campaign rhetoric took on a self-pitying tone. "I am the Jesus Christ of politics," he declared. "I'm a patient victim. I endure everything. I sacrifice myself for everyone." He even promised to abstain from sex until polling day (a true sacrifice, given his chronic womanizing). Astonishingly, such tactics almost paid off, but in the end his coalition lost very narrowly to a center-left group led (once again) by Romano Prodi. Berlusconi's many critics in Italy and around the world issued a collective sigh of relief when the wily entrepreneur was finally ousted, but the relief was mixed with lingering amazement that a sophisticated country like Italy could have allowed a figure like Silvio Berlusconi to come to power in the first place. Some also feared that he might find a way to rise from the dead once again. (And in fact, in April 2008, he did rise again, exploiting a lackluster performance by Prodi to seize the prime ministership for a third time.)

UNITED GERMANY

The united Germany that emerged from the unification negotiations in 1990 was a very different entity from the new nation that Bismarck had orchestrated in 1871. Unlike the so-called Second Reich, the reunified German state of the 1990s came into being not through military victories but through the collapse of the Soviet Empire and the implosion of the GDR. Helmut Kohl's Germany, unlike Bismarck's, was a democracy, and it was firmly embedded in the larger European community. It had no enemies on its borders. Moreover, largely because of American pressure on the USSR, united Germany became a full-fledged member of NATO, just as West Germany had been. Whereas the celebration at Versailles marking Germany's first unification in 1871 had been full of chauvinist bombast and military swagger, the ceremony signaling the merger of West and East Germany, held in the Reichstag on October 3, 1990, was a restrained and sober affair, reflecting Germany's determination to eschew the nationalistic adventurism that had brought so much misery to itself and the world in the past.

One of the first and most difficult questions the new Germany faced was where to locate the national capital. Should it be in Bonn, the West German seat of government since 1949, or ought it move back to Berlin, which had been united Germany's capital from 1871 to 1945? (East Berlin had served as the capital of the GDR from 1949 to 1990, but that status was not fully recognized by the West.) There was much to be said for Bonn. The little Rhineland city, though certainly unprepossessing, was widely associated with West Germany's

Inside the dome of the renovated Reichstag.

orderly transition to democracy and vaunted economic prosperity. Moreover, Bonn was geographically close to the hubs of the European Union and NATO. Berlin, as the pro-Bonn lobby eagerly pointed out, had held sway during the rise of "militaristic Prussia," the disastrous *Weltpolitik* of William II, the failed democratic experiment of Weimar, the moral and political catastrophe of Nazism, and the Stalinist dictatorship of the GDR. The proponents of a move back to Berlin did not deny that their city had a problematical past, but they insisted that by returning to the old capital, the German government could help overcome the divide that had opened up between the two Germanys over the past forty years. As President Richard von Weizäcker, a native Berliner, said, "Only in Berlin do we come from both sides but truly stand as one." When the vote on the capital question was taken in the Bundestag on June 20, 1991, Berlin emerged the victor by a very close margin.

Although Germany was officially united as of October 3, 1990, political, social, economic, and psychological differences between the western and eastern parts of the country remained a potent reality. The euphoria that had accompanied reunification quickly gave way to mutual antagonisms and negative stereotypes. Germans from the western states (so-called Wessis), resenting the higher taxes they had to pay to cover the huge costs of bringing the eastern states up to western standards, decried the eastern Germans (Ossis) as shiftless, backward, and lacking in initiative. The Ossis, for their part, found their western countrymen boastful, aggressive, and insensitive to the special problems that the easterners faced. East German women felt especially aggrieved, for they had sacrificed some of the material benefits and social privileges accorded them by the GDR state. Mourning the demise of a state that had ritually celebrated its female citizens (while also, however, exploiting them), many Ossi women came to see themselves as the biggest losers of reunification. In light of the persistent antagonism between eastern and western Germans, the East German poet Rainer Kurze remarked sadly, "As we razed the Berlin Wall we had no idea that [the barrier] existed also within us." Indeed, the infamous wall had hardly come down before people began speaking of a more formidable "wall in the head."

The deep malaise afflicting the "new states" of the east was fueled by very real socioeconomic inequities. Despite the financial transfers from west to east, the east was not quickly transformed into a "blooming economic landscape," as Chancellor Kohl had promised it would be in the election campaign of 1990. Because of an inability to compete in the new marketplace, many eastern companies had to shut down, resulting in large-scale layoffs. A wholesale privatization of state-owned firms, organized through a government holding company called the Treuhand, brought the dismissal of many more workers. Female workers, as eastern women's organizations quickly pointed out, were losing their jobs even faster than the men. Along with secure jobs, easterners lost various state-supported amenities that were more extensive than the welfare programs obtainable in the west (and now extended to the entire country). Above all, many Ossis felt they had lost their sense of worth and identity in a new environment that was very different from what they had known before. Their frustrations soon found expression in electoral contests. In the Bundestag elections of 1994 the Partei des demokratischen Sozialismus (PDS), composed largely of former Communists from the east, performed well enough in the eastern districts to win thirty seats; in the former East Berlin the PDS won a clear majority.

Besides coping with the demands of the present, the Ossis were obliged to come to grips with the legacy of their Stalinist past. The government of reunified Germany was determined to expose and adjudicate the crimes of the Communist GDR, and it pursued this goal with a much greater zealousness than either of the governments of divided Germany had shown in confronting the Nazi past forty years earlier. With the opening of the voluminous files assembled by the Stasi, the dreaded GDR secret police, a clearer picture emerged of how the domestic intelligence system had worked and who had collaborated with it. Several prominent political and cultural figures who had gained reputations in the GDR for dissidence were now exposed as Stasi collaborators.

In addition to the wrenching social and economic problems attending reunification, Germany found itself flooded by a new wave of immigrants and asylum seekers from the ex-Communist countries and the Third World. In 1991 some two hundred fifty thousand refugees entered the country, and that figure doubled in 1992. Germany now housed 1.4 million refugees, around 8 percent of the world's total. Some of these people were fleeing political persecution in their homelands, but many others simply wanted a better life. Germany was Europe's primary magnet for immigration because of its geographic location, its prosperity, and its relatively liberal asylum laws. Lamentably, the influx of refugees and immigrants generated an upsurge in xenophobia and violence against foreigners, especially (though by no means exclusively) in the eastern states. In the fall of 1991, a band of skinheads in the eastern town of Hoyerswerda attacked Vietnamese and Mozambican "guest workers," who had been imported by the former GDR to do menial labor. In the following summer, thugs attacked the residents of an asylum center in the eastern port of Rostock. Although national leaders condemned these and other antiforeigner attacks, the German government's most significant response to the violence was to tighten its asylum laws. As of July 1993, Germany would not accept asylum seekers who had entered the country through neighboring nations that had been declared politically stable, such as Poland and the Czech Republic. This dramatically reduced the number of asylum seekers, since those two countries had been the major avenues of entry. Of course, the new rule also put a strain on Germany's eastern neighbors, who now had to tighten their own border controls to keep out would-be emigrants to Germany. The stricter asylum laws, combined with a belated get-tough policy toward antiforeigner violence, lowered the number of hate crimes in the second half of the decade, but the task of integrating foreigners still resident in the country remained daunting.

Turkish women in a Berlin park.

This challenge applied especially to Germany's large community of resident Turks, who had lived in the country for years. They and other long-term residents were denied citizenship because for the most part, German law restricted this status to those of "German blood," including thousands of so-called *Volksdeutsche* from the former Soviet Union who generally knew little about the land from which their ancestors had emigrated centuries before. Germany had long been criticized for this policy, which smacked of Nazi practices. Finally, at the end of the decade significant changes in the citizenship laws were made. According to regulations passed in May 1999, any child born in Germany with at least one parent resident in the country for eight years could gain automatic German citizenship. Such an individual could maintain dual citizenship until age twenty-three, at which time he or she had to decide which citizenship to keep. Thus, just in time for the twenty-first century, Germany shifted away from a preoccupation with bloodlines that had disastrously governed its conception of nationhood in years past.

In the months immediately preceding German unification, some foreign leaders, notably Margaret Thatcher and François Mitterrand, had expressed concerns that the country would again become a threat to world peace. During the decade following unification, Germany proved that such fears were unfounded. Among its first foreign policy acts, the new unity government under

Helmut Kohl officially recognized Germany's border line with Poland, thus easing anxieties in that country. Germany went on to provide significant material assistance to Poland and the other new Eastern European democracies. Looking to the West, Germany reaffirmed the Bonn-Paris axis, long one of the linchpins of West German foreign policy. Kohl, who relished his reputation as "the last great European," showed his commitment to European integration by teaming up with Mitterrand to push for a single European currency.

In the realm of international security, the new Germany showed itself, at least initially, to be as cautious and reluctant as the old Federal Republic had been. When the Gulf War broke out in 1990, Bonn elected to make a financial contribution to the allied campaign rather than send troops, as Washington requested. This led to charges that Germany was not pulling its weight in international affairs, that it was acting like "a political dwarf" despite its being "an economic giant." Germany's defense was that it could not afford to be seen acting too assertively so soon after reunification and that in any event its constitution disallowed military engagements outside the NATO area. The majority of the German people supported this policy of reluctance.

One year later, however, Germany summarily decided to recognize Slovenia and Croatia as independent nations, a step that contributed to the breakup of Yugoslavia. Now Germany was widely criticized for acting unilaterally and for throwing its weight around. Yet its bold diplomatic initiatives in the Balkans did not signal a new assertiveness across the board; on the whole, Bonn remained a team player, content to let its senior allies, especially the United States, take the lead in security issues. Again citing constitutional "out of area" restrictions as well as its history of past aggression in the Balkans, Germany refused to participate in the early phases of the UN's peacekeeping mission in that troubled region. However, in July 1994, the Federal Constitutional Court in Karlsruhe ruled that German troops could participate in multinational military operations outside the NATO region, provided the action was sanctioned by the Bundestag. In the following year, German forces joined the UN peacekeeping mission in the Balkans in an auxiliary role, which in 1999 was expanded to include participation in the NATO bombing campaign against Serbia. In justifying this momentous step, the German government argued that the Serbs' "ethnic cleansing" in Kosovo was too reminiscent of the Nazis' crimes to allow Germany to turn a blind eye to this new human catastrophe. Throughout the bombing campaign, which constituted the first time German forces had seen combat since 1945, the Germans were careful to stay within the limits of their mission and to let the Americans and their European allies lead the operation.

In the domestic political arena, as on the international stage, Germany initially hewed closely to the lines set down by West Germany before the fall of the Berlin Wall. This was largely because the long-serving West German chancellor, Helmut Kohl, handily won the top office in the first all-German elections

German Chancellor Helmut Kohl on the campaign trail.

held after reunification. As time went on, it began to appear that the chancellor, who stands six feet two inches and weighs 350 pounds, would be as immovable politically as he was physically. In 1996, he surpassed Konrad Adenauer as postwar Germany's longest-serving leader, and many expected he would ultimately break Bismarck's record of nineteen years in office. However, Kohl's longevity itself became a source of weakness, making him complacent and somewhat aloof from the concerns of ordinary citizens. Moreover, many Germans simply grew tired of having him around. During the throes of reunification he had seemed a welcome anchor amid the swirling currents of change, but before long he came across as inflexible and tired, unable or unwilling to make the adjustments necessary to deal with all the challenges of the new era. Younger Germans in particular found him less appealing than his opponent in the 1998 federal elections, Gerhard Schröder (SPD), who styled himself a "new socialist" and economic modernizer, Germany's answer to Tony Blair. (Having been married four times, Schröder could credibly claim to be a "man of new beginnings.") He won the election and created a new coalition government consisting of the Social Democrats and the Greens, the first such coalition at the national level in German history. As for Kohl, his reputation was much tarnished after he left office by the revelation that he had accepted illegal payments from undisclosed donors to bolster the CDU in its electoral battles in East Germany. He did not help his cause by refusing to name the donors and by comparing criticism of his behavior to the persecution of the Jews under Nazism.

President Bill Clinton
and German Chancellor
Gerhard Schröder (*left*).

Shortly after taking office, Schröder delivered an important speech on the occasion of the sixtieth anniversary of *Kristallnacht* ("night of the broken glass"), the Nazis' brutal anti-Jewish pogrom of November 1938. In his speech the new chancellor said that the Germans must "look ahead without forgetting what happened." He added that with reunification, Germany had finally come of age and felt "neither superior nor inferior to anyone." His comments, while perhaps sounding innocuous enough to most foreigners, were interpreted by some domestic critics as giving license to a dangerous turn in German thinking. "Intellectual nationalism is spreading," warned the late Ignaz Bubis, German Jewry's chief spokesman, "and it is not free of an understated anti-Semitism." Stung by the criticism, Schröder hastily reassured his critics that he and his government had no intention of trying to shrug off the memory of Germany's past crimes. To drive this point home, he threw his support behind the creation of a national monument in the new capital of Berlin to commemorate the Holocaust. This project was extremely controversial for a host of reasons, not least of which was the conviction harbored by many Germans that their nation was being "eternally victimized" because of the Nazi crimes. After years of delay, the Holocaust Memorial finally opened to the public in May 2005. At the opening ceremony, Bundestag president Wolfgang Thierse declared: "Today we open a memorial that recalls Nazi Germany's worst, most terrible crime—the attempt to exterminate an entire people."

Although the new Holocaust Memorial was a potent reminder of Germany's greatest crime, by the time it opened many Germans, from Chancellor Schröder on down, were clearly anxious to throw off the hair shirt in favor of more comfortable attire, preferably in the national colors. In its foreign policy, especially its relationship with the United States, Schröder's Germany had been showing for some time that it was indeed a more "normal" nation, capable of going its own political way. During his campaign for reelection in summer/fall 2002, Schröder went out of his way to criticize President Bush's threat to invade Iraq if Saddam Hussein did not destroy the weapons of mass destruction (WMD) he allegedly had hidden. Schröder called instead for putting more diplomatic pressure on Saddam to allow UN weapons inspectors to return to Iraq to search for the weapons. He added that any "military adventure" in Iraq would have to happen without German participation and that Berlin was also unwilling to help out with its "checkbook," as it had in the Gulf War of 1991. Schröder's position turned out to have great resonance with German voters, who were no more enthusiastic than any other Western Europeans about Bush's Iraqi policy. Schröder's own failings in the economic realm had made his prospects for retaining power uncertain at best, but by strategically separating himself from the widely reviled Bush, he pulled away from his conservative challenger and went on to win the election.

While Chancellor Schröder was departing from traditional German diplomatic practice by openly challenging America on a major foreign policy issue, some of his countrymen were taking a new and more nationalistic line regarding Germany's relationship with its troubled past. Throughout the postwar era, it had been more or less taboo for mainstream "respectable" Germans to speak too openly about German suffering in World War II, for fear that this would look like an effort to evade or mitigate Germany's own guilt. But at the very moment the new Holocaust Memorial was taking its prominent place in Germany's landscape of shameful remembrance, German historians and writers were reminding the world that Germans had been "victims" as well as perpetrators of atrocities during the Hitler era. In a book entitled *Der Brand* (The Fire), historian Jörg Friedrich revisited the firebombing of Dresden by the Royal Air Force in February 1945. He dwelt graphically on the horrific plight of the thousands of civilians who perished in the streets and cellars of that city. Similarly, writer Günther Grass's 2003 novel *Krebsgang* (*Crab Walk*) called attention to the fate of over nine thousand German refugees who drowned in the frozen Baltic following the sinking of the transport ship *Wilhelm Gustloff* by a Soviet submarine in early 1945. Another German victim story that began to get a lot of attention featured the more than 12 million ethnic Germans forcefully expelled from present-day Poland, Russia, and the Czech Republic during and after World War II. Some 1.4 million of these refugees died in the hard trek west. In response to pressure from the expellee lobby in Germany, Schröder promised to establish a commemorative Center against Expulsions.

Despite renewed promises from the chancellor to open up the labor market and promote entrepreneurship, there was not much new in the way of economic growth and revitalization. The great German economic locomotive, far from pulling the rest of Europe down the track, could hardly carry its own freight, and jobs continued to migrate to regions with lower labor costs. German unemployment ran at a post—World War II high of 11.2 percent nationally (and considerably higher in eastern Germany). German universities, once a major spur to economic development, were so underfunded and overcrowded that some of their best faculty members were decamping to America—and even to Britain. Schröder's party, the SPD, steadily lost ground in state parliamentary elections, resulting in the conservative CDU/CSU's gaining control of the Bundesrat, the upper house of the national parliament.

In May 2005, Schröder amazed everyone by calling new elections for September 2005, a year earlier than he had to by law. Since the chancellor's Socialist Party trailed the conservative coalition by as much as 17 percent in national polls, some observers concluded that Schröder must have a political death wish. A more likely explanation for this move was that Schröder wanted a quick election so he would be certain to face Angela Merkel, the conservatives' leading candidate. Merkel, a former Helmut Kohl protégée from eastern Germany, was, to put it mildly, not known for her personal charisma or flair on the campaign trail. Moreover her gender put her at a possible disadvantage in a country that had never elected a woman to the federal chancellorship.

As it turned out, Schröder did run a more effective campaign than Merkel, and he almost beat her. Merkel's coalition's margin of victory was so narrow that the CDU/CSU was obliged to govern in tandem with the SPD in a so-called Grand Coalition. A Grand Coalition had governed only once before in German history, during the chancellorship of Kurt Georg Kiesinger in 1966—69, and the result had been a blossoming of the neo-Nazi right and the terrorist far left. Most observers believed that by the early twenty-first century Germany's centrist democracy was stable enough to resist extremist siren calls. No one could fail to notice, however, that in the 2005 national elections the far left, consisting of the former Communist PDS and a new Linkspartei (Left Party), effectively challenged the moderate SPD for control of the leftist side of the political spectrum. A year later, in regional elections in the eastern states of Brandenburg and Mecklenburg-West Pomerania (Merkel's own constituency), the National Democratic Party, which espoused xenophobic and neo-Nazi views, won seats in the state parliaments.

Many conservatives who backed Merkel's coalition hoped that Germany's first female chancellor would turn out to be a German Margaret Thatcher, a leader who would reverse decades-old policies favoring a heavy state (and union) hand on the levers of economic power. However, the realities of coalition government, combined with the German workforce's addiction to "cuddle capitalism"— generous social benefits and rigorous job protection laws—made this unlikely. And indeed, within months of taking office, Merkel's government proved unable to reform the health care system in a way that might have significantly cut labor costs or eased the federal budget deficit. Unemployment remained as high as ever. Merkel had more success on the world stage. She effectively represented Germany during a trip to China and emerged as a leader in the international effort to pressure Iran to curb its nuclear program. She also did much to improve Germany's troubled relationship with the United States. In summer 2006, she invited President Bush to Stralsrund (Mecklenburg-West Pomerania), where she treated her visitor to a local version of Texas barbeque. Once again, it seemed, Germany was America's best friend on the Continent. Yet even while signaling her intention to work cordially with Bush, Merkel made clear that she had no intention of sending German troops to fight in Iraq.

Germany's ongoing economic woes notwithstanding, the nation under Merkel seemed to be throwing off some of its legendary gloom and pessimism (in a poll taken shortly before the 2005 elections, only 30 percent of the respondents had said they believed they could do something positive to improve their lives). As Germany prepared to host the soccer World Cup in summer 2006, a high percentage of the populace expressed optimism that Germany could do an effective job. And once the German team started actually to win, the national mood turned positively ebullient. With Merkel as their head cheerleader, Germans across the land waved their national colors in a show of unbridled patriotism that would have been frowned upon only a few years earlier. As it happened, some of the World Cup contests, including the final, took place in the giant stadium in Berlin originally built to host the 1936 "Nazi Olympics," but no one seemed to think that that sea of national colors around Berlin during the festival portended a return to the militaristic nationalism of yore.

RUSSIA: RETURN TO AUTOCRACY

In defining its role in the post-Communist era, Germany had many advantages over its sometime rival to the east, Russia. As we have seen, Germany was firmly embedded in the European Union and NATO, and it boasted tested parliamentary institutions, an independent judiciary, a well-regulated banking system, a vibrant stock market, and a sound economy. The new Russia, by contrast, was not part of any alliance system, and its new democratic political institutions and partly privatized economy were extremely fragile, to say the least. If even united Germany had difficulty integrating its formerly Communist eastern states into the world of pluralistic democracy and market capitalism, the new Russia was likely to find this transition much more agonizing.

The daunting challenge of reinventing Russia did not seem to intimidate its new president, Boris Yeltsin. Like a latter-day Peter the Great, he declared his intention to pull his nation into the modern world, whether it liked it or not. In November 1991, Yeltsin appointed two reformers to his cabinet, Yegor Gaidar

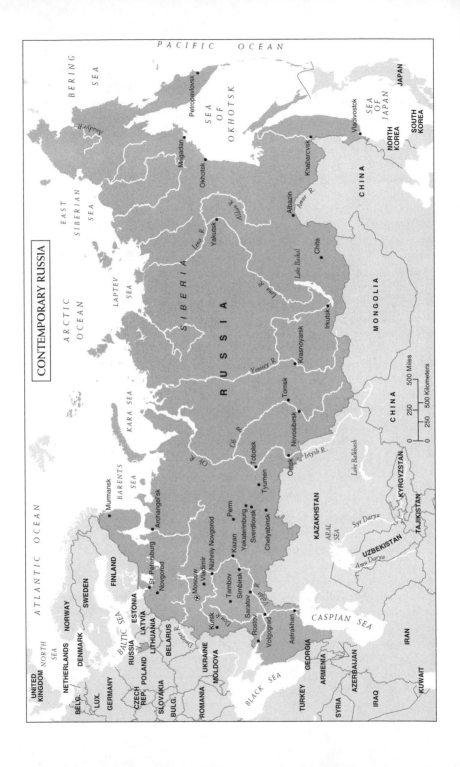

CONTEMPORARY RUSSIA

PACIFIC OCEAN

BERING SEA

SEA OF OKHOTSK

JAPAN

SEA OF JAPAN

NORTH KOREA

SOUTH KOREA

CHINA

EAST SIBERIAN SEA

LAPTEV SEA

ARCTIC OCEAN

KARA SEA

BARENTS SEA

ATLANTIC OCEAN

NORTH SEA

BALTIC SEA

BLACK SEA

CASPIAN SEA

ARAL SEA

Lake Balkhash

Lake Baikal

MONGOLIA

CHINA

KAZAKHSTAN

KYRGYZSTAN

TAJIKISTAN

UZBEKISTAN

Syr Darya

Amu Darya

SIBERIA

RUSSIA

Ob R.

Ob R.

Irtysh R.

Yenisey R.

Lena R.

Lena R.

Aldan R.

Amur R.

Indigirka R.

Don R.

Volga R.

Dnepr R.

Cities and places

Petropavlovsk
Vladivostok
Magadan
Okhotsk
Khabarovsk
Albazin
Chita
Yakutsk
Irkutsk
Krasnoyarsk
Tomsk
Novosibirsk
Omsk
Tobolsk
Tyumen
Murmansk
Archangel'sk
St. Petersburg
Novgorod
Nizhniy Novgorod
Perm
Kazan
Yekaterinburg
Sverdlovsk
Chelyabinsk
Vladimir
Moscow
Tambov
Simbirsk
Saratov
Kursk
Rostov
Volgograd
Astrakhan

Countries

UNITED KINGDOM
NETHERLANDS
BELG.
LUX.
GERMANY
DENMARK
NORWAY
SWEDEN
FINLAND
ESTONIA
LATVIA
LITHUANIA
RUSSIA
POLAND
CZECH REP.
SLOVAKIA
BULG.
ROMANIA
MOLDOVA
UKRAINE
BELARUS
TURKEY
GEORGIA
ARMENIA
AZERBAIJAN
SYRIA
IRAQ
KUWAIT
IRAN

Scale

500 Miles
500 Kilometers
250
0

and Anatoly Chubais. Among their principal duties was the privatization of Russia's vast array of state-run factories, banks, farms, and utilities. The process of privatization began with much fanfare, much talk of purging collectivist plaque from the sclerotic arteries of the Russian economy. It soon became evident, however, that the intended cure was almost as debilitating as the disease. The choicest state firms were quickly bought up by a small clique of insiders, often the same folks who had managed them under the old system. Freed from the Soviet-era practice of retaining employees whether they were needed or not, the new owners threw thousands of workers out on the streets.

Despite the inequities attending Russia's privatization campaign, private enterprise was enthusiastically embraced by many ordinary Russians in the early years of the Yeltsin era. Thousands of hopeful entrepreneurs set up new businesses, and seminars taught by visiting faculty from the Harvard Business School became all the rage. With the spread of private enterprise and an influx of foreign-based banks and companies, cities like Moscow and St. Petersburg (the Soviet-era name Leningrad had been dropped along with Communism) took on a whole new look. A proliferation of Western chain stores and fancy boutiques (all bearing signs in Roman lettering rather than Cyrillic) offered a range of consumer goods hitherto unimaginable. The streets swarmed with late-model Mercedeses, BMWs, and bulky SUVs, the vehicles of choice for the newly rich. Remodeled hotels, such as the Metropol in Moscow, glittered with marble, bronze, and crystal; Armani-suited businessmen and high-priced Eurasian hookers filled their lounges. Another arresting street sight, however, was that of grizzled babushkas hawking trinkets at little corner kiosks. These women were reduced to such straits because their state-funded pensions had been eaten away by skyrocketing inflation.

Outside Russia's large cities, the changes wrought by the new order were rather less evident; in the small towns and villages dotting the steppes and Siberian forests one saw little glitz or glamour. Agriculture, though hardly efficient or prosperous in Soviet days, fell into complete disarray in the Yeltsin era because the old system disintegrated without a new one replacing it. Or, to put it more precisely, fledgling private producers with minimal resources operated alongside vestigial state-run collectives that had lost their market connections and ready access to government subsidies. In some areas, especially those far away from the population centers of western Russia, the rapid decay of state-run farms and the loss of subsidies from Moscow forced the citizenry to revert to a barter economy. Traveling across Siberia in the mid-1990s, the British travel writer Colin Thuberon encountered villagers leaving fields unplowed for lack of fuel for their tractors and fodder for their horses. Instead of farming, they spent their time watching American and Mexican soap operas on television. *Santa Barbara* was a big favorite.

One of the major stumbling blocks on the path to a viable and reasonably equitable market economy—as opposed to the robber baron capitalism that

Russia generated—was rampant corruption at every level of society. Of course, corruption was nothing new in Russia. It had been a fundamental fact of life under the tsars—see Gogol's novel *Dead Souls*—and was equally widespread under the Soviets. Russia's traditional underworld, the *vorovskoi mir* (Thieves' Society), had survived the Bolshevik Revolution to become a major player in the USSR's black-market economy. Shortly after coming to power, Yeltsin announced a "full, head-on assault on crime, bribery, and corruption," but since his government had difficulty paying the wages of its police officers and court officials, these individuals all too often elected to join the criminal bands rather than to combat them.

If Russia's various police and internal security forces did not exactly inspire confidence as bulwarks of order and stability, neither did its army. The Russian military in Yeltsin's era was a pale shadow of the once-proud Red Army that had stood toe to toe with NATO and served as Moscow's primary enforcer in holding its Eastern European empire together. Like the Soviet Union itself, the military had rapidly fallen apart in 1990 and 1991, with the republics of Ukraine, Azerbaijan, and Moldova setting up their own armies. Except for strategic weapons, which were to remain under Moscow's control, all the military hardware that happened to be on the independent republics' territory now belonged to them. A bitter feud erupted between Russia and Ukraine when the latter laid claim to the old Soviet Black Sea fleet, based in Odessa. Russia's Baltic fleet, meanwhile, had to be reduced by 40 percent because of a lack of funds to support it. The ships and submarines lay semimothballed in the harbor of Kaliningrad, leaking their oil and nuclear fuel into the Baltic Sea.

Yeltsin's popularity and stature, which had been immense when he took up the reins as Russia's new president, understandably suffered as the people's frustration mounted over the country's economic woes, lawlessness, and loss of prestige in the world. Opposition to the president crystallized in the Duma, Yeltsin's erstwhile bully pulpit. Heading the charge there were Vice President Aleksandr Rutskoi, an Afghan war veteran and former Yeltsin backer, and Ruban Khasbulatov, the leader of the parliament. Their legislative backers came primarily from the relegalized and revived Communist Party, which hungered for a return to old Soviet sureties, and from the extreme nationalists, who (along with many Communists) deeply resented the collapse of Russia's empire. Many legislators also took umbrage at Yeltsin's autocratic style and his steady buildup of the powers of the presidency. Believing that they had the weight of popular opinion behind them, the dissident parliamentarians began to do all they could to undermine his ongoing campaign for democratic reform. In 1992, they forced him to jettison his principal reformist adviser, Yegor Gaidar.

Frustrated by parliament's obstructionism, Yeltsin decided in September 1992 to disband the Duma and to hold new elections that December. Because this was a highly risky move, the president timed his announcement for a Sunday, September 19, when his legislative rivals would not be at their posts in the

White House. Before he could stage his September surprise, however, word leaked out about the plan, and opposition legislators flocked to the parliament building, which they turned into an enormous bunker. To buttress their position, Rutskoi and Khasbulatov invited in a motley crowd of defenders, including old monarchists, neo-Nazis, and Cossacks, the latter decked out in traditional high boots and furry headgear. The standard of the Romanov family flew next to the hammer and sickle on the roof of the building. Signs hanging from the windows called for the blood of Yeltsin, the blood of Gaidar, and the blood of the Jews. Lee Hockstader of the *Washington Post* described the scene as a "theme park of oddities, a Disneyland of paranoia, a Jurassic Park of menace." The rebels counted on the disgruntled army to come to their aid. Quixotically, they also hoped for endorsements from the Western democracies, but Washington, Paris, and London quickly declared their support for "the democratically elected president." Yeltsin, for his part, at first hesitated to take military action against the rebels, for he was not at all sure that the demoralized army would do his bidding. Instead, he tried to drive the dissidents from their bunker by blasting rock music at them from an armored car parked outside. (The khaki-colored vehicle blasting the music instantly became known as the "Yellow Goebbels.") Undeterred by this sound offensive, Rutskoi and Khasbulatov called upon their followers in the capital to attack the main television station and the office of the mayor. This convinced Yeltsin that he had to act decisively to put down the rebellion. On October 4, he ordered tanks from the Kantemirovsky Division to bombard the White House. To his immense relief, they proceeded enthusiastically to do so. In ordering this action, the president must have been struck by the irony of it all: two years earlier it was he who had been bunkered down in the White House, hoping the troops outside would not try to blast him out. Now, as shells pounded the parliament building, igniting fires inside, a fierce battle broke out between the defenders and troops attempting to storm the place. Teenagers dashed across the battlefield, waving frantically in hopes of attracting the attention of cameramen from CNN. Some 150 people died in the fighting; many of them were bystanders. When the troops finally managed to break into the building and arrest the rebel leaders, the White House (now dubbed the Black House) was pocked with shell holes and darkened with big stains of soot. Of course, this kind of damage could be repaired soon enough; much more difficult to mend were the deep rents in the fabric of Russia's fledgling democracy.

Although the anti-Yeltsin coup of October 1993 ended in failure, it pointed up the strength of resurgent Communist and nationalist currents in Russia. The Duma elections in December of that year, from which Yeltsin had hoped to secure a more pliant parliament, produced instead a more intransigent house. The Communists fared very well, and the party of the ultranationalist candidate Vladimir Zhirinovsky, a vulgar buffoon who had visions of himself as a Russian Hitler, won an astounding 23 percent of the total vote. One of the first acts of the

The Russian parliamentary building (the White House) on fire after shelling by pro-Yeltsin forces during the 1993 coup attempt.

new parliament was to release the October coup leaders, Rutskoi and Khasbulatov, whom Yeltsin then pardoned in hopes of placating the nationalist right.

The president's desire to win over his right-wing critics was a primary factor in bringing on the next major test of Russia's internal cohesion and fragile democratic order: Moscow's protracted campaign to prevent the Caucasian republic of Chechnya, one of the eighty-nine units in the new Russian Federation, from breaking away from the association. The effort to suppress the Chechen rebels, who were determined to create an independent Islamic state, quickly degenerated into a bloody quagmire. Some observers called the Chechen conflict Yeltsin's Vietnam, but a better analogy would be the USSR's Afghan War.

Russia's campaign to squelch Chechnya's independence bid began with a hastily organized invasion in December 1994. The Russian generals promised a quick victory over the "primitive bandits." Right from the outset, however, the invading troops proved to be breathtakingly inept. Lacking any decent maps or intelligence data, the Russians stumbled into one trap after another. They staged attacks with no reconnaissance or backup. Thus, it was not until spring 1995 that they were able to overrun the Chechen capital of Grozny. This hardly constituted a final victory, however, for the rebels simply faded into the surrounding hills, from which they staged periodic raids against the occupiers. Grozny, whose "liberation" had cost some forty thousand Russian and Chechen lives, was now a stinking ruin. Old men who recalled the destruction of Stalingrad in World War II insisted that Grozny looked no better.

As the fighting dragged on with no end in sight, both sides engaged in horrible atrocities, though the Russians, with their contempt for the local populace and their desperate need for an "honorable" end to this nightmare, proved especially vicious. Notorious in this regard were the supposedly crack Interior Ministry troops, who cultivated a Rambo look with piratical head scarves, crossed bandoliers, muscle shirts, and menacing tattoos. They strangled prisoners with barbed wire, buggered them with cattle prods, and shocked them in the testicles with electrodes attached to powerful generators. In April 1995, they massacred dozens of civilians in the village of Samashki. Reports about the atrocities found their way back to central Russia, but they did not generate much outrage. After all, in the eyes of most Russians, the Chechens were little more than a tribe of thieves and murderers.

Understandably, the behavior of Russia's troops did nothing to win the hearts and minds of the Chechen populace, and continued spirited resistance on the part of the rebels, combined with the ongoing military incompetence of the invaders, produced a stalemate. Eventually, after many more months of fruitless fighting, as well as additional atrocities, the two sides drew up a truce agreement in late 1996. By that time, some eighty thousand people had been killed in Chechnya, and the Russian military had suffered higher losses than had the Red Army in Afghanistan. Yet for all its sacrifices, Moscow had not managed to crush the rebels thoroughly or to remove Chechnya as a source of infectious instability in the region. Unable to pull the Chechen thorn from Russia's flank, Yeltsin did his level best to pretend that it simply was not there.

Russian troops take a break during the invasion of the breakaway republic of Chechnya.

The Russian president found it expedient to avert his eyes from the Chechen disaster because he needed to focus on more pressing challenges closer to home. In June 1996, presidential elections were on tap, and "Tsar Boris" faced serious opposition from the Communist Party contender, Genady Zyuganov. (The rightist candidate Zhirinovsky, by contrast, no longer posed much of a threat because his ridiculous antics, which included posing nude in the shower for photographs and licensing his own brand of vodka, had discredited him with too many voters.) The prospects looked very bad for Yeltsin because none of the problems that had plagued the Russian Federation since its foundation had gone away; indeed, they had worsened. The country was in ever-steeper economic decline, corruption flourished, and the government could not meet its financial obligations despite repeated infusions of foreign aid and loans. In light of this bleak situation, some of Yeltsin's aides advised him to use his presidential powers to call off the election. Ever the optimist, however, Yeltsin decided to go ahead with the contest, and he threw himself enthusiastically into the campaign despite bouts of ill health and many a brain-numbing hangover. In addition to his irrepressible populist touch, his main advantage was his rival's total lack of charisma: when Zyuganov spoke, people said, birds fell asleep and dropped from their perches. Another crucial advantage was the support the incumbent enjoyed from newly minted billionaire businessmen like Boris Berezovsky and Vladimir Gusinsky, who fully understood that their continuing prosperity depended on a Yeltsin victory. Finally, the president also had a near monopoly on radio and television advertising, which he did not hesitate to exploit.

Had not Russia's overall situation been so grim, Yeltsin's unique advantages would certainly have resulted in a landslide victory; in the event, he won only 38 percent of the vote and therefore had to face a runoff contest with the next highest vote getter, Zyuganov, who managed 32 percent. Yeltsin won the second contest with 53.8 percent, largely because General Ledbed, who had finished third with 15 percent in the first vote, decided to throw his support behind the president.

Emboldened by his victory, Yeltsin announced a new spate of economic reforms. In March 1998, he sacked his plodding prime minister, Viktor Chernomydrin, and brought in the young reformer Sergei Kiriyenko, who impressed many Russia watchers as a breath of fresh air. Kiriyenko planned to reverse Russia's slide into insolvency by cutting government expenditures and getting serious about collecting taxes. These steps might in fact have had some impact had not Russia gotten caught up in the world financial chaos stemming from the Asian economic collapse of mid-1998. Moscow was forced to devalue the ruble and default on its foreign loans. This of course further damaged the country's shaky credit. The International Monetary Fund (IMF) promptly announced that it would discontinue pouring money down the Russian rathole. Yeltsin's Communist rival, Zyuganov, demanded his resignation. Shifting gears once again, the president fired Kiriyenko and his entire government in August 1998 and reappointed as prime minister his old friend Chernomydrin. However, Chernomydrin's cozy connection to Russia's huge natural gas distributor, Gazprom, made him unacceptable to the Duma, and he had to be dismissed. Hoping to placate his Duma critics, Yeltsin moved Foreign Minister Eugeny Primakov, who had a long Communist pedigree, into the prime minister's office.

Primakov sought to calm domestic discontent by promising to pay back wages to millions of state workers, who had not been paid for months. To reassure Western creditors, he promised to continue with free market reforms. In reality, however, Primakov could make little real progress as long as the corrupt, nepotistic, and unpredictable political system was not thoroughly revamped, a challenge that Yeltsin seemed unable or unwilling to take on. Meanwhile, life became increasingly desperate for many ordinary citizens. In the winter of 1998, eleven people froze to death in Moscow for lack of fuel. Fearing an Africa-style mass famine, the European Union rushed $472 million in food aid to the stricken country.

On January 1, 2000, Yeltsin suddenly resigned the Russian presidency and ceded this office to Vladimir Putin, whom he had appointed prime minister six months earlier. Insiders suggested that Putin got the job mainly because he promised not to pursue Yeltsin and his family in the courts for corruption.

Putin served as acting president until he was elected to the top office in the federal elections of March 26, 2000. At the time of his election, the new Russian president was not very well known in the West. Investigations of his background revealed that he had worked for many years as a KGB operative in Dresden. Following the collapse of the USSR he had served as a civil servant in the St. Petersburg municipal government and then taken over the Federal Security Service, the KGB's domestic successor. Whether or not Putin owed his new job as president to a secret deal with Yeltsin, he certainly represented a departure from his predecessor in terms of personal bearing and habits. Austere and somewhat aloof, he stayed away from the vodka bottle and kept himself in good physical shape with judo and skiing. Upon taking office, he promised to push for more economic reforms, to promote human rights and political freedoms, and to respect the rule of law.

Many of Putin's early actions and policies, however, did not seem to be those of a leader who was determined to create a more liberal, pluralistic, and pro-Western Russia. Indeed, as the former spy settled into the presidency during his first term of office, he increasingly showed that what he had in mind for his country was the gradual abandonment of post-Communist Russia's tentative experiment with democracy.

One of his first actions was to resume Russia's bloody campaign in Chechnya following a series of mysterious apartment house bombings in Moscow that were blamed on Chechen rebels. Despite high body counts on both sides and a new spate of atrocities carried out by Russian troops, the war proved popular at home and helped give Putin the image of a tough guy who would not allow Russia's interests to be trifled with.

In his campaign to restore Russian pride and enhance his own image as a decisive leader, Putin also turned his attention to symbolic issues. Ominously, he ordered the return of the Soviet anthem and reinstated the Soviet red flag for the army. Privately, he had always regretted the collapse of Soviet power, and in various public speeches he now waxed nostalgic about the glories of the Soviet era. "Was there nothing but Stalin's prison camps and repression?" he pointedly asked. "What about the achievements of Soviet science, of the spectacular space flight of cosmonaut Yuri Gagarin, of the art and music of cultural heroes like the composer Dmitri Shostakovich?" Putin seemed to imply that these achievements had come about because the Soviet state had been strong and the people confident in the USSR's world power status.

Of course, symbolic measures alone would hardly have sufficed to strengthen the state, and Putin was quick to take concrete steps to consolidate the power of the executive. He convinced the Duma to grant him the right to fire summarily any of Russia's eighty-nine regional governors for "illegal acts." To ingratiate himself with the military he surrounded himself with former officers and tripled the armed forces' budget. The former KGB man also vastly expanded the powers of the secret service.

Effective criticism of these moves within Russia became increasingly difficult because the Kremlin gradually shut down independent media sources. As early as June 2000, Putin ordered the arrest and incarceration of Vladimir Gusinsky, the head of Media-Most, on charges of corruption. Although Gusinsky had indeed enjoyed a cozy and profitable relationship with the Yeltsin regime, his real crime under Putin was to broadcast critical reports on the Chechnyan War and to back political rivals of the president. In exchange for his eventual release from prison, Gusinsky signed over control of Media-Most to the Kremlin.

Putin also presided over a Kremlin power grab in the all-important energy industry, managing eventually to put most of that vital sector under state control. A key moment here came with the neutralization of oil baron Mikhail Khodorovsky, whose Yukos energy company was Russia's largest private firm. Like Gusinsky, Khodorovsky was imprisoned on charges of corruption, and like Gusinsky he had indeed engaged in shady business practices. However, once again his real crime was a political one—that of funding prodemocracy projects and trying to create an anti-Putin bloc in the Duma. Moreover, Putin found it intolerable that a profitable firm like Yukos stood apart from the vast but less nimble state-owned energy conglomerate. Once Khodorovsky was behind bars (he could have fled abroad but amazingly chose to stay home and face imprisonment), the Kremlin moved in and took over his company.

Putin's rollback of democracy occasioned considerable hand-wringing in the West. In Washington, moreover, Moscow's refusal to relax the 1972 Antiballistic

Missile Treaty to allow America to built a limited antimissile defense caused added consternation. President Bush, tutored about Russia by Condoleezza Rice, his national security adviser and a former academic expert on the Soviet Union, began his first term of office with a negative view of his Russian counterpart. Vice President Dick Cheney's view was even more negative: "Every time I see Putin, I think KGB, KGB, KGB," he said.

From the outset, however, Putin was anxious to develop a positive relationship with Bush, and in January 2001, he proposed a personal meeting with the new American president so that the two men could iron out their differences, man to man. The meeting finally took place in June 2001 in Slovenia. Putin prepared carefully for the encounter. Aware of Bush's evangelical bent, he informed the president that he often wore a cross given him by his mother, a keepsake so special to him that when his dacha burned to the ground a few years back the cross was the only item he retrieved from the ashes. Never mind that this story was pure hokum; it had its intended effect. After the meeting Bush told reporters that he had looked into Putin's eyes and seen his soul—the soul of "an honest and straightforward man." Later, at the G-8 meeting in Genoa, Putin actually let Bush handle the sacred cross, a gesture that Mr. Bush said moved him deeply.

While Bush and Putin may have become soul brothers through personal encounters, what made them geostrategic partners, at least for a time, was the terror attack on America on September 11, 2001. The Russian president was the first foreign leader to telephone Bush with condolences and an offer of support after the attacks. He told Bush that the Russians could fully sympathize with America during its hour of agony because they knew better than anyone else the meaning of Islamic terror. Over the objections of some of his advisers, Putin announced that he would allow U.S. military aircraft to cross Russian airspace on their way to Afghanistan. He also declared that Moscow had no objections to the establishment of American airbases in the former Soviet republics of Central Asia. (In exchange, Washington tacitly agreed not to be too critical of Moscow's brutal actions in its own "war on terror" in Chechnya.)

Although Bush and Putin tried to remain on good personal terms, relations between Washington and Moscow began to cool not long after the 9/11 attacks, and old disagreements between the two nations returned to the fore. To Russia's dismay, Washington withdrew entirely from the ABM Treaty. America also pushed for the expansion of NATO into the former Soviet republics along the Baltic Sea. Putin's continuing crackdown on human rights groups and democracy advocates within Russia brought him censure from various American congressmen. There was also considerable criticism in the American press about a rise of xenophobic nationalism in Russia and the Kremlin's apparent failure to rein in rightist thugs who sometimes attacked foreigners in broad daylight on Moscow's streets. Yet more worrying to Putin's American critics was Moscow's use of its huge natural gas supply as a political weapon to punish Ukraine, whose "Orange Revolution" in 2004 catapulted the pro-Western and anti-Russian Viktor

Yushenko into power. And then, when America went to war against Saddam Hussein in 2003, Bush was deeply disappointed by Putin's open opposition to the Iraq venture, which contrasted sharply to the Russian's stance on America's anti-Taliban operation in Afghanistan. While Bush himself kept his disappointment with Putin somewhat in check, Vice President Cheney openly criticized the Kremlin's domestic and foreign policies in a televised speech in Lithuania. Angered, Putin shot back that Cheney's comments on Russia were about as accurate as his aim as a hunter—a reference, of course, to the vice president's recent maiming of a duck-hunting partner in Wyoming.

When Putin won reelection for a second presidential term in March 2004 he faced no significant opposition. By now the president's own party totally dominated the Duma and had effectively centralized power in the Kremlin. But soon Putin would exploit a terrible tragedy to expand his power even further. In early September 2004 a group of Chechen terrorists took some twelve hundred children and adults hostage in a school building in the southern Russian town of Beslan. In the chaotic and horribly botched effort to free the hostages, hundreds of children, teachers, and parents died. Claiming that he now needed additional powers to fight terrorism, Putin announced the implementation of a plan that had actually been in the works for months: the elimination of the direct election of governors and independent members of parliament. Putin, of course, was not the only world leader who expanded central governmental authority in the name of fighting terror, but his use of the Beslan debacle to cover his push for ever greater autocratic rule seemed particularly egregious. Critics of Russia's flawed democracy under Yeltsin had once labeled the president "Czar Boris," but Putin was showing that he had far better claim to the imperial title than his predecessor.

THE COLLAPSE OF YUGOSLAVIA

World War I began in the Balkans, and it was in this troubled region at the end of the twentieth century that Europe experienced its bloodiest fighting since World War II. The wars of Yugoslav secession not only resurrected old animosities in the Balkans but also revealed the inability or unwillingness of the Western powers to deal quickly and decisively with the new instability and ethnic strife resulting from the breakdown of the Communist system in Eastern Europe. A shaky semblance of order was reestablished in the region only after the United States—reluctantly and belatedly—intervened in the Balkan conflict. The collapse of Yugoslavia thus pointed up one of the home truths of the post-Cold War era: When regional security and human rights were threatened, even on the edge of Europe, the Europeans were unlikely to take strong action unless America led the way.

Although the violent breakup of Yugoslavia exposed deep fissures that had been present in that state's firmament since its creation in 1919, the dissolution

Croatian President Franjo Tudjman (*left*) and Serbian President Slobodan Milošević.

was by no means inevitable. It was the result of specific policies by regional leaders—notably Serbia's Slobodan Milošević and Croatia's Franjo Tudjman—who were more interested in exploiting internal differences than in working to overcome them. Unlike Tito, who had used the Communist Party and Yugoslav Army to stifle stirrings of discontent among the nation's constituent parts, these post-Communist leaders fanned nationalist animosities to enhance their own power. Each claimed that his side was a blameless victim of historical maltreatment. The poisonous rhetoric of ethnic and religious hatred was manipulated to transform neighbors into bitter enemies and to destroy the most internally diverse of the "successor states" built on the ruins of the Austro-Hungarian monarchy.

A symbolic overture to the violent breakup of Yugoslavia occurred on June 28, 1989, when Milošević delivered a speech at the Field of Blackbirds in Kosovo to commemorate the six hundredth anniversary of the Serbs' defeat by the Turks in 1389, a defeat that had ushered in five hundred years of Turkish domination over Serbia. One would think that the Serbs might have been more inclined to forget this moment than to celebrate it, but for them it was a sacred day because their legendary leader, Tsar Lazar, had chosen to fight to the death rather than to capitulate to the Turks; his act thus became a symbol of both

Serbian defiance and victimization. We should also recall that on this same date, in 1914, the Serbian nationalist Gavrilo Princip assassinated Austrian Archduke Francis Ferdinand, thus triggering the outbreak of World War I. Milošević, who had recently transformed himself from a Communist Party hack into a nationalist firebrand, turned the Field of Blackbirds affair into a protest rally against alleged persecution of the Serbian minority in Kosovo by the numerically superior ethnic Albanians. Ostensibly to protect local Serbs, Milošević announced that Belgrade would strip Kosovo of its rights as an autonomous province within Serbia and reassert full Serbian control. The real purpose of this move, however, was to document Milošević's credentials as a Serbian nationalist and to take over Kosovo's vote within the eight-member collective presidency of the Yugoslav Federation. Milošević and his followers saw this rearrangement as only just, since in their eyes Serbia did not enjoy power commensurate with its size and historic contribution to the liberation of the South Slavs from Austrian (and later German) oppression. As he stated at the Field of Blackbirds, "Serbs in their history have never conquered or exploited others. Through two world wars, they have liberated themselves and, when they could, they also helped others to liberate themselves."

Not surprisingly, Milošević's action in Kosovo alarmed the other Yugoslav republics, which saw it as the first step in a campaign to redefine Yugoslavia as Serbia writ large: "Serbo-Slavia." The first republic to respond was Slovenia, which, as we have seen, had already taken the lead in ending the centralized control of the Yugoslav Communist Party. Although it had only 8 percent of the Yugoslav population, Slovenia accounted for 23.5 percent of the country's hard currency exports. Closer in spirit to Vienna than to Belgrade, Slovenia saw itself as the most progressive chip off the old Communist bloc. When Serbia blocked Slovenia's attempt to carve out greater autonomy for itself and the other republics within Yugoslavia, the small northern republic announced its intention to secede entirely from the federation. The Serb-dominated Yugoslav Army (JNA) made an effort to halt the secession, but because it lacked any support within the population of Slovenia, it quickly gave up the struggle. In 1991, Slovenia became an independent state, and it was recognized as such a year later by the Western European nations at the prodding of Germany.

One of the Yugoslav republics that had supported Slovenia's push for a looser confederation was Croatia, which, like Slovenia, felt threatened by Serbian ambitions. In the eyes of Croatian nationalists, Greek Orthodox Serbia was a poor and unsophisticated appendage of Russia, while Catholic Croatia belonged to civilized Central Europe. For many years Croatian nationalism had been taboo in Yugoslavia because of its links to the wartime pro-Nazi Ustachi state. With the demise of Tito's centralized system, however, Croatian nationalist aspirations resurfaced as a potent rival to Serbian claims. Croatia's leader, Tudjman, emerged as a mirror image of Milošević. In his campaign to elevate Croatia's status, Tudjman offered a revised reading of the recent past, claiming that the

Ustachi regime had not killed nearly as many Serbs during World War II as Belgrade contended. At the same time, Tudjman celebrated the Ustachi leader Ante Pavelic as a hero of the Croatian people. Tudjman denied that such initiatives reflected any ethnic animosities on his part, but he increasingly engaged in racist and anti-Serbian rhetoric, declaring on one occasion, "Thank God my wife is not a Jew or a Serb."

With Croatian and Serbian leaders both fanning the flames of nationalist passions, minor interethnic squabbles soon mushroomed into major confrontations. In the summer of 1991, Serbs residing in the heavily Serb part of Croatia known as the Krajina began demonstrating against Croatian control over the police and governmental agencies in that region. When Croatian police units sought to suppress the demonstrations, the Yugoslav army intervened to assist the local Serbs. Suddenly the two largest states of Yugoslavia were locked in a bitter war. Federal army forces and Serb paramilitaries soon overpowered Croatian outposts in the Krajina, asserting control over the whole region by April 1992. Krajina Croats who had lived for generations next to Serbs were forced out of the region in the first of the "ethnic cleansing" operations that were to become one of the ugliest by-products of the Balkan wars.

While fighting was still raging in the Krajina, Serbs also attacked along the Croat-Serb border in eastern Slavonia. Their primary target was the Croatian city of Vukovar, which the Yugoslav Air Force subjected to relentless bombardment. This pretty Danubian city was quickly reduced to a blackened ruin, with corpses stacked in the streets. Croatian patriots called it Croatia's Stalingrad. Croatia responded by launching a campaign of terror against Serb civilians living in Croatian-controlled territory; now it was the Serbs who were being ethnically cleansed.

Yet another focal point in the Serbian-Croatian war was the walled coastal town of Dubrovnik, which Lord Byron had once called the Pearl of the Adriatic. Unlike Vukovar, Dubrovnik was not directly on the Serb-Croat border, and it contained no large ethnic Serb enclave requiring "liberation." Dubrovnik was attacked largely because its beauty and historical significance made it central to the Croatian tourist industry. Day after day Serbian troops fired artillery and tank rounds into the city, damaging medieval buildings that had withstood countless sieges over the centuries.

The plight of Dubrovnik might have been repeated across Croatia had not the Croatians eventually managed to build up a credible military force of their own that could stand toe to toe with the JNA. By early 1992, when it became evident that Croatia could effectively defend what remained of its territory and that the Serbs had won all they could without risking much higher losses, Milošević indicated a readiness to bargain. On behalf of the UN, former U.S. Secretary of State Cyrus Vance brokered a truce that in effect finalized Croatian independence from Yugoslavia. He recommended that twelve thousand five hundred UN peacekeepers be sent to Croatia to oversee the settlement.

Serbian soldiers in Croatia.

The withdrawal of Slovenia and Croatia from Yugoslavia and their subsequent recognition as independent states by the Western European nations prompted the republic of Bosnia and Herzegovina to call a referendum on independence for that multiethnic state. Bosnian Serbs, declaring that they would never live in an independent state in which Muslims and Croatians were numerically dominant, boycotted the vote. When Bosnia and Herzegovina went ahead and declared independence in April 1992, the leader of the Bosnian Serbs, Radovan Karadzić, a egomaniacal former psychiatrist who could have used some shrinking himself, proclaimed a separate Bosnian-Serb state, the Republika Srpska. Immediately thereafter, Bosnian-Serb forces led by a brutal thug named Ratko Mladić, backed up by elements of the JNA, launched military operations in eastern and northern Bosnia designed to "cleanse" that territory of non-Serbs. As if challenged to surpass the atrocities already committed in the Serb-Croat war, these troops embarked on a horrific crusade of rapine, torture, and mass murder. Thousands of Muslim prisoners were shot out of hand or herded into concentration camps, where they were made, on pain of death, to sing Serbian nationalist songs, inflict mutilations on each other, and dig mass graves for their murdered kinfolk.

In early May 1992, Bosnian-Serb forces and their JNA allies smashed into the Bosnian capital of Sarajevo. Karadzić hoped to partition this cosmopolitan city into Serbian and non-Serbian sections, reserving the largest and wealthiest parts for the Serbs. The Serb attackers, however, were able to conquer only certain sections of the town, along with the airport and surrounding mountain heights. From their mountaintop positions (the same mountains, by the way, down which skiers had raced in the 1984 winter Olympic Games), Serb gunners lobbed artillery shells into the city, hoping to pound it into submission. Despite month after month of shelling, Sarajevo held out, and the city's agony, along with graphic reports by Western journalists on the atrocities in the Serb-run concentration camps, finally focused international attention on the tragedy unfolding in Bosnia.

The Western powers were reluctant to intervene in the Bosnian conflict, just as they had hesitated to take action in the Serb-Croat War. To justify their inaction, the Western Europeans (and Americans) trotted out the old myth that interethnic strife was a constant and intractable fact of life in the Balkans. As Lawrence Eagleburger, Washington's ambassador to Belgrade, put it, until these folks "decided to stop killing each other, there's nothing the outside world can do about it." (This perspective was eerily reminiscent of the West's response to the civil unrest in Rwanda, where callous indifference had abetted an enormous human tragedy.) On the other hand, it became increasingly clear that if the Western powers took no action at all in this instance, the people of Sarajevo might starve to death, and additional Bosnian regions might suffer "ethnic cleansing." On May 30, 1995, the UN Security Council finally imposed economic sanctions on Belgrade, and in June of that year UN forces moved to take over the Sarajevo airport so that humanitarian aid could be flown in. These measures, however, did not stop the killing, any more than did an embargo on arms shipments to both sides (this actually helped the Serbs because they already had ample supplies of weapons, while the Bosnians did not). With the butchery continuing unabated, the Western European members of the UN decided to create so-called safe zones in Bosnia and to send in peacekeepers to keep them secure. Significantly, the United States did not participate in this endeavor. Washington did not consider Bosnia vital to American strategic interests. As Secretary of State James Baker famously put it, "We don't have a dog in that fight." The European-staffed peacekeeping forces that were sent to Bosnia—the "Blue Helmets"—were poorly armed and ill equipped, their inadequacies a reflection of the Europeans' ambivalence about their mission and their ongoing inability to come fully to grips with this massive human catastrophe in their own backyard.

The inadequacy of the Western response became horrifyingly evident in the village of Srebrenica, where in July 1995 the worst atrocity of the Bosnian War— indeed, the largest single war crime in Europe since the Second World War— took place directly under the noses of hapless Dutch peacekeepers. With the exception of a brief period in April 1993, Muslim-dominated Srebrenica had managed to elude the grasp of the Bosnian Serbs. Under a peace plan drawn up by Cyrus Vance and former British Foreign Secretary Lord David Owen, this village was supposed to be part of a Muslim province, but the Bosnian Serbs had refused to sign on to the plan. In hopes of keeping the town and its immediate environs free of strife, the UN designated the area as one of its safe zones and dispatched a force of seven thousand Dutch peacekeepers to patrol it. This token force was hardly a deterrent to Milošević and his Bosnian-Serb partners, who envisaged the Srebrenican region as part of the expanded Serbian state they intended to build on the ruins of the old Yugoslavia. On July 6, 1995, Bosnian Serbs launched a full-scale assault on the enclave. They quickly overran the Muslim defenders and the Dutch observation posts, taking thirty Dutch soldiers hostage. Their next move was to bus the women and children out of the area and to lock up most of the men in the local soccer stadium. Over the course of the next few days, these prisoners, most of them noncombatant civilians, were systematically executed. Other men were killed as they tried to flee through the woods. According to a later tabulation by the Red Cross, 7,079 Muslims were murdered in the Srebrenica area. When the killing was over, General Mladić, who had presided over the slaughter, offered up the conquered village as a "present to the Serb nation."

The inability of the Dutch peacekeepers to prevent the massacre at Srebrenica called into question the entire UN operation in Bosnia. It was now apparent that without a greater commitment from the United States, which heretofore had let the European Contact Group nations manage the crisis, the credibility of the UN and the Atlantic alliance might suffer irreparable damage. In summer 1995, therefore, Washington orchestrated a two-pronged military and diplomatic offensive designed to bring the three-year-old Bosnian conflict to an end. NATO planes began hitting Bosnian Serb gun emplacements and troop concentrations around Sarajevo. At the same time, a team of American negotiators led by Assistant Secretary of State Richard Holbrooke shuttled among Belgrade, Zagreb, and Sarajevo, putting pressure on Milošević, Tudjman, and Bosnian President Alija Izebegović to find a diplomatic way out of the bloody impasse.

Washington's leading role in forcing an end to the Bosnian War became especially clear in the final rounds of negotiations, which were held at Wright-Patterson Air Force Base outside Dayton, Ohio, in fall 1995. To prevent the Balkan leaders from denouncing one another in public, the talks were conducted in absolute secrecy. According to Holbrooke, there would be "no history lectures, no bullshit." The talks were difficult, however, as the leaders held very different notions regarding where the ethnic frontiers in Bosnia should be drawn. The meeting might have yielded no agreement had not Milošević been so anxious to get the sanctions lifted that he backed away from the hard-line position of the Bosnian Serbs, who wanted to divide Sarajevo and to hold on to all the lands they had conquered in eastern Bosnia. Using special video game-like machines that simulated the Bosnian topography, Holbrooke and the Balkan leaders finally hammered out a compromise that left Bosnia unified in principle but composed of two distinct entities: a Serbian region based on the Republika Srpska and a Muslim-Croat Federation with its capital in Sarajevo. A NATO-led

Implementation Force (IFOR), bolstered by twenty thousand U.S. troops, would patrol the internal borders to prevent renewed violence and to assist in the repatriation of refugees.

The Dayton Accord was undoubtedly a major accomplishment, but as the implementation process actually took shape, it became evident that the agreement could not turn Bosnia into a viable state or overcome the ethnic divisions that had been deepened by the fighting. Despite the presence of the IFOR troops, refugees attempting to return to their homes were often unable to cross the various lines carved out by the recent war.

Bitter ethnic strife now spread to Kosovo, where the local Serbs had long been demanding a crackdown by Belgrade on Albanian-Kosovar separatists. Having been forced to make major territorial concessions in Bosnia, which had led Bosnian Serbs to denounce him as a "traitor," Milošević was anxious to reassert his nationalist credentials. The ink was hardly dry on the Dayton Accord when he launched a campaign to suppress the Kosovo Liberation Army (KLA), a ragtag guerrilla band dedicated to creating a separate Muslim-Albanian Kosovo nation. In now-familiar tactics, Milošević's security forces stormed through Kosovar villages, murdering anyone suspected of belonging to the KLA and forcing tens of thousands of civilians to flee for their lives into the mountains.

Faced with a new human catastrophe in Kosovo and the threat that the violence there might spread to neighboring Macedonia, which harbored a large community of ethnic Albanians, the Western powers searched frantically for a diplomatic solution. Rejecting the KLA's demand for a fully independent Kosovo, Western negotiators tried to convince the Kosovars to accept extensive autonomy for the province within Serbia, which they offered to guarantee with the presence of a NATO peacekeeping force. (Washington did not join in this offer because President Bill Clinton believed he was too wounded by the Monica Lewinsky scandal to ask the American people to endorse sending American troops.) At the same time, the West put pressure on Milošević to accept the presence of a foreign force on Serb territory. Neither effort made much headway until KLA officials suddenly changed their minds and agreed to autonomy in place of independence at the Rambouillet meeting near Paris in March 1999. The Serbs, however, continued to oppose allowing a NATO force to set foot on the soil of Kosovo, which they considered sacred to their national identity. Having threatened to launch air attacks on Serbian forces in Kosovo and against Serbia itself if Belgrade did not desist from its aggression, NATO was confronted with the choice of following through on this threat or losing serious face—and this on the eve of its fiftieth anniversary, which it was scheduled to celebrate in April. Moreover, popular pressure to act mounted as television viewers in Western Europe and America watched nightly news programs showing thousands of Kosovars being forced from their homes into squalid refugee camps in Macedonia and Albania. In frustration and without any specific war plan or agreed-upon

AUSTRIA

0   50   100 Miles
0   50   100 Kilometers

SLOVENIA

HUNGARY

Danube R.

Zagreb ⊛

Sava R.

CROATIA

VOJVODINA

• Karlovac   • Sisak

Vukovar •   *Danube R.* • Novi Sad

• Bosanski Novi

Bihać   • Prijedor

SERB CORRIDOR

Sava R.

Belgrade ⊛

• Sanski Most

Doboj

Banja Luka   • Brčko

Mrkonjić Grad   Tuzla •   • Zvornik

Jajce   Zenica •   Vlasenica •

Knin •   • Srebrenica

BOSNIA AND HERZEGOVINA   ⊛ Sarajevo

SERBIA

• Split   • Goražde

Mostar •   Foča •   YUGOSLAVIA

ADRIATIC
SEA

MONTENEGRO

• Trebinje

Dubrovnik

KOSOVO

THE DAYTON ACCORD

Podogorica •

Muslim-Croat Federation

Bosnian Serb Republic

--- New interentity boundary line
    per peace agreement

—— Cease-fire line before peace
    agreement

⊚ Serb-held town pending arbitration

ALBANIA

MACEDONIA
(former Yugoslav
Republic)

Kosovo refugees in flight to Macedonia.

"end game" in mind, NATO finally sent its planes and missiles into action against the Serbs on March 12, 1999. Hastily organized though it was, this was the largest Western military campaign since the Gulf War and the first NATO attack on a sovereign state in the alliance's history. Another first was the use of American B-2 Stealth bombers, which flew nonstop from their base in Missouri to drop satellite-guided "smart" bombs on targets in Serbia.

The employment of such high-tech military gadgetry was meant to reduce so-called collateral damage on the ground, as well as to limit casualties to the NATO forces. (The Pentagon feared that the loss of a single pilot would erode popular support for the mission.) In another effort to limit or deter NATO casualties, the fighters and bombers operated at very high altitudes. These tactics indeed averted allied losses (not a single pilot was killed), but they also limited the effectiveness of the bombing, especially that which was aimed at small mobile targets. The NATO bombs smashed bridges and power plants in Serbia but could not prevent Serbian forces in Kosovo from continuing with their brutal business of ethnic cleansing. The "smart weapons," moreover, turned out to be no smarter than the people who set their targets and launched them: sixty Kosovars were killed by a NATO pilot who thought that the refugee column he was bombing was a Serb tank convoy, and an errant American missile destroyed the Chinese embassy in Belgrade because the targeters were using outdated maps.

For all its inadequacies, the NATO bombing campaign certainly did take its toll on Serbia's infrastructure, increasingly making life miserable for the Serb people, whose initial bravado began to crack under the nightly assaults. Fearing that the growing popular frustration might soon turn against his own regime, Milošević finally agreed on June 10 to withdraw his troops from Kosovo. The end might well have come sooner had the West deployed ground troops in addition to the air attacks—or at least not stated from the outset that no ground forces would be used.

The end of Serbian domination of Kosovo also spelled the end for Milošević. In September 2000, he was soundly defeated by the opposition candidate, Vojislav Kostunica. When Milošević nonetheless insisted on a runoff election, protestors took to the streets and demanded that he leave office immediately. Fittingly, the mobs that had brought him to power thirteen years earlier now pushed him out. In October, Milošević relinquished his office. Six months later, the Kostunica government, hoping for an end to UN-mandated sanctions and for economic aid from the West, turned the former dictator over to the Hague Tribunal to stand trial on charges of genocide and war crimes.

Milošević's trial opened in February 2002. It was the most important moment for international justice since the trial of Adolf Eichmann by an Israeli court in 1961. In fact, the Milošević trial was even more pathbreaking because the defendant was the first former head of state in history to face an international war crimes tribunal. (There had been no heads of state on trial at the Nuremberg or Tokyo tribunals following World War II.) Unfortunately, however, as the Milošević trial wore on, it sometimes seemed more akin to low farce than high legal drama. Despite a heart condition that caused delays and suspensions in the proceedings, Milošević insisted on defending himself, which he did with great theatrical flair. He intimidated witnesses and denounced the tribunal for "violating his human rights." The prosecution had difficulty proving that Milošević was personally responsible for atrocities committed by forces led by General Ratko Mladić, who, along with Bosnian Serb leader Radovan Karadzić remained at large in Serbia despite similar indictments for war crimes handed down against them by the Hague Tribunal. In a violation of the principles of open trial, former NATO commander General Wesley Clark was allowed to give testimony in private and with the right to remove from the public record any part of his evidence that Washington considered sensitive to U.S. national interests. (Washington, in fact, largely stayed aloof from the trial because the Bush administration did not recognize the authority of the Hague court.) On March 11, 2006, before any verdict could be rendered, Milošević played a final trick on the court by dropping dead of a heart attack. The day before he died he had sent a letter to the Russian government claiming that he was being poisoned by his jailers.

Milošević was undoubtedly not poisoned, but his poisonous legacy of militant ethnic nationalism and religious separatism lingered on in the bloodstream of the Balkans. In June 2006, following a popular referendum, Montenegro declared its independence from the State Union of Serbia and Montenegro, which had been established in 2003. Montenegrins said they were tired of Serbian bullying. Within rump Serbia, violent attacks on religious minorities, from Muslims to Jehovah's Witnesses, were carried out with little response from the authorities. The Serbian government failed to fulfill repeated promises to turn over Mladić and Karadzić to the Hague Tribunal. Meanwhile, ethnic Albanians in Kosovo stepped up their campaign for an independent state, free of any control from Belgrade. This campaign finally achieved success on February 17, 2008, when leaders in the Kosovar capital of Pristina announced the establishment of the "democratic and multiethnic" Republic of Kosovo. Shortly thereafter, Washington and some EU nations recognized the new state, much to the fury of Serbia and its old ally, Russia.

CHAPTER 17

Europe and the Challenges of Globalization

WHEN THE ISLAMIC TERRORISTS struck New York City and Washington, D.C., on September 11, 2001, many commentators, not just in America, pronounced the dawn of a radical new era in which "everything [had] changed." A mere half-decade after the terrorist attacks, it became apparent that while much had indeed changed—America certainly seemed vulnerable in a new way—the most serious problems facing the world had been building up for a long time. Among those were the challenges of globalization. In fact, many of the features of present-day globalization echoed the ups and downs in the evolution of global capitalism over the last century or so. We should recall that at the beginning of the twentieth century, international trade was booming, the world economy was extensively integrated, technological innovation was revolutionizing communications, and millions of migrants were wandering the earth in search of prosperity. Nevertheless, the Great War of 1914–1918 brought a sudden end to the first era of globalization. The ensuing Great Depression and Second World War caused many to wonder if the good times would ever return. The travails connected with global economic integration in our own era, combined with the possibility of even more devastating terrorist attacks in the future, caused some pundits to forecast the imminent "doom" of globalization as we know it. But of course, the jury is still out in the matter of globalization, just as the longer term implications of 9/11 are yet to be known. As the American journalist Adam Gopnik wrote concerning the collapse of the Twin Towers: "Was this the first Gothic sack of Rome, or Sarajevo 1914, or simply the Manson family to the power of ten?"

Even in the first half-decade or so since the birth of the new century, economic fortunes across the Western world rose and fell in bewildering fashion, and the old dominance of the American dollar in international markets came under increasing pressure as the greenback rapidly lost value relative to the euro, British pound, and Swiss franc. Meanwhile, Europeans and Americans alike struggled to navigate through an economic and financial "perfect storm" generated by a collapse in housing prices (especially in America), a severe credit crunch, and skyrocketing energy and food costs. The economic downturn highlighted the need to deal quickly and systematically with "big picture" crises like climate change and global hunger while simultaneously weakening the will for action in some quarters.

A WIDER AND DEEPER EUROPEAN UNION

In the 1990s and in the first years of the twenty-first century, the countries of Western Europe widened the geographical scope of their international federation and deepened the legal, political, and economic bonds that tied the member states together. This process of transnational integration had been going on in fits and starts since the 1950s, but with these latest developments, "Europe" no longer meant just Western Europe and the "European Community" became the "European Union"—an entity with a much higher degree of internal cohesion. Like so many alterations in the European sociopolitical landscape, these changes came in response to the collapse of Communism and the pressures of globalization—especially the latter. Europe faced increased competition from new trading blocs like the North American Free Trade Association (NAFTA) as well as from that astounding new economic dynamo, China. More than ever, Europe was caught up in economic, social, and environmental processes of pan-European and global dimensions, which required coordinated, multinational responses. The steps taken by the European Union to meet these manifold challenges constituted the world's most advanced experiment in moving beyond the nation-state. Yet at the same time, the program of widening and deepening the union ended up generating considerable resentment among ordinary Europeans—along with a resurgence of nationalistic sentiment.

In December 1991, in the Dutch city of Maastricht, the twelve member states of the European Community met to draw up a revised treaty for the association, which took the new name European Union (EU). It was at this meeting that the union announced its historic decision to create a European Monetary Union (EMU) with a single currency, the euro. The new currency was scheduled to be introduced in 2002. A new European Central Bank, based in Frankfurt, would regulate interest rates and other aspects of the EMU's common financial policy.

Along with the concept of a single currency, the Maastricht Treaty inaugurated a new social protocol, allowing the union to set standards in worker health and safety, mobility of labor, and related issues. Other provisions brought heightened cooperation in the areas of crime prevention, immigration, and asylum policy. Such changes were mandated by a proliferation of international criminal and terrorist organizations whose activities could not be effectively combated by any single state. However, since the member states had very different legal systems and philosophies regarding border security, social welfare, and labor policy,

A poster promoting the anti-Maastricht Treaty campaign waged by Jean-Marie Le Pen and the Front National.

it proved impossible to come up with a uniform set of regulations that every state could accept. Britain in particular was reluctant to surrender control to Brussels in areas it considered crucial to its identity as a sovereign nation. To prevent Britain's rejection of the Maastricht Treaty altogether, the EU allowed London to opt out of some of the social provisions, just as it stayed out of the EMU. To come into law, the treaty required ratification by all the member states, which proved difficult. The Danes, having voted against the treaty in June 1992, accepted it a year later only after some of its provisions had been watered down. The French electorate approved the document by the narrow margin of 51 percent to 49 percent. The treaty finally went into effect on November 1, 1993, ten months later than originally scheduled.

On January 1, 1995, the EU expanded its membership from twelve to fifteen, with the admission of Austria, Finland, and Sweden. These formerly neutral states had previously eschewed membership in the union because of that association's strong ties to NATO, to which all the EU states, except Ireland, belonged. Their accession to the union can be seen as another legacy of the end of the Cold War.

Admitting prosperous states like Austria, Finland, and Sweden to the EU was considerably less controversial than the prospect of bringing in the relatively poor and politically fragile Eastern European states. Having thrown over the dominion of the Soviet Union, these nations (or more precisely, the political and economic elites within these nations) were anxious to "return to Europe," to reclaim their place in a broader community of ideals and standards from which they had been excluded for almost half a century. This ambition provoked an ambivalent response in the West. Western European leaders and opinion makers understood that their nations had a moral imperative to avoid a "second Yalta," a new division of Europe along economic lines. At the same time, however, they realized that if these poor nations were admitted to the union on terms similar to those provided existing members, the costs to the association in the form of sub-sidies and regional assistance programs would likely break the EU budget. There were other concerns as well. The Eastern European states had only recently adopted democratic norms and were struggling to establish Western-style bank-ing systems, legal codes, and law enforcement procedures. Their borders were notoriously porous. For all these reasons, the Western Europeans put off actual admission of the new states for years on end, during which time experts from Brussels descended on the Eastern capitals to coach the natives on how to bring their political, economic, and legal institutions up to EU standards. Finally, in May 2004, the EU officially opened its doors to the ten candidate states that had been alternately cooling their heels and jumping through hoops for over a de-cade. The states in question were Poland, Hungary, the Czech Republic, Slove-nia, Slovakia, Estonia, Latvia, Lithuania, Malta, and Cyprus. Only the latter two nations were not former members of the defunct Soviet empire. (Two other for-mer Warsaw Pact states, Romania and Bulgaria, whose economies and political institutions were yet weaker than those of their neighbors, finally achieved admittance to the EU on January 1, 2007, bringing the total membership to 27.)

In theory, the EU was an association of equals, but the poverty of the new Eastern European members, combined in some cases with relatively high popu-lations (think Poland), prompted the admission of the newcomers on decidedly unequal terms. The EU allowed some of its older members to place quotas on the number of Eastern Europeans who could move west and seek work. In France, one of the states that pressed hardest for the limits, the threat of unchecked migra-tion from the East was graphically summed up in a horror-vision of predatory "Polish plumbers" flocking to France to steal jobs from the native *plombier*. (Poland humorously responded to this scare tactic with a travel poster featuring a buffed-up Polish plumber who says he's staying in Poland and welcomes French tourists to his country.) But perhaps in the end the joke was on Poland after all, for even with the restrictions on migration, so many Poles elected to move west that within two years of joining the EU the country lacked enough workers to undertake the infrastructure improvements that Brussels promised to pay for. Similarly, the EU's notoriously opulent agricultural subsidies were not extended equally to the new Eastern European states. Not only would this have been costly but it would also have helped Eastern farmers compete more effec-tively with their counterparts in the West. And in countless smaller ways, the newest EU citizens were reminded of their second-class status. As one exasperated Czech businessman complained, whenever he flew to London or Paris he was always asked at the airport how much money he had and how long he intended to stay. No wonder, having finally gotten into the club, some Easterners began to question whether membership was such a great deal after all.

The challenges faced by the EU in opening their club to the Eastern European states seemed almost trivial compared to those posed by the possible inclusion of Turkey, which if admitted would be the union's second largest state—and also its poorest. Turkey had applied for EU membership as early as 1987 but for years had not even been given a hearing. By periodically reminding Brussels that it was waiting in the wings, Ankara forced the EU and the Western European governments to think about what it would mean to have a country like Turkey in the Union. In general, that thinking was not very positive, and not only because Turkey was poor and populous. Although Turkey was a democracy, it had a dubious human rights record and a highly problematical legal code. Its military was seen to be too active in politics. Turkey was a member of NATO but it got along terribly with fellow NATO power Greece, an EU state with whom Ankara carried on a long-running battle over the control of Cyprus. Although Turkey was relatively stable and Western-oriented, it bordered troublesome states like Iraq, Syria, and Iran. Most of all, although Turkey was a secular republic, the vast majority of its 70 million inhabitants were Muslims, and the Islamic-leaning Justice and Development Party, which came to power in late 2002, was headed by a politician, Recep Tayyip Erdogan, who had trained as an imam. The fact that Erdogan pushed for Turkey's inclusion in the EU and had promoted major legal reforms, including abolishing the death penalty, seemed less important to many Europeans than the Muslim faith he shared with most of his countrymen: did not Europe have enough Muslims already? it was asked. On occasion, Turkey proved quite adept at hurting its own cause. For example, in late 2003 the Justice Ministry introduced a law allowing a rapist to walk free if he married his victim; the minister justified the law by arguing that "nobody would want to marry a girl who is not a virgin." In 2005, an overzealous prosecutor charged Turkey's most famous novelist, Orhan Pamuk, with the crime of expressing "anti-Turkish sentiment" when he denounced the mass killings of Armenians by the Ottoman Empire in World War I. (The charge was later dropped and Pamuk, who won the Nobel Prize for literature in 2006, himself denounced a new ordinance in France making it illegal to *deny* Turkey's massacre of the Armenians.) Episodes like this reinforced stereotypes in Europe of the Turks as intractably "oriental"—as superficially Westernized heirs of the dreaded Ottomans, against whom Christian Europe had defended itself over the centuries at great cost. It was therefore with gritted teeth and without much prospect of success in the foreseeable future that Brussels finally opened formal "accession talks" with Ankara in October 2005.

By that time, many Turks had turned against the idea of joining the EU. They resented being lectured to by Europeans on the inadequacies of their legal and political institutions. Westernized Turks bristled at the implication that their country was too primitive and too "foreign" to be considered genuinely European. At the same time, many pious Muslims feared that they would have to give up too much of their Islamic soul to join a club that alternately touted its Enlightenment and "Christian" roots. But the possibility that pro-Western Turks might be denied their dream of a partnership with Europe raised an uncomfortable question: would this large Muslim country then look to the East rather than the West? One prominent Turkish official warned that the West would be the big loser if it turned its back on Turkey: "The West would risk losing a vital bridge with the Islamic world at a time when having this bridge is more vital than ever."

In expressing second thoughts over Turkey's application to the EU, one Turkish newspaper columnist asked in June 2005: "If the Europeans are backing out of their own project, then why should we be so enthusiastic?" He was referring to recent "no" votes in France and the Netherlands on referenda to ratify a new European constitution, which was meant both to lay out a practical system of governance for the expanded union and to endow it with ideological purpose.

The constitution that failed its public test in spring 2005 had long been in the making. Beginning in January 2002, a convention of over one hundred delegates met regularly in Brussels. During these meetings, the constitutional framers revealed how fractious Europe remained despite all the noble talk of unity and shared ideals. One significant fault line divided the large nations from the smaller ones over the apportionment of internal powers and budgetary controls. This division came to the fore when France and Germany proposed a new post of president of the European Council, the body that organizes the summits of EU heads of state. The small nations, seeing this as a diabolical plot to turn the EU into a tyranny of the big guys, ganged up to scuttle the proposal. Another subject of fierce contention had to do with the values that might animate the union. A number of delegates, backed by the Vatican, tried to insert a specific reference to Europe's Christian roots into the constitution's preamble. Ultimately this effort failed, and the document that passed out of Brussels was bereft of any sweeping philosophical language concerning moral values.

The biggest failure of the constitutional convention lay not so much in the document it created, which had some commendable features, but in the process by which it was produced. There was no significant effort to include the public or to make the project seem interesting. As a consequence, few in Europe knew that a constitutional convention was in progress, much less had knowledge about the issues being debated.

This failure to engage the public came back to haunt advocates of the new constitution when they tried to get it ratified in all twenty-five member states, which had to happen for the document to come into effect. The rub came when

the Europhiles brought their campaign to France and the Netherlands, two charter members of the original European Common Market. Here the constitution promoters had to contend not so much with opposition to this or that provision but with a generalized hostility toward a huge amorphous bureaucracy over which ordinary citizens had no real influence.

In France, the rejection of the constitution by a margin of ten percentage points was very painful for its high-profile supporters, especially President Chirac; the "non" vote on the constitution was clearly also a "no" to him. In the Netherlands, the rejection was even more decisive—62 percent to 38 percent. In part the Dutch vote reflected widespread fears that smaller nations like the Netherlands were losing influence in the EU and that the constitution would augment that trend. There was also the fear that the EU was becoming more conservative and that a more conservative union might interfere with policies dear to liberal Dutch hearts, such as gay marriage, euthanasia, and easy access to soft drugs. More generally, however, in the Netherlands as in France, the vote on the constitution reflected a pent-up disgust with rule by haughty "Eurocrats" who never had to face elections or to explain how they came up with the increasingly intrusive regulations that governed everything from the size of condoms to the noise levels of power lawnmowers.

In the immediate wake of the no votes on the European constitution, the EU held a summit in which various internal disagreements came to the fore with a new bitterness. Britain's Blair and France's Chirac dueled openly over agricultural subsidies. Blair objected to the huge annual subsidies that Brussels paid to Continental farmers, especially those of France, whom he accused of inefficiency and backwardness. Chirac, for his part, said it was high time to end the annual rebates that Brussels gave Britain (which drew no agricultural subsidies) for the contributions that London made to the common agricultural pot. Responding to Blair's comments about primitive and cosseted French farmers, Chirac huffed that the only contribution Britain had ever made to European agriculture was Mad Cow disease. And he added, "You can't trust a people who cook as badly as that."

The animosity toward the EU awakened by the constitutional votes extended in some measure to the new euro currency, which, having been introduced as planned in January 2002, was by far the most ambitious innovation launched by the union in recent years. Not all the EU states were members of the Euro Zone; the UK, Denmark, and Sweden opted out. The new states that joined in 2004 and 2007 made a commitment to join the EMU at some point, but for the time being none of their economies was sound enough to make the conversion.

Joining this monetary club within a club presupposed not only the desire to do so but the ability to meet strict financial criteria, most notably maintaining annual budget deficits no greater than 3 percent of GDP and an overall national debt no more than 60 percent of GDP. In the original negotiations on the EMU, Germany, which had kept its old deutsche mark sound by avoiding large deficits, insisted on this so-called Stability Pact in order to prevent more profligate nations (like Italy and France) from undermining the new currency by engaging in their usual fiscal irresponsibility. Members of the EMU that failed to meet the Stability Pact requirements in any given year would be subject to sanctions and stiff fines.

As it happened, the transition from the old European currencies to the euro on January 1, 2002, went amazingly smoothly; the problems began later. One of those problems derived from the euro's very success in the international currency market. During the first years of the euro's existence its value hovered below that of the dollar, but as its third birthday approached the euro surpassed the dollar and became the strongest currency on earth. While this development certainly posed a long-term threat to the dollar's traditional status as the world's preferred reserve currency, its immediate effect was to make European goods more expensive in the international market, thereby suppressing exports. Additionally, the EMU's imposition of a "one size fits all" fiscal package on its members proved very problematical because the national economies within the Euro Zone differed significantly with respect to both their absolute strength and their position in the economic cycle. For example, Germany's economy was large but stagnant; Ireland's was relatively small but booming; Portugal lagged far behind in GDP and carried high public debt. Initially the EMU regulations were hardest on the smaller and poorer countries. To get into the EMU—and to stay in—Portugal had to drastically slash public spending, which resulted in increased unemployment and considerable social malaise. Greece, which was already spending far too much on preparations for the 2004 Olympics, resorted to some creative accounting to meet the euro requirements. But in the end it proved to be the big countries that were the worst violators of the Stability Pact. In 2004, France exceeded the annual deficit cap by 1.1 percent. Shortly thereafter Germany, the country that had essentially set up the system, exceeded the limits for both annual budget deficit and overall national debt. When the European Commission began proceedings to punish France and Germany for violating the Stability Pact, these two heavyweights simply refused to accept any sanctions. They also stated that because they expected their economic difficulties to continue—Germany cited the ongoing costs of reunification—they could not commit themselves to meeting the Stability Pact requirements in the future. The smaller states were livid over this high-handed behavior but lacked the clout to do much about it. Meanwhile, looking on from the sidelines at the EMU's tawdry fiscal game, Britain, Denmark, and Sweden reaffirmed their desire to steer clear of it.

The difficulties faced by the EU and the EMU should not obscure the emergence of the expanded union as a true global power, at least in the economic realm. The pre-Maastricht EEC had already been the world's largest trading bloc and wealthiest single market, and the new and expanded EU was much more so. EU-based multinational companies like Nokia, Airbus, BP, and Red Bull rivaled or surpassed U.S. firms in the global marketplace. The EU dispensed more foreign aid to the developing world than did America. Moreover, the peoples of the EU, especially in the core Western European nations, enjoyed the world's highest per capita incomes and the most generous social welfare and health care systems. (These programs were arguably *too* generous, given Europe's aging population; by 2005 the EU had thirty-five people of pensionable age for every one hundred of working age.) Western Europeans had even surpassed Americans in terms of life expectancy and physical stature: the Dutch were the tallest people in the world, trailed closely by the Danes.

But if the EU had indeed emerged as a kind of socioeconomic superpower, was it, as some of its champions claimed, a true "United States of Europe?" The answer is no, although some of the deepening measures of recent years had certainly strengthened Brussels's hand. On the other hand, the very deepening process had spawned renewed disgruntlement and opposition from those who continued to believe that the union's primary role was to be a trading bloc and also from all those factions who believed themselves hurt rather than helped by the policies of "Big Brother Brussels."

As had always been the case with "unified" Europe, the unity was at best partial. The EU continued to lack a common army and a unified defense or foreign policy, and efforts to promote these ideals had not gotten very far. The Iraq war spawned a significant division between those EU governments that to varying degrees supported the 2003 invasion and those that did not. (At the popular level there was considerably more agreement among the EU states that the Iraq war was a bad thing all around.) Despite the rising threat from terrorist groups operating across state borders, the EU lacked a unified law enforcement agency equivalent to the FBI as well as a Europe-wide intelligence agency similar to the CIA. The above-mentioned internal battles over budgets, subsidies, and apportionments of power were even more bitter and divisive than the rows of the 1970s and 1980s had been. On the level of symbols, the EU possessed a flag and an anthem, but few waved the flag and no one seemed to have a clue about the anthem. There was no common language, unless one counted English, which still had a way to go to conquer Eastern Europe (not to mention France). The new euro notes looked suitably "European," but the imposing arches and bridges depicted on them were not renditions of any *actual* structures because the designers were not allowed to "privilege" any one country's cultural patrimony. The images had to be abstractions, rather like European unity itself.

The EU was designed to move Europe beyond the old nationalistic obsessions that had led to so much misery and bloodshed in the "dark" twentieth century, but of course the nationalist impulse had hardly died off—one had only to attend a European Cup soccer match to see that. Although signs of potent nationalism could be found everywhere in Europe, the new Eastern European EU states registered the most intense—and troubling—manifestations of nationalistic fervor Poland fell under the control of Lech and Jaroslav Kaczynski, conservative Catholic twin brothers who distressed Brussels with their jeremiads against secularism, homosexuality, and liberalism and with their demands for a place in the union commensurate with Poland's large population. In Slovakia, the government coalition included two far-right parties that openly preached anti-Semitism. When, in fall 2006, Budapest was overrun by rioters demanding the resignation of Prime Minister Ferenc Gyurcsany, some of the demonstrators carried banners reminiscent of the fascist Iron Cross, which had sided with the Nazis during World War II. In explaining the resurgence of militant populist nationalism in Eastern Europe, one political analyst noted that ordinary people had had no part in either the construction of the political systems that replaced Communism in the early 1990s or the decisions to join the EU. "Most people describe themselves as losers in the change of systems and in joining the EU," reported the analyst in 2006.

WHOSE EUROPE IS IT?

As the post-Maastricht EU struggled to address the problems generated by its expansion, it also wrestled, as the old EEC had done, with the manifold social and security challenges connected to the presence of large immigrant communities in most of its member states. These challenges grew dramatically in the 1990s and the first years of the new century as expanding chaos and chronic poverty in Africa, the Caucasus, the Middle East, and Central Asia sent millions more people clamoring for work and/or sanctuary in Europe. At the same time, the demographic realities in the EU—those low birthrates and aging populations—meant that most EU nations could not function without infusions of outside labor.

The EU's obvious need for labor notwithstanding, the latest influx of foreigners generated renewed resistance among the native populations. The disputes spread to new places, such as Spain, which heretofore had exported rather than imported labor, and to new branches of industry, such as heavy construction and high technology, which heretofore had been able to get by with largely native work forces. In the 1990s, German construction workers rioted over the use of foreign work crews in the refurbishing of the Reichstag building in Berlin. A decade or so later, German chimney sweeps rebelled against the prospect of foreign rivals swooping in from poorer regions to break their monopoly over that tradition-encrusted trade. In Southern Spain, Moroccans and Algerians were

Dublin, 2005. Irish Ferries workers march in protest against a plan to replace native workers with low-paid Eastern European immigrants.

subjected to repeated harassment for allegedly "stealing" the natives' work. In Europe's high-tech industries workers spoke bitterly of being "Bangalored"—that is, displaced from their jobs by low-wage workers in India. Western Europe's right-wing parties took up the anti-immigrant and antiglobalization mantra with a vengeance, hoping to cash in on the growing resentment. Austria's Jörg Haider, a telegenic demagogue, became in the late 1990s a new star of the nativist right, a poster boy of European xenophobia. In France, Jean-Marie Le Pen's daughter, Marine, carried the torch of antiglobalization along with her father. Pin Fortuyn, a flamboyantly gay Dutch populist, generated a fanatical following by tapping into his fellow Hollanders' fears of being swamped by immigrants and overwhelmed by a profusion of pan-European and global institutions.

When populist politicians like Haider, Le Pen, and Fortuyn warned of Europe's being taken over by "aliens" who could not or would not be assimilated, the people they had primarily in mind were immigrants of the Islamic faith whose sizable communities continued to swell through high birthrates and new waves of immigration from Africa, the Middle East, and Southern Asia. Of course, the presence of millions of Muslims in Europe seemed all the more threatening following the terrorist attacks of 9/11 and subsequent attacks (or foiled attacks) by "home-grown" Islamic terrorists in Western Europe. In December 2001, Richard Reid, a British-born Muslim convert, tried to blow up a Miami-bound airliner using a bomb in his shoe. On March 11, 2004, a Spanish cell of Islamic terrorists bombed two trains in Madrid, killing 191 people. On July 7, 2005, four suicide bombers, all British-born Muslims, bombed the London Underground and a bus, killing 52 people. In July 2006, German-based Islamic extremists tried to blow up two trains in northern Germany; had they succeeded, they certainly would have killed hundreds of people.

The horrific actions of European-based Islamic terrorists inflamed anti-Muslim sentiment in Europe. Some critics claimed that Islam as such was a menace and went on to condemn the various efforts in Europe to integrate Muslims (half-hearted as those efforts often were) as misguided and hopeless. The iconoclastic Italian journalist Oriana Fallaci, for example, insisted that her fellow Europeans had been much too tolerant and complacent about the threat posed by Muslims, who were (in her words) "breeding like rats" and rapidly turning Europe into "Eurabia," a colony of Islam. Fallaci's strident voice, as poisonous in its way as that of the Islamic extremists, was no isolated Casandra-call; it found plenty of echoes across Europe.

One very significant echo came from Ayaan Hirsi Ali, a Somali-born Dutch politician who had come to regard the Islamic faith in which she had been reared as absolutely incompatible with modern secular democracy, individual freedom, and gender equality. In collaboration with the Dutch filmmaker Theo van Gogh (a great grandnephew of Vincent), she put together a short film entitled "Submission," whose projection of verses from the Koran onto a naked and

In the aftermath of the terrorist train-bombing in Madrid, a demonstrator holds up a sign reading "We were all on this train."

bruised female body spurred outrage in Holland's Islamic community. On November 2, 2004, a young Moroccan-Dutchman named Mohammed Bouyeri fatally shot van Gogh in broad daylight on an Amsterdam street. In a letter attached by a knife to van Gogh's chest, Bouyeri called for a holy war against all unbelievers and demanded the death of several people by name, including Ayaan Hirsi Ali. (Ironically, although Ali avoided van Gogh's fate, she eventually was expelled from the Netherlands for having lied about her provenance in her application for asylum; she moved on to the United States.)

Blanket denunciations of Islam, whatever their sources, obviously overlooked the reality that the vast majority of European Muslims wanted nothing to do with terrorism. The image of Islam as a monolithic menace also obscured important differences among Europe's Muslim communities with regard to the intensity of their faith and their degree of comfort in secular Europe. On the whole, French Muslims were almost as lax about mosque attendance as French Catholics were about church visits. Germany's Turks also tended toward moderation in the observation of their faith and—more than French Muslims of North African extraction—expressed satisfaction with their adopted country. (Non-Muslim Germans were very gratified to see that many German-Turks waved German colors after victories by the German team in the 2006 World Cup.) In Britain, Muslims from Malaysia and East Africa tended to do better economically and to have fewer reservations about British society than their counterparts from Pakistan and Bangladesh, who were loathe to allow their women to work. The Netherlands' famously liberal culture outraged some local Muslims (Theo van Gogh's murderer was an obvious example), but it also found defenders among some prominent imams and Muslim political leaders who saw virtue in Holland's multicultural values.

And yet, although European Islam was by no means a monolithic threat to secular democracy, a worrisome trend (at least for non-Muslims) was becoming notable among younger Muslims across Europe: a tendency to identify more strongly with the Islamic religion and to express that identification more aggressively. Even Germany's Turks were becoming more fervent in their attachment to Islam. In France, the humiliation and alienation attendant to life in the grim immigrant ghettos led a growing number of young Muslims to adopt more extreme forms of their faith. In Britain, private Islamic schools insisted on a strict separation of the sexes and did not offer admission to non-Muslims. Across Western Europe, more Muslim women and girls donned head scarves or even full Islamic veils, though French public schools banned the scarves and British political leaders spoke out against the full-face veils as "a mark of separation." While frustration over the realities of life for Muslims within Europe played an important role in this growing assertiveness, so of course did anger over Israel's treatment of the Palestinians, Russia's suppression of the Chechnyans, and America's invasion and occupation of Iraq.

European Muslims, it turned out, were also increasingly sensitive to insults (or perceived insults) to their faith. The fact that a number of much-publicized instances of "Islam-abuse" took place on European soil no doubt played a role here. In February 2006, a Danish newspaper published a series of cartoons that mocked the Prophet Muhammad. The cartoons spawned angry demonstrations by Muslims in a number of European cities (though the only lethally violent protests occurred in the Middle East and Africa). Indignation over the cartoons had hardly receded when the newly elected pope, Benedict XVI, roiled the waters further by quoting a medieval Byzantine emperor's statement that

Muhammad had brought "things only evil and inhuman, such as his command to spread by the sword the faith he preached." Muslim anger was especially great in this instance because the offender was the leader of world Catholicism, Islam's historic rival. The pope's hasty denial of any intention to link Islam and violence initially had little effect, and he was obliged to apologize repeatedly and profusely. The spectacle of Pope Benedict falling over himself to placate his Muslim critics ended up alienating some of his own followers, along with secular defenders of free speech, who worried that precious Western values were being sacrificed on the altar of Islamic intolerance. Overall, episodes like these both spurred European Muslims' assertiveness in defense of their faith and heightened concerns among non-Muslims regarding the adaptability of Islam to European society and values.

GREEN DIVIDE: ENVIRONMENTAL POLICIES IN
EUROPE AND THE UNITED STATES

If, in the view of many Europeans, Islamic terrorism constituted the greatest immediate threat to their safety and well-being, managing the environment, above all contending with climate change, emerged as the preeminent longer term challenge of the new era because of the far-reaching implications for the health and survival of the human species. Nevertheless, there was precious little consensus among the governments of the world regarding the severity and exact nature of the environmental crisis, and there was also little agreement about how best to meet the challenges of ongoing environmental degradation. One of the most important lines of division in this domain ran between Western Europe and the United States.

Starting in the mid-1980s, the environmental and energy policies put forth by the main European nations, and by the EC and EU acting as a unit, began to diverge from those championed by Washington. America had pioneered significant domestic environmental legislation in the 1960s and 1970s and was a crucial player in developing the 1987 Montreal Protocol on Ozone Depletion. As the new century and millennium approached, however, European governments and the EU took the lead in pushing for measures to deal with environmental degradation at national, regional, and global levels. As a matter of principle, Europeans increasingly argued that there were environmental assets that money could not buy while Washington tended to assess these issues primarily in terms of costs to business, national competitive advantage and domestic political fallout.

The green divide between the EU and the United States encompassed a variety of contentious issues, from airline "noise pollution" to toxic waste disposal. However, while squabbles over aircraft noise and waste management attracted only minimal interest outside expert environmental circles, the issue of climate change, or "global warming," caught the public's attention virtually everywhere. What generated all the concern was growing scientific evidence that after a brief pause in the mid-twentieth century, the earth's temperature was continuing to rise, and the rise was accelerating. More and more scientists attributed the temperature rise to an increased presence in the atmosphere of "greenhouse gases" like methane and carbon dioxide, which trap the sun's heat close to the earth's surface rather than allowing it to disperse into space. Continued global warming, scientists argued, would lead to shifts in climate zones, rising seas from melting land ice and the polar ice caps, and more extreme weather patterns. In late 2006, a report commissioned by the British government predicted a host of apocalyptic effects from climate change if significant abatement of greenhouse gases did not come soon: these included droughts, flooding, famine, skyrocketing malaria rates, and the extinction of many animal and plant species.

Although some debate continued in the scientific community about the extent of human agency in the latest spate of climate change, in 1997 environmental officials from around the world issued the Kyoto Protocol to the Framework Convention on Climate Change, which called for thirty-five industrialized countries to reduce their greenhouse gas emissions by an average of 5.2 percent of 1990 levels by 2012. To come fully into effect, Kyoto had to be ratified by all the states that had signed it. All the (then) fifteen EU states signed the protocol in 1997, and by May 31, 2002, all these nations had also ratified the agreement. This brought the number of ratifying nations to sixty-one—a figure that increased to one hundred by the end of 2002. The United States was not among that group. President Clinton, prodded by his very "green" vice president Albert Gore, signed the Kyoto Protocol in 1998, but he did not bring the pact up for ratification in the U.S. Senate, where, given Republican domination of that body, the effort certainly would have failed. Republican James Inhofe of Oklahoma, chairman of the Senate's Environment and Public Works Committee, dismissed global warming as "the greatest hoax ever perpetrated on the American people." Clinton's successor, George W. Bush, withdrew America entirely from the Kyoto agreement shortly after taking office. Calling the protocol "fatally flawed," with "unrealistic targets not based on science," he contended that the agreement would impose unacceptable burdens on the American economy and in any event could not work effectively because it did not include major "developing" nations like India and China. (Bush had a point about China: with four-fifths of its power generated by coal, it was expected to pass the United States as the world's biggest emitter of greenhouse gases by 2009. Already it had some of the world's dirtiest air, and one had to wonder whether the athletes competing in the 2008 Beijing Olympics would have to don protective face masks as ordinary citizens of that city often did.) The Bush administration further argued that the best way to deal with global warming issues— should they exist—was to allow businesses to come up with innovative solutions of their own. The Energy Task Force headed by Vice President Cheney advocated an approach that continued to favor traditional energy sources.

A demonstrator in London protesting the Bush administration's refusal to endorse the Kyoto Treaty on climate change.

Despite the nonparticipation in the Kyoto Protocol by the United States, Russia, Australia, and the big developing nations, the EU states decided to stick with their Kyoto emissions-reduction goals, hoping thereby to set a good example for the rest of the world. By late 2006, when environmental officials met for a new UN climate change conference in Nairobi, Kenya, Germany could report emissions reductions of 17 percent, Britain 14 percent, and France 1 percent. Spain and some of the other EU countries registered emissions increases but still hoped to meet their Kyoto targets by 2012 via taxes on carbon-based fuels, energy efficiency regulations, and other steps. In the period between 1990 and 2004, U.S. emissions grew by almost 16 percent, though the growth tapered to 1.3 percent between 2000 and 2004, compared to 2.4 percent overall for forty-one industrialized nations in that same period. America was beginning to make some progress with its private-sector oriented approach, but with 21 percent of total greenhouse gas emissions in 2006, America remained the world's worst offender.

To some degree, the divergence in policy on climate change and other seminal environmental issues reflected the different political cultures that had evolved on opposite sides of the Atlantic. In Europe, environmental parties were represented in several national parliaments and over time had managed to push the mainstream parties in a significantly greener direction. European governments regularly granted tax incentives to environmentally friendly companies while energy bureaucrats devised regulatory regimes designed to limit public and private power consumption. Such policies generally found wide acceptance among national citizenries who tended to see global warming as a genuine threat. According to a Pew Research Center poll taken in June 2006, over 80 percent of Frenchmen and Spaniards said global warming concerned them "a great deal"; slightly over 60 percent of Germans and Britons took this position. In America, the equivalent figure was just under 50 percent, which was actually pretty substantial considering that top officials in the Environmental Protection Agency watered down findings from the agency's own scientists to deemphasize the threat posed by global warming.

Although at the opening of the new millennium Americans continued to consume more energy per capita than any other people in the world, the gap between the United States and Europe with respect to environmental consciousness seemed to be narrowing somewhat. One cause for this trend was escalating gasoline prices, which moved many Americans to rethink their love affair with gas-guzzling SUVs. (Because American carmakers tended to remain behind the learning curve, however, Detroit continued to lose market share to more energy-efficient foreign manufacturers.) California's Austrian-born governor Arnold Schwarzenegger had once personified conspicuous energy consumption by serving as a spokesman for Hummer vehicles, but as the steward of America's largest state, which was also the twelfth largest producer of carbon dioxide emissions in the world, he eventually became a born-again green. By 2004, the governor had given up his Hummers and presided over the nation's strictest carbon dioxide emission standards for automobiles. With respect to global warming, he declared: "I say the debate is over. We know the science. We see the threat. And we know the time for action is now." Thus California took action on its own even as Washington continued to dither. In August 2006, the state legislature passed a bundle of measures designed to achieve a 25 percent reduction in greenhouse gas emissions by 2020. California clearly expected other states to emulate its green example, and at least ten states announced plans to do just that.

At the same time concern was growing about greenhouse gases, the country was becoming alarmed about the national security risks associated with increasing energy dependence on the Middle East, the world's most unstable region. Put more concretely, did it really make sense for America to rely for so much of its oil on one Middle Eastern country, Saudi Arabia, which had produced the majority of the 9/11 terrorists?

PARTING WAYS: THE WAR ON TERROR AND THE CRISIS IN TRANS-ATLANTIC RELATIONS

If 9/11 came to be seen as a kind of secular Judgment Day, introducing a severe time of testing for a suddenly vulnerable and deeply wounded America, the response to this test played out rather differently in the United States and Europe. Sharply divergent approaches to the "war on terror" generated significant tensions between Washington and some of its traditional European partners. Of course, this was not the first time that Europe and the United States had been at odds over how best to respond to threats to Western security; indeed, the disagreements over containing militant Islam echoed in some ways those over fighting Communism during the Cold War.

The trans-Atlantic rift in the war on terror was not apparent in the immediate aftermath of 9/11. On the contrary, expressions of sorrow and solidarity poured in from all over Europe—from national leaders and ordinary citizens alike. European governments quickly announced their support for the invocation of NATO's article 5, the alliance's self-defense clause, according to which any attack against one NATO member was to be treated as an attack against all the other allies. Practically speaking, this meant that the European NATO powers were ready to join in a military coalition to punish the Taliban government in Afghanistan for sheltering the Al-Qaeda terrorists believed to be behind the 9/11 attacks. This was the first time in history that article 5 had been invoked.

Crucially, however, Washington chose to spurn this historic offer of multinational support in favor of a (largely) go-it-alone strategy. The Pentagon made it clear that it did not want to fight another "war by committee," as it had in Kosovo. Thus the only European ally invited to participate actively in the Afghan operation was Britain, which ended up aiding marginally in the preliminary bombing attacks and contributing some Special Forces troops to the subsequent ground campaign. Apart from approving Britain's participation in the venture, Prime Minister Blair's primary role-here was to shore up international support for the undertaking. Although the European governments continued to voice support for the Afghan war, they were miffed over being shunted to the sidelines, and they worried about what Washington's strategy of near-unilateralism in Afghanistan might portend for the further prosecution of the war on terror.

Those worries turned to genuine alarm when it became apparent that the Bush administration planned to use the 9/11 attacks as an opportunity to expand the war on terror to other "rogue states," beginning with Saddam Hussein's Iraq. In late September 2001, shortly before the bombing of Afghanistan began, Deputy Secretary of Defense Paul Wolfowitz told German foreign minister Joschka Fischer that Washington intended to eliminate Saddam Hussein's government once the Taliban and Al-Qaeda were destroyed. Saddam, Wolfowitz insisted, was the modern equivalent of Hitler, a leader so evil and menacing that all efforts to "contain" him were illusory. Saddam's removal, Wolfowitz further intimated, would set the stage for a wholesale alteration of the political equation in the Middle East, which in Washington's view was the only hope for a durable victory in the war on terror.

Even before the Afghan war segued into the invasion of Iraq (without, of course, the capture of Osama bin Laden or the full destruction of the Taliban), European politicians and pundits were expressing reservations about the manner in which Washington was framing the war on terror. President Bush's early reference to a "crusade" against Islamic terrorism rang alarm bells in Europe because it seemed to evoke the old religious clash between Christians and Muslims. Nor were Europeans comfortable with Bush's phrase "Axis of Evil," which sounded a lot like Osama's own terminology for the West and which conjured up a satanic enemy that could not be negotiated with, only fought to the death. "We have to avoid a clash of civilizations at all costs," warned French foreign minister Hubert Vedrine. "One has to avoid falling into this huge trap, this monstrous trap," which Vedrine said had been "conceived by the instigators of the [9/11] assault." While European leaders understood the need for military measures in Afghanistan, some openly wondered whether it was a good idea to conceive the broader campaign against terror as a "war," with military forces taking on the bulk of the job. Having battled terrorists of various stripes for decades on their own soil, Europeans tended to believe that the best counterterrorism work was accomplished through police intelligence and cooperation. And, as some pointed out, since terrorism was the weapon of choice of war's losers, military victory in the classical sense would not make the terrorists disappear; it would only make them multiply.

Europe's (or most of Europe's) reservations about relying primarily on the military to combat terror was part of a broader distrust of things military—a legacy of Europe's own bloody martial past and post–World War II experience of emphasizing the "soft" powers of diplomacy and economic suasion to achieve major foreign policy goals. Europe's lack of a common army and its relatively low levels of defense spending contributed to this trend. America, by contrast, had since World War II relied repeatedly on its military—had often, so to speak, used the marines as its first arm of diplomacy—and although this strategy had not always been successful, the temptation to use the military stick remained intact because the stick was big and handy and because the American people seemed willing to countenance its use provided the national leadership could justify it. (It also helped if the other side could not retaliate too effectively.) On the basis of this historical divergence between Europe and America, the American political commentator Robert Kagan came up with the pithy dichotomy: "Europeans are from Venus and Americans are from Mars." The dichotomy may have been a bit simplistic, but with respect to the use of "hard" power to confront urgent problems, including the threat of terrorism, Americans and Europeans often did seem to be living on different planets.

The Iraq war brought out this divergence much more clearly than the Afghan conflict had done. As is well known, the Bush administration contended that Saddam Hussein posed an imminent threat to world security because he possessed hidden "weapons of mass destruction" (WMD), which he could either use himself or sell to other rogue states or international terrorists. Some members of the Bush administration also contended that Saddam had contributed to the 9/11 attacks. Determined to effect "regime change" in Iraq, Washington put out a call for partners to assist in the operation, though the Pentagon demanded control over any coalition that might be put together and President Bush insisted that the United States would go it alone if need be. Confronted with Washington's call to arms, many of the European governments balked, stating a clear preference to work through the UN to pressure Saddam to allow international weapons inspectors to return to Iraq and make a thorough investigation of the country's arsenal. France went further, however, insisting that "nothing justified [Washington's] envisaged military action." Similarly, Chancellor Schröder of Germany said that he would not support any UN resolution that sanctioned a war. "I will not click my heels in response to orders from Washington," he declared. In response, American Defense Secretary Donald Rumsfeld dismissed France and Germany as "old Europe" (in contrast to the "new" Eastern European nations that expressed a willingness to help remove Saddam), while America's conservative media decried the French as "cheese-eating surrender

Anti-Iraq War protestors in London, 2003.

monkeys" and the Franco-German partnership as an "axis of weasel." In the end, Washington was able to put together a "coalition of the willing" for Iraq, which included small contingents from European nations like Spain, Italy, Denmark, the Netherlands, the Czech Republic, Hungary, Estonia, Latvia, Lithuania, Slovakia, and Poland. However, the only substantial contribution to the effort (apart from America's own) came from Britain. As noted above, Tony Blair made his commitment despite misgivings within his own government and party. He also faced massive opposition from the British populace. In mid-February 2003, an estimated 1 million people, the largest demonstration Britain had ever seen, converged on London to protest against the impending war.

"Operation Iraqi Freedom" began with joint American and British air strikes on Iraq on March 20, 2003. Ground operations commenced on the following day, and though coalition forces encountered significant resistance in some places, by April 9 American troops were able to take control of Baghdad and on April 14 capture Tikrit, Saddam Hussein's tribal homeland. Two weeks later, President Bush stood on the flight deck of the aircraft carrier *Abraham Lincoln*, under a banner proclaiming "Mission Accomplished" and pronounced the end of major combat operations in Iraq.

Bush's secretary of state, General Colin Powell, had warned at the outset of the invasion that Iraq would "crack like a goblet, and it'll be a problem to pick up the pieces." Powell, of course, was soon proven all too prophetic: Iraq was relatively easy to break but very hard to fix. The occupation was lamed from the outset by inadequate planning and insufficient troop levels. It was also distracted by a frenzied search for those "weapons of mass destruction" whose alleged presence was the main justification for the war. Saddam Hussein, who had fled Baghdad upon the arrival of the Americans, was eventually unearthed (literally) by U.S. troops, but his illusive WMD seemed to have vanished into thin air.

The European citizens who opposed the Iraq invasion did not need the failure to find WMD to be convinced that the entire enterprise was unjust and illegal, but their growing belief that the war had been initiated on false pretenses, perhaps downright lies, certainly added fuel to the fires of indignation. The indignation took on signs of hysteria in some instances. In Germany, France, Spain, and Britain, books alleging that Washington itself had masterminded 9/11 to justify attacking Afghanistan and Iraq became best sellers.

European leaders who had contributed forces to the invasion and occupation of Iraq found themselves under increasing attack from outraged citizens and were pressed constantly to justify their policy. This was especially true for Tony Blair, whose dogged defense of the Iraqi venture and his partnership with the American president earned him the contemptuous sobriquet "Bush's poodle." Eventually, as the scene in Iraq degenerated into a bloody quagmire, with various insurgent groups battling coalition troops, sectarian militias battling each other, and atrocities and torture perpetrated by all sides, the "coalition of the willing" became the coalition of the shrinking. Between 2004 and 2006, Spain, the Netherlands, Hungary, Poland, and Italy withdrew their contingents. Needless to say, the European nations that had always steered clear of the Iraqi adventure were less inclined than ever to rethink their policy and contribute to the beleaguered occupation, though they were repeatedly invited to do so by the Bush administration.

Washington had always defended the Iraqi operation as an integral part of the war on terror, but many Europeans, and for that matter a growing number of Americans, argued that the war was a massive distraction from the campaign against Islamic terror, and that indeed it was abetting the terrorists by fueling anti-American sentiment in Muslim lands and bringing thousands of new recruits to the terrorist ranks. Even the British parliament published a report in July 2006 arguing that the war in Iraq was making it harder to fight terrorism effectively.

The Iraq war, however one assessed its legitimacy and logic, was not the only part of the Bush administration's war on terror that strained relations between Washington and Europe. Another area of dispute had to do with the way America treated terrorist suspects. In June 2006, the EU's top justice official was asked by human rights groups to look into allegations that the CIA, in possible collusion with European security officials, had kidnapped suspected terrorists on European soil and held them in secret Eastern European jails before flying them on to countries where they faced torture—a policy Washington called "extraordinary rendition." Although European officials may have played a role in these operations, the chief villain of the piece, in the eyes of Washington's European critics, was an American administration that was willing to violate European law and ignore basic human rights in its fight against terror. In response to these allegations, Washington, in the form of Secretary of State Condoleezza Rice, publicly denied that the United States "transported detainees from one country to another for the purpose of interrogation using torture."

Another bone of contention between Washington and Europe was America's special detention facility at Guantánamo Bay, Cuba, where hundreds of terror suspects were being held indefinitely without having been given trials, regular access to attorneys, or even knowledge of the specific charges against them. While the Bush administration defended the practices at Guantánamo as compatible with international law and absolutely necessary for the war on terror, various European critics (and, once again, many Americans) saw this operation as a gross violation of basic legal norms—indeed, as a form of torture. In June 2006, the EU formally pressed President Bush to close the Guantánamo Bay facility. Tony Blair and German chancellor Angela Merkel personally gave Bush the same advice. (It should be noted, however, that the German government refused for years to accept the repatriation of a Turkish-German terror suspect being held in Guantánamo, thus substantially delaying his release from the prison.)

Widespread indignation over the manner in which Washington conducted its war on terror contributed significantly to an erosion of the American image around the world, not least in Europe. A Pew Research Center poll conducted in spring 2006 found that positive views of the United States had declined markedly across Europe in the past four years. The sense of solidarity with America inspired by the 9/11 attacks had been replaced by distrust, fear, and even loathing. Many Europeans now regarded America's war in Iraq as a greater danger to world peace than North Korea's nuclear weapons program or Iran's nuclear ambitions. America's embassy buildings in European capitals had to be cordoned off behind concrete security barriers and guarded around the clock by local police and U.S. Marines. President Bush could not set foot in Europe without occasioning massive protest demonstrations. Of course, in the years since World War II, American leaders and American policy had often met with opposition from Europeans, but never had the distrust and enmity seemed so deep and wide.

Even serious rifts, however, need not be permanent or irreparably damaging. Nor is it written in stone or in the planetary heavens that Americans over the long run would follow paths significantly different from those of the Europeans in addressing the great problems of the day. At the outset of World War II, when Washington resisted Britain's call to intervene in that conflict, Winston Churchill observed that one could generally count on America to do the right thing—once it had exhausted all the alternatives. At the dawn of the twenty-first century, as a new set of global challenges loomed, the United States and Europe once again needed to be on the same side if those challenges were to be met effectively. One could only hope that the crucial partnership would not come too late.

Suggestions for Further Reading

The printed material on the history of the twentieth century—documentary publications, memoirs, comprehensive histories, historical monographs—would fill a library; the following bibliography is severely selective. It is limited to works published in English. Although the Further Reading compilation for this Sixth Edition retains some of the works of particular significance cited in earlier editions, the list has been extensively pruned to focus on titles of more recent vintage.

GENERAL

Contemporary history poses particular problems for both research and presentation. These are well outlined in Geoffrey Barraclough, *An Introduction to Contemporary History* (1964). More recent surveys include Mark Mazower, *Dark Continent. Europe's Twentieth Century* (1999); Eric Hobsbawm, *The Age of Extremes: A History of the World, 1914–1991* (1994); Peter Conrad, *Modern Times, Modern Places: How Life and Art Were Transformed in a Century of Revolution, Innovation and Radical Change* (1998); Eric D. Weitz, *A Century of Genocide: Utopias of Race and Nation* (2003); Michael Howard, *Liberation or Catastrophe?: Reflections on the History of the Twentieth Century* (2007); and Tony Judt, *Reappraisals: Reflections on the Forgotten Twentieth Century* (2008). A comprehensive examination of women's roles in European society is contained in Bonnie S. Anderson and Judith P. Zinsser, *A History of Their Own. Women in Europe from Prehistory to the Present* (rev. ed., 2000). Paul Kennedy's *The Rise and Fall of the Great Powers: Economic Change and Military Conflict from 1500 to 2000* (1987) examines why great powers, including the present ones, gain and lose power. George L. Mosse, *Fallen Soldiers: Reshaping the Memory of the World Wars* (1990), presents a perceptive study of the consecration of war in the twentieth century. Amy Chu's *Day of Empire. How Hyperpowers Rise to Global Dominance—And Why They Fall* (2007) examines the history of "hyperpowers," (globally dominant empires), including the recent British and American examples. Anthony Pagden's *Worlds at War: The 2,500-Year Struggle Between East and West* (2008) culminates in an examination of present-day Western encounters with Islam against a long historical backdrop.

FROM 1890 TO THE BEGINNING OF THE FIRST
WORLD WAR: GENERAL TRENDS IN THE POLITICAL,
INTELLECTUAL, AND ECONOMIC SCENE

For a lively description of the main features of the political scene in Europe before the First World War, see Barbara W. Tuchman, *The Proud Tower* (1966). The developments and experiences that changed the literary scene after the First World War are analyzed in Robert Wohl, *The Generation of 1914* (1979). Other significant dimensions of the cultural scene are covered in Peter Gay, *Freud: A Life for our Time* (1988); *Wagnerism in European Culture and Politics*, ed. by David C. Large and William Weber (1984); Eugen Weber, *France. Fin-de-Siècle* (1986); David Cannadine, *The Pleasures of the Past: Reflections in Modern British History* (1989); and Peter Gay, *Modernism: The Lure of Heresy* (2007). A survey on the age of imperialism with interesting illustrations will be found in Heinz Gollwitzer, *Europe in the Age of Imperialism 1880–1914* (1969). E. J. Hobsbawm, *The Age of Empire: 1875–1914* (1988), offers a brilliant analysis of the imperial enterprise from a Marxist perspective. More recent studies include Marc Ferro, *Colonization: A Global History* (1997), H. L. Wesseling, *Divide and Rule: The Partition of Africa, 1880–1914* (1996); and Anthony Anghie, *Imperialism, Sovereignty, and the Making of International Law* (2005).

THE GREAT POWERS IN THE LATE NINETEENTH
AND EARLY TWENTIETH CENTURIES

The period before the First World War is discussed in many national studies. For **Britain**, see Max Beloff, *Britain's Liberal Empire, 1897–1921*, vol. I (1970); Roy Jenkins, *Asquith, Portrait of a Man and an Era* (1965); David Cannadine, *Ornamentalism: How the British Saw Their Empire* (2002); Heather Streets, *Martial Races: The Military, Race, and Masculinity in British Imperial Culture, 1857–1914* (2004); and Thomas Weber, *Our Friend "The Enemy": Elite Education in Britain and Germany before World War I* (2008). For the decline of Britain's nobility, see David Cannadine, *The Decline and Fall of the British Aristocracy* (1992). On Britain's greatest city in this era, see Jonathan Schneer, *London 1900: The Imperial Metropolis* (1999); and Judith Walkowitz, *City of Dreadful Delights: Narratives of Sexual Danger in Late Victorian London* (1993).

On **France** in this period, see Eugen Weber's two seminal studies, *The Nationalist Revival in France, 1905–1914* (1959) and *Peasants into Frenchmen: The Modernization of Rural France* (1976). A good cultural study is Charles Rearick, *Pleasures of the Belle-Epoque: Entertainment and Festivity in Turn-of-the-Century France* (1985). For an important dimension of late-nineteenth-century French imperialism, see Robert Lee, *France and the Exploitation of China, 1851–1901: A Study in Economic Imperialism* (1989). On the all-important Dreyfus affair, see Douglas Johnson, *France and the Dreyfus Affair* (1966); and Michael Burns, *Dreyfus: A Family Affair* (1992). On the place of women in turn-of-the-century France, see Mary Louise Roberts, *Disruptive Acts: The New Woman in Fin-de-Siècle France* (2002).

The Wilhelmian period in **Germany** is treated in a number of good biographies of Kaiser Wilhelm II. See, for example, Lamar Cecil, *William II, Prince and Emperor, 1859–1900* (1989) and *William II. Emperor and Exile, 1900–1941* (1996); also John C. G. Rohl,

Wilhelm II: The Kaiser's Personal Monarchy, 1888–1900 (2004). Isabel V. Hull gives an interesting account of the German ruling group in *The Entourage of Kaiser Wilhelm II* (1982). An excellent political history of the period is to be found in Mathew Seligmann, *Germany from Reich to Republic, 1871–1918: Politics, Hierarchy, and Elites* (2000). Germany's greatest imperialist is profiled in Arne Perras's *Carl Peters and German Imperialism, 1856–1918: A Political Biography* (2004). David Blackbourn's *The Conquest of Nature: Water, Landscape, and the Making of Modern* Germany (2006) discusses environmental issues in this period and later. David Blackbourn and Geoff Eley's, *The Peculiarities of German History* (1984) offers a significant reevaluation of the assumptions that have been held to distinguish the course of German history from that of other nations. David Clay Large, *Berlin* (2000), analyzes Berlin's place in imperial Germany and later.

On **Austria-Hungary** and the Habsburgs, see the early seminal study by Robert A. Kann, *The Habsburg Empire: A Study in Integration and Disintegration* (1957). A more recent examination of the imperial collapse is Alan Sked, *The Decline and Fall of the Habsburg Empire, 1815–1918* (2001). Carl Schorske, *Fin-de-Siècle Vienna* (1980), analyzes the intellectual currents that made Vienna a center of the development of modern art. Jacques Kornberg, *Theodor Herz: From Assimilation to Zionism* (1993), looks at the origins of Zionism in the Austrian capital.

For political developments in newly unified **Italy**, see Alexander De Grand, *The Hunchback Tailor: Giovanni Giolitti and Liberal Italy from the Challenge of Mass Politics to the Rise of Fascism, 1882–1922* (2001). On the social tensions that formed an obstacle to the working of democracy, see Richard A. Webster, *Industrial Imperialism in Italy* (1975).

Developments in imperial **Russia** in its last decades are examined in W. Bruce Lincoln, *In War's Dark Shadow: The Russians before the Great War* (1983). Russian imperial ambitions in this era are well described in Theodore R. Weeks's *Nation and State in Late Imperial Russia: Nationalism and Russification on the Western Frontier* (1996). The collapse of the Russian empire is examined in Greg King, *The Fate of the Romanovs* (2003); and Alan Wood, *The Origins of the Russian Revolution, 1861–1917* (2003). Sebag Montefiore's *Young Stalin* (2007) profiles the future dictator at the beginning of his revolutionary career.

DIPLOMATIC EVENTS AND THE FIRST WORLD WAR

The diplomatic history of the thirty-five years before the First World War has been examined in minutest detail because archives of the foreign offices became accessible soon after 1918. The decisive years for the formation of new constellations among the powers are treated in William L. Langer, *The Diplomacy of Imperialism, 1890–1902* (1972). For the crucial developments that created the two opposing coalitions, see also George Kennan, *The Decline of Bismarck's European Order* (1979), and Paul M. Kennedy, *The Rise of Anglo-German Antagonism, 1860–1914* (1980). The question of German responsibility forms a crucial issue in Fritz Fischer, *Germany's Aims in the First World War* (1967), which has aroused a vehement discussion. The history of the war itself has been treated in many memoirs, among them those of Lloyd George and Churchill, and also in studies of military history. John Keegan, *The Face of Battle* (1977), offers a brilliant description of one of the most characteristic military actions: the Battle of the Somme. Keegan's *The First World War* (1998) is the best general account of the war, but see also J. M. Winter, *The Experience of World War I* (1989). Niall Ferguson, *The Pity of War*

(1999), offers controversial views of the war's beginning and end. Eric J. Leed, *No Man's Land: Combat and Identity in World War I* (1979), offers a perceptive analysis of the psychological impact of the war on the soldiers. The relationship between war and economic developments is investigated in Gerald D. Feldman, *Army, Industry and Labor in Germany, 1914–1918* (1966). More recent studies on the war's home front include Broc Millman, *Managing Dissent in First World War Britain* (2000); Jeffrey R. Smith, *A People's War: Germany's Political Revolution, 1913–1918* (2007); Isabel V. Hull, *Absolute Destruction: Military Culture and the Practice of War in Imperial Germany* (2005); and Maureen Healy, *Vienna and the Fall of the Habsburg Empire: Total War and Everyday Life in World War I* (2004). Something of the impact of the war on the minds of those who fought in it is captured in Paul Fussell, *The Great War and Modern Memory* (1975). The best-known and most widely read literary works describing the war are those of Barbusse, Jünger, and Remarque. For the domestic impact of war in Britain, see Arthur Marwick, *The Deluge* (1965). Modris Eksteins, *Rites of Spring: The Great War and the Birth of the Modern Age* (1989), looks at the connections between the war and cultural modernism.

THE INTERWAR PERIOD

The Peace Treaties and Their Failure

For a general discussion of the world that emerged from the First World War, see Gerhard Schulz, *Revolution and Peace Treaties 1917–1920* (1972). The best and most recent general study of the postwar peace conferences in Paris is Margaret MacMillan, *Paris 1919: Six Months that Changed the World* (2002). On the legacy of the Versailles Treaty for the contemporary world, see David A. Andelman, *A Shattered Peace. Versailles 1919 and the Price We Pay Today* (2008). For a study of the efforts to stabilize postwar Europe, see Patrick O. Cohrs, *The Unfinished Peace after World War I: America, Britain, and the Stabilization of Europe, 1919–1932* (2006).

The ideas and interests that influenced and determined the peace settlement have been thoroughly discussed and analyzed by Arno J. Mayer in *Political Origins of the New Diplomacy, 1917–1918* (1959) and *Politics and Diplomacy of Peacemaking: Containment and Counterrevolution at Versailles, 1918–1919* (1967). Sir Harold Nicolson, *Peacemaking, 1919* (1939), gives a report of the peace conference from a human angle. David Clay Large, *Between Two Fires: Europe's Path in the 1930s* (1990), examines the 1930s by looking closely at eight key episodes in that decade.

For a comprehensive treatment of the conduct of foreign affairs during the interwar years, see *The Diplomats, 1919–1939*, ed. by Gordon Craig and Felix Gilbert (1953). For the rise of Fascism in the various European countries, see S. J. Woolf, *European Fascism* (1968), and H. A. Turner, Jr., *Reappraisals of Fascism* (1972). Donald Cameron Watt, *How War Came: The Immediate Origins of the Second World War* (1989), presents a meticulous analysis of the diplomatic events in the two years preceding the war. Anthony Read and David Fisher, *The Deadly Embrace: Hitler, Stalin, and the Nazi–Soviet Pact, 1939–1941* (1988) provides the best account of the German-Soviet alliance.

The Rise of Fascism in Italy

The decade in the course of which Mussolini ended Italian parliamentarism and attained complete power is described by Adrian Lyttelton, *The Seizure of Power: Fascism in Italy 1919–1929* (1973); for a good biography of Mussolini that perhaps overstresses the histrionic aspects of his politics, see Denis Mack Smith, *Mussolini* (1982). The most recent and comprehensive study of Italy in the fascist era is R. J. B. Bosworth, *Mussolini's Italy: Life under the Dictatorship* (2006). Victoria De Grazia, *How Fascism Ruled Women* (1994), examines the plight of women in Mussolini's system.

From Democracy to Nazi Dictatorship in Germany

For a general analysis of the years of parliamentary democracy in Germany, see Eric D. Weitz, *Weimar Germany: Promise and Tragedy* (2007). Richard J. Evans, *The Coming of the Third Reich* (2003) minutely examines the collapse of the Weimar Republic and the early history of the Nazi Party. On the key architect of German foreign policy in this era, see Jonathan Wright, *Gustav Stresemann: Weimar Germany's Greatest Statesman* (2002). For the role of women in this period, see Atina Grossmann *When Biology Became Destiny: Women in Weimar and Nazi Germany* (1984). Grossman's *Reforming Sex: The German Movement for Birth Control and Abortion Reform* (1995), examines the politics of reproduction in Germany from Weimar through the immediate post-World War II period. For intellectual trends that contributed to the rise of the Nazis, see George L. Mosse, *The Crisis of German Ideology* (1964). Henry Ashby Turner, Jr., *German Big Business and the Rise of Hitler* (1985), examines the role of business in the Nazi rise to power. Geoff Eley, *From Unification to Nazism: Reinterpreting the German Past* (1986) and Richard J. Evans, *Rethinking the German History: Nineteenth-Century Germany and the Origins of the Third Reich* (1987) discuss the question of continuity in German history and the place of National Socialism in the German experience. Fritz Stern's *Dreams and Delusions: The Drama of German History* (1987) is a collection of masterly essays that shed much light on how delusions of power led Germans to the tragedy of National Socialism.

On Germany under the Nazis, only a few books will be mentioned, works that throw light on the diverse aspects of the regime. For a comprehensive history containing the latest scholarship, see Richard J. Evans, *The Third Reich in Power* (2005). The best biography of Hitler is now the two-volume work by Ian Kershaw, *Hitler: 1889–1936 Hubris* (1998) and *Hitler: 1936–1945 Nemesis* (2000). For an intriguing study of Hitler interpretations, see Ron Rosenbaum, *Explaining Hitler* (1998). David Schönbaum, *Hitler's Social Revolution* (1980), discusses the structural changes brought about by the Nazi regime. Good comparisons of Hitler's Germany and Soviet Russia can be found in Richard Overy, *The Dictators: Hitler's Germany, Stalin's Russia* (2005), and Robert Gellately, *Lenin, Stalin, and Hitler: The Age of Social Catastrophe* (2007). A very revealing look at daily life inside the Third Reich is provided by the diaries of the German-Jewish intellectual, Viktor Klemperer, *I Will Bear Witness*, 2 vols (1995, 1999). Peter Hoffmann, *History of the German Resistance* (1977) has the most comprehensive treatment of the German opposition to the Nazis. For a collection of essays on the German resistance, see David Clay Large, ed., *Contending with Hitler: Varieties of German Resistance in the Third Reich* (1991). Detlev Peukert, *Inside Nazi Germany: Conformity, Opposition, and Racism in Everyday Life* (1987), shows how ordinary citizens evaded or accepted Nazi policies of oppression. A more recent study of this issue is Eric A. Johnson, *Nazi Terror: The Gestapo, Jews, and Ordinary Germans* (1999). Peter Hayes, *Industry and Ideology: I. G. Farben in the Nazi Era* (1987), presents a meticulously researched study of the role of Germany's largest corporation in the Third Reich. On Munich's role in the rise of Nazism, see David Clay Large, *Where Ghosts Walked: Munich's Road to the Third Reich* (1997). Large's *Nazi Games: The Olympics of 1936* (2007), examines the important role played by the Olympic Games in German and world politics of the 1930s. On the place of environmentalism in the Third Reich, see *How Green Were the Nazis? Nation,*

Environment, and Nature in the Third Reich, edited by Franz-Josef Brüggemeier, Marc Cioc and Thomas Zeller (2005).

The Democracies

For the decade of the 1930s in France, see Eugen Weber. *The Hollow Years: France in the 1930s* (1994). See also William Wiser, *The Twilight Years: Paris in the 1930s* (2000). The intellectual situation is analyzed in James Joll, *Three Intellectuals in Politics* (1965), and in H. S. Hughes, *The Obstructed Path: French Social Thought in the Years of Desperation, 1930–1960* (1968). Robert Soucy, *French Fascism: The Second Wave, 1933–1939* (1995), examines the French right-wing leagues.

On Great Britain, a lively, amusingly prejudiced history of the interwar years is A. J. P. Taylor, *English History, 1914–1945* (1965); the social problems of this period are well presented in Robert Graves and Alan Hodge, *The Long Week-End: A Social History of Great Britain, 1918–1939* (1941); and for a discussion of British policy from the point of view of Labor, see Alan Bullock, *The Life and Times of Ernest Bevin*, vol. I, *Trade Union Leader, 1881–1940* (1960). Britain's failure to adequately rearm in the 1930s is the subject of Christopher Price's *Britain, America, and Rearmament in the 1930s: The Cost of Failure* (2001). For a recent reexamination of the politics and economics of the 1930s in Britain, see Andy Thorpe, *Britain in the 1930s: The Deceptive Decade* (1992). An unforgettable picture of the political and literary scene in England is given in the series of novels by Anthony Powell, collectively titled *A Dance to the Music of Time*, and in the early novels of Evelyn Waugh *Vile Bodies* and *A Handful of Dust*. The British literary scene is also the subject of Samuel Hynes, *The Auden Generation: Literature and Politics in England in the 1930s* (1977).

The Appeasement Policy

Great Britain stands in the middle of the discussion on the appeasement policy. In general, see Maurice Cowling, *The Impact of Hitler: British Politics and British Policy, 1933–1940* (1977). The attitude of the entire group of appeasers emerges brilliantly from A. L. Rowse, *Appeasement: A Study in Political Decline, 1933–1939* (1961). A more recent study of the same subject is N. J. Crowson, *Facing Fascism: The Conservative Party and the European Dictators, 1935–1940* (1997). French appeasement policy is discussed in Yvon Lacaze, *France and Munich: A Study of Decision Making in International Affairs* (1995). On the Soviet Union's concerns regarding the democracies' appeasement policies, see Hugh Ragsdale, *The Soviets, the Munich Crisis, and the Coming of World War II* (2004). A good study of the interpretation and exploitation of the Munich legacy is Jeffrey Record, *The Specter of Munich: Reconsidering the Lessons of Appeasing Hitler* (2007).

The last chance to stop Fascist aggression was lost with the Spanish Civil War. It was an international event but also the climax of internal developments in Spain during the 1920s and 1930s; as such it is presented by Gabriel Jackson, *The Spanish Republic and the Civil War, 1931–1939* (1965). A clear, general account of the war will be found in Hugh Thomas, *The Spanish Civil War* (1961). For the Soviet role in Spain, see Stanley G. Payne, *The Spanish Civil War, the Soviet Union, and Communism* (2004). On leftist intervention in Spain from the democratic West, see R. A. Stradling, *History and Legend: Writing the International Brigades* (2004). For the desperation of the young, produced by the policy of the appeasers, see Peter Stansky and William Abrahams, *Journey to the Frontier: Two Roads to the Spanish Civil War* (1966).

Soviet Russia

For a survey of Russian internal developments, see Martin McCauley, *The Soviet Union since 1917* (1981). The travails of ordinary Soviet citizens is the subject of Katherine Bliss Eaton's *Daily Life in the Soviet Union* (2004). For Stalin as dictator, see, in addition to the above-cited comparative works, Sebag Montefiore, *Stalin: The Court of the Red Tsar* (2003). The opposition that Stalin's rise to power and his policy aroused in Russia and the defeat of his opponents are analyzed by Stephen F. Cohen, *Bukharin and the Bolshevik Revolution* (1974). Ilya Ehrenburg, *Memoirs, 1921–1941* (1964) shows the conditions of intellectual work in Stalin's time. The pressure of ideology and dictatorship on the development and direction of scientific research is outlined by Loren R. Graham, *Science and Philosophy in the Soviet Union* (1972). On Soviet Russia's nuclear policy, see David Holloway, *Stalin and the Bomb* (1994). The best work on Stalin's purges is Robert Conquest, *The Great Terror: Stalin's Purges of the Thirties* (1990). On Soviet agricultural policy, see Sheila Fitzpatrick, *Stalin's Peasants: Resistance and Survival in the Russian Village after Collectivization* (1994).

THE SECOND WORLD WAR

For a general survey, see Peter Calvocoressi and Guy Wint, *Total War: Causes and Courses of the Second World War* (1972). A more recent general account is Gerhard L. Weinberg's magisterial *A World at Arms: A Global History of World War II* (1994). For a comprehensive operational history of the war, see Williamson Murray and Allan R. Millet, *A War to Be Won: Fighting the Second World War* (2000). Ian Kershaw's *Fateful Choices: Ten Decisions that Changed the World, 1940–1941* (2007), examines the crucial political and military decisions that shaped the early phase of the war. The all-important wartime relationship between Churchill and FDR is the subject of Jon Meacham, *Franklin and Winston: An Intimate Portrait of an Epic Friendship* (2003). Laurence Lafore, *The End of Glory; An Interpretation of the Origins of World War II* (1982), provides a good introduction to the extended literature on the outbreak of the war. See also Donald Cameron Watt, *How War Came* (1989).

Almost all the leading statesmen and generals have written memoirs, but it should be mentioned that the memoirs of two of the main actors not only have great historical interest but are also remarkable literary achievements: Winston S. Churchill, *The Second World War*, 6 vols. (1948–1953), and Charles de Gaulle, *The Complete War Memoirs of Charles de Gaulle, 1940–1946*, 3 vols. in one, vol. I trans. by Jonathan Griffin, vols. II and III trans. by Richard Howard (1955–1960).

Older but still useful secondary accounts of the war include Gordon Wright, *The Ordeal of Total War, 1939–1945* (1968); and John Lukacs, *The Last European War, September 1939/December 1941* (1976). See also Angus Calder, *The People's War: Britain 1939–1945* (1969). Another good comprehensive history of World War II is John Keegan, *The Second World War* (1989). America's role in the earlier phases of the European theater of the war is the focus of Rick Atkinson's *An Army at Dawn: The War in North Africa, 1942–1943* (2006), and *The Day of Battle: The War in Sicily and Italy, 1943–1944* (2008). A brilliant recent study of the Red Army at war is Catherine Merridale's *Ivan's War: Life and Death in the Red Army, 1939–1945* (2007). For Stalin's management of the war, see Steven Merritt Miner, *Stalin's Holy War: Religion, Nationalism, and Alliance Politics, 1941–1945* (2003). Paul Fussell's *Wartime: Understanding and Behavior in the Second*

World War (1989), examines the immediate impact of the war on common soldiers and civilians. Mussolini's aims in entering the war and the collapse of an independent Italian policy are described by MacGregor Knox, *Mussolini Unleashed: 1939–1941* (1982). The end of the war comes alive in Hugh R. Trevor-Roper, *The Last Days of Hitler* (1947). Richard Overy, *Why the Allies Won* (1997), analyzes the reasons behind the Allied victory. Other recent studies of the last phases of the fighting in Europe include Max Hastings, *Armageddon: The Battle for Germany, 1944–1945* (2004); and Paul Fussell, *The Boys' Crusade: The American Infantry in Northwestern Europe, 1944–1945* (2004).

Intelligence assumed a role of great importance in the Second World War; in general see F. H. Hinsley et al., *British Intelligence in the Second World War: Its Influence on Strategy and Operations* (1981), and for a personalized and somewhat romanticized presentation of the role of intelligence, see William Stevenson, *A Man Called Intrepid* (1976).

We have a few descriptions of the impact of the war on the people at home. In addition to Calder, mentioned above, see Alexander Werth, *Russia at War, 1941–1945* (1964). R. O. Paxton, *Vichy France: Old Guard and New Order 1940–1944* (1972), analyzes the impact of the German occupation of France, as does Philippe Burrin, *France under the Germans* (1993); and, more recently, Robert Gildea, *Marianne in Chains: In Search of the German Occupation, 1940–1945* (2002). World War II's legacy in postwar France is treated brilliantly in Henry Rousso, *The Haunting Past: History, Memory, and Justice in Contemporary France* (2002). On the war's connections to the Holocaust, see Donald McKale, *Hitler's Shadow War: The Holocaust and World War II* (2002); Jeffrey Herf, *The Jewish Enemy: Nazi Propaganda and the Holocaust* (2006); Ian Kershaw, *Hitler, the Germans, and the Final Solution* (2008); and Mona Sue Weissmark, *Justice Matters: Legacies of the Holocaust and World War II* (2004). A brilliant study of the treatment of local Jews in one Polish village can be found in Jan Gross, *Neighbors: The Destruction of the Jewish Community in Jedwabne, Poland* (2001).

AFTER THE SECOND WORLD WAR

For general surveys, see Walter Laqueur, *Europe since Hitler* (1983) and David Reynolds, *One World Divisible: A Global History since 1945* (2000). A more recent, and very stimulating, survey is Tony Judt, *Postwar: A History of Europe since 1945* (2005). Eric Hobsbawm's *Interesting Times: A Twentieth Century Life* (2002) is devoted primarily to the great historian's experiences in the second half of the twentieth century.

Recent works on the evolution of the Cold War include Martin Walker, *The Cold War: A History* (1993); John Lewis Gaddis, *We Know Now: Rethinking Cold War History* (1997); W. R. Smyser, *From Yalta to Berlin: The Cold War Struggle over Germany* (1999); Detlef Junker, ed., *The United States and Germany in the Era of the Cold War, 1945–1990: A Handbook* (2004); and Martin McCauley, *Russia, America and the Cold War* (2004). Jack F. Matlock's *Reagan and Gorbachev: How the Cold War Ended* (2004) is an insider history by Washington's ambassador to Moscow in the Gorbachev era. Richard K. Betts, *Conflict after the Cold War: Arguments on Causes of War and Peace* (2005) looks at the spate of international conflicts in the immediate wake of the Cold War.

A general survey of the issues faced by Great Britain in the postwar years is Peter Calvocoressi, *The British Experience, 1945–1975* (1978). Kenneth Harris, *Attlee* (1983) describes not only the life of the Labor statesman but also the reforms he and his party enacted. The foreign policy of the Labor government is analyzed in the third volume of the biography of Bevin by Alan Bullock, *Ernest Bevin, Foreign Secretary, 1945–1951* (1984). The third volume of Harold Nicolson, *Diaries and Letters, 1945–1962*, ed. by Nigel Nicolson (1968), gives amusing insight into the British political and social scene in the 1950s. For an analysis of Britain's far-right, see Alan Sykes, *The Radical Right in Britain: Social Imperialism to the BNP* (2005).

The changes in France since the Second World War have been startling. See especially Stanley Hoffman, *Decline or Renewal? France since the 1930s* (1974). Janet Flanner (Genêt), *Paris Journal, 1944–1965*, ed. by William Shawn (1977), gives a lively and concrete account of politics, economic developments, and cultural life. A novel by Simone de Beauvoir, *The Mandarins*, is an interesting reproduction of the intellectual atmosphere in France at the end of the war; the principal figures of the novel, although disguised with different names, are Sartre and Camus. The same figures are scrutinized in Tony Judt, *Past Imperfect French Intellectuals 1944–1955* (1994). Postwar France's difficulties in contending with the legacy of Vichy and the German occupation have been treated in a number of studies, notably Richard J. Golsan, *Memory, the Holocaust and French Justice* (1996); Sarah Farmer, *Martyred Village: Commemorating the 1944 Massacre at Oradour-sur-Glane* (1999); and Alice Kaplan, *The Collaborator: The Trial and Execution of Robert Brasillach* (2000).

The astounding Italian recovery has been carefully studied; see H. Stuart Hughes, *The United States and Italy* (1953), and Muriel Grindrod, *The Rebuilding of Italy: Politics and Economics, 1945–1955* (1955). On the postwar occupation of Germany, see Giles MacDonogh, *After the Reich: The Brutal History of Allied Occupation* (2007). For the complicated relationship between American soldiers and German civilians, see Petra Goedde, *GIs and Germans: Culture, Gender, and Foreign Relations, 1945–1949* (2003). The Soviet occupation zone is treated in Norman M. Naimark, *The Russians in Germany: A History of the Soviet Zone of Occupation* (1995). The Allied treatment of captured Nazi leaders is examined in Richard Overy, *Interrogations: The Nazi Elite in Allied Hands, 1945* (2001); and Norman Goda, *Tales from Spandau: Nazi Criminals and the Cold War* (2008). Atina Grossmann's *Jews, Germans, and Allies: Close Encounters in Occupied Germany* (2007) analyzes the plight of surviving Jews in occupied Germany.

For the emergence of party politics, see Lewis J. Edinger, *Kurt Schumacher, A Study in Personality and Political Behavior* (1965). On West German rearmament, see David Clay Large, *Germans to the Front: West German Rearmament in the Adenauer Era* (1996).

For the situation in Eastern Europe, see Robert Lee Wolff, *The Balkans in Our Time* (1974). A more recent and very comprehensive study of this region is Misha Glenny's *The Balkans: Nationalism, War and the Great Powers, 1804–1999* (2000). The means of establishing and maintaining Russian control in this area are described by Zbigniew K. Brzezinski, *The Soviet Bloc: Unity and Conflict* (1961).

The End of the Colonial Empires

In general, see R. von Albertini, *Decolonization: The Administration and Future of the Colonies, 1919–1960* (1971). For the end of French rule in Africa, see John Talbott, *The War without a Name: France in Algeria, 1954–1962* (1980) and Irwin M. Wall, *France, the United States, and the Algerian War* (2002). An excellent recent study is J. P. D. Dunbabin, *The Post-Imperial Age: The Great Powers and the Wider World* (1994).

Terrorism

In general, see *Social Protest, Violence and Terror in Nineteenth- and Twentieth-Century Europe*, ed. by Wolfgang Mommsen and Gerhard Hirschfeld (1982), which is a collection of essays. *Contemporary Terror: Studies in Sub-State Violence,* ed. by David Carlton and Carlo Schaerf (1981), summarizes in a factual manner developments in the various European countries. Walter Laqueur's *Terrorism* (1977) is a broad, theoretical discussion of the variety of notions involved in the concept. On the most recent terrorist scene, especially Islamic extremism, see Jessica Stern, *Terror in the Name of God. Why Religious Militants Kill* (2003); Fredrik Logewall, ed., *Terrorism and 9/11: A Reader* (2002); Lawrence Wright, *Looming Tower: Al Qaeda and the Road to 9/11* (2006); and Ian Buruma, *Murder in Amsterdam: Liberal Europe, Islam, and the Limits of Tolerance* (2007).

Student Unrest

Basic for the conflict of generations inherent in the student revolt is John R. Gillis, *Youth and History: Tradition and Change in European Age Relations, 1770 to the Present* (1974). For the events in Paris, see the documents in Alain Schnapp and Pierre Vidal-Nacquet, *French Student Uprising: November 1967 to June 1968* (1971). A comprehensive account of the events of 1968 is offered by David Caute, *The Year of the Barricades: A Journey through 1968* (1988).

Eurocommunism

Euro-Communism: Myth or Reality, ed. by Filo ee da Torre, Edward Mortimer, and Jonathan Story (1979), is a careful exploration and evaluation of the rise and role of this movement in the various European countries. For a more recent study, see Adam Ulam, *The Communists: The Story of Power and Lost Illusions, 1948–1991* (1992).

Oil Crisis

The fall 1975 issue of *Daedalus,* Journal of the American Academy of Arts and Sciences, is titled "The Oil Crisis in Perspective." Among the various contributions, the article of Edith Penrose, "The Development of Crisis," deserves particular attention. Walter Laqueur, *Confrontation: The Middle Eastern War and World Politics* (1974), provides a broad historical background. See also Karen R. Merrill, *The Oil Crisis of 1973–1974: A Brief History with Documents* (2007).

Nuclear Weapons and Disarmament

For the development of this problem, Laurence Freedman, *The Evolution of Nuclear Strategy* (1981), is fundamental. A discussion of the main issue and an overview of the recent literature on these issues can be found in Léon Wieseltier, *Nuclear War, Nuclear Peace* (1983). The scope of the nuclear threat is effectively explored in Jonathan Schell, *The Fate of the Earth* (1982). For a study of the diplomatic dimension of the nuclear problem, see George F. Kennan, *The Nuclear Delusion: Soviet-American Relations in the Atomic Age* (1982). Other noteworthy studies include Strobe Talbott, *Deadly Gambits* (1985); McGeorge Bundy, *Danger and Survival: Choices about the Bomb in the First Fifty Years* (1989); Leon V. Sigal, *Nuclear Forces in Europe* (1984); Diana Johnstone, *The Politics of Euromissiles* (1984); and Jeffrey Herf, *War by Other Means; Soviet Power, West German Resistance; and the Battle of the Euromissiles* (1991).

Resurgent Western Europe

Derek W. Urwin, *Western Europe since 1945* (1989), presents a competent general survey. H. Stuart Hughes, *Sophisticated Rebels: The Political Culture of European Dissent* (1988), shows what happened to the revolutionary spirit of 1968 from Paris to Prague.

Stimulating studies on the relationship between Western Europe and the United States are Josef Joffe, *The Limited Partnership: Europe, the United States, and the Burdens of Alliance* (1987); John Palmer, *Europe without America?: The Crisis in Atlantic Relations* (1987); Richard J. Barnet, *The Alliance* (1983); and William Pfaff, *Barbarian Sentiments: How the American Century Ends* (1989). United Europe's emergence as an economic superpower at the end of the twentieth century, and its growing rivalry with the United States, is treated ably in T. R. Reid, *The United States of Europe: The New Superpower and the End of American Supremacy* (2004); Robert Kagan, *Of Paradise and Power: America and Europe in the New World Order* (2003); and John Peterson, *Europe, America, Bush: Transatlantic Relations in the 21ˢᵗ Century* (2003). A penetrating look at the larger world at the dawn of the 21ˢᵗ century is offered by Fareed Zakaria in *The Post-American World* (2008). The impact of the Iraq War on transatlantic relations is treated in Simon Serfaty, *Architects of Delusion: Europe, America, and the Iraq War* (2007).

Problems of immigration and migration in the 1990s are ably discussed in Reginald Appleyard, *International Migration: Challenges for the Nineties* (1991). For the latest developments relating to immigration and migration, see Bill Edgar, *Immigration and Homelessness in Europe* (2004); Peter Wagstaff, ed., *Border Crossings: Mapping Identities in Modern Europe* (2004); Agata Gorny, ed., *Migration in the New Europe: East-West Revisited* (2004); Patrick Ireland, *Becoming Europe: Immigration, Integration, and the Welfare State* (2004). On globalization, see Joseph E. Stiglitz, *Globalization and its Discontents* (2002); and John Baylis, Steve Smith, and Patricia Owens, *The Globalization of World Politics* (2008).

For Thatcher's England, see Peter Jenkins, *Mrs. Thatcher's Revolution* (1988); Hugo Young, *The Iron Lady: A Biography of Margaret Thatcher* (1990); and Juliet S. Thompson and Wayne C. Thompson, *Margaret Thatcher: Prime Minister Indomitable* (1994). On the Tony Blair years, see Con Coughlin, *American Ally: Tony Blair and the War on Terror* (2006); and David Owen, *The Hubris Syndrome: Bush, Blair, and the Intoxication of Power* (2007). For France under Mitterrand, see George Ross, Stanley Hoffmann, and Sylvia Malzacher, eds., *The Mitterrand Experiment: Continuity and Change in Modern France* (1987). The Chirac era is treated in *Chirac's challenge: Liberalization, Europeanization, and Malaise in France,* edited by John T. S. Keller and Martin A. Schain (1996). The modern Italian scene is examined in John Hayraft, *Italian Labyrinth* (1985); Tobias Jones, *The Dark Heart of Italy* (2005); and Alexander Stille, *The Sack of Rome: How a Beautiful Country with a Fabled History and a Storied Culture Was Taken Over by a Man Named Silvio Berlusconi* (2006). A good survey of German developments in the decades following World War II is Henry Ashby Turner, Jr., *The Two Germanys since 1945* (1987). Jeffrey Herf, *Divided Memory: The Nazi Past in the Two Germanys* (1997), treats the very different ways in which the two German states contended with the Nazi legacy. There are a host of excellent studies on the collapse of the GDR, German unification, and Germany's place in the new world order. These include Timothy Garton Ash, *In Europe's Name: Germany and the Divided Continent* (1993); Konrad H. Jarausch, *The Rush to Germany Unity* (1994); Charles S. Maier, *Dissolution: The Crisis of Communism and the End of East Germany* (1997); Philip Zelikow and Condoleezza Rice, *Germany Unified & Europe Transformed* (1995); Andrei S. Markovits and Simon Reich, *The German Predicament: Memory and Power in the New Europe* (1997); Marc Fisher, *After the Wall: Germany, the Germans and the Burdens of History* (1995); Jan-Werner Müller, *Another Country: German Intellectuals, Unification and National Identity* (2000). An intriguing comparison of the new Germany and the new Russia is Angela E. Stent's *Russia and Germany Reborn: Unification, the Soviet Collapse, and the New Europe* (1999). The fascinating career of a key player in the new Germany, Joschka

Fischer, is examined by Paul Hockenous in *Joschka Fischer and the Making of the Berlin Republic* (2007). Germany's first female chancellor is profiled in Clifford W. Mills and Arthur Meier, *Angela Merkel* (2007).

The End of the Soviet Union and the New Russia

For Gorbachev's reforms, see his own treatise, *Perestroika: New Thinking for Our Country and the World* (1987). On the final years of the Soviet power, the collapse of the USSR, and the new Russia, see David Remnick, *Lenin's Tomb: The Last Days of the Soviet Empire* (1993); David Remnick, *Resurrection: The Struggle for a New Russia* (1997); and Dimitri K. Simes, *After the Collapse: Russia Seeks Its Place as a Great Power* (1999). The best study of Russia under Vladimir Putin is Peter Baker and Susan Glasser, *Kremlin Rising: Vladimir Putin's Russia and the End of Revolution* (2006).

The Transformation of Eastern Europe

The best background study for the dramatic changes in Eastern Europe is Joseph Rothschild, *Return to Diversity: A Political History of East Central Europe since World War II* (3d ed., 2000). See also the excellent survey by Misha Glenny, *The Rebirth of History: Eastern Europe in the Age of Democracy* (rev. ed., 1993). On the Solidarity movement in Poland, see Lawrence Weschler, *Solidarity: Poland in the Season of Its Passion* (1982). Hungary's transformation is ably discussed in Charles Gati, *Hungary and the Soviet Bloc* (1988). Timothy Garton Ash has written three excellent collections of essays on events in Eastern and Central Europe in the last three decades of the twentieth century. They are *The Uses of Adversity: Essays on the Fate of Central Europe* (1989); *The Magic Lantern: The Revolution of '89 Witnessed in Warsaw, Budapest, Berlin and Prague* (1990); and *History of the Present: Essays, Sketches, and Dispatches from Europe in the 1990s* (1999). On the violent collapse of Yugoslavia, see Laura Silber and Allan Little, *Yugoslavia: Death of a Nation* (1997); Jan Willem Honig and Norbert Both, *Srebrenica. Record of a Crime* (1997); Roger Cohen, *Hearts Grown Brutal: Sagas of Sarajevo* (1998); and the memoir by Richard Holbrooke, *To End a War* (1998). The disturbing upsurge of xenophobic hatred across Eastern Europe is the subject of Paul Hockenous, *Free to Hate: The Rise of the Right in Post-Communist Eastern Europe* (1993).

Environmentalism and Climate Change

Among the many works on "green" politics in Europe and Europe's response to the challenges of global warming, see F. Muller-Rommel, *Green Parties in National Governments* (2002); Kirstin Dow and Thomas Downing, *The Atlas of Climate Change: Mapping the World's Greatest Challenge* (2006); and Fred Krupp and Miriam Horn, *Earth: The Sequel—The Race to Reinvent Energy and Stop Global Warming* (2008).

Credits

Illustrations Credits

Chapter 1: **p. 4**: Arthaud; **p. 11**: © Corbis; **p. 17**: Hulton Archive; **p. 20**: Hulton Archive; **p. 21**: Snark/Ark Resource, NY; **p. 25**: Mary Evans/The Women's Library; **p. 29**: Bundersarchiv Bild 146/73/36D/14; **p. 31**: Alamy

Chapter 2: **p. 38**: Archives Charmet/The Bridgeman Art Library International; **p. 44**: The Granger Collection, NY; **p. 47**: Mansell/Time Pix; **p. 49**: Hulton Archive; **p. 51**: Hulton Archive; **p. 56**: © Bettmann/Corbis; **p. 62**: Bibliothèque nationale de France; **p. 70**: ullstein bild; **p. 72**: ullstein bild; **p. 76**: ullstein bild; **p. 81**: Popperfoto; **p. 83**: The Granger Collection, NY; **p. 88**: © Bildarchiv Preussischer Kulturbesitz

Chapter 3: **p. 97**: Staatsbibliotek Berlin; **p. 101**: Getty; **p. 106**: © Hulton-Deutsch Collection/Corbis; **p. 108**: Sueddeutscher Verlag Gmbh; **p. 110**: MAN Gutehoffnungshutte; **p. 111**: © E.O. Hoppé/Corbis; **p. 114**: The Warder Collection; **p. 119 (left)**: The Warder Collection; **p. 119 (right)**: Roger-Viollet; **p. 123**: Imperial War Museum; **p. 126**: Alamy; **p. 129**: © Corbis; **p. 132**: The Granger Collection; **p. 133**: Ullstein Verlag; **p. 138**: Roger-Viollet

Chapter 4: **p. 144**: René Dazy Collection; **p. 145**: Hulton Archive; **p. 148**: Hulton Archive; **p. 158**: © Scheufler Collection/Corbis; **p. 164**: Ullstein Verlag; **p. 173**: Staatsbibliotek Berlin; **p. 176**: © Bildarchiv Preussischer Kulturbesitz

Chapter 5: **p. 180**: Bundesarchiv Bild 146/71/91/20; **p. 182**: René Dazy Collection; **p. 190**: akg-images; **p. 195**: Bundesarchiv Bild 102/3490; **p. 204**: © Hulton-Deutsch Collection/Corbis; **p. 223**: ullstein bild; **p. 222**: ullstein bild; **p. 223**: La Documentation Française

Chapter 6: **p. 230**: Science & Society Picture Library; **p. 239**: © Bettmann/Corbis; **p. 242**: Universite de Paris VII; **p. 248**: Bundesarchiv Bild 102/3497A; **p. 253**: ullstein bild; **p. 254**: The Warder Collection; **p. 255**: Bundesarchiv Bild 146/70/83/42; **p. 258**: Sueddeutscher Verlag Gmbh; **p. 259**: Bundesarchiv Bild 146/70/83/42; **p. 263**: © Bettmann/Corbis; **p. 270**: Sueddeutscher Verlag Gmbh

Chapter 7: **p. 275**: Hulton Archive; **p. 284**: Roger-Viollet; **p. 287**: The Warder Collection; **p. 292**: The Warder Collection; **p. 293**: Sueddeutscher Verlag Gmbh; **p. 295**: Yad Vashem; **p. 301**: AP/Wide World Photos

Chapter 8: **p.** 308: ullstein bild; **p.** 309: Stedman Jones/Pix, Inc./Time Life Pictures/Getty Images; **p.** 311: Alamy; **p.** 313: British Information Services; **p.** 321: AP; **p.** 327: Bundesarchiv Bild 101/680/285A/25; **p.** 329: Popperfoto; **p.** 330: ullstein bild; **p.** 332: Bundesarchiv Bild 146/78 Anh. 24/3; **p.** 335: United States Army; **p.** 338: Sovfoto/Eastfoto; **p.** 340: Sueddeutscher Verlag Gmbh

Chapter 9: **p.** 346: Robert Doisneau/Rapho; **p.** 351: © Hulton-Deutsch Collection/Corbis; **p.** 353: Hulton Archive; **p.** 354: AP/Wide World Photos; **p.** 356: Hulton Archive; **p.** 361: United States Information Agency

Chapter 10: **p.** 376: AP; **p.** 380: akg-images; **p.** 383: © dpa/Corbis; **p.** 385: AP/Wide World Photos; **p.** 395: AP/Wide World Photos; **p.** 400: ullstien bild

Chapter 11: **p.** 415: AP/Wide World Photos; **p.** 416: © Manuel Litran/Corbis; **p.** 421: AP/Wide World Photos; **p.** 423: Bundesbildstelle, Berlin; **p.** 428: AP/Wide World Photos; **p.** 434: Sueddeutscher Verlag Gmbh

Chapter 12: **p.** 438: © Bettmann/Corbis; **p.** 441: © Bettmann/Corbis; **p.** 446: AP/Wide World Photos; **p.** 451: © Bettmann/Corbis; **p.** 453: Getty

Chapter 13: **p.** 459: AP/Wide World Photos; **p.** 464: German Information Center; **p.** 468: Bettmann/Corbis; **p.** 471: Marc Riboud/Magnum Photos, Inc.; **p.** 474: AP/Wide World Photos

Chapter 14: **p.** 480: Bettmann/Corbis; **p.** 481: The Warder Collection; **p.** 485: © Reuters/Corbis; **p.** 489: Bettmann/Corbis; **p.** 493: Bettmann/Corbis; **p.** 496: AP; **p.** 499: AP/Wide World Photos; **p.** 501: © Reuters/Corbis

Chapter 15: **p.** 512: Daily Herald/Paddock Publications, Inc.; **p.** 514: © Reuters/Corbis; **p.** 518: AP/Wide World Photos; **p.** 522: Bettmann/Corbis; **p.** 529: © Reuters/Corbis; **p.** 530: © Reuters/Corbis; **p.** 535: © Reuters/Corbis; **p.** 536: © Reuters/Corbis; **p.** 539: © Reuters/Corbis

Chapter 16: **p.** 546: © AFP/Corbis; **p.** 547: Alamy; **p.** 551: © Julian Calder/Corbis; **p.** 552: © AFP/Corbis; **p.** 556: © AFP/Corbis; **p.** 558: © AFP/Corbis; **p.** 561: © David Turnely/Corbis; **p.** 563: © Jim McDonald/Corbis; **p.** 564: © AFP/Corbis; **p.** 572: © Peter Turnley/Corbis; **p.** 573: © Reuters/Corbis; **p.** 579: © Reuters/Corbis; **p.** 582: AP/Wide World Photos; **p.** 587: © AFP/Corbis

Chapter 17: **p.** 592: © Julia Waterlow; Eye Ubiquitous/Corbis; **p.** 600: Charlie Collins/AP Photo; **p.** 602: © Andrea Comas/Reuters/Corbis; **p.** 606: Molly Cooper/Alamy; **p.** 610: © Howard Davies/Corbis

Text Credits

"Spain 1937" (4 lines), copyright 1940 & renewed 1968 by W.H. Auden, from *Collected Poems* by W.H. Auden. Used by permission of Random House, Inc. and Faber & Faber, Ltd.

Index